THE
ECONOMICS
OF THE
WELFARE STATE

Nicholas Barr

Weidenfeld and Nicolson
London

George Weidenfeld & Nicolson Ltd
91 Clapham High Street, London SW4 7TA

ISBN 0 297 78835 3 cased
ISBN 0 297 78836 1 paperback

Photoset by Deltatype, Ellesmere Port, Cheshire
Printed in Great Britain by
Butler & Tanner Ltd
Frome and London

FOR MY MOTHER AND FATHER

Justice is the first virtue of all social institutions, as truth is of systems of thought. A theory however elegant and economic must be rejected or revised if it is untrue; likewise laws and institutions no matter how efficient and well-arranged must be reformed or abolished if they are unjust. [John Rawls, 1971.]

Let us remember that it [*laissez-faire*] is a *practical rule*, and not a doctrine of science; a rule in the main sound, but like most other sound rules, liable to numerous exceptions; above all, a rule which must never for a moment be allowed to stand in the way of any promising proposal of social or industrial reform. [J. E. Cairnes, 1873.]

Contents

Contents

Tables

Figures

Preface

There is a large literature on different aspects of the welfare state and a substantial body of economic theory which bears on the issues involved. One of the main purposes of this book is to draw together these diverse sources into a unified whole. Two general conclusions emerge. First, the issues raised by the welfare state fit very naturally into the conventional theoretical framework used by economists. Second, public involvement in institutions of the general sort which comprise the welfare state (i.e. income support, health care, education and housing) can, for the most part, be justified rather strongly in efficiency terms, quite independent of debates about social justice. To the extent that this is so, it is no longer public involvement *per se* which is controversial but only its precise form and the choice of its distributional objectives.

Throughout the book the main arguments are contrasted with those arising from different perspectives, especially from socialists and from libertarians like Hayek and Friedman. The debate with the latter is particularly fruitful. The difference between their views and a liberal defence of the welfare state rests less on ideology than on economic theory. Specifically, the theory set out in this book assigns a prominent role to technical problems with markets, with particular emphasis on information problems which are largely left out of account in most libertarian writing. These, more than any other theoretical consideration, are crucial to establishing the important efficiency role of the welfare state.

Though written specifically for economics specialists the needs of a diverse readership are kept in mind throughout the book. The early theoretical chapters (3–6) in particular, assume a working knowledge of intermediate microeconomic theory. To help readers with little economics each of these chapters has a non technical appendix, with the aid of which the rest of the book should, for the most part, be intelligible. Algebra is used where necessary to pin down some important concepts precisely; but the results are always explained verbally so that the equations can be skipped by those who are prepared to take their conclusions on trust. As a result the book should be accessible to readers in related academic areas (e.g. social administration, public policy and political economy) and to professionals in such fields as medicine and education. Familiarity with British institutions is not essential; they are described in separate sections which can be consulted as desired. The important arguments do not depend on institutional knowledge and should therefore make sense to readers in (or from) other countries. The principles developed are applicable to all industrialised economies and, where possible, examples and parallels from other countries are given. The Glossary explains the meaning of technical terms, and disentangles some differences of usage in various countries. The central arguments are summarised in Chapters 1 and 15, buttressed by the concluding sections of Chapters 4 (economic and political theory), 11 (income support), 13 (health care and education) and 14 (housing).

The origins of the book lie in lectures given over the years to students at the London School of Economics and in a series of seminars in Tokyo and Osaka under the sponsorship of the Kansai Economic Research Centre. I have been lucky in my audiences – they have never failed to disagree, to challenge and to ask thoroughly awkward questions.

My list of specific debts is large because I launched draft chapters liberally, and my colleagues are generous. My friends and mentors Alan Day and Alan Prest read the complete manuscript in draft, and had a major influence on its final shape. The book as a whole also owes a great deal to Christine Sarson-Gale, who was a splendidly argumentative sounding-board for my ruminations about much of its content, and also contributed substantively to a number of chapters. Many other people have given valuable comments on drafts of one or more chapters: Brian Abel-Smith, Patricia Apps, Tony Atkinson, David De Meza, Howard Glennerster, Gervas Huxley, Kurt Klappholz, Julian Le Grand, Peter Levin, Jane Lewis, Robin Naylor, Joseph Pechman, David Piachaud, Sally Sainsbury, Christine Whitehead and Basil Yamey. Dilia Montes gave helpful research assistance; Hilary Parker typed and retyped with superb efficiency, without fuss, and without ever overshooting a deadline; and Alma Gibbons and her colleagues taught me to use the word processor, and promptly and cheerfully bailed me out of a number of tight corners. I thank them all most warmly without implicating them in errors which remain.

Nicholas Barr
August 1986

PART 1

CONCEPTS

1

Introduction

[The duties of the state are] first . . . that of protecting the society from the violence and invasion of other independent societies; . . . second . . . that of protecting, as far as possible, every member of the society from the injustice or oppression of every other member of it; . . . third . . . that of erecting and maintaining those publick institutions and those publick works which, though they may be in the highest degree advantageous to a great society, are of such a nature, that the profit could never repay the expence to any individual or small number of individuals. [Adam Smith, 1776.]

One of the well-springs of this book has been the exuberant insistence over the years of various of my students and colleagues that economics appears to be largely irrelevant to major issues of social policy. They have a point, and this book is an attempt (with a little help from my friends) both to remedy their grievances and to assert the importance of economics. To help with the former I try to relate economic theory to different notions of social justice and to the historical development of the welfare state. In attempting the latter, two results stand out. First, far from being a subject about which economics has little to say, the issues raised by the welfare state fit very naturally into the framework of economic analysis. Second, the theoretical arguments support the existence of the welfare state not only for the expected equity reasons but also very much in terms of efficiency. This, it turns out, is an area in which economic theory is capable of fairly strong results which can justify the general idea of the welfare state to a surprising extent without resort to ideology.

Given the size of the subject, this book of necessity is an attempt to paint a broad canvas in the hope that readers, even if they do not accept all the answers, will at least be directed to the right battleground. The book addresses two broad questions: what theoretical arguments can justify the existence of the various parts of the welfare state in a modern industrialised economy; and, given these arguments of principle, how sensible (or otherwise) are the specific arrangements in Britain and in other countries?

The approach is best illustrated by two questions which permeate throughout:

(1) What are the *aims* of policy?
(2) By what *methods* are these aims best achieved?

Question 1 is extremely broad-ranging. There is general agreement that the major aims of policy in Western societies include *efficiency* in the use of resources; their distribution in accordance with *equity* or *justice*; and the preservation of *individual freedom*. These aims, however, can be defined in different ways, and may be accorded different weights. To a utilitarian[1] the aim of policy is to maximise total welfare; to Rawls the aim is social justice, defined in a particular way; libertarians make their main aim individual freedom, and socialists their prime concern equality. Beveridge's goal was the conquest of what he called the five giants of Want, Disease, Ignorance, Squalor and Idleness. Harold Macmillan once remarked that a just society should contain both a safety net and a ladder. The answer to question 1 is explicitly normative and largely ideological.

In contrast, it is argued that once question 1 has been answered question 2 is *not* ideological but *technical*, i.e. it raises a *positive* issue. Whether a given aim should be pursued by market allocation or by public provision depends on which of these methods more nearly achieves the chosen aim. Market allocation is neither 'good' nor 'bad' – it is useful in some instances (e.g. private markets for food in Britain are effective in achieving the aim that people should not starve); but in others (it is argued in Chapters 12 and 13 that health care is one) the market mechanism works less well, and public production and allocation can be argued to be more efficient and just. Similarly, public provision is neither good nor bad, but useful in some cases, less so in others. One of the questions throughout is which method is the more useful in different areas of the welfare state.

The distinction between aims and methods is fundamental, and bears reinforcement. Consider two central questions which all societies face:

How much redistribution (of income, wealth, power, etc.) should there be? and

---

[1] Utilitarianism and other theories of society, including those of Rawls and libertarian and socialist writers, are discussed in Chapter 3.

How should the economy best be run (i.e. the market system, central planning, or a mixed economy)?

The first question is clearly ideological and normative; it is an Aims question and so properly the subject of political debate. But *once that question has been answered*, the second question is very largely one of Method (i.e. a positive issue) and more properly the subject of technical than political discussion. This approach is explained in detail in Chapters 3 and 4, and summarised in the concluding section of Chapter 4.

We shall see in Chapter 6 that important concepts like poverty and equality of opportunity are hard, if not impossible, to define in principle, and even harder to measure. The concept of the welfare state similarly defies precise definition, and no attempt is made in this book to offer one (see the Further Reading). Two areas of complication are of special importance. First, the state is not the only source of welfare. Most people find support through the labour market for most of their lives; full employment is thus a major component of welfare broadly defined. In addition to paying wages, firms (individually or on an industry-wide basis, voluntarily or under legal compulsion) may provide for employees in the face of sickness, injury or retirement. Individuals can secure their own well-being through private insurance; and private charities, family and friends also provide welfare. Second, it does not follow that if a service is *financed* by the state it must necessarily be publicly *produced*. It is open to the state to produce a service itself at either central or local level,[1] and to supply it to recipients at no charge (e.g. state education); or to pay for individuals to consume goods produced in the private sector (e.g. free drugs under the national health service); or to give individuals money (either explicitly, or in the form of tax relief) to make their own purchases. The issue of 'privatisation', as we shall see in Chapter 4, is much more complex than is recognised in most public discussion.

Welfare is thus a mosaic, with diversity both in its source and in the manner of its delivery. Nevertheless the state, through various levels of government, is much the most important single agency involved in Britain, and in most industrialised countries; throughout the book the term 'welfare state' can therefore be thought of 'as a shorthand for the state's role in education, health, housing, poor relief, social insurance and other social services' (Ginsburg, 1979, p. 3). In broad terms the welfare state today comprises two sets of institutions, social security (i.e. cash benefits, as defined in the Glossary) and social services (i.e. benefits in kind). Social security is made up of *social*

---

[1] For lack of space, the important topic of central versus local provision will be set largely to one side; see Glennerster (1985) or, for compendious discussion, Foster, Jackman and Perlman (1980).

Table 1.1: Overview of the Welfare State, UK, 1986/7 (est.)

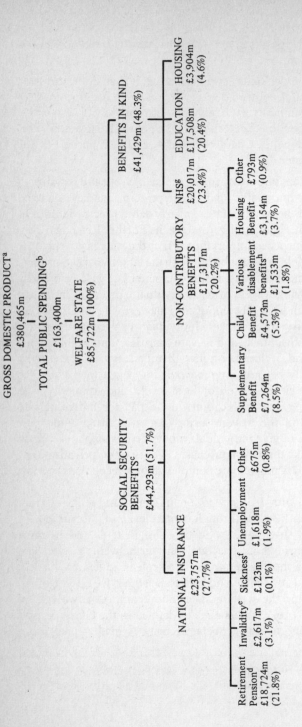

GROSS DOMESTIC PRODUCT[a]
£380,465m

TOTAL PUBLIC SPENDING[b]
£163,400m

WELFARE STATE
£85,722m (100%)

SOCIAL SECURITY BENEFITS[c]
£44,293m (51.7%)

BENEFITS IN KIND
£41,429m (48.3%)

NATIONAL INSURANCE
£23,757m (27.7%)

NON-CONTRIBUTORY BENEFITS
£17,317m (20.2%)

NHS[g] £20,017m (23.4%)

EDUCATION £17,508m (20.4%)

HOUSING £3,904m (4.6%)

Retirement Pension[d] £18,724m (21.8%)

Invalidity[e] £2,617m (3.1%)

Sickness[f] £123m (0.1%)

Unemployment £1,618m (1.9%)

Other £675m (0.8%)

Supplementary Benefit £7,264m (8.5%)

Child Benefit £4,573m (5.3%)

Various disablement benefits[h] £1,533m (1.8%)

Housing Benefit £3,154m (3.7%)

Other £793m (0.9%)

Source: The Government's Expenditure Plans, 1986–87 to 1988–89, Cmnd. 9702-II, Tables 2.12 and 3.15; and Financial Statement and Budget Report, 1986–87, Table 1.2.

Notes: [a]Estimated figure.
[b]Includes current and capital spending and debt interest.
[c]Figure greater than sum of its parts because expenditure in Northern Ireland and on administration has been included.
[d]Includes widows' benefit.
[e]Invalidity benefit and industrial disablement and death benefits.
[f]Excludes statutory sick pay.
[g]Includes personal social services.
[h]Attendance allowance, invalid care allowance, severe disablement allowance and mobility allowance.

insurance, which pays benefits as of right, by virtue of previous contributions, to prevent financial hardship arising out of unemployment, sickness, old age, widowhood or invalidity; and *social assistance*, which helps those in poverty, whether as an exceptional emergency or because they are not covered by social insurance, or as a supplement to social insurance. Social services cover a wide range of activities, including education, medical care, and more general forms of care for the infirm, and mentally and physically handicapped, and for children in need of protection.

In practice the British welfare state can be taken to comprise, at a minimum, the publicly provided benefits (representing about 22.5 per cent of gross domestic product) listed in Table 1.1, together with the contributions which pay for them. Cash benefits are twofold. National insurance is payable to people with an adequate contributions record; benefits cover, *inter alia*, unemployment, sickness (short- and long-term) and retirement, of which the last (over 20 per cent of social spending) is much the largest. Non-contributory benefits include supplementary benefit (paid on the basis of a means test to those with little or no other income) and child benefit (a weekly cash payment to the parent or guardian of every child). The major benefits in kind are the national health service (including personal social services) (approximately 25 per cent of total social spending), education (approximately 20 per cent), and housing (4 per cent, plus substantial additional expenditure on cash assistance with housing costs).

The book is organised in the following way. Part 1 sets the scene, starting in Chapter 2 with a discussion of the historical development of the welfare state in Britain; there is some comparison with other countries, particularly the USA. The next three chapters are the theoretical heart of the book: Chapter 3 discusses various definitions of social justice and their different implications for the welfare state; Chapter 4 sets out the economic theory of state intervention and Chapter 5 the theory of insurance. Chapter 6 discusses problems of definition and measurement. To help readers who are diffident about their theoretical background, the conceptual chapters (3, 4, 5 and 6) each have a non-technical Appendix which summarises the essential material; and technical terms are explained in the Glossary.

Three major threads are developed in Part 1 which run through the rest of the book: the social welfare maximisation problem; alternative definitions of social justice; and measurement problems. The social welfare maximisation problem (set out in Chapter 4) is the conventional starting-point for economic theory. An important theorem states that under appropriate assumptions a competitive market equilibrium will allocate resources efficiently. It is argued that where these conditions hold, the role of the state, if any, is limited to income redistribution; conversely, where these conditions fail, there may be efficiency grounds for intervention in a variety of forms. The second major theme is social justice. The definition chosen will determine the weights assigned to different individuals, with major implications for the form and extent of intervention, e.g. whether people with no income should be supported at subsistence, or at some higher level. The third thread, discussed in Chapter 6, concerns problems of definition and measurement. Many variables are hard to define and, once defined, hard to measure. A crucial and recurrent difficulty is that utility (see the Glossary) is not measurable. This makes it hard both to measure living standards and to compare them. Imperfect information also causes problems, since it is generally difficult to ascertain the extent to which information is lacking. Costs or benefits may similarly be hard to measure.

As far as possible each chapter in Parts 2 and 3 has a similar layout to clarify the structure of the argument. Each chapter discusses in turn: the *aims* of policy; the *methods* by which they might be achieved, i.e. the theoretical arguments about intervention for reasons of efficiency and social justice; *assessment* in the light of this theoretical discussion of the appropriateness (or otherwise) of the British and other systems, including discussion of the empirical literature; and *reform*.

Part 2 analyses cash transfers. Chapter 7 describes the finances of the welfare state. Chapter 8 looks at unemployment, sickness and disability benefits, Chapter 9 at retirement pensions and Chapter 10 at non-contributory benefits, in each case starting with the theory and then assessing the practice. Chapter 11 considers a variety of reforms of income support. Part 3 discusses provision in kind. Chapter 12 analyses the theoretical arguments for public production and allocation of health care and education, and Chapter 13 looks at the effectiveness of the national health service and state education in Britain in comparison with systems in other countries, and discusses alternative ways in which they might be organised. Chapter 14 considers the justification, if any, for state involvement in the housing market.

The conclusions of the book are summarised in Chapter 15. Readers in a hurry can get an idea of the book's approach and its main conclusions by reading Chapter 15 and the concluding sections of Chapters 4 (economic and political theory), 11 (income support), 13 (health care and education) and 14 (housing).

Further Reading

The diversity of sources of welfare is discussed by Glennerster (1985, Ch. 1). On the idea of welfare see Robson (1976), Pinker (1979) and Higgins (1981).

2

The Historical Background

The principle of *laissez-faire* may be safely trusted to in some things but in many more it is wholly inapplicable; and to appeal to it on all occasions savours more of the policy of a parrot than of a statesman or a philosopher. [J. R. McCulloch, 1848.]

The poverty of the poor is the chief cause of that weakness and inefficiency which are the cause of their poverty. [Alfred Marshall, 1885.]

1 Early Days

1.1 POOR RELIEF

The British welfare state is neither the outcome of the Second World War nor simply the creation of the postwar Labour government. Its roots are ancient and complex. Christian charity to relieve poverty has gradually (though even today not wholly) been taken over by state action. And state activity has grown over the years from small scale to large; from local to central; from permissive to mandatory; and from piecemeal to complex and interrelated. From this tangle, however, four events stand out: the *Poor Law Act* of 1601 and the *Poor Law Amendment Act* of 1834 were the main legislative bases of poverty relief before the twentieth century; the *Liberal reforms* of 1906–14 represented a substantial departure from *laissez-faire* capitalism and so can be argued to form the basis of the welfare state; and the *postwar legislation* of 1944–8 set the scene for the welfare state as we know it today.

It should be clear that the question 'how did the welfare state come about?' is vast, so discussion is limited in two important ways. No attempt is made at complete coverage; the story is confined for the most part to the British experience, with only a sideways glance at other countries, notably the USA. The question is also controversial; I shall sketch out the major areas of historical dispute, but make no attempt at resolving them. The chapter is organised chronologically, discussing *seriatim* the period up to the end of the nineteenth century (section 1); the Liberal reforms of 1906–14 (section 2); British developments between the two World Wars (section 3); inter-war poverty relief in the USA (section 4); the Second World War and its immediate aftermath in Britain (section 5); and developments between 1948 and 1985 in Britain and the USA (section 6). Section 7 draws the threads together by considering the forces which created the welfare state.

Among the early motives for public poor relief in Britain were the fear of social disorder and chronic labour shortages in the years after the Black Death of 1348–9. As a result, the state attempted, *inter alia*, to control wages and labour mobility in the Statute of Labourers 1351 and the Poor Law Act 1388. Tudor legislation grew away from this repressive and not very effective regime:

> In 1576 the concept of 'setting the poor on work' was enshrined in statute law where it was to remain for something like three and a half centuries. If the able-bodied required assistance they had to work for it, and in the 1576 Poor Relief Act JPs were instructed to provide a stock of raw materials on which beggars could work in return for the relief they received. [Fraser, 1984, p. 32.]

The 1601 Poor Law Act was built on the 1576 Act, and adopted a twofold approach: each parish was required to assume responsibility for its poor; and different treatment was prescribed for three categories of pauper. The 'impotent poor' (the old and the sick) were to be accommodated in 'almshouses'; the able-bodied were to be given work in a 'house of correction' (not at first a residential workhouse); and idlers who refused to work were to be punished in this 'house of correction'. The idea was that paupers not able to work should be cared for and the able-bodied should be given work; neither regime was intended to be punitive.

This arrangement worked moderately well for nearly two hundred years; but eventually its institutions, locally financed and adapted to a pre-industrial economy, came under increasing pressure from population growth, increased social mobility, industrialisation and economic fluctuations. By 1795 food shortages and inflation resulting from war and bad harvests had spread poverty from the unemployed to those in work, giving rise to various local initiatives, notably the Speenhamland system which supplemented wages with an 'allowance' based on the price of bread. The novelty of these changes was that they extended aid to people in work. Poor relief, whether under the Poor Law *per se* or under a local variant, carried less social stigma than it was later to acquire.

These arrangements soon came under attack. Bentham believed that they caused moral degeneracy among recipients. Malthus argued that poor relief would cause excessive population growth, and Ricardo that it would depress wages and thereby exacerbate poverty. Possibly more important than these theoretical arguments was the escalating cost of relief, partly due to rising prices (especially of bread), and also because of rising unemployment as soldiers returned from the Napoleonic wars. As a result the costs (which were met from local revenues) rose sharply.

The Poor Law Report and the Poor Law Amendment Act 1834 were consequences of this philosophical and financial climate. A Royal Commission was set up in 1832; its Report, which was *laissez-faire* in tone (see the Glossary), was written by Nassau Senior and Edwin Chadwick, a former secretary to Bentham. The intellectual background to the Report, and particularly the position of the Classical economists on the Poor Law, is often misunderstood. It is true that Malthus and Ricardo, worried by population growth and shocked by the earlier effect of the Poor Law, advocated its gradual repeal. But it is *not* the case that Nassau Senior (who was, according to Robbins, more in the mainstream of Classical thought) was against poor relief. In Senior's view, 'the great test which must be applied to any project of state action in regard to relief is the question *whether it has any tendency to increase that which it is proposed to diminish*' (Robbins, 1977, p. 128, his emphasis). Thus, he supported public provision for orphans, the blind and the disabled, including provision of medical treatment and hospitals. He was not in favour of abolishing relief for the able-bodied and their dependants; but here he insisted on the principle of 'less eligibility', i.e. that relief should be limited to an amount and administered in a manner which left the recipient worse off than the employed.

The Poor Law Report was entirely consistent with this approach when it argued that the new system should contain three elements (often referred to as 'the Principles of 1834'): the notion of less eligibility, the workhouse test, and administrative centralisation. Less eligibility was the central doctrine of 1834. It was not intended to apply to the old or sick, but only to the able-bodied whose indigence, it was argued, would be encouraged by higher benefits.[1] The

---

[1] Readers may note more than a passing similarity between these arguments of 150 years ago, and the more recent debates discussed in sections 6 and 7. Some commentators argue that part of the Poor Law spirit persists, e.g. the decline in unemployment benefit relative to other benefits in Britain in the 1980s can be interpreted as a case of less eligibility.

workhouse test (i.e. relief being conditional upon living in the workhouse) was not a principle, but simply a means of enforcing less eligibility. As far as possible, the workhouse would provide a standard of living lower than that of the lowest worker. Additional restrictions were imposed, including the strict segregation of husbands, wives and children. The purpose of centralisation was to avoid local corruption and incompetence; to ensure uniformity; to enhance cost-effectiveness; and to promote labour mobility. The difference between the 1601 Poor Law and the Principles of 1834 is important. The former was intended to give work to the able-bodied without stigma; the latter discouraged claims for relief by making its receipt highly unpleasant and also stigmatising.

The Poor Law Amendment Act followed quickly in the wake of the Poor Law Report. Despite controversy among historians it is now clear that, though the intention of the Act was largely (though in important respects not fully) to implement the recommendations of the Report, the effect of the Act in practice was less than appeared in principle. The Poor Law Commission (in whom the powers of central government were vested) was never able to bend local administration of the Poor Law to its will, particularly in respect of enforcing the workhouse test. But in other respects, it is argued, the implementation of the Act had more unpleasant effects than was intended by its architects (see Bowley, 1937, Pt. II, Ch. 2). Many people were forced to accept the harsh conditions of the workhouse, and many others endured appalling privation to avoid it. Because of its very cruelty, however, the system became over time a force for change, and thus the 1834 Act may be seen as one of the roots of later developments.

1.2 OTHER EARLY SOCIAL LEGISLATION

Notwithstanding the philosophical underpinnings of the Principles of 1834, *laissez-faire* was increasingly eroded over the nineteenth century, particularly in factory legislation and in education and public health. The first Factory Act, passed in 1802, protected women and children by limiting hours and regulating working conditions. Althorp's Factory Act of 1833 tightened the rules and, probably of greater long-run importance, appointed four inspectors to enforce its provisions. The latter was implicit acknowledgement of the right of the state to regulate certain social conditions.

The role of the state in education started more gradually (Fraser, 1984, Ch. 4; West, 1970). Most schools in the early nineteenth century were charitable and reflected the prevailing ethos of social deference, Christian morality and voluntarism. The Sunday school movement had an important role in teaching reading, often with the Bible as the only text. State intervention started in 1833 with a grant to Protestant schools for school building, i.e. as financial help for voluntarism, and from 1847 a grant was paid for a limited scheme of teacher training. As government involvement grew, a Royal Commission was established, though its recommendations were largely superseded by the Education Act 1870, which gave every child the right (at least in principle) to some form of schooling. School Boards were empowered (but not compelled) to provide elementary education, financed by a mixture of central and local revenues. The resulting system was a compromise in which the new board schools coexisted with the voluntary sector. Later developments made elementary school attendance compulsory between five and ten (Mundella's Education Act 1880) and virtually free (the Fee Grant Act 1891).

Thus a process of gradual accretion over the nineteenth century led to a system of primary education which was compulsory and largely publicly funded. Of the many explanations of these changes one in particular is a recurring theme – the *national efficiency* argument, which justified state involvement in education on the grounds that it made labour more productive, thus contributing to economic growth. It is also argued that the 1870 Act was encouraged by the extension of the franchise in 1867, creating a need to educate the growing electorate.

The third breach in *laissez-faire* was in public health (Fraser, 1984, Ch. 3; Finer, 1952, Chs 5, 7 and 8). In the first half of the nineteenth century urbanisation (largely the result of the industrial revolution) and population growth caused cities to grow rapidly, leading to a housing shortage and, connected with it, a sanitation problem. The poor in particular were afflicted by typhus and tuberculosis; and a series of cholera epidemics, being water-borne, attacked everyone, including the middle classes with their ready access to water supplies.

This was the problem. The solution again involves Edwin Chadwick, whose *Report on the Sanitary Conditions of the Labouring Population of Great Britain* (UK, 1842) was remarkable for the high quality of its statistical analysis. Chadwick originally advocated sewage disposal as a public enterprise on the grounds that ill-health, by causing poverty, added to the cost of the Poor Law. The Report, however, included wider grounds for intervention. Its main recommendation (though based on a faulty theory of the transmission of cholera) was that sewage should be separated from other water through the use of glazed pipes. The Report met considerable opposition, both technical and also based on financial, ideological and political arguments. As a result legislation was delayed, and initially ineffective. After several false starts, the Public Health Act 1875 established clear duties for local authorities, and remained the basis of most public health activities until 1936.

This, then, was the situation in the 1870s. The state was slowly becoming involved in increasing areas of social and economic life; but though the Classical economists supported much of the new legislation, the prevailing doctrine was still largely *laissez-faire*.

2 The Liberal Reforms[1]

2.1 THE ORIGINS OF THE REFORMS

The third major development was the period of the Liberal reforms between 1906 and 1914. Historians have debated at length this burst of activity so much at variance with the ideology of the nineteenth-century Liberal Party. Hay (1975) distinguishes three influences in particular which historians regard as underlying the reforms: pressure from below; changed attitudes to welfare provision; and institutional influences.

Pressure from below   There is a measure of agreement that working-class political pressure was one of the origins of the reforms, though the relationship is far from simple. If reform was so popular why was it not a major election issue; and why the long lag between electoral reform in 1867 and social reform in 1906–14? Pelling deals with the problem by denying the premise, arguing that working-class pressure was negligible.

> The members of the working class as a whole, cynical about the character of society as they knew it, were yet fearful of change which would more likely be for the worse than for the better. They advanced into the twentieth century with little expectation of social improvement being engineered by political means, and none at all of the 'welfare state' as we know it today. [1979, p. 18.]

Hobsbawm (1964) argues that it was only unorganised workers who opposed reform. Nor was working-class pressure necessarily important for all the reforms.

Changing attitudes to welfare provision among the political élite arose *inter alia* out of the national efficiency issue. The argument at its simplest was that economic growth depended on a healthy, educated workforce. In dramatic contrast with the Principles of 1834, a speaker in Parliamentary debate could argue: 'The future of the Empire, the triumph of social progress and the freedom of the British race depend not so much upon the strengthening of the

---

[1] This section draws on Hay (1975). See also the Further Reading.

Army as upon fortifying the children of the State for the battle of life' (*Hansard* (Commons), 18 April 1905, col. 539, quoted in Bruce, 1972, pp. 152–3). The influence of the national efficiency arguments is debated. At a minimum they made social reform a politically respectable issue.

A second reason for greater acceptance of intervention was a change in attitudes toward poverty. The social surveys of Booth (1902) and Rowntree (1901) and the study of the health of Boer War recruits yielded much empirical information. The effects of these data on attitudes were complex; they suggested that poverty was more widespread than had been believed, and that not all poverty, even among the able-bodied, was due to moral defect. They also raised doubts about the effectiveness of private philanthropy.[1]

A third influence was the rise of collectivism. The 'Old Liberalism', which was opposed to state intervention, had twofold roots in the 'natural rights' individualist philosophy of writers like Spencer (1884) and in utilitarianism.[2] Between 1860 and 1900, however, several philosophers, though in no sense advocating collectivism, suggested that the traditional definition of individual freedom as absence from coercion was too narrow. It was argued (e.g. Hobson, 1909, Pt. II, Ch. II) that 'positive freedom' should include not only economic freedom but also a measure of economic *security*. It followed that the state, in advancing individual freedom, should adopt an active role in social reform. This was the 'New Liberalism' (see Freeden, 1978), under which social justice and the notion of 'positive' freedom 'provided the means of reconciling individualism and collectivism' (Mowat, 1969, pp. 93–4, quoted in Hay, 1975, p. 36).

In the context of these changing ideas the German example became important. Between 1883 and 1889, largely as a counter to socialist agitation, the German government under Bismarck had created a broad system of social insurance, under which compulsory contributions gave entitlement to a system of guaranteed benefits, thereby removing the threat of the means test and poor-house. The scheme was investigated by Lloyd George, and had a major influence on the form of the National Insurance Act 1911 (discussed below).

Institutional Influences on the reforms included pressure groups such as the Friendly Societies, which represented the idea of working class self-help. It is also argued that bureaucracies like the civil service exerted an independent influence. McDonagh (1960) describes a process whereby, as awareness of a problem grew, a body of experts would be set up to investigate. As a result of its

---

[1] For the view that poverty was 'discovered' much earlier see Himmelfarb (1984).
[2] The important distinction between a natural rights and a utilitarian defence of individual freedom is discussed at length in Chapter 3, which also discusses the ideas of collectivist writers.

findings awareness of the problem increased, and so did the volume of resources devoted to combating it. Experts thus contributed not only to the *manner* in which social problems were tackled, but also to the *range* of issues regarded as the proper province of public policy.

The reforms were central rather than local mainly because of the reluctance of central government (despite several official inquiries) to reform local authority finance in the light of regional inequalities, and the failure of local revenues to rise in step with expenditure.[1] Finally, the reforms were outside the Poor Law partly because the latter was financed locally; partly to side-step the long-established vested interests of local Poor Law institutions; and partly because of popular hostility towards the old system.

2.2 THE NEW MEASURES

Whatever their causes (about which historians will continue to argue) and motives (discussed below), the reforms of 1906–14 were substantial by any standards and particularly so in the context of the times. The new measures concerned children, pensions, unemployment, health and fiscal policy.

Children The Education (Provision of Meals) Act 1906 permitted (but did not compel) local authorities to provide school meals for needy children; the Education (Administrative Provisions) Act 1907 introduced medical inspection of schoolchildren; and the Children Act 1908 made it a punishable offence for parents to neglect their children. The motives for these Acts were partly humanitarian and partly on national efficiency grounds.

Pensions The Old Age Pensions Act 1908

> introduced a new principle into social policy. Hitherto relief had been provided . . . from *local* funds and only after a test of destitution. Now for the first time payments were to be made, as of right, from *national* funds . . . within strict limits of age and means, but with no test of actual destitution. [Bruce, 1972, p. 178, his emphasis.]

The Act introduced a non-contributory pension of five shillings (25 pence) per week for people over 70 whose income was below £31 per year, though it excluded previous recipients of Poor Law relief, and some people on moral grounds.[2]

---

[1] The owner of my borrowed copy of Hay has written 'so what's new?' in the margin.
[2] History is full of small anomalies. An additional reason for the pensions legislation, according to Pelling (1979, p. 11), was '[a] loosening of the Treasury's purse strings [because of] the temporary lull in the naval building race, which was due to the destruction of Russian battleships in the Russo-Japanese War. . . . Thus in a sense it was Admiral Togo, the victor of Tsushima, who laid the groundwork of Old Age Pensions and deserves to be remembered as the architect of the British Welfare State.'

Unemployment and minimum wages   Various earlier proposals to resolve the growing problem of unemployment had met with little success (see Harris, 1972). Any acceptable solution had to meet four criteria (Hay, 1975, pp. 50–1). It had to 'make the minimum alterations in the normal workings of the labour market to satisfy individualists, economists and industrialists'. Second, 'it . . . had to be largely self-financing in order to avoid unacceptable increases in direct taxation or the reintroduction of tariffs'. It had to be separate from the Poor Law to avoid the need to discriminate between the 'deserving' and 'undeserving' poor. Lastly, it had to be sufficiently attractive to head off any socialist threat. The resulting package had three elements: voluntary labour exchanges would assist the normal working of the labour market; there was to be a limited scheme of unemployment insurance; and a Development Fund would finance counter-cyclical public works expenditure, mainly by local authorities.

The scheme of unemployment insurance was limited: it applied only to a narrow range of industries; only workers earning less than £160 per year were covered; and benefits were low to discourage deliberate unemployment. A variety of other industrial legislation, including the Trades Disputes Act and Workmen's Compensation Act in 1906, and the Trade Boards Act 1909, gave the government limited power to set minimum wages. It was recognised that unemployment and sickness were interrelated, so the National Insurance Act 1911 also contained health insurance. The combined package was financed by a weekly contribution of 9d, of which 4d was paid by the worker, the rest by his employer.

Health   Whereas unemployment insurance, according to Hay, was largely the result of working-class pressure, health insurance arose more from considerations of national efficiency. Prior to 1911 there were voluntary hospitals for those who could afford to subscribe to them; for others, Poor Law hospitals offered free and (for the most part) non-stigmatising health care (see Abel-Smith, 1964, Ch. 15). The 1911 Act did little to change these arrangements. Cover was extended only to the breadwinner, who was entitled to a sickness (i.e. cash) benefit, free medical treatment and drugs from a panel doctor, and access to a sanatorium.

Fiscal policy   The fiscal controversies of the period concerned tariffs (which are not the issue here), and progressive income tax. The traditional economic argument was that taxation should be based on the principle of 'equal sacrifice' (implying a poll tax), or of 'equi-proportional sacrifice' (implying a proportional tax). Both approaches ruled out redistribution through the tax system. But by the turn of the century there was limited support for redistribution through tax-financed public expenditure. Edgeworth justified progressive taxation by appeal to the 'least aggregate sacrifice' principle under which *marginal* rather than *total* sacrifice was to be equalised. Equal marginal sacrifice plus the assumption of diminishing marginal utility of income together imply progressive taxation (see Prest and Barr, 1985, Ch. 5, section 1.2).

A different line of argument by people like Hobson (1908) was that monopoly elements resulted in a sub-optimal income distribution which led to underconsumption. By thus attributing unemployment to underconsumption which could be remedied by income redistribution, Hobson foreshadowed Keynes some 30 years before the publication of *The General Theory*. Others, notably the socialists, saw progressive taxation as an issue of social justice, a subject to which we return in Chapter 3.

A brief assessment   In assessing the reforms two hotly debated issues arise: what was their motive (discussed in section 7.1), and were they particularly radical? It can be argued (e.g. Marsh, 1980, p. 17) that the virtually simultaneous introduction of old age pensions, unemployment insurance, sickness benefits and progressive taxation, supported by the interventionist philosophy of the New Liberalism, constituted a fundamental break with earlier economic and political doctrines. However, a closer look at the individual programmes gives a less clear answer. The pension scheme, albeit non-contributory, was to some extent means-tested, and applied only to individuals over 70 who had never received poor relief and were not excluded on moral grounds. Its main purpose, it can be argued, was to improve national competitiveness by weeding out inefficient labour (the national efficiency argument again). Unemployment insurance was based in part on a weekly employee contribution of 4d (i.e. lump-sum and therefore regressive), and applied only to a few relatively skilled workers in some industries. Sickness benefits were financed by the same contribution, with similar coverage; and the health care benefits applied only to the breadwinner.

It can therefore be argued that the reforms were relatively minor and with limited coverage; and that only the pension scheme was substantially redistributive from rich to poor. The New Liberalism, from this viewpoint, was not very new; it still accepted capitalism unquestioningly, and in that sense was only a reinterpretation of the Old Liberalism. As we shall see in section 4 strikingly similar issues arise in considering the novelty (or otherwise) of the 1935 US Social Security Act.

Nor, in conclusion, were the Liberal reforms in any way unique. Germany, as we have seen, had introduced social insurance in the 1880s, motivated in part by fears of social unrest. New Zealand introduced non-contributory pensions in 1898, *inter alia* for reasons of national efficiency, in the face of increased international competition on an economy highly dependent on its exports. By 1908 Denmark, Ireland, Austria, Czechoslovakia and Australia also had social legislation of some sort (Pechman, Aaron and Taussig, 1968, Appendix C; and for more general international comparison Kaim-Caudle, 1973). The Liberal reforms, though one of the earlier examples of nationally organised income support, were not the first; nor did they represent a major discontinuity either with previous arrangements or with developments in other countries.

3 The First World War and the Inter-war Period in Britain

3.1 HOUSING

In contrast with the eventful years between 1906 and 1914 the period thereafter was largely a time of stagnation in social policy, with the important exception of housing. There were also major changes in unemployment insurance (section 3.2). In housing, probably more than any other part of the welfare state, past policies, notably during and after the First World War, have a crucial bearing on current institutions. Before 1914 virtually all housing was provided by the private market. By and large the system worked well for those who could afford it; but for the lowest income groups, particularly in large cities, it led to overcrowding and squalor (Gauldie, 1974). In a strictly technical sense the housing market cleared, but policy-makers found the result unacceptable both for reasons of public health and public order, and for more charitable motives. Early legislation had little effect, mainly because it imposed no *duty* on local authorities to remedy poor housing. Though working-class housing conditions continued to cause concern in the latter part of the century the response was limited mainly to philanthropic efforts (see Merrett, 1979).

By 1918, however, for at least three reasons, housing had become a problem for which existing methods were no longer regarded as adequate. First, there was an acute housing shortage because of falling supply (due to the cessation of building during the First World War, and the deterioration of older property) and rising demand (because people were living longer and marrying earlier; and mobility among young people was increasing). Second, this shortage was regarded as politically too sensitive to be left to private charity and discretionary local action. In 1918 large numbers of soldiers were demobilised, and there were fears of social unrest (the Russian Bolshevik Revolution having occurred in the previous year). Lloyd George's promise in November 1918 'to make Britain a fit country for heroes to live in' was seen as a commitment on which it would have been politically dangerous to renege.

The third reason why housing was thought to warrant government action was because intervention had already occurred, through the imposition of rent control in 1915 as an emergency wartime measure. As we shall see in Chapter 14, rent control is rather like smoking – if one never starts one can do without, but once started it is very hard to give up. By 1918 many people were unable to pay the market price of housing, which had risen sharply because of the shortage; at least as important, controlled rents had already assumed an aura of 'fair' rents. Since immediate decontrol was politically impossible, the government chose to assume some responsibility for people dependent on renting at the lower end of the market, through direct provision of housing at rents equivalent to controlled rents.

The resulting Housing and Town Planning Act 1919 (the Addison Act) contained three provisions: local authorities were invested with the *duty* of remedying housing deficiencies in their areas; house building was to meet *general* needs rather than concentrating only on slum clearance; and the operation received a central government subsidy which underwrote the entire cost of house building in excess of the product of a penny rate.[1] In contrast with nineteenth-century thought, the Act embodied three new principles – central supervision, compulsion and subsidy. It had three long-term effects: the acceptance of the idea of housing as a legitimate area of government intervention in the sense of public production as opposed merely to regulation; the provision of accommodation at a subsidised rent implied a view of housing as a social service; and the service was to be delivered by local authorities. The Act, together with rent control, laid a foundation for housing policy which has lasted to the present.

The Addison Act met with some success. However, generous subsidies, when the capacity of the building industry was already stretched by private sector demand, led inevitably to soaring costs; and when the postwar boom faltered, the resulting public spending cuts (the so-called 'Geddes axe') halted expenditure under the Act. Chamberlain's Housing Act 1923 reduced the subsidy and laid the burden of excessive costs on local revenues. But the subsidy was too small to help the worse-off, and the scheme was used mainly by private builders for moderately priced houses for the middle class and the more affluent section of the working class. The hope that a process of 'filtering up' would free cheaper housing for the less well-off remained unfulfilled, partly because controlled rents reduced housing mobility (a recurring theme). The Labour government of 1924 recognised that the subsidies were failing to reach the people who needed them most (another recurring theme). The Wheatley Act 1924 increased the subsidy on condition that it was used for houses to be let at controlled rents subsidised from local revenues. This stimulated local

---

[1] I.e. the revenue raised by increasing local rates (property taxes) by 1d in the pound.

authority building, and the Wheatley and Chamberlain schemes operated side by side, finally coming to an end in 1933 when it was felt that the housing shortage had been resolved.

To sum up, the First World War and its aftermath saw the introduction of rent control and the provision of subsidised housing by local authorities. But not everyone shared in the gains. Though the overall size of the housing stock increased, there remained a shortage of accommodation at rents the poor could afford. In particular, much local authority housing remained beyond the reach of poorer workers,[1] who still relied largely on the private sector, a fact recognised by the 1938 Housing Act which continued rent control on smaller houses. It can be argued that the continuation of rent control perpetuated the initial shortage; there remained (and remains) little incentive for the private sector to provide rented accommodation for the less well-off. And the continuing story of local authority housing (Chapter 14) is one of considerable subsidy, uneconomic rents and long waiting-lists.

3.2 UNEMPLOYMENT INSURANCE

From 1920 to 1940 unemployment never fell below one million and reached a peak of over three million, in the face of which unemployment insurance *qua* insurance virtually collapsed. The story in many other countries involves similar problems, similar debates and, in broad terms, similar solutions (Kaim-Caudle, 1973). The case of the USA is taken up in section 4.

Developments in the 1920s The Unemployment Insurance Act 1920 extended the 1911 Act to more workers, and also paid an allowance for dependants. It was introduced hastily in the face of rising unemployment after the war, not least among demobilised soldiers. The Act was doomed to failure since rising unemployment inevitably undermined the insurance aspect of the scheme. This led to continual juggling with contribution and benefit levels, and to a series of devices which sought to preserve the fiction of insurance whilst in reality paying uncovenanted benefits (i.e. not paid for by insurance contributions), thereby violating the insurance principle. The payment of uncovenanted benefit out of the insurance fund was partly because the locally financed Poor Law could not cope with mass unemployment and, equally important, because the unemployed strenuously resisted the Poor Law. The realisation grew only slowly that insurance has problems even with short-term unemployment, and is totally inadequate in the face of long-term or mass

---

[1] Though in the 1930s some poorer people obtained local authority housing as a result of slum clearance.

unemployment (a central topic of Chapters 5 and 8).

As a result of the report of the Blanesburgh Committee, two benefits were introduced in 1927. *Standard* benefit was paid as an insurance benefit of indefinite duration to anyone who had made *any* contributions. *Transitional* benefit was payable as of right to those who did not satisfy even the minimal requirements of the insurance scheme, provided that they were 'genuinely seeking work'. Both benefits were paid from the insurance fund. Transitional benefit protected the unemployed from the Poor Law, which was reorganised in 1929, when the powers of the Guardians were transferred to Public Assistance Committees (PACs) run by local authorities.

In 1930 the Labour government changed the regulations for transitional benefit in two ways: they made the benefit a charge on the Consolidated Fund (i.e. general government revenues) rather than the insurance fund; and they relaxed the 'genuinely seeking work' clause. As a result, the numbers receiving transitional benefit doubled within two months, at a cost of £19 million in the scheme's first year, just as the economic crisis came to a head.

The 1931 crisis and the benefit cuts By the late 1920s one strand of policy was concerned with how unemployment benefits should be arranged and financed; another concentrated on the economic crisis more generally, and particularly on how unemployment could be reduced. Economic radicals, most obviously Keynes, with support from the Liberal Party and from various politicians in other parties, favoured expansionary public works expenditure. Economic conservatives like Ramsay MacDonald and his Chancellor Philip Snowden followed the traditional orthodoxy, supporting expenditure cuts, a balanced budget and lower government borrowing.[1] In the 1931 crisis the economic conservatives dominated. The decision to preserve the gold standard by stringent fiscal and monetary policy, particularly a cut in unemployment benefit, split the Labour cabinet and led to the formation of a National Government under Ramsay MacDonald. In the face of expenditure cuts, unemployment and controversy mounted.

The rapid escalation of benefit payments at a time of economic crisis led to immediate action. Benefits were cut by 10 per cent from 17s (85 pence) to 15s 3d (76 pence) in 1931. Standard benefit was limited to 26 weeks, and the administration of transitional benefit (renamed transitional payment) was transferred to the local PACs, though still paid from central funds.

It is a matter of controversy whether *real* benefits fell, since prices had also declined. Between 1921 and 1931 the overall price of consumer goods fell by about 28 per cent, and those of food, clothing and fuel and light by even more.

---

[1] The parallel with the situation fifty years later is striking. It is tempting to ask whether those who believe in Kondratieff (50-year) cycles are perhaps right.

Compared with 1927 (when standard and transitional benefits were introduced) the price of consumer goods fell by 8 per cent, though the price of housing increased by 2 per cent (Feinstein, 1972, Tables 61 and 62). Possibly of greater importance as an explanation of the anger engendered by the cuts was the manner of their implementation. The role of the PACs in this context was crucial, and had ramifications for the relief of poverty which survive to the present. Eligibility for benefit was tightened, though with regional variation which was itself a further cause of anger. The interpretation of the 'genuinely seeking work' condition became harsher. Additionally, from 1931, in sharp contrast with arrangements after 1927, the PACs administered transitional payment on the basis of the stringent Poor Law household means test, which 'like the workhouse before it, was destined to leave an indelible mark on popular culture . . . long after its official demise . . . Receipt of transitional payment through the PACs in effect put the unemployed right back on to the Poor Law' (Fraser, 1984, p. 194).

It is often not appreciated that the desperate plight of many of the unemployed in the 1930s was not typical of the country as a whole. The unemployment rate varied widely between regions, and long-term unemployment was concentrated in a limited number of decaying areas. Whilst the unemployed suffered, living standards rose substantially for those in regular work.

The Unemployment Act 1934 was based on the report of the Holman Gregory Royal Commission in 1932, whose main recommendation was the complete separation of unemployment insurance proper from measures to support the long-term unemployed. The Act, consequently, was divided into two parts. Part I extended compulsory insurance to more workers; restored benefits to their level prior to the 1931 cut; organised contributions on the basis of one-third each from worker, employer and government; and established an independent committee to run the scheme, with responsibility only for those receiving *insurance* benefits. Part II dealt with unemployment assistance for people with no insurance cover, or whose cover had expired. Benefits were paid from general government funds, and run on a *national* basis by the newly established Unemployment Assistance Board. Payment was on the basis of need, in the light of family circumstances. The principle of less eligibility was finally laid to rest. Sixteen years after the end of the First World War, Britain had a system of unemployment relief which worked reasonably smoothly.

The social measures of the 1906–14 period were inadequate for the mass unemployment of the inter-war years. The Widows, Orphans and Old Age Contributory Pensions Act 1925 (extended by a further Act in 1929) introduced the first national scheme of contributory pensions; the 1911 health insurance scheme was enlarged; and there was action on housing. For the most part this legislation was a product of the 1920s. In the 1930s the welfare state was in abeyance, and new measures were little more than crisis management. The main lesson for the future was that *laissez-faire* capitalism could not solve the problem of unemployment – in this area, too, state intervention was necessary. When intervention came, in the form of rearmament and war production, the unemployment problem disappeared – an unhappy way of ending a particularly unhappy period in British social policy.

4 Inter-War Poverty Relief in the USA

4.1 THE ROOTS OF THE 'NEW DEAL'

It is instructive at this stage very briefly[1] to discuss contemporaneous events in the USA, where government involvement in income support (at least at the federal level) began late by international comparison. There was no American equivalent of the Liberal reforms, nor any analogue to the broadening of the British welfare system during and after the First World War. Until 1935 it was accepted that except in times of disaster no able-bodied person need be without work. Public assistance was regarded as charity, and its receipt generally carried social stigma. Until the 1930s such aid as existed came mainly from state and local government, though private schemes also had a limited role. By 1929 approximately 75 per cent of all relief derived from public funds, mostly local. *Until 1933 the federal government paid no grants and organised no programmes for relief or insurance, except for its own employees.* Emergency appropriations were made occasionally in the face of local disasters, but *no federal relief had ever been granted to the unemployed.*

Eligibility requirements and benefit levels varied widely by locality. Common among eligibility rules were: the taking of the 'pauper's oath'; disenfranchisement (in fourteen states); residency requirements; and the condition that recipients live in almshouses (US National Resources and Planning Board, 1942, pp. 26–8). In states where relief was granted to people not living in almshouses, payments were very low; and many localities gave benefits only in kind.

A detailed explanation of why these arrangements changed sharply in the 1930s lies outside the scope of this chapter and is, in any case, a subject of controversy. I shall do no more than set out the main questions. First, why did income support at a national level begin in the USA later than in almost any

---

[1] Lack of space precludes a fuller analysis. See the Further Reading.

other industrialised country[1] and, moreover, at a level which by international standards was low?[2] The arguments are complex (for an overview see Higgins, 1981, Ch. 4). Most writers concentrate on one or more of three sets of factors: the influence of ideology (see section 7.1); the cultural and political heterogeneity of the USA (Gronbjerg, Street and Suttles, 1978; Katznelson, 1978); and the influence of pressure groups (Menscher, 1967; Derthick, 1979; Weaver, 1982, Ch. 4).

A second question is why the 1930s legislation took the shape it did. To a minor extent it was influenced by the experience of other countries, notably Britain, Germany, France, Sweden and Canada. Considerably more important was the desire to head off more radical proposals. Douglas (1925) advocated a system of family allowances for dependants. The Townsend Plan in the early 1930s called for a monthly pension of $150 for everyone over 60. Simultaneously, Huey Long was pursuing his populist campaign to 'share our wealth'. The Social Security Act 1935 was in part 'a compromise measure to blunt the political appeal of the enormously expensive and essentially unworkable Townsend Plan' (Pechman, Aaron and Taussig, 1968, p. 32).

Why, finally, did reform occur when it did? Well before the 1930s, pressures for change were emerging out of various long-run developments, notably technological innovation, the decline of the family farm, and decreasing average household size (see Wilensky and Lebeaux, 1965, pp. 341–8). However, the crisis of the 1930s brought developments to a head. As unemployment mounted after 1929, local expenditure on relief rapidly outstripped declining tax revenues; and emergency assistance by states ran into similar problems, so that federal participation became inevitable. Under Title I of the Emergency Relief and Construction Act 1932, $300 million in federal funds was made available for loans to states to help in their relief efforts.[3]

4.2 THE SOCIAL SECURITY ACT 1935

Between 1933 and 1935 the federal government played an increasing financial and administrative role. The Civilian Conservation Corps, the Public Works Administration, and the Federal Civil Works Administration organised public works; the Federal Surplus Relief Corporation distributed surplus commodities to the needy; and the Federal Emergency Relief Act 1933 created the Federal Emergency Relief Administration to supervise federal grants to states

---

[1] By 1930, 27 countries had public schemes of poverty relief of some sort. Among industrialised countries only Norway, Japan and Switzerland started later than the USA (Pechman, Aaron and Taussig, 1968, Appendix C).

[2] Why, to use a concept first developed by Wilensky and Lebeaux (1965) and subsequently adopted by other writers (see Higgins, 1981, pp. 41–5), did the US adopt a *residual* model of welfare? We return to this issue in section 7.1.

[3] Repayment of these loans was eventually waived.

for unemployment relief. This last had the greatest impact, both at the time and through its influence on subsequent legislation. The use of federal funds gave federal government a measure of influence over the state programmes, in particular on benefit levels and administration, and these features were carried over into the permanent legislation.[1]

The 1935 Social Security Act created what, for the USA, was a broad-ranging scheme. It established two major insurance schemes and three major forms of assistance, administered by a new Social Security Board whose powers and duties were set out in Title VII of the Act.[2]

Federal Old Age Benefits (Title II) were financed by contributions from employees and employers under Title VIII and, as originally envisaged, were to be run largely on actuarial lines with respect to both benefit levels and financing (as we shall see shortly, the latter resolve was not effected).

Federal assistance to states for unemployment compensation was granted under Title III, financed by taxes levied on employers under Title IX. Unlike the pension scheme, which was federal, unemployment insurance was organised by states, which were given wide discretion over the precise form of their arrangements. Though the scheme (being insurance) provided no benefits for individuals currently out of work, this was much the most controversial part of the Act, many employers being bitterly opposed to any form of unemployment compensation. Nevertheless, by 1937 all the states and territories had such a scheme.

Old Age Assistance (Title I) provided for means-tested cash payments to the elderly through federal grants to states with approved schemes. It was envisaged that costs would decline as the insurance benefits under Title II became payable. By 1940 51 jurisdictions offered Old Age Assistance.[3]

Aid to the Blind (Title X) provided federal grants to approved state plans of aid to the needy blind. By 1940 43 states qualified for federal funds.

Aid to Dependent Children (Title IV) paid federal grants to states giving cash assistance to families with needy children 'under the age of 16 [or under the age of 18 if found by the state agency to be regularly attending school] . . . deprived of parental support or care by reason of the death, continued absence from the home, or physical incapacity of a parent.'[4] By 1939 42 jurisdictions

---

[1] For further details of the emergency programmes see US Federal Emergency Relief Administration, 1942; and US National Resources and Planning Board (1942, pp. 26–7).

[2] For the wording of the Act itself see Social Security Act, 14 August 1935, Ch. 531, 49 Statutes at Large 620, or for an edited version, Stevens, 1970, pp. 167–80.

[3] The 48 continental states, plus Washington DC, Alaska and Hawaii.

[4] Social Security Act 1935, Title IV, section 406(a). Phrase in brackets added by an amendment in 1939.

had schemes of this sort which qualified for federal funds.[1]

The 1939 amendments to the Social Security Act stressed its welfare objectives and broadened its scope. The strict actuarial principles of the 1935 legislation were diluted; insurance benefits became payable to dependants of aged recipients, and to widows and children of workers covered by the scheme; payments were to begin in 1940 rather than 1942; benefits were tied to average earnings over a minimum period, thus breaking the link with lifetime contributions; and the earnings test prescribed by the 1935 Act was slightly liberalised before the first benefits were paid.[2] The financial basis of the scheme also changed. The intention of accumulating an actuarially sound fund was abandoned, and benefits to the elderly and their dependants paid almost entirely out of current contributions, i.e. the scheme was organised on a 'pay-as-you-go' rather than a 'funded' basis, an issue discussed at length in Chapter 9.

A brief assessment   To a greater extent than the Liberal reforms the Social Security Act can be criticised as in certain respects a timid measure. The Act, admittedly, was an improvement on earlier arrangements: the range of benefits was broader, the age requirements for retirement more liberal, and the eligibility restrictions on residence and citizenship less stringent; and benefits were paid in cash, this being a condition of the federal contribution to state schemes.

In important respects, however, 'the . . . Act may be reasonably regarded as a conservative legislative solution to a difficult and explosive problem' (Pechman, Aaron and Taussig, 1968, p. 32). First, though the federal government ensured a certain degree of uniformity, state programmes still varied widely in terms of benefit levels and eligibility requirements. Second, the insurance arrangements were severely constrained: in 1940 only about 60 per cent of workers were covered; benefits were intended originally to bear a fairly simple relationship to contributions, thus ruling out any substantial redistribution (though this aspect was relaxed somewhat by the 1939 amendments); and the insurance benefits were subject to an earnings test. Third, the assistance measures were categorical, i.e. they granted aid only to individuals falling into one of the three categories, aged, blind, or dependent child, since it was felt that only these groups should ever require assistance

---

[1] A further eight states (Alaska, Connecticut, Illinois, Kentucky, Mississippi, Nevada, South Dakota and Texas) operated schemes without federal funds (US National Resources and Planning Board, 1942, p. 83).

[2] These changes were based on recommendations in US Advisory Council on Social Security (1938), which contains valuable background information. For details of the legislative history see Myers (1965, Ch. 4) or, more briefly, Pechman, Aaron and Taussig (1968, Appendix B).

during times of high employment.

It is possible, in conclusion, to argue that the historical importance of the original Social Security Act lies less in its precise legislative content, which was in many ways rather conservative, than in the way it gradually brought about public acceptance of income support as a permanent federal institution.

5 The Second World War and Its Aftermath

5.1 WARTIME ACTIVITY

The final climacteric in the development of the welfare state occurred in the years 1940–8. The Second World War was a total war; *everyone's* life was affected, and this, it is argued, led to important changes in attitude. The totality of the war effort forced the British government to adopt powers (e.g. rationing and the direction of labour) on a scale hitherto unknown. It also reduced social distinctions; unlike the divisive unemployment of the 1930s, food shortages and bombs affected all social classes (though not all areas) equally. The pressure of common problems prompted the adoption of common solutions. Attitudes were changed also by increased awareness of social problems as social classes mingled during the war. In the armed services men who would otherwise have led separate lives were thrown together. Evacuation, too,

> was part of the process by which British society came to know itself, as the unkempt, ill-clothed, undernourished and often incontinent children of bombed cities acted as messengers carrying the evidence of the deprivation of urban working-class life into rural homes. [Fraser, 1984, p. 210.]

As well as planning for the future, there was some action on social policy as a direct result of the war, including action on school meals, the transformation of the Unemployment Assistance Board, and dramatic changes in the organisation of health care. As a result of wartime food shortages, school meals and school milk, previously a form of charity, became a normal feature of school life. The needs of wartime diversified the activities of the Unemployment Assistance Board (renamed the Assistance Board). In particular, wartime inflation adversely affected pensioners, and legislation in 1940 allowed the Board to pay supplementary pensions on the basis of need. By 1941 it dealt with ten pensioners to every one unemployed person. It also helped others who fell outside the traditional categories – victims of bombing, evacuees, dependants of prisoners of war, etc. As a direct result of the war the Assistance

Board became a generalised relief agency, and so foreshadowed the National Assistance Board of 1948.

From 1939 onwards there were two sorts of hospital patient. Some received emergency treatment which was free, and financed and organised nationally. Others had to take their turn, as previously, in a voluntary or municipal hospital. Payment in the latter two cases was generally through membership of a contributory scheme to a voluntary hospital, or via a means test (Abel-Smith, 1964, Ch. 26). Initially only military personnel fell into the emergency category, but wartime exigencies extended the services to an ever-widening group of people. This served as an example of large-scale, state-financed health care and also exposed the deficiencies of the old system.

On the planning front the Beveridge Report (UK, 1942) has pride of place. The Report was based on three assumptions: that a scheme of family allowances would be set up; that there would be a comprehensive health care service; and that the state would maintain full employment. The Report envisaged a scheme of social insurance which would be

> all-embracing in scope of persons and of needs. . . . Every person . . . will pay a single security contribution by a stamp on a single insurance document each week. . . . Unemployment benefit, disability benefit [and] retirement pensions after a transitional period . . . will be at the same rate irrespective of previous earnings. [UK, 1942, pp. 9–10.]

Benefits were to be paid also for maternity, and to widows and orphans. Coverage was to be compulsory and (in contrast with the 1935 US Social Security Act) universal in respect of individuals and risk. Flat-rate contributions would give entitlement to flat-rate, subsistence benefits; there would be no means test; and the scheme was to be administered nationally.

The 1944 White Paper, *Social Insurance* (UK, 1944c), accepted most of these recommendations, and became the basis of the National Insurance Act 1946. In the same year two other major White Papers were published. *A National Health Service* (UK, 1944a) envisaged 'a comprehensive service covering every branch of medical and allied activity' providing free treatment on a universal basis, financed out of general taxation. *Employment Policy* (UK, 1944b) was very much a Keynesian document. It committed the government to 'the maintenance of a high and stable level of employment', brought about, where necessary, by counter-cyclical deficit spending. The economic radicals of 1931 had finally come into their own.

The true novelty of the Beveridge proposals, with hindsight, was their replacement of the old, haphazard and piecemeal methods by a coherent *strategy* embracing not only social insurance, but also family allowances, national assistance paid out of central government revenues, the national health service; and (possibly crucially) a presumption of high employment.

The major piece of social legislation during the war was the Education Act 1944, based on Butler's 1943 White Paper (UK, 1943). The Act, which met with strong approval, set the foundation for postwar education. It created a Ministry of Education, whose Minister had the duty of providing a comprehensive national system of what the Act called primary, secondary and further education. Primary and secondary education were to be free up to school-leaving age, which was to be raised to 15 in 1945[1] and to 16 as soon as possible thereafter. An accommodation was made with the voluntary church schools which were, in certain respects, integrated into the state system.

5.2 POLICIES 1946–8

The 1945 Labour government was armed with a large Parliamentary majority and a stack of White Papers, many of which had met with Conservative approval during the wartime coalition. Under the Family Allowance Act 1945 a payment of 5 shillings (25 pence) was made for the second and subsequent children in each family. The benefit was universal and paid out of general tax revenues.

The National Health Service Act 1946, based on the 1944 White Paper, established a national system of comprehensive health care available universally at no charge. The system was financed from general taxation, except for a small proportion from national insurance contributions. The detailed arrangements (Abel-Smith, 1964, Chs. 27–9) involved considerable discussion with the medical profession.

The National Insurance Act 1946 was based on the 1944 White Paper, which in turn followed closely the recommendations of the Beveridge Report. All insured persons were required to buy a weekly stamp (to which the employer also contributed), whose cost varied by age, sex, and marital and employment status. An employed person was eligible for flat-rate benefit under seven heads, including unemployment, maternity, sickness, widowhood, retirement, and a death grant to cover funeral costs. Beveridge had envisaged that it would take 20 years to build up entitlement to a full retirement pension, but in the event the Labour government implemented full pensions from October 1946.

Alongside the National Insurance Act was the National Insurance (Industrial Injuries) Act 1946, which entitled those injured at work to various benefits (usually at a higher rate than sickness benefit), financed by an identifiable component of the national insurance contribution. Because the scheme was compulsory it was possible to pool risks across industries with higher and lower accident rates (see Chapter 5:4.2).

---

[1] The school-leaving age had been set at 14 under Fisher's Education Act 1918.

The National Assistance Act 1948 established a safety net for those whose needs were not covered (or not fully covered) by insurance. The Act, like the other major Acts, was universal in approach. The old Assistance Board became the National Assistance Board. It administered means-tested supplementary allowances to those not in full-time work, whose income was below subsistence. In doing so it assumed the residual functions of the local Public Assistance Committees left over from the Poor Law, which was explicitly repealed by the Act.

The legislation of 1944–8 was, on the whole, successful. If the welfare state has any official birthday it is 5 July 1948, when the provisions of the National Insurance, Industrial Injuries, National Assistance and National Health Service Acts came simultaneously into effect, family allowances and higher pensions having been implemented in 1946. With unemployment below 250,000 the insurance fund made a surplus of £95 million in its first year, but the national health service cost more than anticipated.

There is considerable debate about the importance, or lack of it, of the Second World War in bringing about this legislation. Some writers regard the war as a *sine qua non* for subsequent events (Marshall, 1975; Titmuss, 1976, Ch. 4), others as merely one of a long chain of formative influences.

> The greatest achievement of the 1945–51 Government lay . . . in the firm rounding-off of half a century's constructive work of welfare, and the final shaping of the Welfare State on the lines first laid early in the century on the basis of nineteenth-century experience and investigation. [Bruce, 1972, p. 25.]

Since the issue is not fundamental to the book it is possible, with a clear conscience, to remain agnostic.

6 Recent Developments in Britain and the USA

This section reviews and briefly compares postwar developments in the UK and USA, concentrating mainly on cash benefits. Discussion of health care, education and housing is deferred to the relevant chapters.

Income support in the UK National insurance contributions continued broadly unchanged through the 1950s apart from periodic adjustments as prices and incomes rose. This regime came under pressure. An implication of a self-balancing fund is that total contributions must match total benefits. Since contributions (being flat-rate) could not exceed the reach of a low-income worker, benefits, too, had to be low. This constraint was gradually relaxed, motivated initially by the view that the flat-rate retirement pension was inadequate. So, from 1961 most employees were required to pay an additional, earnings-related pension contribution.

A fundamental change took place under the 1975 Social Security Act, which abolished the weekly stamp for most insured persons, and replaced it from April 1975 with an earnings-related contribution for all employed persons. In October 1985 a system of graduated contributions was introduced, i.e. the contribution rate was reduced for individuals with lower earnings. One of the effects of the changes was to enable the insurance system to redistribute from rich to poor (see Chapters 8 and 9).

National insurance benefits remained unchanged in broad outline for nearly 20 years. The National Insurance Act 1966 introduced an earnings-related supplement to unemployment and sickness benefit for certain employed people. This was abolished in 1982, and sickness benefits reformed in 1983 (see Chapter 8). The National Insurance Act 1971 introduced invalidity benefits for the long-term sick. On the pensions front, as we have seen, a supplementary contribution was levied from 1961, and the resulting increment to pensions became payable gradually in subsequent years. This was a minor change compared with the Social Security Pensions Act 1975, which was one of the most important pieces of social legislation since 1948. During the later 1960s and early 1970s there was much political wrangling over a series of pension proposals, including Labour's 'Crossman plan' and a Conservative scheme by Sir Keith Joseph, neither of which was implemented. The 1975 Act was in certain respects a blend of the two sets of proposals. In a wide-ranging overhaul it considerably extended earnings-related pensions and, for the first time, gave a statutory basis for the indexation of benefits.

The system of family support advocated by Beveridge remained largely intact until the late 1970s. It had two strands: a taxable family allowance for the second and subsequent child in any family, and an income tax allowance for all children. The resulting system was complicated (see Prest and Barr, 1985, Ch. 10, section 3.1) and did not give the greatest benefit to the poorest families (such interrelations between the tax and benefit systems will be a recurring theme). To avoid these difficulties the Child Benefit Act 1975 (a remarkable year for social legislation) abolished family allowances and child tax allowances, and replaced them, with full effect from April 1979, by *child benefit*, a weekly, tax-free cash payment in respect of *all* children in the family, with an additional payment for single parents (see Chapter 10).

Assistance benefits are also discussed in Chapter 10. The National Assistance Board was abolished in 1966, and a Supplementary Benefits Commission with wide discretionary powers established within what was later to become the Department of Health and Social Security. These arrangements remained in force until November 1980 when the Commission was wound up, and its discretionary powers replaced by legally binding regulations. Of greater importance was the large increase over the years in the number of recipients of national assistance/supplementary benefit.

The 1960s saw the 'rediscovery' of poverty (Abel-Smith and Townsend, 1965), including poverty among working families, who were normally not eligible for supplementary benefit. One response was the introduction in 1971 of family income supplement, a cash benefit for working families with children. The scheme's success was limited by problems with take-up (i.e. potentially eligible families not applying), and (again) anomalous interactions between the tax and benefit structures. At certain income levels a family was eligible for family income supplement, but also liable for income tax (Prest and Barr, 1985, p. 315).

More generally, the years after 1960 saw a proliferation of cash assistance benefits. Some directly paralleled the insurance scheme (e.g. pensions for people too old to have an adequate post-1948 contributions record); others were means-tested; and the relation between different benefits, and between benefits generally and the tax system, became highly complex and muddled, raising problems of the 'poverty trap' discussed in detail in Chapter 10:3. By the early 1970s there were over 50 benefits outside national insurance (UK, 1973, pp. 47–8).

A final development was the increasing regulatory role of the state in respect of occupational benefits. Two examples were the conditions imposed on private employers who wished to 'contract out' of the post-1975 pension arrangements (Chapter 9:1), and the requirement that employers administer benefits for short-term sickness after 1983 (Chapter 8:1.2).

Developments in the USA in the 1940s lay outside the social security system. The Full Employment Act 1946, which represented a considerable departure from previous policies, imposed on federal government the (implicitly Keynesian) responsibility for the maintenance of full employment. In the years after 1950 the insurance scheme was steadily broadened to the point where, together with various related programmes, virtually all workers and their dependants were covered. The parallel extension of risks covered is conveniently summarised by the changing name of the scheme: the 1935 Act concentrated on Old Age Insurance (OAI); survivor benefits were added in 1939 (OASI), disablement benefits in 1956 (OASDI), and various health benefits for the elderly and the poor in 1965 (OASDHI).[1]

---

[1] These were amendments, respectively, to Title II of the Social Security Acts of 1939 and 1956; for details see Stevens (1970, pp. 247–9 and 506 *et seq.*). Health care for the aged ('medicare') and the poor ('medicaid') was introduced as Titles XVIII (Health Insurance for the Aged) and XIX (Grants to States for Medical Assistance Programs) in the Social Security Act Amendments 1965 (30 July 1965, 79 Statutes at Large 286). For details see Stevens (1970, pp. 758–75).

The system of earnings-related contributions established by the 1935 Act remained broadly unchanged over the years. The benefit regime was liberalised in several respects: there were proportionately larger increases for lower-income workers (increasing the scheme's redistributive impact); benefits for survivors and dependants were raised relative to those for the insured person (increasing the support given to families); and the rules about the age of retirement were relaxed.

There was considerably less change in the system of assistance benefits. A new benefit, Aid to the Permanently and Totally Disabled, was established in 1950; and Aid to Dependent Children (renamed Aid to Families with Dependent Children) was liberalised in various ways in the 1960s. Of particular note, states were given the option after 1962 of paying benefit not only where the father was absent or disabled, but also where he was unemployed.

Health care for recipients of assistance (so-called 'medicaid') was introduced in 1965, at the same time as its inclusion for the elderly under the main insurance scheme ('medicare'). As we shall see in Chapter 13:1.1 this had major implications for the aggregate cost of health care.

Two events over the postwar period are of particular note: the 'welfare explosion' in the 1960s and 1970s; and the 'rediscovery' of poverty. The welfare explosion was a dramatic expansion in the size and cost of Aid to Families with Dependent Children. The increase was particularly great in the states with the largest cities, especially in New York (where numbers rose from 462,000 in 1963 to 951,000 five years later) and California (where numbers rose from 375,000 to 901,000).

> Governor Reagan complained last night that California's 'permissive' welfare system is encouraging teenaged girls to become pregnant and subsidising hippie communes at poor folks' expense. 'The Age of Aquarius smells a little fishy,' he told a sympathetic audience of conservative Republicans. [*San Francisco Chronicle*, 14 September 1970, p. 37.]

The phenomenon evoked considerable concern, particularly because it coincided with a period of low unemployment and sustained economic growth (see Gordon, 1969; Barr, 1971, Ch. 2; and Barr and Hall, 1981).

Poverty became a major political issue during the 1960s for the first time in thirty years not simply as a defensive response to the escalating numbers receiving assistance, but also for more positive reasons, at least during President Johnson's 'War on Poverty' (see, for instance US, 1969). With hindsight, however, the response to the crisis was long on words but muted in action. There was a measure of support for major reform, and a number of experiments with negative income tax took place (see Chapter 11:2.2), but changes *ex post* were small. President Nixon's Family Assistance Program proposed the abolition of existing assistance schemes and their replacement by a universal system of income supplementation. The McGovern 'Demogrant' advocated what was essentially a large-scale negative income tax. Nothing came of either proposal, partly because of the complexity of the issue, but largely because of a lack of political will in the face of their substantial cost.

The conclusion on the 1960s is that little had changed. Assistance programmes were still categorical, and still varied widely across states. The insurance system had been broadened considerably, but poverty persisted. The view of Wilensky and Lebeaux (1965, pp. xvi–xvii) remained (and remains) true:

> [The] United States is more reluctant than any rich democratic country to make a welfare effort appropriate to its affluence. Our support of national welfare programs is halting; our administration of services for the less privileged is mean. We move toward the welfare state but we do it with ill grace, carping and complaining all the way.

Comparative issues Four strategic issues are the subject of much of the rest of the book: the role of employment; the importance of social insurance; the relation between the benefit and tax systems; and the continued and substantial reliance on means-tested benefits. A high level of employment was seen in both countries as the primary method of income support. The UK government committed itself to such policies in its wartime White Paper (UK, 1944b). The US analogue was the Full Employment Act 1946. The retreat from these commitments in the 1980s is discussed briefly in Chapter 15:2.2.

Social insurance was the major line of defence. The coverage of the 1946 National Insurance Act was broader in three important ways than the Social Security Act as amended in 1939: it dealt with contingencies such as sickness, maternity and burial costs, which were not covered by US legislation; its coverage was virtually universal with respect to individuals; and, as its name implied, it was a *national* scheme (so, too, were assistance payments). In contrast, the US system (apart from federal retirement and disability insurance and, later, health insurance for the elderly) was organised by states, with wide variations in benefit levels and eligibility requirements.

The original intention of both Acts was to emulate private, actuarial insurance as closely as possible, both generally, and particularly in the way pensions were to be paid out of an accumulated fund. But political pressures and favourable demographic and economic trends resulted instead in pensions paid largely out of current contributions, starting in 1940 (USA) and 1946 (UK); and over the years political pressure led to further erosion of the insurance principle as the coverage of both schemes was broadened, and the relation between contributions and benefits relaxed. The overall result, in a

British context, was considerable erosion of the Beveridge strategy. The extent to which such benefits are (or should be, or can be) true insurance is one of the main topics of Chapters 5, 8 and 9.

Tax expenditures (see Chapter 7:1.1) served in both countries to buttress social insurance. Parallel to public pensions, for instance, was the tax relief granted to private schemes. Both methods provide income support for the elderly, though often with very different distributional consequences. That tax expenditures should properly be included in any assessment of income support has long been recognised in the academic literature (for early analyses see Surrey, 1948 and 1958; Titmuss, 1956), though awareness of the issue by politicians has come more slowly. Income tax is relevant also because of the increasing overlap between taxpayers and benefit recipients. Some social insurance benefits are taxable, an issue of acute relevance today when (in sharp contrast with the 1930s and 1940s) most adults are liable for income tax. The overlap is crucial also in connection with income-tested benefits, as we shall see in Chapters 10 and 11.

Reliance on means-tested benefits continued in both countries (and in many others) on a substantial scale despite the existence of wide-ranging social insurance and tax expenditures, and notwithstanding Beveridge's expectation that the assistance measures would become residual. This was partly because in Britain many of the insurance benefits were below the subsistence level established by national assistance/supplementary benefit (thus violating what Beveridge regarded as an essential ingredient of his proposals), and partly because of problems with take-up (see the Glossary). As a result, means-tested assistance continued in both cash (e.g. supplementary benefit, Aid to Families with Dependent Children) and kind (e.g. free medical prescriptions in the UK, 'medicaid' and food stamps in the USA).

The persistence of these benefits, and the large number of people involved, demonstrate that insurance and related measures were only partially successful in abolishing 'want'.[1] Studies in both countries (Abel-Smith and Townsend, 1965; US, 1969) revealed continuing and widespread poverty, partly due to factors outside the direct scope of income support (e.g. racial discrimination). But poverty was also found among the elderly and the unemployed, to whom social insurance was directly relevant.

Finally, as we have seen, there were two substantial differences. There remained a complete absence in the USA of any analogue of child benefit, notwithstanding the many countries which had such arrangements (France

---

[1] This is not to imply that income testing is *necessarily* a sign of a failing system of income support. For an interesting account of the Australian system, which deliberately relies on substantial income testing of most benefits, see Aaron (1984), and for a summary of social security institutions worldwide, US Department of Health and Human Services (1984).

introduced the first scheme before the First World War).[1] Nor was there anything remotely resembling the UK national health service. This remains true in the 1980s.

7 Concluding Issues: from the Past to the Present

7.1 INTERPRETING THE FORCES CREATING THE WELFARE STATE

Given the variety of influences on the welfare state, it is not surprising that there is controversy over which were the most important. The key issue is whether the dominant factor was ideology or the nature of the industrial process. The ideological debate concentrates on the *motives* underlying social legislation. A *liberal* (as defined in Chapter 3:1) interpretation of history attributes the development of the welfare state to the quest for social justice, and sees the events described earlier as progress along a road towards the good society. Fraser (1984, p. 157) writes of Lloyd George's 1909 'People's Budget' that '[here] was the essence of the novel approach: financial policy geared to the social needs of the people; the budget as a tool of social policy.'

Marxists, *per contra*, do not see the welfare state as arising out of a concatenation of disparate events, and certainly not as the result of a quest for social justice. They argue that the primary motive of social legislation has been the protection and preservation of the capitalist system. The welfare state, according to this view, fills two roles; it helps to meet the needs of the capitalist industrial system for a healthy, educated workforce; and it is the 'ransom' paid by the ruling élite to the exploited workforce in an attempt to contain social unrest. To a Marxist, the Liberal reforms were very limited and intended mainly to preserve the existing economic system. Unemployment, sickness and health benefits under the 1911 National Insurance Act applied only to limited classes of worker; and some historians argue that one of the main motives of the 1908 Pension Act (the only substantially redistributive measure) was to weed out of the workforce older men and women whose presence was reducing Britain's industrial efficiency in the face of international competition. These different views of the welfare state are discussed in more detail in Chapter 3:5.3.

Ideology, then, can be argued to have fostered the development of the welfare state either in the quest for social justice or as 'capitalist conspiracy'.

---

[1] For a review and international comparison of family allowances see Bradshaw and Piachaud (1980) and Kahn and Kamerman (1983).

But is ideology actually very important? Recent years have seen the development of the *theory of convergence* based on detailed studies of how welfare states (under whatever name) have arisen in different countries (see the Further Reading). The theory is based on two propositions: first, that all countries, *whatever their dominant ideology*, have over time developed very similar industrial structures (this is the so-called 'logic of industrialism'); and, second, that a welfare state in one form or another is an inevitable concomitant of this industrial structure. The theory therefore bases its argument on technological determinism. At its strongest, it asserts that the dominant force in the development of the welfare state is industrialism and, by implication, that ideology is largely irrelevant.

Ideology or technological determinism? I make no serious attempt to judge the two theories – but a few remarks are in order. The world is a complicated place, and I have a profound suspicion of almost any unicausal explanation of anything: marriages are rarely due *only* to love (or only to money); inflation is rarely caused *only* by monetary phenomena; and the Second World War was not caused only by Hitler, nor only by the Treaty of Versailles. So simply on a priori grounds it can be questioned whether either ideology (liberal or Marxist) or industrialism has a monopoly of truth. Most industrial countries face similar problems of unemployment and pockets of poverty, so it is not surprising that many have adopted broadly similar solutions; the logic of industrialism clearly has some validity.

But ideology also appears to play a part, if only in determining whether a country adopts a *residual* or an *institutional* model of welfare. The former accords welfare a role only when market or family structures break down, the latter regards it as an integral part of modern industrial society (Wilensky and Lebeaux, 1965, pp. 138–9; Higgins, 1981, pp. 41–5). Thus a 'capitalist' country like the USA has (and has always had) a system of income support and social services which is small relative to its population and national income (though it has a wide-ranging system of publicly provided education). A 'socialist' country like Sweden has a highly articulated welfare state; Denmark and New Zealand (which were not highly industrialised) were among the first countries with a public system of old age pensions; and Saskatchewan was the first Canadian province to have publicly organised health insurance.

It is clear, in conclusion, that the forces which created the British (or any other) welfare state are diverse and complex. The question 'how did it come about?' has no easy answer.

7.2 WHAT WAS CREATED?

The nature of what was created, as we have just seen, is a matter of controversy. Is the welfare state a step in the direction of the good society (discussed in detail in Chapter 3:3), an expensive and demeaning road towards totalitarianism (Chapter 3:2), or a cynical device to prop up the capitalist system (Chapter 3:4.2 and 5.3)? Setting these issues to one side, the successes of the post-1948 arrangements are twofold and clear. There is, first, a comprehensive system of income support which has been extended since 1948 in a variety of ways. The insurance arrangements are underpinned by a broad safety net in the form of supplementary benefit, which is organised nationally and for which *everyone* is potentially eligible. Many other countries have considerably less comprehensive systems. The second major success has been the national health service

[which] has brought to all the most obvious and immediate benefits. To many it *is* the Welfare State, and every survey . . . has shown how much it is . . . valued and taken for granted as part and parcel of British life. Serious defects and deficiencies there still are . . . [but] critics, seeing no visible alternative . . . devote their attention to improvement rather than to abolition. [Bruce, 1972, p. 330.]

The failures are also fairly clear. It is striking how many current and prospective problems have their roots or their parallels in the past. The difficulties with unemployment insurance between the wars raised questions about the extent to which unemployment is an insurable risk (see Chapters 5 and 8); the introduction of state pensions in 1908 was motivated in part by demographic problems (Chapter 9); the present antipathy to means testing (Chapters 10 and 11) is strongly influenced by the folk memory of the stringent household means test between the wars; the postwar distributional complexities arising out of the interaction between family allowances and child tax allowances will emerge in many guises; the housing measures during and after the First World War are a direct contributory cause of current difficulties with housing (Chapter 14); and similarly, the exploding costs of medical care in the USA (Chapter 13:1.1) stem in part (though far from wholly) from the introduction of 'medicare' and 'medicaid' in 1965.

Over and above these problems is the fact, despite the relative success of the cash benefit system, that poverty remains. In part this is because the poverty line has moved up as living standards and expectations have risen; but for many the issue is not just one of *relative* poverty, but of uncertainty and harsh discomfort (Mack and Lansley, 1985).

For some, the most important problem of all is the attack on the welfare state in the 1980s. The 'welfare consensus' on both sides of the Atlantic has been threatened (Higgins, 1981, pp. 150–7), though the roots of the attack, at least in America, go back further (Wilensky and Lebeaux, 1965, pp. xxxii–xxxvii). Public expenditure generally, and social spending in particular, have come under close scrutiny. Policy in the UK in the early 1980s included a reduction in unemployment benefits relative to other benefits, less generous indexation, and expenditure cuts in education and housing. The British government declared that a report suggesting large-scale dismantling of the welfare state was a 'dead duck'. However, in the words of a prominent member of the British poverty lobby, 'Dead ducks . . . have a habit of being served in individual pieces' (Lister, 1983, p. 3).

The change in attitude is highlighted by the contrast between the 1944 employment White Paper (UK, 1944b) committing the government to counter-cyclical demand management, and a more recent White Paper on the subject (UK, 1985b), which argued that unemployment should be tackled by reducing inflation, through wage restraint and through job training. The high summer of 1948 has passed. And though no one has a monopoly of wisdom, to some commentators at least, the Principles of 1834 (section 1.1) come rather readily to mind, thereby completing a historical circle.

Further Reading

Good general texts on the historical development of the British welfare state are Bruce (1972), Fraser (1984), Marshall (1975) and Thane (1982). Contemporary discussion of the 'New Liberalism' can be found in Hobson (1909); for recent analysis of economic and political thought at the time see Robbins (1977) and Freeden (1978). For a brief introduction to early poor relief see Rose (1972); on the principle of *laissez-faire* Taylor (1972); and on the Liberal reforms Hay (1975) (brief) or Gilbert (1973) (compendious). The early debates on unemployment are detailed in Harris (1972) and a history of health care prior to 1948 in Abel-Smith (1964). A brief official historical account is given in UK (1985 f, Ch. 3).

The origins of the modern welfare state are discussed explicitly by Harris (1977) (a magisterial biography of Beveridge) and Titmuss (1976) (who stresses the influence of the Second World War). The Beveridge proposals are contained in UK (1942) and those for the national health service in UK (1944a). Detailed historical statistics for the UK from 1855 to 1965 can be found in Feinstein (1972). For the modern institutions see Tolley (1986) (compendious) or (more briefly) UK (1985 f, Ch. 5).

For contemporary accounts of US developments in the 1930s see Douglas (1939), US Federal Emergency Relief Administration (1942) and US National Resources and Planning Board (1942). For retrospective analysis see Altmeyer (1966), Schottland (1963) or Witte (1962), and for later debates Tobin (1968) and US (1969) (a remarkable document). Details of US legislation are given in Stevens (1970).

For differing interpretations of the origins of the welfare state, including discussion of the theory of convergence, see Higgins (1981, Ch. 4) and Mishra (1981, Ch. 3) for a summary, and for specific views Wilensky and Lebeaux (1965) and Rimlinger (1971). A more general international comparison is given in Kaim-Caudle (1973). For a compendious summary of institutions internationally see US Department of Health and Human Services (1984).

3

Political Theory: Social Justice and the State[1]

The fundamental issue [of the welfare state] is not economic. It is moral. . . . The issue is the responsibility of people to manage their own affairs. . . . Is it not the case that while adults manage incomes children receive pocket money? The operation of the welfare state tends to reduce the status of adults to that of children. [Lord Bauer, 1983.]

[The] major evil [of paternalistic programs] is their effect on the fabric of our society. They weaken the family; reduce the incentive to work, save and innovate; reduce the accumulation of capital; and limit our freedom. These are the fundamental standards by which they should be judged. [Milton Friedman, 1980.]

Traditional socialism was largely concerned with the evils of traditional capitalism, and with the need for its overthrow. But today traditional capitalism has been reformed and modified almost out of existence, and it is with a quite different form of society that socialists must now concern themselves. [Anthony Crosland, 1956.]

---

[1] Readers with a limited background in political theory can find the gist of the argument in the Appendix to this chapter.

1 Theories of Society

A society is a co-operative venture for the mutual advantage of its members. It generally contains both an identity of interests and conflicts of interest between individuals and groups. The institutions of any society (e.g. its constitution, laws and social processes) have a profound influence on a person's 'life chances'. The purpose of a theory of society is to offer principles which enable us to choose between different social arrangements. In analysing the welfare state it is helpful to distinguish three broad types of theory: libertarian, liberal, and collectivist.

Libertarians (discussed in section 2) are in many ways the direct descendants of the 'Old Liberalism' of the nineteenth century (Chapter 2:1.1 and 2.1) though, as we shall see, with important differences between 'natural rights' and 'empirical' libertarians. The former (e.g. Nozick) argue that state intervention is *morally wrong* except in very limited circumstances. The latter, including writers like Hayek and Friedman, are the modern inheritors of the Classical liberal tradition;[1] they argue against state intervention not on moral grounds, but because it will *reduce total welfare*. Both groups analyse society in terms of its individual members (as opposed to the group or social class); give heavy weight to individual freedom; and strongly support private property and the market mechanism. As a result, the state's role *vis-à-vis* taxation and redistribution is severely circumscribed.

Liberal theories (section 3) are the modern inheritors of the 'New Liberalism' (Chapter 2:2.1). They find their philosophy in utilitarianism (section 3.1) and in writers like Rawls (section 3.2); their policy advocates in people like Beveridge, Keynes and Galbraith; and their practitioners in politicians like Harold Macmillan and John Kennedy. The theory has three crucial features. First, societies are analysed in terms of their individual members. Second, 'private property in the means of production, distribution and exchange [is] a contingent matter rather than an essential part of the doctrine' (Barry, 1973, p. 166), i.e. the treatment of private property is explicitly regarded not as an end in itself, but as a means towards the achievement of policy goals. Finally, liberal theories contain 'a principle of distribution which could, suitably interpreted and with certain factual assumptions, have egalitarian implications' (*ibid.*), i.e. in certain circumstances income redistribution is an

---

[1] There is a confusing ambiguity in the use of the word 'liberal'. In the nineteenth century it was used as a label for *laissez-faire* thinkers like Bentham and Nassau Senior (Chapter 2:1.1); and today a writer like Friedman, in calling himself a liberal, is using the term in the same way. I shall, throughout, refer to such writers as libertarians, and use the term 'liberal' in the sense described below.

appropriate function of the state. This book, as Chapter 4 will amplify, is firmly in the liberal tradition.

Collectivist theories, too, are varied. *Marxist* theory (section 4.2) draws its philosophy from Marx and its policies from writers like Laski, Strachey and Miliband. The theory sees industrial society as consisting of social classes, defined narrowly in terms of their relation to the means of production. Private property has only a limited role, and the allocation and distribution of resources in accordance with individual need is a primary concern of the state. *Fabian socialists* (section 4.1) present an intermediate case. They derive their philosophy from writers like Tawney, and find their policy advocates in, for example, Crosland and Titmuss, and their practitioners in politicians like Clement Attlee. Though sharing to some extent the egalitarian aims of Marxists, their analysis and methods have much in common with liberal thinking.

In practice the theories blur into one another like the colours of the rainbow, but it is useful for exposition to talk about them as separate entities, especially when contrasting their implications for policy (section 5). Nevertheless, their differences and similarities are complex, and involve subtleties well beyond the scope of one brief chapter. The purpose here is limited to sketching the ideological debate only in outline. Knowledgeable readers will, I hope, be forgiving.

2 Libertarian Views

It is necessary to return briefly to nineteenth-century debates (Chapter 2:1.1 and 2.1). The ideology of *laissez-faire* derived from two quite distinct sets of philosophical arguments. When modern writers like Hayek and Friedman advocate free markets and private property, they follow Hume (1770), Smith (1776), Bentham (1789) and Mill (1863) in doing so on a *utilitarian* or *empirical* basis, out of a belief that such institutions maximise total welfare. Nozick, in contrast, follows Spencer (1884) by defending private property on *moral* grounds, as a *natural right* (see Robbins, 1978, pp. 46 *et seq.*). Though not completely watertight, the distinction between the two views (exemplified by the first two quotes at the head of this chapter) is crucial to debates about policy (section 5), and so merits closer attention.

Natural rights libertarians To Nozick (1974) everyone has the right to distribute the rewards of his own labour. He calls this *Justice in Holdings*, which has three elements. A person is entitled to a holding if he has acquired it

(a) through earnings (so-called justice in acquisition), or (b) through the inheritance of wealth which was itself justly acquired (justice in transfer). Holdings which fall under neither principle cannot be justified, hence (c) government may redistribute holdings acquired illegally (the principle of rectification).

These propositions support the libertarian predilection for a minimalist or 'nightwatchman' state with strictly circumscribed powers: the state can provide one and only one public good, viz. the defence of our person and property, including the enforcement of contracts; but other than correcting past wrongs it has no legitimate distributional role at all. Nozick regards taxation as theft (since it extracts from people money (legitimately acquired) which they would otherwise have allocated in other ways), and also as slavery, in that people are forced to spend part of their time working for government.

Empirical libertarians Hayek's theory has three strands: the primacy of individual freedom; the value of the market mechanism; and the assertion that the pursuit of social justice is not only fruitless (because there is no such thing) but actively harmful because it can (and, he argues, will) end up destroying individual liberty. Freedom to Hayek (1960, Ch. 1) and other libertarians is defined narrowly as absence of coercion or restraint; it includes political liberty, free speech and economic freedom. Coercion is legitimate only in strictly limited cases, such as the protection of individual liberty (*ibid.*, Ch. 9). Individualism is the corollary of freedom, and the two are interdependent;[1] the pursuit of equality will reduce or destroy them (Hayek, 1944).

To Hayek the market is beneficial because it is efficient, and because it protects individual freedom.

> [It is] a procedure which has greatly improved the chances of all to have their wants satisfied, but at the price of all individuals . . . incurring the risk of unmerited failure. With the acceptance of this procedure the *recompense of different groups and individuals becomes exempt from deliberate control*. It is the only procedure yet discovered in which information widely dispersed among millions of men can be effectively utilised for the benefit of all – and used by assuring to all an individual liberty desirable for itself on ethical grounds. [Hayek, 1976, pp. 70–1, my emphasis.]

These advantages arise, according to Hayek, only if prices and wages are allowed to act as signals to individuals as to where to direct their efforts. An individual's reward will be that which induces him to act in the common good; it will often bear no relation either to his individual merit or his need.

Hayek's view of social justice contrasts sharply with that of Rawls. According to Hayek, a given circumstance (e.g. winning the pools, or dying

---

[1] See particularly the explanation of individualism in Hayek (1944, p. 44).

young) can be regarded as good or bad; but it can be described as just or unjust 'only in so far as we hold someone responsible for bringing it about or allowing it to come about' (*ibid.*, p. 31). Thus something is just or unjust *only if it has been caused by the action or inaction of an individual or individuals*. The market, in contrast (*ibid*, pp. 64–5), is an impersonal force like 'Nature', akin to an economic game with winners and losers, whose outcome can be good or bad, but never just or unjust. To Hayek, therefore, the whole notion of social justice is 'a quasi-religious superstition of the kind which we should respectfully leave in peace so long as it merely makes those happy who hold it.' (*ibid.*, p. 66). However, 'the striving for [social justice] will . . . lead to the destruction of the indispensable environment in which the traditional moral values alone can flourish, namely personal freedom' (*ibid.*, p. 67). The reason is that

> the more dependent the position of individuals . . . is seen to become on the actions of government, the more they will insist that the governments aim at some recognizable scheme of distributive justice; and the more governments try to realise some preconceived pattern of desirable distribution, the more they must subject the position of the different individuals . . . to their control. *So long as the belief in 'social justice' governs political action, this process must progressively approach nearer and nearer to a totalitarian system.* [*ibid.*, p. 68, my emphasis.]

Friedman's views are broadly of the same stripe. His primary value is individual freedom. Hence,

> the scope of government must be limited. Its major function must be to protect our freedom both from the enemies outside our gates and from our fellow-citizens: to preserve law and order, to enforce private contracts, to foster competitive markets. Beyond this major function, government may enable us at times to accomplish jointly what we would find it more difficult . . . to accomplish severally. However, any such use of government is fraught with danger. We should not and cannot avoid using government this way. But there should be a clear and large balance of advantages before we do. [1962, pp. 2–3.]

To Friedman and Hayek the state has no distributional role, other than for certain public goods and for strictly limited measures to alleviate destitution.

3 Liberal Theories of Society

3.1 UTILITARIANISM

The utilitarian arguments which form the basis of much of this book derive from the 'New Liberalism' of the early twentieth century (Chapter 2:2.1), which was itself firmly rooted in the nineteenth-century Classical tradition. Thus modern utilitarians have common intellectual roots with empirical libertarians.

The utilitarian aim is to distribute goods so as to maximise the total utility[1] of the members of society. 'Goods' are interpreted broadly to include goods and services, rights, freedoms and political power. Maximising total welfare has two aspects: goods must be produced and allocated *efficiently* (discussed in Chapter 4); and they must be distributed in accordance with *equity* (though not necessarily equally). The equitable distribution is shown in Figure 3.1. Total income to be distributed is *AB*. Individual A's marginal utility (read from left to right) is shown by the line *a–a*, and is assumed to diminish as his income rises. Individual B's marginal utility, which declines from right to left, is shown by the line *b–b*. Total utility is maximised when income is shared equally; A's income is *AC*, and B's is *BC*.

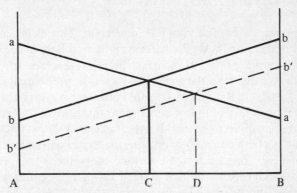

Figure 3.1   *The optimal distribution of income under utilitarianism*

Utilitarianism can therefore justify redistributive activity by the state in pursuit of an egalitarian outcome; but this result depends crucially on two conditions. First, A and B must have identical marginal utility of income functions.[2] If B's marginal utility is shown by *b'–b'*, then the distribution which maximises total welfare is unequal, since A now has an income of *AD*. Second, utilitarianism can fully specify the optimal distribution only where the utility of A and B can be measured cardinally.[3]

---

[1] Synonymously, to maximise total happiness or total welfare.
[2] Strictly, several other (technical) conditions are necessary, i.e. that the underlying social welfare function is symmetric and concave (see Chapter 6:1.2). For further discussion of Paretian utilitarianism and its underlying assumptions see Rowley and Peacock (1975, Ch. 1).
[3] For the definition of cardinal utility see the Glossary.

Various criticisms have been made of this approach. It is asked whether utility is capable of precise definition; whether interpersonal comparison of utility has any meaning; and whose utility counts (e.g. future generations, animals, etc.)? These questions are set to one side to focus on the fundamental criticism, namely that utilitarianism can *sanction injustice* by justifying harm to the least well-off if this maximises total utility. 'The trouble with [utilitarianism] is that maximising the sum of individual utilities is supremely unconcerned with the interpersonal distribution of that sum' (Sen, 1973, p. 16). Formally, suppose that individual B in Figure 3.1 derives less pleasure from life than A because he is disabled. His marginal utility is shown by the line $b'-b'$, and the optimal distribution of goods by point D. Thus B should receive *less* income than A because he is disabled. This outcome is criticised as being unjust.

3.2 RAWLS ON SOCIAL JUSTICE

Rawls in some ways is Nozick's liberal counterpart. Nozick is a natural rights defender of liberty. For Rawls the natural right, and hence the prime aim of institutions, is *social justice*: thus 'each person possesses an inviolability founded on justice that even the welfare of society as a whole cannot override' (1972, p. 2). Justice, to Rawls, has a twofold purpose: it is desirable for its own sake on moral grounds; but also, and importantly, institutions will survive only if they are perceived to be just. Rawls argues that there exists a definition of justice which is both *general* (i.e. not specific to any particular culture), and can be derived by a process which everyone can agree is fair. The resulting principles deal with the distribution of what Rawls calls 'primary goods', i.e. economic goods, and also position, opportunity, skill, liberty and self-respect.

The original position is Rawls's starting-point. He assumes that each person has goals which are facilitated by the possession of these primary goods, and invites us to contemplate a group of rational individuals, each concerned only with his own self-interest, coming together to negotiate the principles of justice. They are free agents in the negotiation, but they must abide by the resulting principles. Rawls thus uses the convention of a *social contract*.

In this situation no discussion between interested parties will yield principles of justice which command universal acceptance. Rawls therefore abstracts the negotiators from their own society by placing them behind a *veil of ignorance*. They are assumed to be well informed about the general facts of the world – psychology, economics, sociology, etc., but each is *deprived of all knowledge about himself*, i.e. of his natural characteristics or endowments, his position in society, and the country or historical period into which he is born. The negotiators seek to advance their own interests, but are unable to distinguish them from anyone else's.

The role of the veil of ignorance is best illustrated by example. To distance ourselves from personal interests we (i.e. citizens through our elected representatives) may decide that aircraft hijackers' demands should never be met, even if innocent lives are lost. We do this in order to save even more lives in the long run; and we establish this doctrine in advance of the event (i.e. behind the veil of ignorance) because if it were our personal loved ones who were kidnapped we would be likely to do anything to save them, irrespective of the possible consequences for others in the future.

The negotiators can consider any principle of justice, e.g. the just action is that which is in the interests of the stronger; or that which ennobles the species; or that which maximises total utility. According to Rawls, the rational negotiator will reject all these definitions because under each he might systematically be underprivileged. The only rational choice is to select principles in terms of what Rawls calls the 'maximin rule' which maximises the position of the least well-off individual or group. The negotiators do this because 'for all they know they may turn out to be the least privileged inhabitants of a country like South Africa' (McCreadie, 1976, p. 117).

The original position, together with the veil of ignorance, plays two distinct roles. First, it is an analytical device, which 'reduc[es] a relatively complex problem, the social choice of the principles of justice, to a more manageable problem, the rational individual choice of principles' (Daniels, 1975, p. xix). Second, and possibly of greater importance, Rawls sees the procedure of rational, self-interested negotiation behind the veil of ignorance as a *moral justification* of the resulting principles – they will be seen to be fair, he argues, because they are selected in a manner which is both rational and fair, hence his term 'justice as fairness'.

The principles of justice which follow are those which Rawls claims would be chosen rationally and unanimously by the negotiators. Because of the veil of ignorance, they will choose to maximise liberty for everyone. Hence:

The First Principle (the 'Liberty Principle'): 'Each person is to have an equal right to the most extensive basic liberty compatible with a similar liberty for others' (Rawls, 1972, p. 60).

The negotiators then turn to the distribution of the other primary goods. Each will reject any principle of distribution which could leave him disadvantaged or exploited.

The negotiators may consider a principle that mandates a thoroughly equal distribution of goods. . . . But they will soon come to realise that they stand to benefit by the introduction of certain inequalities in the distribution of advantages. For example, giving a rural [doctor] an airplane would make him relatively advantaged, but even – and perhaps especially – the least advantaged among the rural populace stand to benefit as a result, and thus should sanction such inequality. [Gorovitz, 1975, p. 281.]

Hence:

The Second Principle (the 'Difference Principle'): 'Social and economic inequalities are to be arranged so that they are both (a) to the greatest benefit of the least advantaged and (b) attached to offices and positions open to all under conditions of fair equality of opportunity' (Rawls, 1972, p. 83).

The possibility of a conflict between the two principles is ruled out by a *Priority Principle*, which gives the first principle absolute priority over the second. A reduction in the liberty of the least well-off cannot be justified even if it is to their economic advantage. In addition, in the second principle he gives priority to part (b) over part (a). Subject to these priorities the two principles can be regarded, more simply, as a special case of a more general conception of justice, in which, 'all social primary goods – liberty and opportunity, income and wealth . . . are to be distributed equally unless an unequal distribution of any or all of these goods is to the advantage of the least favoured' (*ibid.*, p. 303). At its simplest, the distribution of goods between individuals A and B in Figure 3.1 should be that shown by point C unless any other distribution benefits the less advantaged of the two. If goods are not so distributed, then any policy which improves the position of the less well-off would be an improvement according to Rawls.[1,2]

Rawls and utilitarianism   Rawls is an explicit opponent of utilitarianism. He regards it as illogical (inasmuch as it would be rejected by rational negotiators in the original position) and as unjust (in that it can sanction injustice in the interests of maximising total welfare). The two theories can have very different implications. Suppose a given policy change makes at least one person better-off without making anyone else worse-off. This is an increase in Pareto efficiency,[3] and hence desirable to utilitarians even if the individual thus benefited were rich. Rawls's Difference Principle, in contrast, would oppose the policy unless it were also (though not necessarily only) to the advantage of the least well-off. Thus an efficient answer in Paretian terms will not always be a just answer in a Rawlsian sense (though, as argued in Chapter 4:2.2, it may be possible to find a distribution which is both just in a Rawlsian sense *and* Pareto efficient).

---

[1] Under the lexical extension of the difference principle any policy should benefit the worst-off individual; if he/she is indifferent, it should benefit the next worse-off, and so on. Rawls thus admits a policy which benefits *only* the best-off, provided that everyone else is indifferent to it.

[2] Formally, a utilitarian social welfare function (see Chapter 4:1) does not constrain the way individuals are weighted; a Rawlsian social welfare function gives infinite weight to the least-advantaged individual/group.

[3] See Chapter 4:2.1 and the Appendix to Chapter 4, paras 2–4.

Criticisms of Rawls's theory are summarised only briefly. It has been argued that the veil of ignorance would be immobilising, i.e. the negotiators would be unable to make any decisions at all. According to Nisbet (1974, p. 112),

> [the negotiators] don't know much of anything – anything, that is, that we are justified by contemporary psychology in deeming requisite to thought and knowledge of any kind whatever. Nevertheless, Professor Rawls is shortly going to put his happy primitives through feats of cerebration that even the gods might envy. Out of the minds of his homunculi, these epistemological zombies who don't know their names, families, races, generation or societies of origin, are going to come principles of justice and society so vast in implication as to throw all present human societies into a philosopher's limbo.

Miller (1976) (discussed shortly in more detail) similarly argues that removing *all* cultural knowledge will immobilise the negotiators; but failure to do so, though permitting them to make a decision, will result in a culture-bound definition of justice.

Criticisms of the first principle concern Rawls's definition of liberty and his assertion of its primacy. It is argued[1] that Rawls's list of liberties may be too narrow; that the principle of toleration (e.g. of diversity of goals) inherent in Rawls's definition of liberty may reflect class bias; and that some issues are left unresolved, e.g. what liberty should be accorded racists? Additionally, Barry (1973, p. 6) and Hart in Daniels (1975, p. xxx) dispute the priority given to liberty. Poor people might well be willing to trade some liberty for greater social or economic advantage. The second principle is criticised for its crucial dependence on maximin which, it is argued (Letwin, 1983, pp. 22–9; Arrow, 1973), is the optimal outcome only under very restrictive assumptions. It is also criticised by Marxists as being incompatible with any substantial degree of class conflict.

Finally, some writers argue that Rawls has developed not a *general* theory of justice, but a liberal theory. Rawls set out to find an 'Archimedean point' from which a culture-free definition of justice could be derived, but

> in the end the 'Archimedean point' for judging the basic structure of society that Rawls seeks eludes him. Every political theory, and every theory of justice, expresses a particular political and moral perspective. Rawls' achievement, which is considerable, is indeed to have produced *a* theory of justice – a theory of liberal democratic justice. [Lukes, 1972, quoted by Daniels, 1975, p. xvi.]

---

[1] See Daniels (1975, pp. xxviii–xxix) and the chapters therein by Hart, Scanlon, Daniels and Fisk.

Miller's analysis of social justice   Miller (1976) argues that a completely general theory of justice is logically impossible; and that in this respect Rawls was bound to fail. According to Miller, social justice has three distinct elements:

> *rights*, e.g. political liberty, equality before the law;
> *deserts*, i.e. the recognition of each person's actions and qualities;
> *needs*, i.e. the prerequisites for fulfilling individual plans of life.

The 'deserts' aspect implies, ceteris paribus, that someone who works longer hours should receive more pay, and the 'needs' aspect that an individual incapable of work should not be allowed to starve. Though admitting the difficulty of precise theoretical definition, Miller argues that each element is a logically distinct principle embodying a particular type of moral claim.

It is easy to see that rights and deserts can be reconciled (e.g. a man should have the right to keep all his income if he has earned it legally); similarly, rights and needs can be compatible (e.g. a man should be entitled to health care if he is ill). But conflict can arise between desert and need: if I am rich and healthy and you are poor and ill, then either I am taxed (and do not receive my deserts) to pay for your medical treatment, or you receive no treatment (hence your need is not met) so as to protect my deserts.

The essence of Miller's argument is that the definition of social justice depends crucially on the type of society being discussed. In a pure market economy justice will be defined in terms of rights and the requital of deserts. A collectivist defines justice as distribution according to need.

Miller thus argues that the different principles of justice are connected to wider views of society. He criticises utilitarians and Rawls, first, because they take no explicit account of the conflicting claims of rights, deserts and needs, but blur them into a single, indistinct whole. Second, Miller criticises the view implicit in Rawls that there is a single conception of justice upon which everyone's definition will converge, arguing instead that justice comprises conflicting principles, the relative weights attached to which may vary sharply between different societies.

> The whole enterprise of constructing a theory of justice on the basis of choice hypothetically made by individuals abstracted from society is mistaken, because these abstract ciphers lack the prerequisites for developing conceptions of justice. [Miller, 1976, p. 341.]

If they do manage to make choices it must be in terms of culturally acquired attitudes. In short, the negotiators in the original position will be immobilised unless they have some knowledge of the nature of the society for which they are choosing rules of justice. Finally,

> Rawls' individuals are given the attitudes and beliefs of men in modern

market societies, and it is therefore not surprising that the conception of justice they . . . adopt should approximate to the conception . . . dominant in those societies. [*ibid.*, p. 342.]

Hence, he argues, Rawls fails to develop a *general* theory of social justice; such generality is not possible.

4 Collectivist Views

4.1 FABIAN SOCIALISM

Collectivist writers agree on the importance of equality. They regard resources as available for collective use, and consequently favour government action; but they disagree about whether socialist goals can be achieved within a market order. Some writers advocate a mixed economy which blends private enterprise and state intervention; Marxists (discussed in section 4.2) argue that this is not possible; that capitalism is inherently unjust; and that socialism is possible only where the state controls the allocation and distribution of most resources.

Socialist aims vary widely, but three are central – equality, freedom and fraternity. It is recognised that they can clash; and different writers accord them different weight; but together they make up the socialist definition of justice. In Miller's terms the dominant themes are rights and needs, with deserts (though not entirely left out) assigned a smaller role.

There is a measure of agreement (Tawney, 1953 and 1964; Crosland, 1956; and, for a counter-view, Donnison, 1972) that the crucial element of justice is equality, which to socialists is an active concept. Equality of opportunity on its own may be insufficient (Laski, 1967, Ch. 4; Tawney, 1964), since substantial inequality of outcome may persist. Positive equalising measures are needed, though not necessarily complete equality of outcome.

Such emphasis on equality bears closely on Miller's concept of need. Weale points out that 'in some political arguments . . . the assumption is made that to distribute according to need is to satisfy the claims of equality' (1978, p. 67), but suggests (Ch. 5) that the relationship is rather more complicated. For our purposes it is necessary only to note that the concepts of equality and meeting need are closely related, though not logically equivalent.

The socialist concept of freedom is broad. It embraces the free exercise of individual choice (which is possible only if there is no poverty and no substantial inequality of wealth and power), and extends from legal and political relations to economic security. Thus individuals should have some power in relation to their conditions of work, including stability of employment, and should not be subject to the arbitrary power of others. In sharp contrast with libertarian views,

> the socialist believes that freedom is the product of government action rather than government inaction. Only government action through law, economic, social and fiscal policy can redistribute freedom so that its exercise can become a reality for all. [George and Wilding, 1976, p. 66.]

The third major value is fraternity. To a socialist this

> means co-operation rather than competition, an emphasis on duties rather than rights, on the good of the community rather than on the wants of the individual, on altruism rather than self-help. [*ibid.*, p. 66.]

Altruism (e.g. Titmuss, 1970) is a recurring theme in later chapters.

Socialist criticism of the free market starts with the motive given to individuals to pursue personal advantage rather than the general good (see Tawney, 1921), and denies the libertarian assertion that the former brings about the latter. Second, the market is undemocratic, inasmuch as some decisions with widespread effects are taken by a small power élite, and others are left to the arbitrary distributional effects of market forces. Third, the market is unjust because it distributes rewards which are unrelated to individual need or merit, and because the costs of economic change are distributed arbitrarily. Fourth, the free market is not self-regulating; in particular, left to itself, it is unable to maintain full employment. Lastly, the market has not been able to abolish poverty, let alone inequality. In sum,

> production is carried on wastefully and without adequate plan. The commodities and services necessary to the life of the community are never so distributed as to relate to need or to produce a result which maximises their social utility. We build picture palaces when we need houses. We spend on battleships what is wanted for schools. . . . We have, in fact, both the wrong commodities produced, and those produced distributed without regard to social urgency. [Laski, 1967, p. 175.][1]

Socialists are in general agreement over the failings of the free market, and in their choice of aims; but they part company over the best way of achieving them. Though the distinction is far from watertight, and is disputed by some writers, it is useful for exposition to contrast the 'fundamentalists' (largely Marxists), who entirely reject capitalism and its associated pattern of economic and social relations, with the 'revisionists' who hold that the ills of society can

---

[1] Having read this paragraph it is instructive to re-read the quote from Hayek (1976, pp. 70–1) on page 45, on the virtues of the market.

be corrected within a broadly capitalist framework.

Revisionists see two great changes in the capitalist system; first, government today has a large role to play in economic life as well as in other areas; second, the classical entrepreneur has largely disappeared, the ownership of modern corporations being both diffuse and largely separate from the people who manage them. It is argued in consequence (see the quote by Crosland at the head of the chapter) that capitalism has been 'tamed', and that the resulting mixed economy, with an active role for government in the distribution of goods, income and power, is fully compatible with socialist objectives.

4.2 THE MARXISTS

This is not a Marxist book and I am no Marxist writer, so this section seeks only to sketch out as much Marxist thought as is necessary to contrast it with other theories (see the Further Reading). In considering the Marxist view of capitalism we need to turn our minds to three things: the contrast between the Marxist approach and that of conventional economic analysis; its analysis of the exploitation of labour; and its view of the role of government in supporting capitalism.

The Marxist approach differs substantially from that of the classical political economists like Smith (1776) and Ricardo (1817), for whom the production of commodities was largely independent of the society in question. This approach has continued to dominate economic thinking. It is argued that conventional economic theory is applicable to the USA, to Britain, to Sweden, to Yugoslavia and to the Soviet Union; and such economic analysis is seen as almost entirely separate from political and social arrangements. Thus to Sweezy (1942, p. 5), 'economic theorising is primarily a process of constructing and interrelating concepts from which all specifically social content has been drained off'. A key part of Marx's thought, in contrast, is that the economic, political and social structure of a society is determined largely by its dominant *mode of production*. It is argued that the capitalist mode of production will result not only in a particular form of economic organisation, but also (and inevitably) in a particular and inequitable structure of social class and political power.

The exploitation of labour under capitalism is a central tenet of Marxist thought. Conventional economic theory sees individuals as selling their labour services (more or less) freely in a (more or less) competitive market; the wage is established when the demand for labour equals its supply which, under competitive conditions, results in a wage rate equal to the marginal product of labour. Capital, similarly, receives its marginal product which, under competitive conditions and in the long run, is equal to the 'normal' rate of profit plus any premium for risk. Under certain conditions[1] these payments to factors exhaust the product leaving no surplus; thus, it is argued, there is no exploitation. In a Marxist analysis of the labour market this *apparently* free exchange of labour services (called *labour power*) for the wage is seen as a key feature of the capitalist mode of production. But for most people the sale of their labour power is their only means of subsistence, since other methods (e.g. the cultivation of common land) are largely blocked. Thus,

> in the capitalist mode of production the worker is *forced* to sell his/her labour power because he/she has no substantial savings or independent access to the means of production. . . . Hence the relations of production are *enforced* through the institution of the labour market. [Ginsburg, 1979, p. 21, my emphasis.]

Because of this compulsion, the capitalist is able to extract *surplus value* from the labour he employs. Marx's argument is complex, but in essence exploitation arose because the capitalist was obliged to pay only a weekly wage sufficient to support the worker and his family at around subsistence, but could then extract as much output as possible by imposing long working hours. The surplus value is the difference between the value of a worker's output and his wage and is, according to Marx, much greater than that necessary to yield a 'normal' rate of profit. This view, suitably modified to account for wages above subsistence, is held by Marxists today (see Robinson and Eatwell, 1973, pp. 28–9). Individuals whose only source of income is the sale of their labour thus have less power than the (fewer) people with more choice (e.g. because they own wealth and/or have independent access to the means of production). Marx argued that this inequality of power is inevitable in a capitalist society, and consequently the more powerful few are able to exploit labour by extracting its surplus value, hence enjoying a disproportionate share of output.

Because of its exploitative nature, Marx's attitude to capitalism 'was one of total rejection rather than reform and much of his intellectual effort went into proving that the capitalist system was both unworkable and inhuman' (Mishra, 1981, p. 69). The heart of the argument is that the capitalist mode of production causes conflict between one class (the large, poor, exploited working class) and another (the small ruling class, which derives power from wealth and/or political influence), and that conflict between these classes is inherent and inevitable.

---

[1] Euler's theorem states that paying all factors their marginal product will lead to product exhaustion under constant returns to scale. This can occur *either* where the production function exhibits constant returns to scale at all levels of output *or* at the point of minimum long-run average cost.

The role of government in a capitalist society   Given this position, it is necessary to ask why capitalism has survived despite the numerical superiority of the working class. The first reason, according to Marxists, relates to *economic* power, which is concentrated in a small number of hands. The second is the distribution of *political* power. The ruling class dominates government decisions, Marxists argue, both because of its economic power and because members of the economic élite share a common education and social class with the political élite. Accordingly, government in a capitalist society always favours the ruling élite (Miliband, 1969, Chs 4–6). Third, there is the power of the ruling class over *ideas*. The arguments are complex and the details controversial (see Strachey, 1936; Miliband, 1969, Ch. 8). From this prop to capitalism derives the Marxist emphasis on 'consciousness raising'.

All three factors constitute the Marxist explanation of the continuance of capitalism despite class conflict. But there is disagreement whether the resulting structure supports capitalists by furthering the interests *only* of the ruling class, or whether the state, rather more broadly, supports the entire capitalist *system*, with some benefits also for the working class. Gough (1979, pp. 13–14) criticises some Marxist writers for ignoring the effects of class conflict; he argues that in order to protect the capitalist system in the face of working-class pressure the state has extended the benefits of the welfare state, with gains not only for the ruling élite, but for workers as well.

The Marxist state   The next step is to outline the Marxist definition of a just society and the role of government necessary for its achievement. Marxists share the socialist triad of liberty, equality and fraternity, though with some differences in interpretation and in their relative weights. Liberty is a much more active concept than the mere absence of coercion. It cannot exist where economic or political power is distributed unequally, nor where the actions of the state are biased (Laski, 1967, Ch. 4; Miliband, 1969, Ch. 7); freedom, moreover, includes a substantial measure of equality and economic security. To a Marxist, therefore, freedom and equality are two essential and intermingled aspects of social justice. This contrasts very sharply with the liberal perspective, in which the possible conflict between freedom and equality creates the central problem of political economy.

Equality to a Marxist does not necessarily imply complete equalisation. According to Laski (1967, p. 157), 'the urgent claims of all must be met before we can meet the particular needs of some'. Once this basic condition has been met, differences in rewards should depend on effort or ability. It can therefore be argued that the Marxist aim is not one of equality, but of meeting need which, as we have seen (Weale, 1978), is a related but logically distinct objective. In Miller's terms, the Marxist definition of justice is based largely on needs, with rights somewhat secondary and with a small place for deserts.

Finally, we turn to the methods advocated by Marxists for the achievement of these aims. It is clear that their view of society, particularly the emphasis on economic equality and analysis of class conflict, implies a highly active role for government. They stress the importance of nationalising the means of production, both because profits though produced socially generally accrue to a few large shareholders, and because private ownership of productive resources is incompatible with the Marxist definition of freedom. Though not a panacea, nationalisation is regarded as essential to the achievement of Marxist aims, including industrial democracy which is seen as a necessary concomitant of political democracy. An additional purpose is to ensure that industry is run for social rather than private benefit.

Thus a Marxist society would combine public ownership and government planning with wide-scale participation by workers in decisions affecting their lives. Libertarians argue that there is too much planning in the welfare state, Marxists that there is not enough – planning, they argue, far from reducing individual freedom, enhances it. It is quite logical that each side should reach the conclusion it does – planning reduces freedom defined by libertarians as the absence of coercion, but (if successful) enhances freedom defined by socialists to include some guarantee of economic security.

5 Implications for the Role of the State

5.1 THEORETICAL ISSUES

This section compares the theories, and discusses their implications for policy generally (section 5.2) and the welfare state in particular (section 5.3).

Criticisms of liberalism by libertarians centre largely on the definition of individual freedom. The liberal concept includes economic security, so that social justice embraces needs as well as rights and deserts. Libertarians criticise the inclusion of needs (at any rate above subsistence) because the resulting institutions (e.g. taxation) abridge natural rights (Nozick); are part of a slippery slope towards totalitarianism (Hayek); and reduce economic efficiency. Several counter-arguments are possible. The first concerns Hayek's argument that it is not possible to define social justice. As we shall see in Chapter 6, many concepts, including poverty and inequality, are hard, if not impossible, to define; but this does *not* imply that no such phenomena exist. Defenders of Rawls would argue, in addition, that the priority of the liberty principle is explicit protection against the Hayekian slippery slope; and also that redistribution does not violate individual rights where it was agreed behind the veil of ignorance, as part of the social contract.[1]

Criticisms of liberalism by collectivists arise, first, because of the greater collectivist emphasis on needs. Additionally, collectivists adopt a broader definition of freedom. As a case in point, Daniels (1975) criticises Rawls's Liberty Principle, because it underestimates the effect of economic inequality on political liberties; as a result the two principles may be incompatible. Marxists also criticise liberal theories because they leave out class conflict.

Criticisms of libertarianism   There is no opposition by liberals to markets *per se*. But they attack the libertarian emphasis on *free* markets, which can distribute resources unjustly by failing to meet individual need. More specifically, Hayek (1976, pp. 64–5) has a view of markets as a game with winners and losers; but it can be argued that it is a game without rules, like a boxing tournament in which participants are not divided into different classes by weight. To liberals this violates the assumption of equal power on which, *inter alia*, the advantages of a market system depend (see Chapter 4:3.2). Collectivists criticise the libertarian definition of freedom as too narrow, and regard equality and economic security as inseparable aspects of freedom (contrast Hayek, 1944, Ch. 9, and Laski, 1967, p. 520). In addition, Marxists reject the market system entirely.

Criticisms of collectivism   It follows that libertarians entirely reject collectivist views. Attempts to distribute resources equally or in accordance with need are regarded as violations of individual freedom. Liberals criticise collectivist views not because they include need in their definition of social justice, but because they give it pride of place.

5.2 POLICY IMPLICATIONS

Private property is inviolate only to natural rights libertarians like Nozick (1974, Ch. 7), for whom justice in holdings implies total freedom for the individual to allocate as he chooses those resources which he has justly

---

[1] There is at times an opacity about Hayek's arguments about social justice. He states (1976, p. xi) that '[eventually] I perceived that the Emperor had no clothes on, that is, that the term "social justice" was entirely empty and meaningless. . . . The more I tried to give it definite meaning the more it fell apart.' Yet, in discussing Rawls he observes that 'the differences between us seemed more verbal than substantial' (p. xiii). Later, he argues 'that the recognition that in such combinations as "social", "economic" [or] "distributive" . . . justice the term "justice" is wholly empty should not lead us to throw the baby out with the bath water' (p. 100), since if *distributions* cannot be just, *institutions* can. On the latter point Hayek claims that he and Rawls are in agreement.

acquired. To Marxists, resources are available collectively to be distributed according to need, hence their emphasis on public ownership, and the view that 'property is theft' (see Laski, 1967, Chs 5 and 9).

To liberals, private property and public ownership are a pragmatic matter, and government should be free to adopt whichever mix of the two is most helpful in achieving its aims. Rawls maintains that his two principles are compatible with either private or public ownership of resources, or with a mixed economy. Empirical libertarians, as we shall see shortly, accord private property a major but not overriding role; and Fabian socialists allow it a more important role than is the case with Marxists.

Taxation to Nozick means that an individual will work (say) three days a week for himself, and spend two days working compulsorily for the government; to Nozick, therefore, it is taxation, not private property, which is a form of theft. It is, however, mistaken to attribute this view to all libertarians. The necessity of taxation was always acknowledged by the Classical liberals (Robbins, 1978, Ch. 2), albeit with some reluctance because of the consequent interference with liberty. The modern inheritors of this position like Hayek and Friedman concede the necessity of some taxation for the provision of public goods (narrowly defined) and for poverty relief (generally at subsistence).

To collectivist writers (Tawney, 1964, pp. 135–6) taxation for any social purpose is entirely legitimate. Liberals, also, regard taxation as an appropriate means towards policy objectives, though they are concerned about its disincentive effects particularly on labour supply, and more generally with selecting an optimal trade-off between efficiency and social justice (Atkinson and Stiglitz, 1980, Lectures 12–14).

Redistribution Distributive justice is not a problem for everyone. To Marxists, resources are available for collective allocation on the basis of need, which is given clear priority. Natural rights libertarians like Nozick concentrate entirely on rights and deserts. Resources are produced by *individuals*, who thereby acquire the right to allocate them; the question of *societal* allocation does not arise. Distributive justice is therefore removed entirely from the agenda.

Other groups have difficulties with distribution precisely because they are concerned with both desert and need. Empirical libertarians may oppose progressive taxation; but they do not take an absolute line against redistribution in that they accept public action to relieve destitution. Utilitarians favour redistributive activity which increases total welfare, but are concerned about the trade-off with efficiency. Rawls, too, is not a complete egalitarian, since privilege is acceptable where it improves the position of the least well-off.

Public production raises similar arguments. Libertarians countenance provision by the state of at most a limited class of public goods such as law and order, and even those only if no method of private supply can be found (Hayek, 1960, p. 223; Friedman, 1962, Ch. 2). In complete opposition, Marxists regard it as a function of the state to supply all basic goods and services, and to distribute them in accordance with individual need. To liberals the issue of public versus market production and allocation is a pragmatic question of which method is more effective – which is the subject of most of this book.

5.3 ATTITUDES TOWARDS THE WELFARE STATE

The welfare state is a complicated set of institutions, so it is not surprising that attitudes towards it are complicated and often confused.

Natural rights libertarians like Nozick regard a welfare state of any sort as an anathema, seeing its pursuit of the spurious (or immoral) goal of equality as an unacceptable violation of individual liberty.

Empirical libertarians like Hayek and Friedman require careful discussion. Let us return to the distinction (Chapter 2:7.1) between an institutional welfare state, which pursues substantially redistributive goals, and a residual welfare state. The former is strongly opposed by all libertarians as a coercive agency, stifling freedom and individualism, and courting the risk of totalitarianism through the amalgamation of economic and political power under collective planning, in contrast with their separation in a market system. A welfare state of this sort is also seen as creating inefficiency in several ways: it wastes resources because at a zero or subsidised price demand is excessive; resources are used inefficiently because government monopoly is insulated from competition; and the necessary taxation will have costs in terms of efficiency and economic growth.

A residual welfare state has much more limited aims. It is recognised that a free society based on private property and competitive markets is likely to distribute income unequally. Limited state activity may therefore be appropriate to relieve destitution and to provide certain public goods. Empirical libertarians consider this rather austere welfare state as essential to their conception of a civilised society. It is therefore not inconsistent when they attack existing social arrangements in the strongest terms (see Hayek, 1960, and the quote from Friedman at the head of this chapter), but support more limited welfare institutions (Friedman, 1962, Chs 6 and 12).

Liberals and Fabian socialists tend unambiguously to support the welfare state. To Beveridge (1944, p. 254) it was necessary 'to use the powers of the State, so far as may be necessary without any limit whatsoever, in order to avoid the five giant evils'. For most socialist writers, however, the welfare state is not a complete solution to society's ills, but only a step along the way.

. . . while socialists see the welfare state as only the limited and partial achievement of some socialist goals, they are, nevertheless, optimistic about its influence. They see it not as dampening down the political forces making for further social change, but rather as a powerful ally . . . In brief, they see the welfare state as . . . a stepping-stone toward socialism. [George and Wilding, 1976, p. 84.]

It is not surprising that liberals and socialists share some common ground. Robson (1976, p. 17), citing Hobhouse, writes:

The liberal . . . stands for emancipation, and is the inheritor of a long tradition of those who have fought for liberty, who have struggled against government and its laws or against society because they crushed human development. . . . The socialist stands for solidarity of society, for mutual responsibility and the duty of the strong to aid the weak. . . . On this analysis the ideals of the liberal and socialist were seen as complementary rather than conflicting.

Marxists disagree strongly among themselves. Is the welfare state (a) *only* an instrument of capitalist oppression, or does it (b) *also* represent a progressive outcome of working-class pressure? Under the first view, the welfare state is at best irrelevant, a 'ransom' paid by the dominant class, and an institution dealing with symptoms rather than causes of economic and social problems; at worst, the welfare state is actively malign, in that it sustains the capitalist system. O'Connor (1973) sees the state as promoting economic growth (the 'accumulation' function) and enhancing social harmony (the 'legitimation' function). The accumulation function includes the reproduction of labour power (e.g. the health and education aspect of the welfare state); continued accumulation of capital (i.e. the maintenance of profits sufficient to maintain a high level of investment); and consumption sufficient to absorb the output of the capitalist system. The legitimation function relates to the political and social requirements of capitalism:

social control . . . has to do with the maintenance of order and the reduction of social conflict and tension. From the viewpoint of the ruling classes this often means reducing the workers' hostility towards the capitalist regime. [Mishra, 1981, p. 82.]

This, according to some Marxists, is the major purpose of the welfare state.

Other Marxist writers see the welfare state as serving the interests of the capitalist class *and* those of workers. A central insight (see Gintis and Bowles, 1982) is the contradictory position of the welfare state in a modern capitalist economy; the former is based on rights (e.g. of citizenship) and needs, the latter recognises claims on resources based on deserts (e.g. through the ownership of property). Thus Gough (1979) sees the state not as a neutral umpire, nor as acting *merely* in the interests of the capitalist class (as opposed to the capitalist *system*), but as responding to pressure: from the working class to meet needs and extend rights; and from capital to perform the accumulation function. Ginsburg, too, recognises the importance of class conflict in the development of the welfare state, but argues that though the demands of the working class have produced important material gains, 'those demands have been processed and responded to in such a form that, far from posing a threat to capital, they have deepened its acceptance and extended its survival' (1979, p. 19).

The welfare state thus has contradictory functions.

It simultaneously embodies tendencies to enhance social welfare, to develop the powers of individuals, to exert social control over the blind play of market forces; and tendencies to repress and control people, to adapt them to the requirements of the capitalist economy. [Gough, 1979, p. 12.]

As a result it is not surprising that some Marxists have ambivalent attitudes. Is the welfare state an

agency of repression, or a system for enlarging human needs and mitigating the rigours of the free-market economy? An aid to capitalist accumulation and profits or a 'social wage' to be defended and enlarged like the money in your pay packet? Capitalist fraud or working-class victory? [*ibid.*, p. 11.]

Whether the welfare state contributes to justice is clearly a matter of perspective, and hence susceptible of no definitive answer. Miller (1976, pp. 343–4) admits that

readers with a yearning for Rawlsian 'moral geometry' may . . find this [conclusion] disappointing. Can there be no conclusive arguments in political theory, and, moreover, arguments of universal validity that hold good across social and historical barriers? This is indeed a pleasant prospect, but since there seems little hope of it being realised, I conclude that we shall have to make do with more modest results.

It is, nevertheless, instructive to end with a few words on who can usefully talk with whom, and about what. It is not possible to enter debate with natural rights defenders of free markets and the nightwatchman state, save by disputing their values, nor really with Marxists, to whom the evils of the market system are axiomatic. But dialogue *is* possible between empirical libertarians, liberals and Fabian socialists and would (I suspect) be particularly fruitful between the first two. Writers like Hayek and Friedman share common roots in nineteenth-century Classical liberalism with the largely utilitarian arguments of this book. Their position rests less on an ethical, than on a theoretical and empirical view about the institutions likely to maximise total utility. The distinction is vital. The issues dividing a liberal defence of the welfare state from the views of empirical libertarians are not moral but largely factual. The main thrust of the argument is that technical problems with markets as both a theoretical and an empirical matter are much more pervasive than Hayek and Friedman allow. These are the grounds of the debate; the theoretical heart of the argument is the subject of Chapter 4.

Further Reading

Libertarian ideas are set out in Nozick (1974) (a natural rights defence), Hayek (1944, 1960 and 1976) and Friedman (1962 and 1980). The intellectual roots of these ideas are discussed by Robbins (1978). For a libertarian critique of egalitarianism see the essays in Letwin (1983).

The liberal approach is analysed by Barry (1973) and Miller (1976). For an introduction to Rawls (1972) see Gorovitz (1975) (one of the best teaching articles I have read, and one to which readers are most warmly referred). For more detailed commentary see the contributions in Daniels (1975); for liberal critiques Barry (1973) and Miller (1976); and for cogent libertarian criticism Nisbet (1974). McCreadie (1976) offers an interesting application to the UK national health service.

A simple introduction to socialist thought (and also to the other theories of society) is given by George and Wilding (1976), and discussion in greater depth by Laski (1967), Miliband (1969), Crosland (1956) and Tawney (1964) (a defence of equality).

The classic exposition of Marxist economic theory is Sweezy (1942); for a simple introduction see Robinson and Eatwell (1973) and Fine (1975) and for more complete discussion Mandel (1976), Harrison (1978) and Desai (1979). Marxist attitudes to the welfare state are discussed by Gough (1979), Ginsburg (1979) and Mishra (1981).

Appendix: Non-Technical Summary of Chapter 3

1 Chapter 3 discusses various theories of society – libertarianism, utilitarianism, Rawlsian arguments and socialism. In practice the theories blur into each other like the colours of the rainbow – but it is useful for exposition to talk about them as separate entities.

Libertarian Theories

2 To libertarians (section 2), as their name implies, the primary aim of institutions is individual liberty, and the best method of achieving its economic dimension is through the operation of private markets. *Natural rights libertarians* like Nozick (1974) defend a minimal (or 'night-watchman') state on ethical grounds, *empirical libertarians* like Hayek and Friedman out of a belief that such a regime will maximise total welfare. For natural rights libertarians the state has no legitimate distributional role at all; to empirical libertarians its distributional activities are very strictly circumscribed.

3 Hayek argues in addition that the pursuit of social justice is not only fruitless because there is no such thing, but also dangerous because it will destroy the market order which is both efficient and the only guarantee of personal freedom. According to Hayek (1976) a given circumstance is just or unjust only if it has been caused by the action/inaction of a *named* individual or individuals. The outcome of impersonal forces ('Nature') can be good or bad, but never just or unjust. The market is seen as an impersonal force, akin to an economic game with winners and losers, and so the market-determined distribution of goods can be neither just nor unjust. The notion of social justice therefore has no meaning. Its quest, however, is dangerous, according to Hayek, because once governments start to interfere with the market-determined distribution a process is set in motion which progressively approaches totalitarianism.

Liberal Theories

4 Liberal theories (section 3), e.g. utilitarianism and writers like Rawls, contrast with libertarian views first by allowing the state a greater distributional role, and second through a weaker presumption that the free market is necessarily the best means of production and distribution. The treatment of property rights is not an end in itself, as with libertarians, but a means towards the achievement of stated policy aims. In certain circumstances this can justify a mixed economy.

5 The utilitarian aim is to distribute goods so as to maximise the total utility

65

of society's members (section 3.1). Where individuals have identical marginal utility of income functions this occurs when income is shared equally (Figure 3.1). Utilitarianism thus enables statements to be made about the optimal distribution of goods (which in certain circumstances can be egalitarian), and so legitimates a redistributive role for the state.

6 This approach is criticised by Rawls and others because it can justify harm to the least well-off individual or group, if this raises total utility.

7 Rawls, in contrast, makes justice the primary aim of policy (section 3.2) (for a very clear introduction see Gorovitz, 1975). Rawls defines social justice in terms of two principles, the first dealing with the distribution of liberty, the second with that of other goods. Taken together they imply that all goods (interpreted broadly to include liberty and opportunity) should be distributed equally unless an unequal distribution is to the advantage of the least well-off individual or group. No policy should be undertaken, according to Rawls, unless it benefits also (though not necessarily only) the least well-off. Again, there is a legitimate, and generally egalitarian, redistributive role for the state.

8 The theories of utilitarians and Rawls can have different policy implications. Suppose a given policy change makes at least one person better-off without making anyone worse-off. This is a Pareto improvement (see Chapter 4:2.1); hence utilitarians would regard the policy as desirable even if the individual thus benefited were rich. Rawls's principles of justice would oppose the policy unless it were also to the advantage of the least well-off. Thus an efficient answer in a Paretian sense is not always just in a Rawlsian sense (see Chapter 4:2.2).

Socialist Theories

9 The main socialist aims are equality, freedom and fraternity. These values can conflict, and different writers accord them different weight. But there is general agreement about the importance of equality, which is closely related (though not logically equivalent) to the further socialist aim of meeting need.

10 Despite agreement about their aims, and in their diagnosis of the failings of the free market, socialists are divided over how best to achieve them, most fundamentally over the role, if any, of the market system.

11 Some socialists (section 4.1) argue that institutional changes, not least the enlarged role of government in economic life, have greatly reduced the evils of capitalism and made it possible to harness the market system to socialist goals. Adherents of this view accept a role for private property and the market mechanism, though modified in both cases by state intervention, i.e. like liberals they feel that their aims are likely to be best achieved by some sort of mixed economy.

12 Other socialists, e.g. Marxists (section 4.2), argue that private ownership and the market system are inherently in conflict with socialist aims. In particular they regard the market as exploitative and therefore incompatible with equality. Marxists therefore reject capitalism outright, whether or not it makes up part of a mixed economy, and give the state a primary role in production and allocation, as well as in distribution and redistribution.

Attitudes towards the Welfare State

13 The appropriate role of the state depends crucially on the underlying theory of society (sections 5.1 and 5.2), as also will attitudes towards the welfare state (section 5.3).

14 Natural rights libertarians reject all but minimal intervention and are unambiguously hostile to the welfare state, which they regard as a coercive agency which stifles freedom and individualism, and encourages waste and inefficiency in pursuit of the spurious and dangerous goal of social justice.

15 Empirical libertarians have a broadly similar attitude towards a large-scale welfare state with substantial redistributive goals. They do, however, recognise that a free society based on private property and competitive markets is likely to distribute income unequally, and are therefore prepared to support an austere welfare state whose primary aim is the relief of destitution.

16 The main support for the welfare state comes from liberals and some socialists, in the latter case unreservedly, because it is seen as an equalising force. For liberals its existence is a contingent question: they support the institutions of the welfare state where (and only where) they contribute more than alternative arrangements to the achievement of society's aims. In such cases their support is unreserved.

17 Marxists are generally hostile to the welfare state, though with some controversy. 'Hardline' commentators regard it as an actively malign agency which serves *only* (or mainly) as an instrument of social control, to protect the continued existence of the capitalist system. Other writers argue that, though the welfare state is indeed a 'ransom' paid by the dominant class, it *also* represents a genuine improvement in working-class conditions.

18 Finally, who can talk with whom, and about what? No debate is possible between liberals and natural rights libertarians on the one hand, or Marxists on the other. Debate *is*, however, possible between liberals and libertarians like Hayek and Friedman, who argue less from a moral position than from an empirical view about the the institutions likely to maximise total utility. The main thrust of this book is that technical

problems with markets, as both a theoretical and an empirical matter, are much more pervasive than Hayek and Friedman allow – in other words, the issues which separate a liberal defence of the welfare state from the views of empirical libertarians are at least as much factual as ideological.

4

Economic Theory 1:
State Intervention[1]

Every individual . . . generally . . . neither intends to promote the public interest, nor knows by how much he is promoting it. By preferring the support of domestic to that of foreign industry he intends only his own security; and by directing that industry in such a manner as its produce may be of the greatest value, he intends only his own gain, and he is in this, as in many other cases, led by an invisible hand to promote an end which was no part of his intention. [Adam Smith, 1776.]

[The] market needs a place, and the market needs to be kept in its place. It must be given enough scope to accomplish the many things it does well. It limits the power of bureaucracy, . . . responds reliably to the signals transmitted by consumers and producers. . . . Most important, the prizes in the market-place provide the incentives for work effort and productive contribution. . . . For such reasons I cheered the market; but I could not give it more than two cheers. The tyranny of the dollar yardstick restrained my enthusiasm. [Arthur M. Okun, 1975.]

---

[1] Non-technical readers can find the gist of the argument in the Appendix to this chapter.

1 The Formal Structure of the Problem

We now change gear sharply and move from the world of political philosophy to economic theory. The main aim is to develop a framework which addresses the question of why the state does (or should) produce and/or allocate some goods like health care and education, but leaves others like food for the most part to the private market. The main issues concern economic efficiency and social justice. Section 1 sets out the formal structure of the problem. Section 2 shows that the efficiency aim is common to all theories of society, but that redistributive goals depend crucially on what definition of social justice is chosen. The next step (section 3) is to consider the circumstances in which the market will allocate efficiently, and appropriate forms of intervention in their absence. The pursuit of social justice (section 4) raises such questions as: why does cash redistribution occur; should it be voluntary; should it be in cash or in kind; and what role (if any) should the state adopt to bring about equal access to goods and services, or to foster equality of opportunity or outcome? As a precursor to policy discussion in later chapters, section 5 sets out the logic of what has come to be known as 'privatisation'. Section 6 pulls together the main threads running through Chapters 3 and 4, by setting out the theoretical argument of the book, and establishing the areas of debate with its opponents, particularly libertarian writers like Hayek and Friedman.

The conventional starting-point for economic theory is the social welfare maximisation problem. The aim of policy is to maximise social welfare subject to the three basic constraints of tastes, technology and resources,[1] i.e.

Maximise:	$W = W(U^A, U^B)$	Social welfare function	(4.1)
Subject to:	$U^A = U^A(X^A, Y^A)$	} Tastes	(4.2)
	$U^B = U^B(X^B, Y^B)$		(4.3)
	$X = X(K^X, L^X)$	} Technology	(4.4)
	$Y = Y(K^Y, L^Y)$		(4.5)
	$K^X + K^Y = \bar{K}$	} Resources	(4.6)
	$L^X + L^Y = \bar{L}$		(4.7)

The aim in equation (4.1) is to maximise social welfare, W, as a function of the utilities of individuals A and B, U^A and U^B (i.e. the problem is a *joint* maximisation of efficiency and social justice). The constraints of tastes, technology and resources are shown by equations (4.2) to (4.7). The utilities of individuals A and B are constrained by their consumption of goods X and Y (equations (4.2) and (4.3)); and consumption is constrained by equations (4.4)

---

[1] This formulation is taken from Layard and Walters (1978, Ch. 1).

and (4.5), which show the production functions for X and Y in terms of the inputs of capital, K and labour, L; the inputs used to produce X and Y are constrained by the total availability of capital and labour, $\bar{K}$ and $\bar{L}$ (equations (4.6) and (4.7)).

The problem as formulated relates to a *first-best economy*. This implies one of two situations: either there is no impediment to efficiency, and also an optimal distribution of endowments; or it is possible for government to counter problems of inefficiency or maldistribution with first-best policies (e.g. via lump-sum taxation). An important theorem discussed in section 3 establishes the (first-best) assumptions under which a competitive market will allocate resources efficiently; and it is argued that where these conditions hold, the state has no role except (possibly) a distributional one.

The conditions, however, are stringent, as is the assumption that lump-sum taxation is feasible. A *second-best economy* faces additional constraint(s) due, for instance, to technical problems or to social institutions. Imperfect information is a recurring theme, e.g. if U^A is not well defined with respect to X^A. As a result, unrestricted markets may be inefficient or inequitable, and intervention may be appropriate. Another problem concerns externalities. If U^A depends on (say) X^B we have a consumption externality which constitutes a constraint additional to those in equations (4.2) to (4.7). This may justify intervention in one of a number of forms. We return to these issues in sections 3 and 4.[1]

2 Why Economic Efficiency is One of the Aims of Policy

2.1 THE CONCEPT OF ECONOMIC EFFICIENCY[2]

Since the concept of efficiency is fundamental to the whole book, this brief and very elementary introduction is included in the main body of the chapter rather than relegated to the Appendix. Technical readers should proceed directly to section 2.2.

Broadly speaking, economic efficiency[3] is about making the best use of limited resources given people's tastes. It concerns both the production and

---

[1] For a compendious survey of the literature on first- and second-best analysis within the social welfare maximisation framework see Atkinson and Stiglitz (1980, Lectures 11–14) and the references therein; and for a wide-ranging collection of articles Atkinson (1982).

[2] Non-technical readers should consult (in ascending order of difficulty) the relevant chapters (see the following footnotes) in Le Grand and Robinson (1984a) or Laidler (1981).

[3] Referred to synonymously as Pareto efficiency, Pareto optimality or allocative efficiency.

allocation of goods. This involves the choice of an *output bundle*

$$X^\star = (X_1, X_2, \ldots, X_n) \tag{4.8}$$

(where X_i is the output of the ith good) with the property that any deviations from these quantities will make at least one person worse off. The intuition of this efficient output bundle is shown at its simplest in a partial equilibrium framework in Figure 4.1. The optimal quantity of any good, ceteris paribus, is that at which the value placed by society on the marginal unit equals its marginal social cost.[1]

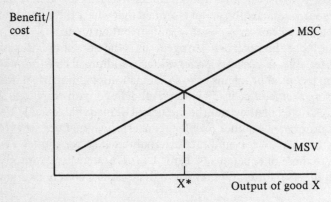

Figure 4.1   *Pareto optimal output: the simple case*

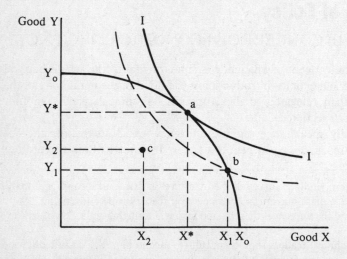

Figure 4.2   *A simple general equilibrium representation of Pareto optimal output*

---

[1] For a clear and simple exposition see Le Grand and Robinson (1984a, Ch. 1).

For a general equilibrium three conditions must hold simultaneously.

(1) *Efficiency in production*: factor proportions should be optimal so as to obtain the maximum output from given inputs, i.e. production is at a point on the transformation curve Y_0-X_0 in Figure 4.2, which shows the maximum quantities of the two goods which can be produced with available resources. Formally, this requires the marginal rate of factor substitution to be equal in the production of all goods.

(2) *Efficiency in product mix*: the output bundle should be optimal given existing production technology and consumer tastes. Formally, production is not at *any* point on the transformation curve in Figure 4.2, but at the specific point *a*, at which the ratio of marginal production costs (i.e. the slope of the transformation curve) is equal to the ratio of marginal rates of substitution in consumption (i.e. the slope of the 'social' indifference curve, I–I).

(3) *Efficiency in consumption*: the resulting output should be allocated so as to maximise utility – in formal terms, the marginal rate of substitution must be equal for all individuals.[1]

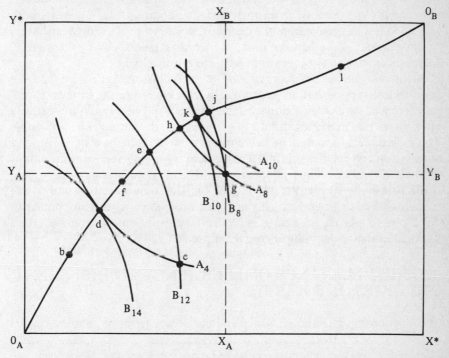

Figure 4.3   *The Edgeworth box (distribution)*

---

[1] See in ascending order of formality Laidler, 1981, Ch. 18; Layard and Walters, 1978, Ch. 1; and Varian, 1984, Ch. 5.

The meaning of the third condition is analysed further in the Edgeworth box in Figure 4.3. The size of the box shows the total output to be divided between individuals A and B, $O_A - X^\star$ of good X and $O_A - Y^\star$ of good Y, where the quantities $X^\star$ and $Y^\star$ are those taken from Figure 4.2 (hence fulfilling efficiency in production and in product mix). The output allocated to A is measured from the origin O_A, and that to B from O_B; at point g the two individuals share output equally. The contract curve, represented by the line $O_A - O_B$, shows those combinations of X and Y at which the marginal rate of substitution between the two goods is the same for both individuals. Any movement away from the contract curve makes at least one person worse off. Hence any point on the contract curve constitutes an efficient allocation.

The concept of a *Pareto improvement* is important for the analysis which follows. Suppose the initial allocation is shown by point c; then individual A on indifference curve A_4 is 'poor' and B on indifference curve B_{12} 'rich'. If trade moves the allocation to point d, then B is better-off (he has moved to the higher indifference curve B_{14}) and A is no worse-off; this is a Pareto improvement. Similarly, a move to the allocation shown by e makes A better off without harming B; and a move to an intermediate allocation like f benefits both parties. Thus any move from the distribution shown by c to any distribution on the contract curve between d and e, including points d and e themselves, increases efficiency and constitutes a Pareto improvement.[1]

A different concept, *administrative efficiency*, is illustrated in Figure 4.2.[2] We have seen that point b is not economically efficient, since the broken 'social' indifference curve passing through b lies below I–I; but b is administratively efficient, in that movement from b to a, increasing the output of Y, is possible only by reducing the output of X. Point c, in contrast, is both economically and administratively inefficient, since a movement from c to a increases the output of *both* X and Y. Thus all points inside the transformation curve are administratively inefficient; all points on the transformation curve are administratively efficient, but only point a is economically efficient. Similarly, only points on the contract curve in Figure 4.3 are efficient. The next question is which of these allocations is socially optimal.

2.2 THE RELEVANCE OF EFFICIENCY TO DIFFERENT THEORIES OF SOCIETY

The relationship between efficiency and social welfare at its simplest can be

---

[1] For an amusing and informative example taken from a prisoner of war camp see Radford (1945).
[2] Also synonymously called non-economic efficiency, non-allocative efficiency, X-efficiency or engineering efficiency.

illustrated in terms of Figure 4.3.[1,2] We have seen that a move from point *c* to a point like *e* is a Pareto improvement. The next step is to show that this is not just a utilitarian result. In each case two questions are considered: (a) given an initial sub-optimal allocation, what constitutes a welfare improvement; and (b) what is the optimal distribution of goods, i.e. what allocation is both efficient and socially just? Two results are established: economic efficiency, in the sense of a movement to an appropriate subset of the contract curve, is an important aim under *all* the definitions of social justice discussed in Chapter 3; and in a first-best economy no distribution can be socially just unless it is also efficient.

The fixed factor case assumes an Edgeworth box of given size, and also that the conditions for efficiency in production and in product mix hold. This is equivalent to discussing a first-best solution.

Libertarianism:[3] welfare is increased by any Pareto improvement, which to writers like Nozick is the *only* source of welfare gain. Thus a movement from *c* in Figure 4.3 to any point on the contract curve between points *d* and *e* (including the end points) increases welfare.

Natural rights libertarians have little to say about the optimal distribution of goods. If the initial distribution is at *c* then any point on the contract curve between *d* and *e* is optimal, provided that *c* accords with Nozick's idea of justice in holdings, and that the movement from *c* to the contract curve is the result of individual utility maximisation through voluntary trading in a competitive market system. More generally, depending on the initial distribution, any point on the contract curve can be an optimum. Empirical libertarians like Hayek and Friedman support this conclusion, save that they accept redistributive activity up to (but not beyond) a guarantee of subsistence, i.e. any point on the contract curve can be an optimum between points *b* and *l*, if these show subsistence for individuals A and B, respectively.

Utilitarians aim to maximise total utility. Again, any Pareto improvement, such as a move from *c* to the contract curve between (and including) points *d* and *e*, will increase welfare.

Is any point on the contract curve superior to any other, i.e. do movements *along* the contract curve raise welfare? The utilitarian answer, which is often

---

[1] The issue can be approached also via a utility possibility frontier, which can be derived as a simple transformation of the contract curve in Figure 4.3; see Brown and Jackson (1982, Ch. 1) or, for a fuller treatment, Atkinson and Stiglitz (1980, Lecture 11.2).

[2] These can be murky waters. This section (and Barr, 1985, from which it largely derives) abstracts from a number of potential problems – for a critique of the whole welfarist approach see Sen (1979, especially section VI).

[3] The libertarian theory of society is discussed in Chapter 3:2. Utilitarianism, Rawls and socialism are discussed in Chapter 3, sections 3.1, 3.2 and 4, respectively, and in the Appendix to Chapter 3.

misunderstood, depends on whether utility is ordinally or cardinally measurable (see the Glossary). When utility is cardinally measurable and A and B have identical marginal utility of income functions (as in Figure 3.1), welfare is maximised by starting from an equal distribution of goods, shown by point g in Figure 4.3. From this egalitarian endowment Pareto improvement is possible; under the stated assumptions total utility will be highest at point k. Individuals A and B are on indifference curves A_{10} and B_{10}, respectively; each enjoys ten units of utility (because utility is cardinally measurable); and (because marginal utility of income declines) total utility is lower at all other points on the contract curve. In these circumstances a move *along* the contract curve from a point like e towards k constitutes a utilitarian welfare improvement.

This egalitarian outcome, however, depends on A and B having identical marginal utility of income functions. If A is a gloomy guy and B is a cheerful chappie, social welfare is maximised at a point like d, and with roles reversed at a point like l. The same logic applies when utility is measurable only ordinally but here, though we know that the optimum distribution is at a point like k (or d or l), we cannot say which point because we cannot compare the utility of the two individuals. The latter conclusion, it is important to note, is fundamentally different from the libertarian argument that there is no ethical difference between points on the curve like d, k and l.

Rawls's aim is to distribute resources in accordance with social justice. Starting again from point c, a movement to e is a Rawlsian improvement (RI) because it benefits the less advantaged individual A. But a movement from c to d, though a Pareto improvement (PI) is *not* RI because it violates Rawls's principle that matters are to be arranged to the benefit of the least advantaged. A movement from c to a point between d and e is RI (and PI), because it benefits A at least to some extent. In addition, a movement from c to points between (and including) e and k, though it is not PI (since individual B is made worse-off), is RI because it benefits the less advantaged A. Hence a movement from c to the contract curve between d and e, *including* points d and e is PI; RI excludes point d^1 and includes points between e and k. The conclusion is that if we are off the contract curve at a point like c, there will always be a subset of the contract curve which is RI. Thus, in a first-best economy *all Rawlsian socially just distributions lie on the contract curve*.

According to Rawls, goods should be distributed equally, unless any other distribution benefits the least well-off. Hence the just distribution is generally point g, and the optimum outcome point k, i.e. a single, known and (generally) egalitarian point. Any movement along the contract curve towards k is an unambiguous improvement.

---

[1] Unless the lexical extension to the Difference Principle applies (see p.50, footnote 1).

Socialism: under one interpretation resources are to be shared equally. A movement from *c* to *e* raises the welfare of (poor) individual A, thereby reducing relative inequality. Such a move is a socialist improvement (SI). But a movement from *c* to *d* helps only (rich) individual B. If output is fixed (i.e. ruling out the case where B uses the extra resources to bring about economic growth to the advantage of A), this increases relative inequality and is therefore not SI. A movement from *c* to an intermediate point like *f* is arguable. I shall define (though others may disagree) SI to refer to any movement which increases individual A's *relative share* of output, thereby reducing inequality. Suppose *f* is the point on the contract curve at which A's relative share is the same as at *c*. We can then interpret as SI a movement from *c* to any point on the contract curve between (and including) *e* and *k*, and arguably also to any point between *e* and *f* (excluding point *f* itself). *SI is thus a subset of RI*, and all first-best solutions which are just in a socialist sense lie on the contract curve; and, like Rawls, socialists will favour any movement along the contract curve towards *k*.

Relaxing the fixed factor supply assumption complicates matters because of the resulting need, in the absence of lump-sum taxation, to analyse policies in a second-best economy. It is a standard proposition (Atkinson and Stiglitz, 1980, p. 343) that lump-sum transfers, being based on characteristics exogenous to the taxpayer, can bring about any desired distribution of income or goods without efficiency loss. Taxes related to income, however, (including any indirect tax whose payment rises with income) are not lump-sum, and generally cause inefficiency, *inter alia* through their effect on individual labour supply. But attempts to achieve social justice (such as a movement from *e* to *k* in Figure 4.3) generally require redistribution; and this involves taxation which, by the definition of its aim, must be income-related. As a result, any practicable system of taxation may restrict factor supply, reduce output and cause inefficiency in production and/or product mix. Thus there may be a trade-off between efficiency and equity.

This trade-off is analysed formally in the optimal taxation literature[1] in terms of the social welfare maximisation framework set out in section 1. The distribution which jointly optimises efficiency and social justice depends on two sets of factors: the efficiency costs of redistribution (mainly a technical matter depending, *inter alia*, on the compensated elasticity of factor supply); and the relative weights attached to efficiency and equity (which is primarily an ideological issue).

When account is taken of the efficiency impact of redistribution it may not be possible, for instance, to move from point *c* to point *e*. The only feasible

---

[1] See Atkinson and Stiglitz, 1980, Lecture 11; or, for a simple introduction, Brown and Jackson, 1982, Ch. 20.

possibilities might be:

(1) A movement to a point like *b*, which is efficient and leaves total production unaffected but which, in most theories of society, is less just than the distribution shown by *c*; or

(2) A movement to a distribution less unequal than *b*. In this case redistributive taxation will cause efficiency losses, generally by reducing output (i.e. attempts to move from *c* towards *e* will shrink the size of the box in Figure 4.3).

In the face of this trade-off there will be different views about the desirability of an increase in efficiency, which will not be seen as a welfare gain if its equity cost is 'too' high. To some libertarians equity has a zero weight; a movement from *c* to *b* will therefore increase both efficiency and welfare. To utilitarians the weight given to social justice is an open question. A given efficiency gain may or may not increase welfare; and the utilitarian optimum will not necessarily be efficient (i.e. utilitarians are prepared to sacrifice some efficiency in the interests of greater justice). Rawlsians and socialists gave social justice a higher weight, and will therefore generally accept a higher efficiency cost to achieve a just distribution. Note, however, that no theory of society gives social justice complete priority. Even a Marxist would resist the pursuit of distributional objectives if the resulting efficiency costs reduced output to zero.

Conclusions focus particularly on the relationship between efficiency and social welfare. The overall conclusion is that the analysis of this chapter is general in its application.

Conclusion 1: the meaning of efficiency (e.g. a movement from point *c* to a point on the contract curve) is the same in all theories of society.

Conclusion 2: welfare improvements: welfare is increased under all the theories of society by a movement from a point like *c* to an appropriate subset of the contract curve. Additionally, a movement from *c* to a point between *e* and *f* (excluding *f*) is SI *and* RI *and* PI. *Efficiency gains of this sort raise social welfare under all the theories of society discussed in Chapter 3.*[1] Where such a movement is feasible, this conclusion is valid whether factor supply is fixed or variable.

Conclusion 3: the optimal distribution in a first-best economy: for any of the theories of society discussed earlier *all first-best socially just distributions are also Pareto-efficient.* Efficiency in this case is a necessary condition for social justice.

---

[1] Note that this does *not* imply that the definition of efficiency is value-free. Pareto efficiency is generally considered to embrace two value-judgements: (a) social welfare is increased if one person is made better-off and nobody worse-off, and (b) that individuals are the best judge of their own welfare; see Le Grand (1984), and Rowley and Peacock (1975, Ch. 1). The assertion here is that a subset of Pareto improvements, though not value-free, is consistent with all the theories of society discussed in Chapter 3.

Conclusion 4: the optimal distribution in a second-best economy: in this case an increase in efficiency may be possible only at the expense of social justice. Whether such an efficiency gain raises social welfare depends on the relative weights accorded efficiency and equity, weights which will generally vary with different theories of society. Thus, the second-best optimum distribution may be a point which is not Pareto-efficient.

3 Intervention for Reasons of Efficiency

3.1 TYPES OF INTERVENTION

Discussion so far has concerned the *aims* of policy. The next step is to consider *methods*. This section discusses the circumstances in which market allocation is efficient and, if not, the types of intervention which might be justified. The analysis here (and for most of the book) looks mainly at static efficiency, though in later chapters issues of economic growth (i.e. dynamic efficiency) are discussed where relevant.

The state can intervene in four ways: regulation, finance and public production, which all involve direct interference in the market mechanism, and cash transfers, which may have indirect effects.

Regulation The state interferes with the free market through a large number of regulations. Some (e.g. concerning alcohol sales or shop opening hours) have more to do with social values than economics. But many are acutely relevant to the efficient and/or equitable operation of markets, especially where knowledge is imperfect. Regulation of *quality* is concerned mainly with the supply side, e.g. hygiene laws relating to the production and sale of food and drugs; laws forbidding unqualified people to practise medicine; and consumer protection legislation generally. Regulation of *quantity* more often affects individual demand, e.g. the requirement to attend school; mandatory automobile insurance; and compulsory social insurance contributions.

Finance involves subsidies (or taxes) applied either to the *prices* of specific commodities or to the *incomes* of individuals. Price subsidies affect economic activity by changing the slope of the budget constraint facing individuals and firms. They can be partial (e.g. for public transport or local authority housing) or total (e.g. free drugs for the elderly in Britain, and under medicare in the USA). Similarly, prices can be affected by a variety of taxes (e.g. on pollution or congestion). Income subsidies raise different issues which are discussed shortly.

Public production   Though regulation and finance modify market outcomes, they leave the basic mechanism largely intact. Alternatively, the state can take over the supply side by producing goods and services itself; in such cases the state owns the capital inputs (e.g. school buildings and equipment) and employs the necessary labour (e.g. teachers). Other (more or less pure) examples are national defence and (in Britain) the national health service. It is important to be clear that finance and production are entirely separate forms of intervention, both intellectually and in practice. The distinction is of considerable relevance to the issue of 'privatisation', discussed in section 5.

Cash transfers (i.e. income subsidies) can be tied to specific types of expenditure (e.g. education vouchers or housing benefit) or untied (e.g. social security benefits). First-best transfers take the form of a lump sum, and therefore affect economic activity by changing the incomes of individuals, with no extra-market effect on product or factor prices. As we saw in section 2.2, however, redistributive transfers in practice are not of this sort, and so cannot be regarded in efficiency terms as wholly neutral.

3.2 EFFICIENCY ARGUMENTS FOR INTERVENTION

This section is in some respects the theoretical heart of the book. The so-called *Invisible Hand theorem* asserts that the market-clearing set of outputs, X_M, will be the efficient output bundle $X^\star$, in equation (4.8) if and only if a number of assumptions hold. These (henceforth collectively called the *standard assumptions*) concern perfect information, perfect competition, and the absence of market failures, which are discussed in turn. The Invisible Hand theorem asserts that a market allocation will automatically be efficient if and only if the standard assumptions *all* hold. In this case there is no justification for intervention on efficiency grounds. But if one or more of the assumptions is violated the resulting market equilibrium will generally be inefficient, and state intervention in one of the forms described above may be appropriate.

Perfect Information

The quality of information available to individuals and firms is a topic with a recent and rapidly growing literature, and an issue of central importance to arguments about the welfare state. Simple analysis implicitly assumes that consumers are informed about what goods are available and about their nature. The assumption can fail, *inter alia*, in two important ways: economic agents may have imperfect knowledge of the *quality* of goods and/or their *prices*. This realisation has produced a literature on how quality variations can interact with market institutions (e.g. 'lemons', signalling); and since information may be costly to acquire, the implications of search (e.g. for a higher wage or lower price) have been explored (see the Further Reading at the end of Chapter 5). Complete information requires at least three types of knowledge: about the quality and nature of the product, about prices, and about the future.

Quality   The assumption that economic agents have perfect knowledge about the nature of the product (including factors) implies that individuals have well-defined indifference maps, and firms, similarly, well-defined isoquants. This is plausible for some goods, e.g. food, but less so for technically complex commodities. When the assumption fails, the market itself can sometimes solve the problem by supplying the information necessary for rational decisions. When I buy a house I do not know whether it is structurally sound, but I can buy the information by hiring the services of a surveyor. More generally, information is available from a large number of specialist publications. In such cases intervention is unnecessary.

Other types of information failure may justify regulation. Consumers usually have sufficient knowledge about the characteristics of food to choose a reasonably balanced diet, but may be imperfectly informed about the conditions in which the food was prepared. The state therefore intervenes with hygiene laws, whose effect is to improve consumer information, thereby increasing efficiency. Where the information failure is small, regulation may suffice. But serious failures may justify public production and/or allocation. Chapter 12 argues that it is unrealistic to postulate rational choice in many areas of health care; nor, since the subject is inherently technical, will consumers always be able to acquire the necessary knowledge. In these circumstances, there *may* be a justification for public production and allocation.

Price   Rational choice requires also that agents are perfectly informed about prices, i.e. that they face a well-defined budget constraint. This is plausible for commodities like clothes, less so for things like car repairs. Where the assumption fails, the market, again, may supply the necessary information, e.g. a house or a piece of jewellery can be professionally valued. In such cases the services of the valuer improve knowledge about prices, and so increase efficiency. Where the market does not resolve the problem, state intervention via regulation may be necessary, for instance a requirement to issue price lists.

It should be noted that rational choice depends on both indifference/ isoquant map and budget constraint; hence perfect information is needed about the nature of the product *and* about prices – neither on its own is sufficient.

The future   Intertemporal utility maximisation requires perfect information also about the future. I know that I will need food this week and again next week, and shop accordingly; but I do not know how much furniture I will consume over the next ten years nor how many cars, because I do not know whether my house will catch fire or my car be involved in an accident. In such cases, the market solution is to offer insurance, which gives me certainty since any losses I suffer will be made good by the insurance company. However, as discussed in Chapter 5, technical problems (due largely to information failures in insurance markets) can make private insurance inefficient or impossible. In these circumstances public production might be appropriate.

Perfect Competition

The second major assumption of the Invisible Hand theorem concerns perfect competition in product and factor markets, and also (and importantly) in capital markets. The assumption has two essential features: economic agents must be price takers; and they must have equal power.

Price-taking implies a large number of individuals and firms, with no entry barriers in any market. The assumption can fail, e.g. in the presence of monopoly, monopsony or oligopoly, and appropriate intervention can increase efficiency. Monopoly does not *per se* justify public production. It is a standard proposition (Hirschleifer, 1980, pp. 348 *et seq.*) that a monopolist can be given an incentive to produce the efficient output either through the imposition of a maximum price (i.e. regulation) or via an appropriate per unit subsidy (with or without the addition of a lump-sum tax). Where imperfect competition takes the form of oligopoly other forms of regulation might be appropriate (e.g. the Monopolies and Mergers Commission in the UK and anti-trust legislation in the USA).

It is conventionally argued, not least by writers like Hayek and Friedman, that the advantages of competition are the maximisation of consumer choice (i.e. consumer sovereignty) and the minimisation of cost. Without perfect information, however, agents are unable to exercise their choice rationally; nor can they tell whether competitive cost reductions are associated with an unacceptable reduction in quality. An important conclusion follows – that *the efficiency advantages of competition are contingent on perfect information*.

Equal power is not violated if some individuals have higher incomes than others and so have more 'dollar votes'. In all other respects agents must have equal power – there can be no discrimination. The assumption is frequently breached, and hard to correct. In some areas (e.g. safety legislation in factories) the state intervenes through regulation. Others, such as having friends in high places (which socialists regard as a major cause of inequality), have no easy solution; nor does outright discrimination, e.g. by race or sex. Legislation (i.e. regulation) in these areas has met with only limited success.

No Market Failures

This assumption can be violated in three major ways: public goods, external effects, and increasing returns to scale. These concepts, especially the second, arise frequently in the following chapters. They are discussed in more detail in the Appendix.

Pure public goods exhibit three technical characteristics, non-rivalness in consumption, non-excludability and non-rejectability, which together imply that the market is likely to produce inefficiently, if at all. Once a public good is produced, non-excludability makes it impossible to prevent people from using it, hence it is not possible to levy charges (this is the *free-rider* problem); in such cases the market may fail entirely. Non-rivalness implies that the marginal cost of an extra user (though *not* of an extra unit of output) is zero. The efficient price should therefore be based on individual marginal valuations of the good, i.e. on perfect price discrimination; where this is not possible, the market is likely to be inefficient. If a public good is to be provided at all, the appropriate form of intervention is generally public production.[1]

External effects are a closely related phenomenon. They arise when an act of agent A imposes costs or confers benefits on agent B for which no compensation from A to B, or payment from B to A takes place. More formally, a technological externality arises when A's utility or production function is interrelated with B's. It is a standard proposition[2] that in the presence of an external cost the market-clearing output will generally exceed the efficient output, and vice versa for an external benefit. Where property rights are unambiguous the problem can sometimes be resolved by the market itself through negotiation between the parties concerned (Coase, 1960), but this is not always possible, for instance where property rights are not enforceable (e.g. air pollution), or where transactions costs are high because large numbers of people are involved (e.g. traffic congestion). In such cases, intervention may be warranted in one of two generic forms: regulation, or an appropriate Pigovian tax or subsidy. The choice of method depends on a complex of factors. Taxation/subsidy is the usual solution if the intention is marginally to change levels of consumption or production. But regulation may be useful where the aim is to enforce at least a minimum level of some activity (e.g. compulsory automobile insurance); or to restrict it below some maximum (e.g. mandatory

---

[1] For further details see Prest and Barr, 1985, Ch. 3, sections 2.2 and 2.3; Brown and Jackson, 1982, Ch. 3; or Musgrave and Musgrave, 1984, Ch. 3. The classic exposition of the theory of public goods is Samuelson (1954).

[2] For an excellent simple treatment of the welfare effects of externalities see Le Grand and Robinson, 1984a, Ch. 2; for more advanced discussion see Layard and Walters, 1978, Ch. 6; and Varian, 1984, Ch. 7.3.

pollution controls); or where measurement problems prevent assessment of the appropriate tax/subsidy.[1]

Increasing returns to scale at all levels of output imply that average cost will exceed marginal cost, as in Figure 4.4. The consequent long-run losses will drive competitive firms from the industry, which will either become monopolised or (if even a monopolist makes losses) will cease to exist at all. Intervention can take one of two forms. The industry could remain private, buttressed by an appropriate lump-sum subsidy, $(AC_0 - P_0)X_0$ in Figure 4.4;[2] or it could be nationalised and similarly subsidised. The appropriate intervention, therefore, is subsidy or public production or both.

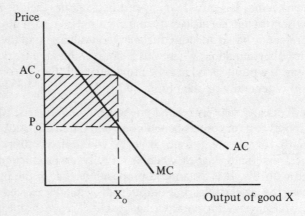

Figure 4.4 *The loss resulting from marginal cost pricing under increasing returns to scale*

It is important to be clear about what has been said, and what not said, about the size of the public sector. Discussion has concerned the circumstances in which goods and services are produced more efficiently in either sector. But the size of the public sector depends not only on these supply-side considerations, but also on demand. If there are only two goods, food (produced privately) and education (produced publicly), the optimal size of the public sector will depend on preferences over food and education, and will vary over time and across countries, depending *inter alia* on tastes.

---

[1] For discussion in the context of environmental issues see Baumol and Oates (1979).
[2] Though the taxation necessary to finance the subsidy would itself be distortionary unless levied on a lump-sum basis.

3.3 EXAMPLES OF INTERVENTION ON EFFICIENCY GROUNDS

By and large the market for food conforms with the standard assumptions. People generally have sufficient information to buy a balanced diet; food prices are well known; and most people know roughly how much they will need over a given period. Food production and (especially) distribution are competitive; and there are no major market failures. A possible violation is ignorance about the conditions under which food is produced, so the state intervenes with hygiene regulations. These enhance consumer information, leaving the private market to operate efficiently. There are no serious advocates of a national food service.

With health care, in sharp contrast, most of the assumptions fail (as discussed in detail in Chapter 12:3.1). Consumer information can be highly imperfect, since much medical treatment is complex and technical. In addition, knowledge of prices is scant. Nobody knows how much health care they will need and, as shown in Chapters 5 and 12, there are major technical (again, largely information) problems with private medical insurance. It is also argued that health care is not competitive. Finally, some medical care can generate externalities. What type of intervention is then appropriate? Information failures and the lack of competition can justify regulation; the externality can justify subsidies; and a strong (though not overriding) argument for public production and allocation arises out of the serious problems with both consumer information and private insurance.

It is instructive to apply these arguments also to past or present public enterprises well outside the welfare state, like railways, electricity, telephones, steel, coal, airlines and other candidates for nationalisation as have been implemented elsewhere, such as banking and insurance.

The issues can be encapsulated by observing (a) that market allocation is more efficient, ceteris paribus, the greater the extent to which the standard assumptions hold; and (b) that administrative allocation (e.g. by the state) is more effective, ceteris paribus, the smaller the divergence in individual tastes. Thus food, which conforms with (a) but conflicts with (b), is a clear case for market allocation; for defence, and arguably for health care, the situation is reversed, thereby lending plausibility to an allocative role for the state.

4 Intervention for Reasons of Social Justice

4.1 WHY DOES REDISTRIBUTION OCCUR?

Different definitions of social justice (or equity) were discussed in Chapter 3.

The main questions in this section are different, namely why does redistribution occur; should it be in cash or kind; and is there enough redistribution?

Coerced redistribution   There are three broad explanations of why redistribution occurs, corresponding very roughly with libertarian, liberal and Marxist theories. The arguments of Downs (1957) and Tullock (1970) though not explicitly libertarian, have something of that flavour.[1] In both theories the 'poor', acting as individuals or as part of a coalition, use their voting power to enforce redistribution from the 'rich'. Downs assumes that politicians seek office for reasons of income, status and power, and therefore choose policies which maximise the votes they receive at the next election; and that citizens vote for the party whose programme promises them the highest expected utility. Since the income distribution in most countries contains relatively few people with high incomes and many with lower incomes, governments maximise votes by redistributing from the rich, thereby gaining the (many more) votes of those with lower incomes.

The logic of this argument is that the system will redistribute towards equality. That equality is not reached is attributed to three countervailing pressures: fear of the efficiency losses (especially the labour supply disincentive) of high taxation; the fact that the rich generally have more power and can to some extent protect themselves; and the fact that the poor might want some inequality to remain, in the hope that they might some day themselves be rich.

Tullock assumes that policy is based on the wishes of the majority, and discusses how different income groups might form voting coalitions. In particular, he notes that any coalition of at least 51 per cent of the electorate must contain not only the very poor but also many in the middle-income group. His theory therefore offers an explanation of the commonly observed phenomenon (Le Grand, 1982) that public expenditure on the poor is often lower than on the middle-income group (which tends, for example, to make more intensive use of the educational system).

Voluntary redistribution   According to Downs and Tullock redistribution is motivated by selfishness and enforced by political coercion. Hochman and Rodgers (1969), in contrast, recognise the possibility of generous (or even altruistic) motives. Their theory seeks to explain both voluntary giving, and the fact that people with high incomes may vote for political parties which propose to tax them more heavily to finance redistributive policies. At the heart of this approach lies the notion that individual welfares are interdependent.

The simplest explanation of *voluntary* redistribution is a breakdown in the

---

[1] See also Buchanan and Tullock (1962), and for a non-technical introduction Tullock (1976).

assumption of no externalities. Assume a two-person world with representative 'rich' and 'poor' individuals, R and P. If R is concerned with P's utility as well as with his own, both may gain by a gift from R to P. Where redistribution makes some people better-off without making anyone worse-off, transfers from rich to poor may be justified on quasi-efficiency grounds.[1]

Formal analysis: in the simplest case R and P each has a utility function which is dependent only on his own income. Thus

$$U^R = f(Y^R) \tag{4.9}$$
$$\text{and} \quad U^P = f(Y^P) \tag{4.10}$$

where U^R and U^P are the utilities of the rich and the poor man, respectively, and Y^R and Y^P their incomes. But now suppose that R's utility depends not only on his own income, but also on P's. Then,

$$U^R = f(Y^R, Y^P), f_1 > 0, f_2 \geq 0 \tag{4.11}$$

where f_1 and f_2 are the partial derivatives of U^R with respect to Y^R and Y^P, respectively. There is an externality inasmuch as, ceteris paribus, R's utility rises with P's income.[2] In this situation redistribution from rich to poor can be rational: it will raise P's utility (because his income goes up) and also R's utility (because of the increase in P's income) so long as

$$\frac{\partial U^R}{\partial Y^P} > \left| \frac{\partial U^R}{\partial Y^R} \right| \tag{4.12}$$

where the first term shows the increase in R's utility as a result of the increase in P's income, and the second the reduction in R's utility because of the reduction in his own income. Voluntary redistribution from R to P will be rational so long as the first term exceeds the second.

Criticisms of voluntarism: this approach leaves no distributional role for the state through compulsory taxation unless voluntarism can be shown to be sub-optimal. Two such arguments have been proposed. The first concerns the problem of free riders, which can arise when the model is extended from the two-person case to the *n*-person. Suppose that it is not the income of specific *individual* poor people which affects the utility of the rich, but the *overall* distribution, which then displays all the characteristics of a public good.

Each individual in society faces the same income distribution. No one can be

---

[1] For a fuller exposition see Hochman and Rodgers (1969); also the Comments by Meyer and Shipley (1970), Musgrave (1970), and Goldfarb (1970); and the Reply by Hochman and Rodgers (1970). A similar approach treats the size distribution of income as a public good; see Thurow (1971).

[2] In formal terms we are relaxing the assumption that the social welfare function is additive, see Chapter 6:1.2.

deprived of the benefits flowing from any particular income distribution. My consumption of whatever benefits occur is not rival with your consumption. In short, the income distribution meets all the tests of a pure public good. Exclusion is impossible; consumption is non-rival; each individual must consume the same quantity. The same problems also occur. *Each individual has a vested interest in disguising his preferences concerning his desired income to avoid paying his optimal share of the necessary transfer payments.* [Thurow, 1971, pp. 328–9, my emphasis.]

Hence,

it can be argued that private charity is insufficient because the benefits from it accrue to people other than those who make the gifts. . . . [We] might . . . be willing to contribute to the relief of poverty, *provided* everyone else did. [Friedman, 1962, p. 191, his emphasis.]

Thus it may be rational for the rich to vote for redistributive taxation, which is compulsory and so avoids free riding.[1,2] I shall refer to this as 'voluntary compulsion'. Since it is, up to a point, imposed by the rich upon themselves this is a very different argument from the 'coercion via the ballot box' of Downs and Tullock.

A second and completely separate criticism of voluntarism is that if redistribution were *only* that which the rich volunteered, it might be sub-optimal even in the absence of free riders. Suppose the initial situation is shown by point *d* in Figure 4.3, and the social welfare maximising distribution by point *k* (as it would for Rawls or a socialist). The rich might be prepared through voluntarism to move the distribution from *d* to *f*, or through compulsory taxation to *e*. But if the income externality is 'exhausted' at *e* then a movement to *k*, though possibly raising *total* utility, would reduce the utility of the rich. In such a case voluntary transfers would be insufficient to bring about the egalitarian distribution advocated, for example, by socialists.

It follows, in conclusion, that voluntary redistribution *alone* will be sub-optimal unless one believes *both* that free-riding is not a problem *and* that the optimal amount of redistribution is that which the rich wish to volunteer.

Marxists, as we saw in Chapter 3:5.3, view redistribution as the outcome of two sets of forces: the needs of the capitalist system for an educated and healthy workforce, and as a response to class conflict. On the latter point Marxists argue

---

[1] Attempts have been made to defend voluntarism against the free-rider argument. As yet the issue is unsettled. See Sugden (1982 and 1984), and subsequent discussion by Collard (1983) and Sugden (1983a). For a simple introduction to the literature see Sugden (1983b).
[2] Many charitable organisations now attempt to reduce free-riding by assigning (e.g.) a specific, named family to the giver.

that the state will act to preserve the capitalist system, and will enact redistributive policies if that is necessary to prevent social unrest. Crudely, redistribution is motivated by the self-interest of the ruling class, as the necessary 'ransom' to protect its long-run interests.

4.2 SHOULD REDISTRIBUTION BE IN CASH OR KIND?

What, if any, are the arguments for redistribution in kind (i.e. transferring commodites directly to the poor at zero or non-market prices)? We have seen that if the standard assumptions all hold, markets will allocate efficiently, in which case equity aims are generally best pursued through cash transfers (though subject to the caveat that redistributive taxation is itself a potential source of inefficiency). This suggests that the use of in-kind transfers for distributional purposes is appropriate only where they are also justified on *efficiency* grounds. I shall argue that this proposition is generally valid, with the exception of one counter-argument, again based on voting, which suggests that in some circumstances it may be politically easier to redistribute in kind (e.g. to give the poor free education rather than the money to buy it).

Formal analysis: in equation (4.11), the utility of the rich person depends both on his own income, and that of the poor man. But suppose the externality is caused not by P's *income* but by his *consumption*. Then,

$$U^R = f(Y^R, C^P) \qquad (4.13)$$

where C^P is P's consumption. However, not all increases in C^P will necessarily raise the utility of the rich – consumption of alcohol by the poor might fail to do so. It is necessary to disaggregate so that,

$$C^P = G^P + B^P \qquad (4.14)$$

where G^P is 'good' consumption by the poor (children's clothing, basic food), and B^P is 'bad' consumption (whisky, welfare, Cadillacs), where 'good' and 'bad' are defined by the rich.

From equations (4.13) and (4.14) we have

$$U^R = f(Y^R, G^P, B^P) f_1 > 0, f_2 \geqslant 0, f_3 \leqslant 0 \qquad (4.15)$$

where f_1, f_2 and f_3 are the partial derivatives of U^R with respect to Y^R, G^P and B^P, respectively. R's utility increases with his own income, and with 'good' consumption by P, but decreases with P's 'bad' consumption. In this situation, transfers of 'good' consumption take place as long as

$$\frac{\partial U^R}{\partial G^P} > \left| \frac{\partial U^R}{\partial Y^R} \right| \qquad (4.16)$$

where the first term shows the increase in R's utility resulting from the increase in P's 'good' consumption, and the second is the decrease in R's utility because of the decrease in his own income.

Merit goods are defined as commodities in respect of which the state overrides consumer sovereignty, e.g. school education is compulsory, irrespective of the wishes of parents or children.[1] If the standard assumptions hold there is no efficiency justification for merit goods. Figure 4.5 shows how their existence can be explained by a consumption externality. Suppose individual P initially faces the budget constraint $Y_P - Y_P$ and maximises utility by choosing point a. Now compare a cash transfer with a compulsory in-kind transfer. Suppose that the cash transfer shifts P's budget constraint outward to $Y_1 - Y_1$ so that he maximises utility at point b. Alternatively, a compulsory transfer of $Y_P - Y_2$ units of education shifts P's budget constraint to $Y_2 - Y_2$, and utility is maximised at c. Given the choice, a rational poor person will favour the in-kind transfer, since c is on a higher indifference curve than b.

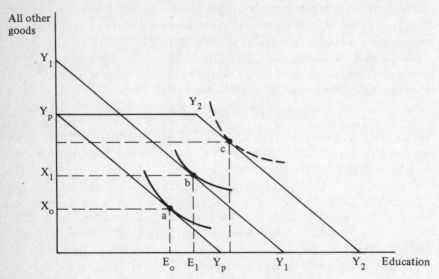

Figure 4.5 *Redistribution in cash and kind*

Now consider matters from the viewpoint of individual R. It is clear that the in-kind transfer is the more costly (i.e. measuring along the horizontal axis, the in-kind transfer consists of $Y_P - Y_2$ units of education, whereas the cash transfer buys only $Y_P - Y_1$ units). However, though R gives up more *income* to finance the in-kind transfer, he might give up less *utility*. In the presence of a consumption externality, an income transfer can reduce the utility of the rich

---

[1] For further discussion see Musgrave and Musgrave, 1984, Ch. 4.

both *per se* and because it might be used by the poor to finance 'bad' consumption. Transfers in kind, though costing more in financial terms, have the advantage from R's point of view that they are entirely 'good' consumption. If f_2 in equation (4.15) is large and positive, and f_3 large and negative, then R too might prefer the in-kind transfer.

In this case social welfare might be higher with in-kind transfers, despite the absence of any efficiency reasons for public production or allocation, simply because both rich and poor prefer it that way. This runs counter to the conventional argument that cash transfers are usually more efficient.

4.3 HORIZONTAL EQUITY

Discussion thus far has concentrated on *vertical equity*, i.e. the redistribution of income or consumption from rich to poor. Social justice also involves *horizontal equity*, which concerns goals like minimum standards for certain goods and services, or equal access to them, and equality of opportunity.[1]

Minimum standards are a form of regulation, and can therefore be justified only by the failure of one or more of the standard assumptions. This can occur in three ways. Where agents have imperfect information they are generally unable to make rational choices; a case can be made on this basis for minimum standards in schools and hospitals. Second, if agents have unequal power they might not be able to enforce their decisions; this justifies, for example, regulations about safety standards at work. Finally, there may be externalities. If my house has inadequate sewage disposal the resulting public health hazard is an argument for appropriate building codes.[2]

If the standard assumptions hold, however, consumers are able to make rational choices, and to enforce them, provided they have sufficient income to do so. In such cases, concern with the quality of consumption should manifest itself in cash redistribution rather than minimum standards except, possibly, in the presence of consumption externalities. The latter, however, is a dangerous argument, since minimum standards imposed on the poor 'for their own good' (i.e. 'good' consumption) may end up harming the poor if pitched at a higher level than is justified in efficiency terms (see Chapter 14:5.2 for discussion of housing standards).

---

[1] For the place of horizontal equity in the social welfare maximisation framework of section 1, see King (1983).

[2] In the light of these theoretical arguments it is noteworthy that much early social legislation in Britain was concerned with factory conditions and public health, see Chapter 2:1.2.

Equal access Where the standard assumptions hold, the only cause of unequal access is shortage of income, for which the appropriate remedy is generally cash redistribution. But action to ensure equal access may be justified in particular by the failure of the assumptions of perfect information and equal power.[1] A case in point is 'know-how', inequality of which is a major cause of inequality generally. Know-how includes understanding the value of education; knowing your entitlements under the national health service; knowing your legal rights; and also, more generally, your social and professional contacts. In the face of such inequality the state can intervene through regulation (e.g. legislation against discrimination); through subsidy (e.g. legal aid for people with low incomes); or through public production (e.g. the provision of compulsory, free education, which is supposed to be of an equal standard for all).

Equality of opportunity is closely related to equal access. We return to the issue in some detail in Chapter 6:3.1.

The horizontal equity argument should not be overstated. Where the standard assumptions hold, any problems of unacceptable standards or unequal access are generally *income distribution problems*. If so, minimum standards and institutional action to ensure equal access are likely to be inappropriate; the state can best ensure equal access to consumption of an acceptable standard by cash redistribution which, in this case, serves both efficiency and social justice.

4.4 IS THERE ENOUGH REDISTRIBUTION?

We saw in section 2.2 that social justice is concerned with movements along the contract curve towards the optimal distribution. What is that distribution; and have we achieved it?

Libertarians[2] see the optimal distribution as the result of competitive market forces on legally acquired endowments. They support the relief of destitution through voluntary charity, which writers like Nozick regard as the *only* legitimate method, all redistributive taxation being coercive. It follows from earlier discussion that if the free-rider problem is non-trivial, voluntary giving will be sub-optimal even in libertarian terms. Empirical libertarians like Hayek and Friedman allow taxation to bring incomes up to (but not beyond) subsistence if voluntary giving fails to do so, not least because of the free-rider problem, which Friedman explicitly accepts (see the quote on page 88.)

---

[1] For a theoretical analysis of how the failure of the equal power assumption leads to discrimination against women, see Apps (1981).

[2] See p. 75, footnote 3.

However, most libertarians argue that benefits are too high, and therefore that we have *too much* redistribution. This is precisely the conclusion of Downs and Tullock, discussed earlier.

Utilitarians are unsure which distribution maximises social welfare, because of the impossibility of measuring utility cardinally. They are therefore unclear whether there has been too much redistribution or not enough.

Rawls argues unequivocally that goods should be distributed equally unless any other distribution is to the advantage of the least well-off. This is not the actual situation, and therefore there has been too little redistribution. Rawls would disagree with the Downs–Tullock argument that democratic politics have resulted in excessive redistribution, arguing that voting and other political activity in practice takes place *outside* the veil of ignorance. Negotiation is therefore hindered by special pleading, particularly because the rich generally have greater power. The resulting distribution is nowhere near the Rawlsian optimum.

Socialists, too, are clear that their goal of equality has not been reached. A Marxist would argue that no other outcome is possible within the present economic system because capitalism can preserve itself only by using the power of the ruling class to exploit workers. To a Marxist equality under capitalism is a contradiction in terms.

5 From Theory Towards Policy: The Issue of Privatisation

The concept of privatisation is considerably more complicated than most participants in recent debate have realised. It is important to be clear that *finance* and *public production* (discussed in section 3.1) are entirely separate forms of intervention, both conceptually and in practice. A good can be financed publicly or privately, and it can be produced in either sector; thus there are four cases. A commodity like food is generally financed and produced in the private sector (Box (1) of Table 4.1); at the other extreme, most school education is produced publicly and paid out of tax revenues (Box (4)). Two intermediate cases are frequently overlooked. In Britain goods like domestic gas and electricity are produced in the public sector but, with some exceptions, are financed by charges on the private sector (Box (2)). Other goods are produced privately but sold to the public sector, including part of university output and many of the material inputs to the national health service, e.g. drugs, blankets. Those who favour privatisation have at the back of their minds a movement from Box (4) to Box (1)). But, more generally, it can be defined as any movement up and/or to the left in Table 4.1.

Table 4.1: An Overview of Public and Private Provision[a]

		PRODUCTION	
		Private	Public
FINANCE	Private	**(1)** Food	**(2)** Domestic gas (in the UK) Electricity (in the UK) Her Majesty's Stationery Office
		PRIVATISATION	
	Public	**(3)** NHS inputs (eg drugs, blankets, etc) Universities (in the UK) Education vouchers Military equipment	**(4)** Health care under the NHS Primary and secondary education National defence

NOTE: [a]The examples in boxes 1–4 are only approximate.

This analysis, unfortunately, is so over-simplified as to be of little use for our purposes. In reality, markets are virtually never purely private: food is subject to regulation about quality, and its price is distorted *inter alia* by agricultural subsidies; and it may be purchased out of transfer income (e.g. social security benefits), or provided without charge (e.g. free school meals). Nor are there many pure cases of free public provision, e.g. charges are levied under the national health service for prescriptions and dentistry.

To clarify the situation, even keeping matters as simple as possible, it is necessary to distinguish not only (a) in which sector *production* takes place and (b) which sector *finances* it, but also the influence of *regulation* on decisions about production and consumption, in particular on (c) the total quantity produced of any good and (d) how much each individual consumer will receive. These are illustrated in Table 4.2, though the analysis is still far from exhaustive. The first part shows different examples of private production. Line

(1) (which corresponds to Box (1) in Table 4.1) shows the pure private case, e.g. food purchased out of non-transfer income. Production is private, and total supply determined by producers; individuals decide how much to consume, and pay for it themselves. Line (2) is identical except that individual consumption is financed by the state. The simplest case is food purchased out of transfer income; other examples are food stamps, medicare and medicaid in the USA. Line (3) illustrates a private market subject to regulation. In line (3)(a) the individual consumption decision is made by the state (mandatory automobile insurance, statutory sick pay);[1] in line (3)(b) the state puts a ceiling on total production, though allocation to individuals remains private (very roughly the case of health care in Canada). Line 4 illustrates private production modified by both regulation and finance (i.e. roughly Box (3) in Table 4.1). In line (4)(a) production decisions are wholly private (e.g. education vouchers). Line (4)(b) shows the case where allocation and finance are wholly public, but production itself takes place in the private sector (national health service inputs like blankets and X-ray machines, certain types of military equipment).

The second half of the Table looks at public production. In line (5)(a) output is produced in the public sector but allocated and financed privately (domestic gas, electricity, Her Majesty's Stationery Office); in line (5)(b) supply is determined publicly, but demand decisions and finance are private (pay beds in health service hospitals). These cases approximate Box (2) in Table 4.1. Line (6) illustrates public production and allocation with private finance, e.g. social insurance. Line (7) illustrates public production and finance, though the individual consumption decision is private, e.g. secondary education after minimum school-leaving age. The case of pure public production is shown in line (8) (i.e. Box (4) in Table 4.1); examples include (as approximations) compulsory school education, the national health service and national defence.

We can now see what privatisation means. Libertarians favour private production under column (1), producer and consumer sovereignty under columns (2) and (3) and private finance under column (4). They would therefore choose line (1) or, failing that, the private market underwritten by cash transfers, shown in line (2). Privatisation can therefore be seen as an upward movement in the table from a lower line to a higher.

The issues How, then, should specific proposals for privatisation be analysed? It was argued in section 3 that regulation, finance or public production may increase efficiency where the standard assumptions fail. Conversely, where they all hold there are no efficiency grounds for intervention in private markets, and distributional objectives are generally best approached through cash transfers.

---

[1] Statutory sick pay is described in Chapter 8:1.2.

Table 4.2: Public and Private Provision: A More Complete View[a]

TYPE OF ALLOCATION	PRODUC-TION (1)	REGULATION		FINANCE (4)	EXAMPLES
		Decision about Total Production (2)	Decision about Individual Consumption (3)		
(1) Pure private (= Box 1 in Table 4.1)	PRIVATE	PRIVATE	PRIVATE	PRIVATE	food purchased out of non-transfer income
(2) Private market plus state finance (income subsidy)	Private	Private	Private	Public	all consumption of privately produced goods purchased out transfer income; food stamps; medicare & medicaid (USA)
(3) Private market plus regulation					
(a) regulation of individual consumption	Private	Private	Public	Private	mandatory car insurance; statutory sick pay
(b) regulation of total supply	Private	Public	Private	Private	health care (Canada, approx)
(4) Private production, state regulation and finance (= Box 3 in Table 4.1)					
(a) supply wholly private	Private	Private	Public	Public	education vouchers
(b) total supply determined by state	Private	Public	Public	Public	inputs for NHS & national defence
(5) Public production, private allocation and finance (= Box 2 in Table 4.1)					
(a) total supply determined by private demand	Public	Private	Private	Private	gas, electricity, HMSO NHS pay beds
(b) supply wholly public	Public	Public	Private	Private	
(6) Public apart from private finance	Public	Public	Public	Private	national insurance (UK), health care insurance (Canada approx)
(7) Public apart from private consumption decision	Public	Public	Private	Public	secondary education after age 16
(8) Pure public (= Box 4 in Table 4.1)	PUBLIC	PUBLIC	PUBLIC	Public	NHS, national defence

Note: [a] The examples are only approximate.

The issues raised by the privatisation debate (see the Further Reading) fall naturally into this framework. It is necessary, in the case of any particular activity, to consider the extent to which it conforms with the necessary assumptions. And in this context information problems assume considerable importance. Because of technological change over the century the optimal scale of many types of industry is large; and in any large organisation information (i.e. management) problems are likely to arise whether the industry is public or private. It is therefore not surprising that 'the fundamental problems concerned with the control of public utilities are very similar, irrespective of whether they are in the public or private sectors' (Webb, 1984, p. 99).

Whatever the answers about privatisation (and they are rarely clear-cut) the technical dimension of the analysis should not be obscured by ideology,[1] an observation which leads naturally to the final part of the chapter.

6 Conclusion: Economic and Political Theory

6.1 ACHIEVING POLICY AIMS: A LIBERAL VIEW

This section brings together the analysis of Chapters 3 and 4. The vital distinction between the *aims* of policy and the *methods* available to achieve them should by now be clear. Aims include social justice and economic efficiency: the definition of social justice will vary with different theories of society (Chapter 3); economic efficiency has broadly the same meaning in all theories of society (section 2). Methods embrace cash transfers and direct intervention in the market through regulation, finance and public production. The resulting form of economic organisation, at one extreme, is the free market (with or without redistribution) and, at the other, central planning and public production of all basic goods and services (with or without charges). In between are different types of mixed economy involving both private markets (with or without intervention in the form of regulation and finance) and public production.

The central argument of this book is that the proper place of ideology is in the choice of aims, particularly in the definition of social justice and in its trade-off with economic efficiency; but *once these aims have been agreed* the choice of

---

[1] As an example of how ideology can bias logic, note the tendency for proponents of free markets to regard 'managers' as 'good' and 'administrators' as 'bad' ('bureaucrats' being a term of abuse for everyone). In many respects, however, managers, administrators and bureaucrats all do broadly the same job and face similar problems. Calling them by different names with differing emotive connotations does little to advance the argument.

method should be regarded as a *technical* issue rather than an ideological one. Whether a particular good or service is provided publicly or privately should be decided on the basis of which method more nearly achieves the aims of social justice and economic efficiency; and government intervention, similarly, should take place not on the basis of doctrinaire views about methods, but only if the achievement of policy aims is thereby enhanced. In the sense that the issue of market versus state provision is a contingent matter rather than an item of dogma this book is firmly in the liberal tradition.[1]

How, then, should we choose between different methods? The analysis of section 3 suggests:

Proposition 1: efficiency: where one or more of the standard assumptions fail, state intervention in the form of regulation, finance or public production may increase economic efficiency. If none of the assumptions fails, efficiency is generally achieved best with no intervention.

Turning to social justice, assume that there is no consumption externality in the utility functions of the rich (section 4.2). Then:

Proposition 2: social justice:
(a) Only efficiency arguments can justify intervention other than cash redistribution. If no such efficiency justification exists, the interests of social justice are likely to be served best by *income* transfers.
(b) But if there exist arguments which suggest that efficiency will be furthered by public production and allocation of any good or service, then social justice can be enhanced by *in-kind* transfers (e.g. redistribution via free education or health care).

There are three possible exceptions to Proposition 2. The first is the consumption externality argument, which offers a justification of sorts for transfers in kind even where there are no efficiency grounds for public production or allocation. The second concerns the role of giving. There is no *technical* argument against having a market for babies. But most societies rule this out on ethical grounds. It is argued, for instance, that health care might more appropriately be regarded as a gift than a purchase, and Titmuss (1970) makes a cogent argument for blood to be treated in this way.

The optimal taxation literature offers the third exception (see Bos, 1984). The taxation necessary to finance income transfers may reduce labour supply; if so, a given distributional objective *may* be possible at lower efficiency cost by subsidising the *prices* of goods consumed by the poor. The result requires (a) that such goods are consumed only (or mainly) by the poor, and (b) that their

---

[1] For a classic defence of the mixed economy on broadly similar grounds see Okun (1975).

consumption is not strongly complementary to leisure.

From a purely theoretical viewpoint, this suggests that the two propositions can be criticised for their 'piecemeal' approach, i.e. for discussing conformity with the standard assumptions in a given area whilst implicitly assuming that they hold in all other areas. This ignores second-best considerations (Lipsey and Lancaster, 1956). Several defences are possible. First, in a limited number of cases the approach is *theoretically* valid (Davis and Whinston, 1965). Second, the measurement problems involved in applying any other approach to policy are intractable, so that 'the rules of first-best optimality, coupled with the caveat of second-best . . . constitute part of the fund of guidelines from which good, if not perfect, policy might be formulated' (Winch, 1971). Third, none of the areas covered by the welfare state conforms very closely with the two conditions in the previous paragraph.

Finally, I want to nail a line of argument which I regard as wholly fallacious. In one form it runs, 'We must have a national health service because otherwise the poor could not afford adequate health care' – an argument which does the cause of its proponents little service. The fallacy is that if inability to pay were the *only* difficulty there would not be a *market allocation problem* with health care but an *income distribution problem*, which could be solved by cash transfers as currently with food. The justification for the national health service, as argued in Chapter 12, lies not in Proposition 2(a) (which applies to food) but in Proposition 2(b).

Even more woolly is the assertion that, 'We must have a national health service because everybody has a right to health care.' The fallacy lies in the word 'because'. It is just as plausible to argue that everybody has a right to good nutrition, yet there are few advocates of a national food service. The statement confuses aims with methods. There is wide acceptance of the value that people have a right to adequate nutrition and health care. These are *aims*; but the existence of these rights does not, *per se*, have any implications for the best method of achieving them. As we shall see, there are good reasons why Britain has a national health service but not a national food service – entitlement to food and health care, however, is not one of them.

6.2 THE DEBATE WITH LIBERTARIANS

Propositions 1 and 2 would meet with general agreement from liberals and Fabian socialists. Marxists would reject them for the reasons discussed in Chapter 3:5. They accept the idea of social justice, but argue that too little has been done to achieve it. The efficiency arguments embodied in Proposition 1 are in large measure rejected on the grounds that the market system, though possibly in some respects efficient, is the fundamental *cause* of the failure to achieve social justice. We return to this issue in Chapter 15:2.1.

The debate with empirical libertarians like Hayek and Friedman is in many ways the most interesting and, given current policy concerns, the most relevant. The less interesting part of the argument is ideological. Libertarians reject almost in their entirety the social justice arguments of section 4, and in consequence reject Proposition 2. Hayek argues (Chapter 3:2) that there is no such thing as social justice, and that its quest risks eventual totalitarianism. Libertarians argue that there is too much redistribution, and that redistribution in kind is even more dangerous than transfers in cash. Taken as an ideological view little counter-argument is possible, save to assert a different set of values.

The debate over efficiency is much more important. As we saw in Chapter 3:2 empirical libertarians are the direct descendants of Classical liberalism (compare the views in Friedman (1962, Ch. 2) on the role of the state with those of Adam Smith quoted at the head of Chapter 1). Writers like Hayek and Friedman therefore admit a limited role for the state in the presence of market failures like externalities and public goods; and both accept a very restricted welfare state. Beyond this, however, both would resist the efficiency arguments of section 3. State intervention, it is argued, is often the *cause* of imperfect information rather than its result (e.g. if there were a competitive market for health care people would acquire better information, in part because market institutions would arise to supply it). They support intervention to break monopolies or near-monopolies in product and (particularly) factor markets, and argue that domestic monopolies of tradeable goods need not be a problem if there are no barriers to foreign trade. As a result they argue that state intervention is excessive.

In sum, libertarians like Hayek and Friedman accept the analytical framework of section 3, but interpret facts differently. To that extent the debate is empirical. But it is also (and importantly) theoretical. What is not in dispute is the aim of maximising social welfare, nor the existence of imperfections in the form of monopolies, externalities, public goods and increasing returns to scale. The critical difference, as suggested in section 3, is that Hayek and Friedman greatly underestimate technical problems with markets, and can be criticised in particular for the failure of their analysis systematically to take account of information problems. These afflict consumers of increasingly complex products, and managers of increasingly large-scale enterprises, and they include technical – again largely information – problems in insurance markets (Chapter 5). The existence of information problems, more than any other theoretical consideration, suggests that a properly designed welfare state is much more than an instrument of social justice. It also has a major efficiency role.

Further Reading

The most comprehensive treatment of the subject-matter of this chapter is Atkinson and Stiglitz (1980, Lectures 11–18). For a gentler introduction to the economic theory of markets and welfare economics see Le Grand and Robinson (1984a, Chs 1 and 2) (elementary); Laidler (1981, Chs 18 and 19); Brown and Jackson (1982, Chs 2–4); Musgrave and Musgrave (1984, Chs 3–6) (intermediate, non-mathematical); and Layard and Walters (1978, Chs 1–3) or Varian (1984, Chs 5–8) (somewhat more advanced). For a lucid, non-technical discussion of efficiency, equity and their trade-off see Okun (1975) (a classic, and strongly recommended defence of the mixed economy). References to the literature on information problems are given in the Further Reading at the end of Chapter 5.

For a simple introduction to the theory of externalities see Le Grand and Robinson (1984a, Ch. 2), and for fuller discussion of market failures Prest and Barr (1985, Ch. 3), Layard and Walters (1978, Ch. 6) and Musgrave and Musgrave *op. cit.* A complete technical account of the optimal taxation literature and the trade-off between efficiency and equity is given by Atkinson and Stiglitz *op. cit.*; for less technical discussion see Brown and Jackson (1982, Ch. 20).

Different definitions of equity are discussed in Chapter 3; for an excellent brief summary see also Le Grand (1984). A non-technical introduction to the theory of coerced redistribution through the ballot box is given by Tullock (1976), and in more complete form by Downs (1957) and Tullock (1970). The theory of voluntary (Pareto optimal) redistribution is developed by Hochman and Rodgers (1969); see also Thurow (1971). For general discussion of the economics of charity see Sugden (1983b) (a simple introduction), and for a more complete treatment Sugden (1982 and 1984) and the discussion in Collard (1983) and Sugden (1983a).

Privatisation is the subject of a rapidly growing literature. Minford (1984b) favours radical privatisation. For argument about the welfare state, and about public enterprise generally, see the contributions in Le Grand and Robinson (1984b) and Steel and Heald (1984). More general discussion is contained in Beesley and Littlechild (1983) and Peacock (1984). The relative efficiency of public and private enterprise is discussed by Caves and Christensen (1980) and Pryke (1982). For an analysis of UK government policy see Kay and Thompson (1986) and the Comment by Brittan (1986).

Appendix: Non-technical Summary of Chapter 4

1 Chapter 4 sets out the economic theory of state intervention, with particular emphasis on why intervention might foster efficiency and/or social justice (also referred to as equity).

The Concept of Economic Efficiency

2 The efficient (or Pareto optimal) output of any good (section 2.1) is the quantity which maximises the excess of benefits over costs. This is the output $Q^\star$ in Figure 4.1 at which the value placed by society on the marginal unit of output equals its marginal social cost (for an excellent exposition see Le Grand and Robinson, 1984a, pp. 3–9).

3 A Pareto improvement (i.e. an increase in efficiency) takes place if any change in production or distribution makes one person better-off without making anyone else worse-off.

4 Section 2.2 shows that an increase in efficiency can raise welfare under *any* of the theories of society discussed in Chapter 3. The aim of efficiency is therefore common to all these ideologies, though the weight attached to it will vary when its achievement conflicts with distributional goals.

Intervention for Reasons of Efficiency

5 The state can intervene in four ways (section 3.1). **Regulation** mainly concerns the quality of supply (e.g. hygiene laws relating to food, minimum building standards) and regulation of individual demand (e.g. the legal requirement to attend school, compulsory membership of national insurance). **Finance** can involve subsidies (or taxes) which change the price of specific commodities. Subsidies can be partial (e.g. local authority housing) or total (e.g. free drugs under the national health service). **Public production** covers national defence, education and (in Britain) most health care. These three types of intervention all involve direct interference in the market mechanism. **Cash transfers** do not do so directly, but enable recipients to buy goods of their choice at market prices, e.g. elderly people receive a retirement pension with which they buy food.

6 **The Invisible Hand theorem** asserts that markets are automatically efficient if and only if a number of assumptions hold (section 3.2). These conditions (collectively called the **standard assumptions**) are discussed in paragraphs 7–16 below, which, together with paragraphs 22–6, summarise the theoretical heart of the book. The conditions relate to perfect information, perfect competition and the absence of market failures.

7 **Perfect information** implies, first, that consumers and firms should be well

informed about the nature of the product, and also about prices. This is plausible for some goods (e.g. food and clothing), less so for others (e.g. health care). Where the assumption fails, several solutions are possible: the market itself may develop institutions to supply information (e.g. professional valuers, consumer magazines); or the state may respond with regulations (e.g. hygiene laws in the case of food); where information problems are serious the market might be so inefficient that public production might be a better answer.

8 Individuals need perfect information also about the future, so as to make rational choices over time. This is broadly true of food (since I know that I will need to eat tomorrow, next week, next month); it is not true with motor cars, because I do not know whether my car will be involved in an accident. The market can frequently cope with this sort of uncertainty through the mechanism of insurance (the main topic of Chapter 5). But private insurance can be inefficient or impossible for technical reasons; some risks (e.g. unemployment) are not insurable, largely because of information problems in the insurance market. In such cases public production may be necessary for reasons of efficiency.

9 **Perfect competition** must apply in all input and output markets and also to capital markets (i.e. access to borrowing). Two conditions must hold: individuals must be price takers; and they must have equal power.

10 Price taking implies free entry and exit into/from an industry with a large number of consumers and firms, none of whom individually is able to influence market prices. Where the assumption fails (e.g. in the case of a monopoly) intervention generally involves regulation (e.g. a price ceiling) or an appropriate mix of taxation and subsidy.

11 Equal power is violated by any difference (apart from differences in individual incomes) in the ability of individuals to choose their consumption. The assumption rules out all forms of discrimination; where it fails, solutions (to the extent that they exist) are usually based on regulation.

12 **Market failures** arise in three forms: public goods, external effects and increasing returns to scale.

13 **Public goods** in their pure form exhibit three technical characteristics: non-rivalness in consumption, non-excludability, and non-rejectability. Private (i.e. 'normal') goods are rival in consumption in the sense that if I buy a cheese sandwich there will be one sandwich less available for everyone else; excludability means that I can be prevented from consuming the cheese sandwich until I have paid for it; and rejectability implies that I do not have to eat it unless I wish to. Not all goods display these characteristics, the classic example being national defence. If the Royal Air Force is circling over Britain the arrival of an additional person does not reduce the amount of defence available to everyone else (non-rivalness in

consumption); nor is it possible to exclude the new arrival by saying that the bombs will be allowed to fall on him until he has paid his taxes (non-excludability); nor is the individual able to reject the defence on the grounds of pacifist beliefs (non-rejectability). Similar considerations apply wholly or in part to roads, public parks and television broadcast signals.

14 In discussing public goods, an important distinction should be noted. For a private good the marginal cost associated with an extra *unit of output* and the marginal cost of an *extra user* are one and the same thing – if it costs £1 to produce an extra cheese sandwich, it also costs £1 to provide for an extra cheese-sandwich-consumer. But this identity does not hold for public goods – for example, the marginal cost of an extra hour's broadcasting is positive and generally large, whereas the marginal cost of an extra viewer is zero. This has important implications. If a public good is provided at all, non-excludability makes it impossible to charge for it (this is the **free-rider** problem); in such cases the market will generally fail entirely. Non-rivalness implies that the marginal cost of an extra user (though *not* of an extra unit of output) is zero, and therefore the efficient price should be based not on costs, but on the value placed by each individual on an extra unit of consumption. Since this is impractical, the market is likely to produce an inefficient output. Thus the market is either inefficient, or fails altogether; if the good is to be provided at all it will generally have to be publicly produced.

15 **External effects** arise when an act of individual A imposes costs or confers benefits on individual B, for which no compensation from A to B or payment from B to A takes place or, more formally, when A's utility or production function is interrelated with B's. The effect of externalities is to create a divergence between private and social costs and benefits. As a result, the market output in the presence of an external cost will generally exceed the efficient output, Q^* in Figure 4.1, and vice versa for an external benefit. On occasion the market can resolve this inefficiency itself. Coase (1960) shows that where the law assigns unambiguous and enforceable property rights the externality problem may be solved by negotiation between the parties concerned. But this is not always possible, for instance where property rights are not enforceable (e.g. air pollution) or where large numbers of people are involved (e.g. traffic congestion). In this case intervention may be justified either through regulation (e.g. mandatory filtering equipment) or via an appropriate tax (sometimes referred to as a Pigovian tax) on the activity generating the external cost (see Le Grand and Robinson, 1984a, Ch. 2).

16 **Increasing returns to scale** arise when doubling all inputs leads to more than twice the output. If a production function exhibits increasing returns to scale at all levels of output, average cost will always exceed marginal cost

as in Figure 4.4 (p. 84). It follows that at an output of Q_0 the marginal cost price p_0 is less than average cost, AC_0; hence competitive pricing results in an inherent loss shown by the shaded area. If firms in a competitive industry make long-run losses they will leave the industry, which will either become monopolised or, if even a monopolist is unable to make a profit, will cease to exist. The result, therefore, is a sub-optimal output or a failure by the market to produce at all. Two solutions are possible: paying firms a lump-sum subsidy equal to the loss associated with competitive pricing; or nationalising the industry and paying an identical subsidy. The appropriate intervention is therefore subsidy or public production, or both.

17 The market will allocate efficiently only when *all* the assumptions in paragraphs 7–16 hold, in which case no intervention on efficiency grounds is necessary. Where one or more of the assumptions fails it is necessary in each case to consider which type of intervention (regulation, finance or public production) is most likely to improve efficiency.

Intervention for Reasons of Social Justice

18 Section 4.1 sets out three explanations of why redistribution occurs. To libertarians it is enforced on the rich by the voting power of the poor. Utilitarians argue that the rich may *choose* out of altruistic motives to vote for political parties which propose to tax them more heavily to finance redistributive policies. Marxists explain redistribution partly in terms of the needs of the capitalist system for an educated and healthy workforce, and partly as an attempt to reduce class conflict; in either case redistribution is motivated by the self-interest of the rich.

19 In certain circumstances it may be politically easier to make direct in-kind transfers, e.g. education. The formal analysis (based on the idea of a consumption externality) is shown by the voting model in section 4.2. Suppose the utility (see the Glossary) of a representative rich individual, R, rises with his own consumption, and also with the consumption of a representative poor man, P. In particular, suppose that R's utility rises with 'good' consumption by P (e.g. education), but falls with P's 'bad' consumption (e.g. whisky), where 'good' and 'bad' are defined by R. In this circumstance it might be rational for R to offer P an education costing (say) £1000, but to offer a cash transfer of only £200 (since P might spend the latter in part on 'bad' consumption). Faced with these offers, P might prefer the in-kind transfer to the lower cash sum (see Figure 4.5 on p. 90), i.e. both rich *and* poor might vote for compulsory in-kind transfers.

Privatisation

20 The term 'privatisation' is considerably more complicated than most of its

users realise (section 5). As a first approximation, commodities like food are *produced* and *financed* privately whereas, at the opposite extreme, most education is produced in the public sector and paid for out of tax revenues. But intermediate cases are possible (Table 4.1). Some goods are publicly produced, but are financed by user charges (e.g. electricity); others are paid from tax revenues but produced in the private sector (e.g. drugs supplied free under the national health service).

21 Matters become considerably more complicated when regulation is included. It is then necessary to distinguish not only the sector in which (a) production and (b) finance take place, but also who decides (c) how much in total of any good will be produced and (d) how much each individual consumer will receive. Some of these cases are set out in Table 4.2.

Achieving the Aims of Policy

22 Section 6 draws together the main arguments of Chapters 3 and 4 by making the distinction between the *aims* of policy and the *methods* available to achieve them. Aims embrace social justice and economic efficiency; methods include cash transfers and direct interference in the market through regulation, finance or public production.

23 The central argument of this book is that the proper place of ideology is in the choice of aims, particularly the definition of social justice and its trade-off with economic efficiency; but once these aims have been agreed, the choice of method should be regarded as a *technical* issue, not an ideological one. Whether a commodity like health care is produced publicly or privately should be decided on the basis of which method more nearly achieves previously agreed aims. A rationale for choosing between the different methods is given in section 6.1 in the form of two propositions.

24 **Proposition 1: efficiency**: where one or more of the standard assumptions fail, state intervention in the form of regulation, finance or public production may increase economic efficiency. If none of the assumptions fail, the efficiency aim is generally achieved best by the market with no intervention.

Subject to minor qualifications it is possible to argue:

25 **Proposition 2: social justice**
(a) Only efficiency arguments can justify intervention other than cash redistribution. If no such efficiency justification exists, the interests of social justice are best served by *income* transfers;
(b) But if there exist arguments which suggest that efficiency will be furthered by public production and allocation of any good or service, then social justice can be enhanced by *in-kind* transfers (e.g. redistribution in the form of free education or health care).

26 The two propositions make the issue of market versus state production and allocation a contingent matter, placing this book firmly in the liberal tradition (as defined in Chapter 3:1). The debate between this book and libertarian writers like Hayek and Friedman is joined in section 6.2.

5

Economic Theory 2: Insurance[1]

Insurance, *n*. An ingenious modern game of chance in which the player is permitted to enjoy the comfortable conviction that he is beating the man who keeps the table. [Ambrose Bierce, 1842–1914.]

1 Introduction

It is possible to buy insurance against a wide variety of common mishaps like burglary, death, or car accidents; against losses caused by bad weather; and for holiday deposits lost through illness. It is even possible to buy life insurance for one's dog or cat.[2] On the face of it this is all a bit curious, since the published accounts of insurance companies show that they usually make a profit. A representative individual thus receives less in benefit in the long run than he pays in contributions.

This gives rise to two questions: why do people insure voluntarily, e.g. against burglary; and under what conditions will the private market provide insurance? These questions concerning, respectively, the demand and supply sides of the insurance market are discussed in sections 2 and 3. It is also important to consider the circumstances in which a market equilibrium will exist, and will be efficient (section 4).

---

[1] Non-technical readers can find the gist of the argument in the Appendix to this chapter.

[2] 'Dogs and Cats Get Cover from the Pru', *The Times*, 3 November 1981.

The analysis of insurance markets pre-dates the more general interest in the economics of information, but many of the problems which arise are examples of a more general class of information problem (see the Further Reading). The parallels will be noted as we proceed. But since the purpose of the chapter is to set out only as much of the theory of insurance as is necessary to discuss the welfare state, I shall keep to the basics.

2 The Demand for Insurance

2.1 THE INDIVIDUAL'S DEMAND

Why might a rational individual choose to insure when the expected payout is less than his premium payments? The answer, if he is risk-averse, is that uncertainty *per se* causes disutility; hence certainty is a commodity yielding positive marginal utility, for which he will pay a positive price. The formal argument starts with the definition of a risk-averse individual as someone with diminishing marginal utility of income, as shown in Figure 5.1.[1] Suppose there is a 'bad' outcome, y_1, yielding utility $U(y_1)$, and a 'good' outcome, y_2, yielding

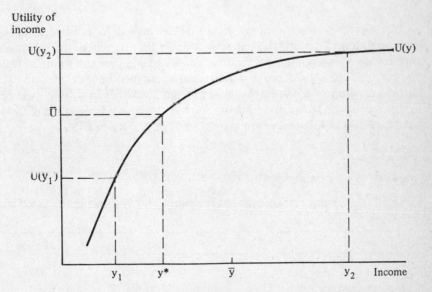

Figure 5.1   *The demand for insurance by a risk-averse individual*

[1] A good, simple introduction is Laidler (1981, Ch. 7); see also the Further Reading.

utility $U(y_2)$, occurring with probabilities p_1 and p_2, respectively. The individual's expected income, and expected utility are:

Expected income: $E(y) = \bar{y} = p_1 y_1 + p_2 y_2$ (5.1)
Expected utility: $E(U) = \bar{U} = p_1 U(y_1) + p_2 U(y_2)$ (5.2)

If $p_1 = p_2 = \frac{1}{2}$, expected income, $\bar{y}$, is midway between y_1 and y_2, (if $y_1 = £100$, and $y_2 = £1000$, then $\bar{y} = £550$); and expected utility, $\bar{U}$, is midway between $U(y_1)$ and $U(y_2)$.

It is important to realise that a risk-averse individual can obtain the utility $\bar{U}$ in two entirely different ways. First, as the *expected* utility from an uncertain income of y_1 or y_2. Note that the individual never receives $\bar{y}$; each year he receives *either* y_1 *or* y_2, with corresponding utilities $U(y_1)$ and $U(y_2)$; the expected (or average) outcome is $\bar{y}$. Second, he could obtain $\bar{U}$ from a *certain* income $y^\star$, as shown directly by the utility function in Figure 5.1. A rational individual will therefore be indifferent between an income $y^\star$ with certainty and an expected income $\bar{y}$ arising from uncertain outcomes y_1 and y_2. The total value of certainty (including consumer surplus) is thus

$$V = \bar{y} - y^\star \tag{5.3}$$

and a rational individual will pay a net price, ϕ, so long as:

$$\phi \leqslant V \tag{5.4}$$

The *net* price of insurance, ϕ, should be carefully distinguished from the gross premium. The difference is shown in Table 5.1, where the insurance company charges an annual premium of £550, and compensates for up to £900 of lost income. In a 'good' year the individual has an income of £1000, and pays a gross premium of £550, leaving a net income of £450. In a 'bad' year his income is £100; he pays a premium of £550 but receives compensation of £900. Thus the effect of insurance is to guarantee a net income of £450.

Table 5.1: Gross and Net Insurance Premiums, and Net Income in Good and Bad Years

	Good Year	*Bad Year*
(1) Income	£1000	£100
(2) Insurance premium	£550	£550
(3) Insurance benefit	–	£900
(4) Net Income ((1) − (2) + (3))	£450	£450
(5) Net Premium ((2) − (4))	£100	£100

The net premium, ϕ, is the difference between the gross premium and the average payout. The latter is the individual's expected loss

$$E(L) = pL \qquad (5.5)$$

defined as the size of the loss, L, times the probability, p, that it will occur. Thus the net price of insurance is

$$\phi = \Pi - pL \qquad (5.6)$$

where Π is the gross premium. In the example, the individual's expected loss is £450; so £450 of the gross premium can be regarded as a form of saving to cover his own losses over the long run. The *net* price of insurance is £100, which the individual will pay so long as it does not exceed the value to him of certainty, V, in equation (5.3). We return to the calculation of insurance premiums in section 3.1.

2.2 THE NATURE OF THE PRODUCT: INSURANCE AS A MECHANISM FOR POOLING RISK

The twin intellectual bases of insurance are the law of large numbers and gains from trade. Under the former, *individuals* may face uncertainty, but society can face approximate certainty, i.e. I do not know whether I will die this year, but the death rate for men aged 25 to 45 is known and stable. It is the relative certainty about the *aggregate* probability resulting from the law of large numbers which opens up to individuals the possibility of exploiting gains from trade by agreeing to pool risks.

This can be shown formally.[1] Suppose each individual's income is a random variable y with mean, μ, and variance, $\text{var}(y)$; there are N such individuals with incomes $y_1, y_2 \ldots y_N$, respectively. We assume:

(i)   all individuals face the same probability distribution of outcomes;
(ii) y, μ and $\text{var}(y)$ for each individual are independent of those for every other individual (e.g. fire hazard or burglary, but *not* crop failure).

In the absence of insurance, the variance (i.e. risk) facing the ith individual is $\text{var}(y_i)$. Now suppose all N individuals put their income into a pool agreeing that each will receive

$$\bar{y} = \frac{1}{N}(y_1 + y_2 + \ldots + y_N) \qquad (5.7)$$

This pooling is a form of insurance. The variance for society is

$$\text{var}(y_1 + y_2 + \ldots + y_N) = N \, \text{var}(y)$$

---

[1] This presentation is drawn from Layard and Walters (1978, Ch. 13).

since all incomes are independent and have the same variance. But the variance for the *individual* is smaller. He receives the average income, $\bar{y}$ in equation (5.7) and

$$\text{var}(\bar{y}) = \text{var}\left(\frac{y_1}{N} + \frac{y_2}{N} + \ldots + \frac{y_N}{N}\right)$$

$$= N\,\text{var}\left(\frac{y}{N}\right)$$

$$= \frac{\text{var}(y)}{N} \to 0, \text{ as } N \to \infty \tag{5.8}$$

Equation (5.8) shows that if N identically distributed and independent incomes are pooled, the variance of average income (and hence the risk to the individual) tends to zero as N tends to infinity. By 'trading' (i.e. pooling) individuals can acquire certainty.

2.3 AN EXAMPLE: ANNUITIES

Annuities (i.e. an annual income stream) are another form of pooling. An individual could buy an income of £y per year for n years by paying a lump sum, A, equal to its present value, i.e.

$$A = y + \frac{y}{1+r} + \frac{y}{(1+r)^2} + \ldots + \frac{y}{(1+r)^{n-1}} \tag{5.9}$$

where r is the rate of interest.[1] More generally, the capital cost of a given income stream is

$$A = f(y, n, r) \tag{5.10}$$

Consider someone with £50,000 accumulated in pension contributions over his working life. He could finance his retirement (12 years on average, for a 65-year-old man in Britain) by consuming this lump sum at a rate of say £5000 per year; but he thereby risks outliving his savings. He can avoid this uncertainty by buying an annuity, which is a form of insurance in which he exchanges £50,000 and an uncertain lifespan for an annual income of £y, with certainty and for life. He is, in effect, making a bet with the insurance company – if he hands over the lump sum and immediately drops dead, he loses (because he receives

---

[1] A simple exposition of the present value formula is given in Lipsey (1983, Ch. 28); for further detail see Layard and Walters (1978, Ch. 12), Brown and Jackson (1982, Ch. 8), or Musgrave and Musgrave (1984, Ch. 8). For a complete treatment of cost-benefit analysis including discussion of the discount rate see Mishan (1982).

back less than the lump sum), but if he lives to 98, he wins. This arrangement is exactly analogous to income-pooling. All retired persons put their lump sums into a pool and draw the average income; those who live longer draw more than those who die younger, but the fund can pay for the long-lived because it is based on average life expectancy. The process is both technically feasible and with low transactions costs, because the aggregate distribution of age at death is known and stable.

How large is the annuity? Equation (5.10) can be rewritten as

$$y = g(A, n, r) \tag{5.11}$$

which shows that the annual payment, £y, for a given lump sum, A, depends on the insurance company's view of n (the applicant's life expectancy) and r (its expected interest rate).

Life expectancy   The insurance company pays a lower annual income the longer it expects to pay benefit. This depends on four broad factors.

Age: the younger a person the longer, on average, he has to live and the smaller the annuity he is offered in respect of a given lump sum.

Sex: on average women live longer than men. Thus, other things being equal, a woman will receive a smaller annuity than a man. In practice, many pension schemes pool across men and women for annuity calculations; this raises a number of important equity issues (see Chapter 9:4.2).

Health: we should expect an insurance company to be interested in an individual's health. But since it is easier to detect health problems than to prove their absence, there is usually more interest in an applicant's health for life insurance than for annuity purposes, the more so because in the latter case early death is to the company's advantage. Insurance companies therefore usually pool across health for annuities, but not for life insurance.

Marital status: where an annuity is payable also to a surviving spouse, the age difference between husband and wife becomes relevant. If I retire at 65, and my wife is considerably younger, she is likely to outlive me by many years, in which case the payout period, n, is longer, and the annuity correspondingly smaller. However, where schemes are compulsory (e.g. a pension scheme for schoolteachers), insurance companies usually pool across men aged 65 irrespective of the age of their wives. This is feasible because for the *group* the average age difference is predictable.[1]

The rate of interest   If changes in the price level are not to affect the real value of an annuity, it is necessary to base calculations on the real rate of interest (i.e. the excess of the nominal interest rate over the rate of inflation). This is a

---

[1] The fact that such schemes are compulsory is important – this aspect is dealt with in more detail in sections 3.2 and 4.2.

difficult variable to predict; estimates based on past data (Barr, 1975c) suggest that the long-run real rate of return is often not more than 1 per cent.

Suppose an individual has accumulated a lump sum of £50,000, and the insurance company expects him to live for 12 years ($n = 12$) and anticipates a real rate of interest of one per cent ($r = 0.01$). The actuarial value of an annuity is obtained by substituting these values into equation (5.11) to obtain a value for y. The subject of annuities in the context of pension finance is a major topic in Chapter 9.

3 The Supply Side

3.1 THE SUPPLY OF INSURANCE

This part of the chapter discusses the price at which the private market will supply insurance, and then turns to a number of technical problems.

The actuarial premium   Suppose that I insure the contents of my house for £1000, when the probability of being burgled is 1 per cent. From equation (5.5) my expected loss is the product of the insured loss, L, and the probability, p, that the loss will occur. The insurance company knows that on average it will have to pay out £10 per year (i.e. 1 per cent of £1000). The actuarial premium, Π, is then defined as:

$$\Pi = pL + T \qquad (5.12)$$

where pL is the individual's expected loss, and T the insurance company's transactions costs, including administrative costs (e.g. sending an expert to assess the damage) and normal profit. Π is the price at which insurance will be supplied in a competitive market.

Conditions for private insurance   The actuarial premium in equation (5.12) rests on a number of conditions on the probability, p. Some are strictly technical; others bring us directly back to the issue of perfect information. Problems under either head can make private insurance inefficient or impossible.

Private insurance requires, first, that the probability of the insured event for any individual is *independent* of that for anyone else. This condition is necessary because insurance depends on the existence in a given period of a predictable number of winners and losers. If, in the extreme, individual probabilities were completely related, then if one person suffered a loss so too would everyone else; actuarial insurance is clearly not able to cope with this situation. An important example (discussed in Chapter 9:3.1) concerns inflation which, if it affects any one member of an actuarial pension scheme, will affect all.

The second condition is that the relevant probability must be *less than one*. If not, equation (5.12) simplifies to:

$$\Pi = L + T > L \qquad (5.13)$$

and the actuarial premium exceeds the insured loss. I might, for example, have to pay a premium of £1500 to insure against burglary losses of £1000. Private insurance will not be offered because there will be no demand for it. In economic terms there is no possibility of spreading risk, and hence no gains from trade. This problem can arise for the chronically or congenitally sick, where the probability of ill-health is equal to one unless insurance is taken out *before* the condition is diagnosed. Medical insurance policies usually exclude treatment for pre-existing conditions precisely because the probability of needing treatment is too high to insure. Similarly, it may be difficult to buy insurance against burglary in high-risk areas.

We have seen (Chapter 4:3.2) that market efficiency requires perfect information, which applies to insurance as to any other commodity. But suppliers of insurance may have imperfect information in a number of ways. Thus (condition 3), the probability must be *known or estimable*. Where the assumption fails, the carrier (i.e. the insurance company) is unable to calculate a premium from equation (5.12), making private insurance impossible. Thus, private markets are generally unable to offer insurance against future inflation, *inter alia* because the probability distribution of different levels of future price change cannot be estimated.

Further problems are caused by asymmetric information, where the supplier of insurance has less information than the customer. Thus (conditions 4 and 5), there should be *no adverse selection*, and *no moral hazard*. The former arises where the purchaser is able to conceal from the carrier the fact that he is a high risk; the latter (slightly to over-simplify) occurs where the customer can costlessly manipulate the probability of the insured event without the supplier's knowledge. Both problems require further discussion.

3.2 ASYMMETRIC INFORMATION

Adverse selection is a manifestation in insurance markets of the more general concept of 'lemons' (Akerlof, 1970). The purchaser of insurance may have a much better idea than the supplier of whether he is a 'lemon' (i.e. a poor risk). Suppose there are N_H high-risk individuals and N_L low-risk, for whom the relevant probabilities are p_H and p_L. The efficient premiums are

$$\Pi_L = p_L L + T \qquad (5.14)$$
$$\Pi_H = p_H L + T \qquad (5.15)$$

for low- and high-risk individuals, respectively. But if the supplier cannot distinguish high- and low-risk customers (i.e. high risks can hide the fact), then premiums must be based on the *average* expected loss:

$$\Pi = \left[p_H \frac{N_H}{N_H + N_L} + p_L \frac{N_L}{N_H + N_L} \right] L + T \tag{5.16}$$

If low risks buy less cover and high risks more at an average premium, Π, the resulting policies are less efficient than would exist if individually tailored policies, Π_L and Π_H, were possible. Additionally, if low risks drop out altogether and p_H tends to 1, insurance becomes impossible. The theory of where market equilibrium will be established has not been fully worked out.[1] An interesting issue (discussed in section 4.2) is whether it is always necessary to charge different premiums on the basis of differing risks.

Examples of adverse selection arise in medical insurance, where it may be possible for people to conceal facts about their health. Insurance companies try to guard against the problem by asking potential customers to disclose 'any other relevant fact'.[2]

Moral hazard   At its strongest, the no moral hazard condition requires that both the probability, p, and the insured loss, L, should be exogenous to the individual. Slightly less stringently, moral hazard can be avoided so long as individuals can influence p or L only at a cost to themselves greater than the expected gain from so doing. Where the assumption fails, customers can affect the carrier's liability without its knowledge. In analysing the consequences, it is useful to consider p and L separately.

Probability endogenous: individuals can frequently influence the probability of an insured event. In the context of unemployment insurance (Chapter 8:2.2) a problem arises if individuals can affect either the likelihood or the duration of unemployment. Another example is pregnancy, which can be influenced by individual action, and may be the result of choice. In the latter case (Chapter 12:3.1), the probability cannot be regarded as wholly exogenous, and private medical insurance will usually exclude the costs of a normal pregnancy (though the extra costs of complications are often covered because the probability of *complications* is exogenous).

In some instances, the problem is more apparent than real. In the case of life

---

[1] In some circumstances high-risk individuals are compelled to reveal themselves (e.g. bad drivers have accidents and so make frequent insurance claims). In these cases the market mechanism can take some account of the additional information. See Akerlof (1970) and Rothschild and Stiglitz (1976).

[2] Where such facts are not disclosed, the carrier may refuse to pay benefit. The carrier is usually the judge of what constitutes a 'relevant fact'.

insurance it is possible to influence the probability of dying; but this poses no problem for insurance markets, because the cost to the individual of committing suicide prevents its use solely as a device for collecting insurance benefits. Companies usually find it sufficient to refuse benefit during the first year of the policy (this is to prevent people who have decided to commit suicide from taking out a large insurance policy before doing so, i.e. to counter adverse selection rather than moral hazard).

Moral hazard, therefore, causes no inefficiency where the costs to the individual of manipulating the probability are higher than his expected gain. In addition, the problem can sometimes be side-stepped where insurance is compulsory. A woman will not become pregnant just because the medical costs are covered by insurance; but if she intended to have a child, she would take out insurance before doing so (this latter problem also embraces adverse selection). But where all workers in (say) the steel industry are compelled to join a particular medical insurance scheme, the supplier will know the expected number of births per 1000 families and can calculate premiums accordingly. In contrast, if insurance were voluntary a disproportionate number of intending parents might join.

Where there is no compulsion, and individuals can control at small cost the probability, p, in equation (5.12), the insurance company will be able to calculate neither the expected loss nor the actuarial premium. In such cases the private market is generally unable to offer insurance.

Endogenous size of loss: in a number of cases the individual can influence not the probability of the insured event, but the size of the resulting loss. Where an insurance company pays all medical costs, neither patient nor doctor is constrained by the patient's ability to pay. The marginal private cost of health care is zero for both doctor and patient, even though social cost is positive. The results of this type of moral hazard (often referred to as the *third-party payment problem*) are twofold: because of the divergence between private and social costs, consumption of health care (and consequently the insurance payout) is larger than is efficient (Chapter 12:3.1); and there is upward pressure on insurance premiums.

Similarly, suppose automobile insurance pays for all car repairs. I then have an incentive to drive recklessly (i.e. p endogenous), and also to have my car repaired lavishly (e.g. a respray where touching up the paintwork would suffice). Again, inefficiency arises in the form of overconsumption.

Where the probability is endogenous, private insurance may fail altogether. Where it is the loss which is endogenous the problem is not one of non-existence, but of inefficiency. Moral hazard thus causes a fundamental problem: the more and better the insurance provided, the less individuals have to bear the full consequences of their actions, and the less, therefore, the incentive to economise on consumption. A number of devices try to reduce the problem. *Coinsurance* shares the loss between the individual and the carrier (e.g. car drivers who make frequent claims usually pay higher premiums). *Deductions*, commonly found in medical insurance and car insurance, discourage excessive claims by making the policy-holder pay the first £X of any claim. *Inspection* is frequently used for damage claims (e.g. for house contents or automobile repairs); in this case the carrier inspects the damage and pays benefit only in respect of what it regards as the true insured loss.

In analytical terms, adverse selection and moral hazard are both examples of information failure. Neither problem would arise if the insurance company could 'get inside the head' of insured persons (i.e. could read their thoughts), and hence could verify their risk status, and see whether they were manipulating the relevant probability (i.e. behaving differently from the way they would behave in the absence of insurance).

4 The Insurance Market as a Whole

4.1 THE EXISTENCE AND EFFICIENCY OF PRIVATE INSURANCE MARKETS

The existence of private insurance markets requires three conditions.
  (1) There must be positive demand. From equation (5.3) this requires that

$$V = \bar{y} - y^\star > 0$$

This condition holds only if some individuals are risk-averse.
  (2) It must be technically possible to supply insurance, i.e. none of the problems discussed previously must make private insurance impossible.
  (3) It must be possible for insurance to be supplied at a price which the individual is prepared to pay. Equation (5.6) defines the net premium as

$$\phi = \Pi - pL$$

Thus, from equation (5.4), a market for insurance exists only if

$$V \geqslant \Pi - pL$$

i.e. (from equations (5.3) and (5.12)) only if

$$\bar{y} - y^\star \geqslant T \qquad (5.17)$$

Thus insurance can be supplied at an acceptable price only where the individual's risk-aversion (represented by the difference between $\bar{y}$ and $y^\star$) is sufficient to cover the carrier's administrative costs and normal profit.

These three conditions hold for the examples of private insurance in section 1. Consider the case of the vicar who wants to insure against the loss to the parish if it rains on the day of the church fete. Since he wants to insure, it follows that he is risk-averse, hence the demand condition holds. Nor are there technical problems on the supply side; the probability of rain on a given day is known and less than one; there is no adverse selection (since the vicar cannot hide rainfall statistics from the insurance company) and no moral hazard (since he cannot influence the weather). Finally, administrative costs are low, since it is easy to establish whether or not the weather was bad, and so insurance can be provided at a low net price.

Efficiency   It was argued in Chapter 4 that an unrestricted private market allocates resources efficiently only if the standard assumptions hold. These assumptions apply equally to insurance.

Perfect information is relevant to those who buy insurance, and to the companies supplying it. Because of the multiplicity of insurance policies, individuals do not usually have perfect information; but, as in similar cases, the market has developed institutions – insurance brokers – to provide it. Suppliers must have perfect information about the overall probability of an insured event; and information must be symmetric.

Perfect competition provides consumers with their desired type and mix of insurance, and ensures that suppliers make no long-run excess profits.

No market failures: the relevant market failure is externalities. These can arise in the presence of adverse selection, one of whose effects is to impose external costs on low-risk individuals. A further cause of externalities is the third-party payment problem, which will generally create a divergence between private and social costs.

Where these assumptions fail, private insurance (a) may be inefficient, and (b) may not be supplied at all. Both types of problem are acutely relevant to unemployment insurance (Chapter 8:2.2), to the protection of pensions against inflation (Chapter 9:3.1) and to medical insurance (Chapter 12:3.1).

4.2 OTHER ASPECTS

Premium differentials   A question which arises from the earlier discussion of adverse selection is whether efficiency requires that differences in individual probabilities should *always* result in different premiums. Suppose I am burgled more often than my brother. This could be because I am unlucky (a *random* difference), or because I live in London, which has a high crime rate, and he lives in the country (a *systematic* difference).

To define more precisely what we mean by random and systematic differences suppose that individual probabilities can vary randomly, i.e.

$$p_i = \bar{p} + \epsilon_i \tag{5.18}$$

where p_i, the probability of the ith individual being burgled, comprises a 'true' or average probability, $\bar{p}$, and a random component, ϵ. If ϵ is truly random, and hence has a zero mean, the average probability, $\bar{p}$, is simply the mean of the observed probabilities, p_i. Thus, over N individuals

$$\bar{p} = \frac{1}{N} \sum_i p_i \tag{5.19}$$

Now consider two groups of individuals: $p_{11}, p_{12}, \ldots, p_{1M}$ are the probabilities facing the M individuals in group 1, and $p_{21}, p_{22}, \ldots, p_{2N}$ those of the N people in group 2. From (5.19) we can calculate the average probability for individuals in group 1, $\bar{p}_1$, and similarly for group 2. We can then say:

(1) if $\bar{p}_1 = \bar{p}_2$ any difference in probabilties between individuals in the two groups is *random*;

(2) if $\bar{p}_1$ is significantly greater than $\bar{p}_2$ differences in the probabilities are *systematic*. It is then appropriate to talk of high- and low-risk individuals, with average probabilities $p_H (= \bar{p}_1)$ and $p_L (= \bar{p}_2)$, respectively.

We can sum up:

Conclusion 1: the efficient price of insurance should not reflect *random* differences in probabilities;

Conclusion 2: but where the decision to insure is voluntary, efficiency requires that suppliers should seek to discover who is high- and who low-risk, and charge premiums accordingly, as in equations (5.14) and (5.15).

In contrast, where insurance is compulsory, it might be possible to pool high- and low-risk individuals and charge everyone the average premium (equation (5.16)), since low-risk people cannot choose not to insure. This approach raises important issues, so it is instructive to consider some examples.

The 1946 National Insurance Act (Chapter 2:5) applied pooling explicitly to both individuals and risks. All employed men of working age paid the same lump-sum contribution to buy entitlement, *inter alia*, to the same unemployment benefit, even though some groups (e.g. doctors) were much less likely to be unemployed than others (e.g. construction workers). All individuals paid an average premium as in equation (5.16); and because contributions were compulsory it was not possible for overcharged low-risk individuals to opt out. Analytically, the low-risk group paid an actuarial premium (equation (5.14)) plus an unavoidable lump-sum tax, and the high-risk group paid an actuarial premium shown by equation (5.15) and received a lump-sum transfer. Thus a system which charges a compulsory average premium irrespective of risk can alleviate problems of adverse selection; it might, however, cause secondary inefficiency, e.g. charging everyone the same premium for industrial injury insurance might lead to inefficient expansion of risky industries.

Another example (Chapter 9:4.2) is the pooling of men and women in pension schemes, despite the fact that on average women live longer. Again, the broken link between premiums and individual probabilities causes little inefficiency in insurance markets *per se*, though it might have an efficiency impact on the relative wages of men and women and/or on the relative size of the male and female workforce. In contrast, automobile insurance is also compulsory, but there is no pooling across groups – people with worse accident records generally pay higher premiums. We can therefore add

Conclusion 3: if insurance is compulsory then charging all categories of risk the same premium causes little inefficiency in *insurance* markets, though it might cause inefficiency in related activities.

Fallacious equity arguments appear in a number of guises. The first is that insurance is inequitable because it redistributes from those who do not make claims to those who do. This assertion merits little discussion. The whole point of insurance is that people do not know whether they will need to claim (i.e. whether the 'good' or the 'bad' outcome will occur). A rational risk-averter increases his utility by choosing a lower income with certainty (y^* in Figure 5.1), in preference to the higher expected income, $\bar{y}$. Insurance can bring about this increase in utility precisely because the individual is a net contributor in a 'good' year and a net beneficiary in a 'bad' year.

A second fallacious argument is that 'private insurance is inequitable because the poor cannot afford adequate cover'. This proposition can be attacked in a number of ways. First, if the *only* difficulty is that the poor cannot afford enough, then the problem is not one of market allocation but of income distribution, and can be solved by cash redistribution. Second, who decides what level of cover is 'adequate'? Public provision on these grounds can be justified only where there are efficiency problems with private insurance, or if the poor have imperfect information. The arguments developed earlier, in particular the two propositions in Chapter 4:6.1, apply equally to insurance.

Further Reading

The economics of uncertainty is set out in simple form in Laidler (1981, Ch. 7) and in slightly more detail and somewhat more formally in Layard and Walters (1978, Ch. 13) and Varian (1984, Ch. 3). A useful textbook is by McKenna (1986). Market equilibrium is analysed by Rothschild and Stiglitz (1976). On moral hazard and adverse selection see Pauly (1974), and the classic article by Arrow (1963) (which discusses medical insurance).

On information problems more generally see Varian (1984, Ch. 8) and Arrow (1974) for overviews, Akerlof (1970) on 'lemons', and Spence (1973) on signalling. Diamond and Rothschild (1978) collect a number of major papers on uncertainty and related information problems.

Appendix: Non-technical Summary of Chapter 5

1 Chapter 5 discusses the demand and supply of insurance, and some problems which can arise on the supply side of a private insurance market.

The Demand and Supply of Insurance

2 Uncertainty reduces the utility of an individual who is risk-averse; hence certainty has a positive marginal value, and a risk-averse individual will be prepared to pay a positive price for it. When I take out insurance the commodity I am buying is certainty (e.g. that if my car is stolen it will be replaced). The formal argument is presented in section 2.1.

3 The supply of insurance is discussed in section 3.1. Suppose that the probability, p, of being burgled is 1 per cent; and that if I am burgled my loss, L, will be £1000. On average, therefore, I can expect a loss of £1000 once every 100 years. In annual terms my expected loss is $p \times L = 1$ per cent $\times$ £1000 = £10, i.e. the insurance company knows that on average it will have to pay me £10 per year. Formally, an **actuarial premium**, Π, is defined as

$$\Pi = pL + T \qquad (5.12)$$

where pL is the expected loss of the individual buying insurance, and T is the insurance company's administrative costs and normal profit. Π is the price at which insurance will be supplied in a competitive market.

Technical Problems on the Supply Side

4 Private insurance will be inefficient or non-existent unless the probability, p, in equation (5.12) meets five conditions (sections 3.1 and 3.2). First, the probability of a given individual being (e.g.) burgled must be **independent** of the probability of anyone else being burgled. What this means (roughly speaking) is that insurance depends for its financial viability on the existence in any year of a predictable number of winners and losers.

5 Second, p must be **less than one**. If $p=1$ it is certain that my car will be stolen; hence there is no possibility of spreading risks, and the insurance premium will equal or exceed the cost of a new car. This problem can arise for the chronically or congenitally ill, for whom the probability of ill-health equals one unless insurance is taken out *before* the condition is diagnosed.

6 A third condition is that p must be **known or estimable**. If it is not, insurance companies will be unable to calculate an actuarial premium, and private insurance will be impossible. Thus the private market is generally unable to supply insurance against future inflation because the probability

123

of different levels of future price increases cannot be estimated.

7 Fourth, there must be **no adverse selection**, which arises when a purchaser is able to conceal from the insurance company the fact that he is a poor risk. If the insurance company cannot distinguish high- and low-risk customers it will have to charge everyone the same premium, based on the average risk. As a result, low-risk individuals will face an inefficiently high premium and may choose not to insure even though, at an actuarial premium, it would be efficient for them to do so. This problem arises particularly in the case of medical insurance for the elderly.

8 Finally, there must be **no moral hazard**. The problem can arise in two ways: first, where the customer is able costlessly to manipulate the probability p in equation (5.12) that the insured event will occur; and second, where the customer can manipulate the size of the loss, L. The latter difficulty is conventionally called the **third-party payment problem**.

9 There are numerous ways in which consumers can manipulate the relevant probability. The chances of developing appendicitis are beyond individual control, and so medical insurance for this sort of complaint is generally possible. In contrast, the probability of becoming pregnant, or visits to one's family doctor, can both be influenced by individual actions and are therefore generally not well covered by private medical insurance. Where the problem is serious, the supplier is unable to calculate the actuarial premium, and private insurance is impossible.

10 The third-party payment problem does not make insurance impossible, but causes overconsumption. The problem is particularly relevant to health care. If an individual's insurance pays all medical costs, then health care is 'free' to the patient. Similarly, on the supply side, the doctor knows that the insurance company will pay his charges; he is therefore not constrained by the patient's ability to pay. As a result, both doctor and patient can act as though the cost of health care were zero. This is inefficient: it causes overconsumption and creates upward pressure on insurance premiums.

11 The problems discussed in paragraphs 4–10 can cause inefficiency, and may make private insurance impossible. Both difficulties are relevant to unemployment insurance (Chapter 8:2.2), to the protection of pensions against inflation (Chapter 9:3.1) and to medical insurance (Chapter 12:3.1).

6

Problems of Definition and Measurement[1]

To criticise inequality and to desire equality is not . . . to cherish the romantic illusion that men are equal in character and intelligence. It is to hold that, while their natural endowments differ profoundly, it is the mark of a civilised society to aim at eliminating such inequalities as have their source, not in individual differences, but in its own organization. [R. H. Tawney, 1964.]

Common prosperity cannot and never will mean absolute egalitarianism or that all members of society become better off simultaneously at the same speed. . . . Such thinking would lead to common poverty. [People's Republic of China, Central Committee's Decision on Reform of the Economic System, 1984.]

1 Measuring Welfare

1.1 INDIVIDUAL WELFARE

Measurement problems are a recurring theme. They are illustrated here in the context of poverty (section 2) and inequality (sections 3 and 4), the reduction of

---

[1] Non-technical readers may omit sections 1.2, 4.1 and 4.2. The gist of the argument is in the Appendix to this chapter.

which, it is widely agreed, is among the aims of the welfare state. This raises two sets of issues: how do we define poverty and inequality; and how do we measure them in principle and in practice? To answer these questions it is necessary to start with the definition and measurement of welfare for individuals and for society as a whole.

Defining Individual Income

Wealth and income The theoretical concept of income is complex and the literature vast (see the Further Reading). For present purposes it is possible to simplify matters by considering income as the flow deriving from a stock of wealth. Individual wealth can arise, broadly, in three forms. *Physical wealth* consists of consumer durables like houses, machines (e.g. cars, television sets), Picassos, and Persian rugs. *Financial wealth* includes shares, government bonds, and bank accounts.[1] *Human capital* is wealth embodied in individuals as a result of skill and training, and has two quite separate sources: it is the result of past investment in education and training (which is what most people mean when they talk loosely of human capital); but it also arises from 'natural talent'. The latter requires explanation. Obvious examples are musicians like Yehudi Menuhin or footballers like Pele, whom most of us could not emulate however much training we had. The concept, however, is much broader. The talent of a road-sweeper, for example, consists mainly of muscle and an ability to put up with simple routine; and a major item under this head is the ability to walk, dress, wash oneself, etc. (which forms of human capital are denied to the severely disabled).

Each type of wealth yields a flow of income. Physical wealth produces non-money income in the form of a flow of services, e.g. housing, or televisual services, but can also yield money income (e.g. a house to a landlord, or an automobile to a taxi-driver). Financial wealth yields money income, e.g. the annual flow of interest from a £1000 bank account. Human capital produces income in several forms. Suppose an individual divides his time between 'work' and 'leisure'.[2] When he is working, his human capital yields money income (i.e. wages), and non-money income like job satisfaction (which can be positive or negative); and when not working, he receives non-money income through the enjoyment of leisure (again positive or negative), and also in the form of own production (household chores, gardening, etc.).

---

[1] It is legitimate to include both physical and financial wealth for *individuals*. But for wealth as a whole, care is needed to avoid double counting, which would arise if, for example, Ford factories and Ford shares were both included in the definition of wealth.
[2] The distinction between work and leisure is increasingly regarded as suspect (see, for instance, Apps, 1981). But it does no harm to retain the distinction for present purposes, and makes the exposition clearer.

Full income, Y_F, consists of the flow of services from *all* individual wealth, i.e. money income, Y_M, plus all forms of non-money income, Y_N. In short,

$$Y_F = Y_M + Y_N \qquad (6.1)$$

where money income comprises wage and non-wage money income (e.g. dividends and interest),[1] and non-money income includes job satisfaction, the flow of services from physical wealth, the value of own production and, importantly, the enjoyment of leisure.[2] For given prices, full income thus defined is a measure of an individual's *opportunity set*. The word 'opportunity' is crucial. The opportunity set measures the individual's potential power to consume goods (including leisure) whether or not *ex post* he chooses to do so (for the central importance of choice in assessing individual welfare, see Le Grand, 1984). Full income is thus a form of generalised budget constraint, and so a natural variable in terms of which to measure poverty and inequality.

The logic of the theoretical argument is completed by observing that if we assume given prices and identical tastes, there is a one:one correspondence between an individual's full income as defined in equation (6.1) and his utility. Whether or not we adopt the stringent assumption of identical tastes it is possible by defining full income as the return to *all* forms of individual wealth to construct a measure of individual consumption opportunities in a way which makes theoretical sense.

The Haig–Simons definition   The next step is to see how this theoretical approach might be put into practice. The classic definition of individual income is by Simons (1938, p. 50), also called the Haig–Simons definition:

> Personal income may be defined as the algebraic sum of (1) the market value of rights exercised in consumption and (2) the change in the value of the store of property rights between the beginning and the end of the period.

More simply, 'income in a given period is the amount a person could have spent while maintaining his wealth intact' (Atkinson, 1983, p. 39). The word 'could' is important. My income is increased if my *potential* to consume is raised, whether or not I actually choose to consume more.

The Haig–Simons definition has twofold importance: it indicates how income might be measured in practice; and it is comprehensive (and therefore theoretically sound) because it includes the following types of income which are omitted from conventional definitions, e.g. for tax purposes.

---

[1] This definition leaves unanswered the difficult question of whether, and to what extent, capital gains should be included in income. See Prest and Barr, 1985, Ch. 13, section 4.

[2] For the importance of leisure in the definition of income see Atkinson and Stiglitz, 1980, pp. 260–1.

Non-pecuniary benefits from work include the consumption of work-related goods. Where such 'fringe benefits' are marketable (e.g. a chauffeur-driven car) they can be valued fairly easily. But problems arise where benefits are non-marketable and/or a mixture of 'work' and 'leisure'. Is a business trip abroad pure work, or leisure in disguise, or a mixture of the two? And how should 'enjoyment' of the trip be valued? A further benefit is job satisfaction, whose measurement raises obvious problems. All these non-pecuniary benefits are part of 'rights exercised in consumption', and their market value forms part of the Haig–Simons definition.

Income in the form of non-market goods includes goods I have produced myself (e.g. building an extension to my house) which could in principle be part of market production, and also the consumption of unpaid services produced by others within the household sector (e.g. cooking, cleaning, child-minding).[1] Both forms of activity give rights over consumption, and their market value is properly included in the Haig–Simons definition. Income under this head also includes leisure, whose value to an individual is not less than the earnings thereby forgone, £X. These rights over consumption are no less income for being exercised over £X of leisure rather than £X of goods, and are properly included in a strict interpretation of Haig–Simons.

Imputed rent is the market value of the services of consumer durables, notably owner-occupied houses, whose importance has already been stressed.

Capital gains and losses, according to Haig–Simons, are part of income since they constitute a change in the value of the store of property rights. An individual with a £1000 asset which appreciates over the period to £1100 would be able (assuming no inflation) to spend an extra £100 without reducing his wealth. Thus capital gains should be included as part of income *in the period in which they accrue*, whether or not they are realised; and capital losses should similarly be deducted from income.

Measuring Individual Income

The next step is to consider how a theoretically sound definition of income might in practice be measured. This raises three sets of problems.

How do we measure income? A version of Haig–Simons which might be workable is the sum of wage income, non-wage money income, fringe benefits, imputed rent and realised capital gains. But this measure deviates from full income as defined in equation (6.1) through the omission of job satisfaction, extra-market production and forgone income taken as leisure, and also because capital gains are not measured as they accrue. Further problems arise in attributing to individuals the benefits of publicly provided goods and services

---

[1] In formal terms these two sorts of activity correspond to production for own consumption and production for trade within the household sector (see Apps, 1981).

(e.g. education, health care, roads).

Because non-money income is largely unmeasurable, it is necessary to focus on money income. This would not matter if money income were a good proxy for full income, but in practice the proportion of income arising in non-money form varies widely and unsystematically across individuals.[1] Non-observability of parts of full income prevents a complete characterisation of the individual opportunity set, and forces us to use the unreliable yardstick of money income. The notion of full income is useful less as a guide to policy, than as an explanation of why conventional definitions of poverty and inequality in terms of money income have only limited validity as measures of individual welfare.

The income unit, i.e. whose income is being measured? This raises the two separate questions of how to define an income unit, and how to compare units of different sizes. The latter issue of 'adult equivalents' is discussed in section 3.3. On the first, consider a household consisting of a man, a woman and two children, whose only source of income is £10,000, earned by the man. Regarded as a family, two adults and two children share an income of £10,000; no one is poor; nor is there necessarily substantial inequality. But if the man is regarded as a separate unit (as for income tax purposes if he and the woman are not married), then the woman and child have no income; they will be counted as poor; and there will be substantial measured inequality. The narrower the definition of the income unit, the greater are measured poverty and inequality.

The problem is more intractable than it seems. At its heart lies another measurement problem – the impossibility of measuring income flows *within* a household. In the example just discussed, the real focus of interest is the extent to which income is shared; since this is unobservable we note instead the observable but not strictly relevant fact that the man and woman are married, and thereby infer (rightly or wrongly) that income is shared.[2]

Over what time-period is income measured? Problems arise here because income does not in practice flow continuously. Consider a salesman who earns £200 per week in commission but receives no wage; during the year he works 50 weeks, earning £10,000, and in the remaining two weeks, because of illness, earns nothing. If income is measured over a year he is not poor, but on a weekly basis he is poor for two weeks. For some purposes (e.g. setting a level for student support) it might be appropriate to use a long-run notion like permanent income. In other circumstances the answer might be different. If a

---

[1] See, for instance, Layard *et al.* (1978, Ch. 2).

[2] Further discussion of defining income and income units is contained in the literature on the taxation of husband and wife. For recent contributions see Barr (1980), Hurley (1985), UK (1986b) and for a brief summary Prest and Barr (1985, Ch. 13, section 2).

student with no family to help him, and no job with which to support himself, applied for assistance during the summer vacation, it would not be very helpful to refuse benefit because he had a high expected lifetime income. In cases of immediate need, the relevant definition of income is usually short-run.[1]

1.2 SOCIAL WELFARE

Similar arguments apply at an aggregate level. A comprehensive measure of national income would include both money and non-money income as the following speech by Robert Kennedy illustrates:[2]

> We cannot measure . . . national achievement by the gross national product. For the gross national product includes air pollution and advertising for cigarettes, and ambulances to clear our highways of carnage. . . . It swells with equipment for the police to put down riots in our cities; and though it is not diminished by the damage these riots do, still it goes up as slums are rebuilt on their ashes. . . . And if the gross national product includes all this, there is much that it does not comprehend. It does not allow for the health of our families, the quality of their education or the joy of their play. . . . It allows neither for the justice in our courts, nor for the justice of our dealings with each other. . . . It measures everything, in short, except that which makes life worth while.

More formally, the *social welfare function* in equation (4.1) is the explicit relation between aggregate welfare and the welfare of the individuals who make up society. If U^i, the utility of the ith individual, depends on his income (appropriately defined), y^i, then social welfare, W, can be expressed as

$$W = W(U^1(y^1), U^2(y^2), \ldots, U^n(y^n)) \tag{6.2}$$

or, more simply, as $\qquad W = W(y^1, y^2, \ldots, y^n) \tag{6.3}$

Thus $y^1, \ldots, y^n$ measure the welfare individually of each of the n members of society; these are aggregated into a measure of social welfare through the function W. Social welfare functions are categorised in terms of their properties (see Cowell, 1977, pp. 41–50), an explanation of which is a necessary prelude to the discussion of aggregate inequality in section 4.[3]

Property 1: Non-decreasing: formally, let social welfare in state A be $W_A = W(y^1, y^2, \ldots, y^{iA}, \ldots, y^n)$ and in state B $W_B = W(y^1, y^2, \ldots, y^{iB}, \ldots, y^n)$.

---

[1] For further discussion, see Atkinson (1983, Ch. 3.2).
[2] See Newfield (1978, pp. 59–60). The speech was made in Detroit in May 1967.
[3] Non-technical readers can proceed directly to section 2.

In other words, the distribution in states A and B differs only because the ith individual has a higher income in state B than in state A. Then a social welfare function is non-decreasing if and only if

$$W_B \geqslant W_A \text{ if } y^{iB} \geqslant y^{iA} \tag{6.4}$$

Non-decreasing implies that if any individual's income rises, social welfare cannot decrease.

Property 2: Symmetric: a social welfare function is symmetric if

$$W(y^1, y^2, \ldots, y^n) = W(y^2, y^1, \ldots, y^n) = \ldots$$
$$= W(y^n, \ldots, y^2, y^1) \tag{6.5}$$

Social welfare depends on the distribution of income, but not on who gets which income, i.e. social welfare is unchanged if two people 'swap' incomes. This is equivalent to assuming that all individuals have identical utility functions.

Property 3: Additive: a social welfare function is additive if

$$W(y^1, y^2, \ldots, y^n) = \sum_{i=1}^{n} U^i(y^i) = U^1(y^1) + U^2(y^2) + \ldots + U^n(y^n) \tag{6.6}$$

This is the utilitarian social welfare function, under which social welfare is simply the sum of the utilities experienced individually by members of society. Additivity implies that a person's utility will be independent of everyone else's income – a strong assumption which rules out the possibility of welfare interdependence discussed in Chapter 4:4.1. It also rests uneasily with the relative definition of poverty discussed shortly.

These three properties, taken together, have important implications. If a social welfare function is non-decreasing, symmetrical and additive it has the general form

$$W = \sum_{i=1}^{n} U(y^i) = U(y^1) + U(y^2) + \ldots + U(y^n) \tag{6.7}$$

where: (a) (in contrast with equation (6.6)) U is the same for each individual (a consequence of symmetry); and (b) $U(y^i)$ increases with y^i (because the social welfare function is non-decreasing).

Equation (6.7) makes it possible to use $U(y^i)$ as an index of social welfare. If there is an increase in the income of the ith individual, the increase in social welfare will be

$$U'(y^i) = \frac{dU(y^i)}{dy^i} \geqslant 0 \tag{6.8}$$

The welfare index $U(y^i)$ is *not* an ordinary utility function. It shows the *social* marginal valuation or *welfare weight* of changes in the ith person's income. To show why $U'(y^i)$ is the welfare weight, consider a tax/transfer scheme which leads to a series of (small) changes in individual incomes, $\Delta y^1, \Delta y^2, \ldots, \Delta y^n$. The resulting change in social welfare is the total differential ΔW; and if the social welfare function takes the simple form of equation (6.7), then

$$\Delta W = U'(y^1)\Delta y^1 + U'(y^2)\Delta y^2 + \ldots + U'(y^n)\Delta y^n \qquad (6.9)$$

and the terms $U'(y^i)$ act as a system of weights when summing the effects of the scheme on social welfare. The next step is to discuss what value the weights might take. This brings us to:

Property 4: Concave: a social welfare function is concave if the welfare weight always decreases as y^i increases, i.e. concavity implies diminishing social marginal utility of income. A £1 increase in income raises social welfare more if it goes to a poor than to a rich person; thus a small redistribution from rich to poor raises social welfare. For some purposes it is useful to know how concave a social welfare function is, i.e. how rapidly the welfare weight falls as an individual's income rises. Thus:

Property 5: Constant relative inequality aversion: a social welfare function has constant relative inequality aversion (or constant elasticity) if the utility index $U(y^i)$ has the specific form

$$U(y^i) = \frac{1}{1-\varepsilon} y^{i(1-\varepsilon)} \qquad (6.10)$$

where ϵ is a non-negative *inequality aversion parameter*. The welfare index in equation (6.10) has the property that the proportional decrease in the welfare weight for a given proportional increase in income is the same at all income levels. A 1 per cent increase in an individual's income reduces his welfare weight by ϵ per cent whatever his income (i.e. the 1 per cent increase can be from £100 to £101 or from £10,000 to £10,100). The larger is ϵ, the more rapid is the decline in the welfare weight as income rises, hence the name 'inequality aversion parameter'. We return to these issues in more detail in section 4.2.

2 Poverty

2.1 DEFINING POVERTY

This section discusses various attempts to define poverty (section 2.1); makes the important distinction between poverty and inequality (section 2.2); and considers the measurement of poverty (section 2.3).

Indicators of poverty Attempts to construct an objective (i.e. value-free) poverty line face a series of largely intractable problems. Individual consumption opportunities should be measured in terms of full (i.e. money plus non-money) income. Since this is not possible it is necessary to turn to more measurable indicators. Three approaches have commonly been used: actual consumption of a specific bundle of goods; total expenditure; and total money income. Each has its difficulties, of which the following is the barest of summaries (for further discussion see Atkinson, 1986, section 2.1). The first approach requires a definition of the appropriate consumption bundle; and when that difficult task has been accomplished leads to a multi-dimensional (and hence complex) definition of poverty. The expenditure measure requires adjustment for inefficient spending.

Money income is a flawed measure of individual welfare, and is one of the major causes of the somewhat unhappy intellectual state of analytical definitions of poverty.[1] Three problems were discussed in section 1.1: the unsystematic relation between money income and full income; the definition of the income unit; and the time-period over which income is measured. None of these has an unambiguous answer, so that any definition of poverty in terms of money income is likely to be somewhat arbitrary, a point reinforced in section 3.2.

All three measures – consumption, expenditure and income – face an additional and major problem. They all look only at *ex post* magnitudes, without regard to the (possibly crucial) influence of choice *ex ante* (see the discussion of full income on p. 127). I may eat no meat and have low expenditure and income, and so be poor according to all three measures. But if by choice I am a vegetarian ascetic, then my opportunity set (i.e. my *potential* living standard) may exceed the poverty line.

Defining a poverty line would raise major difficulties even if all problems with measurable indicators had been solved. In particular, should poverty be regarded as an absolute or a relative concept? With an *absolute* definition a person is poor if his money income is too low to keep him alive and healthy. Early studies (see the Further Reading) attempted to define poverty 'objectively' by reference to basic nutritional requirements. There are serious objections to this approach. People have different nutritional requirements even in the absence of special medical diets, so that no universally applicable

---

[1] For the most compendious recent UK work see Townsend (1979), and for a trenchant critique Piachaud (1981). See also the Further Reading.

standard is possible; nor is it reasonable to expect people to fill these requirements at minimum cost. Philosophically, the idea of an absolute poverty line stems from times when it was natural to think in subsistence terms, but this can be argued to be out of place (at least in developed countries) when people live well above subsistence, and where the concept of deprivation is applied to emotional and cultural standards as well as to physical ones.

Under a *relative* definition, with deceptive simplicity, a person is regarded as poor if he or she feels poor. The definition of poverty will vary by time and place according to prevailing living standards, and whether or not a person feels poor will depend in part on what he sees around him (see Runciman, 1972). It can be argued (though there is no way in which the hypothesis can formally be tested) that the riots in America's inner cities in the late 1960s were caused not only by the poverty of black residents, but also by the contrast implied by television advertisements for gleaming kitchens and automatic garage door openers, aimed at middle-class whites living only five miles away.

An absolute poverty line will remain fixed at subsistence; with a relative definition it will tend to rise with living standards generally. In the latter case it is argued (Townsend, 1979) that a person is poor if he or she cannot participate in 'normal' life, i.e. poverty is related to social stratification. Thus a person without access to television is culturally deprived, and a poverty budget should include at any rate a black-and-white television set. Similarly, it might be argued in the near future that a child is deprived if he or she does not have his/her own pocket-computer.

A different line of argument for real increases in the poverty line is that over time incomes rise; hence the demand for inferior goods falls, and they tend to disappear from the market.

> The paradox of affluence is that [it] actually creates, as a by-product, a new poverty. . . . [Thus,] more people have cars, so that buses carry fewer passengers at higher fares, and services are cut. More householders have washing-machines, so launderettes for the rest are fewer and seedier. The more people who have central heating, the harder and dearer it becomes, as the number of coal merchants dwindles, for the others to buy coal. [*Sunday Times*, 19 September 1982.]

In such cases it is necessary to raise the poverty line so that people can buy the next cheapest substitute (for further discussion see Sen, 1983).

Formally, an absolute definition of poverty is more appropriate the greater the extent to which the utility of rich and poor depend only on their own incomes, and a relative definition the greater the extent of income externalities. Suppose the relevant utility functions are

$$U^R = f(Y^R) \tag{6.11}$$
$$U^P = f(Y^P) \tag{6.12}$$

where U^R and U^P are the utilities of a representative rich and poor person, respectively, and Y^R and Y^P their incomes. This is the case implied by an additive social welfare function (equation (6.6)), and an absolute definition of poverty might be appropriate. But if the utility functions are

$$U^R = f(Y^R, Y^P) f_1 > 0, f_2 > 0 \tag{6.13}$$
$$U^P = f(Y^R, Y^P) f_1 < 0, f_2 > 0 \tag{6.14}$$

(where f_1 and f_2 are the partial derivatives of utility with respect to Y^R and Y^P, respectively) we have an income externality, as discussed in Chapter 4:4.1, and both rich and poor might prefer a poverty line which rose over time.

To conclude, the definition of poverty, like the definition of a just distribution, is less a matter of positive economics than of social convention, and of the underlying notion of social justice (embodied formally in the welfare weights of the social welfare function). A definition of poverty in terms of money income may be widely accepted, but analytically is inevitably somewhat arbitrary.

2.2 POVERTY AND INEQUALITY

Absolute poverty and inequality are two quite separate concepts which should not be confused. Absolute poverty refers to a standard of living below some benchmark. The undotted income distribution in Figure 6.1 shows a substantial number of poor people (i.e. the area A), a large number of middle

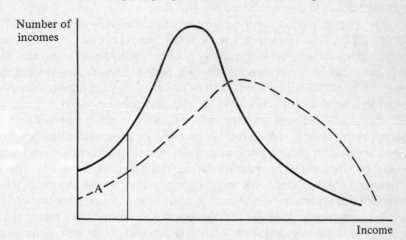

Figure 6.1   *Poverty and inequality*

incomes and few high incomes. Inequality is concerned not with the absolute living standard of the poor, but with the *differences* between income groups; the dotted distribution shows more inequality (but less absolute poverty) than the undotted one. Various measures of this dispersion are discussed in section 4.

The difference between poverty and inequality is illustrated more fully in Table 6.1, which shows the average income in two societies of the poor (the lowest two-thirds of incomes), the rich (the top third), and the average income of rich and poor together. In society 1 the poor have an average income of £3600, which is one-third of the average income of the rich, £10,800. In society 2 (which is identical in all respects except income) the average income of the poor, £5000, is one-quarter of the average income of the rich, £20,000. In society 2 the poor have a higher standard of living than in society 1 (i.e. there is less absolute poverty), but are further behind both the average income, and the standard of living of the rich (i.e. there is more inequality).

Table 6.1: Poverty and Inequality in Two Different Societies

	Society 1	Society 2
Average income of the poor	£3600	£5000
(⅔ of population)	(⅓ income of rich)	(¼ income of rich)
Average income of the rich		
(⅓ of population)	£10,800	£20,000
Average income of rich and		
poor together	£6000	£10,000

It is instructive to ask which society the poor would choose. Suppose a representative poor person has the utility function shown by equation (6.12); his utility depends on his own income, and his rational choice is society 2. In contrast, with equation (6.14), his utility increases with his own income but decreases as that of the representative rich person rises. If the externality (shown by f_1) is sufficiently strong, it will be rational for a poor person to choose society 1 in which the difference between rich and poor is smaller.

The distinction between poverty and inequality is important because it might not be possible to reduce *both*. A supply-side argument is that poverty can be alleviated by reducing the taxation of the rich, thereby encouraging economic growth and making possible further redistribution from rich to poor (i.e. reducing the top rates of tax might change society 1 into society 2). The relevance of this argument (whose truth is ultimately an empirical question) is its implicit assumption that the real enemy is absolute poverty rather than inequality, i.e. it assumes an individual utility function of the form of equation (6.12).

In contrast, it was stated at a Labour Party Conference in the early 1970s that any subsequent Labour government would introduce a wealth tax to 'squeeze the rich until the pips squeak'. Such a statement implicitly assumes that inequality rather than poverty is the main enemy, i.e. that the utility of the poor is shown by equation (6.14). But if the argument of the previous paragraph is true, then any attack on inequality might aggravate absolute poverty through the effect of higher taxation in reducing economic growth and hence the size of the tax base (i.e. attacking inequality might convert society 2 into society 1). The policy conclusion is not that attacks on inequality *will* increase absolute poverty, but that they might, making it important to be clear about which is the focus of attention.

2.3 MEASURING POVERTY

Empirical definitions of the poverty line   We have seen that poverty is hard to define without a measure of full income. But policy-makers cannot refuse to establish a poverty line on the grounds that there exists a conceptual impasse; and it is possible to infer roughly what the state thinks by looking at what it does. First, is poverty regarded as absolute or relative? With an absolute definition, the poverty line, as represented, for instance, by the level of long-term supplementary benefit (i.e. 'welfare'), would have about the same real value today as in 1948 when the Beveridge arrangements came into effect, i.e. the benefit would have been uprated in line with price changes. In fact, for most of the period, benefits kept pace with changes in pre-tax average earnings,[1] so in practice poverty has been treated as a relative concept. As an example, between 1948 and 1982 nominal, pre-tax average earnings rose some twentyfold, and so did the long-term supplementary benefit scale rate.

Turning to the other questions posed earlier, the definition of the income unit for cash benefit purposes is fairly broad, in that the incomes of individuals living together will usually be aggregated, irrespective of their marital status.[2] In comparing families of different sizes, the poverty line has been set at about 20 per cent of pre-tax average earnings for a single person, at around 30 per cent for a married couple, and at 40–45 per cent for a family of four. Thus the implied adult equivalents (see section 3.3) for a single individual, a couple and a family of four are 100, 150 and about 200, respectively. Finally, the time-

---

[1] Since the real burden of taxation rose substantially over the postwar period this implies that the real level of benefits *rose* relative to *post-tax* average earnings.

[2] The treatment of cohabitation has always generated considerable heat and not very much light. For further discussion of this problem area, see CPAG (1986a), and Lynes (1981). For more general discussion of the choice of income unit see Fiegehen and Lansley (1976).

period over which income is measured for awarding cash benefits is frequently
short. For some benefits it is necessary only to show that one has no current
income; for others evidence of the previous five weeks' income is required.

These are the state's answers to the various definitional questions (for further
detail, see Barr,.1981). They are valid to the extent that over the years they have
acquired the force of social convention, but they should not be regarded as
having any particular intellectual merit.

Measuring the extent of poverty raises two major questions: how much
poverty is there; and who are the poor? Since it is not possible to define poverty
even for an individual, it is not surprising that the first question has no
unambiguous answer. The simplest measure of aggregate poverty is the *head
count*. Suppose that the poverty line is set at £X per week. One can then ask how
many people are poor in terms of that definition. Even this simple question
cannot be answered readily. It is not possible to use the number of recipients of
supplementary benefit as an estimate of the poor population. Not everyone who
is eligible for benefit receives it; and recipients are an unknown proportion of
those potentially eligible, so that it is not possible to scale up the number of
recipients into an estimate of the poor population.[1] On this definition, the
number of poor people in Britain is larger than the number receiving
supplementary benefit (4.7 million[2] in 1985), but without additional information we do not know how much greater. As a result, estimates have to be
constructed from sample surveys, which suggest that in the early 1980s there
were between 5 and 10 million poor people in Britain.[3]

The head count, even were an accurate figure to be obtained, gives at best a
partial picture. It fails to indicate by how much people fall below the poverty
line. Even worse, a transfer of £100 from someone well below the poverty line to
someone only £50 below *reduces* poverty as measured by the head count. In part
because of this deficiency, a second measure, the *poverty gap* (see Beckerman,
1979) is sometimes used. This considers the total shortfall from the poverty
line, divided by the poverty line or by total income. The former gives an
approximate measure of the average depth of poverty, the latter of the relative
cost of relieving it. Both approaches have been criticised, *inter alia* by Sen
(1976) who suggests an alternative aggregate index, though this, too, has been
criticised. The general conclusion is that a definitive aggregate measure of
poverty is not possible – for surveys see Atkinson (1986, section 2.2)

[1] The issue of these so-called 'take-up rates' is discussed in more detail in Chapter 10:3.
[2] This figure refers to the number of *recipients*. When account is taken of their
dependants the total number supported wholly or in part by supplementary benefit was
about 70 per cent higher.
[3] For a summary of various results, see Hemming (1984, p. 53), and Townsend (1979).
For international comparison, see Roberti (1978).

and Foster (1984).

A further dimension of poverty is its *duration*. If most people experience poverty only as a short-term phenomenon, the problem is smaller than if large numbers suffer near permanent poverty. In practice, long-term poverty is substantial (Layard *et al.*, 1978), and compounded by the extent to which it is transmitted across generations. Atkinson, Maynard and Trinder (1983) found that nearly half of their sample of poor people came from poor parents (see also Meade (1974) and in a US context Brittain (1977 and 1978)).

Finally, and very briefly, who are the poor? Not surprisingly they comprise disproportionately: the elderly; the unemployed; those with health problems (particularly long-term); large families; single- (usually female-) parent families; and racial minorities. In recent years in Britain, however, poverty has become more common also among working families. Discussion of empirical evidence is resumed in Chapter 10:3.3.

3 Inequality 1: Individuals and Families

3.1 DEFINING EQUALITY AND INEQUALITY

Different definitions of equality   This section discusses equality (as with poverty it turns out that no wholly satisfactory definition is possible), and then turns to inequality between individuals (section 3.2) and families (section 3.3). The first question is: equality of what? In principle the answer is easy – individuals are equal if they face identical opportunity sets. But full income cannot be measured, so matters in practice are more complex. Le Grand (1982, pp. 14–15) distinguishes five possible definitions. The simplest, *equality of final income*, implies that individuals are equal if they have the same level of money income plus income in kind. But complications arise in measuring income in kind. Should there be *equality of public expenditure* (i.e. expenditure on (say) health care is the same for everybody); or *equality of use* (e.g. everyone is allocated the same quantity of health care), or *equality of cost* (e.g. everyone faces the same cost of using the national health service, which implies that people visiting their doctor should be compensated for any lost earnings); or *equality of outcome* (e.g. health care is allocated so that, as far as possible, everyone enjoys equally good health)? All have valid claims as definitions of equality; all are different.

Similar problems arise when we try to define equality of opportunity. An individual's income according to Atkinson and Stiglitz (1980, p. 267) depends on three sets of factors: his *endowments* (e.g. of human capital or inherited wealth); his *tastes* with respect to work and leisure, consumption and saving, risk, etc.; and his *luck*, inasmuch as the outcome of choices is often stochastic. Thus two individuals with identical tastes and opportunity sets may experience very different outcomes – 'some people work for a firm that goes bankrupt; some people invest early in Rank Xerox' (*ibid.*).

Equality of opportunity is best approached in several steps.

First step: equality of opportunity exists if

$$Y_F = K \text{ for all } i \quad i = 1, 2, \ldots, N \tag{6.15}$$

where Y_F is full income as defined in equation (6.1), and includes a time dimension. Equation (6.15) states that full income should be the same for all N individuals in society. The obvious problem is that no account is taken of the stochastic element in individual income. Equality of opportunity implies that people should have an equal *chance*, i.e. it is an expected value not an absolute value which should be equal. Hence:

Second step: equal opportunity can be said to exist if

$$E(Y_F) = K \text{ for all } i \tag{6.16}$$

Here equality of opportunity requires only that expected income should be the same for all individuals. This is an adequate definition of equality of opportunity in terms of *full* income, which captures all aspects of the individual opportunity set. In practice, however, measurement problems force us to use money income, which varies not only with the individual opportunity set, but also with individual tastes; and differences in income for the latter reason (as we shall see in section 3.2) need not imply inequality. Hence, if Y is money income:

Third step: equal opportunity exists if

$$E(Y|T_i) = K \text{ for all } D_i \tag{6.17}$$

Equation (6.17) requires explanation. Some characteristics may affect money income without causing inequality; these include any differences in individual choice which are the result of differences in tastes, and so are referred to as T (taste) characteristics. But if money income varies systematically with other characteristics (e.g. social class, race, sex, parental money income), we would regard society as unequal; these are the D (discrimination) characteristics. Equation (6.17) states that equality of opportunity exists if the expected value of money income is the same for all individuals with given T characteristics, but must be invariant to their D characteristics.

At first glance equation (6.17) seems to offer a workable (and possibly even a measurable) definition of equality of opportunity. But it contains two strategic difficulties concerning (a) the definition of Y, and (b) the distinction between the T and D characteristics. The use of money income as an indicator of welfare raises problems even if we control for age and tastes. There are two issues. First, equality of opportunity must apply both to cash income and to income in kind. We have seen that Le Grand distinguishes various definitions of equality (of public expenditure, of use, of cost and of outcome); each has a claim as a definition of equality yet, when discussing distribution in kind, each can be different. Equation (6.17) is no longer unambiguous. Second, defining inequality narrowly in terms of material well-being conceals its social and political dimensions (Runciman, 1972, Ch. 3). These aspects can be analysed in economic terms as violations of the perfect information and equal power assumptions (Chapter 4:3.2), but they stand in their own right as independent sources of inequality.

Even if full income were measurable, there remains the problem of distinguishing a T from a D characteristic. There is general agreement that social class, race and sex are D characteristics; and it can be argued that laziness or a long time horizon are T characteristics. But what about 'natural ability'? If ability is entirely exogenous (i.e. 'innate') one might argue that differences in ability are the luck of the draw, giving rise to the stochastic element of Y. Society might choose to take no action where people do well out of their gifts (e.g. the state does not confiscate the high incomes of musicians or athletes), but may compensate those who have done badly (e.g. someone with a congenital health problem). A completely different case arises if ability is at least partly endogenous, e.g. induced by differences in the quality of education. Ability is then in part a D characteristic, and positive discrimination might be justified.

Thus people can be unequal for two entirely different reasons. Where incomes differ because of discrimination, one can argue that society is unfair; and appropriate remedial action might involve trying to change the structure of society. In contrast, inequality of money income can arise purely because of random differences in people's luck (i.e. 'life' can be unfair). This is captured by the stochastic element in equation (6.17). Bad luck may require remedial action, but does not imply that society is unfair.[1]

The last word should go to Okun (1975, p. 76, reprinted in Atkinson, 1980), who summarises the problem with customary eloquence and a plea for action.

> The concept of equality of opportunity is far more elusive than that of equality of income. . . . [It] is rooted in the notion of a fair race where people are even at the starting line. But . . . it is hard to find the starting line. Differences in natural abilities are generally accepted as relevant character-istics that are being tested in the race rather than as unfair headstarts and handicaps. At the other extreme, success that depends on whom you know

---

[1] For further discussion, see Klappholz (1972).

rather than what you know is a clear case of inequality of opportunity. And it seems particularly unfair when the real issue is whom your father knows.

The inheritance of natural abilities is on one side of the line of unequal opportunity, and the advantages of a family position are clearly on the other. But much of the territory is unsettled.

3.2 MEASURING INEQUALITY BETWEEN INDIVIDUALS

Inequality between individuals is best approached by considering A and B, with money incomes of £10,000 and £5000, respectively, and asking why they might in fact be *equal*. There are three reasons why differences in money income might have no bearing on an individual's opportunity set, and so be irrelevant to issues of equality.

Different choices can cause differences in money incomes in two ways. A and B have *different tastes about money income* if they have different leisure preferences. Suppose A likes fast cars and nightclubs, and B likes walking across the hills with his dog. A (with money-intensive consumption preferences) might choose to work longer hours; and B might work fewer hours (i.e. enjoy more leisure) and/or choose work with more job satisfaction (i.e. higher non-money income). Both A and B are maximising their utility, and there is no case for regarding them as unequal simply because one has higher money income. Second, there can be *differences in acquired skills*: suppose A has chosen to forgo income early in life in order to acquire skills, whilst B has not. A's higher income is a return to his investment in human capital. Again there is no reason to suppose that there is any inequality provided (and the proviso is crucial) that A and B had the *same opportunity*, including access to information, to acquire skills (for further discussion see Le Grand, 1984).

Age Suppose A earns twice as much as B because he is 40 years old and highly skilled, whereas B is 20 years old and an apprentice. Suppose, further, that when B is 40 he will earn as much as A does now. In this case, the difference in money income is simply a life-cycle effect, and no long-term issue of inequality arises.[1]

---

[1] The need to control for age is particularly important in analysing the distribution of wealth. Consider an equal society, in which everyone has identical earnings, of which 5 per cent are saved to finance his/her retirement. The resulting wealth distribution would be highly unequal, since young people would have no wealth (because they had not yet started to save); people aged 98 would have very little wealth (because they would have spent all their savings); and people aged 64 would have substantial wealth (because they had been saving all their working lives and had yet to start dissaving).

The time dimension If A and B have fluctuating incomes, A might earn £10,000 and B £5000 this year, with the positions reversed next year. Taking the two years together, there is no inequality. More generally, inequality is greater if it is perpetuated across generations, i.e. if a rich person systematically has rich descendants and a poor person poor ones (see the Further Reading).

It is possible also to ask the question in reverse. Suppose A and B each have money income of £10,000. That does not necessarily mean that they are equal. They might face different price levels; more importantly, A might have a larger family than B and so, it might be argued, has a lower standard of living. This raises issues of how to compare families of different sizes.

The conclusion is that money income is a misleading indicator of inequality. *This does not imply that there is no inequality in society – just that money income is bad at measuring it.*

3.3 MEASURING INEQUALITY BETWEEN FAMILIES

If it is not possible to compare the living standards of two individuals, we are likely to make even less headway with families of different sizes. Families with the same standard of living are said to have 'equivalent' incomes, from which can be derived equivalence scales which say, for instance, that a family consisting of a man, wife and two children has an 'adult equivalent' of 2½, i.e. the family needs 2½ times the income of a single person to have an 'equivalent' standard of living. Putting the issue a different way, suppose A has a money income of £10,000 and is married; if the couple then has a child, what increase in money income is necessary to leave them as well off as before?

The problem inherent in the question is illustrated by the following two arguments. The *per capita money income argument* states that if a couple has a child, then per capita income in the household falls, and the couple will need a *higher* money income to maintain their standard of living. The *utility argument*, along revealed preference lines, asserts that a couple will have a child by choice only if it raises their utility; thus where two people with perfect information (admittedly a strong assumption) have a child by choice, their utility is increased, and they can maintain a given standard of living with a *lower* money income.[1]

It follows that the question as posed (i.e. if a couple has a child, by how much must its money income be increased to leave it as well-off as before?) implies an assumption that parents' living standards depend only on their consumption level, ruling out the possibility that they might derive utility from the child.

---

[1] Note that couples may be prepared to pay large amounts to adoption agencies or for medical treatment to cure infertility.

This should be borne in mind when considering the conventional analysis of adult equivalents, typified by McClements (1977 and 1978, Ch. 3), which accepts this stringent assumption rather uncritically.[1]

Figure 6.2, taken from McClements (1978, p. 47), illustrates the conventional approach. Consider two couples, A (with one child) and B (with no child) under the following assumptions:

(1) each family consumes two commodities, food and housing;
(2) a child eats 50 per cent of the food eaten by a couple but needs no more housing (this is unrealistic but highlights the analysis);
(3) utility depends *only* on the consumption of food and housing (as we have seen, this is a highly restrictive assumption); and
(4) if a couple has a child their indifference map does not change; hence neither does their consumption pattern except in response to a change in relative prices (this is another restrictive assumption).

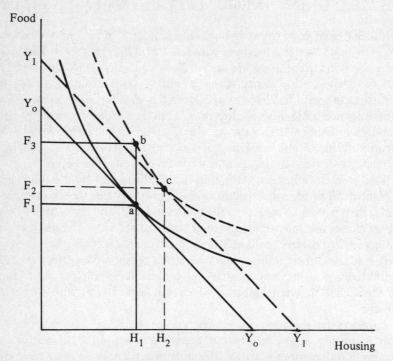

Figure 6.2   *The cost of maintaining an 'equivalent' standard of living for different families*

---

[1] For a simple introduction see Atkinson (1983, Ch. 3.3). The literature on adult equivalents is large – see the Further Reading.

Childless couple B faces the budget constraint Y_0–Y_0 with the unbroken indifference curve, and maximises utility at point a (F_1, H_1). Because of assumption (2), at the same level of housing, H_1, couple A with one child needs F_3 ($=1.5F_1$) of food to achieve the same standard of living as couple B. This is shown by point b (F_3, H_1) on the dotted indifference curve. With the given relative prices couple A can reach the living standard shown by this indifference curve at point c, at a lower cost than at b.

Given the earlier assumptions, the following incomes are equivalent:

Couple B (childless): $Y^B = p_F F_1 + P_H H_1$ $\qquad\qquad\qquad$ (6.18)

Couple A: $\qquad\qquad\quad Y^A = p_F F_2 + P_H H_2$

$\qquad\qquad\qquad\qquad\quad < 1.5 P_F F_1 + P_H H_1$ $\qquad\qquad$ (6.19)

where Y^A and Y^B are the money incomes of couples A and B, respectively, and p_H and p_F are the prices of housing and food. It is not necessary to compensate a couple fully for the extra food consumed by their child because, under the stated assumptions, raising food standards for the couple with a child costs 1.5 times as much as a similar increase for the childless couple, whereas a given increase in housing standards costs the same for each couple. This is equivalent to a 50 per cent increase in food prices for the couple with a child, and leads to a substitution of (now relatively cheaper) housing.

These conclusions rest crucially on the assumptions, not only the minor assumption that a child will eat half as much as a couple but, more importantly, that the couple derives no utility from the child, and does not change its consumption pattern. The first requires that the indifference curve for the couple with a child must lie outside that for the childless couple to maintain a given standard of living, and the second constrains the movement to a 50 per cent vertical upward shift. The two assumptions together ensure that the equivalent money income will always be higher for the couple with a child. This might be realistic for a low-income family; but the utility argument might well be more plausible for families well above the poverty line.

4 Inequality 2: Aggregate Measures

4.1 THE DESCRIPTIVE APPROACH

This section discusses the measurement of inequality in society as a whole, starting with simple representations of the income distribution, and proceeding to more complex measures and a brief review of empirical studies. The aim is to construct a scalar representation of income differences within a given population. Ideally it would take on values between zero (if everyone had the same income) and one (if one person had all the income). This would enable us to answer questions like: how much inequality is there in Britain today? Is it less than ten years ago? Is it less than in the USA? Any such overall measure of inequality rests on two ingredients:

(a) What is the unit defined to be equal or unequal, e.g. the individual, family or household? Here we talk only of 'individuals' and abstract from issues of household size and definition.
(b) Inequality of what, e.g. income, wealth, power? The literature generally looks at 'income', which usually means money income.

An inequality measure combines knowledge of the 'incomes' of 'individuals', though we shall see that its usefulness is qualified both by measurement problems (e.g. the use of household money income) and by conceptual difficulties.

The frequency distribution and associated measures The simplest starting-point is the *frequency distribution*, which shows the number of income recipients at each level of income. It can be represented as a continuous function as in Figure 6.1, or as a histogram. The frequency distribution has the advantage of being simple and easy to interpret, especially in the middle-income ranges. But it is weak at the tails: the left-hand tail should include negative incomes (e.g. business losses), and the right-hand tail has been severely truncated.

A simple yet dramatic way of representing the income distribution is *Pen's parade*,[1] in which each person (i.e. income recipient) marches past the onlooker. The parade takes an hour, and each person's height corresponds to his/her pre-tax income (a person with average income having average height). This representation is vivid; it shows up the tails well; and we can see not only the distribution, but also who is where in it. It does not, however, lend itself to quantification.

Several measures of inequality based on the frequency distribution are discussed in detail by Sen (1973, Ch. 2) and Cowell (1977, Ch. 2). This section discusses only the most important. A natural way of trying to capture aggregate inequality is by a summary measure of dispersion like the *variance*,

$$V = \frac{1}{n} \sum_{i=1}^{n} (y^i - \mu)^2 \tag{6.20}$$

where y^i is the money income of the ith individual, μ is average income, and where there are n income recipients. The advantage of the variance is that it

---

[1] See Pen (1971) in Atkinson (1980, pp. 47–55) for an entertaining (and non-technical) description of the income distribution.

considers the whole distribution, and that measured inequality is reduced by any redistribution which brings an individual's income closer to the mean. Its main disadvantage is its sensitivity to the absolute level of income; if all incomes double (or are expressed in dollars at an exchange rate of $2 = £1) there is no change in inequality, but V quadruples.

This problem is avoided by the *coefficient of variation* defined as

$$C = \frac{V^{1/2}}{\mu} \qquad (6.21)$$

which is the variance normalised on average income. The advantage of C is its independence of scale. But it has a number of difficulties, not least that it is neutral to the income level at which transfers take place, i.e. transferring £100 from an individual with an income of £1000 to one with an income of £500 has the same effect on C as a £100 transfer from a person with an income of £1 million to one with £999,500. If we want to give greater weight to transfers to lower incomes, one procedure is to take some transformation which staggers income levels. The logarithm achieves this. The variance of the logarithm of income has the added advantage of scale independence (if income (say) doubles, this simply adds a constant to all logarithms of income, which cancel when calculating deviations from the mean). For this reason the *variance of the logarithm of income*

$$H = \frac{1}{n} \sum_{i=1}^{n} (\log y^i - \log \mu)^2 = \frac{1}{n} \sum_{i=1}^{n} \log\left(\frac{y_i}{\mu}\right)^2 \qquad (6.22)$$

has often been proposed as an inequality measure. H has the advantages that it is invariant to the absolute level of income, is sensitive to income transfers at all income levels, but gives greater weight to transfers to lower incomes. There are also disadvantages. The measure (in common with V and C) considers only differences of income from the mean; and it squares those differences. Both procedures are somewhat arbitrary. In addition, the logarithmic transformation increasingly contracts higher incomes so that, as a measure of social welfare, H may not be concave at higher income levels, i.e. H can *rise* in the face of some transfers from rich to less rich.[1]

The Lorenz curve was devised explicitly as a representation of inequality. Though the diagram is old (Lorenz, 1905) it is a powerful device, intimately connected with an important theorem by Atkinson discussed in section 4.2. In Figure 6.3 the horizontal axis shows the per cent of income recipients

---

[1] Concavity and other properties of social welfare functions were discussed in section 1.2.

(individuals or households), the vertical axis the share of total income. The Lorenz curve is shown by the line 0–*a*–B. Each point shows the share of total income received by the *lowest x* per cent of income recipients; thus point *a* shows that the bottom 40 per cent of individuals receives 17 per cent of income.

It should be clear that the Lorenz curve will coincide with the diagonal 0–B if income is distributed completely equally (because only then will the lowest 50 per cent of individuals receive 50 per cent of total income, and so on); and the greater the degree of inequality the further the curve will lie from the diagonal. If the Lorenz curve for the UK lies entirely inside that for the Netherlands (Figure 6.4A) we can say that income inequality is lower in the UK; but where the curves cross (Figure 6.4B) an ambiguity arises. Lorenz curves thus give only a partial ordering of outcomes.[1]

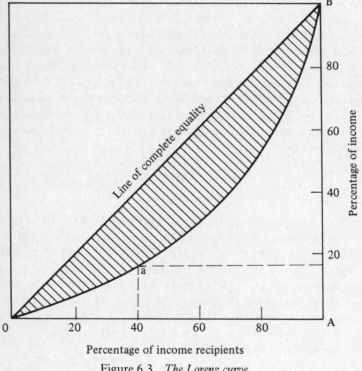

Percentage of income recipients

Figure 6.3   *The Lorenz curve*

[1] For an interesting attempt at least partly to resolve the ambiguity see Shorrocks (1983). He constructs a 'generalised Lorenz curve' by scaling up the conventional Lorenz curve by the mean of the income distribution. Whilst the measure is often successful at resolving ambiguity, it does so only because of strong assumptions about the weight given to absolute living standards. Weakening these assumptions greatly reduces the ambiguity-resolving power of the construct.

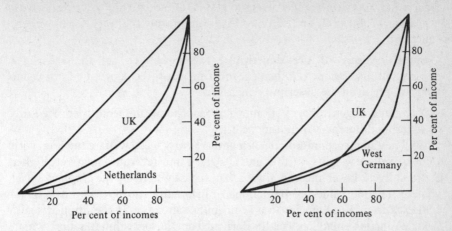

Figure 6.4A and B   *Lorenz curves for the UK, the Netherlands and West Germany*
(Source: Atkinson (1970), non-mathematical summary, in Atkinson (1980, p. 41).)

The Gini coefficient is based on the Lorenz curve; diagrammatically it is the ratio of the shaded area in Figure 6.3 to the triangle 0AB. If incomes are distributed completely equally it will be zero; and if one person has all the income it will be unity. Formally, the Gini coefficient is defined as half of the arithmetic average of the absolute differences between *all* pairs of incomes, the total then being normalised on mean income:

$$G = \frac{1}{2n^2\mu} \sum_{i=1}^{n} \sum_{j=1}^{n} |y^i - y^j| \qquad (6.23)$$

This can also be written (Sen, 1973, p. 31) as

$$G = 1 + \frac{1}{n} - \frac{2}{n^2\mu}(y^1 + 2y^2 + \ldots + ny^n) \qquad (6.24)$$

for $y^1 \geqslant y^2 \geqslant \ldots \geqslant y^n$

The Gini coefficient has several advantages. It is independent of the absolute level of income (like C and H); it avoids the arbitrary squaring procedure of V, C and H; and it compares each income not with the mean (like V, C and H), but with each other income, as equation (6.23) makes clear. Its disadvantages are twofold. It gives ambiguous results when comparing distributions for which the Lorenz curves cross. The second disadvantage is more subtle, and we return to it later. Formulation (6.24) shows that the Gini coefficient is a weighted sum of people's incomes, with the weights determined solely by the person's *rank-order* in the distribution. Thus y^1 (the highest income) enters the

149

term in brackets with a relative weight of $1, y^2$ (the second highest income) with a relative weight of 2, and so on. This is an entirely arbitrary social welfare function.

General critique of the descriptive measures To set the scene for subsequent discussion, it is helpful to bring out three conceptual criticisms which apply to all the descriptive measures.

(1) They lack generality. V, C and H all incorporate the arbitrary procedures of squaring differences from the mean.

(2) They all incorporate an *implicit* and *arbitrary* social welfare function with built-in welfare weights. With V and C a given transfer from a relatively higher to a relatively lower income always has the same effect; the implied social welfare function values all reductions in inequality equally, even if redistribution is from a millionaire to a semi-millionaire. For H the implied social welfare function embodies weights derived from the logarithm function, which again might not be one's chosen weights. The social welfare function underlying the Gini coefficient, as equation (6.24) shows, embraces weights based on rank order.

(3) At best the descriptive measures give only a partial ordering of outcomes. This is obviously true of intersecting Lorenz curves and hence of the Gini coefficient. The same problem arises with the other measures.[1]

4.2 EXPLICITLY NORMATIVE INEQUALITY MEASURES

Normative measures start explicitly from a social welfare function. This section discusses in order an important theorem by Atkinson, its implications, and the Atkinson inequality measure and its interpretation.[2]

The Atkinson theorem on Lorenz ranking is remarkable for its generality.[3] Assume

(1) States A and B have income distributions given by $(y^{1A}, y^{2A}, \ldots, y^{nA})$ and $(y^{1B}, y^{2B}, \ldots, y^{nB})$, respectively;

(2) Total income is the same in states A and B;

---

[1] For trenchant criticism of virtually all summary measures see Wiles (1974, especially pp. 7–12). He advocates the semi-decile ratio (i.e. the ratio of the average income of someone in the top 5 per cent of incomes to the corresponding average for the lowest 5 per cent) as the least bad summary statistic.

[2] Other approaches, by Dalton (1920) and Theil (1967), are discussed by Sen (1973, Ch. 2) and Cowell (1977, Ch. 3).

[3] For a simple introduction see Atkinson (1983, pp. 54–9). See also the Further Reading.

(3) W is a social welfare function which is non-decreasing, symmetric, additive and concave (see section 1.2).

Then: the Lorenz curve for B lies wholly inside the Lorenz curve for A *if and only if* $W_B > W_A$ for *every* social welfare function with the four properties listed in assumption (3).

To amplify, the theorem tells us:

(1) If the Lorenz curve for B lies wholly inside that for A, then: (a) welfare in state B is higher than in state A; we can say this *without knowing what the social welfare function is*; (b) the income distribution is unambiguously more equal in state B; (c) the Gini coefficient compares distributions unambiguously; and (d) all the conventional summary measures (e.g. V, C and H) give the same result.

(2) Conversely, if social welfare is higher in state B, then we know that Lorenz curve B must lie strictly inside Lorenz curve A.

(3) As a corollary, if Lorenz curves cross: (a) we cannot say whether inequality is greater in state A or B; (b) the Gini coefficient gives an ambiguous comparison; and (c) different inequality measures give different results.

These conclusions link the (descriptive) Lorenz curve to the explicitly normative world of the social welfare function. But the result is still not sufficient, both because not all Lorenz curves are non-intersecting, and because we still want a *numerical* measure of inequality. Atkinson approaches the issue by considering the Lorenz curves in Figure 6.4. The theorem enables us to say unambiguously that the distribution of income is less unequal in the UK than in the Netherlands. Figure 6.4B shows that the share of lower incomes is higher in West Germany than in the UK, but at higher incomes there is less inequality in the UK. By inspection, the area between the Lorenz curve and the diagonal is greater for West Germany than the UK, so that the Gini coefficient will show that the UK is *less* unequal than West Germany. But a measure which gives greater weight to lower incomes will show that the UK is *more* unequal.

Atkinson draws two major conclusions:

(1) Where Lorenz curves cross it is necessary to compare one income group with another. Thus the degree of inequality cannot in general be compared without introducing values about the distribution in the form of welfare weights for different income levels. This should be done *explicitly* via a social welfare function, in contrast with descriptive measures, which all embody implicit but unstated weights;

(2) Only where Lorenz curves do not intersect is it possible (subject to assumption (3) of the theorem) to avoid the necessity of explicit welfare weights; in this case all the descriptive measures will agree.

The Atkinson inequality measure considers distributional values explicitly. It is based on a social welfare function with the five properties discussed in section 1.2, i.e. non-decreasing, symmetric, additive, concave and with constant relative inequality aversion, ϵ, as in equation (6.10), as an explicit represent-ation of distributional values. The Atkinson measure is given by

$$A = 1 - \left[\sum_{i=1}^{n} \left(\frac{y_i}{\mu} \right)^{1-\varepsilon} f(y^i) \right]^{1/(1-\epsilon)} \qquad \varepsilon \neq 1 \qquad (6.25)$$

where y^i is the income of individuals in the ith income range (n ranges altogether), $f(y^i)$ is the proportion of the population with incomes in the ith range, and μ is mean income. A will be zero *either* if $y^i = \mu$ for all i (i.e. if income is equally distributed), *or* if $\epsilon = 0$ (i.e. if policy is concerned only with the absolute level of income, not its distribution). The greater the deviation of y^i from μ and/or the higher the value of ϵ the greater the value of A.

There is a natural connection between ϵ and the theories of society discussed in Chapter 3. If $\epsilon = 0$ society is indifferent to inequality, and A will be zero. If $\epsilon = \infty$ society is concerned only with the position of the lowest individual or income group, as advocated by Rawls. Socialists, too, would choose a high value. Utilitarians set no a priori limits, but would choose the value which maximised total welfare. In general the place of ϵ between the two extremes determines the importance of redistribution from richer to poorer. It should be clear from equation (6.25) that the deviation of y^i from μ is weighted by the exponent $(1-\epsilon)$, rather than the arbitrary squaring formula of V, C and H.

The meaning of ϵ is shown by Atkinson's 'mental experiment', subsequently elaborated as Okun's 'leaky bucket'. Consider taking £100 from a rich man and giving a proportion £x to a poor man, the rest leaking away in efficiency losses (disincentives, administration). How far can x fall (i.e. how leaky can the bucket be) before we no longer regard the redistribution as desirable? The answer determines ϵ.[1] The higher is ϵ, the lower x can be (i.e. the more egalitarian the view, the more 'leakiness' is tolerable): if $\epsilon=1$ it is fair to take £100 from a rich person and give £50 to a poor person; if $\epsilon=2$ it is sufficient if the poor man receives £25.

The Atkinson measure can be interpreted both as an inequality measure and as an index of the potential welfare gains from redistribution. Consider the proportion of present total income necessary to achieve the same level of welfare if it were equally distributed. If $A = 0.3$, we can say that if income were equally distributed we should need only (100% − 30% =) 70% of present national income to achieve the same level of social welfare. Alternatively, the gain from redistributing to equality is equivalent to raising national income by 30 per cent. The welfare gain is higher (a) the greater value of ϵ, and (b) the

---

[1] ϵ is determined from the formula $1/x = 2\epsilon$; see Atkinson, 1983, p. 58.

more unequal the pre-existing distribution.

Table 6.2 (taken from Atkinson, 1970) shows the value of A for the UK, the Netherlands and West Germany. Measured inequality is greater the higher is ϵ; consequently the welfare gains from redistribution to complete equality in the UK rise from 12 per cent of national income when $\epsilon = 0.5$ to 43 per cent when $\epsilon = 2$. The table also shows that inequality in the Netherlands is unambiguously greater than in the UK for all values of ϵ, as the non-intersecting Lorenz curves in Figure 6.4A show. West Germany is more unequal than the UK for $\epsilon < 3$; but when inequality aversion is high, West Germany is less unequal because of its greater equality at lower incomes.

Table 6.2: Values of the Atkinson Inequality Measure for the UK, the Netherlands and West Germany

Value of ϵ	UK	Netherlands	West Germany
0.5	0.12	0.15	0.17
1.0	0.24	0.29	0.29
1.5	0.34	0.42	0.38
2.0	0.43	0.52	0.45
3.0	0.55	0.66	0.54

Source: Atkinson (1970), non-mathematical summary, in Atkinson (1980, p. 42).

The Atkinson measure thus has powerful advantages. Conventional measures like the Gini coefficient obscure the fact that a complete ranking of states is possible only where the form of the social welfare function is specified; and the social welfare functions implicit in conventional measures are often arbitrary, if not unacceptable. The Atkinson measure avoids both difficulties – a complete ranking of states is possible, though precise knowledge of the social welfare function is unnecessary.

The main criticism of the measure is not operational but philosophical, namely its basis on an additive, individualistic social welfare function, i.e. on the assumption that social welfare is a (more or less) simple sum of individual utilities. Writers like Sen (1973, pp. 47–53 and 1979) criticise this feature, and argue that the social valuation of the welfare of individuals should allow for the sort of welfare interdependence discussed in Chapter 4:4.1.

4.3 INEQUALITY: SOME EMPIRICAL RESULTS

Problems with empirical work on the distribution of income are ubiquitous.
(1) Virtually all studies are based on the current money income of households or tax units. This procedure raises serious difficulties for all inequality

153

measures:

(a) It fails to include non-money income (section 1.1) and is therefore inherently a poor measure of individual opportunity sets. Additionally, cross- country comparisons may omit certain dimensions of inequality, e.g. differences in political freedom.

(b) It fails to exclude differences in money income which have no bearing on inequality, e.g. life-cycle factors and individual choice (section 3.2).

(c) Adjustments for differences in the size and composition of different households, where they are attempted at all, face the problems described in section 3.3.

(2) Summary measures of inequality raise the following conceptual problems:

(a) Conventional measures are subject to the criticisms set out at the end of section 4.1.

(b) The Atkinson measure is based on the assumption of additivity.

(c) Trends over time need to be interpreted in the light of structural change. For example, an increase in the size of a poor group, e.g. students or old people, will appear to increase inequality even though the position of each student or pensioner is unchanged.

(3) Data problems:

(a) Information on income by type or level of income, or type of recipient might be scant.

(b) The definition of income might change over time, or be incompatible with those of other countries.

(c) Estimation is generally based on income classes, and so neglects dispersion within each class; the use of more disaggregated data generally increases measured inequality.

Some results   The fact that empirical work faces problems does not mean that it is not useful, merely that considerable care is needed in interpreting its results. So this bare summary should be regarded as no more than indicative, and subject to qualifications (for which see the studies themselves).

Soltow (1968), in a study of long-run changes in the UK, drew Lorenz curves for 1688, 1801–3 and 1867, which showed that inequality decreased for lower incomes, but increased for higher incomes. It follows that whether inequality increased or decreased depends on the relative weights attached to higher and lower incomes (the Gini coefficients for the three periods were 55 per cent, 56 per cent and 52 per cent, respectively). The Lorenz curve for 1962/3 was strictly inside the other three; the Gini coefficient was 34 per cent. From this and other evidence Soltow tentatively concluded that overall inequality did not change in the eighteenth and nineteenth centuries; that only since about the First World War has there been a decrease in inequality; and that the decrease since then has been substantial. These findings have not been without their critics (see the Further Reading).

The size distribution of money income in the UK in the 1960s was investigated by Nicholson (1974, pp. 78–82), and that for the postwar period as a whole by the Royal Commission on the Distribution of Income and Wealth (UK, 1979a, Ch. 2, reprinted in part in Atkinson, 1980, pp. 71–8). The Royal Commission found that between 1949 and 1977 the share of the top 1 per cent fell from 6.4 per cent of after-tax income to 3.5 per cent, and of the top 10 per cent from 27.1 per cent to 22.4 per cent. But this was balanced by the increased share of the other groups in the top half of the distribution. As a result, the income share of the bottom 50 per cent rose very little, from 26.5 per cent to 27.6 per cent; and the top 10 per cent in 1976/7 received almost as much income after tax as the bottom 50 per cent. The impression of a decline in inequality is misleading. The fall in the Gini coefficient from 35.5 per cent in 1949 to 31.5 per cent in 1976/7 was mainly because of reduced inequality at the top of the distribution. Atkinson (1980, p. 45) sounds yet another warning about summary measures; the Gini coefficient fell from 35.5 per cent in 1949 to 33.9 per cent in 1970/1, but the share of the bottom 50 per cent *fell* slightly from 26.5 per cent to 26.1 per cent (on the same problem see Wiles, 1974, pp. 7–12).

Inequality can occur also through access to goods in kind, as we saw in section 3.1. Le Grand (1982) analyses the use made by different income groups of health care, education and housing, and concludes that the UK institutions for alleviating inequality are less successful than is sometimes supposed. We return to this issue in greater detail in Chapter 7:4.2 and Chapters 13 and 14.

The problems which arise in measuring inequality in one country, or comparing it over time, are bad enough. They are compounded when attempting to make comparisons across countries, mainly because the definitions of income and income recipients are frequently inconsistent (see Lydall, 1979). Some international comparisons by the Royal Commission on the Distribution of Income and Wealth[1] considered the distribution of income in eight countries. The main conclusions (and they should be regarded as very tentative) are that on almost any definition of income and of recipient the UK has a less unequal distribution, and the USA, Canada and West Germany a more unequal distribution. Australia, Sweden and the Republic of Ireland also tend to have less inequality, while France and (on some definitions) Japan have more.

Problems are even more complex in countries like those in eastern Europe where prices are often not market prices (e.g. subsidised food), and income is often received in kind (e.g. free holidays). An attempt at least partially to navigate these shoals can be found in Wiles (1974).

Empirical studies of the distribution of wealth (see the Further Reading) also

---

[1] UK (1977a, Ch. 6), reprinted in part in Atkinson (1980, pp. 79–99). See also Stark (1977).

face serious difficulties. Some are conceptual, e.g. what should be included in personal wealth. Others are measurement problems, e.g. the valuation of estates at death. Many are problems of both concept and measurement, e.g. whether accrued pension rights should be included as part of personal wealth and, if so, how they should be valued; or how the distribution of estates at death might be grossed up to give a picture of the wealth holdings of the living.

Further Reading

For an overview of the problems of defining and measuring income, poverty and inequality see Atkinson (1983) (compendious and non-mathematical), and for wide-ranging collections of recent contributions Atkinson (1980 and 1987).

The classic works on defining and measuring income are Fisher (1930, pp. 3–35), Simons (1938, pp. 41–58), Hicks (1946, pp. 171–81) and Kaldor (1955, pp. 54–78).

The classic historical studies of poverty are by Booth (1902) and Rowntree (1901); for follow-up studies see Rowntree (1941) and Rowntree and Lavers (1951); for an assessment Briggs (1961); and for careful re-working and updating Atkinson, Maynard and Trinder (1983). For more recent discussion of the definition and measurement of poverty see Fiegehen and Lansley (1976), Fiegehen *et al.* (1977), Townsend (1979), Piachaud (1981) (a critique of Townsend), and Sen (1983). Orshansky (1965) discusses the calculation of a poverty line for the USA. For attempts to quantify poverty in aggregate see Beckerman (1979), Sen (1976) and Foster (1984) (a survey of the literature). For detailed studies of low incomes in the UK see Fiegehen *et al.* (1977), Layard *et al.* (1978), Berthoud *et al.* (1981), Beckerman and Clark (1982), and Mack and Lansley (1985); for a similar study of US data see Danziger, Haveman and Plotnick (1984).

The meaning of 'equality' is discussed by Okun (1975, Ch. 3) and Le Grand (1982 and 1984). On the theory of the intergenerational transmission of inequality see Bowles (1973); Arrow (1971) examines the impact of job discrimination; more general aspects of the inheritance of inequality are discussed by Meade (1974), and in a US context by Brittain (1977 and 1978) (the articles by Bowles, Arrow and Meade are reprinted in Atkinson (1980)). For a simple introduction to the literature on adult equivalents see Atkinson (1983, Ch. 3), and McClements (1978, Ch. 3). For detailed studies see Prais and Houthakker (1955) (see also Muellbauer, 1980); Singh and Nagar (1973); McClements (1977) (see also Muellbauer, 1979); and Muellbauer (1977). A study based on US data is given in Lazear and Michael (1980). For critical reviews of the literature see Nicholson (1976) and Deaton and Muellbauer (1980).

Aggregate inequality is illuminated in Pen (1971) (reprinted in Atkinson, 1980), and discussed more generally by Atkinson (1983). For a discussion of inequality measures see Sen (1973, Ch. 2) and Cowell (1977, Ch. 2); the latter contains a useful introduction to social welfare functions. The classic article on the Atkinson inequality measure is Atkinson (1970), reprinted with a non-mathematical summary in Atkinson (1980, pp. 23–43) (for a simple introduction see Atkinson (1983, pp. 54–9). For the 'leaky bucket' experiment see Okun (1975, pp. 91–100) (another piece of vintage Okun to which the reader is warmly recommended), and for a witty and highly critical review of most inequality measures Wiles (1974).

For an account of the difficulties of empirical work see Lydall (1979). Empirical analysis of the UK income distribution over the long run is given by Soltow (1968) (for a critique see Williamson (1980) and Lindert and Williamson (1982 and 1983)). For studies of more recent years see Nicholson (1974) and the Royal Commission on the Distribution of Income and Wealth (UK, 1979a). For international comparisons see the Royal Commission on the Distribution of Income and Wealth (UK, 1977a) and Stark (1977).

Estimates of the distribution of wealth are given in Atkinson (1974), Atkinson and Harrison (1978), and Brittain (1978) (a study of the US); Harrison (1979) looks at the distribution of wealth in ten countries.

Appendix: Non-technical Summary of Chapter 6

1 Chapter 6 discusses problems which arise in defining and measuring the key concepts of income, poverty and inequality.

Income

2 The only theoretically sound definition of individual income (section 1.1) is **full income**, Y_F, which consists of money income, Y_M, plus all non-money income, Y_N (e.g. job satisfaction, the value of services from housing and consumer durables, the value of own production, and the enjoyment of leisure), i.e.

$$Y_F = Y_M + Y_N \qquad (6.1)$$

The inclusion of non-money income, including the enjoyment of leisure, is crucial. Full income defined this way is a broad measure of an individual's *potential* consumption, i.e. of his power to consume goods (including leisure) if he so chooses. As such it is a form of generalised budget constraint.

3 The measurement of income (section 1.1) is bedevilled by several sets of problems. First, money income is used as a proxy for full income because it is not possible to measure most forms of non-money income. The fact that there is no systematic relation between Y_M and Y_N makes money income an unreliable yardstick of consumption opportunities, and therein lies the origin of many of the problems of defining and measuring poverty and inequality. A second difficulty concerns the definition of the unit whose income we are measuring, e.g. whom does the income unit include, and how should the incomes of families of different sizes be treated? Finally, over what time period should income be measured? The conclusion is that a theoretically sound definition of income faces intractable measurement problems.

Poverty

4 In principle poverty should be defined in terms of full income. Its measurement therefore faces all the problems described in para. 3. But even if these were solved it would still be necessary to decide whether poverty (however measured) should be defined in absolute or relative terms (section 2.1). **Absolute poverty** means that a person's money income is too low to keep him alive and healthy. Early studies hoped in this way to measure poverty 'objectively', an approach now out of favour, at least in developed economies. **Relative poverty** implies that a person is poor if his/

her standard of living deviates substantially from the average of the society in which he lives, i.e. if he cannot participate in 'normal' life.

5 Poverty (in an absolute sense) and inequality are two entirely separate concepts (section 2.2). Absolute poverty relates to a standard of living below some benchmark, inequality to the *difference* between the incomes of poor and non-poor. The distinction is important because policies aimed at one might aggravate the other. It is therefore necessary to be clear whether poverty or inequality is the main focus of attention.

Inequality

6 **Equality of opportunity** (section 3.1) would be hard to define even if full income could be measured. The main problem is to decide which causes of income differences reflect inequality. Systematic differences due to race, sex or social class are generally regarded as examples of inequality. But ambiguity can arise when differences are due to 'natural ability', depending on whether or not it is influenced by differences in the quality of education. Equality of opportunity does not, however, rule out random differences in income (i.e. luck).

7 These problems are compounded because in practice it is necessary to use money income as a proxy for individual welfare. Differences in money income can overstate inequality between individuals A and B for at least three reasons (section 3.2): they may have different tastes and hence have made different choices (e.g. about leisure); they may be at different stages in their life cycle (e.g. A fully trained, B an apprentice); and the difference in their incomes may be the result of random fluctuations. Other factors can understate inequality. None of this implies that there is no inequality in society – just that money income is bad at measuring it.

8 Further problems arise when comparing the incomes of families of different sizes (section 3.3). One argument is that if a couple has a child, per capita household income will fall; it follows that larger households need higher money income than smaller households to maintain an 'equivalent' standard of living. Alternatively, if a couple has a child by choice, it can be argued that though per capita money income falls the couple's *utility* rises because otherwise they would not have had the child. In the latter case a larger household does not necessarily need a higher money income to maintain a given living standard. Again, the problem arises because it is not possible to measure full income; and again there is no practical solution.

9 Section 4 discusses measures of the overall degree of inequality in society. These measures, to the extent that they are valid, enable us to compare inequality in Britain today with inequality ten years ago, or with inequality in the USA.

159

10 A widely used measure is the **Lorenz curve** (section 4.1). In Figure 6.3 the horizontal axis shows the per cent of individuals/households, the vertical axis the per cent of total income. The Lorenz curve is shown by the line 0–*a*–B. Each point on the curve shows the share of total income received by the *lowest x* per cent of individuals. Thus point *a* shows that the bottom 40 per cent of individuals receives 17 per cent of income. If income is distributed completely equally the Lorenz curve will coincide with the diagonal (i.e. the lowest 50 per cent of individuals receive 50 per cent of income, and so on). Thus the greater the degree of inequality, the further the Lorenz curve will be from the diagonal, and vice versa. The **Gini coefficient** is an inequality measure based on the Lorenz curve; diagrammatically it is the ratio of the shaded area in Figure 6.3 to the triangle 0AB. It follows that the Gini coefficient will vary between zero (if income is distributed completely equally) and one (if one person has all the income).

11 The use of the Gini coefficient as a measure of inequality is subject to a variety of criticisms (section 4.3). First, it is based on the current money income of individuals or households: this omits all non-money income (paras 2 and 3); it fails to exclude differences in money income which have no bearing on inequality, e.g. life-cycle factors and individual choice (para. 7); and it faces difficulties over differences in household size (para. 8). Second, the data on money income are not always accurate, complete or consistent over time or across countries. Finally, the Gini coefficient raises a number of conceptual problems. These are discussed in section 4.2 together with the Atkinson inequality measure, which treats inequality in a more sophisticated way, and hence avoids some of the problems of the Gini coefficient.

12 The main message of para. 11 for non-technical readers is that the Gini coefficient, though widely used and useful in some circumstances, is in no way definitive as a measure of overall inequality.

PART 2

CASH BENEFITS

┌─────────┐
│   7   │
└─────────┘

Financing the Welfare State

Taxes, after all, are the dues that we pay for the privileges of membership in an organised society. [Franklin D. Roosevelt, 1936.]

Thrift should be the guiding principle in our government expenditure. [Mao Tse-tung, 1893–1976.]

1 The Structure of the UK Government Accounts

1.1 CONCEPTUAL ISSUES

This chapter discusses the finances of the welfare state, and is somewhat more institutional than the rest of the book. The subject is vast, and this brief account does little more than scratch the surface (see the Further Reading). National insurance and other cash benefits are discussed in section 2, and the rest of the welfare state, mainly the national health service, education and housing, in section 3. Section 4 considers a number of important methodological issues. This section describes the structure of UK[1] government accounts, as a

---

[1] Hitherto the terms Britain and the UK have been used interchangeably. Henceforth (particularly when talking about statistical data) they will be used more precisely, viz. Britain (or Great Britain) consists of England, with Wales and Scotland (Act of Union with Scotland 1706). The United Kingdom (UK) is Great Britain and Northern Ireland (Act of Union with Ireland 1800; Government of Ireland Act 1920).

163

backdrop to which it is necessary at least briefly to list a number of conceptual points.

The boundaries of the public sector have to be established, *inter alia* between the government sector and public corporations, and between government on the one hand and companies and the personal sector on the other. This task is much more complex than is apparent (Prest and Barr, 1985, Ch. 8). It is not possible to define such boundaries unambiguously; careful judgement is needed; and any definition, however carefully constructed, will be open to criticism.

Levels of government activity The most obvious distinction is between central and local government. For instance, total spending by central and local government is *not* the simple sum of their respective expenditures. Part of central expenditure is a grant to local authorities, which then forms part of local spending. In producing overall public sector accounts it is necessary to avoid this sort of double counting, hence the combined figures in Table 7.1 contain no item for central government grants to local authorities.

Government activity on current, capital and financial account It is necessary to distinguish receipts on current account (mainly from taxes on income and expenditure); receipts on capital account (e.g. from capital taxation and the sale of capital assets); and financial receipts (mainly the revenue from government borrowing). Similar distinctions arise on the expenditure side.

Types of government expenditure It is vital to distinguish absorption of goods and services from transfer payments. To illustrate, public spending on education comprises:

(1) Absorption of goods and services, which includes (a) current expenditure (i.e. public consumption in the form of teachers' salaries, etc.); and (b) capital expenditure (i.e. public investment such as the costs of building new schools).

(2) Transfer payments, which include (a) current grants to the personal sector (e.g. student educational grants); and (b) capital grants to the private sector (e.g. contributions to the cost of university building).[1]

Chapter 4:3.1 set out the four generic forms of state intervention – regulation, tax/subsidy, public production and cash transfers. Government absorption of goods and services (as in (1) above) corresponds with public production. Transfer payments take two very different forms. The first is explicit transfers, as in (2) above, which also include all state cash benefits. Second there are:

---

[1] These are transfer payments from the viewpoint of government because universities are regarded as part of the private sector.

Tax expenditures, i.e. implicit public expenditure in the form of tax reliefs. Cash assistance to help poor tenants with their rent is an explicit transfer, mortgage interest tax relief for owner-occupiers an implicit transfer. Both serve similar purposes, i.e. assisting with accommodation costs, and both ultimately make up part of private sector spending. Tax relief for private pensions is similarly a form of transfer.[1] But tax expenditures do not appear in conventional public spending figures; and their distributional implications have been criticised. Both issues assume special relevance in the context of pensions (Chapter 9) and housing (Chapter 14) (for detailed discussion see the Further Reading).

1.2 GOVERNMENT REVENUE AND EXPENDITURE

The revenue proposals of government are set out each year in the Budget, and more formally in the *Financial Statement and Budget Report* and the Finance Bill. The details of the central government accounts described in Prest and Barr (1985, Ch. 9) need no repetition here, save to note the long-standing principle of British public finance, that in general all central government revenues, whatever their source, are paid into the *Consolidated Fund*, from which all central government expenditure is made. The only major exception is the *National Insurance Fund*, which is discussed in section 2.2.

Most of the income of a local authority is paid into its *Rate Fund*, whose revenue derives from two main sources: a grant from central government (i.e. from the Consolidated Fund), whose complexities lie well outside the scope of this book; and local rates, i.e. a tax levied on the rental value of property. There is also a rate rebate scheme as part of housing benefit (Chapter 10:1), which subsidises the rate bills of individuals with low incomes. For present purposes the most important aspect of local finance is the size of the central government grant (about 42 per cent of total local spending in 1986/7), which raises major issues for the relationship between central and local government, particularly in the light of developments like 'rate capping' (i.e. tight control by central government of the revenue-raising powers of local government) (see the Further Reading).

Table 7.1 gives an overview of the income and expenditure of government. The three main blocks of revenue relate to central government, national insurance contributions and local government. Central government revenue in 1986/7 was £111.9 billion, mainly from current taxation. Taxes on income, administered by the Inland Revenue, raised £52.8 billion, nearly three-quarters from income tax, making it the largest single revenue source. Taxes on expenditure, mostly administered by Customs and Excise, raised £46.3 billion.

---

[1] Though valuation problems may arise – see UK Board of Inland Revenue (1983).

Table 7.1: Income and Expenditure of Central and Local Government, UK, 1986/7 (est.) (£million)

REVENUE

	(1)	(2)	(3)	(4)
CENTRAL GOVERNMENT				
Taxes on income				
Income tax	38,700			
Corporation tax	12,100			
Other	2,000			
		52,800		
Taxes on expenditure				
VAT	20,700			
Taxes on alcohol, tobacco and hydrocarbon oils	16,400			
Other	9,200			
		46,300		
Taxes on capital		2,800		
			101,900	
Other central government revenue				
Rents		300		
Dividends and interest		3,200		
Other		6,500		
(Grants to local authorities)		(−14,860)		
			10,000	
TOTAL CENTRAL GOVERNMENT REVENUE				111,900
NATIONAL INSURANCE CONTRIBUTIONS				26,200
LOCAL GOVERNMENT				
Local authority rates			15,600	
Other current revenue				
Rents		2,900		
Dividends and interest		600		
Other		−1,300		
(Grants from central government)		(14,860)		
			2,200	
TOTAL LOCAL GOVERNMENT REVENUE				17,800
TOTAL GENERAL GOVERNMENT RECEIPTS				155,900
GENERAL GOVERNMENT BORROWING REQUIREMENT				7,500
GENERAL GOVERNMENT RECEIPTS AND BORROWING				163,400

Sources: *Financial Statement and Budget Report, 1986–87*, Tables 1.2 and 6.5; and *The Government's Expenditure Plans, 1986–87 to 1988–89*, Cmnd 9702-II, Table 2.8 and p. 341, para. 9.
Notes: [a]See Table 14.1 for a breakdown of this total.
         [b]See Table 13.2 for a breakdown of this total.

EXPENDITURE

	Central government (1)	Local government (2)	Certain Public Corporation Expenditure (3)	Total (4)
SPENDING BY PROGRAMME				
Defence	18,525	–	–	18,525
Foreign and Commonwealth Office	1,920	–	39	1,959
European Community	652	–	–	652
Agriculture, Fisheries and Food	2,003	152	14	2,170
Trade and Industry	1,379	70	133	1,581
Energy	791	–	−677	115
Employment	3,625	102	4	3,741
Transport	1,308	2,331	1,169	4,809
DOE – Housing	1,236	1,480	36	2,752[a,e]
DOE – Other Environmental Services	379	3,105	138	3,622
Home Office	1,523	4,026	–	5,549
Education and Science	2,469	11,850	–	14,319[b,e]
Arts and Libraries	321	412	–	733
DHSS – Health and personal social services	15,094	2,604	27	17,724[c,e]
DHSS – Social Security[g]	39,725	3,207	–	42,932[d,f]
Scotland	3,298	3,784	491	7,573
Wales	1,384	1,434	86	2,904
Northern Ireland	3,464	640	416	4,521
Chancellor's Departments	2,003	–	6	2,008
Other Departments	1,526	–	–	1,526
Reserve	4,500	–	–	4,500
Central privatisation proceeds	−4,750	–	–	4,750
Adjustments	−400	–	–	−400
PLANNING TOTAL	101,986	35,198	1,882	139,100
GENERAL GOVERNMENT DEBT INTEREST				18,200
NATIONAL ACCOUNTS ADJUSTMENTS				6,100
GENERAL GOVERNMENT EXPENDITURE				163,400

[c] See Table 13.1 for a breakdown of this total.
[d] See Table 7.5 for a breakdown of this total.
[e] Excludes expenditure in Scotland, Wales and Northern Ireland.
[f] Excludes expenditure in Northern Ireland.
[g] Social security comprises expenditure on all contributory and non-contributory cash benefits.

In addition to tax revenues, central government also received £10 billion, *inter alia* from rents, dividends and interest.[1] National insurance contributions (£26.2 billion) are discussed in more detail in section 2.

Local government receipts were £17.8 billion, mainly from local rates (the only tax levied by local authorities) of £15.6 billion. Rents, mainly from local authority housing, raised another £2.9 billion. In addition, there is the central government grant (£14.9 billion in 1986/7), mainly the rate support grant and a subsidy to each authority's Housing Revenue Account. To avoid double counting, this intra-governmental transfer is omitted from the totals.

Total current and capital receipts were £155.9 billion, to which are added financial receipts (i.e. public sector borrowing) of £7.5 billion, bringing the total revenue of all levels of government to £163.4 billion.

The spending proposals of government are set out each year in a public expenditure White Paper (UK, 1986a) and debated by Parliament. There has been much discussion over the years about the planning of public spending and its control (see the Further Reading), in part because of the increased costs of the welfare state. The Public Expenditure White Paper in its current format gives a detailed breakdown of public spending,[2] and is the source of Table 7.1 and many of the later tables.

The 1986/7 planning total for expenditure was £139.1 billion, £102 billion (almost 75 per cent) by central government, and £59.9 billion in the form of transfers (UK, 1986a, Table 2.10), to which must be added £18.2 billion interest on the national debt. Total expenditure in national account terms was £163.4 billion. Much the largest programme was social security (£42.9 billion), mainly by central government, almost entirely on national insurance and other cash benefits.[3] Defence spending was £18.5 billion, and health and personal social services £17.7 billion, also mainly by central government. Spending on education was £14.3 billion, mainly by local government; and expenditure on housing was £2.8 billion, with substantial involvement by both levels of

---

[1] This £10 billion does *not* include proceeds from the sale of assets, which appear as a negative item on the *expenditure* side in the government accounts; for criticism see Barr (1986).

[2] The Public Expenditure White Papers have been the subject of considerable criticism. Since 1980 planning has been in 'cash' terms, i.e. departments are allocated a specific sum, irrespective of subsequent price changes. This makes planning of *expenditure* easier, but creates great difficulties for *volume* planning (i.e. for resource allocation) – see Glennerster, 1985, pp. 25 *et seq*.

[3] As explained in the Glossary, there is an unfortunate ambiguity in the use of the term 'social security'. In the USA it generally refers only to retirement benefits; in British usage it refers to *all* contributory and non-contributory cash benefits. The term will be avoided where possible. Where its use is inevitable it will be used in the British sense.

government, to which must be added all cash transfers connected with housing.[1] Spending under most of these heads was in reality somewhat higher, since expenditure on, for example, education in Scotland, Wales and Northern Ireland is included in the totals for those countries.

One point to emerge immediately is the sheer size of the welfare state, however defined (and it consists at a minimum of cash benefits, health, education and housing). In Table 7.2 these are divided into social services (approximating to the last three) and current grants to the personal sector (approximating cash payments). Figures are given also for defence and debt interest in current and constant prices in 1920, 1948 and 1986/7. There is always room for differences in judgement about the definition of the welfare state; and the price index is subject to the usual caveats; the figures should therefore be regarded as no more than indicative (for further discussion see Heald, 1983, Ch. 2). Several broad results emerge:

(1) The welfare state has assumed an increasing proportion of public spending; in 1920 it absorbed about 28 per cent of total government expenditure, only marginally greater than debt interest payments and about 1¾ times defence spending; the picture had not changed greatly by 1948; but by 1986/7 the welfare state made up over half of public spending, and over four times the expenditure on either defence or debt interest.

(2) Government spending doubled as a percentage of gross national product, from about 21 per cent in 1920 to nearly 43 per cent in 1986/7.

(3) A consequence is the sharp increase in the welfare state as a percentage of gross national product, from under 6 per cent in 1920 to 10 per cent in 1948, and to 22.5 per cent in 1986/7.

(4) In real terms (1948 prices), expenditure on the welfare state rose from £420 million in 1920 to £1195 million in 1948 and to £6233 million in 1986/7, representing a 15-fold increase since 1920, and a fivefold real increase since 1948. The resulting expenditure, however, (at least as far as cash benefits are concerned) is still well below the European average as a proportion of national income (Glennerster, 1985, p. 218; Newman, 1985).

2 Cash Benefits

2.1 INDIVIDUAL NATIONAL INSURANCE CONTRIBUTIONS

Current arrangements are the outcome of various changes since 1948 (Chapter

---

[1] Disaggregated figures are given in Tables 7.5 (cash benefits), 13.1 (health), 13.2 (education) and 14.1 (housing).

Table 7.2: Gross National Product and Spending by Central and Local Government, UK, 1920, 1948 and 1986/7

ITEM	1920				1948				1986/7			
	£m current prices (1)	£m 1948 prices (2)	% of government spending (3)	% of GNP (4)	£m current prices (5)	£m 1948 prices (6)	% of government spending (7)	% of GNP (8)	£m current prices (9)	£m 1948 prices (10)	% of government spending (11)	% of GNP (12)
DEFENCE (military & civil)	186	234	16	3.3	743	743	19	6.3	18,525	1,347	11	4.9
SOCIAL SERVICES (current expenditure on goods and services)	169 }	420	28	5.9	541 }	1,195	31	10.1	41,429 }	6,233	52	22.5
CURRENT GRANTS TO THE PERSONAL SECTOR	165 }				654 }				44,293 }			
DEBT INTEREST	320	402	27	5.6	553	553	14	4.7	18,200	1,323	11	4.8
TOTAL GOVERNMENT CURRENT SPENDING	1,182	1,485	100	20.8	3,862	3,862	100	32.6	163,400	11,880	100	42.9
GROSS NATIONAL PRODUCT (market prices)	5,688	7,146	–	100	11,837	11,837	–	100	380,465	27,662	–	100

Sources: Feinstein (1972), Tables 12, 13, 33, 35 and 61; *National Income and Expenditure* (1957, Tables 1, 36 and 39); *Monthly Digest of Statistics*, various issues; and Table 7.1.

2:6). There are three types of contributor for national insurance purposes: employed persons, the self-employed and the non-employed, as summarised in Table 7.3.[1]

Table 7.3: National Insurance Contribution Rates 1986/7

CLASS 1 (employed earners, not contracted out)	Employee (1)	Employer (2)
Contribution on all earnings where total weekly earnings are		
below £38.00	–	–
between £38.00 and £59.99	5%	5%
between £60.00 and £94.99	7%	7%
between £95.00 and £139.99	9%	9%
between £140.00 and £285.00		10.45%
in excess of £285.00	9% of £285	10.45% of all earnings

CLASS 2 (self-employed, flat-rate)	
Self-employed persons with profits in excess of £2075 per year	Flat-rate contribution of £3.75 per week

CLASS 3 (voluntary contributions by non-employed persons)	
Non-employed persons	Flat-rate contribution of £3.65 per week

CLASS 4 (self-employed, earnings related)	
Self-employed persons with profits in excess of £4450 per year	6.3% of profits between £4450 and £14,820 per year[a]

Note: [a] Half of the Class 4 contribution is deductible for income tax purposes.

Employed persons (i.e. most wage and salary earners) involve Class 1 contributions by both employee and employer. The employee contribution was 9 per cent of earnings (all figures relate to 1986/7) up to the *upper earnings limit* (£285 per week), with various exceptions: an individual with weekly earnings below £95 paid a reduced percentage rate (Table 7.3), and no contribution at all if earnings were below the *lower earnings limit* (£38 per week); and an individual who was contracted out of the state earnings-related pension scheme (Chapter 9:1) paid contributions at a reduced rate.

A full contribution year requires a total contribution of at least that due on 50

---

[1] For compendious details of these institutions see Tolley (1986, Chs 3 and 4).

times the lower earnings limit. An individual receiving unemployment benefit, if he or she would otherwise fall below this minimum, is given a *credit*, i.e. no contribution is paid, but future benefits are awarded as though the appropriate percentage contribution had been made on earnings equal to the lower earnings limit. At one time a married woman could opt out of most of her contribution (thereby losing entitlement to most benefits), but this option is no longer generally available.

Two features of these arrangements should be noted immediately. First, in contrast with income tax, the appropriate contribution rate is applied to *total* earnings, not just to earnings in the relevant range. Thus someone earning £94 per week pays an employee contribution of 7 per cent of £94, i.e. £6.58; but if earnings rise by £1 he pays 9 per cent of £95, i.e. £8.55. An extra £1 of earnings could therefore cost £1.97 in extra national insurance contributions, plus an additional 29 pence in income tax, i.e. a marginal tax rate of 226 per cent. This has implications for incentives in the context of the poverty trap (see the Glossary), as discussed in Chapter 10:3.

Second, unlike income tax and the other types of national insurance contribution, the income limit for Class 1 contributions operates strictly on a week-by-week basis. Thus, someone earning £38.10 in some weeks and £37.50 in others would pay contributions in weeks where earnings were £38.10, even if his average for the year were under £38. These contributions are not refundable, in sharp contrast with the operation of income tax in similar circumstances. Uneasy relationships like this have generated pressure for an integrated system of income tax and national insurance contributions (Chapter 11:3.2).

The basic employer Class 1 contribution in 1986/7 was 10.45 per cent of the employee's gross weekly earnings. Before October 1985, no contribution was payable on earnings above the upper earnings limit; thereafter, though the limit remained in force for the employee contribution, employers paid the full 10.45 per cent, however high the employee's earnings. For lower earnings the employer contribution was payable at a lower percentage rate in the same way as the employee contribution (Table 7.3); and a lower contribution was payable in respect of contracted-out employees.

Both employee and employer Class 1 contributions are collected together with income tax. They help to pay for national insurance benefits; and part of the contribution is channelled to the national health service.

The self-employed pay both Class 2 and Class 4 contributions. The Class 2 contribution is flat-rate (£3.75 in 1986/7) paid, as of old, in the form of a weekly stamp. Class 4 contributions are a percentage (6.3 per cent in 1986/7) of a self-employed person's profits between certain limits, collected by the Inland Revenue as part of the individual's income tax assessment. Since October

1985, half of the Class 4 contribution is deductible for income tax purposes. Class 2 and 4 contributions do not entitle a self-employed person to the full range of benefits available to an employee. There is no unemployment benefit, no earnings-related retirement pension, and no entitlement to redundancy pay.

A person who is both employed and self-employed is potentially liable to pay Class 1, Class 2 and Class 4 contributions, subject to an annual ceiling on total contributions. The details are complex (see Tolley, 1986, para. 3.35).

The non-employed, broadly, are not current members of the labour force, e.g. students, or married women who are not employed or self-employed. To maintain an unbroken contributions record, such a person is permitted (but not compelled) to pay a flat-rate Class 3 contribution (£3.65 per week in 1986/ 7).[1] The payment of Class 3 contributions gives no right to immediate benefit, but may enhance entitlement in the future.

Thus virtually all adult workers and a substantial number of the non-employed pay national insurance contributions, which go into the National Insurance Fund rather than the Consolidated Fund. Formally, therefore, national insurance is a contributory scheme. But it is argued in Chapters 8:3.1 and 9:5.1 that the contributory principle has been so eroded since Beveridge's original scheme that it can be doubted whether this is any longer the case.

2.2 THE NATIONAL INSURANCE FUND

National insurance benefits are paid from the National Insurance Fund, and all other central government benefits from the Consolidated Fund. The distinction is important for operational purposes and for understanding the structure of government accounts, but has rather less economic significance.

Revenue   On the revenue side the relation between the two funds is fairly straightforward. The income of the National Insurance Fund arises from a small number of clearly defined sources; virtually all other central government revenues go into the Consolidated Fund. The main revenues of the National Insurance Fund (Table 7.4) are from the various classes of insured persons, from a grant from the Consolidated Fund and from interest receipts. In 1984/5 total net contributions were £19 billion, the great bulk from Class 1 contributions. The central government contribution was £2.6 billion. The details are complex, but in essence the National Insurance Fund received a

---

[1] An exception is a woman (or in certain circumstances a man) staying at home to look after young children; she is normally able to avoid breaks in her contribution record without paying Class 3 contributions because she receives home responsibility protection; see Chapter 9:1.

Table 7.4: Account of the National Insurance Fund, UK, 1984/5 (£million)

REVENUE AND EXPENDITURE

REVENUE
Contributions

Class 1 (employed earners)	18,655.9	
Class 2 (self-employed flat-rate)	336.7	
Class 3 (voluntary contributors)	24.6	
Class 4 (self-employed earnings-related)	208.1	
Other	242.6	
Total gross contributions	19,467.9	
Less employers' recoveries in respect of statutory sick pay	−468.0	
Total net contributions		18,999.9
Supplement from Consolidated Fund		2,597.0
Interest receipts		520.5
Other		1.2
TOTAL REVENUE		22,118.5

EXPENDITURE

Benefits	20,925.7
Administration, etc.	819.2
Current surplus	373.7
TOTAL EXPENDITURE	22,118.5

BALANCE OF FUND

BALANCE AT BEGINNING OF YEAR	4,603.8
EXCESS OF RECEIPTS OVER PAYMENTS	373.7
BALANCE AT END OF YEAR	4,977.5

Source: *National Insurance Fund: Account 1984–85*, (HMSO, 1985), pp. 4 and 6.

supplement from the Consolidated Fund, equal to a given percentage (11 per cent in 1984/5) of its revenue from contributions from insured persons on the assumption that there was no contracting out.[1]

---

[1] The details of contracting out are discussed in Chapter 9:1.

The interest item (£521 million in 1984/5) is earned on current revenue and on the accumulated surplus (nearly £5 billion in 1984/5) shown at the bottom of the table. At various times there has been debate about the proper role of the Fund, though a surplus of some sort is desirable for a number of reasons: to bridge short-term imbalances (the end-year balance represents about twelve weeks' outgoings); to cushion a growing increase in contribution rates to finance pensions; and to assist with public sector borrowing (which last aspect has drawn a certain amount of political fire). Whether the Fund should be organised on actuarial lines (i.e. have a reserve sufficient to pay all expected future liabilities) is a major topic of Chapter 9.

Two general points should be noted. First (Table 7.1) total contributions in 1986/7 were £26.2 billion; hence revenue of the National Insurance Fund was nearly 25 per cent of central government revenue from all other sources, and larger than any other revenue source except income tax. In effect there is a third estate alongside the Inland Revenue and Customs and Excise. Second, this revenue does not go through the normal budgetary process of central government. Although administered by the Department of Health and Social Security, the accounts of the National Insurance Fund are kept separate from the general accounts. Changes in the rates of contribution or benefit may be announced in Parliament separately from the Budget, and are debated on separate occasions (though national insurance has not been immune from attempts to contain public spending).

Expenditure   On the expenditure side matters are less tidy. In principle benefits from the National Insurance Fund (e.g. for unemployment) are paid only to individuals with an appropriate contributions record, whilst similar benefits paid from the Consolidated Fund are awarded on the basis of other criteria, such as income (supplementary benefit) or number of children (child benefit). In practice, however, there are many linkages and interactions, because many individuals receive benefits from both sources, so that it is often necessary to discuss them together.

Expenditure on cash benefits is set out in Table 7.5. Much the largest is the retirement pension (£17.9 billion in 1986/7, or three-quarters of all contributory benefits). This does not include pensions outside the scope of national insurance (listed in the second half of the table), such as war pensions and pensions for people who retired too soon after 1948 to be entitled to a national insurance pension. The remaining insurance benefits cover unemployment, sickness (i.e. relatively short-run health problems), invalidity (i.e. long-term and permanent health problems) and widowhood. Total spending on the insurance benefits was £23.8 billion.

Expenditure on non-contributory benefits in 1986/7 was £17.3 billion, of which nearly 70 per cent was on supplementary benefit (£7.3 billion) and child

Table 7.5: Cash Benefits, UK, 1986/7 (est.) (£million)

CONTRIBUTORY BENEFITS (i.e those paid from the National Insurance Fund)		
Retirement pensions (including lump-sum payments)		17,882
Widows' benefit etc.		842
Unemployment benefit		1,618
Sickness benefit		123
Invalidity benefit		2,217
Industrial injuries benefits		472
Maternity allowance and child special allowance		185
Death grant		18
		23,757
NON-CONTRIBUTORY BENEFITS (i.e. those paid from the Consolidated Fund)		
Non-contributory retirement pension (including lump-sum payments)		45
War pensions		572
Attendance allowance and invalid care allowance		766
Severe disablement allowance		260
Mobility allowance		507
Supplementary benefit		
Supplementary pension	997	
Supplementary allowances	6,267	
		7,264
Child benefit		4,573
Family income supplement		158
Maternity grant		18
Housing benefit rent rebates and allowances		3,154
		17,317
ADMINISTRATION		
Contributory benefits (including costs of collecting contributions)		856
Non-contributory benefits		879
Housing benefit		123
		1,858
TOTAL PROGRAMME		42,932
NORTHERN IRISH EXPENDITURE		1,361
TOTAL SOCIAL SECURITY BENEFITS		44,293

Source: *The Government's Expenditure Plans, 1986–87 to 1988–89*, Cmnd. 9702-II, Tables 2.12 and 3.15.

benefit (£4.6 billion). Supplementary benefit is payable to pensioners (supplementary pension) and others (supplementary allowance) whose income after receipt of all other benefits is still below the poverty line; it thus constitutes the final 'safety net' on the cash side of the welfare state. Child benefit is a tax-free cash payment in respect of each child, payable weekly to (usually) the mother; an additional sum is payable to single parents. Both benefits are discussed in Chapter 10. Housing benefit (£3.2 billion) assists low income tenants, and figures prominently in Chapter 14.

3 Benefits in Kind

This section surveys very briefly the finances of the national health service, of the state educational system, and of local authority housing (for details see the Further Reading). As we shall see in Chapter 13:1 the original intention of the national health service that all health care should be free has largely been realised. Medical attention is generally free, with the exception of certain items (e.g. prescriptions) for which charges, generally below full cost, apply to some people. About 11 per cent of national health service expenditure is financed by national insurance contributions, and 3 per cent from the charges just mentioned (UK, 1986a, chart 3.14.4). The remaining 86 per cent comes from general taxation. Table 7.1 shows that total spending in 1986/7 was £17.7 billion, £15.1 billion by central government (mainly on the health service), and £2.6 billion by local authorities (mainly on the personal social services) (for further detail see Table 13.1). The national health service, clearly, is not a contributory scheme, and any assessment of its finances must discuss the tax system as a whole (see section 4).

State education (discussed in Chapter 13:2) is supplied largely without charge. Historically it was both produced and financed locally, and it is still the case today that by far the greater part of educational expenditure is by local government. Table 7.1 shows that spending on education and related activities was £14.3 billion (for further detail see Table 13.2), over 80 per cent of it by local authorities. However, because of central government grants this implies, on average, that some 42 per cent of educational finance derives indirectly from the Consolidated Fund. I shall abstract from most of the central versus local debates as they apply to education (and the national health service and local authority housing) and discuss education for the most part as a non-contributory scheme financed from general taxation, and differing from the national health service only to the extent that there is a larger role for local government (see the Further Reading).

Table 7.1 shows that net expenditure on housing in 1986/7 was £2.8 billion, with substantial involvement by both central and local government (see Table 14.1 for further detail). This figure *understates* public involvement in housing: first, it is a net figure, and therefore excludes capital receipts from the sale of housing and land; second, it omits other forms of housing expenditure, e.g. housing benefit, which appear as part of spending on cash benefits; third, the tax relief for owner-occupiers, like all tax expenditures, is an invisible item in government accounts (they serve simply to reduce the revenue from income tax in Table 7.1). The importance of tax expenditures in any systematic analysis of public spending is emphasised by their scale. Mortgage interest tax relief in 1985/6 amounted to £4750 million (UK, 1986a, Table 2.24), considerably more than total direct expenditure (and even larger if capital gains tax relief is included). Housing expenditure thus broadly defined is set out in Table 14.2.

In 1985 about 30 per cent of households lived in local authority housing. For Britain as a whole, local authority rents never covered current housing costs, the shortfall (which declined in the 1980s) coming from local taxation and a central subsidy. Thus local authority housing is financed partly out of 'contributions' (i.e. rents), partly out of local taxation and partly from the Consolidated Fund. The system has caused considerable controversy over the years; it is assessed in Chapter 14.

4 Assessing the Welfare State

4.1 INCIDENCE CONSIDERATIONS

Assessing the efficiency and redistributive impacts of the welfare state is a vast undertaking which raises both methodological and measurement problems (see Atkinson and Stiglitz, 1980, Lecture 9), and one on which little more than a start has been made. This section limits itself to outlining some of the issues of principle, leaving more detailed discussion to later chapters. Two aspects assume special relevance: the notion of tax incidence; and the importance of considering benefits and taxes together.

The simple tax incidence argument is illustrated in Figure 7.1, which analyses the partial equilibrium incidence of a housing subsidy. Suppose the housing market is in equilibrium at price, p_0, and quantity, X_0. A specific rent subsidy shifts the supply curve vertically downwards to S−subsidy; this reduces the price paid by the tenant from p_0 to p_1 (i.e. only a small reduction), and increases the price received by the landlord substantially from p_0 to p_2. The result is that if landlords are rich and tenants poor (not that this is necessarily the case), then a seemingly redistributive housing subsidy might of itself be regressive. Similarly, suppose that labour is supplied inelastically to the market (empirically plausible for primary workers).[1] A reduction in income tax or the national insurance contribution can be analysed as a labour subsidy, and Figure 7.1 shows how the subsidy reduces unit wage costs to the employer from p_0 to p_1 (since p_1 is on the demand curve for labour), and increases the wage received by the employee from p_0 to p_2 (since p_2 is on the labour supply curve). In this case the tax reduction benefits mainly the employee. But the result is reversed where labour supply is elastic.

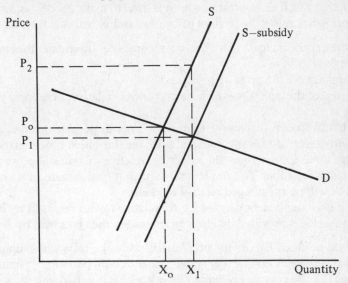

Figure 7.1   *Partial equilibrium incidence of a subsidy*

The general equilibrium incidence argument   However, to be sure of the efficiency of any policy, or of its redistributive effects, it is necessary also to see how the *general* equilibrium of production, consumption and distribution is affected. There has been some work on applied general equilibrium analysis (see the Further Reading), though none yet on the impact of the welfare state.

The discussion of incidence concentrates on the effect, ceteris paribus, of tax/expenditure changes on the relative position of different income groups. The crucial words are ceteris paribus and the *relative* position of individuals or groups (see Prest and Barr, 1985, pp. 101–5). The ceteris paribus condition is

---

[1] The primary labour force consists of 'breadwinners', i.e. people who would normally be in the labour force full-time; it consists traditionally of men and unmarried women below retiring age. The secondary labour force consists of people who are not *necessarily* full-time members of the labour force, e.g. people under 18, people past retiring age and married women.

important because we are trying to separate the distributional effect of a given change in tax (or expenditure) from any other change in the system. This makes it necessary in principle to introduce a countervailing tax which is (a) distributionally neutral and (b) keeps the budget balance unchanged. It should be clear that this procedure is fraught with difficulty.

Assuming that this can be done by one means or another, the effect of a tax change on the relative position of different income groups will depend on several sets of factors. Suppose individual A sells factor m, which is used to make good x, and B sells factor n, which is used to make good y; and suppose that a tax change raises the relative price of x. Individual A is then better-off:

(1) the greater the increase in his pre-tax income (i.e. the greater the rise in the relative price of m);
(2) the smaller are the taxes he pays; and
(3) the greater the extent to which he consumes (relatively cheaper) y rather than x.

The first two items together determine A's net disposable income, and are often jointly referred to as the 'sources' side; the third item concerns the 'uses' side. The three factors show the effect on relative incomes of a tax change considered in isolation. To complete the distributional picture, it is crucial to add that A will be advantaged relative to B also:

(4) the greater the benefit derived by A (relative to that received by B) from goods/services provided by government out of the taxes paid by A and B.

It should be clear that discussion of distributional effects which limits itself to tax changes *simpliciter* (i.e. (2) above) looks at only part of the picture, and one which may be completely altered by other changes, particularly under (3) and (4).

4.2 REDISTRIBUTION: A PRELIMINARY DISCUSSION

The meaning of progressivity is illustrated by an individual's average tax rate, i.e. his tax bill as a proportion of his total income. A tax is progressive if the average rate is higher for someone with a higher income. Suppose that an individual can earn £2500 tax-free per year, and pays tax at a marginal rate of 30 per cent on anything above this. Someone earning £2500 pays no tax; someone earning £5000 pays £750 (15 per cent of his income); and someone with £10,000 pays £2250 in tax (22.5 per cent of his income). Thus the tax (which is a stylised version of the UK system) is progressive, even though most people face the same marginal rate of 30 per cent.[1]

In assessing the progressivity of a tax it is necessary, in addition to its formal

---

[1] Whether the degree of progression is the *right* one is an entirely different question.

structure, to know the number of people affected, and also the extent to which the formal tax rates apply in practice. Thus a tax of 30 per cent on income up to £20,000 and 100 per cent thereafter may sound highly progressive, but if nobody has income in excess of £20,000 then in practice the tax is proportional. On the second point, a tax is less progressive than it appears if the highest rates are never applied, i.e. if tax evasion is proportionately more frequent at higher incomes.

Considering taxes and benefits together   The discussion in section 4.1 suggests two implications. First, in assessing the way the welfare state is financed, it may be necessary to consider simultaneously a variety of taxes contributing to the Consolidated Fund, the National Insurance Fund and local revenues. Suppose a government tries to help the poor by increasing the employer national insurance contribution relative to the employee contribution. The discussion underlying Figure 7.1 suggests that it is of no analytical consequence whether a tax is imposed on the buyer or seller. In the case of national insurance, it is therefore (except in the very short term) the *combined* employer and employee contribution which matters; any attempt to increase one and reduce the other is little more than window dressing.

Second, it is frequently the *overall* system which is important. The issue is complex (see Prest (1968), Peacock and Shannon (1968), and the Further Reading), but for present purposes the crucial point is that taxation and expenditure should be considered together. At its simplest, a scheme which uses a proportional tax to subsidise mink coats will usually be regressive; the same tax used to finance poor relief is likely to be progressive.

In principle the logic is simple. Consider a commodity (e.g. health care) which is publicly supplied without charge, and financed by a specific contribution. This arrangement is redistributive from rich to poor *if (rich) individual A pays more in contributions than (poor) B, if each consumes the same quantity; it is also progressive if A consumes twice as much as B, but pays more than twice as much in contributions*.

In practice matters are more complicated because it is hard to identify precisely which contributions/taxes have paid for the commodity, i.e. which tax(es) would be reduced or abolished if it were no longer publicly supplied. It might be argued that health care is redistributive so long as A (who consumes twice as much as B) pays more than twice as much in taxes. But this implicitly assumes that health care is financed by a proportionate share of all taxes. The definition in the previous paragraph must therefore be qualified: health care is financed progressively if A consumes twice as much as B, but pays more than twice as much in whatever taxes are used to finance it.

Redistributive implications   These various aspects must all be borne in mind in considering the extent to which the welfare state is financed progressively.

This is done for unemployment and sick pay in Chapter 8:3.2, for pensions in Chapter 9:5.2 and for the major non-contributory benefits in Chapter 10:3.3. It is concluded that these benefits all redistribute from rich to poor to a greater or lesser extent, particularly in recent years, when a variety of changes in contribution conditions have corrected many of the perverse redistributive effects described by Kincaid (1975, Ch. 5). According to Nicholson (1974, Table 3) national insurance benefits and supplementary benefit in 1970 reduced the Gini coefficient by over 5 per cent.

The redistributive effects of the national health service and the educational system are discussed in Chapter 13:1.2 and 2.2, and of local authority housing in Chapter 14:4. It was traditionally thought that all three systems redistributed from rich to poor, but Le Grand (1982) argues the contrary. The core of his argument is that though these benefits are financed progressively, in that the rich pay more towards them in taxes and contributions than the poor, they may be used even more progressively so that the overall result can be regressive. For example, if the rich pay twice as much in taxes as the poor to finance university education, but use it proportionately five times as much, then it is not the rich who subsidise the poor, but the other way round.

Thus there is a limited presumption that at least the cash side of the welfare state is progressive. But any such view is rendered somewhat tentative by incidence considerations; by conceptual difficulties (e.g. the validity of the Gini coefficient); and by measurement and data problems.

Similar caveats are necessary in interpreting the state of affairs in other countries. Danziger and Plotnick (1977) found that cash transfers in the USA in 1970 reduced the Gini coefficient from 47.7 per cent to 40.8 per cent. Estimates for the same year by Smolensky *et al.* (1977) showed that cash benefits reduced the Gini coefficient from 44.4 per cent to 39.8 per cent, and the inclusion of in-kind transfers to 37.1 per cent. The latter is likely to be an overestimate, partly because the in-kind transfers were valued at taxpayer cost rather than at their cash equivalent to recipients, and partly because no account was taken of the possibility of differential usage which led Le Grand to his somewhat startling conclusion for the UK. US events in the 1980s are examined by Danziger, Haveman and Plotnick (1984) and Pechman (1985). All these issues are discussed in more detail in the following chapters.

Further Reading

The most complete and up-to-date account of the finances of the welfare state is by Glennerster (1985). For an historical perspective see Peacock and Wiseman (1967).

Conceptual problems with government accounts are discussed in Prest and Barr

(1985, Chs 8 and 9). On the concept and measurement of tax expenditures see McDaniel and Surrey (1984), Surrey and McDaniel (1985) and, in a UK context, Willis and Hardwick (1978).

For data on public spending see *The Government's Expenditure Plans* (The Public Expenditure White Paper), and for taxation the *Financial Statement and Budget Report*. For general data see *National Income and Expenditure* (the 'Blue Book'). All are published annually by HMSO.

On the planning and control of public expenditure see Prest and Barr (1985, Ch. 9, section 3) and Glennerster (1985, Ch. 2). More general issues of the growth of taxation and expenditure are discussed by Heald (1983). On the finance of local government see UK (1976), Foster, Jackman and Perlman (1980), Prest and Barr (1985, Chs 10 and 20) and Glennerster (1985, Chs 2 and 3).

The institutions of national insurance contributions (and other state benefits) are described in Prest and Barr (1985, Ch. 10), and in detail in Tolley (1986), published annually. On the finances of the national health service, personal social services and education see Glennerster (1985, Chs 8, 9 and 10), and of housing *ibid.*, Ch. 11, and UK Department of the Environment (1977a, b, c, d).

The theory of tax incidence is set out in Prest and Barr (1985, Ch. 5, section 2), Brown and Jackson (1982, Chs 11 and 12) and Musgrave and Musgrave (1984, Chs 12–14). For empirical studies see Aaron and Pechman (1981) and Pechman (1985). The pioneering work on applied general equilibrium analysis is Harberger (1962); for later developments see Piggott and Whalley (1985 and 1986).

For methodological discussion of the distribution of public expenditure see Prest (1968), Peacock and Shannon (1968), O'Higgins (1980), Stephenson (1980) and Le Grand (1985). For empirical analysis of redistribution (and its pitfalls) see Nicholson (1974), Le Grand (1982), and UK (1985j) for the UK, and for the US Danziger and Plotnick (1977), Smolensky *et al.* (1977) and Danziger, Haveman and Plotnick (1984).

8

Contributory Benefits 1:
Unemployment, Sickness and Disability

The plan covers all citizens without upper income limit, but has
regard to their different ways of life; it is a plan all-embracing in
scope of persons and of needs. [Beveridge Report, 1942.]

1 Introduction and Institutions

1.1 THE ISSUES

Aims and methods   The main aim of cash benefits, historically, has been the
relief of destitution, i.e. the prevention of *absolute* poverty (see the Glossary).
Motives have been controversial, ranging from altruism to capitalist
oppression (Chapters 2:7.1, 3:5.3 and 4:4.1), but with widespread agreement
about the aim itself. More controversially, two additional aims have come
increasingly to be recognised during the twentieth century: the protection of
accustomed living standards and the reduction of inequality.[1] The need for
income support arises because earnings can be interrupted or reduced for a
number of reasons, in particular by stochastic contingencies (e.g. unemploy-

---

[1] These aims are in no way exhaustive, though they are the only ones discussed
systematically in this chapter. Other aims which have been mentioned include the social
recognition of unremunerative but important tasks (e.g. caring for children or the
elderly or disabled within the family), and social solidarity.

ment or ill-health), or by life-cycle effects (e.g. retirement or the presence of dependent children).

The methods available for income protection vary enormously, but schemes can usefully be classified into three types – private, public and mixed. Pure private arrangements include voluntary charity and the voluntary purchase of actuarial insurance. Mixed schemes involve public participation in private arrangements through regulation (e.g. minimum standards for private insurance) and/or through finance. The latter frequently takes the form of tax expenditures (Chapter 7:1.1), e.g. tax relief for private pension contributions. Public schemes embrace two generic forms of institution: *social assistance*, which is financed from taxation, and usually awarded on the basis of a means test, and *social insurance*, under which benefits are conditional on previous contributions.

Which method is preferred depends in part on how the aims of cash benefits are interpreted, which in turn depends on political perspective. Libertarians make a sharp distinction between two forms of income transfer: under actuarial insurance an individual provides for his *own* benefits through his previous contributions; under a non-contributory scheme, his benefits are paid by *others*. In the former case an individual may legitimately choose any desired benefit, provided he pays an actuarial premium; in the latter, the aim of cash transfers should be to prevent *absolute* poverty, i.e. benefits should be at subsistence. To a libertarian the preferred methods for achieving these aims are voluntary private insurance and private charity, respectively. Socialists see income transfers as contributing to their egalitarian aims, and therefore favour publicly organised transfers to prevent *relative* poverty and to reduce inequality.

Liberals take an intermediate line. We saw in Chapter 6:2.1 that poverty cannot be defined analytically, so its definition is largely ideological. The alleviation of poverty, however defined, can be via insurance (private or public, voluntary or compulsory); through cash transfers out of tax revenues; via private charity; or through whatever mix of these approaches best meets stated aims. The pros and cons of these methods are the subject of Part 2 of the book. This chapter looks at social insurance; retirement pensions raise a number of separate issues which are discussed in Chapter 9. Chapter 10 looks at non-contributory benefits (i.e. social assistance), and Chapter 11 discusses possible reforms.

Questions about national insurance are of two sorts. The first (section 2) is whether it should be national (i.e. publicly provided). This in turn raises questions about the circumstances in which people insure voluntarily, and those where it might be appropriate for the state to make insurance compulsory and/or to provide insurance itself. The second issue (section 3) is the effectiveness of the existing system, including its effects on work effort and saving. Where necessary, different benefits are discussed separately. The major conclusions about cash benefits are set out at the end of Chapter 11.

Non-economic arguments   Three types of argument are commonly adduced to justify publicly provided cash transfers. The first is that 'the state has a duty to protect its less fortunate members' or that 'everyone has a right to protection from catastrophic income loss'. Both value-judgements are widely accepted. Both, however, beg the crucial question of *how* individuals are most effectively helped. It is precisely this issue which is the main subject of this chapter and the next. The second type of argument is that 'without national insurance the poor could not afford adequate cover'. The weakness of this position was discussed in Chapter 4:6.1. If there are no technical problems with private insurance, the market can supply it efficiently; in such cases, distributive aims are generally best achieved through cash transfers.

A third argument is that 'it is immoral for insurance companies to profit from people's misfortunes'. This is tenable as a value-judgement. But it has been argued (Chapter 4:6.1) that the question of public versus private production and allocation is less a moral issue than a technical one. Hence insurance against income loss should be publicly provided if that is more efficient and/or just; but where private insurance is more efficient, equity aims can generally be achieved through cash transfers. We do not, after all, say that food should be publicly provided because it is immoral for food manufacturers to exploit the fact that without it people would starve.

1.2 INSTITUTIONS

In institutional terms, national insurance refers to benefits payable to individuals with the necessary contributions record; in economic terms it is an insurance scheme against income loss due to events like unemployment, ill-health or old age. The development of the Beveridge system after 1948 was discussed in Chapter 2:6, and contribution arrangements in Chapter 7:2.1. This section summarises current benefit institutions (for detailed discussion see Tolley (1986) and the Further Reading).

Unemployment benefit is paid at a flat rate (£30.80 per week in 1986/7 for someone with a full contributions record), and is included in taxable income. Claimants must be willing and able to work. Benefit is payable for up to one year at which time, if not earlier, the individual becomes eligible for supplementary benefit (Chapter 10:1). Where entitlement to the insurance benefit is exhausted, individuals must work for at least 13 weeks at a minimum of 16 hours per week to qualify for further benefit.

Statutory sick pay   Compensation for sickness operated similarly until 1983, when the Social Security and Housing Benefits Act 1982 transferred to employers the administration of short-term sickness benefits (for details of the debate and an early assessment see Prest, 1983). Under the scheme, as amended, employees are eligible for statutory sick pay for up to 28 weeks in a tax year, which covers the vast majority of health-related absences. Benefits are partly earnings-related, at weekly rates (in 1986/7) of £31.60, £39.20 and £46.75, depending on previous earnings. Various groups are excluded, *inter alia* those below the lower earnings limit, the self-employed, and people over pensionable age. In addition, benefit is not payable in respect of the first three days of absence from work. A medical certificate is required only where sickness lasts more than seven days; for shorter absences a system of self-certification operates.

Statutory sickness payments are made by employers, who simply deduct such disbursements from their monthly return of national insurance contributions. The benefit is, in effect, paid from the National Insurance Fund.[1] Far from privatising sick pay (as had originally been intended), the main effects of the changes were the transfer of administration from the Department of Health and Social Security to employers, and also the greater administrative ease of subjecting such benefit to tax and national insurance contributions. From a financial viewpoint, compensation for sickness remains firmly in the public sector.

Sickness benefit applies to individuals not covered by statutory sick pay. The benefit is flat-rate, tax-free, and payable for up to 28 weeks. Once entitlement to statutory sick pay or sickness benefit runs out after 28 weeks, recipients are eligible for invalidity benefit (discussed below).

The contribution conditions for unemployment and sickness benefit are complex. To qualify for full unemployment or sickness benefit, an individual must have paid at least the minimum contribution (Chapter 7:2.1) in the complete tax year preceding the calendar year in which the interruption of employment occurred. Where contributions fall short of this minimum but exceed half, benefit is paid on a sliding scale. In sharp contrast, there is no contribution condition for statutory sick pay.

Since 1971, coverage has been extended in various ways to people suffering from long-term illness. **Invalidity benefit** pays a tax-free pension, which

---

[1] Formally, it appears as a negative item in the *revenue* of the National Insurance Fund (see Table 7.4). The only obvious advantage of such an accounting fiction is the apparent reduction in public spending which thereby results. Tax expenditures have a similar effect; see Barr (1986).

Table 8.1: The Main National Insurance Benefit Rates, 1986/7[a]

RETIREMENT BENEFITS	
Basic state retirement pension	
single person	£38.70[T] per week
married couple	£61.95[T]
State earnings-related pension	earnings-related
Non-contributary retirement pension	
single person	£23.25[T]
married woman	£13.90[T]
WIDOW'S BENEFIT	
Widow's allowance (first 26 weeks)	£54.20[T]
Widowed mother's allowance	£38.70[T]
Widow's pension	£38.70[T]
UNEMPLOYMENT BENEFIT	
single person	£30.80[T]
married couple	£49.80[T]
SICKNESS BENEFIT	
single person	£29.45
married couple	£47.65
INVALIDITY BENEFITS	
Invalidity pension	£38.70
Invalidity allowance (in addition to	
invalidity pension)	£2.60–£8.15[b]
Severe disablement allowance	£23.25
MATERNITY BENEFITS	
Maternity grant	£25.00 (single payment)
Maternity allowance	£29.45
DEATH BENEFITS	
Death grant for an adult	£30.00 (single payment)
Death grant for persons under 18	£9.00–£22.50 (single payment)
INDUSTRIAL INJURIES BENEFIT	
Disablement benefit (100 per cent rate)	£63.20
Death benefit	
first 26 weeks	£54.20[T]
thereafter for spouse who is disabled,	
elderly or looking after children	£39.25[T]
otherwise	£11.61[T]
MISCELLANEOUS BENEFITS	
Child's special allowance (in addition	
to child benefit)	£8.05 per week
Guardian's allowance (in addition to	
child benefit)	£8.05

Source: *Hansard*, 24 February 1986, cols 691–98.

Notes:

[a]Benefit rates are those in force from July 1986.

[b]Benefit is tax-free except when paid as an addition to retirement pension.

[T]Benefit chargeable to income tax. Exceptionally, for the 1986/7 tax year only, the *increase* in retirement benefits and widow's benefit in July 1986 was tax-free.

replaces statutory sick pay or sickness benefit after 28 weeks. An additional payment, **invalidity allowance**, is made where incapacity began more than five years before pensionable age.

Severe disablement allowance, introduced by the Health and Social Security Act 1984 to replace an earlier benefit, applies to those with insufficient contributions to qualify for invalidity benefit. Entitlement is based on several factors, including age and the degree of incapacity (see Tolley, 1986, Ch. 10). Of the many other non-contributory benefits for the disabled, the two most important are the **attendance allowance**, which is paid in respect of people who require frequent, prolonged or continual assistance or supervision, and the **mobility allowance** for people who are unable or virtually unable to walk, but who are able to go out and so make use of the allowance.

From Table 7.5, the total cost of these benefits in 1986/7 was £1618 million for unemployment benefit, £123 million for sickness benefit,[1] and £2217 million for invalidity benefit. These three benefits, together with retirement and widows' pensions, make up over 95 per cent of direct national insurance disbursements. The remainder comprise a wide variety of smaller benefits, the rates of some of which are shown in Table 8.1.

Maternity benefits arise in two forms. The *maternity grant* is a once-and-for-all tax-free payment of £25, intended to help with the general expenses of having a baby. The *maternity allowance* is a weekly tax-free payment to a working mother, based on her own contributions record. For a woman with a full contribution record it is payable for up to 18 weeks, but not in any period in which the claimant does paid work. From April 1987, maternity allowance is to be replaced for many women by *statutory maternity pay*, whose structure and administration is similar to statutory sick pay.

Death Maternity benefits take care of the cradle. The death grant was supposed to provide the grave; but inflation has entirely eroded its ability to do so, and the benefit is to be abolished.

Industrial injury benefit applies to all employed earners. Three types of benefit are payable in respect of an industrial accident or disease. *Statutory sick pay/ sickness benefit* is payable without contribution condition for up to 28 weeks of absence from work. *Industrial disablement benefit*, in contrast, is payable (a) for the entire duration, whether temporary or permanent, of any loss of faculty, and (b) whether or not the person is unable to work. Benefit is payable when statutory sick pay/sickness benefit ceases, or from three days after the accident

---

[1] Disbursements in respect of statutory sick pay in 1984/5 amounted to £468 million – see the revenue side of Table 7.4.

if there is no incapacity for work. Various additional payments can be made where injury is exceptionally severe.[1] *Death benefits* are paid when a worker dies as the result of an industrial accident or disease. The widow (in some circumstances the widower) receives a pension (£54.20 per week in 1986/7) for 26 weeks, and thereafter, if she satisfies a number of additional conditions, a lower pension for life, or until she remarries.[2]

Two additional national insurance benefits specifically concern children. **Child's special allowance** is payable to a woman who is divorced and has not remarried, upon the death of her former husband, where she has a child to whose support he previously contributed at least 25p a week. The allowance (£8.05 per week in 1986/7) is paid for each child, in addition to child benefit. Second is the **guardian's allowance**. Where the parents of a child are dead, and at least one satisfies a nationality or residence condition, anyone who looks after a child as part of his or her family and receives child benefit may qualify for a guardian's allowance.

Increases for dependants   The level of many of these benefits may be increased if the beneficiary has dependants (adult or child). In the latter case, child benefit is normally payable in addition.

The level of almost all benefits is regularly reviewed. Most are uprated according to statutory formula; some are increased on an ad hoc basis; most are increased annually. A rare exception is the death grant, which was set at £20 in 1949, and raised to its present level of £30 in 1967. The 'cradle to grave' claim is less realistic than once it was.

2 Theoretical Arguments for State Intervention

2.1 EFFICIENCY 1: REGULATION

Are efficiency and social justice assisted by state involvement in insurance markets? In particular, would individuals in a private market buy the *socially* efficient quantity of insurance against the causes of income loss covered by national insurance? This breaks down into three separate questions: (a) Why do people insure at all? (b) Why does the state make membership of national insurance compulsory? (c) Why does the state provide such insurance itself?

The first question was answered in Chapter 5 – a rational risk-averse

---

[1] For details see Tolley (1986, paras 18.19–18.24).
[2] Under changes foreshadowed in UK (1985k, paras 5.10–5.15) the widow's benefit for the first 26 weeks is to be replaced by a tax-free lump-sum payment of £1000.

individual will insure voluntarily so long as the value of certainty exceeds the net cost of insurance. Why, second, is membership of national insurance compulsory? The standard argument for voluntarism is that it is efficient for an individual to make his own decision so long as he bears fully the costs of so doing. If I do not insure my Picasso, society would regard this as my prerogative. Similarly, it might be argued that I should be free not to insure against income loss because of unemployment or ill-health; if I then lose my job and starve that is my fault.

The flaw in the voluntarism argument in this case is that it overlooks the external costs which non-insurance can impose on others. Suppose someone chooses not to insure, and then loses his job. If society bails him out by paying a non-contributory benefit, the external cost falls upon the taxpayer. Alternatively, if he is given no help he starves, which imposes costs on others in a variety of ways. First, non-insurance may bring about not only his own starvation, but also that of his/her dependants. There are also broader costs, including the excess of the individual's lost output over his consumption; any resulting increase in crime; and the financial costs of disposing of his body, or the health hazards if it were left where it fell. Additionally, though more arguably, it is possible to specify a psychic externality, where people do not like the idea of a society which allows people to starve. If so, the individual's death from starvation imposes external costs by reducing the utility of others directly.[1]

Where an activity causes an external cost, one form of intervention is a Pigovian tax.[2] Here, however, the aim is not marginally to influence consumption decisions through marginal price changes, but to prevent non-insurance. Making insurance compulsory (i.e. regulation) is likely to be a more effective way of achieving this.

In sum, the major efficiency argument for compulsory membership (which applies equally to the smaller national insurance benefits), is that uninsured losses due to unemployment, illness, industrial injury, maternity or death may impose costs on others, including dependants like spouses and children. There is an analogy with automobile insurance, which is also compulsory in most countries. But, quite correctly on efficiency grounds, compulsion is limited to

---

[1] Some activities impose unambiguous external costs, e.g. air pollution. In other cases a given activity by individual A may or may not impose costs on B, depending on B's utility function. Whether or not my late night trumpet playing is a cost to my neighbour depends *inter alia* on his taste in music. It might similarly be argued that the psychic cost imposed on society by my starvation would not arise if members of society had different utility functions. These issues are addressed by Sen (1970).

[2] See, in ascending order of completeness, the Glossary, the Appendix to Chapter 4, para. 15 and/or Chapter 4:3.2.

insurance to cover the damage I might inflict on *others*. I can choose whether to take out insurance to cover damage to my *own* car or person.

2.2 EFFICIENCY 2: PUBLIC PROVISION

To continue the analogy, the state makes car insurance compulsory, but does not supply insurance itself. Why then, does it provide national insurance? This question brings us back to the discussion in Chapter 5:4.1 of the circumstances in which private insurance markets are efficient. In particular, we need to look at the supply conditions, namely that the probability of the insured event must be independent across individuals, must be less than one, and known or estimable, known equally to all parties (i.e. no adverse selection), and exogenous (i.e. no moral hazard). Efficiency arguments about the appropriateness of public provision hinge on whether these five assumptions hold in the cases of unemployment and sick pay insurance, etc.

Unemployment insurance   We need to consider each assumption separately.

(1) Whether individual probabilities of becoming or remaining unemployed are independent is a matter of high controversy. Simple Keynesian theory suggests that unemployment reduces demand and contributes to further unemployment. Those who believe in a natural rate of unemployment deny this conclusion except in the short run. Individual probabilities may be partly correlated, though this problem alone is unlikely to make private insurance impossible.

(2) The overall probability of being unemployed is less than one, though for some sectors of the labour force, such as unskilled young people, it may be too high for private insurance to be viable. An additional problem is how private schemes could cope with unemployed school-leavers.

(3) The average probability of being unemployed is well known – it is simply the aggregate unemployment rate. There is also considerable knowledge of the probability of unemployment for sub-groups of the labour force.

(4) There is no major problem of adverse selection. A private unemployment insurance company could ask about an applicant's previous employment record.

(5) Much the greatest problem with private unemployment insurance is moral hazard. The insured individual may be able to influence the probability of being unemployed in two ways. First he can influence the *stock* of unemployment by bringing about his own redundancy ('I'll work for you this week for nothing if you'll then make me redundant'). Second, and of much greater importance, he can influence the *duration* of unemployment. As we shall see (section 3.1) the relationship between the level of benefits and the rate

of unemployment is hotly disputed. There is some agreement that the higher the replacement rate (i.e. the ratio of income when unemployed to net income when in work), the longer a rational individual is likely to spend on job search, though much less agreement about whether this increases unemployment overall.

To say that individuals with insurance devote more time to job search is not *necessarily* to imply inefficiency. In principle, the efficient duration of unemployment for the ith individual, x_i, is that period which he would rationally choose if he had to finance his unemployment from accumulated savings or by borrowing in a perfect capital market. Inefficiency arises when an individual chooses to be unemployed for longer than x_i because insurance has reduced the marginal cost to him of so doing. It was for this reason that Beveridge insisted on full employment, because 'the only satisfactory test of unemployment is an offer of work' (UK, 1942, p. 163).

We saw in Chapter 5:3.1 that an actuarial premium is calculated as

$$\Pi_i = p_i L + T \tag{8.1}$$

where p_i is the probability of the ith individual becoming or remaining unemployed, L is the unemployment benefit, and T the carrier's transactions cost. Moral hazard of the sort described above means that p_i can be manipulated by the insured individual, making it impossible for the insurance company to calculate a premium. An academically scurrilous but nevertheless telling argument is the observation that if private insurance is possible anywhere, then it is likely to exist in the USA – and I am not aware of any substantial private unemployment insurance scheme, either in the USA or elsewhere.[1] Since unemployment does not accord well with the model of actuarial insurance it is not surprising that earlier schemes, under the 1911 National Insurance Act and during the 1920s, ran into trouble (Chapter 2:2.2 and 3.2).

Moral hazard thus renders impossible the private supply of insurance. Two major conclusions follow:

(a) If income support is to exist for the unemployed, it will almost certainly have to be publicly provided (it is hard to envision private charity on a sufficient scale, except in times of very high employment, i.e. when the problem is minimal). The libertarian predilection for private markets and voluntarism is

---

[1] It is true that in Sweden the system of unemployment insurance is notionally private. But in practice, though its administration is largely private, over 90 per cent of the funding is public, and the system is hedged by extensive regulation. Individuals without cover (for whatever reason) are eligible for publicly provided assistance (i.e. non-insurance) benefits. The system is therefore more usefully regarded as a public scheme whose administration has been hived off to the private sector (cf. statutory sick pay in the UK).

likely, in this instance, to be untenable. Publicly provided unemployment benefits can be supported on *efficiency* grounds because of information problems in insurance markets, problems of which no mention is made in Hayek's (1960, Ch. 19) attack on publicly provided benefits.

(b) The resulting institutions will not (because they cannot) be actuarial insurance. They will generally be tax/transfers of one sort or another; but whatever they are, they are not insurance.

Sickness insurance Asking the same questions about sickness insurance, the individual probabilities of absence from work because of ill-health are unrelated, except during a major epidemic (i.e. the likelihood of my missing work for health reasons is independent of your state of health). Except for the chronically ill, the probability of absence is less than one, and can be estimated. There is no problem of adverse selection, since a private insurance company could ask about an applicant's previous health and absenteeism. Nor is there a serious problem of moral hazard. The probability of missing work is broadly exogenous, since making oneself genuinely ill is costly, and pretended illness can usually be policed by requiring claimants to provide a doctor's certificate.

Thus there is no substantial technical difficulty with private sick pay insurance, and such institutions exist in many countries. The only efficiency justification for public provision is through a two-step argument:

(a) There are economies of scale to be derived from running unemployment and sick pay insurance jointly. It is administratively cheaper to collect both contributions simultaneously; and, if a claimant is genuinely unemployed *or* ill, it may avoid the need to decide which of the two is applicable.

(b) Unemployment benefits must be publicly provided for technical reasons.

Given (b) it follows from (a) that there are at least administrative savings to be made by running a public sick pay scheme alongside unemployment insurance.

The smaller national insurance benefits Voluntary maternity insurance may face problems of adverse selection (i.e. only women intending to become pregnant would insure), making private supply impossible. However, as we saw in Chapter 5:4.2, compulsion can side-step this problem. Thus, if maternity insurance is compulsory, it would not necessarily have to be publicly provided.

The death grant is intended to cover funeral costs. All we are talking about here is a form of life insurance, with which the private market is well able to cope. Similar arguments apply to the child's special allowance and guardian's allowance, which are payable when one or both parents are dead, and also to increases for dependants more generally. If private insurance is feasible for the individual, it is also feasible for his/her dependants (e.g. we saw in Chapter 5:2.3 how an annuity can cover a spouse).

In the case of industrial injury insurance, again, there is no strong argument for public provision. The probability of injury is independent across individuals, less than one, and can be estimated. Nor do serious problems arise with adverse selection or moral hazard (for instance, it would not generally pay an individual deliberately to injure himself). It is true that some occupations are riskier than others, but this simply means that private insurance would require higher premiums for riskier occupations.

In all these cases there are sound reasons for compulsion, but no need for public provision. Counter-arguments to the latter position are that there might be administrative economies if all social benefits were organised together; and there might be administrative difficulties in enforcing compulsion if supply were private. The issue of public versus private pensions is deferred to Chapter 9:3.1.

Two other arguments have been put forward at various times to explain or justify public provision of national insurance. Marxists argue (Chapter 3:5.3) that such institutions are a form of social control, whose main aim is to prevent social unrest. This argument may *explain* the existence of national insurance, but it does not necessarily *justify* it. In particular, it does not establish why we have publicly organised insurance rather than (say) simple cash transfers. It is sometimes also argued, along Keynesian lines, that national insurance generally, and unemployment benefit in particular, is a built-in stabiliser. But asserting that this is a consequence (albeit a beneficial one), again, does not necessarily *justify* national insurance.

2.3 SOCIAL JUSTICE

What are the equity arguments for publicly provided insurance? Horizontal equity concerns such goals as minimum standards for certain commodities and/or equal access to them. It was argued in Chapter 4:4.3 that these occur automatically where the assumptions of perfect information and equal power hold, in which case horizontal equity grounds for intervention are very limited. This line of argument lends little support to public provision of national insurance. Individuals can acquire information about different insurance policies, as they do currently for car insurance with the advice, if necessary, of the various automobile associations. Should protection be necessary there is a case for regulation of standards, as for food; but analogously this is not an argument for provision.

It is true that power is not distributed equally among individuals. This can be a major problem for health care and education, but is not likely to be serious in this case. Where insurance markets are competitive what matters is not whether individuals have more or less power, but whether they are able to pay an actuarial premium. In the case of car insurance, premiums are generally related to age and previous driving record, but there is no evidence of a systematic relationship between premiums and social class. Similarly there is no reason to expect substantial discrimination with unemployment and sick pay insurance, and a fortiori with the smaller benefits.

Vertical equity concerns redistribution from rich to poor. The standard argument, that 'the state must provide insurance, because otherwise the poor would not be able to afford adequate cover' is false (section 1.1). A somewhat more subtle variant is that private insurance cannot redistribute from rich to poor, only from 'lucky' to 'unlucky', and therefore insurance should be publicly provided to redistribute income. Again, the key argument in Chapter 4:6.1 suggests that without efficiency reasons for provision, distributive goals should be pursued via cash transfers except, possibly, in the presence of consumption externalities (Chapter 4:4.2). In this case, the rich may want the poor to consume insurance, and so impose it as a merit good; and the poor may feel less stigmatised by receiving 'insurance benefit' than 'welfare'. Both reasons offer an explanation (though not necessarily a justification) of public provision for reasons of vertical equity.

Finally, it can be argued (Chapters 4:6.1 and 5:4.2) that to the extent that there are *efficiency* grounds for making membership of national insurance compulsory, it is not inappropriate to finance the scheme so as to redistribute from rich to poor. We return to this issue in the next section.

3 An Assessment of the National Insurance System

3.1 EFFICIENCY AND INCENTIVES

Arguments of Principle

This part of the chapter briefly assesses the UK system in the light of earlier theoretical argument. Most of the issues are empirical, but we start with two a priori issues: should national insurance be national (i.e. publicly provided); and is it insurance?

Should it be national? The efficiency arguments rest on externalities, justifying compulsion, and technical (mainly information) failures on the supply side of the insurance market, justifying provision of the major benefits, though with a somewhat weaker argument for sick pay insurance than for the other schemes. If we ignore consumption externalities, the main equity arguments are (a) that the poor may feel less stigmatised by insurance, and (b) that if insurance is publicly provided for efficiency reasons, it can then be used as a redistributive device. These arguments are compelling. Some areas could, indeed, be returned to the private sector, as considered for short-term sick pay (Prest, 1983). However, unemployment is an uninsurable risk and, as argued in Chapter 9, so is inflation, with major efficiency implications for public involvement with pensions. Since unemployment benefits and pensions comprise over 80 per cent of national insurance expenditure, if we ask 'Should national insurance be national?' the short answer is yes.

Over the years there has been much confusion about the purposes of social insurance. There are good reasons for thinking of it both as a technical instrument for dealing with market failure *and* as a redistributive device. But the two cases are argued on very different grounds, and should be carefully distinguished.

Is it insurance?   This implies a series of further questions.

(1) Are contributions geared to risk? From Chapter 7:2.1, the answer is no. In the scheme envisaged by Beveridge, contributions were to be geared to the *average* risk, as shown in equation (5.16), and adverse selection avoided by making membership compulsory. This principle was violated because retirement pensions from 1946 onwards were not actuarial (see Chapter 9); because from 1975 contributions by the employed (Class 1) and self-employed (Class 4) were related not to average risk but to the contributor's income; and because of the existence of credits for the unemployed, and for a parent who stays at home to look after young children or the disabled. In the latter two cases, compulsion avoids the worst of the efficiency losses associated with adverse selection, but the resulting system is very different from the way voluntary, private insurance would operate.

(2) Is the scheme funded? Again, the answer is no. As discussed in Chapter 9, state pensions, unlike private ones, make no provision for future liabilities. In addition, contributions (i.e. insurance premiums) do not even cover *current costs*, in that the National Insurance Fund receives a non trivial contribution from the Consolidated Fund (see Table 7.4).

(3) Are rights to benefit dependent only on the occurrence of the insured event? The answer again is no. Benefits (but not contributions) are higher where the contributor has dependants; and contributions and benefits taken together are redistributive from rich to poor. In both respects national insurance is more generous than true insurance. It is less generous in that the retirement pension is generally withdrawn quite rapidly if an individual has any earnings (Chapter 9:1), i.e. pensions in the five years after normal retirement are, in effect, subject to a means test. All three features conflict with strict actuarial principles. Elsewhere, additional restrictions may be imposed,

e.g. 'workfare' in various American states requires recipients of unemployment and related benefits to undertake work or training.

The conclusion is that national insurance is not actuarial insurance at all. Indeed, in the case of unemployment, as we saw in section 2.2, no other result is possible. Instead, it is a transfer scheme which mimics private insurance by levying contributions (i.e. taxes) from those who are able to pay them, and awarding benefits to those who are regarded as appropriate recipients (e.g. the sick, unemployed and retired). This has been very obvious since 1975, when the national insurance contribution for most people became earnings-related and therefore analytically equivalent to an income tax.

The Quantity and Type of Insurance

Chapter 5:4.1 described the conditions under which the private market will provide the efficient quantity and type of insurance. Many of the arguments in this chapter and the next suggest that these conditions fail for insurance against income loss due in particular to unemployment, and partly also to old age. But to argue that markets are inefficient is not to imply that public institutions will necessarily do better. This raises three sets of what are ultimately empirical issues: should benefits be based on actuarial contributions; does the state provide the optimal quantity and type of insurance; and what are the scheme's incentive effects?

Should benefits be based on actuarial premiums?   Compulsory membership avoids inefficiency in insurance markets caused by adverse selection (Chapter 5:4.2). There might, however, be secondary inefficiency in other markets, e.g. compulsory unemployment insurance at a standard contribution rate subsidises industries with higher unemployment. To what extent this artificially enlarges them at the expense of other industries is unknown.

Whether or not the insurance principle should be retained is therefore controversial. If compulsion and non-actuarial premiums cause little or no secondary inefficiency, there would be no efficiency problem if the National Insurance Fund were abolished and benefits paid from the Consolidated Fund like supplementary and child benefit. However, if national insurance is a fiction it is at least a benign fiction. Recipients might well feel less stigmatised by a benefit to which they are 'entitled' by virtue of previous contributions (the popular hatred of the Poor Law being one of the important reasons why Beveridge favoured insurance over a scheme financed by general taxation). To that extent, dressing up income support to look like true insurance, though not technically necessary, can be argued to increase social welfare.

Does the state provide the optimum quantity of insurance?   Where insurance is compulsory and publicly provided, inefficiency arises if the state, through misperception of individual preferences or for other reasons, constructs a larger or smaller than optimal scheme. In a first-best world, the *i*th individual (assumed rational and risk-averse) will choose to insure against a loss L_i for which he pays the actuarial premium shown in equation (8.1). All N individuals make this utility maximising decision, resulting in a vector of optimal insurance purchases

$$(L_1, L_2, \ldots, L_N) \qquad (8.2)$$

The L_i vary across individuals depending *inter alia* on their risk-aversion.

Will national insurance offer these optimal quantities? The answer must be no, because the insurance offered will be some sort of average which does not cater for differences in individual tastes. Even so, national insurance is likely to be less inefficient than the free market outcome, partly because risks like unemployment are uninsurable, and because individuals can buy additional insurance against risks like sickness and disability. The comparison between the relative efficiency of a market equilibrium under imperfect information (in this case particularly moral hazard) and compulsory public provision is complex (see Arrow, 1970; Pauly, 1974; and Rothschild and Stiglitz, 1976) and somewhat inconclusive. What can be said (albeit arguably) is that there is no solid evidence to suggest that the cover offered by national insurance, plus voluntary private arrangements, differs *substantially* from the notional optimum in equation (8.2).

Administrative aspects   Considerable effort has been devoted to computerisation, and the streamlining of procedures. Administrative cost was low for long-term benefits (1.5 per cent of expenditure on retirement pensions in 1983/4), but higher at 9 per cent for unemployment benefits (UK, 1986a, Table 3.15.18). A different question is whether contributions and benefits are correct. There is no evidence of systematic maladministration (UK Department of Health and Social Security, 1982; Brown, 1975, Ch. 4), though the system has been accused of being cumbersome (Dilnot, Kay and Morris, 1984, Ch. 2). However, complaints, often justifiable, about the way benefits are administered in particular instances (National Consumer Council, 1984) indicate room (some would say considerable room) for further improvement.

Incentive Issues

In discussing the incentive effects of social insurance two questions predominate: is the system itself a contributory cause of unemployment; and does it reduce the rate of saving and capital accumulation (the latter issue being particularly relevant in the case of pensions)?

Are unemployment benefits a contributory cause of unemployment?   The discussion of moral hazard in section 2.2 has already hinted at this issue. With a high replacement rate (i.e. the ratio of income when unemployed to post-tax and transfer income in work) the low paid may be scarcely worse-off (and possibly, in the short run, better-off) when out of work. This it is argued (Parker, 1982; Minford *et al.*, 1985) creates an 'unemployment trap', whereby an unemployed individual has no financial incentive to seek work (this should be contrasted with the 'poverty trap' (Chapter 10:3.2), under which an individual doing at least some work is given no incentive to work longer hours).

The logic of the disincentive argument is appealingly straightforward. Simple theory suggests that higher replacement rates tend to reduce work effort which is financially motivated. This view, it is claimed, is supported empirically by the sharp rise after 1966 (when the earnings-related supplement to unemployment benefit was introduced) in both replacement rate and unemployment rate. Reality, however, is less simple: people may not work solely for monetary gain; the replacement rate is far from easy to measure (Hemming, 1984, pp. 97–107); only one in six of the unemployed met the contribution conditions for the earnings-related supplement, which therefore had a much smaller impact on replacement rates than was commonly supposed (Atkinson and Flemming, 1978); and the UK replacement rate is by no means high by international standards (United Nations, 1982, Table 1.1.19).

The quantitative literature is large, complex and controversial (for surveys see Atkinson, 1986, section 5.3 and 1987, Ch. 8). Early studies used aggregate time-series data (Maki and Spindler, 1975 for the UK; Grubel and Maki, 1976 for the US), and found that benefits exerted a substantial upward effect on the level of unemployment. The advantage of the time-series approach is its apparent ability to analyse the effects of a policy change. But in practice it is difficult to separate these effects from other influences on unemployment, not least because aggregate data necessitate such devices as representative individuals, replacement rates based on average benefit levels and average tax rates, and so on, which obscure most of the variation between individuals.

Cross-section data have the great advantage of being a much richer source of information on the large differences between individuals. This makes it possible to estimate the determinants of unemployment with greater precision than the aggregate data allow. The general conclusion of the cross-section studies (see the Further Reading) is that though the duration of unemployment is likely to be slightly greater at higher replacement rates, the magnitude of the effect is not large.

This consensus, however, conceals a rich collection of difficulties, both of principle and measurement. The major methodological problem with cross-section analysis is its attempt to extrapolate from individual behaviour to the aggregate economy, a procedure which is valid only where individual responses are not interdependent. Suppose that as someone with a high replacement rate I am very choosy about accepting a new job. If everyone else's behaviour is independent of mine this will increase unemployment. But if behaviour is interdependent, my choosiness simply means that someone else takes the job I have rejected. In this case the replacement rate determines *who* is unemployed, but not total unemployment. Cross-section analysis does not enable us, as an empirical matter, to distinguish the two cases.

The treatment of benefits also raises substantial problems. Institutional complexities, in particular the interaction of the tax and benefit systems, make it difficult to estimate benefits accurately. One approach is to estimate the individual's potential entitlement; the difficulty here is that the sample may not contain sufficient information (e.g. past contribution records) to make this procedure accurate. Alternatively, it is possible to use actual benefit receipts. This avoids complexity, but causes statistical difficulties where unobserved individual characteristics influence *both* the level of benefit *and* the probability of accepting a particular job offer, e.g. if I am lazy (unobserved) I may have a poor employment record and consequently receive less benefit *and* be less keen to accept a new job. An added problem is the time dimension, which static data are not able to capture (Hamermesh, 1979 and 1980); for instance, I may decide to accept a job offer not because my replacement rate is low, but because my entitlement to benefit is about to expire. At least one major study (Atkinson *et al.*, 1984) argues that if benefits are measured correctly there is no effect of benefits on duration. In view of these difficulties it is not surprising that the precision of the estimates (as measured, for instance, by the statistical significance of estimated coefficients) is often low even by cross-section standards.

The general conclusion, which applies equally to cross-section and time-series studies, is that they lack robustness with respect to the definition of variables, the choice of sample and time period, and the specification of the estimated equation. The simplicity of the original argument disappears the deeper one digs – and the more we learn the greater the complications of which we are made aware. In short, the hypothesis that unemployment benefits exert a substantial upward effect on the level of unemployment receives little empirical support.

Disability benefits and labour supply are also a controversial relationship. Some writers (Parsons, 1980; Halpern and Hausman, 1985) conclude that disability payments substantially reduce US labour force participation. But the Parsons results are not robust, and are criticised in a number of respects by Haveman and Wolfe (1984) (see also Haveman, Wolfe and Warlick, 1984), who conclude that the effect, though statistically significant, is small.

Pensions and labour supply may also be related if pensions induce early retirement. In addition, it is argued that publicly provided pensions, financed out of tax revenues, may reduce savings, capital accumulation and economic growth. These issues are discussed in Chapter 9:5.

3.2 EQUITY ISSUES

Horizontal equity It can be argued that national insurance gives everyone equal access to income support. One of the major themes of the Beveridge Report was that national insurance should be comprehensive, unified and compulsory. This aim has been achieved in that there is no evidence of discrimination in the payment of benefits, nor of substantial maladministration.

However, not all groups receive equal coverage, despite Beveridge's intention to the contrary. Fifty years ago most single-parent families resulted from widowhood, which therefore received extensive coverage, especially where there were young children. It is argued that this group (which today comprises only one in six single-parent families in Britain) is treated generously relative to families separated by other causes, such as divorce. The difficulty (and the prominence of the latter group among the poor) arises largely because benefits are conditioned on cause (e.g. widowhood) rather than outcome (i.e. being a single parent).

Disability benefits have also been criticised. Again, individuals facing similar problems do not necessarily receive similar benefits. Under plausible assumptions a single man will receive twice as much if 100 per cent disabled in an industrial accident than with identical disabilities from a non-industrial cause (Hemming, 1984, p. 119). The topic of compensation generally was discussed by a Royal Commission (UK, 1978c), but there has been little change in piecemeal institutions, despite considerable pressure for a system of unified income support for all forms of disability, irrespective of cause (Disability Alliance, 1975; Disablement Income Group, 1979).

There is also criticism that the relative treatment of men and women can be inequitable (e.g. for certain benefits it is the husband in a two-parent family who must apply).

Vertical equity raises two sets of questions. First, how redistributive is national insurance? The major difficulties include conceptual problems (Chapter 7:4) and many of the measurement problems discussed in Chapter 6. A definitive answer would require general equilibrium analysis of the joint incidence of contributions and benefits. No such work exists, so we must be content with more rough-and-ready answers. National insurance contributions for most people rise disproportionately with income for all except the highest earners. The state pension is redistributive from rich to poor (Chapter 9:5.2). Unemployment benefits are also redistributive, inasmuch as those with lower incomes pay smaller contributions, generally for fewer weeks, and receive unemployment benefit more frequently than someone with a higher income. Sick pay is redistributive to the extent that claims are more common amongst the lower paid. According to Nicholson (1974, Table 3.3) pensions reduced the Gini coefficient in 1970 by 3.58 per cent, unemployment benefits by 0.2 per cent and the system of sickness benefits then in operation by 0.58 per cent. Changes since then, notably the introduction of earnings-related contributions and the abolition of the earnings-related supplement for unemployment and sickness benefit, have tended to increase these redistributive effects (see the Further Reading at the end of Chapter 7).

Another aspect of vertical equity is whether benefits are pitched at the right level. This, in turn, raises two further questions. First, is the level of benefit that which would have been chosen by a hypothetically perfectly informed, rational individual making a voluntary decision about his insurance cover? This is the issue, discussed earlier, of whether national insurance provides the efficient quantity of insurance. Second, we need to consider the level of insurance benefits relative to the poverty line. Since poverty cannot be defined in any wholly satisfactory way (Chapter 6:2.1) the poverty line, as manifested, for instance, by the supplementary benefit scale rate (Chapter 10:1) has status only as a social convention. If this is regarded as an appropriate poverty line, it follows that the main national insurance benefits, which are generally less than supplementary benefit, are too low. We return to the subject in Chapter 10:3.1.

Further Reading

A compendious and up-to-date account of institutions (including legal sources) is published annually by Tolley (1986), and in somewhat less detail by CPAG (1986h). A brief official account of the system in 1985 is given in UK (1985f, Ch. 5), and a critique of existing arrangements by Dilnot, Kay and Morris (1984, Ch. 2). For a simple introduction to income support generally see International Labour Office (1984a).

On the theory of insurance see the Further Reading at the end of Chapter 5, and on unemployment/sickness insurance Creedy and Disney (1985, Chs 6–8).

A good general reference on the economics of labour supply is Brown (1983a). For empirical analysis of the causes of unemployment see Minford *et al.* (1985); see also Nickell's (1984) critique of an earlier version and Minford's (1984a) reply. The main time-series studies of the effects of unemployment benefit on labour supply are Maki and Spindler (1975) for the UK and Grubel and Maki (1976) for the US. The main cross-section studies are Nickell (1979a, b), Atkinson *et al.* (1984) and, for the US, Feldstein and Poterba (1984). For a cohort study see Narendranathan, Nickell and Stern (1985). The cross-section literature is reviewed by Lancaster and Nickell (1980), Atkinson (1981) and Atkinson *et al.* (1984), and for the US by Hamermesh (1977) and Danziger, Haveman and Plotnick (1981). Both the cross-section and time-series literature is surveyed by Atkinson (1986, section 5.3 and 1987, Chs 8 and 9). For an ambitious attempt to estimate the labour supply effects of income transfers generally see Wolfe *et al.* (1984).

A general discussion of disability benefits is contained in Walker and Townsend (1981). The main empirical studies of labour supply effects are Parsons (1980), Halpern and Hausman (1985) and (critical of Parsons) Haveman and Wolfe (1984). For a brief survey see Atkinson (1986, section 5.2).

For a (somewhat depressing) account of the difficulties of reforming the system even in a relatively minor way see Prest (1983).

On the distributional impact of national insurance see the Further Reading at the end of Chapter 7.

9

Contributory Benefits 2: Retirement Pensions

'You are old, Father William,' the young man said,
'And your pension has almost run out;
And yet you insist that funding is safe
It's no wonder you're all up the spout.'

'In my youth,' Father William replied to his son,
'They told me my savings would grow;
But, now that I'm perfectly sure I have none,
I'd prefer you to Pay as I Go.'

[With apologies to Lewis Carroll]

1 Introduction and Institutions

The main purpose of retirement pensions is to prevent poverty in old age and (at least partly) to protect the living standards to which pensioners have become accustomed. The questions which arise broadly parallel those of Chapter 8. Section 2 discusses different methods of organising pension schemes, and their pros and cons; the efficiency and equity arguments for state intervention, and the effects of different types of intervention are analysed in sections 3 and 4; and national insurance pensions and related benefits are assessed in section 5.

The 1975 Social Security Pensions Act was one of the most important pieces

205

of social security legislation since the National Insurance Act 1946 (Chapter 2:6), and is the basis of the current arrangements described here. A number of proposed reforms, which will affect people retiring after the end of the century, are discussed in section 5.1 (for references on current and future institutions see the Further Reading).

The contributions side was discussed in Chapter 7:2.1. To qualify for a full pension an individual must generally have contributed to the current (i.e. 1975) scheme for at least 20 years, and either to the current scheme or its predecessor (i.e. the 1948 scheme) for at least 49 years (men) or 44 years (women). Where this requirement is not met, pension is awarded on a sliding scale. In contrast with previous legislation, *home responsibility protection* ensures that years spent by a parent at home looking after children or a disabled dependant will not usually result in loss of pension. Thus a woman who drops out of the labour force for 15 years to look after her children has to work for only 29 years (i.e. 44 *minus* 15) to qualify for a full pension.

On the benefits side, the major provisions of the 1975 Act (as subsequently amended) may be summarised as follows:[1]

(1) The weekly pension consists of two components, the *basic component* (which is flat-rate) and the *earnings-related*[2] component.

(2) The basic component for a single person is approximately equal to the lower earnings limit,[3] which is set at about one-quarter of national average earnings (£35.50 in 1985/6).[4] For earnings below this level the basic component is reduced pound for pound with earnings.

(3) The earnings-related component for a person with a full contributions record is calculated as 25p of pension per pound of earnings between the lower earnings limit and a ceiling equal to the upper earnings limit.

(4) The pension is based on the individual's best 20 years, thus improving pensions by omitting years in which earnings were low.

(5) The same pension formula applies to men and women, though pensionable age is 65 for men and 60 for women.[5]

(6) The scheme will reach maturity in 1998. Each year of contribution gives entitlement to earnings-related pension equal to 1¼ per cent of the excess of earnings (or the ceiling, whichever is the lower) over the lower earnings limit. Thus, a person who has contributed for 20 years will receive an earnings-

---

[1] Several major changes to these arrangements, to take effect after 2000, were under discussion in 1986; the most important are listed in section 5.1.

[2] Also referred to as the state earnings-related pension scheme (SERPS).

[3] The lower and upper earnings limits are explained in Chapter 7:2.1.

[4] The actual calculations are done on an annual basis, but achieve the same effect as the (simpler) weekly description in the text.

[5] This age differential is under increasing pressure – see section 5.2.

related pension of 25 per cent (i.e. 20 × 1¼ per cent) of the relevant earnings, in addition to the flat-rate pension.

(7) A man receives an increase in his pension if he is married unless his wife has a pension in her own right, in which case she receives the full pension to which she is entitled on the basis of her earnings. Where a couple has two contribution records, the surviving spouse receives the basic pension plus *both* earnings-related components, up to the maximum which could have been earned by a single person.

(8) From 1975 the basic component was uprated each year in line with the increase in average earnings or the increase in prices, whichever was the greater. This caused a number of problems, and legislation in 1980 changed the formula so that the *mandatory* uprating reflected only price increases. The earnings-related component is protected in two ways. First, the earnings on which the pension is calculated are revalued each year in line with the general movement of earnings, so that the earnings-related pension, when first awarded, reflects the 20 years of highest *real* earnings. Second, the earnings-related component, once in payment, is uprated each year at least with increases in the price level.

(9) The pensions of people who work beyond pensionable age are increased by 7.5 per cent (in real terms) for each year by which pension is deferred. This has important implications, to which we return in section 5.2.

(10) Membership of the flat-rate scheme is compulsory. But it is possible to contract out of the earnings-related component by belonging to an occupational (i.e. private) scheme which offers a *guaranteed minimum pension*. Such a scheme must meet stringent conditions but, broadly, should pay at least the pension offered by the state scheme to someone with an identical earnings record. In sharp contrast with any past arrangements, the state will index in line with price changes the guaranteed minimum pension paid under approved private schemes. The important issues this raises are discussed in section 3.

Let us take a specific example of the scheme at maturity (but assuming 1987 data for simplicity). Suppose someone retires with a full contributions record, and with average earnings over his best 20 years of £200 per week (roughly the 1987 average). If he were single he would receive a basic pension of £38.70 per week, plus one-quarter of the excess of his average earnings (£200) over the lower earnings limit (£38). His earnings-related pension would therefore be £40.50 per week and the total pension £79.20.

Entitlement to pension is unaffected by limited weekly earnings (up to £75 in 1986/7). Thereafter, for men under 70 (women under 65) pension is rapidly withdrawn. Anyone with earnings even remotely approaching the national average receives no pension at all, and is therefore more or less forced to defer retirement.

Many individuals and couples receiving a national insurance pension are eligible also for supplementary benefit (Chapter 10:1), including automatic entitlement to various other benefits such as housing benefit. One of the main purposes of the 1975 scheme was to reduce the numbers receiving both retirement pension and long-term supplementary benefit. Historically this has been a serious problem; in 1984 out of 9.7 million national insurance pensioners almost one in five also received supplementary pension.

Widowhood Provision for widows (and in restricted circumstances for widowers) takes three forms. *Widow's allowance* is paid for 26 weeks after the husband's death to a widow who is under 60 when her husband dies or, if over that age, if her husband was not a retirement pensioner. There may be additional payments for dependent children. *Widowed mother's allowance* is payable to a widow with at least one qualifying child when her widow's allowance ends after 26 weeks, but is subject to more stringent contribution conditions. *Widow's pension* is payable to a widow over 40 after the termination of her widow's allowance or widowed mother's allowance. For widows between 40 and 50, the pension is payable at a reduced rate.[1]

All the pension schemes discussed so far are dependent on a national insurance contributions record. In addition, there is a **non-contributory retirement pension**, primarily for people who retired too soon after 1948 to have made adequate contributions. Anyone who is 80 or over and is not receiving a national insurance pension, or is receiving one at a low rate, may qualify for a non-contributory pension. As its name implies it is not a national insurance benefit, and is paid out of the Consolidated Fund.

Private pension schemes vary widely: some are voluntary, some compulsory; some are contributory, others not; some cover all workers in an occupation, others only senior personnel (the so-called 'top-hat' schemes); some, but by no means all, meet the conditions for contracting out of the state scheme; and a few allow pension rights to be transferred to a new job; virtually none offers anything close to complete indexation against inflation. Most occupational schemes have only two features in common. First, almost all are funded.[2] Second, most qualify for tax relief in a variety of forms, i.e. private pensions receive public support in the form of tax expenditures (Chapter 7:1.1), though with serious valuation problems (UK Board of Inland Revenue, 1983). Given this variety, no attempt is made to summarise private schemes (see UK, 1981) save to note that their coverage has grown substantially over the years, from about 25 per cent of employees in 1954 to not far short of 50 per cent in 1979.[3]

---

[1] A number of changes are foreshadowed (UK, 1985k, paras 5.10–5.15), including the replacement of widow's allowance by a tax-free lump-sum payment of £1000; widowed mother's allowance and widow's pension would be paid from the outset of widowhood.

[2] The organisation of funded pension schemes is explained in section 2.

[3] For an analysis of private pension schemes in the USA see Munnell (1982).

2 Methods of Organising Pensions

The economics of pension schemes can be confusing because writers easily become bemused by its *financial* aspects (i.e. analysis of insurance companies' portfolios of financial assets). I shall try to simplify matters by concentrating on the essential *economic* issues (i.e. the production and consumption of goods and services).

From an individual viewpoint, the economic function of pensions is to redistribute consumption over time. By contributing to a pension scheme an individual consumes today less than he produces, so as to continue to consume when he has retired and is no longer producing. In principle, an individual can transfer consumption over time in two ways: by storing current production; or by acquiring a claim to future production.

One way of ensuring future consumption is to set aside part of current production for future use, e.g. by digging a hole in one's back garden and adding to its contents each year tins of baked beans, shoe-laces, and soap powder. Though this is the only way Robinson Crusoe could guarantee consumption in retirement, the method in practice leaves much to be desired. Storing current production is costly in terms of the potential return to savings forgone, and also because storage costs for many commodities are high. A second problem is uncertainty in a variety of ways: what quantities to store; what new goods might become available; and how one's tastes might change. Third, some services can be transferred over time by storing the physical wealth which generates them (e.g. it is possible to store housing services by being an owner-occupier); but it is not possible, even in principle, to store services deriving from human capital, such as haircuts or, very important in old age, medical services. Organising pensions by storing current production on a large scale is therefore a non-starter.

The alternative is for individuals to exchange current production for a claim on future output. There are two broad ways in which I might do this: by saving part of my wages each week I could build up a pile of *money*, which I would exchange for goods produced by younger people after my retirement; or I could obtain a *promise* that I would receive my share of goods produced by others after my retirement. The promise could be from my son ('don't worry, Dad, I'll look after you when you're old'), or from government: '[The Government's] policy on pensions is to secure better benefits for all pensioners, present and future.' (UK, 1974, p. iii). The two most common ways of organising pensions broadly parallel these two sorts of claim on future production. So-called *funded* or money-buying schemes follow the first,

Pay-As-You-Go or unfunded schemes the second.[1]

Funded and Pay-As-You-Go schemes In a funded scheme (frequently organised in the private sector by insurance companies), contributions are invested in a variety of financial assets, the return on which is credited to its members. When an individual retires, the pension fund will be holding all his/her past contributions, together with the interest and dividends earned on them. This usually amounts to a large lump sum which is converted into an annuity (Chapter 5:2.3). The annuity is then the individual's pension. Funding, therefore, is simply a method of accumulating money, which is exchanged for goods at some later date. Most occupational schemes are of this type.

Funded schemes have two major implications: they always have sufficient reserves to pay all outstanding financial liabilities (since an individual's entitlement is simply his past contributions plus the interest earned on them); and a representative individual, or a generation as a whole, gets out of a funded scheme no more than he has put in, i.e. with funding, a generation is constrained by its own past savings. Other implications emerge throughout the chapter.

Pay-As-You-Go (PAYG) schemes are usually run by the state. They are contractarian in nature, based on the fact that the state has no need to accumulate funds in anticipation of future pension claims, but can tax the working population to pay the pensions of the retired generation. Almost all state pension schemes today are PAYG, the only major exceptions being Sweden and Japan (see Rosa, 1982).

From an economic viewpoint PAYG can be looked at in several ways. As an individual contributor, my claim to a pension is based on a promise from the state that if I pay contributions now I will be given a pension in the future. The terms of the promise are fairly precise; they were set out in some detail in section 1. From an aggregate viewpoint, the state is simply raising taxes from one group of individuals, and transferring the revenues thereby derived to another. State-run PAYG schemes, from this perspective, are no different from explicit income transfers like child benefit.

The major implication of the PAYG system is that it relaxes the constraint

---

[1] There are other ways of organising pension schemes. The so-called *book* method makes advance provision for pensions on the company's balance sheet in the same way as provision is made for any other deferred liability (e.g. future tax payments). Money is not transferred out of the company (as it is with funded schemes) but is retained for use by the company. At the same time a reserve is set up in the balance sheet to reflect the estimated liability. In *cash* terms there is little difference between book reserving and Pay-As-You-Go. Funding and Pay-As-You-Go are thus the two generic methods of organising pensions, and discussion is confined to them.

that the benefits received by any generation must be matched by its own contributions. Samuelson (1958) showed that with a PAYG scheme it is possible in principle for *every* generation to receive more in pensions than it paid in contributions, provided that real income rises steadily; this is likely when there is technological progress and/or steady population growth.

Preliminary comparison PAYG schemes have three advantages: they are generally able to protect pensions in payment against inflation; they can generally increase the *real* value of pensions in line with economic growth; and full pension rights can be built up quickly, since pensions are paid not by one's own previous contributions, but by those of the current workforce. These points are illustrated in Table 9.1. In period 1 the total income of the workforce is £1000, so that a contribution rate of 10 per cent yields £100. Suppose by period 2 prices and earnings have risen by 100 per cent (column 2). A contribution of 10 per cent now yields £200, which has a purchasing power of £100 at the old price level, and so maintains the real value of pensions in the face of inflation. Alternatively, suppose (column 3) that economic growth raises earnings to £2000, while prices stay at their original level. In this case the 10 per cent contribution rate has a *real* yield of £200, and so it is possible to double the real value of pensions.

Table 9.1: Financing a Pay-As-You-Go Pension Scheme in the Presence of Inflation and Growth

	PERIOD 1	PERIOD 2 (Inflation)	PERIOD 2 (Growth)
	(1)	(2)	(3)
(1) Total income of workforce	£1000	£2000	£2000
(2) Price index	100	200	100
(3) Pension contribution rate	10%	10%	10%
(4) Available for pensions	£100	£200	£200
(5) Real value of pensions ($=$(line (4)/line (2))$\times 100$)	£100	£100	£200

Against these undoubted advantages must be offset the major problem that PAYG is sensitive to any change in the age structure of the population which reduces the workforce relative to the number of dependants. The crucial variable is the so-called *dependency ratio*,

$$\frac{P}{W} \tag{9.1}$$

where P is the number of pensioners and W the number of workers. Influences like increased longevity raise the number of pensioners, and longer education reduces the size of the workforce. Lowering the retirement age simultaneously reduces the workforce and increases the number of pensioners. Finally, as we shall see, any large 'bulge' in the birth rate can cause serious difficulties.

Another claimed disadvantage of PAYG finance is that it makes pensioners dependent on the future workforce. This is true. But, as we shall see in section 3.2, the same is true of funded schemes. In both cases pensioners are dependent on future generations, since both schemes build pensions round claims on future production, rather than by storing current production.

The disadvantages of funded schemes tend to mirror the advantages of PAYG. Starting with inflation, it is important to distinguish (a) pensions in build-up, when contributions are still being paid, and (b) pensions in payment. Funded schemes can generally cope with inflation during the build-up of pension rights, and with a given rate of *anticipated* inflation once the pension is in payment. But they do not cope well with unanticipated inflation during the pay-out period. The reason is straightforward. A pensioner under a funded scheme builds up over his working life a capital sum, which he exchanges upon retirement for an annuity. From equation (5.11) the size of the annuity depends not only on the lump sum, but also on the *real* rate of interest facing the insurance company (i.e. the excess of the nominal interest rate over the rate of inflation). Where inflation is correctly anticipated, nominal interest rates, and hence also the nominal annuity payment, can be adjusted to take account of inflation. But where inflation after retirement is higher than expected, a pure funded scheme is generally unable to index benefits, e.g. widows on fixed incomes suffered a drastic reduction in the real value of their pensions during the years of high inflation in the mid-1970s.[1]

It should be noted that the relative ability of PAYG and funding to cope with inflation is due less to the method of finance *per se* than to the fact that in many instances only the state can guarantee indexed amounts. Funded schemes can cope with inflation if their assets are indexed by the state, e.g. where the state sells indexed gilts or where it underwrites directly the indexation component once funded pensions are in payment.[2] However, the part of the return which compensates for inflation is paid out of current tax revenues, i.e. on a PAYG basis. More generally, any receipts of funded schemes deriving from current

---

[1] See for instance, 'Lady Spencer Churchill; Why She and Others Like Her Deserve All the Help They Can Get', *The Times*, 24 February 1977.

[2] As discussed in section 1, the latter is the current situation in the UK in respect of the guaranteed minimum pension received by individuals who have contracted out of the state earnings-related pension scheme. The UK government also sells indexed bonds (see p. 225, footnote 1).

tax revenues, whether the return to indexed bonds or the tax advantages they currently enjoy, constitute a PAYG element in such schemes.

In principle, an individual can insure against uncertainty. We saw in Chapter 5 how private insurance works in the case of burglary, which suggests the possibility that individuals insure against inflation. This is one of the issues considered in section 3.1 – it turns out that such an escape route is generally not possible without state intervention.

For similar reasons it is not possible for funded schemes substantially to increase the real value of pensions in line with economic growth which occurs after a pensioner's retirement. Finally, it takes a long time to build up full pension rights in a funded scheme, because it takes an individual many years to build up a lump sum sufficiently large to generate an annuity which will support him/her fully in retirement.

Against these disadvantages, it is often claimed that funding has the major advantage of being insensitive to changes in the dependency ratio. The argument is that a funded scheme always has sufficient resources to pay the pensions of its members, since the present value of a representative pension stream exactly equals past contributions, plus interest. It is true that a funded scheme will have sufficient resources to pay all *money* claims against it; but it does *not* follow that funding, on that account, offers pensioners better protection against demographic change. This controversial topic is addressed in detail in sections 3.2 and 5.1.

3 Efficiency Arguments for State Intervention

3.1 PUBLIC VERSUS PRIVATE PROVISION

Section 3.1 discusses efficiency aspects of public versus private provision, and section 3.2 looks at the PAYG versus funding controversy. Social justice is considered in section 4.

Efficiency requires that individuals buy the *socially* efficient *real* level of pension. The theoretical conditions under which private insurance markets achieve this result were discussed in Chapter 5:4.1. The three major policy issues are why people insure at all, why the state makes membership of a pension scheme compulsory, and why it provides retirement pensions itself.

We know that a rational, risk-averse individual will pay pension contributions (i.e. buy insurance) so long as their net cost does not exceed the value to him of the certainty he thereby derives (Chapter 5:2.1). Membership is compulsory because of the external costs which arise if an individual does not buy pension rights (Chapter 8:2.1). The issue of public provision is more

213

complicated. The private market provides pensions efficiently only if the standard assumptions of perfect information, perfect competition and no market failures hold. On the demand side it is not unreasonable to postulate perfect information, not because individuals are necessarily able to acquire it themselves, but because they could purchase it from an insurance broker. On the supply side it is necessary to consider separately the five technical conditions (Chapter 5:3) which must hold if the private market is to supply insurance efficiently.

The probability of living to a given age for pensioner A is independent of that for pensioner B; and the probability is known and less than one. Data on mortality rates are reliable in all industrialised countries. Nor is there any problem of adverse selection – by and large people do not know when they are going to die. Moral hazard is not a problem either; suicide is costly to the individual, and works in the insurance company's favour.

The initial conclusion, therefore, is that there is no technical problem with private pension provision. This, however, overlooks inflation. An individual can purchase a future consumption bundle which is efficient in terms of quantity and quality only if he is able to guarantee the *real* value of his future pension. This can occur without intervention only if the private market can supply insurance against unanticipated inflation. Such insurance is not possible for two important reasons. First, the probability of pensioner A experiencing a given rate of inflation is *not* independent of that for pensioner B – the rate of inflation facing one pensioner will (by and large) face them all. There is no possibility of winners compensating losers and so insurance is impossible. In addition, the probability distribution of different future levels of inflation is neither known nor estimable.[1] Private inflation insurance is therefore not possible, hence there are no funded, wholly private schemes which offer fully indexed pensions.

This technical problem with private inflation insurance gives an efficiency argument, at a minimum, for state intervention to assist private schemes with the costs of unanticipated inflation once pensions are in payment. The state is able to offer such a guarantee because it can use current tax revenues on a PAYG basis. This will introduce a PAYG element into even the purest funded scheme. It should be clear that an indemnity against inflation, if publicly provided, is not true insurance (because it cannot be), but simply a form of tax/transfer. Since efficiency requires individuals to make decisions about the real value of the pension they purchase, and since the appropriate guarantees against inflation can be given only by the state on a PAYG basis, there is a cast-iron efficiency argument for at least some public involvement with pensions.

---

[1] Inflation is not a problem for (say) car repairs, because automobile insurance, unlike pensions, is financed by *current* premiums.

Whether this should stop at the provision of inflation indemnities for private markets, or whether the state should step in to provide pensions itself on either a PAYG or a mixed funded/PAYG basis, is an open issue upon which most of the rest of the chapter has a bearing.

3.2 FUNDING VERSUS PAY-AS-YOU-GO: THEORETICAL ARGUMENTS

The demographic problem Having established the case for at least some public involvement, the next question is whether any state scheme should be funded or PAYG and, in particular, what are the relative merits of the two methods in the face of demographic change. This issue is analysed by Barr (1979), on which this section draws heavily.[1] The problem has become important, as shown in Figure 9.1, because of the peak in the UK birth rate in the 1940s, and the secondary bulge of the mid-1960s. These cohorts of 'bulge' babies will retire between 2010 and 2030, and if the fall in the birth rate after 1964 persists will have to be supported in old age by the much smaller succeeding generations. Specifically, in 1985 there were 2.3 national insurance contributors for each pensioner; the projected figure for 2035 is 1.6 (UK, 1985k, para. 1.12; see also the Further Reading).

The problem is compounded by the increases in the earnings-related

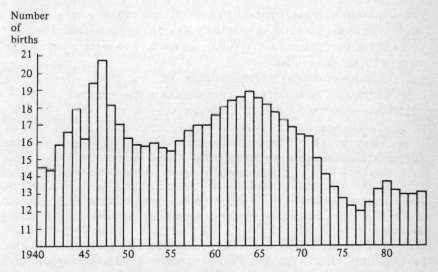

Figure 9.1 *Live births per 1000 population, 1940–84* (Source: *Annual Abstract of Statistics*, various years.)

---

[1] The analysis is similar in spirit to Samuelson (1958).

pension under the 1975 Act (see section 1). Even with the reforms fore-shadowed in UK (1985k) (see section 5.1) a worker with an average contributions record will receive a pension almost twice the current flat-rate benefit.

The demographic problem is not confined to Britain. A startlingly similar pattern exists in the USA (see Munnell in Pechman, 1983, pp. 84–5) and in most of the EEC countries, including Belgium, Denmark, Germany, Italy and the Netherlands, and also in Australia, New Zealand and Japan.[1] Much of the industrialised world thus faces the potentially explosive problem, on present trends, of an ageing population with heavy retirements after about 2010.

The widely held (but false) view that funded schemes are inherently 'safer' than PAYG is an example of the fallacy of composition.[2] For *individuals* the economic function of a pension scheme is to transfer consumption over time. But (ruling out the case where current output is stored in holes in people's gardens) this is not possible for society as a whole; the consumption of pensioners as a group is produced by the next generation of workers. From an *aggregate* viewpoint, the economic function of pension schemes is to divide total production between workers and pensioners, i.e. to reduce the consumption of workers so that sufficient output remains for pensioners. Once this point is understood it becomes clear why PAYG and funded schemes, which are both simply ways of dividing output between workers and pensioners, should not fare very differently in the face of demographic change.

The simple model highlights the argument under strong assumptions. These simplify the analysis without substantially altering the conclusion. They are:

(1) Output per head remains constant over time, and is the same whether pensions are funded or PAYG.

(2) The number of workers remains constant.

(3) Wages are fixed in real terms, pensions in nominal terms.[3]

(4) There is no trade with other countries.

---

[1] This is a remarkable fact. Why should countries as different as Denmark (Protestant and highly industrialised) have a pattern of birth rates which is very similar to Italy (Catholic and with some largely unindustrialised parts). Australia which escaped much of the recession of the 1970s nevertheless has a declining birth rate. And Japan faces exactly the same problem despite large differences in religion, social organisation and patterns of industry. No one has yet given a satisfactory explanation of this striking similarity.

[2] It is a fallacy of composition to assume that because something is true for an individual it will *necessarily* be true on aggregate. For instance, if I stand on my seat in the theatre I will get a better view, but if everybody does so nobody will get a better view. See Samuelson (1980, p. 11).

[3] This assumption, like the others, is relaxed later. But empirically it is not much of an exaggeration for occupational pensions – see the report by the National Association of Pension Funds in *The Guardian*, 26 June 1979.

The simplest case is illustrated by the first column of Table 9.2. There are ten workers who produce an output of 1000. Assume that there are no taxes, so that the workers receive the whole of their output; and assume that each unit costs £1. Now suppose that workers use 900 units of output for current consumption, and set the remaining 100 units aside for their retirement. Pension provision can then take two forms. Workers can sell 100 units of output for £100 to the current generation of pensioners, who are able to buy it with their own past savings. The current generation of workers saves the money, and uses it when it retires to buy the non-consumption of the then workforce. This, at its simplest, is how funded schemes operate.[1] Alternatively, in a PAYG world, 100 units of output are transferred from workers to current pensioners via a 10 per cent tax on the workforce, so that it can afford to consume only 900. When the current workforce retires it would in turn receive 100 units of output.

Table 9.2: Output and Consumption with Workforces of Different Sizes

| | PERIOD 1 | PERIOD 2 (constant productivity) | PERIOD 2 (doubled productivity) |
	(1)	(2)	(3)
Size of workforce	10	5	5
Total output=total income of the workforce	1000	500	1000
Workers' consumption	900	450	900
Workers' non-consumption	100	50	100

Note: Output is measured in physical units.

Under the stated assumptions both schemes can continue indefinitely and both lead to the same result. Three conclusions emerge: (a) pensioners can consume only what workers produce but do not consume; (b) pensioners always depend on succeeding generations to provide the labour to produce the goods which they consume; and (c) under the stated assumptions PAYG and funding lead to identical results.

The effects of a decline in the workforce The previous assumptions stand,

---

[1] In practice things can be more complicated: contributions can come from employers and the government as well as from workers; and contributions may not be entirely at the expense of workers' consumption. These factors complicate the analysis but do not change the logic of the underlying argument.

217

except that the labour force halves. This case is shown in the second column of Table 9.2. With output per worker unchanged (by assumption) output has halved to 500, and workers' consumption to 450, leaving 50 units of output for pensions. Under PAYG, the 10 per cent tax mentioned above leads to exactly this result. With a funded scheme matters are more complicated. The current generation of pensioners is taken to be the previous workforce of ten in column 1, which has accumulated sufficient funds to buy an output of 100 at the initial price of £1 per unit. If the savings habits of workers do not change, total expenditure will be £450 by workers on current consumption, plus £100 by pensioners out of accumulated funds. The total of £550 is greater than the value at current prices of output of 500. Whilst pensioners get their £100 in *money* safely transferred to their retirement they will not necessarily receive 100 units of *consumption*.

In economic terms, if there is a large accumulation of pension funds when the workforce is declining, the high level of spending by pensioners out of their accumulated savings will reduce the rate of saving in the economy, and possibly lead to aggregate dissaving. Net pensioner consumption (i.e. the excess of pensioner consumption over any pensioner production) is greater than saving by workers (i.e. the excess of workers' production over their consumption at current prices); and at full employment this causes demand inflation, which erodes the purchasing power of pensioners' accumulated funds, and hence their consumption. The precise mechanism of this inflationary process is spelled out in Barr (1979), which shows that if the labour force halves then, under the stated assumptions, output will halve, the price level double, and pensioner consumption halve. In the extreme, it does me no good to accumulate a huge fund if on the day I retire the last of the workforce boards ship for Australia – I will have plenty of five-pound notes, but no mechanism for transforming them into consumption.[1]

Relaxing the assumptions Suppose first that workers' wages are not necessarily indexed, nor pensions necessarily fixed in money terms. If the labour force halves (the other assumptions remaining in force), output will halve (column 2 of Table 9.2). This output can be divided between workers and pensioners in different ways; but their joint demand is constrained by total supply. The relative shares of the two groups will depend on such factors as their political and bargaining strengths, i.e. whether pensioners are more powerful lobbying for current tax revenues (PAYG) or as the owners of capital. There is no difference of principle between the two methods, only a practical issue.

Suppose, next, that productivity doubles, but is unaffected by the method of

---

[1] Australia would be unlikely to allow me to buy Australian goods with pounds in this sort of situation.

pension finance. If the other assumptions still hold, a smaller workforce of five can now produce the same output as previously produced by ten (column 3). Workers can consume 900, leaving 100 for pensioners. The system is in equilibrium, in this case because supply has adjusted. In a world of funding, the growth in output makes possible sufficient extra saving by the smaller workforce to match dissaving by the larger group of pensioners. Under PAYG a tax at an unchanged rate of 10 per cent enables government to transfer to pensioners the 100 units of output promised to them.

Relaxing the demographic assumptions is straightforward. Suppose that the decline in the working-age population is entirely offset by increases in the labour force participation of women, and in the retirement age. In this case, column 1 of Table 9.2 applies in period 2, notwithstanding demographic change. The problem is entirely resolved, again on the supply side, for both types of pension scheme, for the same reason as in the previous paragraph. A similar conclusion arises from any combination of increased productivity and labour force participation which prevents output from falling.

Finally, it is in principle possible to maintain the consumption of both workers and pensioners with goods produced abroad, provided the country has sufficient overseas assets to do so. This could be done with publicly owned stocks of foreign currency (PAYG) or with foreign assets accumulated by pension funds.

Two conclusions emerge.

(1) If changes in productivity and labour force participation are independent of the method of finance, then relaxing the assumptions does not change the previous results. In particular, it remains the case that funding and PAYG are not substantially different in their ability to cope with demographic change. This should not be surprising. The task of both schemes is to reduce workers' consumption; PAYG does this by taxing workers, funding by forcing (or allowing) them to save. The only difference is that PAYG makes explicit the notion that pensions involve current resources.

(2) The crucial variable is *output*. A decline in the labour force causes problems for any pension scheme only if it causes a fall in output; the problem is solved to the extent that this can be prevented.

The choice between PAYG and funding in the face of demographic change is therefore relevant only to the extent that funding (as is sometimes argued) systematically causes output to be higher. This is a matter of considerable controversy both theoretically and empirically, and is the main topic of section 5.1.

Other aspects This section digresses briefly to a number of other issues dividing the proponents of PAYG and funding, mainly to make clear that they have little or nothing to do with the central issue of paying for pensions. The main arguments are that funded schemes are safer, give more freedom, and impose greater financial discipline.

The question of safety, as we have seen, turns on whether pensioners as a group are better able to fight for their share of national output as recipients of current tax revenues or as the owners of capital. The PAYG mechanism makes clear both the quarrel over output shares and the dependence of pensioners on the next generation of workers. Funding hides both issues, but does not remove them. It is, indeed, possible for the state to break promises made earlier under a PAYG scheme. But funded schemes are equally vulnerable, and equally political – consider, for instance, the reaction to any proposal to withdraw the tax advantages currently granted to pension funds.[1]

As a practical matter the national insurance retirement pension has approximately tripled in *real* terms since 1948. Funded benefits have usually failed to keep up with inflation. A study by the Government Actuary cited in Kincaid (1975, p. 130) reported that where occupational schemes raised pensions after retirement, the average increase in the ten years to 1971 was 2.5 per cent a year, whilst prices rose on average by 4.5 per cent. Another survey suggested that not more than 5 per cent of members of private schemes received an index-linked pension.[2]

A related, libertarian-type argument asserts that taxes in a PAYG world curtail individual liberty. The counter-argument is that the issue of freedom is raised not by PAYG versus funding but by compulsion versus voluntarism. A compulsory funded scheme would give no more freedom than current arrangements.

A final argument is that funding imposes greater financial discipline. With PAYG the state makes promises now, but may not have to pay anything till later (e.g. increases under the 1975 Act are not fully payable until 1998); thus the immediate revenue charge is negligible relative to the annual value of the potential future liability. With funding, promises of higher future benefits must be matched immediately by increased contributions. Though factually true, these are not necessarily arguments against PAYG. Many would regard as one of the great *advantages* of PAYG its ability to increase benefits rapidly should there be the political will to do so. To say that PAYG is 'unsound'

---

[1] Whilst on the subject, it should not be imagined that even storing current output at the bottom of one's garden gives complete protection against *all* contingencies. The state can always expropriate such output either explicitly, or by a tax on individual wealth or, more subtly, by engineering inflation and imposing a non-indexed capital gains tax on an accruals basis. In similar vein, funded schemes run a potential risk of state direction of their investment portfolios.

[2] The survey was conducted by the National Association of Pension Funds. See *The Guardian*, 26 June 1979.

because it is open to abuse is hardly conclusive – the same argument can be applied to motor vehicles or pain-killing drugs.

A related view is that PAYG is dangerous because it can be used profligately to redistribute income. To some, however, the ability to redistribute income is one of the great advantages of PAYG. Which argument one adopts depends largely on views about social justice, to which we turn next.

4 Social Justice

4.1 PUBLIC VERSUS PRIVATE PROVISION

This section, which closely parallels Chapter 8:2.3, and consequently is brief, considers the equity arguments for public provision of pensions. Horizontal equity concerns goals like a guaranteed minimum standard of some commodities, or equal access to them. These occur without intervention (Chapter 4:4.3) where individuals have perfect information and equal power, a line of argument which lends little support to public provision of pensions. If individuals do not have perfect information they would generally be able to buy it. At most there is a case for regulation of minimum standards. The fact that individuals do not have equal power lends further support to minimum standards but, again, there is no argument for public provision.

We have already discussed in Chapter 8:2.3 and elsewhere the weakness of the vertical equity argument that the state should provide pensions because otherwise the poor could not afford them. The earlier conclusions apply equally here – that public provision solely to foster redistribution is justified only by a consumption externality, where the rich confer pensions on the poor as a merit good and/or where the poor themselves prefer 'insurance benefits' to explicit transfers.

Consumption externalities apart, equity reasons for public provision must appeal to efficiency arguments. These arise out of the inability of the private market to supply inflation insurance, which gives an efficiency justification for public provision at least of the indexation component of pensions, and possibly (depending on the outcome of the funding versus PAYG debate) of the entire pension. As we have seen (Chapter 4:6.1), once a commodity is publicly provided on *efficiency* grounds, it is not inappropriate to finance it redistributively; and the fact that membership is compulsory implies (Chapter 5:4.2) that premiums based on income rather than individual risk need not cause problems of adverse selection. These efficiency arguments for compulsion and public provision, taken together, suggest that using publicly organised pensions for distributional purposes does not necessarily cause substantial efficiency losses.

221

4.2 THE REDISTRIBUTIVE EFFECTS OF PENSIONS

A pension scheme, depending on its precise construction, can redistribute income from young to old, from rich to poor, and from men to women. It is necessary to consider PAYG and funded schemes, and in each case to ask three questions: is such redistribution possible; is it inevitable; and to what extent does it occur in practice?

Redistribution from young to old PAYG finance enables a generation as a whole to receive more than the sum of its past contributions. Thus redistribution from the young workforce to the retired generation is *possible*. But it is not *inevitable*, since a PAYG scheme could be organised to pay actuarial benefits. *In practice*, as we shall see in section 5.2, there has been substantial redistribution from young to old in many countries over the past 40 years.

With funded schemes it is necessary to consider separately the cases of stable and unstable price levels. In a world with no inflation the funded benefits of any generation are constrained by its past contributions, rendering redistribution from young to old impossible. The effect of unanticipated inflation is to bring about unintended redistribution from old to young (and vice versa for unanticipated price deflation).

Redistribution from rich to poor can, and usually does, occur with PAYG pensions. In many state schemes (including those in Britain and the USA) there is *formula redistribution*, in that individual B with half the income of individual A will generally pay half the contribution, but receive a pension which is more than half of A's. This effect is partially offset by *differential mortality*, to the extent that the rich live longer than the poor. But redistribution is not inevitable – it is possible to organise a PAYG scheme in which pensions are proportional to contributions.

It might be possible to devise a (compulsory) funded scheme which redistributed from rich to poor. But where membership is voluntary, the present value of the annuity received by a representative individual must equal the lump-sum he has accumulated over his working years. This implies, ceteris paribus, that pensions must be proportional to contributions, thus ruling out systematic redistribution.

Redistribution from men to women The following are all statements of fact referring to the UK:

(1) The normal retiring age for men is 65, at which age a man has a life expectancy of 77. The average man is thus retired for 12 years.

(2) The normal retiring age for women is 60, at which age women have a life expectancy of 80, so that the average woman is retired for 20 years.

(3) It is therefore $20/12 = 1\frac{2}{3}$ times as expensive to provide a given weekly pension for a woman as for a man.

(4) If men and women pay equal contributions and receive equal weekly benefits, then redistribution takes place from men to women. Since women live longer than men, abolishing the differential retirement age would reduce the subsidy but would not eliminate it.

Redistribution from men to women occurs for these reasons in both funded and PAYG schemes. The phenomenon is widespread, but is particularly strong in the UK, which is almost alone in having a lower retiring age for women (a subject to which we return in section 5.2). Two issues arise: is such redistribution inevitable, and is it desirable? On the first point, one could devise a scheme (PAYG or funded) in which women received benefits related to their longevity. A woman could receive a lower weekly/monthly pension than a man with an identical contributions record, i.e. a definition of equity as a pension stream of equal present value. Alternatively, women could pay a higher contribution, and receive the same weekly/monthly pension as men, i.e. equity consists of women receiving a pension stream with a higher present value, matched by a larger contributions stream. Thus there are two definitions of equity: equal present value or equal weekly value. Either is defensible; but they are different – hence the equity problem.

Redistribution from men to women in pensions, though not inevitable, is almost universal, partly from a belief that any differential is a form of discrimination. A decision by the US Supreme Court (1978) declared differential pensions unconstitutional even if calculated actuarially (i.e. on the basis of equation (5.11)).[1] Nor is such redistribution necessarily undesirable. Analytically, it occurs because women pay the same premiums as men, despite being (from the insurer's viewpoint) worse risks because they live longer. As we saw in Chapter 5:4.2, efficiency generally requires that premiums should be proportional to risk; where insurance is compulsory, however, low-risk individuals are not able to opt out, and charging the same premium for all categories of risk does not cause adverse selection. It is possible that secondary inefficiency might arise, e.g. the possible distortion of labour supply decisions which non-actuarial contributions might cause. To the extent that this is not a substantial problem, the decision whether all classes of risk should pay the same premium can be made mainly on equity grounds. Thus some compulsory schemes do not match premium with risk (unemployment benefits), whilst others do (e.g. automobile insurance).[2]

---

[1] Though tenable on equity grounds, the decision was based on a total failure to understand the nature of insurance.

[2] Women have sometimes been required to pay higher medical insurance premiums than men of the same age ('Weaker Sex Should Pay More for Health Insurance, Judge Rules', *The Times*, 16 August 1985, p. 3).

5 An Assessment of National Insurance Retirement Pensions

5.1 EFFICIENCY AND INCENTIVES

Background Questions

This section asks whether the national insurance pension scheme is efficient and equitable, starting with the a priori questions of Chapter 8:3.1: should pensions be national (i.e. publicly provided); and are they insurance?

Should they be national? The efficiency arguments for state pensions rest on externalities, justifying compulsion, and technical failures in the insurance market, justifying public provision at a minimum of indexation. There is no serious disagreement that it should be compulsory for people to belong to a pension scheme, at least up to some minimum level, nor that economic efficiency requires choices about future consumption levels. Decisions about pensions are therefore more efficient if inflation can be ignored, but only the state can offer inflation insurance (i.e. indexation). Thus there is a largely uncontentious role for public provision at least of indexed assets for use by private, funded schemes.[1] The efficiency argument for public provision of the whole pension is less clear-cut.[2]

Are they insurance? Chapter 8:3.1 pointed out that national insurance contributions are not geared to risk; that the pension scheme is not funded; and that rights to benefit are not determined solely by the occurrence of the insured event. In addition, as we shall see in section 5.2, the scheme effects considerable redistribution, and offers credits for people at home looking after young children, and for the unemployed. These arrangements are a considerable departure from the Beveridge scheme, whose lump-sum contributions and benefits ruled out redistribution from rich to poor (assuming, for example, equal life expectancy); and since the original proposals were for a funded scheme they would also have ruled out redistribution from young to old. It can be argued that the present scheme has moved so far from the original concept that it is no longer a contributory scheme, but more of a tax/transfer scheme. Whether or not this is an advantage is debatable.

---

[1] The role of the state *vis-à-vis* indexation is generally accepted even by writers who oppose public provision of any pension above a basic minimum – see, for instance, Morgan (1984, p. 74).

[2] For comprehensive discussion of these issues see the reports of an Australian Committee on the subject (National Superannuation Committee of Inquiry, 1976 and 1977).

Turning to the quantity and type of pension (see Chapter 8:3.1 for parallel discussion of unemployment and sickness benefit), two questions arise.

Should benefits be based on actuarial premiums? The key issue is the extent to which non-actuarial premiums cause secondary inefficiency by distorting labour supply decisions where individuals are compelled to buy a different quantity of insurance from that which they would voluntarily have chosen. No empirical answer exists to this question.

Does the state provide the optimal quantity and type of pension? Only tentative answers are possible. But inflation raises far more serious problems for pensions than for unemployment and sickness insurance, and so requires separate discussion. The state has long been active in indexing pensions. Barr (1981) shows that from 1948 to 1975 the basic pension was in practice indexed to average pre-tax earnings though there was no legal requirement for this. Since 1975 annual uprating at least in line with price changes has been mandatory; and the government has indemnified certain private, funded schemes against inflation (section 1). In addition, since 1981, the state has issued indexed bonds for use *inter alia* by private pension funds.[1]

It can be argued that the increasing role of the state in indexing public and private pensions has contributed to the relative certainty with which individuals can plan for the future, and has therefore increased efficiency, albeit imperfectly because the state scheme makes no allowance for different degrees of risk-aversion between individuals. But there have been a number of problems of implementation, not least in the years between 1975 and 1980, when the indexation formula gave an unintended upward bias to the real value of the basic flat-rate pension (a similar problem arose in the USA). For this and other reasons some writers (see Hemming and Kay, 1982a, p. 46) argue that the pension system is larger than would voluntarily be chosen.

Incentive Issues

Pensions, saving and economic growth There is a large and controversial literature on two major incentive issues: does PAYG restrict saving and output growth; and do pensions reduce labour supply? It is often regarded as self-evident that saving, and hence economic growth, will be higher with funding than under PAYG. But this assertion requires at least three major qualifications. First, it is in any case only while a fund is *building up* that saving might

---

[1] To give a very simplified version, an ordinary 10-year government bond sold in 1987 for £100 would pay (say) £10 interest per year and repay the £100 loan in 1997. A similar indexed bond would make a lower interest payment each year, but would repay in 1997 not £100 but the initial sum indexed for changes in the price level. If prices had doubled over the period, the bondholder would receive £200 plus interest (also indexed) in 1997.

be higher. It should be clear from column 1 of Table 9.2 that in the long run workers save 100 and pensioners dissave 100, so that net saving is zero.

The second qualification is that opinion is very divided as to whether funding increases saving even during the build-up phase (see the Further Reading). The issue was discussed long ago by Sidney and Beatrice Webb in the context of the 1908 Old Age Pensions Act (Chapter 2:2.2). They reported that 'some of our witnesses . . . have taken the view . . . that such non-contributory pensions would be likely to discourage thrift and saving' (Webb and Webb, 1909, p. 334). Current debate was reopened by Feldstein (1974). He argued that PAYG financing, particularly if pensions are higher than actuarially justified, reduces saving, but that any inducement to early retirement (discussed below) would tend to increase savings to pay for a longer retirement after a shorter working-life. The issue is therefore theoretically indeterminate. His empirical work, based on time-series data, concluded that the US social security (i.e. pension) scheme (which is PAYG) reduced personal saving by about 50 per cent, thereby reducing the capital stock by 38 per cent below what it would have been in the absence of the social security system.

Aaron (1982) sets out three theoretical models of the determinants of saving: the life-cycle model (which rules out bequests); the multi-generational model (which allows bequests); and the short-horizon model (which relaxes the assumption that individuals make rational lifetime plans based on (more or less) full information). Barro (1974 and 1978) criticises Feldstein's use of a life-cycle model, in which an increase in PAYG benefits *must* in theory reduce savings, and points out that in a multi-generational model increased benefits could instead increase bequests (and hence not reduce savings). Aaron (1982, p. 28) summarises the theoretical debate by observing,

> that a person determined to find a respected theoretical argument to support a preconception will find one, and that a person without preconceptions will find a bewildering diversity of answers in economic theory about whether social security [i.e. pensions] is more likely to raise or to lower consumption or labor supply.

> To get by this theoretical impasse, one turns with hope to the empirical research. . . . As will become clear, most of these hopes remain unfulfilled.

Feldstein's empirical work was also criticised: additional variables such as the unemployment rate or a measure of permanent income tended to reduce the effect on saving, and to destroy its statistical significance; and the results were highly sensitive to the time-period over which the relation was estimated. The results were finally discredited by Leimer and Lesnoy (1982) who found an important error in some of Feldstein's data. They also pointed out that the results are very sensitive to the way in which people are assumed to form expectations. The latter point, borne out by subsequent simulations by

Auerbach and Kotlikoff (1981), gives rise to the conclusion that *any result is possible*. Aaron (1982, p. 45) concludes that 'it would be pointless to continue the time-series debate, even if better data should become available'. Cross-section results, too, are inconclusive (*ibid.*, pp. 45–50).

The third qualification is that an increase in saving does not *necessarily* raise output. There are not one, but three links in the argument that future output will be higher with funding than with PAYG: (a) funding leads to a higher rate of saving in the build-up period than PAYG, (b) this higher saving is translated into more/higher quality investment than would otherwise occur, and (c) this investment leads to an increase in output. The last two links need not hold, and so converting the national insurance scheme on to a funded basis may not improve matters. According to Rosa (1982, p. 212) the experiences of Sweden and Japan in running state funded schemes

> offer powerful evidence that this option may only invite squandering capital funds in wasteful, low-yield investments [which] should give pause to anyone proposing similar accumulations elsewhere.

The Government Actuary makes the same point in a more agnostic way, by admitting that he is 'not in a position to judge whether . . . pension fund money is more capable than other money of being deployed in accordance with the long-term national interest' (UK, 1978b, para. 25). All three links have to hold before it can be asserted that funding will lead to greater increases in output than PAYG. At best the assertion is not proven.

Pensions and labour supply The question here is whether pensions (either PAYG or funded) reduce aggregate labour supply. The problems are similar to those which beset empirical analysis of the labour supply effects of unemployment benefits (Chapter 8:3.1). On the contributions side, the theoretical analysis of taxation on work effort is generally accepted (see Atkinson and Stiglitz, 1980, pp. 23–61, or Brown, 1983a). The effect of national insurance contributions is to drive a wedge between gross and net money wages. If workers discount future benefits entirely, contributions have the same effect as an income tax; at the other extreme, where future benefits bear an actuarial relationship to contributions, and are perceived to do so, national insurance contributions are not a tax but simply the price of insurance which, like any other price, has little if any distortionary effect on labour supply.

The impact of future benefits, on the other hand, is much harder to analyse. They are payable only in certain contingencies, can be changed by legislation, and will depend on, for example, marital status; and it is not possible to borrow against future benefits, which must therefore be weighted by the probability that each type of benefit will be received at some given future date. The weighted benefits must then be discounted to present value using the market rate of interest or, for people who cannot borrow as much as they wish, at a personal rate of time preference. Similar problems arise (see section 5.2) in valuing pension rights considered as part of personal wealth.

As a result, modelling the effect of pensions on labour supply is complex. Some studies conclude that pensions (both public and private) reduce labour supply (for the UK Zabalza and Piachaud, 1981; for the US Boskin, 1977; Boskin and Hurd, 1978; and Diamond and Hausman, 1984). Others argue that pensions have little or no effect on work effort (Gordon and Blinder, 1980; Hamermesh, 1984; and Burtless and Moffitt, 1984). Up to a point the conflicting results can be explained *inter alia* by differences in model specification, different treatment of benefits and taxes, and different choice of samples (see Atkinson, 1986, section 5.1). To a considerable extent, however, the issue is not only unresolved, but may remain so. A study by Mitchell and Fields (1981) used a single body of survey data in four different (and plausible) ways, and found that the US social security scheme induced workers to retire earlier, or later, or left the retirement decision unaffected.

It is important to be clear that the issue of labour supply, though highly significant, is entirely separate from the PAYG versus funding controversy. Though different methods of organising pensions may influence the rate of saving, it is most unlikely that the method of finance *per se* will affect work effort. An individual will base his labour supply decision on the size of his future pension, on the terms on which he can buy it, and on the range of choice he is allowed. His decision might be affected by uncertainty but, if he is rational, he is unlikely to care whether his income in retirement derives from tax revenues or from a pension fund. The issue of PAYG and funding is relevant to labour supply decisions only to the extent that perceptions about certainty might differ between the two methods; and if pensions (of whatever sort) do induce retirement the simplest solution is to raise the retirement age and/or to give greater financial incentives to defer retirement.

Dealing with Future Problems

Possible policies in the face of the demographic problem   We saw earlier that the Eurotoddlers of the 1950s and 60s will cause a sharp rise in the dependency ratio when they retire in the years after 2010. Any solution to the declining population of working age must either reduce demand and/or increase supply. This implies one (or more) of three outcomes. Demand can be reduced (a) by increasing contributions, thereby reducing the average consumption of workers, and/or (b) by reducing benefits, thereby reducing the average consumption of pensioners.

Alternatively, on the supply side, both workers and pensioners can have the consumption they currently expect, so long as (c) output rises sufficiently to maintain average consumption per head (hence the emphasis in section 3.2 on the key role of output). In theory, this involves either or both of two strategies. *Increased output per worker* can arise from increases in the quantity and quality of capital, and from increases in the quality of labour. *Increased numbers of workers* can arise from increased labour force participation by those of working age; from an increase in the retirement age; and/or by importing labour (e.g. 'guest-workers').

In practice, supply-side policies in the face of a declining workforce should therefore include some or all of the following.

(1) Policies to increase the capital stock and its quality, e.g. robots (which have the added advantage of not requiring pensions). We must be clear, strange though the idea may sound at present, that we are talking about an era of potential labour *shortage*, hence the importance of labour-saving capital.

(2) Increased investment in labour through education and training.

(3) Increasing labour force participation by reducing the unemployment rate and by encouraging more married women to join the labour force (e.g. by providing more child day-care facilities).

(4) Raising the retirement age. A two-year increase for men from 65 to 67, with no increase in pensions, is an implicit reduction in benefits of about 15 per cent, but with the advantage that it works not by reducing living standards in retirement, but by reducing the average duration of retirement. A policy of this sort has already been announced in the USA for the years after 2000. In Britain it would also be possible (and desirable – see section 5.2) to abolish the anomalous differential retirement age of men and women.

(5) Importing labour through immigration. (It has been suggested that a uniquely British solution would be to absorb the (mostly young) population of Hong Kong in 1997, when the colony's lease returns to China.)

To what extent is funding a solution? Funding is clearly irrelevant to policies (2)–(5), which can all be pursued by *direct* methods. If funding makes any difference, it can only be if it (a) leads successively to an increase in saving, in investment, and in output (i.e. policy (1)), *and* (b) does so more effectively than any other method of garnering resources and channelling them into productive investment. The stringency of these conditions should be clear from earlier discussion. The evidence on (a), both theoretically and empirically, is mixed, inconclusive and highly controversial, and that on (b) is unlikely to be less so. The funding versus PAYG controversy can therefore be argued rather to miss the point, by concentrating on a method of increasing output which is both indirect (viz. the three steps in (a)), and debatable. Since the issue is one of economic growth, it seems easier and more reliable to adopt direct methods of effecting policies (1)–(5).

We saw in Chapter 5:2.2 that it is possible to insure against uncertainty as an individual, but not on aggregate. Both funding and PAYG offer *individuals* certainty over their future, but it does not follow that either method can reduce uncertainty for society as a whole. The future is full of uncertainties, which affect pension schemes, just as they affect most other institutions. It should not, therefore, be surprising that there is little to choose between PAYG and funding in this respect. To imagine that funded schemes are substantially better in the face of uncertainty is to fall for crude mythology.

Proposed reform   There has properly been widespread concern (Hemming and Kay, 1982b) over the prospective cost of the state earnings-related pension scheme (SERPS); but it is unwise to be dogmatic, since the outcome depends crucially on growth rates over the next 40 years. A proposal (UK, 1985d) to abolish SERPS was criticised both in Parliament (UK, 1985h) and more widely, and a subsequent White Paper put forward a demand-side strategy with two elements: a reduction in the earnings-related pension for those retiring after 2000; and encouragement for occupational schemes.

The major proposed changes to the state scheme (UK, 1985k, Ch. 2) would modify the arrangements described in section 1 as follows. The earnings-related component would be reduced to 20p (rather than 25p) per pound of earnings between the lower and upper earnings limits, the change to be phased in for those retiring after 2000. The calculation would be based on lifetime average earnings (not the best 20 years), with safeguards for those currently eligible for home responsibility protection. The surviving spouse would inherit up to half, rather than all, his/her spouse's earnings-related pension.

Occupational schemes were changed in several ways: the 1985 Social Security Act gave added protection to people leaving a scheme early and/or transferring to a new scheme; contracting out would be liberalised in a number of respects; and, as an explicit cost-saving measure, occupational schemes contracted out of the state scheme would be made responsible for indexing the guaranteed minimum pension (section 1) in respect of the first 3 per cent of inflation each year.

The details of any scheme are liable to criticism. For instance, calculating benefits over lifetime averages, rather than the best 20 years, works to the disadvantage of people with fluctuating incomes (disproportionately the less well-off, and in particular women). However, if the SERPS promises are thought to be too generous, then the strategy of making the promise less generous is much more sensible than the earlier proposal to scrap SERPS and rely on private, funded schemes. The arrangements described in section 1 were the result of nearly two decades of debate (Chapter 2:6), with a considerable measure of all-party support for the final outcome. Little has changed since 1975, save that the scheme has probably turned out to be unrealistically generous, given likely demographic trends and their effect on output. The proposed changes should reduce the most acute cost (i.e. demand-side) pressures, particularly if buttressed by supply-side policies (1)–(5), listed above. In the US, similar changes, in the form of future increases in contribution rates and in the retirement age, have already been announced.

5.2 EQUITY ISSUES

The discussion in Chapter 8:3.2 of the equity of national insurance applies equally to pensions. This section concentrates on a number of other issues.

Redistribution from young to old The real purchasing power of the basic state pension in the UK increased about threefold in the 30 years to the early 1980s, and far exceeds that to which pensioners are actuarially entitled. In the USA people retiring in recent years received a social security pension at least twice their actuarial entitlement (Rosen, 1982, pp. 152–3). Whether this is more equitable than a funded scheme with no such redistributive possibilities is a matter of judgement.

Redistribution from men to women can occur in both funded and PAYG schemes as a consequence of differential life expectancy (section 4.2). This type of redistribution is particularly strong in Britain, which is virtually alone in having a lower retirement age for women. The differential started in 1940, when the retirement age for women was reduced to 60, partly because of a campaign by women's organisations.[1] The measure accorded well with prevailing and earlier views about the role of married women, 'the great bulk of whom are fortunately in this country free at all ages to devote their attention to the care of their household' (General Report of the 1911 Census (p. 161), quoted by Hunt (1981)).

The redistribution arising from the differential retirement age is inequitable for at least two reasons. First is the anomaly whereby a woman who retires at 65 will receive a higher pension than a 65-year-old man with an identical contributions record, because she has worked beyond her normal retirement age.[2] Second is the discrimination against women who would prefer to work longer. A court verdict in 1986 made it harder for employers to compel a woman to retire at 60,[3] and the government has foreshadowed legal changes to

---

[1] The Old Age Pensions Act 1908 established a common retirement age of 70. It was reduced to 65 under the Old Age and Widows and Orphans Contributory Pensions Act 1925. For details of the events leading to the change in 1940 see Thane (1982, p. 245).
[2] The real pension is increased by 7.5 per cent for each year of work beyond normal retiring age (section 1); thus a woman retiring at 65 receives a pension 37.5 per cent higher than that of an identical 65-year-old man.
[3] 'EEC Court Backs Woman over Retirement Age', *The Times*, 27 February 1986, p. 1.

give men and women doing similar work the right to retire at the same age.[1] Demographic pressures suggest that retirement on a full pension for men and women at a common age of 65 (or possibly higher) is plausible.[2]

Were this indefensible anomaly to be removed, the transfer from men to women would be reduced but not eliminated. What, if anything, could or should be done about it? The argument that the transfer to women's pensions is justified because women are discriminated against in the labour market is weak because it suggests that two wrongs make a right. A more honest argument for the transfer is its retention as an explicit equity objective. As we have seen (section 4.1) this is defensible, since compulsory membership means that the subsidy will not cause inefficiency in insurance markets through adverse selection. This being the case, it can be argued as a matter of general policy that one should recognise the fact of a transfer from men to women, but having recognised it simply to leave it at that.

Redistribution from rich to poor The system of benefits (section 1) and contributions (Chapter 7:2.1) together imply considerable formula redistribution (see section 4.2). At its simplest, from Table 7.3, someone with weekly earnings of £50 pays a 5 per cent contribution (i.e. £2.50), and someone earning £250 pays 9 per cent (i.e. £22.50). If each received only the basic pension, the 'poor' person would receive nine times as much pension per pound of contribution. Because of the earnings-related component, the effect is not as strong as the example suggests, but ceteris paribus there is still redistribution from rich to poor.

Other factors, however, work in the opposite direction. First, there is differential mortality, in that the better-off have a greater life expectancy (and hence collect their pensions longer) and, a related phenomenon, tend to stay in education longer (and hence start to pay contributions later). Second, it is disproportionately the better-off who contract out of the state scheme, and this, too, significantly reduces its redistributive impact.[3]

---

[1] 'Equal Age for Retirement', *The Times*, 23 May 1986, p. 1.

[2] The possibility of a common retirement age of 60 can be ruled out because of its cost. It has been estimated, even with the current dependency ratio, that common retirement at 60 would raise the cost of the national insurance retirement pension by about 40 per cent, i.e. by some 2 per cent of GDP. In any case, many people would retire later out of choice. In the USA political pressure led to the Age Discrimination in Employment Act 1978, which enables (but does not compel) broad classes of people to defer retirement until the age of 70.

[3] Contracting out raises other important issues, including its impact on finances. The extent to which reliance on private sector earnings-related pensions will save the state money in the long run depends on a complex of factors, including the size of the current revenue loss to the state in terms of lower contribution receipts; the rate of economic growth; and the cost on public funds of indexing the guaranteed minimum pension paid by private schemes. See Creedy (1982, Ch. 6), Creedy and Disney (1985, Ch. 4) and Hemming (1984, pp. 131–5).

The overall redistributive effect is therefore complex, and results are far from definitive. Nicholson (1974, Table 3.3) found that in 1970 the national insurance retirement pension reduced the Gini coefficient in Britain by 3.58 per cent. The subsequent introduction of earnings-related contributions (and a fortiori with graduated contributions) has strengthened this effect. Similar features are found in the pension schemes of many other countries (see the Further Reading).

Other aspects Redistribution also takes place between households of different sizes. From Table 8.1, the basic pension for a married man is 60 per cent higher than for a single person making the same contribution; in the USA the comparable figure is 50 per cent (Rosen, 1982, p. 153).

Finally, note should be taken of the important relation between accrued pension rights and the distribution of personal wealth. Because pension rights are distributed more equally than most other forms of non-human wealth, the overall wealth distribution is more equal when they are included. The size of the effect, however, is controversial, depending on (a) precisely which types of pension wealth are included (e.g. how should national insurance pension rights be treated?), and (b) the valuation placed on any particular entitlement to a future income stream. The latter problem is particularly intractable.[1]

5.3 CONCLUSION

Empirical investigation suggests that funding is likely to make little difference, if any, to growth rates. The funding solution is indirect in its mechanism, controversial in its outcome, and likely in any case to have only a second-order effect; it would, therefore, be highly dangerous to imagine that, simply by embracing funding, the demographic problem would be solved. In addition, efficiency arguments of principle point strongly towards a public role at least for indexation. The efficiency case for substantial public, PAYG involvement is therefore strong. Such an argument accepts that it is appropriate for people to use the state as a collective institution for saving and insurance where it is able to perform these functions more cheaply and efficiently than any private alternative.

Aaron (1982) contrasts these findings, which give no conclusive evidence that PAYG schemes have deleterious efficiency effects, with the strong evidence that their equity impact is beneficial, i.e. that they have greatly improved the economic status of the elderly. He concludes that decisions about

---

[1] The valuation problems involved were discussed briefly in section 5.1 See also UK (1975, pp. 665–75) for the problems of valuing an indexed pension, and UK (1979a, Ch. 4).

the future of state pensions should therefore be made mainly on equity grounds.

Further Reading

Details of UK institutions are set out in Tolley (1986) (comprehensive, and includes references to the legislation), and CPAG (1986b) (both published annually). For an analysis of the Social Security Pensions Act 1975 see Barr (1975a). For proposed changes in the UK system see UK (1985k). Systems abroad are discussed by Lynes (1986) (France), Munnell (1982) (private schemes in the USA) and Rosa (1982).

For an introduction to the theoretical issues underlying pension finance see Samuelson (1958) and Barr (1979); for the prospective demographic picture Ermisch (1980 and 1983) and UK (1985k, para. 1.12); and for international discussion of policy Rosa (1982).

The incentive effects of pensions concern (a) saving and economic growth and (b) labour supply. For empirical analysis of the former see Feldstein (1974 and 1979) for pro-funding arguments, and for a survey of the literature and a counter-view Aaron (1982, Ch. 4). Other useful surveys are Danziger, Haveman and Plotnick (1981) and Atkinson (1986, section 5.6). On labour supply see Zabalza and Piachaud (1981) for the UK, and for the US Boskin and Hurd (1978) and various of the chapters in Aaron and Burtless (1984). For surveys of the literature on labour supply see Aaron (1982, Ch. 5), Danziger, Haveman and Plotnick (1981), and Atkinson (1986, section 5.1).

Discussion of the prospective costs of the UK state earnings-related pension is contained in Hemming and Kay (1982b) and UK (1985f, Ch. 2).

The distributional effects of national insurance pensions are estimated by Nicholson (1974). For US analysis see Aaron (1982, Ch. 6) and Danziger, van der Gaag, Smolensky and Taussig (1984). See also the Further Reading at the end of Chapter 7.

The literature on the distribution of wealth is surveyed in Atkinson (1980, Pt. 4) and (1983, Chs 7 and 8). Specific discussion of pension rights as part of wealth is contained in UK (1979a, Ch. 4) and UK (1975, pp. 665–75).

10

Non-Contributory Benefits

Poverty is a great enemy to human happiness; it certainly destroys liberty, and it makes some virtues impracticable, and others extremely difficult. [Samuel Johnson, 1709–1794.]

1 Introduction and Institutions

Non-contributory benefits are many and diverse. Their only common feature is that they are all paid out of general taxation rather than from the National Insurance Fund. The main schemes listed in Table 7.5 are buttressed by many smaller benefits. They differ widely: some are administered centrally, some locally; some are mandatory, others discretionary; some take the form of cash grants for specific purposes (higher education awards for students), others serve to reduce the price of specific commodities (rent subsidies), others make certain goods available without charge (free medical prescriptions). In many cases the distinction between benefits in cash and kind becomes blurred, though for the purposes of this book, it is not necessary to dwell on them.

The aims of these benefits, as set out in Chapter 8:1.1, are the prevention of absolute poverty and, more controversially, the protection of living standards and the reduction of inequality. This chapter considers the extent to which non-contributory benefits contribute to the achievement of these aims, starting with the institutions of four of the most important: supplementary benefit, housing benefit, child benefit, and family income supplement (for details see the Further Reading). Subsequent sections consider the arguments for state intervention, and assess the efficiency and equity of the current system, including a brief survey of empirical evidence. Some of these arrangements are due to be modified in the later 1980s (UK, 1985k), as discussed briefly in Chapter 11:4, with changes in particular to supplementary benefit (to be re-named Income Support) and family income supplement (to be re-named Family Credit).

Supplementary benefit is the final safety net, when family income from all other sources falls below a specified minimum. Expenditure is large (£7264 million in 1986/7, Table 7.5), exceeding that on any other benefit except the national insurance pension. The numbers involved are also large: in early 1985 there were over 4.7 million recipients of whom some four-fifths were either pensioners and widows (1.7 million) or unemployed (2 million). The scheme has changed in various ways since 1948 (Chapter 2:6) and its details are complex. Where a benefit is intended to supplement people's incomes there are bound to be complications in its interactions with other income sources. Discussion here is restricted to the simplest cases.

Supplementary benefit is awarded as *supplementary pension* to those over pension age and *supplementary allowance* to anyone else. Benefit is calculated by setting *requirements* against *resources*. If the latter are less than the former the difference is paid as benefit. Additionally, supplementary benefit acts as a 'passport' to other benefits, including housing benefit, free prescriptions and dental treatment, and free school meals. The scheme is usefully discussed under three heads: eligibility; benefits for those with no income or capital; and the treatment of income.

Eligibility: anyone aged 16 or over who is not in full-time work may be eligible for supplementary benefit, whether or not he or she has a national insurance record or is receiving national insurance benefit. For those under pensionable age the benefit officer has the power to make the benefit conditional on registering for work, though this rule is not applied to the sick, to single parents of children under 16, to blind people not used to working outside the home, and to certain other groups.

Benefits for those with no income or capital: the determination of benefit in any particular case rests on two considerations: how much benefit is awarded to a family with no other income; and how this award is affected by any income the family has, corresponding to the 'requirements' and 'resources' aspects of supplementary benefit.

Normal requirements are calculated according to scale rates laid down by law, which vary according to the numbers and ages of dependants. Housing costs are generally excluded, since recipients of supplementary benefit are normally entitled automatically to housing benefit (discussed below). The scale rates for 1986/7 are shown in Table 10.1. The long-term rate is paid to recipients of supplementary pension, and to those who have been receiving a supplementary allowance and have not been required to register for work for the last 52 weeks. A higher rate of benefit is payable where the householder or a dependant is over 80 or blind.

Additional requirements consist of regular weekly payments to cover particular expenses, including the cost of special diets, extra heating costs, help in the home and nursing help. Where the relevant regulations are satisfied, the benefit officer *must* authorise the additional payment. Beneficiaries may also receive single payments for what the law calls an 'exceptional need', e.g. clothing, baby things, furniture, housing repairs, the conditions for which are set out in considerable detail in the regulations.

The treatment of income: the resources element calculates income for the purposes of supplementary benefit, the underlying principle being that all income is included unless it is specifically 'disregarded'. Though the

Table 10.1: Supplementary Benefit Scale Rates, 1986/7[a] (Partial listing)

SCALE RATE	ORDINARY RATE £s per week	LONG-TERM RATE £s per week
Husband and wife	48.40	60.65
Single householder	29.80	37.90
Any other person aged:		
18 and over	23.85	30.35
16–17	18.40	23.25
11–15	15.30[b]	15.30[b]
under 11	10.20[b]	10.20[b]

ADDITIONAL REQUIREMENTS	LOWER RATE	HIGHER RATE
Heating	2.20	5.55
Central heating	2.20	4.40
Estate central heating	4.40	8.80
Blind addition	1.25	
Diet	1.60, 3.70 or 10.65	
Laundry	excess over 55p/week	

Source: *Hansard*, 24 February 1986, cols 691–99.

Notes: [a]Benefit rates are those in force from July 1986.

[b]Child benefit and child benefit increase are, in effect, deducted from these rates.

regulations for disregards are complex (Tolley, 1986, Ch. 15), the following income is *ignored* for the purposes of establishing entitlement: £4 per week earned by the claimant plus £4 per week by his/her spouse if he/she is working; in the case of a single parent, in addition, half of his/her earnings between £4 and £20 per week; housing benefit; mobility allowance; and attendance allowance. A variety of other disregards relate to such income as education maintenance allowances, maternity and death grants, and the first £4 from most other sources.

Disregards apart, *all* income is included in family resources, in particular: most national insurance benefits including retirement and unemployment and sickness benefit; industrial injury benefit; child benefit; and family income supplement. For supplementary benefit purposes the relevant magnitude is 'net' earnings after tax and national insurance contributions, and after allowing for work expenses, including fares and child-minding costs. The ability to deduct these expenses contrasts sharply with the rules applicable for income tax purposes.

Complications can easily arise in defining the types of income which are disregarded or included; in the interactions when claimants or their families have several different sources of income; and in the calculation of work expenses. In addition, any capital owned by the individual or family may affect entitlement. The value of an owner-occupied house is ignored entirely. Other capital, including savings, redundancy payments and some tax rebates, is ignored if it does not exceed an upper limit (£3000 in 1986/7). Those with capital in excess of the limit are not normally eligible for benefit.

A family's benefit is calculated as the difference between its requirements and its resources. If requirements are estimated at £80 and resources at £20 per week, benefit will normally be £60. At the margin an extra pound of earnings therefore costs £1 of benefit, in economic terms a 100 per cent implicit tax rate. Thus the implicit tax on disregarded income is 0 per cent, on certain earnings of single parents 50 per cent, and on all other income including most national insurance benefits 100 per cent. Supplementary benefit can therefore be thought of as 'topping up' family income from whatever source to bring it up to a basic minimum.

Housing benefit was introduced in 1983 under the Social Security and Housing Benefit Act 1982 to replace earlier arrangements. It includes assistance with rents for tenants in private and public sector accommodation, assistance with rates (see the Glossary) and some assistance to owner-occupiers. The amount of benefit generally depends on the claimant's gross income (including that of his/her spouse), household size, and the amount of rent and rates.

Housing benefit is administered by local authorities. For individuals receiving supplementary benefit (so-called 'certificated' cases) the Department of Health and Social Security automatically notifies the relevant local authority of the claimant's circumstances. Housing benefit is then awarded in different forms depending on housing status. The rent and rates of a tenant are normally met in full.[1] The rent of local authority tenants is usually paid on their behalf (i.e. those whose rent is paid in full receive no cash, and pay no rent); the rates of all householders in receipt of housing benefit are similarly paid directly on their behalf. Owner-occupiers receive assistance with their rates under housing benefit in the same way as tenants. If they receive supplementary benefit they are eligible also for assistance with their mortgage interest payments, which are normally paid in full (though no help is given with capital repayments).

Individuals not in receipt of supplementary benefit are also potentially eligible for housing benefit (these are the so-called 'standard' cases). Housing benefit for such claimants works as described above, with the following differences: standard cases have to make explicit application to their local authority, in contrast with the automatic procedure for certificated cases; rent and rates, depending on the claimant's income, are not necessarily paid in full; and owner-occupiers are eligible for assistance with their rates, but not with mortgage interest payments (see the Further Reading).

Child benefit is not a national insurance benefit though, like most cash benefits, it is administered by the Department of Health and Social Security. The current scheme replaced child tax allowances and family allowances from 1979 (Chapter 2:6), and cost £4573 million in 1986/7 (Table 7.5). Child benefit consists of a tax-free weekly payment (£7.10 in 1986/7) in respect of each child (under 16, or under 19 if in full-time education) in the family. The benefit is payable to the person responsible for a child, either someone with whom the child is living, or someone who contributes to the support of a child living elsewhere. When a child lives with both parents the mother has title to the benefit.

Some single parents are eligible also for **child benefit increase**, payable in 1986/7 at a rate of £4.60 per week for the first or only child. In principle all single parents are eligible, except for those who already receive certain long-term national insurance benefits.

In contrast with the combination of child tax allowances and family allowances, child benefit is administratively much less cumbersome, and is worth the same to everyone whatever their income. The benefit is part of a gradual trend towards standardising support for children. Schemes of this sort

---

[1] A 1985 White Paper (UK, 1985k) foreshadowed the possibility that rates might no longer be paid in full, even for those receiving supplementary benefit.

exist in many countries – for surveys see Kahn and Kamerman (1983) and Bradshaw and Piachaud (1980).

Family income supplement is payable to the head of a low-income family who is normally engaged in full-time paid work, and where there is at least one dependent child. The benefit is payable to families whose normal gross weekly income is below a prescribed amount determined by Parliament (£98.60 in 1986/7 for a family with one child under 11, increasing by £11.65 for each additional such child, and by larger amounts for older children). The amount payable is half the difference between a family's gross income and the prescribed amount, subject to a maximum weekly payment.

In the case of a married couple, or a man and woman living together, it is the man who must be in full-time work (at least 30 hours per week, or 24 hours for a single parent), and it is he who must make the claim. An award will normally be made for 52 weeks, and once made will not be affected by any increase in income during the period. Recipient families are automatically entitled to the same variety of additional benefits as those receiving supplementary benefit.

Other schemes range over educational benefits (e.g. free school meals, clothing grants); health benefits (free prescriptions, free welfare milk and vitamins); benefits for the disabled and handicapped (e.g. the fares to work scheme); employment and job-training benefits; help for the elderly (e.g. meals on wheels); legal aid; and help for the homeless. There are at least 50 schemes of this sort (for details see the Further Reading).

2 Theoretical Arguments for State Intervention

Efficiency and social justice   Non-contributory benefits cover three broad categories of people. First are those whose national insurance (despite compulsory membership) leaves them in poverty. Someone who is unemployed and receiving full unemployment benefit might still be below the poverty line, especially if he/she has a large family. Such a person is eligible also for supplementary benefit. Second are those without national insurance cover because they have exhausted their entitlement, or because they never had any (e.g. a school-leaver, or a recently divorced woman with no recent contributions). Such individuals have to rely on supplementary benefit, and possibly also child benefit. Finally, there are those whose reason for poverty is not covered by national insurance, e.g. the parent of a large family in full-time, low-paid work, who has to rely on child benefit and family income supplement.

None of these categories can readily be dealt with by private insurance; and none except the first can be helped by raising national insurance benefits or by extending their coverage. Much poverty is associated with children and/or high housing costs, neither of which is an insurable risk. Two conclusions emerge: *private* insurance is not possible in most of these cases; nor is extending *national* insurance a complete answer.

The state could, of course, do nothing, and let people face the risk of starvation but, even ignoring equity arguments, this would have a variety of *efficiency* costs including social unrest/crime among those facing starvation; the death by starvation of dependants including children (the future labour force); and the fact that malnutrition causes poor health, thereby raising health care costs and lowering the capacity of adults to work and of children to absorb education. These costs (cf. the nineteenth-century national efficiency arguments in Chapter 2:2.1) give efficiency grounds for the relief of poverty.

From the viewpoint of social justice, libertarians incline towards private charity where poverty is caused by a non-insurable risk. However, we saw in Chapter 4:4.1 that various difficulties, including the free-rider problem, might cause voluntary giving to be inefficiently low even by libertarian standards. Thus writers like Friedman and Hayek do not oppose subsistence payments out of public funds, though they favour every inducement to encourage people to work (the modern incarnation of 'less eligibility' (Chapter 2:1.1)). Socialists, in contrast, argue for generous benefits paid on the basis of need, to advance their egalitarian objectives.

Thus there are solid arguments of both efficiency and social justice for public provision of subsistence benefits on a non-insurance basis. Whether they should be higher than subsistence is a matter of judgement.

Criteria for assessing redistributive schemes How effective are non-contributory benefits at relieving poverty? This question was tackled for national insurance benefits (and will be for health care, education and housing) in terms of their efficiency and equity. But for redistributive schemes the argument is illuminated by three somewhat different criteria which cut across the efficiency/equity distinction.

The level of benefits: does the scheme under consideration give recipients a socially acceptable standard of living? This involves, first, *money benefits*: does the scheme pay enough to enable the purchase of an adequate consumption bundle? Second the issue of *stigma*: for any given level of money support a person's living standard (in utility terms) is reduced to the extent that he/she feels stigmatised by receiving benefit.

The focus of benefits: again there are two issues. An ideal scheme will have no gaps, i.e. benefits will go to everyone who needs them. Failure can arise either because *eligibility rules* prevent some needy groups from applying, or because *take-up* is less than 100 per cent. In the latter case, on the demand side eligible claimants may not apply, either for lack of information or because of stigma; on the supply side an eligible person may apply but be refused, either in error or because of discrimination. Second, an ideal scheme might wish to avoid 'leakages', i.e. benefits should go *only* to those who need them. This reduces the cost of the scheme, but may involve high implicit tax rates and the poverty trap (see the Glossary).

The cost criterion embraces the benefits themselves and also the cost of administration.

These three criteria interact in important ways which emerge in subsequent discussion. Cost constrains the freedom to have high benefits. There is an important interaction between cost and the level of benefit: as we shall see, increasing (say) supplementary benefit by x per cent is likely to increase cost by much more than x per cent. A further interaction is between cost and focus: again it transpires that reducing the rate at which benefits are withdrawn as family income rises, disproportionately affects costs.

3 An Assessment of Non-Contributory Benefits

3.1 SUPPLEMENTARY BENEFIT

Level Are benefits high enough to relieve poverty? With an absolute definition (Chapter 6:2.1) the answer is generally yes, in that nobody starves,[1] and also because between 1948 and 1980 real benefits rose in line with pre-tax average earnings (Chapter 6:2.3). With a relative definition, no unambiguous answer is possible.

Stigma reduces the utility associated with a given level of benefit, though with controversy over the form of the effect and its strength (see Deacon and Bradshaw, 1983). The limited empirical evidence is discussed in section 3.3. Given the popular hatred of the stringent household means test between the wars (Chapter 2:3.2), it is argued that many recipients feel stigmatised either by the receipt of benefit *per se*, or by the effect on their self-esteem of the investigations necessary to establish eligibility.

Focus First, are there gaps? The eligibility rules for supplementary benefit are broad, reflecting its status as benefit of last resort. France has no comparable scheme, neither does the US for non-waged adults without children. However,

---

[1] But there has been increasing concern in recent years about the incidence of hypothermia among the elderly. For discussion of whether the level of supplementary benefit is too low see Cooke and Baldwin (1984).

though empirical evidence (discussed in section 3.3) is not precise, a sizeable proportion of those eligible do not receive benefit (i.e. take-up is incomplete). On the demand side an unknown number do not apply. On the supply side, not all eligible applicants are awarded benefit, for instance if a benefit officer attributes to the regulations a harsher interpretation than was intended, or is unaware of certain entitlements (on the latter, see Berthoud, 1984). Such difficulties cannot entirely be avoided, but there is little evidence of systematic discrimination in the enforcement of rules (e.g. by race) in the award of supplementary benefit.[1]

The second aspect of the focus criterion concerns 'leakages', i.e. the extent to which benefit is withheld from those who do not need it. Viewed narrowly, supplementary benefit scores well in this respect. Once a recipient family has used up its small disregard (section 1), it loses £1 of benefit for every pound of additional net earnings which, in effect, imposes a 100 per cent implicit tax rate on earnings. This focuses benefits very sharply indeed.[2] Figure 10.1 shows in stylised form the combination of leisure and income available to a recipient of supplementary benefit with an initial endowment at b of 24 hours of leisure. The line ab shows his/her earning opportunities.[3] Suppose a scheme is now introduced under which income is not allowed to fall below $0c$. This is shown by the line cde. An individual choosing 24 hours of leisure will receive an income of $0c = be$. If he works, the first £4 (say) of net earnings is disregarded, and spendable income rises above the supplementary benefit level, as shown by the line eg. But once his disregards are exhausted, he loses benefit pound for pound with earnings, and so his spendable income is fixed, as shown by the dashed line fg. This is equivalent to an implicit marginal tax of 100 per cent, in the sense that all extra earnings are 'taxed away' by the loss of benefit: it is impossible for recipients to raise their net disposable income; it also removes all financial incentive to work. Where people work solely to earn money, the budget constraint collapses to the two segments af and ge. No one who works only for money will choose a point on the segment fg (since at point g the individual has the same income as at f, but more leisure). If a person receives £50 in supplementary benefit, which he loses pound for pound with earnings above £4, then fg covers earnings from £4 to at least £54. This strong potential

---

[1] Two qualifications are necessary. First, the rules themselves might be discriminatory (e.g. towards women). Second, it is claimed that some racial discrimination in the award of benefits has occurred (CPAG, 1984). For evidence of systematic racial discrimination in some US cities in awarding benefits under Aid to Families with Dependent Children in the 1960s see Barr and Hall (1975).

[2] Over a limited range of income the rate of withdrawal for single-parent families is 50 per cent – see section 1.

[3] For details of this theoretical apparatus consult any standard microeconomic text, e.g. Laidler (1981, Ch. 5) or Brown (1983a, Chs 1 and 2).

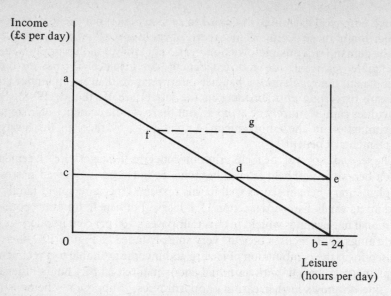

Figure 10.1 *Stylised representation of the budget constraint under supplementary benefit*

labour supply disincentive is the price of focusing benefit sharply on those in need.

The labour supply disincentive is one of the major economic criticisms of supplementary benefit. An individual who works only for money will choose either to be on the segment *af* (i.e. earning enough to be off supplementary benefit), or at a point on the line *ge* (i.e. earning under £4 per week). By its very construction, supplementary benefit almost forces people into one of two extreme categories, of being fully self-sufficient or almost completely dependent on the state, a conjecture supported by US evidence (Barr and Hall, 1981). There is no real provision for people who, though not self-sufficient, are able at least partly to support themselves. Such people are rarely apparent because the system almost forces them into full dependence. The very fact of focusing benefits sharply on those in need brings about one of the worst features of supplementary benefit – its tendency to be strongly divisive between the self-supporting and the dependent. The qualitative direction of the disincentive is clear, but there is controversy about its empirical magnitude, to which we return in section 3.3.

Cost   In 1985 the number of recipients was 4.7 million (and nearly 8 million when account is taken of dependants); in addition, the long-term benefit rate has more or less kept pace with pre-tax average earnings. For both reasons costs have risen sharply over the years; and as the amount handed over to the poor has increased so have administrative costs. When national insurance was introduced in 1948 it was thought that eventually everyone would be self-supporting through work or insurance, and that national assistance (as it was then called) would dwindle. But over time the number of recipients grew, as did the complications. The number of officials required to administer supplementary benefit approximately tripled between 1966 and 1980.[1] It was argued (UK Department of Health and Social Security, 1978a) that a tailor-made service with various extra allowances could no longer be administered effectively. The formal codification of supplementary benefit in 1980 (Chapter 2:6) simplified administration very little. As a result, supplementary benefit disbursements in 1986/7 were £7264 million (Table 7.5), to which must be added administrative costs of around 11.5 per cent of these payments (the comparable figure for the national insurance pension was 1.5 per cent) (UK, 1986a, Table 3.15.18). Are these benefits affordable? The answer must be yes, since they are actually paid. But the possibility of enhancing the scheme is clearly limited.

The scope for improvement is reduced by interactions between the three criteria. First, could benefits be increased? Suppose a family of given size receives £50 per week, which is reduced pound for pound with earnings (disregards are ignored for simplicity). Doubling benefit from £50 to £100 would roughly double the cost of benefits to existing recipients (i.e. by assumption those earning less than £50 per week); but in addition, more people (by assumption those earning between £50 and £100) would become eligible. Another possible improvement would be to reduce the rate at which benefits are withdrawn as earnings rise. This would increase the transfer receipts of families with other income; and it might reduce stigma, inasmuch as means-testing (the main cause of stigma) could be reduced. Unfortunately, the room for manoeuvre in this direction is limited. Returning to the example above, with a 100 per cent implicit tax rate only those earning below £50 are eligible; with a 50 per cent rate anyone earning below £100 is eligible. Halving the tax rate, like doubling the benefit level, raises costs both by increasing benefits to existing recipients and by increasing the number of potential beneficiaries (see Levy (1979) for empirical verification in a US context). The increase in costs associated with either change is accentuated by the shape of Britain's income distribution. The number of people with incomes between 1 and 1½ times the supplementary benefit level is large, correspondingly reducing the scope for increasing benefits.

---

[1] In 1984 the total number of officials at the Department of Health and Social Security was 80,000.

3.2 OTHER INCOME-RELATED BENEFITS

How the Poverty Trap Arises

The poverty trap can arise also for people not in receipt of supplementary benefit, who lose benefit under a variety of other schemes. Someone whose earnings rise by £1 can lose 50 pence of family income supplement, over 15 pence of housing benefit,[1] and possibly also entitlement to free medical prescriptions, etc.; in addition, the earner may have to pay income tax and national insurance contributions. It is argued (Prest, 1970; Piachaud, 1971; Parker, 1982) that when these losses are added up the resulting implicit tax rate can approach, or exceed, 100 per cent.

When discussing the measurement of poverty (Chapter 6:2.3), the three important questions concerned how many people were poor (the 'head count'), by how much they fell below the poverty line (the 'poverty gap'), and for how long they remained there. In the case of the poverty trap, analogously, we need to ask how high are implicit tax rates; how many people do they affect; and for how long do they apply or not apply?

How high are implicit tax rates? The principal elements of the poverty trap are shown in Table 10.2, which refers to 1982. Earnings between £42 and £47 per week were subject in principle to a combined tax/withdrawal rate of around 75 per cent, rising to over 100 per cent for weekly earnings between £47 and £82; earnings above £82 faced a combined rate of over 60 per cent. The ill-effects of such tax rates are twofold. First, low-income families cannot raise their net income. In early 1986 (Dilnot and Stark, 1986, Table 1) four-person families with pre-transfer earnings between £70 and £145 per week all had spendable income, after taxes and benefits, of between £117 and £122 (cf. the range of hours *fg* in Figure 10.1). The second ill-effect is that high tax rates bring about a strong substitution effect against work effort, and so are potentially a major labour supply disincentive.

A complete analysis, however, must take account of several complications. The first is the complexity of the benefit formulae.[2] Table 10.2 is highly simplified. When additional benefits are introduced, implicit tax rates can vary more widely. At the point at which entitlement to free school meals was lost, the tax rate in 1982 could reach nearly 300 per cent, i.e. an extra pound of earnings could cost nearly £3 in taxes and lost benefit (UK, 1983b, p. 201). In addition, the interactions between different benefits in calculating entitlement to each is complex. The structure of implicit tax rates facing any particular

---

[1] These schemes were described briefly in section 1.

[2] See Lynes (1984) for an example of the complications which can arise in calculating entitlement to family income supplement, depending on the time of year the application is made.

Table 10.2: How the Poverty Trap Arises in a Simple Case, April 1982[a]

	Per cent	Per cent
EARNINGS BETWEEN £42 and £47 per week		
Extra national insurance contributions	8.75	
Withdrawal of family income supplement	50	
Loss of rent and rate rebates		
(at higher withdrawal rate)	16.5	
TOTAL THEORETICAL LOSS, £42–£47		75.25
EARNINGS BETWEEN £47 and £80 per week[b]		
Extra income tax	30	
Extra national insurance contributions	8.75	
Withdrawal of family income supplement	50	
Loss of rent and rate rebates		
(at higher withdrawal rate)	16.5	
TOTAL THEORETICAL LOSS, £47–£80		105.25
EARNINGS BETWEEN £80 and £82 per week		
Extra income tax	30	
Extra national insurance contributions	8.75	
Withdrawal of family income supplement	50	
Loss of rent and rate rebates		
(at lower withdrawal rate)	11.5	
TOTAL THEORETICAL LOSS, £80–£82		100.25
EARNINGS BETWEEN £82 and £130 per week[c]		
Extra income tax	30	
Extra national insurance contributions	8.75	
Loss of rent and rate rebates		
(at lower withdrawal rate)	23	
TOTAL THEORETICAL LOSS, £82–£130		61.75

Source: House of Commons, Treasury and Civil Service Committee Sub-Committee, Session 1982–83, *The Structure of Personal Income Taxation and Income Support*, Minutes of Evidence, HC 20-I, pp. 197–8.

Notes: [a]The figures relate to a married couple with two children and with particular rent and rates in April 1982.

[b]Income tax liability in 1982 started at £47 per week.

[c]Entitlement to family income supplement in 1982 ceased at £82 per week.

family will depend both on its size and composition, and on the precise mix of benefits it receives.

This brings us to a second set of complications. Table 10.2 describes a simplified case for a so-called 'typical' family. To assess the impact of the poverty trap, however, we also need to know *how many* families face such rates, i.e. how many families of different sizes and types there are at each income level; which benefits they actually receive (the take-up question); and which margin we are discussing, that for the primary or a secondary earner. The empirical literature is discussed in section 3.3.

Mitigating Factors

The third complication concerns the *length of time* over which people face or do not face these tax rates. Here, fortunately, there are mitigating factors, the most important of which are the existence of fixed-period awards, and the fact that most benefits are uprated annually.

The logic of fixed-period awards   Family income supplement (and hence also the benefits to which it is a 'passport', such as free school meals and free prescriptions) is granted on the basis of five weeks' pay slips, and the award is made for 12 months, during which the authorities need not be informed of any increases in family income. A family which is awarded £20 a week receives a book of 52 vouchers for £20 each, which can be encashed week by week.

The main reason why benefits are awarded for a full year is the administrative convenience of not having to reassess a family each time its income changes. This administrative practice has a substantial impact on implicit tax rates. Any increase in earnings which occurs during an award period does not result in any immediate loss of benefit, and so the marginal tax rate is zero, at least in the short run. And even if an increase in earnings is permanent, so that benefits at some future date are assessed on the basis of a higher income, any loss of benefit which occurs not at the time of the increase in earnings, but only later, is likely at least partly to be discounted, and hence to be less of a disincentive.

Table 10.2 shows that a family earning an extra pound could lose up to £1.05 in benefit. This figure must now be reinterpreted. It is certainly the case that family A will receive £1.05 less in benefit than family B if its earnings are one pound higher. Thus the high implicit tax rates apply cross-sectionally. Our interest, however, is the impact on family A's benefits of an increase in its earnings. This is a time-series question, and from this perspective the poverty trap is mitigated in two ways: because of fixed-period awards an increase in earnings may cause no loss of benefit, at least in the short run; in addition, benefits will generally have been uprated by the end of the award period, taking much of the sting out of reassessment. The moral of the story is the important economic impact of administrative practice.

Formal analysis   The effect of fixed-period awards in reducing the perceived tax effect of the withdrawal of benefits is of sufficient importance to merit more formal analysis (non-technical readers can skip the equations). Consider the value of an income stream of £1 per year subject to a tax rate, t. In perpetuity this is worth[1]

$$P = \int_0^\infty (1-t)e^{-rv}dv = \frac{1-t}{r} \tag{10.1}$$

where $v = $ time, and r can be interpreted either as the rate of interest or as a marginal rate of time preference (both interpretations will be discussed).

If no tax is imposed until the end of the current award period (here till the end of year 1), then the present value of the income stream is P (from equation (10.1)) *plus* the value of the first year's tax remission, t.

$$P' = P + t = \frac{1-t+rt}{r} = \frac{1-t(1-r)}{r} \tag{10.2}$$

Comparing equation (10.2) with (10.1) shows that the effect of not levying any tax for the first year is to 'write down' the effect of the tax by a factor $(1-r)$, i.e. the effective burden of the tax is only $(1-r)$ times the nominal burden. Interpreted as a rate of interest, the tax not paid in the first year (£t) can be invested to yield £rt in each successive year, to pay part of each year's tax bill. Interpreted as a rate of time preference, the more heavily the future is discounted, the lower is the perceived burden of the tax.

Equation (10.2) applies strictly only when tax is unpaid for a full year. More generally, suppose that earnings increase when a fraction k, $0 < k \leqslant 1$, of the year has already passed. Then only £$(1-k)$ is earned during the current award period, and the present value of the income stream if fully taxed is

$$P_k = \int_k^\infty (1-t)e^{-rv}dv = \frac{1-t}{r}e^{-rk} \tag{10.3}$$

But if no tax is levied till the end of the first period then the present value of the income stream is P_k *plus* the value of the first year's tax remission:

---

[1] Since for any constant, A

$$\int_0^\infty Ae^{-rv}dv = -\frac{A}{r}\left[e^{-rv}\right]_0^\infty = \frac{A}{r}$$

$$P'_k = P_k + \int_k^1 te^{-rv}\, dv \tag{10.4}$$

Evaluating and simplifying

$$P'_k = \frac{e^{-rk}}{r} - \frac{te^{-r}}{r} \tag{10.5}$$

The first term is the present value of an untaxed unit increase in income starting a fraction, k, through the first period; the smaller is k the larger the value of the pay increase. The second term is the perceived present value of the tax burden where the tax is imposed only after the end of the first period, and is lower the higher is r. Thus the higher the individual's marginal rate of time preference the greater the tendency for the loss of future benefits to be discounted.

Major implications Fixed-period awards can have profound policy implications. They enable the poor to raise their net income more easily, since benefit need not be lost at the time earnings rise. To that extent the tendency for families to be trapped in poverty is less acute than the traditional view suggests. Second, labour supply incentives may be improved. Temporary changes in earnings (e.g. overtime at Christmas) will not affect benefits; and even where increases are expected to persist, the tax rate relevant to labour supply decisions is that *perceived* by recipients which, from equations (10.2) and (10.5), will depend on their time preference. This is almost certainly high, both because their income is low and because any increase in earnings may only be temporary. A poor worker is unlikely to reject an opportunity to increase his earnings because it might cost him benefit six months later.

There is little systematic evidence on rates of time preference, but it is possible to make inferences. In Canada it normally takes about two months to process a claim for a tax refund. In order to get the money immediately, some people (before the practice was made illegal) would sell their title to a refund for between 30 and 70 per cent of its face value (Community Income Tax Service, 1976). The sale of a title to \$100 in two months time for \$70 now implies a marginal rate of time preference of 600 per cent per year. From the second term in equation (10.5), $r = 6$ implies

$$t\frac{e^{-r}}{r} = 0.0004t$$

– in other words the perceived tax burden is almost zero. Even with less extreme cases the tax burden is reduced to under 40 per cent of its nominal value when $r = 100$ per cent, and to under 7 per cent when $r = 200$ per cent. If such rates of time preference are general, the tax effects of benefits withdrawn only some months after earnings have increased are likely to be heavily discounted, thereby considerably reducing disincentives.

In addition to their beneficial impact on (a) family poverty and (b) labour supply, fixed-period awards have two further advantages. If taxes are fully discounted, the withdrawal of benefits as income rises is analytically equivalent to a lump-sum tax collected at some time in the future, with all the welfare properties of lump-sum taxation. Second, fixed-period awards ameliorate the dilemma faced by public policy between the desire to preserve incentives by keeping tax rates low, and the need to reduce costs by focusing benefits sharply on those in need (hence withdrawing benefits rapidly as income rises). Fixed-period awards cushion the impact of high rates of withdrawal, whilst avoiding the huge expenditure which would be involved in substantially reducing them. Incentives are thus partly preserved, and the trade-off between cost and incentives rendered less acute.

3.3 EMPIRICAL ISSUES AND EVIDENCE

The empirical literature on non-contributory benefits is surveyed by Danziger, Haveman and Plotnick (1981) and Atkinson (1986, section 5). Two issues predominate: their effectiveness in relieving poverty, and their incentive effects.

The Effectiveness of Non-contributory Benefits in Relieving Poverty

The level of benefits   The question here is whether benefits are sufficiently high to relieve poverty (assuming, initially, that people claim all the benefits to which they are entitled). For Britain, at least until 1980, the answer must be a qualified yes. Two points are noteworthy about the supplementary benefit scale rate: it is set at 100 per cent of a notional poverty line, rather than some fraction; and between 1948 and 1980 it retained its relativity to pre-tax average earnings, and hence rose relative to post-tax earnings (Barr, 1981). As a result Beckerman (1979) found that cash benefits reduced the number of people below the supplementary benefit poverty line from 22.7 per cent of the population before all transfers to 3.3 per cent, and reduced the income gap (i.e. the aggregate shortfall of incomes below the poverty line) from £5.9 billion per year to £0.25 billion.[1] Though no quantitative evidence is yet available it seems likely that the position deteriorated in the 1980s.

The American record is less impressive. Danziger, Haveman and Plotnick

---

[1] The concepts and problems involved in defining a poverty line and measuring the extent of poverty are discussed in Chapter 6:2.

(1984) show that in 1983 cash benefits reduced the poverty count (as defined by the official poverty line) from 24 per cent of the population pre-transfer to 15.2 per cent, and to between 10 and 13 per cent if transfers in kind are included. This is partly because there is no automatic relation between the official US poverty line (which is federal) and benefit levels (which are usually set by states).

Living standards in utility terms depend not only on cash benefits, but also on the extent of stigma. Empirical studies are inconclusive mainly because stigma is not the only influence on take-up (another crucial variable being the extent to which claimants are aware of their potential entitlement). Serious statistical problems arise in attempting to separate two influences so different and so hard to measure (see Warlick, 1981; Moffitt, 1983; Duncan, 1984).

The focus of benefits First, do benefits go to those who need them? This boils down mainly to take-up. The best recent estimates for supplementary benefit (Atkinson, 1984a and 1987, Ch. 10) are that over the period 1973–81 24–35 per cent of families over pensionable age were non-claimants.[1] For families of working age the corresponding range was 21–30 per cent. Take-up is generally higher among those entitled to greater benefits (*ibid.*); in 1981 about 85 per cent of supplementary benefit was claimed relative to estimated expenditure with (hypothetical) full take-up. For family income supplement the consensus about take-up is 45–55 per cent of potentially eligible families, nowhere near the initial target of 85 per cent.

In the USA, take-up of the main income-tested benefit, Aid to Families with Dependent Children, though low in the late 1960s (see the official study by Projector and Murray, 1978), increased considerably, largely because of positive action by administrators and rights workers. It is estimated that by 1977 take-up of the basic scheme was 94 per cent, and of the unemployed-parent scheme 72 per cent.

Drawing the threads together, cash benefits may fail to relieve poverty for three sets of reasons: (a) the absolute level of benefits may be too low; (b) coverage may be inadequate for certain groups, in the sense that they are poor but not eligible for benefit; and (c) take-up may be incomplete either (on the demand side) because of ignorance about entitlement, or stigma or (on the supply side) out of maladministration and/or discrimination. In Britain (b) applies in the case of working families (Abel-Smith and Townsend, 1965) and some single-parent families, and (c) applies particularly to the elderly. In the US problems arise under all three heads.

---

[1] See also Berthoud (1984) on problems with take-up; and for problems during a cold winter, 'Heating Aid Fails Nine Pensioners out of Ten', *Sunday Times*, 2 March 1986, p. 4.

The second aspect of focus is the extent to which benefits are restricted to the poor. This raises two questions: how high are implicit tax rates, and how many people face them? The complexity of these issues was stressed in section 3.2; and further complications arise where tax rates are determined by the actual operation of the system, which may differ substantially from the scheme on paper. Barr and Hall (1975) found that in 1967 in almost all major US cities the measurement of income by welfare caseworkers reduced the implicit tax rates embodied in Aid to Families with Dependent Children considerably below the 100 per cent rate specified in the regulations. In the UK Deacon and Bradshaw (1983) estimate that in the early 1980s up to 12 million people received at least one income-tested benefit. Of these, according to government figures (based on work by Atkinson which investigated a large sample of individual families), about 600,000 tax units in 1980 faced marginal tax rates of over 50 per cent, of whom 120,000 faced marginal rates of 70 per cent and over (UK, 1983a, Table 15 – see also Chapter 11:3.2).

Where implicit tax rates, as imposed by the *de facto* operation of benefit systems, are high and are faced by substantial numbers the problem of the poverty trap with its inequities and disincentives becomes important. Where tax rates are low, the issue arises of benefits paid to those who do not 'need' them. This is Beckerman's concept of 'target efficiency', estimated more recently by Dilnot, Kay and Morris (1984, Table 2.4). Their conclusion, that 100 per cent of supplementary benefit expenditure in 1981 went to those below the poverty line, is almost tautologous given that (a) poverty is defined in terms of the supplementary benefit level, and (b) supplementary benefit incorporates a 100 per cent withdrawal rate. For family income supplement and rent and rate rebates the corresponding figure was 35.5 per cent, i.e. 62.5 per cent of these benefits went to families with pre-transfer incomes *above* the supplementary benefit level, or were payments in excess of those necessary to bring incomes to that level. For cash benefits as a whole, 54 per cent of disbursements went to 'poor' families, i.e. to those whose post-transfer income did not exceed the poverty line.

It is not clear how these figures should be interpreted. Dilnot *et al.* take them to imply that the system is 'wasteful' in that benefits 'leak out' to the non-poor. But to the extent that the harsher aspects of the poverty trap are thereby alleviated, the leakages may have benefits in incentive as well as in equity terms (it being remembered that recipients with incomes just above the supplementary benefit level can hardly be regarded as comfortably off).

Finally, in assessing the effectiveness of income transfers in relieving poverty, we should remind ourselves of major and unavoidable methodological questions. First, there are the many problems in defining the poverty line, the unit of receipt, and the distribution of income within that unit (Chapter 6:2.1).

Second, is the value placed by recipients on the transfers: the value of cash benefits may be reduced by stigma, and that placed on in-kind transfers may be less than their market price (though see Chapter 4:4.2). Third, and possibly of greatest intractability, is the incidence of the transfers (Chapter 7:4.1). Calculations assume (because no other procedure is practicable) that a family's pre-transfer income is that which it would have been in the absence of any system of income support. This is, to say the least, a strong assumption. Similarly, it is assumed that benefits paid to those in work, including family income supplement and child benefit, have no effect on wage rates.

Incentive Effects

When turning to the incentive effects of cash transfers the waters are, if anything, even murkier. The incentive effects of unemployment benefits (Chapter 8:3.1) and pensions (Chapter 9:5.1) are closely linked with the present discussion, which is consequently brief. In the context of income-related benefits the main empirical questions are: what are their labour supply effects, and what are their effects on family formation?

Labour supply   A heroic study (Wolfe *et al.*, 1984, Table 6) concludes that in the US in 1981 a 10 per cent increase in income-related transfers would have reduced hours worked by recipients by 3½–4 per cent; for insurance-type transfers the comparable figure was about 2 per cent. Barr and Hall (1981) in a study of Aid to Families with Dependent Children in 1967, though not an explicit study of labour supply, found that recipients responded rationally to the budget constraint they faced, suggesting a negative relationship between benefit levels and labour supply. Levy (1979) shows that attempts to improve labour supply incentives may be successful for existing recipients in the US; but labour supply overall may fall because benefits (being now more attractive) induce non-recipients to decrease their work effort and join the programme. This is precisely the reason (section 3.1) why lowering the tax rate implicit in supplementary benefit is likely to be costly. All such conclusions, however (and particularly numerical estimates of labour supply elasticities) should be read alongside the caveats in Chapter 8:3.1 about the empirical literature on unemployment benefits.

Effects on family formation   Income support may affect family formation in various ways. Research has concentrated on the US welfare system, and the extent to which it gives families an incentive to split up. In particular, it has been argued that the sharp rise in the number of black female-headed households after 1960 was causally related to the increase in real benefits under Aid to Families with Dependent Children. Various studies, both time-series and cross-section, have investigated the question but, as with stigma, conclusions vary widely. Honig (1974) (see also Minarik and Goldfarb, 1976, and Honig, 1976) using 1960 data found a positive relationship between benefit levels and the proportion of female-headed families, with a stronger effect for non-white families. Barr and Hall (1981), using 1967 data, found that race exerted no independent effect on welfare dependency (though this does not rule out the possibility that black and white family formation were equally affected by increasing benefit levels). Yet other studies have failed to find any significant effects. The literature is surveyed by Atkinson (1986, section 5.5).

3.4 CONCLUSION

Britain's income distribution, like that in almost all industrialised countries, is heavily skewed towards lower incomes. We want to support the poor (the level criterion), but the income distribution makes it inevitable that benefits must be withdrawn fairly rapidly if limited resources (the cost criterion) are to be focused on the most needy. This focus can be achieved in various ways: benefit can be withdrawn as family income rises, either immediately (supplementary benefit) or eventually (family income supplement); or it can be removed when an individual's status changes (e.g. the loss of unemployment benefit upon resumption of work, or loss of child benefit when a child reaches the age of 16). Whatever the method, a poverty trap in one form or another is largely inevitable, an observation which brings us naturally to Chapter 11.

Further Reading

The most comprehensive (and up-to-date) summaries of the institutions of non-contributory benefits are published annually by Tolley (1986) (which includes references to legislation) and CPAG (1986a, b). Further detail and analysis of supplementary benefits is given in Lynes (1981). A number of reform proposals are set out in UK (1985k).

For comment and criticism see Meade (1978, Ch. 5), Atkinson (1983, Ch. 11), UK (1983a) and Dilnot, Kay and Morris (1984, Ch. 2). The construction and operation of housing benefit is assessed by Hemming and Hills (1983), Hemming (1984, Ch. 7), Kemp (1984) and Glennerster (1985, Ch. 11); for an official view see UK (1985g).

The empirical literature on the incentive effects of income support schemes, and on their effectiveness in alleviating poverty is vast. Two excellent and compendious surveys are Danziger, Haveman and Plotnick (1981) and Atkinson (1986, especially section 5) (see also Atkinson, 1987, Chs 10–12). On redistributive effects see the Further Reading at the end of Chapter 7.

11

Strategies for Reform

If a free society cannot help the many who are poor, it cannot save the few who are rich. [John F. Kennedy, 1961.]

1 Approaches to Income Support

The last three chapters discussed the cash side of the welfare state in some detail. This chapter considers more generally the pros and cons of different forms of income support; it is not a discussion of specific reform proposals (UK, 1985k; UK, 1986b), but of different *strategies*. The starting-point is how most usefully to identify the poor. Two approaches stand out. Benefits can be conditioned on *income* (i.e. means-tested), the archetypal example being the sort of negative income tax discussed in section 2. Alternatively, they can be conditioned on the *characteristics* of recipients through categorical schemes which award benefits on the basis, for example, of being unemployed, sick or retired. This is the so-called 'Back to Beveridge' strategy, discussed in section 3. Section 4 considers mixed strategies. Section 5 summarises the major conclusions to emerge from Chapters 8 to 11.

The distinction between categorical and non-categorical schemes is important. The former stress the *causes* of poverty, and institute programmes for specific groups. Historically, it was thought that most people would be self-supporting through work, or through insurance against income loss due to unemployment, sickness or old age; and that the few who fell outside these groups could be categorised into the disabled, the blind, etc. Underlying this

256

approach is the distinction between the 'deserving' poor (e.g. widows with young children) and the 'undeserving'. Such thinking lay behind the Poor Law, and permeated much of the 1930s New Deal legislation in the USA. The Beveridge Report, though liberal in its attitude, distinguished eight 'reasonable' causes of poverty (UK, 1942, pp. 124–5).

Non-categorical schemes, in contrast, regard recipients as belonging to a spectrum which includes the self-supporting, the very poor and a large number in between. Such schemes concentrate on outcome rather than cause, and classification is made only in terms of need. The approach is attractive because there are few gaps through which 'difficult' cases can fall, but has the disadvantage of requiring a means test in one form or another.

A common thread throughout the chapter is that there are no easy solutions to poverty in countries with relatively large numbers of people with low incomes. This is not an argument against increased redistribution, but a warning that it will not be brought about without an awareness of the difficulties involved. Advocates of redistribution serve their cause ill by espousing simplistic and infeasible solutions.

2 The Negative Income Tax Approach

2.1 THE IDEA

Negative income taxation is the archetype of cash support conditioned on an income test. This section discusses the way such schemes work, and considers briefly a British proposal which came close to implementation in the mid-1970s. Section 2.2 discusses large-scale negative income taxation, and section 2.3 a possible role for a small-scale scheme as part of a package of wider reform.

The principle is easily outlined in terms of the UK income tax system, shown in simplified form in Figure 11.1A by the line OBA: individual income is tax free up to $£B$; thereafter it is taxed at t per cent. Suppose that $B = £2000$ and $t = 35$ per cent. The simplest negative income tax is shown by the line G_0BA: if an individual's income is above £2000 he pays tax of 35 per cent of the excess over £2000; if it is below £2000 he *receives* 35 per cent of the shortfall below £2000. Someone with an income of £2500 pays 35 per cent of £500, i.e. £175, while an individual with an income of £1500 receives £175. More generally, it is possible to have a different tax rate above and below the break-even income (shown by the line G_1BA), and a higher breakeven for larger families.

Formally, the simplest negative income tax relates the individual's tax bill, T, (positive or negative) to his income, Y, as

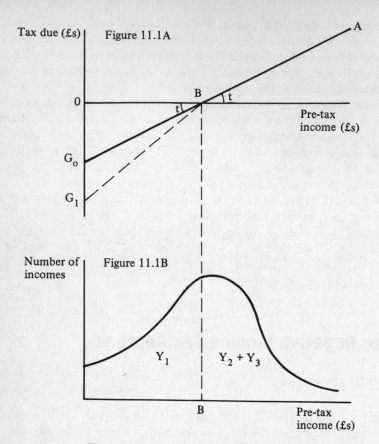

Figure 11.1   *The cost of negative income tax*

$$T = t(Y - B) \qquad (11.1)$$

where t is the tax rate applied above and below the break-even income, B, as shown by the line G_0BA. It is often more useful to think of the system in a different way: an individual with zero income receives 35 per cent of the amount by which his income falls below £2000, i.e. £700; from equation (11.1) it is entirely equivalent to give *everyone* a transfer of £700, and to tax *all* other income at 35 per cent. Thus

$$T = tY - G \qquad (11.2)$$

where $G = tB$ is a lump-sum transfer to the individual, who then pays tax at a rate, t, on all his other income, Y. Similarly, an individual could be given a larger transfer, say G_1 in Figure 11.1A, and taxed at 50 per cent on the first £B of his income and 35 per cent thereafter. A scheme which gives everyone a lump sum, and taxes all other income goes under the generic name of a *social dividend scheme*. Equations (11.1) and (11.2) show that social dividend schemes and negative income taxes are exactly equivalent. Such arrangements have been given various names, like minimum income guarantee, reverse income tax, and guaranteed income schemes. Analytically they are identical. All are completely identified by two features: the size of the transfer, G, to an individual with no income, and the tax structure applied to any other income.

The tax credit scheme of the early 1970s (discussed in section 2.3) is an example of the social dividend approach.[1] It proposed weekly tax credits (at 1972 prices) of £4 per single person, £6 per couple and £2 per child; all other income was to be taxed at 30 per cent (with higher rates for the highest incomes). For people with low earnings the tax credit was greater than their tax liability, thus raising take-home pay above gross pay. Certain groups were excluded, notably the self-employed and people below the poverty line, the latter because they almost certainly already received some sort of income support, thereby (it was argued) complicating the administration of cash assistance if they received some of their income as tax-credit and the rest (e.g.) as supplementary benefit.

2.2 AN ASSESSMENT OF LARGE-SCALE NEGATIVE INCOME TAX SCHEMES

Negative income tax schemes have attracted widespread support (see the Further Reading): from libertarians because cash transfers are compatible with market allocation, and so can loosen what they see as the stranglehold of in-kind transfers under the welfare state; and from socialists because the scheme guarantees everyone at least a minimum income as a right of citizenship and without a means test. Additionally, it is claimed that negative income tax will boost take-up, reduce stigma and, by bringing all individuals under a single umbrella, enable government to be better informed about the economic condition of the population. Possibly the most important claims are that negative income tax can solve two major problems – the poverty trap, and the failure of the welfare state substantially to redistribute income.

Why then, despite such widespread support, has no country adopted a large-scale scheme? The short answer, for a nation with an income distribution like Britain's, is its cost; this implies a large increase in tax rates, which aggravates the poverty trap and/or creates labour supply disincentives.

---

[1] For the proposals see UK (1972a), for various assessments UK (1973), Prest (1973), Barr and Roper (1974) and for a counter-view Atkinson (1973).

Issues of Cost

A useful starting-point is the distinction between a small-scale scheme, which offers a low guaranteed income like G_0 in Figure 11.1A, and a large-scale scheme giving a higher transfer like G_1. Under the first, the cost is not large, and no high tax rates are necessary; but the guaranteed income is low, so no substantial help is given to the poor, and the need for additional benefits remains. If negative income tax is the sole anti-poverty device it is necessary to have a high guaranteed income like G_1; this raises problems of cost, as illustrated in Figure 11.1. The intercept, G_0, and slope, t, of negative income tax completely characterise the position of an individual or family. But the cost of the scheme and its redistributive strength depend *both* on the tax/benefit function *and* on the size distribution of income. The society shown in Figure 11.1B contains many poor people with income less than B, and relatively few rich people; consequently, the cost of the scheme shown in Figure 11.1A will be higher because of the larger number of net beneficiaries relative to net contributors, than in a richer country (i.e. one in which the left-hand tail, Y_1, is smaller).

The logic of the cost issue　Estimates for 1972 (Barr 1973 and 1975b) suggest that a scheme which paid a universal transfer at the supplementary benefit level would require close to a threefold increase in the average burden of income tax from 20 per cent of personal income to 50–60 per cent. Atkinson (1983, p. 275) illustrates the point: if the guaranteed income for an average family is x per cent of average income, and if income tax currently raises y per cent of average income for purposes other than income support, then the average income tax rate must be $x+y$. With plausible values for x and y (Atkinson suggests 35 per cent and 15 per cent), the *average* rate of *income* tax (i.e. ignoring all indirect taxes, etc.) is at least 50 per cent.

Why are large-scale schemes so costly? The intuitive answer is that 'ordinary' income tax has to raise revenue to finance benefits *only* (or largely) for poor people, whereas negative income tax pays benefit to *everyone*. The resulting increase in taxation can be viewed in two ways: either because higher gross benefit payments require higher taxation, or because higher taxes are necessary to claw back benefits paid to rich people. The effect of universal benefits is to raise at least some marginal tax rates, even if the average tax rate (inclusive of benefits) is unchanged.

It is necessary, however, to dig deeper. Consider the society shown in Table 11.1 with five poor individuals (assumed to have no income) and ten rich people (whose income is £10,000 per year) as shown in lines (1) and (2). The tax base (i.e. pre-transfer personal income) is £100,000 (line (3)), and the tax threshold £4000 under income tax and £0 under negative income tax (line (4)). The poverty line, by assumption, is £4000 per year (line (5)). Under 'ordinary'

Table 11.1: Hypothetical Effect of Negative Income Tax on Tax Rates[a]

	'ORDINARY' INCOME TAX AND BENEFITS		NEGATIVE INCOME TAX	
	Poor Individual (1)	Rich Individual (2)	Poor Individual (3)	Rich Individual (4)
ASSUMPTIONS				
(1) Number of individuals	5	10	5	10
(2) Pre-transfer income of each individual (per year)	0	£10,000	0	£10,000
(3) Tax base (= total pre-transfer personal income)	10 × £10,000 = £100,000	10 × £10,000 = £100,000	10 × £10,000 = £100,000	10 × £10,000 = £100,000
(4) Tax threshold	£4000	£4000	£0	£0
(5) Poverty line (per year)	£4000	£4000	£4000	£4000
(6a) Cash transfer to each *poor* individual under income tax	£4000	0		
(6b) Guaranteed income to *all* individuals under negative income tax			£4000	£4000
IMPLICATIONS				
(7) Total cost of income support (line (1) × line (6))	5 × £4000 = £20,000		15 × £4000 = £60,000	
(8) Total taxable income (from lines (3) and (4))	10 × (£10,000−£4000)=£60,000		10 × £10,000 = £100,000	
(9) Tax rate on taxable income (from lines (7) and (8))	£20,000/£60,000 = 33⅓%		£60,000/£100,000 = 60%	
(10) Post-transfer income	£4000	£4000+(1−⅓)£6000 = £8000	£4000	£4000+(1−.6)£10,000 = £8000
(11) Average tax rate on personal income (from lines (7) and (3))	£20,000/£100,000 = 20%		£60,000/£100,000 = 60%	

Note: [a] Assumptions:
1) Taxation levied only to finance cash transfers.
2) No transactions costs.

income tax (columns (1) and (2)), £4000 is transferred to each of the five poor individuals in the form of 'welfare' benefits; rich individuals receive no transfer (line (6a)). The total cost of the scheme is £20,000 (line (7)), requiring a tax rate on income above the threshold of 33⅓ per cent (lines (8) and (9))); post-transfer incomes of poor and rich are £4000 and £8000, respectively (line (10)). Under an otherwise identical negative income tax (columns (3) and (4)), both poor *and* rich receive a transfer of £4000 (line (6b)). The cost of the scheme is £60,000, requiring a tax rate on all income of 60 per cent (lines (7)–(9)). Post-transfer incomes of rich and poor are identical to the income tax case: poor individuals have £4000; rich individuals each receive £4000 but have to pay £6000 in tax, leaving a net income of £8000. The introduction of a negative income tax with a uniform tax rate has had no effect on post-transfer incomes but, by tripling the cost of income support, has tripled the average tax rate (line 11) to ensure that rich individuals still pay £2000 net tax despite receiving an initial transfer of £4000.

However, Table 11.1 to some extent hides the fact that negative income tax may not increase taxation *per se*, so much as *replace implicit by explicit taxation* (see the Glossary on implicit tax rates). There are two cases. In the first, both the level of benefits and their coverage remain unchanged under negative income tax, as in Table 11.1. Identical recipients receive identical benefits; total net expenditure is unchanged; no increase in net revenue is necessary; and nobody's post-transfer income has changed. Negative income tax has produced an exact mimic of the previous system by a different administrative mechanism: nothing has been done to relieve poverty; and the poverty trap and labour supply disincentives are unchanged. The only difference is that in Table 11.1 someone whose income rises from £0 to £10,000 under income tax will (a) lose £4000 via implicit taxation, and (b) pay an additional £2000 in explicit income tax; under negative income tax he pays £6000 in explicit tax. The only effect of negative income tax in this case is to make *all* withdrawal of benefit part of *explicit* taxation. From one perspective this is more a difference of form than of substance; from another it forecloses the possibility of minimising incentive effects through devices like fixed period awards (Chapter 10:3.2), or the conditioning of benefits not on income but, for example, on health or employment status.

A second, and very different, case arises where net benefits and/or coverage are increased by negative income tax. This raises the net income of at least some poor people; but net expenditure rises, necessitating an increase in taxation over and above the replacement of implicit by explicit taxation.

The logic of what is happening is seen most easily in terms of two hypothetical states of the world, in which benefits are paid *only* to the poor (state A), or are paid to *everyone* (state B). Then:

(1) *Total tax revenue*: gross expenditure, and hence on a revenue-neutral basis also gross tax revenues, must be higher in state B than state A.

(2) *Average tax rate* (ATR): if tax revenues are greater in state B then ATR must be higher.

(3) *Marginal tax rates* (MTR): if ATR is higher, then MTR must be higher for at least some groups. There are two polar cases: *either* the increase in MTR is concentrated wholly on the poor, in which case (a) the poverty trap is institutionalised and (b) there is a potential labour supply problem for the poor; *or* the increase in MTR is concentrated wholly on the rich, in which case (a) the poverty trap is in principle 'solved', but (b) there is a potential labour supply problem for the rich.

Thus negative income tax inevitably raises explicit tax rates.

Formal analysis The cost of any scheme is the tax/benefit function in Figure 11.1A weighted by the income distribution in Figure 11.1B (non-technical readers can skip the equations). Thus:

$$C = AG - \int_0^\infty t(Y)D(Y)dY \tag{11.3}$$

where: G = the guaranteed income per individual/ family
   A = the total number of individuals/families
   Y = personal income
   $t(Y)$ is the tax function (given in Figure 11.1A by the tax parameter, t), and
   $D(Y)$ is the distribution of pre-tax income (given in Figure 11.1B).

Any issue of cost boils down to an empirical question about the elements of equation (11.3). For a given population, A; transfer, G, and tax function, $t(Y)$, the cost of the scheme and its redistributive strength depend on the size distribution of pre-tax personal income $D(Y)$, and in particular on the relative size of the left-hand tail of Figure 11.1B.

Within this framework it is possible (see Darr, 1975b) to estimate the cost of different tax regimes – 'ordinary' income tax and two variants of negative income tax. Each of the systems comprises two elements – gross expenditure and gross revenue. For income tax gross expenditure consists of total spending on cash benefits, S, and all remaining expenditure, R, out of income tax revenue. R, in other words, is the required surplus of income tax over expenditure on cash benefits. Under a large-scale negative income tax, S is omitted (since all existing cash benefits are, by assumption, abolished), and gross expenditure consists of R and the cost of the guaranteed income payments, AG in equation (11.3). On the revenue side, total personal income, Y, is split into three components: Y_1 is the income of 'poor' individuals/

families with pre-transfer income below the tax threshold (i.e. the left-hand tail of Figure 11.1B); Y_2 is income below the tax threshold of families whose total income exceeds the tax threshold (equivalent to the personal allowances under income tax); and Y_3 is income above the tax threshold. Formally,

$$Y_1 = \int_0^B D(Y)dY$$

$$Y_2 + Y_3 = \int_B^\infty D(Y)dY \tag{11.4}$$

where B is the income tax threshold. Attention is focused on a very simple form of the tax function, $t(Y)$ in equation (11.3), with tax rates t_1 and t_2 applying, respectively, to income above and below the tax threshold.

Income tax is shown by the line $0BA$ in Figure 11.2. Gross expenditure consists of cash benefits, S, plus the required surplus, R. On the revenue side, income below the tax threshold, $Y_1 + Y_2$, is not taxed (i.e. $t_1 = 0$); income above the threshold, Y_3, is taxed at the basic rate of income tax (including national insurance contributions), $\bar{t}$. Thus a simplified version of income tax is

$$C_1 = S + R - \bar{t}Y_3 \tag{11.5}$$

where, by definition, $C_1 = 0$.

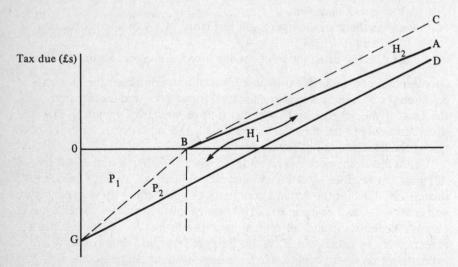

Figure 11.2   *The redistributive effects of negative income tax*

Dual-rate negative income tax consists on the expenditure side of the gross cost of the guaranteed income, AG (replacing existing cash benefits, S), and the required surplus, R. On the revenue side, taxes are levied at rates t_1 and t_2 on the relevant parts of the tax base, as shown by the line GBC in Figure 11.2. Dual-rate negative income tax is constructed so as to keep benefits in the hands of the poor by ensuring that all benefits are taxed away by the time the tax threshold, B, is reached. A benefit of £40 and a threshold of £50 implies that $t_1 = 40/50 = 0.8$, i.e. the restriction

$$t_1 = \frac{G}{B} \qquad (11.6)$$

and the cost of the system is

$$C_2 = AG + R - \frac{G}{B}(Y_1 + Y_2) - t_2 Y_3 \qquad (11.7)$$

Compared with income tax, the poor gain an amount related to the area P_1 in Figure 11.2.[1] Since all benefits are taxed away by the time the tax threshold is reached, the rich are invariant between the two systems if the tax rate on income above the threshold remains unchanged. But, as drawn, the dual-rate scheme imposes a higher rate than income tax above the tax threshold (i.e. BC has a steeper slope than BA), so the rich lose an amount related to the area H_2. Benefits remain in the hands of the poor.

Single-rate negative income tax is a special case where the same tax rate is levied on all income. Thus $t_1 = t_2$, and from equation (11.7)

$$C_3 = AG + R - t_2 Y \qquad (11.8)$$

where by definition (from Figure 11.1B and equation (11.4))

$$Y = \int_0^\infty D(Y)dY = Y_1 + Y_2 + Y_3 \qquad (11.9)$$

If the constraint of revenue neutrality is relaxed, this system is illustrated by the line GD in Figure 11.2. Income below the tax threshold is now taxed at the lower rate, t_2, so in comparison with income tax the poor gain an amount related to the area $P_1 + P_2$. As drawn, the rich gain H_1.[2] In this scheme, therefore, some benefit spills over to the rich, a result which remains true even if the single tax rate is chosen to ensure revenue neutrality.

A final and important point is the relation between the tax rate t under the single-rate scheme and the dual rates t_1 and t_2, on the assumption that the schemes cost the same. From equations (11.7), (11.8) and (11.9) the tax yields under the two schemes are equal if

$$tY = t_1(Y_1 + Y_2) + t_2 Y_3 \qquad (11.10)$$

---

[1] Understood as weighted by the appropriate section of the income distribution.
[2] Again weighted by the appropriate section of the income distribution.

Hence the relation between the single and dual rates is given by

$$t = \theta t_1 + (1 - \theta) t_2 \tag{11.11}$$

where

$$\theta = \frac{Y_1 + Y_2}{Y} \tag{11.12}$$

Two important implications follow from equation (11.11). First, t can be thought of as the marginal rate applied to all income; *or* as a weighted average of the dual rates; *or*, more generally, as the average of any set of marginal rates with the same tax yield. Second, if t_1 is higher than t_2 (which is likely if the poverty trap is a problem) then t is higher the larger is θ, i.e. the smaller is Y_3 as a proportion of total income.

Major implications The foregoing apparatus demonstrates some earlier results more precisely. Equation (11.6) shows that under the dual-rate scheme the tax rate, t_1, on low income rises *pari passu* with the level of benefits. Thus negative income tax recreates the poverty trap in another form. The first conclusion, therefore, is that *with the dual-rate scheme (which keeps all benefits in the hands of the poor) the more successfully poverty is alleviated the more serious becomes the problem of the poverty trap*. The situation is no different from that under the present system of cash benefits.

The solution to the poverty trap is to withdraw benefits more slowly, in which case the break-even income rises above the tax threshold. This is the case under the single-rate scheme, which lowers the marginal tax rate on the poor. But from equation (11.7) if the poor pay lower taxes on Y_1 then the rich pay lower taxes on Y_2. It follows, on an equi-cost basis, that more revenue will have to be collected from Y_3. Thus, for a given guaranteed income, *the poverty trap can be alleviated only by increased taxation of the rich*. This, as we shall see, can cause labour supply problems.

The last result is emphasised by equation (11.11), which shows that the average tax rate t (whether thought of as a single rate of tax applied to all income, or as the weighted average of a set of marginal rates) will be higher the smaller is Y_3 as a proportion of the tax base. This gives rise to a fundamental (but often overlooked) conclusion – that for a given level of benefit *it is the shape of the income distribution which 'creates' the poverty trap – changing the system of cash transfers will not solve the problem so long as benefits are conditioned on income*.

Negative income tax thus increases tax rates at some or all levels of income: it institutionalises the poverty trap and/or leads to higher tax rates on incomes above the poverty line. The only offsetting advantage is that the high tax rates on low income are at least systematic, in contrast with the often arbitrary pattern of the current system. In a country with Britain's income distribution the level of benefits and their cost can be reconciled only by the imposition of punitive taxation. This raises two consequential problems: the focus of benefits, as we shall see shortly, is far from sharp despite the presence of high tax rates, and there is potentially a serious labour supply problem.

Consequential Issues

Labour supply It is possible to draw on two sets of evidence. Econometric studies (e.g. Hall, 1973; Pencavel, 1984) broadly confirm the conclusions of attitude surveys (Break, 1957a, b; Brown and Levin, 1974) that the labour supply of primary workers is wage inelastic. This might be taken to suggest that the introduction of a negative income tax would have no substantial effect on work effort, but several major caveats are necessary. First, labour supply estimates, being based on actual data, are derived for the most part from tax rates between 25 and 40 per cent; their conclusions are therefore valid only for tax rates within this range. The pitfalls of making predictions far outside the range of data on which estimates are based are well known. Second, it was found by Hall and others in the USA, and confirmed for the UK (Greenhalgh, 1977) that the supply elasticity of secondary workers (married women, teenagers, people past retiring age) can be substantial. Finally, there is the effect of perceptions on behaviour. The withdrawal of means-tested benefits as income rises can impose a 100 per cent implicit tax. Negative income taxation makes the tax explicit; and if taxation is thereby made more visible labour supply disincentives might be strengthened.

A second source of evidence is a series of negative income tax experiments in the USA in the years after 1968. The main one, informally called the New Jersey Experiment, involved more than 1300 families, who received a guaranteed income between 50 and 125 per cent of the poverty line, and faced tax rates of between 30 and 70 per cent. The experiment spawned a vast literature (see the Further Reading). The initial consensus was that the data offered little evidence of substantial reductions in the labour supply of household heads. A number of doubts were subsequently raised: the conclusions applied for the most part only to primary workers, and the labour supply responses of participants may have been influenced by the limited duration of the experiment.

Redistributive effects Negative income taxation has implications for both horizontal and vertical equity. A large-scale scheme paying benefits at the supplementary benefit level can improve horizontal equity in two ways: it can increase take-up, and it can reduce stigma, because there is no longer a benefit system for the poor and a tax system for the non-poor, but one system in which everyone is treated similarly.

On vertical equity (i.e. the issue of focus) negative income tax scores less well. At first glance it might appear that by benefiting the poor at the expense of the non-poor, it is strongly redistributive. This is not necessarily so. The cost of negative income tax, as we have seen, depends *inter alia* on the size distribution of income. So too does the redistributive strength of any particular scheme (i.e. the amount redistributed from those above to those below the break-even income), simply because a 1 per cent increase in the average tax rate raises more revenue for redistribution to the poor the greater the proportion of taxpayers who are non-poor.

Barr (1975b, pp. 38–44) shows that in a country with an income distribution like Britain's, negative income tax will not be a strong redistributor for two reasons. First, as benefits are increased, the average tax rate has to be raised to finance them. Second, there are many people with low incomes and relatively few with high incomes; the tax increase necessary to finance a high guaranteed income therefore falls substantially on those with low and average incomes, thus clawing back a substantial proportion of the benefit to the poor. In consequence the redistributive effects, though not trivial, are muted.

Conclusion 1   Given (a) the shape of the UK income distribution, (b) current benefit levels and (c) the fact that labour supply is potentially endogenous, two results follow. First, a universal negative income tax will be very costly; this will necessitate high tax rates which are likely to cause labour supply problems. Second, negative income taxation will not be a strong redistributor.

2.3 THE ROLE OF A SMALL-SCALE NEGATIVE INCOME TAX

Given this conclusion, there are two ways of proceeding: one is the 'Back to Beveridge' approach discussed in the next section; the other is to retain the idea of a negative income tax, but to make it small-scale and combine it with other schemes of income support.

Universal tax-credits   A small-scale scheme will not, by definition, solve poverty, and is therefore relevant to poverty relief only if it makes other redistributive schemes more effective. The starting-point is the tax-credit proposals described earlier. The scheme would have paid a weekly tax-credit, and taxed all other income at 30 per cent;[1] but it would have excluded the self-employed and, more importantly, the poor. The original proposals (UK, 1972a) as modified by Parliamentary discussion, were feasible and would have been implemented but for the General Election of February 1974. Further-

---

[1] Except that those with higher incomes would have paid a higher marginal tax rate, as at present under income tax.

more, it would have cost only an extra £112 million (UK, 1973, Vol. II, p. 424) plus the cost of additional administration to make the scheme universal. Thus, a universal tax-credit scheme (i.e. a small-scale negative income tax) is financially feasible if the credits are chosen to supplement existing arrangements rather than to supplant them. For this purpose a tax-credit worth roughly the same as the income tax personal allowance would suffice.

How useful would such a scheme be? We saw in Chapter 6:2.3 that one of the major difficulties in identifying and counting the poor lies in the fact that the Inland Revenue knows very little about them. The key feature of a universal tax-credit scheme is not that it would *per se* help the poor greatly (because the credit would be small), but that for the first time the whole population would be brought under the Inland Revenue umbrella. This would make it possible (Barr and Roper, 1974) to use computers to search out the poor (discussed shortly), thereby increasing the take-up of means-tested benefits. The strategy is to use a universal negative income tax not to *solve* poverty, but to enhance the effectiveness of benefits aimed specifically at the poor.

A scheme of this sort, as well as improving take-up, would alleviate the poverty trap in two ways. First, the tax-credits being universal, all other cash benefits become devices only for 'topping up' income, rather than mechanisms for total income support. This has the important advantage that the tax implicit in supplementary benefit and similar schemes will apply over a shorter range of income. Suppose a family receives £50 in supplementary benefit; under the present system (ignoring disregards) it faces a 100 per cent implicit tax on the first £50 of its net earnings. But if its weekly tax-credit were £30 it would receive only £20 in supplementary benefit, and so face a 100 per cent tax rate on only the first £20 of net earnings. As a second improvement, fixed-period awards (Chapter 10:3.2) would further reduce the poverty trap. A family in receipt of a £30 tax-credit, if awarded housing benefit of £10 per week for six months, would receive £40 per week *irrespective of income*. Thus, by the back door, one is able to achieve the desirable result of paying a larger credit to families with low incomes. There was much pressure for such an arrangement at the time the tax-credit proposals were under consideration, but the Inland Revenue insisted that the resulting variety of marginal tax rates at the lower end of the income distribution would be an administrative nightmare (UK, 1973, Vol. II, p. 3, para. 12). The scheme just described would be no more complex than existing arrangements from an administrative viewpoint, and if adequately computerised could be considerably simpler.

Administrative aspects It would be highly desirable, as a start, if existing means-tested benefits were rationalised. This should include standardising the definition of income used in assessing different benefits; standardising eligibility requirements (e.g. by extending the current system whereby families receiving supplementary benefit or family income supplement are automatically entitled to various other benefits); merging some benefits; and where possible making use of fixed-period awards.

As a second aspect of administration, computerisation of both tax and benefit systems is needed. Income tax is computerised in many (if not most) industrialised countries, and is scheduled nationwide in the UK for the late 1980s (the tax-credit scheme was to have been computerised from its inception). The importance of computerisation is that it enables a universal tax-credit scheme to be used as a search device to seek out the poor.[1]

It is also possible to computerise the calculation of eligibility and benefit entitlement. The starting-point is an all-purpose application form seeking the minimum information necessary to calculate benefits under all relevant schemes. The form should be capable of completion by members of the public; it is unlikely to be much longer than that which has to be filled in for *each* scheme at present. Computer programs have already been written and tested, into which the information from the all-purpose application is fed, and whose output is a list of *all* benefits to which the family is entitled, and the amount of benefit payable under each. The importance of computerising the benefit side is in speeding up administration and making it easier to apply for benefit, thereby increasing both accuracy and take-up.

The resulting scheme would require an enormous amount of detailed development work, but would look broadly as follows. First, it would be open to anyone, at any time, to apply for benefit using the all-purpose application just described. In addition, because the tax-credits are universal, the tax authorities could combine their knowledge of (in theory) *everyone's* income with their computerised tax system to compile at the end of each tax year a list of all tax units with income below some specified amount. This list would be passed to the Department of Health and Social Security. Everyone on the list would have a low income; but not everyone would be poor, e.g. a highly paid person who had started working in Britain only during the last month of the tax year would (legitimately) have a low income for tax purposes, but would not be poor. The Department of Health and Social Security would weed out the non-poor by sending each tax unit on the list an all-purpose benefit application form (completion of which would be *voluntary*). Completed returns would be processed, and benefit assessed, by computer.

If people could speedily ascertain their entitlement to *all* benefits with a

---

[1] There would be other advantages. Computerisation makes possible self-assessment for income tax, which in turn makes it administratively feasible to dispense with the long basic rate band and replace it (if one so desires) by a structure of smoothly rising marginal tax rates. This is a somewhat technical administrative argument, but one with important policy implications – for details see Barr, James and Prest (1977).

single application, they would be more likely to apply; and if they did not apply, the 100 per cent survey of taxpayer incomes, even if conducted only annually, would take on average no more than six months (and at the outside slightly over a year) to 'catch' them. The result, almost certainly, is take-up rates substantially above those achieved at present.

It might be argued that the use of computers would make (especially) the benefit system more impersonal. The counter-argument is that in a *well-designed* system computers would do what they are good at (viz. complicated arithmetic), leaving benefit officers free to do what they are (or should be) good at, namely dealing with people.

Conclusion 2 The proper role of a universal negative income tax is not as a major redistributor of income, but as a *search device* to discover low-income families. Take-up rates for means-tested benefits could thereby be substantially raised. In addition, the guaranteed income need be no higher than the value of current income tax personal allowances; hence the scheme does not raise benefit levels but only take-up rates; thus costs are not excessive, minimising problems with the poverty trap.

3 The 'Back to Beveridge' Approach

3.1 THE IDEA

Negative income taxation seeks to raise low incomes by paying benefits conditioned on income. The so-called 'Back to Beveridge' strategy makes benefits conditional on other characteristics, e.g. being unemployed, ill or retired, or having children. In its pure form, benefit is payable only on the basis of criteria like these; the issue of means testing does not arise.

The Meade proposals are a recent example of this approach (see also International Labour Office, 1984b). Meade (1978) argues that the existing system fails to prevent poverty because the main national insurance benefits and child benefit are below the poverty line defined by supplementary benefit, thus violating a key Beveridge principle. His proposed reforms concentrate on rectifying this problem. They are: (a) raising all national insurance benefits to the supplementary benefit level; (b) the payment of child benefit at the supplementary benefit level; (c) the payment of additional benefits (to one-parent families, the disabled, etc.); and (d) the phasing out of many means-tested benefits. Income tax should be harmonised with the reformed system, in particular, (e) the income tax threshold should be raised to the supplementary benefit level.

271

Proposals of this sort can alleviate the poverty trap in two important ways (for a detailed critique of the Meade arguments see Prest, 1979). First, the major benefits are at or above the poverty line, thus reducing the number of people receiving supplementary benefit and facing its 100 per cent implicit tax. Second, these benefits are not affected by changes in income, but only by a change in the recipient's category, e.g. the loss of unemployment benefit upon resumption of work. This does not remove the poverty trap so much as side-step it by concentrating the entire tax effect on the change in status.

The logic of the approach, in addition to alleviating the poverty trap, has important and much wider implications, which are worth exploring by way of a simple example. Assume:

(1) only redheads are poor;
(2) all redheads are poor;
(3) there is no hair dyeing technology.

In these circumstances it would be possible completely to eliminate poverty (as defined by the poverty line) by paying a redhead benefit. Additionally (and crucially), because benefits go *only* to the poor no substantial increase in tax rates is necessary.

These results follow for two reasons. First, having red hair is a necessary condition for poverty (assumption (1)); were this not the case a redhead benefit would leave gaps by failing to cover poor people who did not have red hair. It is also a sufficient condition (assumption 2)); were this not the case, benefits would 'leak out' to redheads who were not poor. Thus having red hair is perfectly correlated with poverty. Second, having red hair is wholly exogenous to the individual (assumption (3)). The ideal characteristics on which to condition benefits are therefore *exogenous correlates* of poverty.

What would this strategy imply in practice? Empirically, the major correlates of poverty are: unemployment; ill-health (sickness and disability); large families; single-parent families; old age; and high housing costs. Benefits paid to people in these categories would embrace the great majority of the poor. How exogenous are these characteristics? The endogeneity of the level and duration of unemployment is highly controversial (Chapter 8:3.1). With ill-health, the problem is less acute because genuine ill-health is costly to the individual, and also because policing is possible through certification procedures. The incidence of large families is exogenous with respect to benefits unless decisions to have children are influenced by the existence of child benefit and supplementary benefit; and similarly, the occurrence of single-parent families is exogenous unless the decision by parents to separate is substantially influenced by the existence of cash benefits (see the discussion in Chapter 10:3.3 of the empirical literature on family formation). A crucial issue in this context is whether having children/separating is more strongly endogenous than labour supply. Turning to old age, reaching retirement age is entirely beyond the individual's control. Individuals may choose voluntarily to defer retirement, but this works in the 'right' direction by increasing labour supply. Housing costs are far from exogenous under any system which, like housing benefit, bases assistance on *actual* costs. Matters could be improved if assistance were related to a regional index of *average* housing costs (see Chapter 14:5.2).

Some comments on the exogenous correlates approach are necessary. First, as we have seen, the strategy offers the possibility of side-stepping the poverty trap by concentrating the entire loss of benefit on a change of category (e.g. accepting a job, or regaining health). Exogeneity in this context is clearly crucial.

Second, some individuals with incomes below the poverty line will fall outside the characteristics just described (i.e. the characteristics are not a necessary condition for poverty). For this group at least, a residual income tested scheme would be necessary. There will also be people within the six categories (hence qualifying for benefit) whose pre-transfer income is above the poverty line (i.e. the categories are not a sufficient condition for poverty). For this reason there is a case for making all benefits taxable in the same way as earned income.

Finally, it should be noted that the exogenous correlates approach can, at least in part, be organised through the institutions of social insurance (as currently for unemployment, ill-health and old age), but does not have to be (e.g. child benefit). The issue of whether some forms of income support are dressed up as insurance therefore remains open.

3.2 COMBATING THE POVERTY TRAP

A recent example of the exogenous correlates approach (UK, 1983a and b)[1] differs from most previous studies by basing its work not on an analysis of so-called 'typical' families but on a detailed study of a large sample of actual families. Such disaggregation makes it possible to show not only how the poverty trap arises, but also how many people it affects. This section draws out some of the more important strands of the argument.

Reforming national insurance contributions   The starting-point for reform according to the Report is to iron out various anomalies by integrating income tax and national insurance contributions (UK, 1983a, paras 8.1, 8.2 and 8.10;

---

[1] Referred to colloquially as the 'Meacher Report'. It is referred to here for convenience as 'the Report', though for Parliamentary reasons it does not have that status.

for more recent discussion see UK, 1986b, Chs 6 and 7). The existing system has two main problems. First, as we saw in Chapter 7:2.1, the lower earnings limit for national insurance contributions (£38 per week in 1986/7) is an *exemption* not an *allowance*; thus someone earning £37.50 pays no contribution, but someone earning £38 pays a contribution of 5 per cent of the *whole* £38, i.e. £1.90. Second, the contribution is levied on a week-by-week basis, so that someone earning £37.50 one week and £38.50 the next pays less than someone (with the same total income) earning £38 each week. Both features contrast sharply with the operation of income tax.

To avoid these anomalies the Report suggested that the two taxes be integrated. National insurance contributions were to have an *allowance* equal to the income tax personal allowance (thereby forgoing revenue), and the upper earnings limit was to be abolished (thereby gaining revenue). The former effect was the stronger; on a revenue neutral basis the combined income tax/national insurance contribution would have had to be around 41¼ per cent.

Income tax thresholds   It is often argued that one way of mitigating the poverty trap is to raise the threshold of income tax. The first major conclusion of the Report was that this view is fallacious. The reason is simple: of 100 people taken out of tax by an increase in the threshold, 43 are pensioners (for whom incentive issues are largely irrelevant), nearly half are secondary workers, and only eight are earning household heads (Kay, 1984). As a result, an increase in the tax threshold, financed in the Report's 'Package A' by an increase in the rate of integrated income tax/national insurance contribution, left virtually unchanged the number of household heads facing marginal tax rates of over 50 per cent (UK, 1983a, para. 12.15).

Benefit levels   A much more fruitful strategy, the Report concluded, was to improve existing benefits. Thus the broad thrust of 'Package C' (UK, 1983a, paras 12.7 and 12.20) on the benefit side was (a) to increase sharply both child benefit and the increase for single parents, and (b) to increase retirement pensions. Because some gaps would remain, the coverage of supplementary benefit was to be extended slightly; and to prevent too much 'leakage' to the non-poor, child benefit was to be taxed as earned income (as pensions are already). These increases were to be financed by abolishing the income tax married man's allowance and, in effect, by allowing mortgage interest to be deducted only at the basic rate of income tax.

The effect of these changes would be to increase the incomes of families with children and of the elderly, for the most part through benefits which are categorical rather than conditioned on income, thereby considerably reducing the number of people requiring means-tested benefits. As a result, the number of household heads facing marginal tax rates in excess of 50 per cent would be substantially reduced from 590,000 to 280,000, and the number with marginal tax rates in excess of 70 per cent from 110,000 to 50,000 (UK, 1983a, para. 12.20).

The approach embodied in the package thus reduces the poverty trap. In addition it is likely to have beneficial incentive effects, since the criteria on which benefits are awarded are largely exogenous to recipients (or, at least, are more exogenous than labour supply). To the extent that this is the case: (a) poverty is reduced (an equity gain); and (b) because costs are manageable, poverty trap tax rates can be reduced, thus improving labour supply incentives (an efficiency gain).

4 Mixed Strategies

Sections 2 and 3 discussed the two strategies for the most part in isolation. As a guide to practical policy, however, neither on its own is likely to succeed. Benefits conditioned on income generally run into problems of high tax rates; and pure categorical schemes face intractable problems of gaps in coverage, benefits 'leaking' to the non-poor, and problems with defining and administering borderline cases. The most likely path for reform is a judicious combination of the two approaches. One example, as we saw in section 2.3, is a small-scale, universal negative income tax with additional benefits for the poor; the latter could be conditioned either on income, or on the characteristics of recipients.

The main purpose of this chapter has been to set out the logic of different strategies for reform, so no attempt is made here to go beyond listing some of the many reform proposals which have appeared recently (for a brief survey see Atkinson, 1984c). Some tend more towards conditioning benefits on income. The Institute for Fiscal Studies proposals (Dilnot, Kay and Morris, 1984) advocate a substantial integration of income taxation with benefits, whereby virtually all national insurance benefits and child benefit are replaced by a series of income-tested benefits with a high rate of withdrawal (in some instances over 80 per cent) at low incomes. The package, though clearing up some of what Dilnot *et al.* regarded as the worst difficulties of present arrangements, has had its severe critics (Piachaud, 1984; O'Kelly, 1985), not least over its administrative feasibility.

The proposals of the Basic Income Research Group (based on an earlier scheme in UK, 1983b, pp. 420–53) are more obviously a negative income tax. The scheme has several variants, of which the most promising pays a guaranteed income which varies with family characteristics (e.g. extra payments are made for sickness, disability and old age). Some versions have the additional desirable characteristic that benefit is invariant to age (if below pensionable age), sex, marital status and employment status, thus minimising distortions in respect of labour market decisions and family formation. In many ways this scheme is a universal negative income tax whose guaranteed income varies with the characteristics of recipients (and hence is very much a blend of the two approaches). Nevertheless, most versions of the scheme require a tax rate of 70 per cent or more on low incomes.

The most fully articulated 'Back to Beveridge' scheme is that discussed in section 3.2. The incomes of many of the poor would be raised by increasing child benefit and the national insurance pension. For recipients with pre-transfer incomes above the tax threshold these would be taxable at around 40 per cent (the rate of the proposed integrated income tax/national insurance contribution). A not dissimilar set of proposals is made in National Consumer Council (1984).

A major overhaul of existing arrangements was suggested in a government consultative document (UK, 1985d) with several companion volumes (UK, 1985e, f, g), and a more circumspect set of proposals in a subsequent White Paper (UK, 1985k). The proposed changes to the state pension scheme were discussed in Chapter 9:5.1. Other proposals in the White Paper concerned a series of fairly complex changes to supplementary benefit (which was to be renamed Income Support), and a major extension of family income supplement (to be renamed Family Credit). A detailed assessment of these proposals lies outside the remit of this chapter. Some of the suggestions represent undoubted improvement, e.g. the partial move towards standardising the definition of income used in assessing benefits; and the choice of income definition under which marginal tax rates (though remaining high) are systematically kept below 100 per cent, thus removing the most glaring discontinuities in the present structure of withdrawal rates. Other parts of the proposals, however, have been heavily criticised (for initial assessments see the Further Reading).

5 Conclusion: Cash Benefits

This section brings together the main conclusions of Part 2 of the book. The primary aims of cash benefits are the prevention of absolute poverty, the protection of living standards and the reduction of inequality, of which only the first is non-controversial. Their achievement requires two sorts of mechanism. *Self-help* is necessary for people who are self-supporting on a lifetime basis but need a system which can reallocate income over time to iron out discontinuities. *Vertical redistribution* is necessary for those who are unable to support themselves over their lifetime as a whole.

The menu of methods of self-help includes private insurance and state activity, the latter in the form of publicly provided (i.e. social) insurance, or through transfers out of current tax revenues (social assistance). Vertical redistribution can be achieved by private charity, or through publicly organised transfers out of tax revenues (note that actuarial insurance cannot systematically redistribute from rich to poor). The respective merits of these methods can be summarised as follows.

Public versus private insurance The private market cannot always supply the efficient quantity and type of insurance against all causes of income loss.

(a) Because non-insurance may cause an externality, there is an efficiency argument for making some forms of insurance compulsory (Chapter 8:2.1).

(b) Private insurance in several important areas will be inefficient or non-existent: private unemployment insurance is not possible, mainly because of moral hazard (Chapter 8:2.2); and pure private pension insurance is likely to be inefficient because inflation is not an insurable risk (Chapter 9:3.1). This gives an efficiency justification for public provision of unemployment benefit and, at a minimum, provision on a PAYG basis of the indexation component of pension schemes. The efficiency arguments for public provision of sickness benefits and the smaller national insurance benefits are weaker.

Pension finance No definitive answer is possible.

(a) Theoretical and empirical analysis of the effects of pension schemes on saving and labour supply have produced conflicting and inconclusive results (Chapter 9:5.1).

(b) Moving national insurance pensions on to a funded basis will not by itself solve the future problem of pension finance (Chapter 9:5.1). The important changes are those which act to increase national output directly: through investment in new technology and improvements in the quality of labour (both of which increase productivity per worker); and through increased labour force participation, including a considerable reduction in unemployment, increased participation by women, and later retirement.

(c) The choice between PAYG and funding depends mainly on one's views about income redistribution and financial flexibility (Chapter 9:3.2 and 5.3)

The insurance principle – is it possible, necessary or desirable? It is *possible* for the state to create institutions similar to private, actuarial insurance, e.g. the original Beveridge concept of flat-rate contributions based on average risk, giving entitlement to flat-rate benefits. For non-insurable risks (unemployment, inflation) these merely mimic private institutions but are not true insurance. It does not follow that insurance-type institutions are *necessary*. If membership of an insurance scheme is compulsory it is possible, without the likelihood of substantial inefficiency, to charge premiums which are not based upon individual risk (Chapter 8:3.1).

It is an open question whether adherence to the insurance principle in a state scheme is *desirable* (Chapter 8:3.1). Social assistance has the advantage of flexibility, since entitlement to benefit does not depend on a contributions record; the corresponding disadvantages are that benefits conditioned on income may be stigmatising, and can cause a poverty trap (Chapter 10:3). Social insurance, whilst less flexible, may have advantages because it side-steps the poverty trap (Chapter 11:3); because individuals might perceive contributions differently from taxes, with correspondingly different labour supply effects; and because recipients might feel less stigmatised by benefits conditioned on previous contributions rather than on an income test.

It should be noted, however, that these advantages depend only on the *perceived* basis of benefits on contributions. It may be advantageous to adopt a fiction of insurance without the reality. From a strictly rational viewpoint, the compulsory nature of contributions makes it irrelevant whether they are treated as insurance premiums or as earmarked taxation. In the face of uninsurable risks, benefits must be publicly organised, and financed on a non-actuarial basis, even if they are dressed up as insurance (Chapter 8:2.2).

Vertical redistribution In part because of the free-rider problem, redistribution through private charity is likely to be sub-optimal even from a libertarian perspective and a fortiori from a Rawlsian or socialist viewpoint (Chapter 4:4.1). Thus at least some publicly organised redistribution through the tax system can be justified under any theory of society, though with considerable disagreement about how much (Chapter 4:2.2 and 4.4). Any such redistribution will be constrained by the size distribution of income (Chapter 11:2.2).

National insurance in Britain Present arrangements (a) are more a tax-transfer scheme than true insurance (Chapter 8:3.1), and (b) (subject to qualifications) redistribute from rich to poor, from young to old, and from men to women (Chapters 8:3.2 and 9:5.2). Because the scheme is compulsory, (a) and (b) can be argued to cause no *major* inefficiency apart from a potential labour supply disincentive – an issue on which evidence to date is inconclusive (Chapter 8:3.1).

Non-contributory benefits in Britain
(a) Supplementary benefit is withdrawn rapidly as the income of recipients rises, thereby containing costs and focusing benefits on those with the lowest incomes. The price of these advantages is the poverty trap, which makes it difficult for families to increase their standard of living, and therefore creates a labour supply disincentive (Chapter 10:3.1).

(b) Families not in receipt of supplementary benefit may also face a poverty trap arising out of the withdrawal of other benefits for which entitlement is determined by an income test. Awarding benefit for a fixed period can mitigate the worst labour supply effects, but the complexity of the existing system makes firm conclusions difficult (Chapter 10:3.2).

Reform

(a) The arguments about the desirability of maintaining an insurance fiction are finely balanced, and depend more on how contributions are perceived than on their analytical characteristics (Chapter 8:3.1).

(b) Benefits conditioned on income (whether means-tested explicitly or in the form of a large-scale negative income tax) suffer from the necessity of high tax rates to finance them. This causes a poverty trap with major efficiency and equity costs.

(c) For this reason large-scale negative income tax schemes cannot solve poverty on their own. Their cost is a consequence not of the negative income tax mechanism *per se* but of (i) the existing size distribution of income, (ii) the poverty line chosen, and (iii) the empirical fact that labour supply is not exogenous (Chapter 11:2.2).

(d) Benefits conditioned on characteristics other than income can circumvent some of these difficulties, particularly if the criteria are exogenous to the recipient and highly correlated with poverty. This 'Back to Beveridge' approach offers some hope of improvement whether or not the contribution principle is retained (Chapter 11:3). The most hopeful route for reform is probably a careful blend of the two approaches (Chapter 11:4).

(e) Reform is likely to be hampered by the political difficulties which can beset even small changes (Prest, 1983), and by the major difficulties of theory, measurement and methodology (Chapters 8:3.1, 9:5.1 and 10:3.3) which face empirical work.

What are the implications for policy of these largely technical arguments? The preferred libertarian methods of voluntary private insurance and voluntary charity rather fall by the wayside. Private insurance will frequently be inefficient, not primarily because people are unable to make rational decisions but because of technical problems on the supply side. Libertarians might therefore concede an element of compulsion in view of the externality caused by non-insurance (Chapter 8:2.1), and allow in addition a limited role for non-actuarial, tax-financed transfers to raise to subsistence those incomes which remain low despite private charity. This will be especially relevant to non-insurable risks. Libertarians criticise national insurance as exceeding the scope necessary to achieve this limited purpose, thereby curtailing the freedom of taxpayers to make their own decisions.

Socialists favour public organisation of cash transfers, financed by progressive taxation; benefits should be awarded on the basis of need, and should be above subsistence so as to reduce inequality. Whether insurable risks are dealt with out of tax revenues or by publicly organised insurance (and in the latter case whether a formal contribution should be levied) is an area of debate. However, many socialists abhor means testing, partly because of the poverty trap and partly as a legacy of the Poor Law. In the absence of a universal guaranteed income this brings us back to insurance, at which point there is some convergence between socialist and liberal views.

Further Reading

There is a huge literature on negative income taxation. For specific proposals see UK (1972a) (a government proposal), Christopher *et al.* (1970) (tending to the libertarian) and for a cogent liberal appeal Meade (1972). In the US context see Tobin, Pechman and Mieszkowski (1967), Green (1967), Tobin (1968) and Aaron (1973). On the costs of negative income tax see Barr (1975b) and Atkinson (1984b) (the latter is reprinted in Atkinson, 1987, Ch. 16).

One of the best accounts of the US negative income tax experiments, including details of the experimental design and an analysis of the labour supply responses, can be found in the contributions to Pechman and Timpane (1975). For a briefer review see Haveman and Watts (1977), and for an account of the experiments in rural areas, Palmer and Pechman (1978).

The best statement of the 'Back to Beveridge' arguments can be found in Meade (1978, Ch. 13) and UK (1983a).

Recent proposals for reform can be found in Dilnot, Kay and Morris (1984) and the basic income proposals (see UK, 1983b, pp. 420–53) (both of which rely heavily on income testing). Schemes based more on the characteristics of recipients are UK (1983a, especially paras 12.7 and 12.20) and National Consumer Council (1984).

Government proposals are set out in UK (1985k). For assessment of these, and earlier proposals in UK (1985d, e, f, g), see Davis *et al.* (1985a, b) (qualified support), Berthoud (1986) (qualified opposition), CPAG (1985b) (unqualified opposition) and for a Parliamentary view, UK (1985h).

PART 3

BENEFITS IN KIND

12

Health Care and Education 1: Arguments of Principle

Risk varies inversely with knowledge. [Irving Fisher, 1930.]

Man is the most versatile of all forms of capital. [Irving Fisher, 1930.]

1 Introduction

The questions   Three intellectual threads run through this book: the social welfare maximisation problem, issues of social justice, and problems of definition and measurement. The discussion of cash benefits was concerned mainly with the first two; in the case of benefits in kind the third assumes a special importance. Many of the arguments about health care and education turn crucially on the measurement of private and social costs and benefits, and also on the extent to which it is reasonable to assume perfect information.

Health care and education are discussed side by side because the intellectual issues they raise are in many ways similar. But the subject is vast and can in no way be encompassed in two chapters, so I shall be eclectic. The main questions asked are: how efficient/just is a competitive market for health care/education likely to be (the issue of 'privatisation'); to what extent would public production and allocation be more efficient/just; and would any intermediate system involving both public and private sectors perform better than either of the pure cases? There is some very limited discussion of the personal social

283

services, but a number of other important issues receive little mention, including health care and education production functions and the detailed finances of health care and education (see the Further Reading).

Section 2 looks at the aims of policy in respect of health care and education; the next two sections discuss methods of achieving them, in particular *why* the state intervenes (section 3) and *how* in theory it might intervene so as jointly to maximise efficiency and equity (section 4). Chapter 13 assesses the reality, and looks at various proposals for reform.

Non-economic arguments To clarify the approach, it is useful to remind ourselves of some arguments whose weakness was discussed earlier. Bad economic arguments about state intervention are generally of two sorts: either they fail to understand the nature and limitations of market allocation; or they confuse aims and methods. A common libertarian position is that health care is an 'ordinary' commodity which (like any other) should be distributed in accordance with income, tastes and relative prices; if we do not like the distribution of health care we should change the distribution of income. It is argued below that this is a mistake of the first kind.

Arguments which confuse aims and methods were discussed in Chapter 4:6.1. The view that 'health care/education/housing are basic rights *and therefore* should be provided by the state' is illogical because the words 'and therefore' simply do not follow from the initial premise. If health care etc. are basic rights then so is food, which is provided well enough by the private sector. For the same reason, the argument that 'health care, etc. should be publicly provided because otherwise the poor could not afford them' does not stand up. Poverty may justify cash transfers but is not, without considerable qualification, a justification for public provision.

The same arguments can be viewed from the political perspectives discussed in Chapter 3. Socialists believe that goods like health care, education and housing should be provided collectively. This view is tenable as a value-judgement, but the consequent policies are unlikely to be successful unless they go with rather than against the grain of economy theory. It is argued here that health care can successfully be provided publicly, mostly without direct charge, but we shall see in Chapter 14 that the same cannot be said of housing. Libertarians argue that virtually all goods, including health care, education and housing, should be supplied privately because collective provision is both inefficient and a violation of individual liberty. This view, again, is workable in practice only if it accords with economic theory. Markets can fail entirely (unemployment insurance) or be inefficient (many forms of health care insurance) – devout hopes are not enough. Liberals reject both lines of argument because each makes the *method* of provision (market or state) a primary *aim*. It is argued in Chapter 4:6.1 that a better approach is to choose aims on the basis of personal values and ideology, and then to select on *technical* grounds whichever method best achieves them.

Institutions For the purpose of this chapter, virtually no institutional knowledge is necessary (see Chapter 13:1.1 and 2.1). As a good approximation, the national health service (NHS) is financed out of central government revenues, and health care (with minor exceptions) is provided publicly and without charge, both for treatment by a general practitioner (i.e. family doctor) and for hospital in- and out-patient treatment. Hospital doctors and nurses in the NHS are paid a salary. Family doctors are paid in a complex way reflecting *inter alia* the numbers and ages of their patients. Throughout the NHS very little payment is on a fee-for-service basis. There is also a small private sector (about 5 per cent of total expenditure on health care).

Education is compulsory to age 16. Primary (age 5 to 11) and secondary education (age 11 to 18) are provided publicly and without charge. There is also a small private sector (again, about 5 per cent of the total). So-called further education is available beyond 16. For the most part these are all public sector institutions funded by a mixture of central and local revenues. In contrast, university education is privately *produced* but largely (though latterly to a decreasing extent) *financed* publicly out of central and local funds.[1]

2 Aims

2.1 CONCEPTS

Social welfare is maximised by the joint pursuit of economic efficiency[2] and social justice (or equity). This section outlines the meaning of these ideas as they apply to health care and education, and then turns to the more difficult problem of measuring them. The fact that health care and education are important does not mean that they are not economic commodities. Resources devoted to medical uses are not available for other purposes. There is a trade-off: if we spent nothing on health some people would die unnecessarily of trivial complaints; if we spent the whole of national income on health care there would be no food, and we would all die of starvation. The optimal quantity clearly lies somewhere between — in principle where the value gained from the last unit of health care (or education) is equal to the marginal value which would be

---

[1] The distinction between public and private production and finance is set out in detail in Chapter 4:5.

[2] The concept of economic efficiency is defined in Chapter 4:2.1.

derived from the alternative use to which the resources involved could be put. This is the quantity X^* in Figure 4.1.

Efficiency in this sense must apply to two separate issues: the overall size of the health care/education system as a proportion of gross national product (I shall call this the *macro* efficiency issue); and the allocation of resources to different uses *within* health care/education (the issue of *micro* efficiency), so as to produce the optimal quantity, quality and mix.

The concept of equity, as we have seen (Chapters 4:4 and 6:3.1), is more elusive.[1] Le Grand (1982, pp. 14–15) distinguishes four definitions of equity in consumption: equality of public expenditure, equality of use, equality of cost, and equality of final outcome. Two definitions are of particular interest. Equality of use implies that everyone should receive the same quantity; the problem is that people differ in their medical requirements, and in the extent to which they choose to consume education, or are able to benefit from it. Equality of outcome implies an unequal allocation such that everyone enjoys an equal state of health or level of educational attainment. Whether or not such an aim is thought desirable, it is not fully feasible.

To avoid some of these difficulties, equity will be defined as a form of *equality of opportunity* as described in Chapter 6:3.1 (especially equation (6.17)). This does not mean that individuals can necessarily obtain as much health care or education as they want (since health care resources are scarce it is probable that no system could satisfy everyone's wants). But it does mean that any individual should receive as much health care as anyone else in the same *medical* condition, regardless of any factors which are thought to be irrelevant, e.g. income. Similarly, for education it implies that if individuals A and B have similar tastes and ability they should receive the same education, irrespective of extraneous considerations. This definition of equity has at least the merit that it apportions scarcity in a just way.

Once we have decided the efficient level of production of health care and education and its equitable distribution, the remaining question is who should pay for it, i.e. to what extent is it appropriate to finance health care or education progressively? This is an issue of vertical equity discussed in Chapter 4:4.1. It was argued in Chapter 4:6.1 that if health care is allocated efficiently by the market then equity aims are generally best achieved through cash transfers. But where health care is publicly produced and allocated for *efficiency* reasons,

---

[1] According to the White Paper on the founding of the national health service, 'the Government . . . want to ensure that in the future every man and woman and child can rely on getting . . . the best medical and other facilities available; that their getting them shall not depend on whether they can pay for them or on any other factor irrelevant to real need' (UK, 1944a). McLachlan and Maynard (1982a, p. 521) correctly find these statements 'vague and Utopian'.

it may be appropriate to finance it out of progressive taxation; if so, it is possible, though not inevitable (Chapter 13:1.2 and 2.2) that in-kind transfers will redistribute from rich to poor.

2.2 MEASURING COSTS AND BENEFITS

Health Care

The concept of efficiency is well understood. But attempts to make it operational by measuring costs and benefits (Abel-Smith, 1983; Aaron and Schwartz, 1984) must of necessity be somewhat rough-and-ready because of serious measurement problems, particularly in the quantification of benefits. The total cost of the NHS and its component parts is readily available (see Table 13.1). The costs of different types of treatment are harder to establish, *inter alia* because of the familiar problem of apportioning overheads and the need to distinguish short- and long-run marginal costs, but these problems are not insurmountable.

On the benefit side there are three very major problems. First, there is the tremendous difficulty involved in measuring health itself (Culyer, 1983; Hunt *et al.*, 1980; Office of Health Economics, 1985). To the extent that this is possible, the second problem is how to value an improvement in an individual's health. The difficulties are highlighted in the extensive literature on placing a monetary value on human life (see the Further Reading). Such attempts are sometimes regarded as distasteful or immoral. But all sorts of policies affect the risks faced by individuals, and hence on aggregate the number of deaths. Many accident victims would be saved if they could receive medical attention rapidly; nevertheless, we do not have casualty departments on every corner, nor ambulances constantly patrolling the streets. Thus we are not prepared to spend infinite sums of money to save one life. The question therefore arises of how much we should be prepared to spend to reduce the risk of death by 1 per cent or, more generally, to reduce the extent or duration of ill health, given that such efforts are at the expense of education, food, etc.

The difficulty is obvious once we realise that the benefits of improved health are twofold. There are (or may be) *output benefits*, i.e. the increased output/income of the individual whose affliction is reduced or removed. This is hard enough to measure. In addition, there are intractable problems in measuring the *utility benefits* arising from any reduction in the physical and emotional suffering of the patient and his/her family.

Even were it possible to measure the benefits from an improvement in health, a third, and even greater problem remains – that of measuring the extent to which any reduction in suffering or output loss is directly *caused* by medical care. A patient's complete recovery could be due entirely to the treatment he has received; it could also be due, wholly or in part, to his natural recuperative powers. It is increasingly accepted that a patient's powers of physical recovery and his/her psychological make-up can be related. The influence of these intangible factors (e.g. the 'will to live') is crucial, but impossible to measure; and if it is ignored we will tend to overestimate the benefits of health care.

Given these difficulties, cost-benefit studies of medical care (see Cullis and West, 1979, Ch. 8) are of necessity somewhat limited in their scope. They are useful as far as they go; but they do not go very far; nor is progress likely to be easy. Partly because of these problems, the more limited technique of cost-effectiveness studies tackles a narrower issue by considering a specific medical condition (Piachaud, 1972; Williams, 1985), and examining the costs of alternative forms of treatment. Here answers are possible largely because no attempt is made to measure benefits.

Education

Measuring the costs and benefits of education raises similar questions, but even greater problems. As with health care, the cost side presents no insurmountable problems. We know the direct costs of the state educational system and its components (Table 13.2). The problem of apportioning overheads is the same as for health care. In addition, for individuals past school-leaving age, it is necessary to include an estimate of forgone earnings as a measure of the output lost by their withdrawal from the labour market, taking into account the wage they would have received and the likelihood of their finding a job.

There are major difficulties in measuring benefits. First, what precisely do we mean by a good education (analogous to the problem of measuring health)? Second, is education causally related to increased productivity, or is it just a 'screening' device (see below)? Third, the social benefits of education may exceed those to the individual recipient, raising issues of externalities. Finally, it is necessary to consider the use of educational resources not only at a point in time (the issue of static efficiency), but also the impact of education on economic growth (dynamic efficiency). These issues are discussed in turn in the context of a simple human capital model.

The human capital model attempts to explain the demand for education which, like health care, brings the individual both production and utility benefits. It is argued, in the case of the former, that an individual who acquires more education becomes more skilful and productive. This approach sees education as a form of investment, analogous to improving machinery. From the individual viewpoint, such investment is profitable to the extent that it increases future income by more than its initial costs (including forgone earnings). Empirically there is a strong correlation between an individual's education and his lifetime earnings (see Psacharopoulos, 1975). The overall pattern summarised by Blaug is that 'within a few years after leaving school . . . better educated people earn more than less educated people; their advantage continues to widen with age and . . . the favourable differential persists until retirement' (1970, p. 27).

Utility benefits can arise, first, because the individual may derive utility from the educational process itself (i.e. education might have consumption benefits in the present as well as investment benefits in the future). Second, the individual return to education includes not only higher financial rewards but also non-money returns in the form of job satisfaction and the enjoyment of leisure. None of these is measurable.

To clarify and summarise the *individual* return to education it is helpful to set out formally the individual investment decision. The initial assumptions of the simplest human capital model are:

(1) Education raises the individual's marginal product in the future and therefore his future money income;
(2) This increase in money income is the *only* benefit from education, i.e. we rule out consumption benefits and future non-money returns.

If B_t is the benefit to the individual from an extra year's education, and r is his personal rate of time preference, the *gross present value* (GPV) to the individual[1] of an additional year of education is

$$\text{GPV} = \frac{B_1}{1+r} + \frac{B_2}{(1+r)^2} + \ldots + \frac{B_N}{(1+r)^N} \qquad (12.1)$$

The *net present value* (NPV) is

$$\text{NPV} = \sum_{t=0}^{N} \frac{B_t}{(1+r)^t} - C_0 \qquad (12.2)$$

where C_0 is the cost of an additional year of education (including forgone earnings). The individual will continue to acquire education so long as $GPV > C_0$, i.e. up to the point where $NPV = 0$. This is the level of education Q_0 in Figure 12.1, where the marginal private value (MPV) of education is the marginal gross present value from equation (12.1), and the marginal private cost (MPC) is the cost of education to the individual.

Relaxing the second assumption does not change the flavour of the results. Consumption benefits reduce C_0 in equation (12.2), and non-money returns

---

[1] A simple exposition of the present value formula is given in Lipsey (1983, Ch. 28). For a more complete treatment of cost-benefit analysis see Brown and Jackson (1982, Ch. 8), Musgrave and Musgrave (1984, Ch. 8) and Mishan (1982).

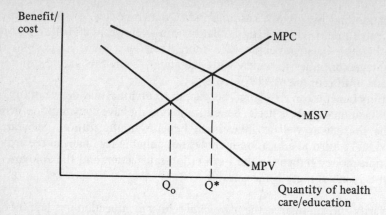

Figure 12.1 *A simple human capital model of the individual decision to invest in health care/education*

increase B_t in equations (12.1) and (12.2). Either phenomenon increases the quantity of education an individual will choose to acquire.

The screening hypothesis It might seem, therefore, that by measuring the money income benefits (though not the utility benefits) to the individual we can establish a lower bound on the production benefits of education. This is valid if we are prepared to assume that education is *causally* related to increases in individual income through increases in individual productivity. This is the strong first assumption made above. In contrast, the screening hypothesis (see the Further Reading) argues that education is *associated* with increases, but does not cause them. The distribution of earnings is the result of a complex interaction of factors including sex, race, family circumstances, natural ability and the quantity and quality of education (Blaug, 1970, pp. 32–46). The screening hypothesis is a special case which argues that education beyond a basic level does not increase individual productivity. Instead, it is assumed at its simplest that firms seek high-ability workers but are unable, prior to employing them, to distinguish them from those with low ability.[1] Individuals therefore have an incentive to make themselves distinctive by some sort of signal. According to the screening hypothesis education fills exactly this function. By and large it is high-ability individuals who perform well in the educational system. Educational achievement is therefore correlated with higher productivity but does not cause it, and hence is no more than a screening or signalling device to prospective employers, which it is in the *individual's* (though not necessarily in society's) interests to acquire. Just as an individual's

---

[1] Analytically the problem is identical to adverse selection – see Chapter 5:3.2, Atkinson and Stiglitz (1980, pp. 359–60), and the Further Reading.

good health may be due more to innate powers of recovery than to health care so, according to this view, is productivity the result of natural ability rather than post-primary education.

The conclusion from the individual viewpoint is that it is possible to measure the money income benefits (but not the utility benefits) *associated* with different levels of education; but the *causal* relationship is much less clear. The screening hypothesis leaves the individual's decision to invest unaffected, and so leads to the same result as the human capital model. But, to the extent that it is true, screening has profound implications for the *socially* optimal level of investment in education, to which we turn next.

External benefits[1] Setting the screening hypothesis to one side for the moment, education can create benefits to society over and above those to the individual in two ways: production benefits and broader social benefits. On the first, education may make a worker more productive; it may also enable him/her to raise the productivity of others. For example, individual A can communicate in writing with individual B only because *B* can read; B's education therefore raises A's productivity/utility. Individuals may also become more adaptable and better able to keep up with technological change. The economic spin-offs of higher education and a more mobile educated populace are relevant in this context. It is not surprising that much new 'high tech' industry is concentrated round clusters of universities, e.g. Cambridge (Mass.) and Cambridge (England). Measuring these benefits is difficult, not least because it is hard to separate the effects of education from other determinants of productivity, e.g. natural ability and the quantity and quality of capital equipment.

Education may also have broader benefits. First, there are *family benefits*. Schools viewed as a child-minding institution can create output benefits by enabling parents to work in the market sector (thereby raising their output and earnings) or in the household sector (thereby raising their output but not their earnings). Schools can also create utility benefits by enabling parents to enjoy more leisure. The value of these child-minding benefits could in principle be measured by what parents would be prepared to pay a child-minder.[2] Education may also create *cultural benefits* external to the recipient in at least two ways. A common cultural experience (music, art, literature) may foster communication generally, both at the time and in the future. In addition, there may be neighbourhood effects; the mechanics of taking children to school,

---

[1] See Chapter 4:3.2 and/or the Appendix to Chapter 4, para. 15.
[2] Whilst education clearly creates family benefits, it is arguable whether such benefits are external. In a world where parents make voluntary decisions about their children's education and pay the full market price for it, no issue of externalities arises. Where education is compulsory and provided free the issue is less clear-cut.

parent–teacher associations, etc. bring people into contact and may foster shared attitudes locally. Education in this context can be regarded as part of the socialisation process, as a device which fosters social cohesion, though measurement problems are intractable.

As a result, if education (a) increases individual productivity and (b) creates external production benefits, then the amount of education chosen by an individual in a market system, Q_0 in Figure 12.1, will generally be *less* than the optimal amount, Q^*, an issue discussed in more detail in section 3.2. However, if the claims of the screening hypothesis are valid then education leads to (but does not *cause*) an increase in individual income, but does not raise output. In this case individuals may acquire *more* education than is socially optimal.

Rate of return studies, despite these difficulties, have attempted to measure the benefits of education. The rate of return to education, r_0, is that rate of interest which equates the present value of the stream of future benefits in equation (12.2) to the initial cost of acquiring an additional unit of education. In other words, r_0 is the rate of interest which reduces the *net* present value of additional education to zero. It is vital to distinguish the private rate of return (which determines individual decisions) from the social rate (which is the relevant variable for efficient resource allocation).

Psacharopoulos (1973 and 1980) estimates the private and social rates of return to different levels of education across countries. Two conclusions emerge: the rate of return is highest for primary education, and then declines; and the private rate of return exceeds the social rate at all levels of education (mainly because in all countries education subsidies reduce costs to the individual but not to society). These results must be heavily qualified. First, they are based on *money* returns. No account is (or can be) taken of the consumption value of education, nor of its non-money returns in the form (especially) of job satisfaction. Where these factors are present, empirical estimates *understate* both private and social benefits to an unknown extent. Second, such estimates can measure only the *association* between education and earnings. But to the extent that the screening hypothesis is true the causal link is weakened, in which case the measured social (though not the private) benefits of post-primary education will be *overstated* by an unknown amount. The estimation of rates of return, in short, is a heroic undertaking.

The relationship between education and economic growth, for these and other reasons, remains unclear. The rate of growth of output in any country depends on the increase in the quantity and quality of its capital stock; on the increase in quantity and quality of its labour force; and on a variety of non-economic factors. Education affects only one of these, the quality of the labour force. The problem is to separate the quantitative effect of this variable given the influence of all the others. Despite a great deal of work, little progress has been made. Much of the early literature is summarised by Blaug (1970, Ch. 3). About the only firm conclusion to emerge is the unsurprising one that no country has experienced a substantial degree of economic development without first achieving a level of basic literacy in a substantial proportion of its population (various estimates agree that 40 per cent is about the minimum for 'take-off'). Beyond this, little has been established, Denison's (1962, 1967 and 1969) monumental work notwithstanding.

The conclusion to which this leads is simple but depressing. The efficiency aim is clear enough in principle for both health care and education, but measurement problems make definitive empirical answers unlikely, if not impossible. The definition of equity is more elusive but, as we shall see in Chapter 13:1.2 and 2.2, empirical work has made some headway.

3 Methods 1: Theoretical Arguments for State Intervention

3.1 EFFICIENCY ARGUMENTS FOR INTERVENTION: HEALTH CARE

This section considers the efficiency and equity arguments for public involvement in health care and education, i.e. the theoretical question of *why* the state intervenes. Private markets allocate efficiently only if the *standard assumptions* hold, i.e. perfect information, perfect competition and no market failures such as external effects (Chapter 4:3.2, and the Appendix to Chapter 4, paragraphs 5–17). The underlying question is why health care is 'different' from equally vital commodities like food (and similarly in section 3.2 for education). Early literature was concerned with characteristics of the demand for medical care; later work concentrated more on the supply side, particularly on the behaviour of doctors individually, and on the medical profession as a corporate entity. A third, and completely different, set of arguments (section 3.3) centres on the notion of altruism which, it is asserted, has particular relevance to health care.

Information problems   It is useful to start by asking whether medical care conforms with the standard assumptions (see Arrow, 1963 and Culyer, 1971a). First, are individuals perfectly informed about the nature of the product (in analytical terms is their indifference map well defined)? The answer, clearly, is no. Many people are unknowingly ill, particularly the elderly (Williamson *et al.*, 1964), and those with ailments like diabetes (Israel and Teeling-Smith,

1967; Florey, 1982) and hypertension (Hart, 1970) which can be largely without symptoms in their early stages. In addition, individuals are often ignorant about which types of treatment are available, and about the outcome of different treatments (which is often probabilistic). Furthermore, what little the patient knows is generally learned from a doctor (i.e. the supplier of health care services); and many types of treatment (e.g. setting a broken leg) are not repeated so that much of what a patient learns is of little future use.

There are other areas in which the consumer knows little and has to rely on the supplier for information (e.g. hi-fi, used cars). But in these cases it is usually possible to buy information (e.g. consumer magazines, or a report by the Automobile Association), and legislation offers increasing consumer protection.[1] With medical care the costs of mistaken choice are usually greater and less reversible than with most other commodities; an individual generally does not have time to shop around if his condition is acute; doctors are frequently reluctant to offer assessments of colleagues; and consumers frequently lack the information to weigh one doctor's advice against another's. Finally, health and health care have strongly emotive connotations, e.g. ignorance may in part be a consequence of fear, superstition, etc.

To a considerable extent, therefore, consumers lack the information necessary for rational choice; and even if teaching and information facilities existed, health care is inherently a technical subject, so that there is a limit to what consumers could understand without themselves becoming doctors. The problem is exacerbated by the existence of groups who would not be able to make use of information even if they had it, such as the mentally handicapped and victims of road accidents.

To say that there is ignorance need not *ipso facto* be evidence of inefficiency. Information may be costly, and its acquisition therefore inefficient if the resulting gain is small. Some degree of ignorance may well be optimal, though almost certainly less than would prevail under a private health care market.

If consumers are to make rational choices they need to have the necessary information, and also the power to enforce their decisions. Efficiency therefore requires equal power, in the sense that there should be no constraint on the ability of individuals to consume health care (or education) other than differences in their money income, i.e. people may have different incomes, but there should be no discrimination. This assumption was presented in Chapter 4:3.2 as a precondition of perfect competition, but the issue is closely related to perfect information and so fits naturally into the discussion at this point. In the context of health care and education, power consists largely of knowledge about their uses and benefits; knowledge about one's rights in respect of the

---

[1] It has been suggested that a consumer magazine about medicine might be called *Which Doctor?* (letter in *The Times*, 25 April 1986).

NHS and the educational system; and the ability and confidence to be articulate. It is somewhat implausible to imagine that this is the state of affairs for all consumers, though in the final analysis the issue is empirical.

Because of imperfect information and unequal power, consumers will choose inefficiently, though there is room for debate about the extent of the problem (this is one of the key issues in any discussion of health care). It is also not clear whether the result will be under- or over-consumption. If the 'true' marginal private valuation in Figure 12.2 is shown by the curve MPV, consumer ignorance can result in demand curves D1 (underconsumption) or D2 (overconsumption). In addition, where knowledge and power are systematically related to socio-economic status, there is also inequity (section 3.3).

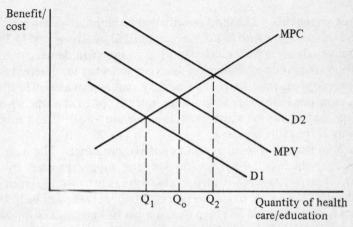

Figure 12.2   *The effects of consumer ignorance on individual demand for health care/ education*

What solutions exist? The provision of information on a scale sufficient for rational individual choice may be too costly, in which case decisions about treatment must be delegated to doctors. Minimal intervention takes the form of regulation, e.g. only individuals with approved qualifications are allowed to practise medicine. But where the information problem is serious the performance of the market may be so inefficient that more extensive state involvement, either through substantial regulation of private production, or through public production and allocation, might be a better solution. We return to this issue in section 4.1.

A separate issue is whether consumers are adequately informed about prices (formally, whether their budget constraint is well defined). Here, again, it can be argued that most consumers are ignorant of what a particular form of treatment 'should' cost; and, because a great deal of medical care is not repeated, information often has no future use. Nor would it help if consumers were well informed about prices. Rational choice requires simultaneous knowledge *both* of prices *and* of the nature of the product (i.e. of both budget constraint and indifference map); knowledge of prices without adequate information about different types of treatment will not ensure efficiency.

The result is inefficiency of the type discussed above, and summarised in Figure 12.2. If the *only* problem were inadequate information about prices the appropriate intervention would be regulation, either in the form of a published price list or through price controls. But where information about the nature of the product is imperfect, ignorance about prices adds further weight to the argument for more substantial state involvement.

Insurance arguments   The third information assumption – knowledge about the future – clearly fails with health care, as stressed by Arrow (1963). Patients do not know when, or how much, health care they will demand; they lack information about the probabilities of different outcomes for different types of treatment, and about the relative efficiency of different providers of health care; and they consume health care services infrequently, often at a time when their judgement and ability to acquire information are small. The problem of uncertainty is therefore serious.

In many instances the market solution is insurance. The real issue, therefore, is whether the private market can supply medical insurance efficiently. This, we saw in Chapter 5:3.1, requires five technical conditions: the probability of needing treatment (see equation (5.12)) must be independent across individuals, and less than one; it must be known or estimable; and there must be no substantial problem of adverse selection or moral hazard (the last three conditions adding up to perfect information on the part of the insurance company). The extent to which these hold for health care is discussed by Arrow (1963, 1965, and 1968), Pauly (1968) and Crew (1969).

Looking at the first condition, the probabilities of different individuals requiring treatment are independent except during major epidemics. Second, the probability of requiring treatment of a particular type over a given period is less than unity for ailments like appendicitis or a broken leg. But the condition fails for chronic medical problems (e.g. diabetes) arising before an insurance policy is taken out, and a fortiori for congenital problems.[1] In the absence of insurance starting before birth, the private market generally fails to cover these cases.

---

[1] A related (but different) point is that treatment of long-term illness is generally expensive, so that competitive pressures act to reduce premiums at the expense of long-term coverage.

The probabilities relevant to health care insurance are generally estimable, but problems arise both of adverse selection and moral hazard (Chapter 5:3.2). Adverse selection occurs where an individual is able to conceal from the insurance company that he is a bad risk. In this situation the market either provides an inefficient quantity of insurance or fails to provide it at all. Akerlof (1970, pp. 492–3) asks why Americans over 65 cannot easily buy medical insurance, and concludes

> that as the price [of insurance] rises the people who insure themselves will be those who are increasingly certain that they will need the insurance; for error in medical check-ups, doctors' sympathy with older patients, and so on make it much easier for the applicant to assess the risks involved than the insurance company.

One way to finesse the problem, as we saw in Chapter 5:4.2, is to make it compulsory for people to belong to an approved insurance scheme.

Moral hazard can arise in two ways: patients may be able to influence either the probability of requiring medical treatment, or its cost. Taking the probability issue first, individuals do not usually injure themselves deliberately so as to qualify for medical treatment (though they might drive more recklessly if they know that their medical costs will be borne by the insurer). But both the decision to consult one's family doctor and pregnancy can be matters of *choice* which lead to the consumption of medical services. As a result, many voluntary, private medical insurance schemes offer only limited cover for

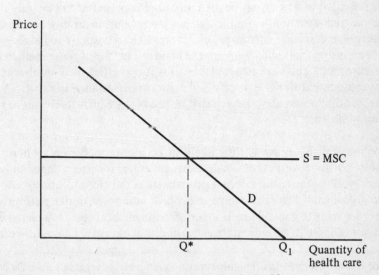

Figure 12.3 *A simple market for health care*

consultations with general practitioners and for the cost of a normal pregnancy, since both are substantially controlled by the individual (though in the latter case the costs of complications may be fully covered because (unlike the original pregnancy) they are exogenous to the mother).

A second type of moral hazard arises where consumers can influence the cost of treatment. This is the *third-party payment* problem. It has two sources: the fact that the insurance company is largely divorced from the decisions of doctor and patient; and the fact that the doctor is paid a fee for service. Suppose medical insurance covers all costs. Health care is then 'free' to the patient; and the supplier is not constrained by the patient's demand curve. Patient and doctor both face zero *private* costs, even though the *social* costs of health care are positive and frequently large, and both have an incentive to consume all health care which yields *any* private benefit.[1] The result is overconsumption, i.e. Q_1, greater than the efficient outcome, Q^* in Figure 12.3.

Devices like coinsurance, deductions and inspection (Chapter 5:3.2) are used to counteract the worst effects of moral hazard, but are at best only partial solutions. Deductions make the patient pay a fixed cost, but do nothing to raise the *marginal* cost of health care; with a coinsurance rate of (say) 10 per cent, the patient's private marginal cost is only 10 per cent of marginal social cost. Neither device on its own prevents overconsumption. Nor, typically, are administrative methods like inspection of medical bills generally sufficient to curtail demand to the efficient level.

One additional problem requires discussion – that of transactions costs. We saw earlier (equation (5.17)) that insurance, even if efficient on the supply side, can be provided at a price which the individual is prepared to pay only if his degree of risk-aversion is sufficient to cover the insurance company's administrative costs and normal profit. If transactions costs are too high, some risk-averse individuals will choose not to insure. This is not *per se* inefficient if high transactions costs are unavoidable. But it *is* inefficient if an alternative system could avoid them, e.g. private health care insurance in the USA has high accounting costs; these are avoided by the NHS which rarely has to send patients a bill.

Private medical insurance is thus likely to be highly inefficient. There will generally be no coverage or inadequate coverage for the congenitally or chronically ill (because the relevant probability is too close to unity), and for the old (because of fears of adverse selection); and cover under pure private schemes for visits to general practitioners and the medical costs associated with pregnancy is likely to be limited (because of moral hazard). These difficulties,

---

[1] For an argument suggesting that this effect, though real, is exaggerated see De Meza (1983).

plus the problem which can arise if transactions costs are high, all lead to *underconsumption*. Third-party payments cause *overconsumption*.

There are several lines of attack on these problems. Minimal intervention involves several types of regulation. Insurance could be compulsory to prevent the externalities caused by non-insurance (Chapter 8:2.1), with cover starting before birth to cope with the congenitally and chronically ill. It might also be necessary to prevent insurance companies from withholding cover from high-risk individuals, and also to regulate conditions under which they could increase premiums. These latter points would alleviate the problem of adverse selection. Moral hazard would have to be left to dubiously effective devices like coinsurance, or to different types of insurance, like health maintenance organisations (discussed in section 4.1).

A more radical approach is publicly provided insurance, at least for those groups for which the private market caters less well (though such schemes in practice would almost certainly be no more than a 'mimic' of true insurance – cf. the discussion of unemployment benefits in Chapter 8:2.2 and 3.1). The most radical solution is to abandon the model of actuarial insurance because it does not fit health care very well, and replace it either by state *finance* of all medical care on a non-insurance basis (e.g. out of taxation), or by public *production* of health care services which could then be supplied free, or at a price related to patients' ability to pay.

The remaining assumptions   The assumption of equal power was discussed earlier. The next step is to consider the applicability of perfect competition, i.e. whether the markets for inputs like skilled manpower and drugs are competitive. In the case of doctors there are two issues: is the number of doctors restricted below its efficient level; and do doctors maximise profits, or have they other goals? It has long been argued that medical associations may artificially restrict the number of doctors. For instance, per capita real income in the USA is about twice that in Britain; and the number of telephones, televisions and cars per head is also about double the UK level. Yet the number of doctors per capita in the USA is less than one-third higher than in Britain. This could be because health in the USA is better, or because each US doctor is able to supply more health care than his UK counterpart because he/she has more advanced equipment; or because the US has fewer people willing or able to become doctors; or that the number allowed to train is artificially restricted. Only the last argument bears empirical scrutiny. If it is true, the result is underconsumption.

The element of monopoly power resulting from barriers to entry is an old argument (see Friedman and Kuznets, 1945). Recent analysis focuses more on the behaviour of doctors. It is not argued that they act like the profit-maximising monopolist of elementary textbooks, but rather that they pursue several goals. It is suggested that a doctor's reputation depends more on the assessment of his/her fellow professionals than on direct evaluation by the consumer, and that the approval of colleagues is more easily achieved in the development of more advanced techniques (e.g. heart transplants). Thus, it is argued, there is a bias towards certain glamorous types of health care. Doctors' behaviour is then determined jointly by this type of motive, and by their economic environment. As we have seen, doctors do not generally face the costs of their production decisions, but are reimbursed by insurance companies which generally do not question their activities. There is no budget constraint facing doctors individually; and on aggregate they are constrained only by the willingness of consumers to pay insurance premiums.

These arguments, if true, point towards economic inefficiency in the form of oversupply of health care generally. In addition, the *composition* of that supply is distorted in favour of glamorous areas, and against low prestige activities (e.g. general practice, occupational health). The consensus today seems to be that the underprovision resulting from an undersupply of doctors is probably more than offset by the behaviour of individual doctors (of the *distribution* of that health care more will be said later). It seems that the best that can be said of the market system is that two different forms of monopoly behaviour may to some extent cancel each other out. This 'two wrongs make a right' line of argument cannot be said to be very convincing.

What solutions exist for this non-competitive behaviour? At a minimum, regulation is required on standards (e.g. doctors must have approved qualifications). In addition, some regulation of prices and possibly also monitoring of doctors' activities might be appropriate. Another potential solution is the libertarian approach (see the Further Reading) of removing entry barriers to medical practice, thereby enhancing competitiveness on the supply side and largely removing the need for state intervention of the type just described. This solution, however, may be more apparent than real. The advantages of competition are that it increases consumer choice and minimises costs. However, as we saw in Chapter 4:3.2, an increase in the range of choices is desirable only where consumers are sufficiently well informed to choose between them, which is frequently not the case with health care; and if competitive forces push down prices consumers, for the same reason, will be unable to assess whether quality has declined, and if so whether they want the lower quality product at the lower price. The counter-argument to the proponents of market systems for health care is that *the advantages of competition are contingent on perfect information*.

The conclusion is that supply-side deviations from competitive behaviour are likely to cause inefficiency, but removing restrictions to competition is unlikely *on its own* to improve economic welfare.

The remaining assumptions concern externalities and increasing returns to scale. The literature on health care distinguishes two sorts of externality: 'caring' externalities, such that my utility is reduced if you receive less health care than I think you should (these are a matter more of the *distribution* of health care than the efficiency of its production – see section 3.3); and technological externalities.[1] The latter arise mainly via communicable diseases (e.g. if I am vaccinated against polio I benefit, and also confer a benefit on you because you cannot now catch polio from me), though in the context of today's medical technology these externalities, though real, are only a small fraction of the total value of health care. It is a standard proposition that technological external benefits, if uncorrected, cause underconsumption by creating a divergence between private and social benefits (Figure 12.1). The problem can be solved in a variety of ways, the most relevant here being regulation (e.g. making vaccination compulsory) or a Pigovian subsidy (see the Glossary). Externalities are not *per se* a justification for public production and allocation.

It is sometimes argued that health care is subject to increasing returns to scale (Chapter 4:3.2 and Figure 4.4). Were this the case, health care would be a natural monopoly which, if uncorrected, would lead to underconsumption. The theoretical solution is to regulate the industry (e.g. by setting a maximum price supporting the competitive output, and paying a lump-sum subsidy to make up the resultant losses), or to nationalise the industry. However, the range of output over which health care exhibits increasing returns to scale is small even with today's large-scale technology. So the problem is unlikely to arise except, possibly, in sparsely populated areas.

3.2 EFFICIENCY ARGUMENTS FOR INTERVENTION: EDUCATION

The arguments about the conformity of education with the standard assumptions parallel those for health care, so discussion is brief.

Perfect information Do consumers of education have perfect information about the nature of the product (i.e. are indifference maps well defined), about prices (i.e. do they know their budget constraint), and about the future? Knowledge of the nature of the product is certainly not perfect. Children (the immediate consumers) are not well informed. In a market system decisions are therefore left to parents, at least for early education. But parental preferences can cause inefficiency in two ways: they might themselves have imperfect information; or they might not consider the child's best interests but those of

---

[1] On the definition and effects of externalities, and possible remedies, see Chapter 4:3.2, and/or the Appendix to Chapter 4, para. 15.

the family as a whole, themselves included. The issue is further complicated because the notion of 'the product' in education is much more elusive than with health care. What constitutes a good education varies enormously between families, e.g. its subject-matter, the role of discipline, the place of religion and its type (see Coons and Sugarman, 1978).

Such complexities make it difficult even for intelligent, well-educated young adults to make rational decisions – how many students make a *fully* informed choice of university and of subjects studied? In addition, consumers of education are likely to differ in the extent of their confidence and articulateness (the issue of unequal power). The result of these factors is inefficiency, though both its extent and direction (see Figure 12.2) are open to debate. But it is likely that imperfect information leads to underconsumption, particularly by the lowest socio-economic groups (see section 3.3).

Solutions can take several forms. In contrast with health care, the market itself might supply information, e.g. advisory centres, or a 'Good Schools Guide' which included each school's performance in public examinations. But it can be argued that where children or their families have imperfect information and/or where families cannot be relied on to act in their best interests, there is an efficiency argument for intervention, particularly in the form of regulation. This would embrace mandatory school attendance (discussed below), and the establishment of minimum standards and inspection to ensure conformity with those standards. Only if the information problem is regarded as major is there an argument on this account for public production and allocation.

A second issue is the extent to which consumers or their families are well informed about prices. If education were privately produced this information would be provided by the market. But, as with health care, it should be remembered that improved knowledge of prices will increase efficiency only where consumers are well informed also in other respects. If intervention on efficiency grounds were thought necessary it would take the form of publishing a list of school fees, or regulating them.

The problem of information about the future is minor. Parents know that their children will need education at least until minimum school-leaving age. In a market system they would make financial provision for their children's education out of current income, out of savings or, if they were uncertain of their future income or lifespan, by taking out an endowment policy the proceeds of which could be used to pay school fees in the future. Uncertainty (as opposed to poverty) raises no substantial problems in this context.

Perfect competition The proposition that the advantages of a competitive market for health care are contingent on perfect information is equally applicable here. But the information problem is arguably less severe for education, so this section is not concerned with the desirability of competition, but with its feasibility. Two issues arise: the supply of education, and the availability through the private market of finance for education.

There is no reason why schools in cities should not act competitively. But a rural school may have a local monopoly and, if run to maximise profits, would underprovide. The standard solution is price regulation (Chapter 4:3.2). Education finance raises different issues. From an efficiency viewpoint we do not normally worry if an individual cannot afford more than x units of a good. If a student cannot afford smoked salmon and therefore buys none there are no *efficiency* implications. But if an individual cannot afford an adequate diet and suffers malnutrition then, as well as equity costs, there are efficiency losses in the form of external costs to others. Similar losses arise if an individual cannot afford to buy the socially efficient amount of education, e.g. basic literacy and numeracy. With perfect capital markets children could finance their own education by borrowing against their future earnings. But capital markets are not perfect; students seeking to borrow money can usually offer only human capital as collateral, whereas lending institutions usually require physical capital or financial wealth. In a pure market system this would result in underconsumption, giving an efficiency (as well as a possible equity) justi-fication for intervention. This could take several forms: the state could act as guarantor for loans made by private institutions to children for educational purposes; it could provide loan finance itself; or it might choose to subsidise education.

Market failures Education is not a public good; nor does it generally face increasing returns to scale. But we saw in section 2.2 that education can create two sorts of external benefit: production benefits relate to productivity and economic growth; cultural benefits include social cohesion. The strength of these effects is hard to measure, but they cannot on that account be ignored. Intervention can involve regulation in the form of compulsory attendance at school until age 16 to prevent underconsumption (see the analogous argument for compulsory membership of an unemployment insurance scheme in Chapter 8:2.1); and an appropriate Pigovian subsidy (see the Glossary) could in principle achieve a similar effect.

3.3 EQUITY ARGUMENTS FOR INTERVENTION

Horizontal equity was discussed in Chapter 4:4.3 in terms of perfect information (which is necessary for rational decisions) and equal power (which is necessary to enforce those decisions). Both may be lacking for consumers of education and (particularly) health care. Equity issues arise most acutely where these problems systematically affect the lower socio-economic groups most strongly (a likely occurrence if information is costly to acquire). Thus parents with little education may have less information than better-educated parents in making decisions about their children; in addition, they may be less able to make use of any information they acquire. In such cases intervention in the following forms may improve equity as well as efficiency.

Regulation would be concerned, on the input side, with the professional qualifications of doctors, nurses, social workers and teachers; with drugs; with school meals; with buildings; and with school attendance. Regulation of output would include inspection in both public and private sectors of schools, hospitals and personal social services.

Where imperfect information causes underconsumption a subsidy might be applied either to prices (e.g. free medical prescriptions) or to incomes. Income subsidies usually take the form of cash transfers (e.g. supplementary benefit); but education vouchers (Chapter 13:2.3) can be thought of as a form of tied transfer; so too can student educational grants. In most circumstances price subsidies cost less than income subsidies (Culyer, 1980, pp. 71–6; Lindsay, 1969). This is because if the price of (say) health care is subsidised, consumption will increase via both income *and* substitution effects; with an income subsidy only the income effect operates, so a larger subsidy is generally needed to bring about a given increase in consumption.

Where problems of inadequate information and inequality of power are serious, efficiency and equity may jointly be maximised by public allocation and/or production. In broad terms this depends on two factors: whether the private or public sector is more efficient at producing health care and education; and whether policing of standards is more effective in one sector or the other. This issue is discussed in section 4.

Vertical equity concerns the extent to which health care does or should redistribute from rich to poor, and similarly for education. We saw in Chapter 7:4 that (subject to various caveats) publicly provided health care is redistributive if (rich) individual A pays more tax contributions to its costs than (poor) B where each consumes the same quantity, and also if A consumes twice as much as B but pays more than twice as much in contributions. Why might this be thought desirable – why, in other words, might people care about the distribution of health care and education *per se*? A formal explanation is given by the voting model discussed in Chapter 4:4.2. Suppose the utility of a representative rich individual, R, rises with his own consumption and also with the consumption of a representative poor man, P. In particular, suppose that R's utility rises with 'good' consumption by P (e.g. health care or education) but falls with P's 'bad' consumption, e.g. whisky. This is a consumption externality of the type described by equation (4.15). It might therefore be rational for R to make an in-kind transfer to P of health care or education costing (say) £300, but to offer a cash transfer of only £100 (since P might spend the latter on 'bad' consumption). Given these offers, P might prefer the in-kind transfer to the lower cash amount (see Figure 4.5). If the difference between the two offers is sufficiently large, both rich *and* poor might vote for compulsory in-kind transfers of health care and education.

It is worth delving more deeply into the nature of the consumption externality. 'Good' consumption by the poor can raise the utility of the rich for two entirely different reasons. The rich might vote for transfers to the poor of health care/education for reasons of efficiency/self-interest. They might believe that a healthy, educated workforce fosters economic growth; or that increased health care and education for the poor raises their productivity and/or reduces the cost of caring for them; or that such transfers prevent social unrest. This is the 'national efficiency' argument (Chapter 2:2.1) which gives rise to the Marxist interpretation of the welfare state (Chapter 3:5.3). A completely different explanation is that some rich individuals care about the distribution of health care and education for reasons of *altruism* (Lindsay, 1969; Culyer, 1980, Ch. 3).

Thus, alongside efficiency arguments for public production and allocation, there may be powerful equity motives which make it politically easier to make transfers in kind. The rich may favour them for either selfish or altruistic reasons; and the poor may prefer them, either because the in-kind transfer is more generous than the cash offer for which they might realistically hope, and/ or because they feel less stigmatised by receiving benefits in kind than in the form of means-tested cash transfers.

The voting model explains why *some* transfers of health care and education take place. But is the amount transferred *optimal*? This was discussed in Chapter 4:4.4. Libertarians support in-kind transfers (if at all) only as *voluntary* action by the rich, but not as a result of coercion by the poor via the ballot box (Chapter 4:4.1); they therefore argue that redistribution under the existing system is greater than optimal. Socialists support in-kind transfers for their own sake, because they increase equality (this is especially relevant to education), and argue that redistribution of health care and education is almost certainly sub-optimal.

The role of giving   Previous discussion suggested two reasons for intervention to enhance equity: inadequacies of information or power may justify intervention to foster horizontal equity; and consumption externalities can explain in-kind transfers. The role of giving raises a third set of arguments. The analysis so far has treated health care and education as commodities to which the standard economic arguments apply. But most societies, for generally accepted ethical reasons, decree that certain commodities, which in principle are readily marketable, should be excluded from the usual economic calculus.

Thus, there is a free market for the purchase and sale of cattle but, in most countries, no similar market for babies, for wives or for slaves. Titmuss (1970) argues that for ethical and philosophical reasons there should similarly be no market for blood, which should be donated to recipients. This, he argues, is a morally superior method of distribution.

Two questions arise: how valid are Titmuss's views about blood; and to what extent do these arguments generalise to other commodities? Whether blood should be given rather than allocated by the market is ultimately one of social values, so that no answer is unambiguously right or wrong. But Titmuss's views are rightly respected on moral grounds, and also because certain characteristics of blood make its allocation as a gift both feasible and (arguably) also efficient. The reasons for the latter view are threefold: the opportunity cost of the *act* of giving blood (e.g. the time and discomfort) is small; and that of losing a pint of blood effectively zero; furthermore, blood donation can create an altruistic externality, inasmuch as donors often experience a utility gain, not from the act of giving but from the thought of the benefit the blood will confer on others. These considerations together suggest that the marginal social cost of blood is likely to be low, and may be zero. In this case giving might be both morally superior *and* efficient.

This makes blood a special case, so that it is dangerous indiscriminately to generalise the notion of giving into areas like health care and education (a mistake of which Titmuss himself was never guilty). The main reason is that the marginal social cost of health care is positive and often large. It is therefore an economic commodity. If a doctor spends more time with one patient he/she will have less time to spend with others; and resources devoted to health care are at the expense of other uses (contrast the case of blood, the giving of which has virtually no opportunity cost to the donor, and which (*pace* Dracula) cannot be used for other than medical purposes).[1] Thus, voluntary giving of health care and education, even if regarded as morally superior, will generally run into major allocative problems which do not arise with blood (though see Sugden, 1984).

4 Methods 2: Types of Intervention

4.1 HEALTH CARE

Section 3 discussed *why* the state might intervene. The next question is *how*

---

[1] Though resources used in *processing and storing* blood do have alternative uses and hence a positive opportunity cost.

best it might do so. Since the aim is jointly to maximise efficiency and equity they are discussed together. Three broad types of regime are considered for health care, and in section 4.2 for education: market production and allocation (with or without income transfers); public production and allocation; and intermediate strategies. The analysis of market production is closely linked to the issue of 'privatisation' discussed in Chapter 4:5, which should be read alongside this section (see especially Table 4.2 which is referred to extensively in this chapter and the next). The main focus at this stage is the theoretical argument about different forms of organisation; policy issues are deferred to Chapter 13.

Medical technology used to be cheap, so that health care could be treated as a basic right like voting privileges, but costly advances are making this approach unsustainable.

> The policy of meeting medical need, which once entailed little social waste, now threatens to cause considerable waste, largely through the provision of services that are medically needed (the benefit to the patient is positive), demanded (because marginal cost to the patient is zero or very low), and supplied (because providers are fully reimbursed or are indifferent between low- and high-benefit care), but that provide benefits worth less . . . than social cost. [Aaron, 1981a, p. 25.]

Because of rising costs the issue of macro efficiency (i.e. expenditure on health care as a proportion of national income) has become increasingly important in all industrial economies (Chapter 13:1.1). It is therefore of more than usual importance to be dispassionate in considering methods of allocation.

Pure market provision   Some writers (see the Further Reading) argue that health care is similar to food. On the demand side, consumers have preferences which they should be allowed to translate into their utility-maximising consumption pattern. Supply will adjust to these preferences more efficiently if it is competitive. Government intervention destroys the fit between demand and supply, and the destruction is greatest if intervention takes the form of public production. Writers of this ilk favour privatisation to the greatest extent possible, i.e. ideally line (1) in Table 4.2, or for low-income families line (2).

We saw in section 3.1 that health care comes nowhere near conformity with the standard assumptions, so that unrestricted market allocation is not a theoretically promising approach. But analysis of the pure market case is important to an understanding of the problems raised by health care. To focus the argument, discussion concentrates on two simple cases, initially assuming away non-competitive supply-side behaviour, and concentrating in particular on the problems of imperfect information on the demand side of the product market and the supply side of the insurance market.

Case 1: Assume initially that there is no insurance, so that consumption is constrained by price. In the presence of consumer ignorance (and to some extent also because of unequal power) the demand curve is not properly defined, but 'wobbly' as shown in Figure 12.2, so that the market-clearing quantity can be above or below the optimum. Uncorrected externalities lead to underconsumption, and non-competitive supply-side behaviour to under- or over-consumption, depending on what it is that doctors seek to maximise. The result is inefficiency in the total volume of resources (i.e. macro inefficiency), possibly substantial, though with no clear presumption of its direction, and also micro inefficiency (i.e. the allocation of resources to different types of health care). There is also considerable inequity; the distribution of health care is determined by inequalities in the income distribution; and these inequalities are heightened where knowledge and power are correlated with income (so that the poor are the least informed), and also by the absence of insurance and perfect capital markets. The overall result is likely to be substantial *underconsumption* of health care.

Case 2: Assume that health insurance pays all medical bills in full. Consumption is no longer constrained by price, and is therefore determined mainly by the supplier; as a result the indeterminacy of the patient's demand curve is less important. On the supply side, the doctor has no incentive to ration demand to the efficient quantity Q^* in Figure 12.3. Both patient and doctor can behave as though the cost of health care were zero, leading to consumption Q_1. From an efficiency viewpoint, this system leads unambiguously to *overconsumption*, since third-party payments give neither side of the market an incentive to moderate its consumption.[1] There is also inequity, inasmuch as some individuals are unable to buy insurance (the old, the chronically ill, etc.), and others cannot afford insurance premiums which overconsumption has raised to an inefficiently high level.

These arguments, it should be noted, do not necessarily apply on the input side. There is no reason why many material inputs should not be privately produced, e.g. food products (the NHS does not grow its own vegetables), drugs, beds, towels, X-ray machines and so on. Some inputs of services might also be privately produced, e.g. food or laundry, provided that the costs of quality control are not excessive.

Mixed public/private involvement To what extent might health care be based on mixed public/private involvement so as to avoid the worst problems of pure private provision? The desirability of such a package depends on two factors: would it be more efficient/equitable than any other method including

---

[1] There might be some pressures to economy, e.g. from employers who pay health care insurance premiums on behalf of their employees.

the NHS; and might it be politically more acceptable than NHS-type arrangements (as might be the case, for instance, in the USA)? To be feasible it would have to be constructed out of various theoretical ingredients, relating to (a) production and (b) finance.

Production: the supply of medical treatment in a private market is crucially influenced by fee for service and third-party payments. The result, as we saw above, is that the market output, Q_1 in Figure 12.3 exceeds the efficient output Q^*. Third-party payments create a divergence between private and social costs and benefits, and hence cause a particular kind of externality. These, we know, can be dealt with in a number of ways, of which two are of special relevance. First, output could be restricted to Q^* by *regulation*; this would involve policing doctors' decisions, either by administrative means or through the imposition of a budget constraint (e.g. line (3)(b) in Table 4.2).

Alternatively, it is possible to *internalise the externality* by merging the activities of doctor and insurance company, thereby forcing doctors to face the social marginal cost of the treatment they prescribe. The outstanding example of this approach is the notion of a *health maintenance organisation* of the type now found increasingly in the USA (see Chapter 13:1.3 for more extensive discussion). The essence of a health maintenance organisation in this context is that *doctors* provide the insurance; as a result the externality is internalised and there is no longer an incentive to over-prescribe. It might be possible by one of these methods to constrain private production to its efficient level.

Finance could then be organised in one of two generic ways. One possibility is private finance plus residual state finance. 'Easy' cases (i.e. the insurable conditions of non-poor individuals) are financed by private insurance subject to regulation in two ways: there would be minimum standards of coverage, and insurance would be compulsory because of the externality caused by non-insurance (see Chapter 8:2.1). Two difficulties arise: non-insurable risks, and the poor. The former, as we saw in section 3.1, include congenital and chronic health problems, the medical needs of the elderly, visits to general practitioners and pregnancy. The state could deal with these cases *either* by subsidising private insurance premiums through an explicit subsidy or via an untied cash transfer; *or* by paying the full cost of treatment through a residual public insurance scheme, or out of tax revenues. The poor could be assisted similarly. This approach raises a number of serious problems: there is the difficulty of defining borderlines, both as between the types of health care problem which qualify for state assistance, and over the income level below which the poor are subsidised; policing would be necessary to prevent oversupply; and the familiar poverty trap could arise for the poor.

A second possibility is state finance. Here the state pays medical bills either through a public health care insurance scheme, membership of which is compulsory, or out of tax revenues. An analytically equivalent arrangement is compulsory membership of regulated, private, non-profit insurance institutions acting, in effect, as agents of the state. The advantages of this arrangement are twofold: the scheme's compulsory nature makes it possible with no efficiency loss to gear premiums to ability to pay, rather than to risk (Chapter 5:4.2); and its universal coverage (with respect both to individuals and type of illness) avoids problems with borderlines. It is important, however, to be clear that such institutions, to the extent that they avoid the gaps of private schemes, are less like actuarial insurance and more like earmarked taxation (cf. Chapter 8:2.2 for the case of unemployment benefits). The disadvantage of this approach is that considerable policing is necessary to prevent oversupply.

These considerations suggest two coherent mixed strategies. Suppose that health care is *produced* by health maintenance organisations of some kind; that membership is compulsory for all individuals; and that insurance premiums are *financed* by individuals (in the case of the poor out of transfer incomes). This arrangement has the flavour of line (3)(a) in Table 4.2. Alternatively, suppose health care is produced privately, but not by health maintenance organisations; payment is made by the state (either directly or through publicly provided or regulated health care insurance); and total output is controlled by the state either directly or via a global budget constraint. This mechanism follows the general thrust of line (3)(b) for health care *per se* and of line (6) for health care insurance. Policy aspects of such arrangements are discussed in Chapter 13:1.3.

Public production, allocation and finance   To justify this arrangement requires consideration of the different elements of line (8) in Table 4.2. Consumer sovereignty is appropriate where information is sufficient for rational choice, a process which may be assisted by regulation of quality. In the case of health care it can be argued that the patient's information is often so imperfect that the individual consumption decision is best made on his behalf by an expert (column (3)).[1] The argument for publicly financed health care (column (4)) rests on the problems just discussed of private insurance, viz. the imperfect information of insurance companies (which contributes to the third-party payment problem), and the fact that not all medical conditions are insurable. The third-party payment problem can also justify public production as a method of controlling the resulting large and inefficient increases in the output of health care (Chapter 13:1.1). More formally, the imperfect information of consumers justifies control of *quality*, and that of insurance companies control of *quantity* (column (2)). Both forms of policing might be more effective if production itself were public (column (1)).

---

[1] There is a wealth of literature on the question of whether patient or doctor knows best. For further references and a review of the literature see Illsley (1980, Chs 5 and 6).

The argument for public production and allocation thus turns in a crucial though complex way on the issue of information. To justify this arrangement, however, it is necessary to show not only that the conditions for market efficiency fail, but also that public production and allocation are less inefficient than any alternative arrangement. The first point is relatively easy to establish, the second less so.

Because of information problems the NHS strategy can be regarded as feasible – an institution which arose historically largely for equity reasons works because it goes with the grain of *efficiency* considerations. The strategy has four cornerstones. Dealing with demand-side problems, (a) treatment is decided by doctors, largely solving the difficulties caused by consumer ignorance; and (b) health care is financed (mostly) out of tax revenues, and is (mostly) free at the point of use. These features avoid the problems of gaps in insurance cover by abandoning the insurance principle even as a fiction; and medical care is made available without stigma to the poor. On the supply side, (c) doctors receive little or no fee for service, thus reducing third-party payment incentives to oversupply; and (d) health care is explicitly rationed, in part by administrative means, and partly by the existence of a budget constraint for the NHS as a whole. The idea, at least in principle, is to restrict consumption to the quantity Q^* in Figure 12.3. Furthermore, once it is estalished that public production and allocation are justifiable on efficiency grounds, it is legitimate to finance health care so as to further distributional aims (Chapter 4:6.1). In theory, therefore, the strategy is feasible in both efficiency and equity terms. The practice is assessed in Chapter 13:1.

4.2 EDUCATION

The theoretical arguments raised by education largely parallel those for health care. The main differences are that the problem of information (though not of unequal power) may be less acute; that the problems raised by private medical insurance are not relevant; and that the issue of capital markets (and probably also of external effects) is probably of greater importance.

Pure market provision (i.e. lines (1) or (2) of Table 4.2). Critics of public provision (see the Further Reading) ideally wish to see education produced, allocated and financed privately. But recognising some of the difficulties described earlier, their policy proposals (Chapter 13:2.3) are of private production, with mixed public/private finance and some regulation.

The argument against market production and allocation of education is the failure of many of the assumptions necessary for market efficiency. Regulation can be justified by imperfect information and unequal power, and the presence of externalities and local monopolies. Subsidies can be justified by externalities, and subsidies or the provision of loan guarantees (or of loans themselves) by capital market imperfections. The issue of public production rests largely on the extent of information problems. It should be clear that a pure market system is likely to be highly inefficient, and also inequitable to the extent that knowledge, power and access to capital markets are correlated with socio-economic status. Unrestricted market provision of education is theoretically implausible and, in practice, does not exist in any country.

Mixed public/private involvement (e.g. line (4)(a) in Table 4.2). The issue is whether it is possible to devise an efficient and equitable package whereby the state regulates education and subsidises it wholly or in part, but where production takes place in the private sector. This is the way universities operate in many countries, and proposals to extend these arrangements to schools (e.g. so-called 'voucher' schemes) are discussed in Chapter 13:2.3.

Several ingredients are necessary for this approach to be efficient and equitable. The state would have to regulate education in one or more of the following areas: mandatory school attendance to some minimum age; the range of syllabuses; minimum qualifications for teachers; certification of schools (i.e. would an individual need permission to start a school?); inspection to ensure an adequate quality of service; and fee levels (i.e. should schools be allowed to charge what they like?). Though the principle of regulation is accepted, commentators disagree widely as to how far it should go.

Subsidies to education may be justifiable for both efficiency and equity reasons. In a libertarian world individuals pay for the private benefits they receive from education, but are subsidised to the extent that external benefits are thereby conferred upon others.[1] This degree of subsidy might, however, be insufficient. Individuals from lower socio-economic groups might face imperfect capital markets; in addition they (and their families) might systematically have poorer information about the benefits of education and/or be reluctant to incur large debts. Any resulting tendency to underconsumption suggests a larger subsidy than the externality argument implies, and maybe a 100 per cent subsidy, at least for school education. Additionally, if the subsidy is only partial, it may be necessary on both efficiency and equity grounds for the state to provide loan capital.

Private production is likely to be efficient only if its quality is adequately policed. Libertarians dispute this view, arguing that dissatisfied parents could move their child to another school, and also that if a private school has a bad reputation it will go out of business. The weakness of this line of argument is twofold. First, parents may not have sufficient information to realise that their

---

[1] Note that this approach is logically incompatible with the screening hypothesis (section 2.2).

child is being badly educated or, if they do, may not have the confidence to do anything about it. Second, education is not a repeatable experiment. It is true that a restaurant which provides bad service will go out of business; its former clients will have suffered nothing worse than a bad meal, and can spend the rest of their lives going to better restaurants. But the application of this argument to education makes an unfounded leap in logic. Education is in large measure a once-and-for-all experience; a child who has had a year or two of bad education may never recover. In addition, a child may face a high emotional cost (changing friends, etc.) in changing school. A more apt analogy is a restaurant which gives unknowing customers food so bad that it might cause permanent ill health.

Finally, private consumption decisions are likely to be efficient and equitable only if families have sufficient information, and if they use it in the child's best interests. The issue of whether the state or the family is better qualified to make educational decisions in the name of an individual child is controversial to say the least. Some parents, maybe disproportionately in the higher socio-economic groups, are capable of more informed decisions than the state; others make poorer decisions. If the quality of parental choice is systematically related to socio-economic status, and the effect is strong, then private allocation can be argued to be less equitable than state allocation, irrespective of the balance of argument about efficiency. It is not surprising that the advocates of parental choice almost invariably belong to the higher socio-economic groups.

Public production, allocation and finance   (i.e. line (8) in Table 4.2). The question is whether public funding, together with public production and (to a large extent) allocation is less inefficient and inequitable than the sort of arrangements just described. The allocation issue should be argued on the basis of perceptions about imperfect information and social cohesion, and that of public production on whether it is, or is not, likely to be more efficient than the private market. These issues, we have seen, turn crucially on the answers to two questions. First, do parents *on average* make better or worse decisions than the state about their children's education? Second, if the quality of parental choice varies systematically with socio-economic status, how do we weigh the relative claims of middle-class children and their parents to be allowed private choice, against those of children in lower socio-economic groups, whose interests might be served better by the state? The answer to the first question is empirical. The answer to the second depends on one's political stance. Libertarians argue that state allocation interferes with parental freedom and therefore reject it. To socialists the aim of equality is paramount; the claim of children from poorer families therefore takes priority, and state allocation is preferred. Liberals try to recognise the claims of both groups. This involves a system either of public allocation which takes account of stated parental preferences (this is the way the system set up under the 1944 Education Act is supposed to work), or of parental choice subject to careful scrutiny.

The a priori arguments about the public/private provision of education are more finely balanced than those about health care.[1] But it is fair to say that the failures of the assumptions necessary for market efficiency are sufficiently strong to make public production, allocation and finance, at least of school education, a tenable strategy. To the extent that this is the case on efficiency grounds, it is appropriate to finance education redistributively for reasons of social justice (Chapter 4:6.1).

Finally, since education is not a homogeneous whole, it is necessary to ask whether the same answers apply to all types of education. For instance, should there be one set of answers for compulsory education and another for education beyond the minimum school-leaving age; should some types of education be free and others not; should some be financed by partial or total grants, or by loans; and if the latter, on what terms should the loan be made or repaid? These and other questions are discussed in Chapter 13:2.

4.3 THE PERSONAL SOCIAL SERVICES

Lack of space precludes all but an introductory mention of the personal social services (see the Further Reading). They cover four main areas: residential care for children, the elderly and the mentally and physically handicapped; day care for the same groups; domiciliary assistance (e.g. home help and 'meals on wheels'); and fieldwork, mainly the activities of social workers. Present arrangements derive largely from the Seebohm Report (UK, 1968a).

The personal social services are the responsibility of local authorities, but for historical reasons (Younghusband, 1978) are a complex mixture of public and private involvement. Many services are produced by local authorities themselves but, to a much greater extent than health care or education, production also takes place outside the public sector. There are many voluntary bodies (Dr Barnardo Homes, Chiswick Family Rescue, charitable homes for the elderly); and services are also produced in the personal sector (e.g. fostering) and in the private, profit-making sector (e.g. private old people's homes). Local authorities buy services from all three sources.

The finance of social services is almost as complex. Private revenue sources include voluntary donations to charitable bodies, and various charges levied by local authorities. Public funding derives in part from local revenues and,

---

[1] It is therefore curious that in practice the educational systems of different countries vary much *less* than their systems of health care. In particular it is surprising from an *economic* point of view that school education in the USA is publicly produced, allocated and financed (i.e. line (8) in Table 4.2).

latterly, also out of the NHS budget, the combination being referred to as *joint financing* (see Wistow, 1983). *Public* expenditure on personal social services (under 1 per cent of gross domestic product – see Table 13.1) is tiny compared with health care and education, but is buttressed to a largely unknown extent by private resources of money and time.

The purpose of social services, broadly, is to fill the gaps between the other parts of the welfare state. They exist to help those who cannot help themselves, and come into operation when care within the family breaks down or needs support. Some people suffer physical and mental handicaps, including the problems of old age; children need care if they have no family to provide it, or if their family cannot provide it adequately; single parents, immigrants and the unemployed and poor may find it difficult to keep a home together. In some instances specific individuals need care, in others whole families (see Pizzey's (1974) moving account of battered wives and their families).

It is the characteristics of the clients more than the nature of the product which is relevant to the public/private debate about social services. First, many recipients and/or their families have inadequate information and power, with implications for both production and allocation. The issue of *allocation* turns crucially on whether individuals or the local authority have better information and/or are better able to protect the interests of recipients in choosing the quantity and type of care. The question of *production* depends on whether quality control via regulation and inspection of privately produced services can be effective at reasonable cost; if not, public production could be more efficient and equitable.

A second aspect of the client group is (usually) their poverty, so that the *finance* of social services will generally have to be public. This can cause inefficiency in either sector. With public production, caseworkers do not generally have to face the social costs of the care they prescribe. One experimental solution is to give each social worker a 'shadow budget' (Davies *et al.*, 1983). Privately produced services can cause third-party payment problems, as exemplified by the boom in 'welfare for profit' nursing homes and other social services in the USA as a result of the Title XX amendment to the Social Security Act 1974 (see the Further Reading).

It should be clear, in conclusion, that substantial public involvement is likely to be needed; and that the theoretical analysis of health care and education is equally applicable in this context.

Further Reading

On the nature of health care, including problems with insurance, see Arrow (1963) (the classic article) and Culyer (1971a). Abel-Smith (1983) discusses the measurement of efficiency in health care. On the human capital approach see Grossman (1972), and for a critique and extension Dowie (1975). The literature on production and cost functions is set out in Cullis and West (1979, Chs 6 and 7) (a good general text on the economics of health).

The literature on valuing life is summarised by Cullis and West (1979, Ch. 9) and Marin (1983). On the need for such information see Schelling (1968). The human capital approach to valuing life is exemplified by Dawson (1967) and the 'willingness to pay' approach by Jones-Lee (1969) and, more formally, by Acton (1973). Marin and Psacharopoulos (1982) attempt to make the latter approach operational. For critiques see Mishan (1971) and Broome (1978), and for an overview Jones-Lee (1976).

The case for market provision of health care and education is set out by Lees (1961) (health care only), Seldon (1981), Friedman and Friedman (1980, Chs 4 and 6), and Minford (1984b); for a critique see Bosanquet (1983, Chs 11 and 12). On the role of giving, the classic work is Titmuss (1970).

For an overview of the personal social services see Glennerster (1985, Ch. 9). Present institutions go back to the Seebohm Report (UK, 1968a); on the allocation of social workers' time see UK Department of Health and Social Security (1978b). Joint financing is assessed by Wistow (1983); Barr and Carrier (1978) give a case-study comparison of costs in the public sector and a voluntary institution. On controlling the quantity of services, Davies *et al.* (1983) set out a micro-budgeting approach; on 'welfare for profit' see Gilbert (1983) and Russell (1983, pp. 119–20). The quality of service can be deficient in both private and public sectors – see UK (1978a) for an example of the latter. Mayer and Timms (1970) discuss possible conflicts between the wishes of client and social worker.

The best general book on the economics of education is Blaug (1970). On the vast literature on the theory of human capital and its application see Blaug (Ch. 1) for an excellent introduction; the classic work is Becker (1975). The screening hypothesis is discussed by Layard and Psacharopoulos (1974), Stiglitz (1975), Layard and Walters (1978, pp. 386–9), and Varian (1984, Ch. 8). See also the Further Reading on the theoretical literature on information problems at the end of Chapter 5.

On the institutions of the NHS and the educational system see the Further Reading at the end of Chapter 13.

13

Health Care and Education 2: Assessment and Reform

That any sane nation, having observed that you could provide for the supply of bread by giving bakers a pecuniary interest in baking for you, should go on to give a surgeon a pecuniary interest in cutting off your leg, is enough to make one despair of political humanity. [George Bernard Shaw, 1911.]

All that is spent during many years in opening the means of higher education to the masses would be well paid for if it called out one more Newton or Darwin, Shakespeare or Beethoven. [Alfred Marshall, 1885]

1 The National Health Service and Private Health Care

1.1 INSTITUTIONS

This part of the chapter starts with an overview of the institutions of the National Health Service (NHS) and of private health care, and then attempts to assess the extent to which the NHS meets the aims of efficiency and social justice (section 1.2); section 1.3 discusses a variety of reforms. The second part of the chapter follows the same procedure for the educational system. The main

317

conclusions of Chapters 12 and 13 are summarised in section 3.

Two points should be made immediately. First, expenditure on the NHS (around 6 per cent of national income) is low by international standards. However, expenditure has risen since the mid-1970s for several reasons. There was a 'bulge' in the birth rate in 1948 and another in the mid-1960s (Figure 9.1). The number of old people has increased, intensifying the demand on facilities (in 1983/4 health and personal social services expenditure per person over 75 was nearly eight times that on someone aged 16–64 (UK, 1986a, Chart 3.14.6)). Costly new techniques have led to increased expectations. The relative price effect has also acted to raise the cost of health care services by more than the average increase in prices.[1]

A second feature of the NHS, notwithstanding the problems discussed later, is its popularity. In the words of two American commentators,

> the NHS promised high quality medical care to the acutely ill and increasingly delivered on that promise. It unquestionably spared patients the fear of financial ruin from medical bills. As a result, it became and remained one of the most popular institutions in Britain, second only to the Crown and a close second at that. [Aaron and Schwartz, 1984, p. 14.]

The Operation of the National Health Service

The NHS in England[2] is the responsibility of the Secretary of State for Social Services. He/she is answerable to Parliament, and is responsible for the Department of Health and Social Security. Under the Department are 14 Regional Health Authorities, whose function is twofold: to plan health care in the light of local needs, subject to a regional budget total set by central government; and to allocate resources to the second-tier bodies, the District Health Authorities, whose main task is to organise hospital and community health services in their areas. Primary health care (in particular family doctors) forms an entirely separate structure organised by Family Practitioner Committees appointed by the Secretary of State. The administrative structure has seen considerable change in recent years, with a major reform in 1974 and

---

[1] The relative price effect measures the extent to which the price of commodities like health care tend to rise faster than prices generally. There are two reasons: first, throughout the economy the price of labour tends to rise faster than the general price level (i.e. real earnings rise); and second, health care has a higher than average direct labour content, about three-quarters of NHS current spending being on directly employed staff (UK, 1986a, Ch. 3.14, para. 35). The same broadly, is true of education. For details of the relative price effect, see UK, (1972c, paras 68–71) and Rees and Thompson (1972).

[2] The Secretaries of State for Scotland, Wales and Northern Ireland are responsible *inter alia* for the NHS in those countries.

another in 1982, and remains the subject of criticism (see point (12) on p. 331).

However, the main concern of this chapter is the economics, not the administration, of the NHS. Discussion is organised round the four areas highlighted in Table 4.2: the production of health care; the individual consumption decision (i.e. how the system works from the viewpoint of the consumer); finance; and the aggregate production decision (i.e. budget setting).

Production of health care under the NHS has a tripartite structure of primary health care, hospitals, and community health care. The main element in primary health care is the system of general practitioners (i.e. family doctors). Every member of the community is registered with a general practitioner (GP), who deals with straightforward complaints and chronic conditions, and when necessary refers patients to hospital and specialist services. In the latter case the GP acts both as a guide (to steer patients to the appropriate specialist) and as a filter (to prevent trivial complaints being taken to a specialist). GPs also have a role in preventive medicine, including immunisation, family planning, cervical screening, etc.

The employment status of GPs is complex. Technically they are self-employed professionals under contract to the local Family Practitioner Committee, though the central Medical Practitioners Committee has limited powers to prevent the establishment of new practices in well-provided areas. Remuneration is also complex. Somewhat to simplify, GPs receive three forms of payment. First, there are various allowances, mainly a basic practice allowance to cover running costs, plus other allowances, e.g. if the practice is in an under-doctored area. Second, they receive a capitation payment of £X for each person on their register, where X is higher for older people. Third, there is a variety of other payments, *inter alia* for certain forms of preventive health care (UK, 1986c, Appendix 2). The key point, and one to which we return, is that with few exceptions (notably payments to dentists, and for some types of preventive care to GPs), payment throughout the NHS takes the form more of a *salary* than fee for service.

The other major types of primary medical care are dentistry, pharmaceutical services and ophthalmic services, all of which fall under the aegis of the local Family Practitioner Committee. In England about 14,000 dentists work as independent contractors to their local Family Practitioner Committee, by whom they are paid a fee for service on an agreed scale, net of the consumer charges they levy (also on an agreed scale) (UK, 1986c, Appendix 2). Pharmacists dispense drugs, dressings etc. as prescribed by doctors, for which they are paid (plus a profit margin, but net of the consumer charges discussed below) by the local Family Practitioner Committee.

319

Table 13.1: Health and Personal Social Services, UK, 1986/7 (est.) (£million)

	Current spending	Capital spending	Total
NATIONAL HEALTH SERVICE			
Hospital and community health services	10,366	765	
Family practitioner services	3,899	11	
Central health services	500	17	
Charges	−479		
			15,078
PERSONAL SOCIAL SERVICES			
Local authority services	2,941	79	
Central government services	14		
Charges	−419		
			2,614
OTHER			29
TOTAL PROGRAMME			17,721
EXPENDITURE IN			
Scotland			2,443
Wales			1,115
Northern Ireland			738
TOTAL HEALTH AND PERSONAL SOCIAL SERVICES			22,017

Source: *The Government's Expenditure Plans, 1986–87 to 1988–89*, Cmnd. 9702-II, Tables 2.12 and 3.14.

Hospitals absorb over two-thirds of the resources of the NHS (Table 13.1). There are about 2800 NHS hospitals, covering the full range of medical care. The hospital sector in England directly employs over 800,000 people, including 41,000 medical personnel, over 400,000 nurses and 73,000 professional technical staff such as radiographers (UK, 1986a, Table 3.14.4).

Hospital doctors are paid a salary rather than a fee for service though, as discussed below, they are able to combine salaried work for the NHS with private practice. The organisation of NHS hospitals differs from that in most other countries. The contrast with the USA is made by Aaron and Schwartz.

[An NHS] hospital is a quasi-feudal enterprise, ruled largely by a peerage of senior physicians (consultants) who usually work only at one hospital and derive most or all of their income from salary. Each has junior physicians assigned to him, and each has a . . . number of beds to which he can admit patients. . . . Consultants are responsible . . . for the disposal of all the hospital's resources. The typical British hospital administrator, unlike his US counterpart, has little power or authority. . . . Thus consultants, whose personal salaries and positions are unaffected directly by budgetary vicissitudes, must parcel out the meager rations allotted through the health district. They have every incentive to do so amicably, for they are part of a select medical club whose members must work together, usually for the rest of their professional lives. That each has only a limited personal economic stake in the outcome of the allocations facilitates such co-operation. [1984, p. 20.]

The third branch of the NHS is the Community Health Service, which has three functions: preventive health services, including health education, health visiting, screening and vaccination programmes, and maternity and child welfare clinics; liaison with the local authority, especially over matters of public health; and co-operation with personal social services departments, so that wherever possible health and personal care can be dealt with together.

The individual consumption decision As a first approximation, all health care under the NHS is free, except for the charges described below. The main source of health care for most people is their GP. Individuals are free to register with any NHS GP in their area who is prepared to add them to his/her list of patients. Anyone who wishes, for whatever reason, to change to another GP may do so. No charge is made for consultations or for home visits. The GP prescribes treatment or, in more complicated/serious cases, refers the patient to an NHS hospital.

Where a GP prescribes drugs, the patient has in principle to pay the pharmacist a fixed charge per item, e.g. per bottle of tablets. The charge in 1986 was £2.20, having risen steeply since 1979,[1] though broad classes of people are exempt, e.g. children, expectant mothers, old people, certain chronically ill individuals, and people with low incomes (Tolley, 1986, Ch. 8). These groups include about 50 per cent of individuals, disproportionately those who make the greatest use of drugs. There is continued controversy over prescription charges, which are regarded by some as an anomaly in an otherwise largely free health service, and by others as a useful check on wasteful usage (see Cooper, 1985). As in many other countries, Britain's drug bill has increased sharply in recent years.

Individuals are also free to choose their dentist. In the past dental treatment was heavily subsidised, but by the mid-1980s charges came much closer to the full cost of treatment, though check-ups *per se* remained free, and broad classes of people were exempt from charges.

---

[1] A charge of 5 pence was introduced in 1952; in early 1979 it was 20 pence.

A patient is usually referred to hospital by his/her GP, but in emergencies this procedure is bypassed. All hospital treatment under the NHS is free, including test procedures, consultations with doctors, nursing, drugs and intensive care, whatever the type of complaint and however long the hospital stay. All the facilities of the NHS are available to anyone living in Britain, with the exception of temporary residents (i.e. those staying in the country for less than six months).

Finance   The finances of the NHS are discussed in detail by Glennerster (1985, Ch. 8) (see also Aaron and Schwartz, 1984, pp. 17–21). For our purposes it is necessary to observe only that of the total cost of the NHS shown in Table 13.1, 86 per cent came from general (mainly central government) tax revenues, and 11 per cent from national insurance contributions. Thus some 97 per cent of the NHS was financed out of taxation, and only about 3 per cent from charges (UK, 1986a, Chart 3.14.4).

The aggregate production decision (i.e. setting budget limits). The annual budget for the NHS as a whole is determined in the same way as the budget for national defence or any other government service, as the result of negotiation between the Treasury and spending departments, as modified by subsequent discussion in Cabinet (Prest and Barr, 1985, Ch. 9; Glennerster 1985, Chs 2–4). The figure which emerges is a global budget for the NHS as a whole, which is divided between the relevant Secretaries of State. The division of the total among the 14 English Regional Health Authorities is partly at the discretion of the Secretary of State for Social Services, but is also constrained by formulae designed to improve the geographical distribution of health care resources.[1] Each regional authority divides its total between the District Health Authorities. The allocation of funds to major projects (e.g. building a new hospital) is normally made at the Regional level; most decisions about day-to-day expenditure are made at the District level. The procedure is therefore largely one of 'top down' allocation, substantially constrained by expenditure in previous years.

Private Health Care

Alongside the NHS is a system of private health care. Individuals can consult GPs privately (in which case they pay his/her fees and the full cost of any drugs), and/or obtain treatment in a private hospital or in a 'pay bed' in an NHS hospital, whether or not the original consultation with the GP was private. Though it has grown somewhat in recent years the private sector

---

[1] E.g. as a result of the report of the Resource Allocation Working Party (UK Department of Health and Social Security, 1976a) – see p. 329, point (10).

remains small, involving about 5 per cent of total expenditure on doctors and hospital in-patient care, and about 2 per cent of hospital beds. It is used mainly by those wanting the convenience of a private room or (more contentiously) by those faced with a long wait for treatment under the NHS.

Most private health care is financed by voluntary insurance, which is cheap in Britain for four reasons (Aaron and Schwartz, 1984, p. 23): most patients use an NHS GP even if they see a consultant privately; the NHS provides a back-up in cases where patients present complications with which private hospitals are not equipped to deal; people with private insurance are usually young and employed (their health care insurance is often a fringe benefit of their job), and hence low risk; finally, health care is cheaper in Britain than, for example, the USA, not least because British doctors and nurses are paid less.

The relationship between private health care and the NHS is a source of substantial and continuing controversy. NHS hospitals have specialist consultants who are the head of the medical hierarchy. They are contracted to work for the NHS, but can choose whether to do so full-time or part-time. Most of them elect for the part-time option and practise in their consultative capacity both as part of the NHS and privately.[1] The existence of 'pay beds' within the NHS has aroused the greatest controversy. It is argued that people with money can jump the queue without necessarily paying the full economic cost of treatment, and many regard this as inequitable. Others argue that private patients bring extra income to some consultants, and to ban private practice by NHS employees would result in large and costly pay demands, and possibly the loss of highly skilled specialists. Efforts have been made to separate private provision from public, but the issue is a political football. Speedy resolution is unlikely.

International Comparisons

Before turning to an assessment of the NHS it is helpful to have some perspective on the organisation and problems of systems elsewhere. In very broad terms all industrialised countries adopt one of three models of health care provision. (a) private production financed by private insurance, e.g. the USA; (b) private production financed by public (or quasi-public) insurance, e.g. France, Germany, Canada and (approximately) Japan; or (c) public production financed by the state on a non-insurance basis, e.g. the UK.

These systems are discussed in detail in McLachlan and Maynard (1982a). Two major conclusions emerge: the pervasiveness of regulation in *all* health care systems; and a dramatic escalation of health care costs in most countries.

---

[1] Consultants choosing the full-time option are allowed to earn up to 10 per cent of their income from private practice.

The latter point is echoed by Aaron (1981a) and Abel-Smith (1984 and 1985). Despite the variety of systems, there is considerable similarity in the difficulties they face. The most important arise out of the third-party payment problem (Chapter 12:3.1). Doctors are the ultimate allocators of resources. But because they are paid by the insurance scheme or the taxpayer, they have no incentive to evaluate costs and benefits at the margin, causing inefficiency in allocating resources to different areas of medical care (i.e. micro inefficiency discussed in Chapter 12:2.1). If doctors are paid a fee for service (as in most systems of private production) they have a further incentive to oversupply; too many resources are devoted to health care in total (i.e. macro inefficiency), and costs rise.

Since fee for service paid by a third party is the most common way of paying doctors it is not surprising, despite the variety of their institutions, that most countries have experienced a dramatic escalation in health care expenditures. The point is vital. According to the contributors to McLachlan and Maynard (1982a):

> The rising costs of medical care and, as a result, the problems of expenditures and cost containment . . . is of major concern in the Federal Republic of Germany. [p. 235.]

> . . . moves for a closer control to check the growth of expenditure [on health care in France] which is alarmingly high. [p. 267.]

> In the US cost containment is the major driving-force behind legislative and private sector health strategies. Faced with intolerable deficits, the Congress appears determined to end its open-ended commitments to low income groups and the aged. Similarly, employers are increasingly determined to control health care costs. [p. 333.]

Nor is the problem confined to Western countries.

> The cost of medical care in Japan has risen very rapidly. . . . The rate of increase has also grown steadily and so has, as a result, the percentage of the gross national product absorbed by medical care. [Chester and Ichien, 1983, p. 23; see also Noumi, 1983.]

The editors conclude that

> however much health systems and policies may seem to differ from country to country all current policies have one major aim, cost containment which is an omnibus description of policies . . . to contain not just *unit costs* but also *total* expenditure in both public and private sectors. [McLachlan and Maynard, 1982a, p. 13, their emphasis.]

Of the countries covered by McLachlan and Maynard only two have not suffered a cost explosion: the UK, largely because of Parliamentary control of public expenditure;[1] and Canada, which imposes a global budget constraint at a provincial level on the expenditure of its public health insurance scheme.

The situation in the USA is a textbook example. The system until the mid-1960s (as a rough approximation) was one of private production financed by private health care insurance (for historical analysis see Anderson (1968) and Russell (1980, pp. 171–8)). But problems arose, and as a response medicare (for the old) and medicaid (for the poor) were introduced in the mid-1960s. The modification they introduced was simple: the poor and old continued to receive private treatment; but their medical bills were now paid out of federal/state funds. The effect of these unlimited third-party payments was entirely predictable: federal spending on health care rose from $13 billion in 1970 to $74 billion in 1982 (i.e. 2½ times more rapidly than price increases), and is projected to increase to $134–$144 billion in 1988 (Russell, 1983, pp. 116–17). As a result, health care became the fourth largest item of federal expenditure after income support, defence, and debt interest.

There are two possible arguments against the assertion that these cost escalations are caused by inadequately policed third-party payments. One is to argue that the USA has a greater taste for health care than (say) Britain (i.e. demand is higher in the USA); the other is that American citizens suffer more health problems than the British (i.e. need is greater in the USA). If the former, we would expect high-spending countries to enjoy better health; if the latter, that they suffer more illness. Neither phenomenon is the case (Culyer, 1976, Ch. 10; Aaron and Schwartz, 1984, pp. 12–13).

What solutions have been tried in the face of this common problem? The first is regulation over the quantity and quality of medical care. According to McLachlan and Maynard such regulation is inescapable, even in private schemes: 'insurance based systems are subject to regulations and controls similar (and sometimes greater) in effect to those that apply [in the UK]' (1982a, p. 12). Consequently,

> privatisation of health care finances will lead to extensive private regulatory behaviour . . . [which] will eventually restrict the freedom of the professions and hospitals to fix the prices, quantities and qualities of the care they provide. [1982b, p. 38.]

A variety of solutions has been tried in the USA. There have been attempts to increase competition, so as to drive down costs. The difficulty with this solution (Chapter 12:3.1) is that the benefits of competition are contingent upon perfect information, an assumption which is largely untenable for health

---

[1] The ability of the NHS to act as a monopoly buyer is another contributory factor.

care. Second, the USA has introduced 'cost-sharing', i.e. coinsurance (Russell, 1983, pp. 124–9). This is just another name for consumer charges. The problem here is that charges high enough to reduce demand substantially are likely to cause equity problems. Finally, Congress has abandoned the principle that health care should be provided on the basis of need *irrespective of cost* by the introduction of budget limits; and federal matching grants to states were reduced at the margin for medicare and medicaid in the early 1980s. These measures met with some limited success in reducing expenditure, though without in any way altering the scale of the overall problem (for an assessment, see Holahan, 1984).

The most successful method of restricting supply to around its efficient level has been the imposition of budget limits either on public expenditure (Britain) or on insurance disbursements (Canada). This is an important conclusion because the demand for health care will increase in the future not only with advances in medical technology but also because of the problem (discussed in Chapter 9) of ageing populations in all industrialised countries.

1.2 ASSESSMENT

Efficiency, as discussed in Chapter 12:2.1, can be defined in principle but is hard to measure, mainly because of difficulties in measuring (a) the benefits of health care as opposed to other activities (the *macro* efficiency issue), and (b) the relative benefits in different areas of health care (*micro* efficiency). Quantitative work on the former is non-existent and on the latter is scant (Cullis and West, 1979, Ch. 8; Aaron and Schwartz, 1984, Ch. 7), so discussion is to some extent a mixture of a priori argument with only a small leavening of empirical evidence. Consideration is given initially to the efficiency advantages of the NHS, first advantages in principle, then in practice; to criticisms of the NHS which I regard as invalid; and to valid criticisms. The NHS has at least four efficiency advantages in principle.

(1) *Supply-side incentives* to economise on the use of resources arise, first, from the way renumeration is organised. Doctors are not generally paid a fee for service. Thus there is no financial incentive to oversupply, a point indirectly confirmed by recent evidence (UK, 1986d) of unnecessary treatment by dentists (who *are* paid a fee for service). There is no argument of principle against paying doctors a high salary – the crucial point in this context is that it is *fixed*. In the case of GPs these incentives may go too far, since the capitation payment system (page 319) gives GPs an incentive to increase the size of their lists, but to decrease the time spent with any one patient. To that extent there is an incentive for GPs either to *undersupply* or to pass patients to the hospital

sector. This argument should not be overstated, however, since a patient who feels he/she is not receiving adequate attention from his/her GP can transfer to the list of another doctor, thereby reducing the original GP's income.[1]

A second form of constraint is the NHS budget (a macro efficiency point), coupled with the control exercised by the NHS over doctors' behaviour and the traditions of the medical profession in Britain. The overall result is that there is no financial incentive to supply excessive medical care, Q_1 in Figure 12.3, rather than the socially optimal quantity Q^*; this is true both for health care as a whole and for different types of treatment, though with a question mark over the possibility of undersupply by GPs.

(2) *The individual consumption decision* The decision about treatment is generally made by doctors. This reduces the problem of imperfect information. In addition, the patient is more likely to trust a doctor's decision based on clinical judgement unclouded by financial motives.

(3) *Finance* for the most part is out of general tax revenues, thereby avoiding problems in insurance markets, such as high probabilities of requiring treatment, adverse selection and moral hazard (Chapter 5:3 and Chapter 12:3.1 and 4.1). To the extent that taxes are based on ability to pay there are also equity advantages, discussed below.

(4) *Treatment is free* at the point of use in most cases. This encourages early diagnosis and reduces the externality problem (which would reduce consumption from Q^* to Q_0 in Figure 12.1), and also has equity advantages.

The system has advantages also in practical terms.

(5) *Macro efficiency* The NHS is cheap by international standards. It currently absorbs 6 per cent of national income; the US figure is approximately twice as large. Yet according to Aaron and Schwartz, '[these] large differences in per capita average medical expenditures between the two countries are not associated with large differences in life expectancy' (1984, p. 13). According to Klein (1984, p. 15), 'the NHS seems to be a remarkably successful instrument for making the rationing of scarce resources socially and politically acceptable'.

(6) *Micro efficiency* We shall see shortly that the NHS is not above criticism for the way it allocates resources to different areas of health care. But it also has advantages. Because of its unified structure and because payment is not generally based on fee for service,

the NHS has shown a greater ability than insurance-based systems to

---

[1] It can therefore be argued that the capitation element of GPs' pay under the NHS approximates to a voucher system.

substitute medical time; to make use of the team approach and to provide a framework in which choices can be made between hospital and community care. Substitution can be seen in hospitals in the wide responsibility of the ward sister and outside the hospital in the roles of the district nurse and the health visitor. [Bosanquet, 1983, p. 154.]

Additionally, the unified structure of the NHS enables action to be taken on overall medical priorities (see points (10) and (11) below) in a way which is largely impossible with market-based systems. For a compendious study which lends considerable support to the NHS, see the Report of the Royal Commission (UK, 1979b).

Two criticisms are made of the NHS (particularly in the USA) which do not hold water.

(7) *The NHS is a monopoly* The first argument is that customers have no choice. This is not the case. They are free to choose (and change) their GP; to ask for a second opinion; or to opt for private medical care. A different argument is that the NHS devotes too many resources to bureaucracy. In fact, the NHS bureaucracy, like those in the health care systems of most countries, has increased. But it remains small by international standards. Administrative costs in the USA in the late 1970s were 5.3 per cent of total current expenditure (OECD, 1977, quoted in Bosanquet, 1983, p. 156). The NHS figure was 2.6 per cent, in part because the NHS devotes virtually no resources to billing patients. A further counter-argument is that centralisation can have positive advantages by making it possible to set out priorities, and by enabling the NHS to negotiate low prices for drugs.

(8) *Work effort* Doctors, it is argued, work less hard if they are not paid a fee for service and/or the best and most innovative individuals will be lost to the profession (this is the issue of *dynamic* efficiency). There are two lines of attack on this position. It assumes uncritically that labour supply is motivated solely by financial gain, but loses plausibility if one allows for non-money wages and a tradition of service. Many professionals are paid salaries, e.g. academics, lawyers and accountants who are employed rather than self-employed, yet it is not argued that they should be paid a fee for service. Though difficult to prove, it might be argued that Britain attracts to the medical profession individuals who gain substantial job satisfaction, whilst countries with private systems attract those with more strongly financial motives; if so, it does not follow that the latter group is either more able or harder working. A second counter-argument is that even if work effort/innovation *is* substantially motivated by high pay, it might well suffice to base remuneration on high salaries rather than fee for service.

To rebut these arguments is not to say that no criticism is possible.

(9) *Macro inefficiency* Many commentators argue that too few resources in total are devoted to the NHS. Budget restrictions (see Bosanquet, 1982) have aggravated waiting-lists for non-urgent (and some urgent) treatment; and many hospital buildings are old. Pro-market writers argue that the NHS *causes* too few resources to be devoted to medical care; but international comparison suggests that private systems lead to excessive consumption which regulation has only partly curtailed. The appropriate solution if the NHS has too few resources (about which there is widespread agreement), is to relax the budget restrictions rather than substantially to alter the system.

Micro inefficiency arises in two important ways.

(10) *Micro inefficiency in the spatial allocation of resources* NHS resources are geographically misallocated, especially hospitals, whose location is largely a matter of historical accident. The Resource Allocation Working Party (RAWP) (UK, Department of Health and Social Security, 1976a) made specific proposals for geographical reallocation on the basis of such criteria as the size and demographic structure of the population in an area, health indicators such as local mortality and fertility, and gaps in existing provision. The overall effect of the recommendations was that resources should be shifted away from London and the south-east of England. Subsequent policy reduced measured inequality (relative to a target index of 100, the best-provided region in 1977 was at 118 and the worst-off at 90; in 1985 the figures were 108 and 96). In a time of restricted budgets, however, the policy was controversial, and facilities in London came under increasing pressure.[1]

(11) *Micro inefficiency in the allocation of resources to different types of health care* Though doctors within the NHS face few financial incentives likely to cause *systematic* misallocation, problems remain, partly where shared financial responsibility between central and local government creates perverse incentives (Glennerster, 1985, Ch. 9), and partly because of the implicit nature of decision criteria. Because of widespread complaint that 'unfashionable' areas like geriatric care and treatment of the mentally ill were under-funded, priorities between different types of health care and different client groups were reconsidered (UK, Department of Health and Social Security, 1976b), and resources slightly shifted from acute services and maternity care (the latter in the light of the falling birth rate) towards services for the elderly, the mentally ill and handicapped, and children.

Why does the NHS not always allocate its limited budget with maximum

---

[1] See 'Emergency Case for the Capital' *The Times*, 12 May 1986, p. 10 and for more general assessment, Glennerster (1985, Ch. 8), and Bosanquet and Townsend (1980, pp. 211–19).

efficiency? One answer is that it lacks a clear objective and the information necessary to implement it. Aaron and Schwartz (1984, Ch. 7) identify various criteria which influence the allocation of resources within the NHS. The six most important are:

(i)   Age: there is less rationing of health care for children than for adults, partly because such investment yields benefits over a longer time period than medical care for an older person (a technical consideration), and partly because people have strong emotions about children (a social value).

(ii)   The costs of alternatives to medical care: medical treatment is more likely if treating a patient costs less than not doing so.

(iii) Dread diseases like cancer receive more resources, ceteris paribus, even though treatment may do little to prolong life.

(iv)   The more visible a disability, the more likely it is to be treated.

(v)   Total cost: the smaller is the total cost of treatment (*not* the smaller the ratio of costs to benefits) the greater the likelihood that treatment will be given.

(vi)   The need for capital funds: the lower the capital overheads the more likely, ceteris paribus, that treatment will be offered.

Two conclusions follow. Only the first two criteria accord with strict economic rationality; the next two can be justified, if at all, only on the grounds of the weights society attaches to different types of disease; the last two are unambiguously irrational. The second conclusion is that all these criteria are the result of weights which are *implicit*, and are largely those of *doctors*. The fundamental efficiency criticism of the NHS is that it has no clear-cut, explicit objective. The point is discussed by Culyer (1976, Ch. 7), who argues that the NHS should allocate health care on the basis of 'need' – and much of his argument is concerned with providing an operational definition. One way of doing so, he suggests, is to define an index of need in terms of factors such as time already spent waiting for treatment; urgency, based on the level of a patient's health (i.e. how ill), and its rate of change (i.e. how rapidly the condition is deteriorating); the number of his/her dependants; and whether the condition affects his/her livelihood. The factors of which account is taken in defining need and their relative weights should, he argues, be determined by *society* (e.g. by Parliament) and not by the medical profession alone. The concern of doctors should be to *evaluate* need on the basis of criteria already laid down. This would enhance efficiency, whilst simultaneously introducing elements of public choice into health care.

This approach requires two sorts of information: first, quantitative estimates of the costs and output benefits of different types of treatment (a technical question); and a set of weights to be applied to relevant non-medical criteria (e.g. whether the patient has dependants), which is almost entirely a social or political matter. Both sorts of information are relevant to the construction of systems which explicitly encourage efficient resource use. An important tool in this context is micro budgeting (Bevan, 1984; Enthoven, 1985, and, as applied to personal social services, Davies *et al.*, 1983), under which each hospital (and possibly each individual department within a hospital) is given a notional budget, and doctors are faced with appropriate shadow prices. This suggests a carefully defined research agenda of the sort laid out by McLachlan and Maynard (1982a, pp. 548–53). Thus a major efficiency criticism of the NHS (it is equally a criticism of other health care systems) is that it assembles and uses *too little information*.

(12) *Administrative inefficiency* The argument that the NHS has a dis-proportionate number of bureaucrats does not stand up (point (7)). There has, however, been a continuing problem over administrative co-ordination. After several official reports (UK, 1962, 1968b, 1970, 1972b) there was some improvement, though administrative reform in 1974 was widely regarded as unsatisfactory (UK, 1979b; UK Department of Health and Social Security, 1979). After another round of reform in 1982 the appointment of professional managers was suggested (UK Department of Health and Social Security, 1983). There is also some evidence (UK, National Audit Office, 1985) that nursing staff could be used more efficiently.

Equity, as we saw in Chapter 4:2.2 and 4.3, cannot be defined unambiguously, but depends on political values; in addition (Chapter 6:3.1), the definition of equality is fraught with ambiguities. For present purposes horizontal equity is defined in terms of equality of opportunity in respect of health care, as set out in Chapter 12:2.1. Thus individuals A and B with identical medical conditions should receive equal health care unless other relevant differences exist (e.g. one of them has young or old dependants); irrelevant considerations (e.g. that A is rich and B poor) should make no difference. How closely does the NHS approximate this ideal? Though there is room for disagreement, the equity advantages of the NHS can be listed as follows.

(13) *The unimportance of income* The quantity of health care an individual receives is largely (though as we shall see not wholly) unconstrained by his/her income. No one is denied health care because of poverty; and no one goes in fear of financial ruin as a result of expensive medical treatment. The latter is a particular problem in countries where not only health care but also health insurance is private (e.g. the USA).

(14) *The distribution of health care* is less unequal than in many other countries (but see point (17), below).

(15) *The system accords with British notions of social justice* (McCreadie, 1976), and is highly popular politically (Halpern, 1985).

Equity criticisms are twofold.

(16) *Health care resources are distributed unequally by region*, though less so than hitherto, as discussed in point (10).

(17) *Health care resources are distributed unequally across socio-economic groups* Three issues arise: the empirical facts; the explanation of those facts; and implications for policy. Le Grand (1982, Ch. 3) finds that inequalities of outcome persist; over a wide variety of indicators the higher socio-economic groups enjoy better health and longer life than lower groups. His second conclusion, which confirms the findings of the Black Report (Black, 1980, Ch. 4), is that the NHS does not achieve equality of use:

> The evidence suggests that the top socio-economic group receives 40 per cent more NHS expenditure per person reporting illness than the bottom one. Moreover, this almost certainly underestimates the overall inequality in the consumption of medical care, partly because of biasses in the method of calculation and partly because the estimates ignore care that is privately financed. [Le Grand, 1982, p. 46.]

This result can be explained (see Figure 13.1) in terms of two sets of factors. The *benefits* of health care perceived by the lower socio-economic groups (MPV_P) may be lower than those of the rich (MPV_R), e.g. if the poor have worse information; or the poor might rationally place a lower value on health (e.g. where someone's life is miserable smoking might genuinely be one of his/her few pleasures); or the actual benefits to poorer people might be lower if doctors treat them with less care and compassion than middle-class patients. Probably of greater importance, the poor face higher *costs* of health care. Since treatment is free the main cost is time. Travel time is generally higher for less-advantaged people, who more often have to rely on public transport, and who may have further to travel. Once at the hospital or GP's consulting-room, waiting time may be longer, e.g. because middle-class people with easier access to a telephone more often make an appointment. Finally, the cost of each hour's wait is generally higher for the poor, who more often lose pay if they spend a morning in a hospital out-patient clinic, a cost not faced by people on salaries. These factors taken together can explain why in practice Q_R in Figure 13.1 is 40 per cent higher than Q_P.

What implications can be drawn from these facts? To say that the NHS has not achieved its objective of equal treatment for equal need (from which assertion few would dissent) does not mean *ipso facto* that the NHS has not been an equalising force. First, the NHS cannot be regarded as a failure unless an alternative system of health care is more equalising. All the evidence

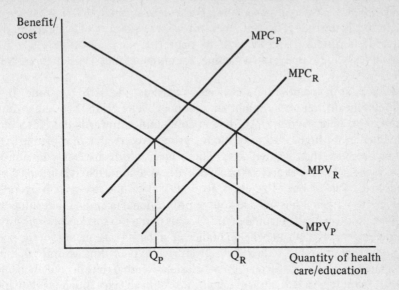

Figure 13.1   *Differences in the costs and benefits of health care/education by socioeconomic group*

suggests the contrary. The distribution of health care in Britain is more equal than in most other countries, and almost certainly more equal than it would be in the absence of the NHS (whatever the alternative system).

The second reason why the NHS, despite unequal usage, can be an equalising force emerges when expenditure is discussed not in isolation but, more properly, in conjunction with the taxation which finances it (Chapter 7:4.2). The argument is important, and worth spelling out. Suppose that the pre-transfer incomes of poor and rich are 20 and 80; that all income is taxed away by the state to provide free goods and services; and that the rich receive twice as many goods and services as the (equally numerous) poor. As a result, the post-transfer incomes of poor and rich are 33⅓ and 66⅔, respectively. From the perspective of expenditure, the rich receive twice as much as the poor, suggesting that public allocation as an equalising force has failed. But when expenditure and taxation are considered together the picture is very different: the income of the poor has been raised both absolutely from 20 to 33⅓, and relatively, from one-quarter of that enjoyed by the rich to one-half. On either count, the system taken as a whole is equalising.

(18) *Redistributive effects of the NHS* To what extent is the NHS thus financed progressively? In practice, measurement raises almost insuperable problems, *inter alia* because of the difficulty of measuring the incidence of taxes

and benefits, but the *logic* is clear (Chapter 7:4.2, as qualified by Chapter 7:4.1). If individual A contributes on average (say) twice as much as B in whatever tax is used to pay for the NHS, but receives the same quantity of health care, then the NHS redistributes from rich to poor (i.e. is progressive). But if A contributes twice as much but consumes four times as much as B then the NHS is regressive.

We have seen (point (17)) that, ceteris paribus, the 'rich' consume 40 per cent more health care per capita than the 'poor'. The NHS thus redistributes from rich to poor if on average the tax contribution towards the NHS of an individual in the highest socio-economic group exceeds that of someone in the lowest by more than 40 per cent. The crucial words are 'tax contribution towards the NHS'. The NHS is progressive if we assume that it is financed by a progressive tax, or out of taxation generally (since the tax system overall is progressive). Even if it is financed out of proportional taxation the result is still likely to hold, since the income of individuals in the top socio-economic group is on average more than 40 per cent higher than the average income of the poor. To argue that the NHS redistributes from rich to poor thus assumes that it is not financed specifically by regressive taxation, i.e. that the effect of abolishing the NHS would be a reduction in income tax, or in all taxes, but not a reduction only in tobacco taxation.

Additionally, even if the redistributive effect is weak, the NHS is still an equalising force if it reduces inequality more than any alternative system. The most plausible conclusion is not that the NHS has failed, but that it is not as strong an equalising force as some of its supporters had hoped. This suggests that the aims of egalitarians are likely to be served better by keeping and improving the NHS than by replacing it.

1.3 REFORM

No system of health care can be perfect. The real issue is to choose the least inefficient and inequitable form of organisation. Four sets of reform are considered: radical privatisation; the possible role of health maintenance organisations; a system of privately produced but publicly funded medical care; and possible improvements to the NHS.

Radical privatisation The failure of virtually all the standard assumptions[1] (Chapter 12:3.1) suggests a priori that an unrestricted private market (i.e. lines (1) or (2) in Table 4.2) is likely to be highly inefficient for technical (i.e. non-ideological) reasons (Chapter 12:4.1), and also inconsistent with many people's

---

[1] I.e. the assumptions necessary for the market to allocate efficiently – see Chapter 4:3.2, or the Appendix to Chapter 4, paras 6–17.

perceptions of social justice (Chapter 12:3.3). This view, as we saw in section 1.1, is confirmed by empirical observation. Countries which have adopted ad hoc modifications to private health care systems have typically experienced sharp and unexpected cost increases. Nor does it follow that the private sector produces better quality health care than the NHS.[1]

An additional argument concerns the possible effects of the recent rapid growth in private medical care in Britain. So long as private treatment is only a marginal activity it can serve as a useful device for enhancing consumer choice and alleviating excess demand. But if the private sector were to grow beyond a certain (unknown) size it is possible that 'the most demanding consumers of health care [would] exit from the public sector so diminishing the political voice for more spending in the public sector' (Klein, 1984, pp. 23–4). This, it is argued, could lead to a two-tier system – high quality private medicine for the better-off, and low quality treatment under the NHS for the poor. Such an outcome would tend to have two effects. It would shift medical resources from the poor to the rich; whether this is desirable depends on one's definition of social justice. In addition, if the private health care sector becomes large, it is likely to run into all the problems faced by other countries, as typified by the US experience.

If radical privatisation is not the answer, what package of reforms might be feasible? The main conclusion of the theoretical discussion in Chapter 12 is that it is not possible to make health care efficient and equitable by ad hoc tinkering with private markets. What is needed is a carefully thought out *strategy*. Since virtually all health care is financed by third parties (i.e. insurance companies or the taxpayer) the marginal cost to the consumer is zero, and he will generally demand an inefficiently high quantity, Q_1 in Figure 12.3. The heart of the issue is therefore the rationing of treatment to $Q^\star$. In principle this can be done in two ways: (a) by making doctors face the marginal social cost of health care; or (b) by imposing a budget constraint on total expenditure. The next two mixed public/private packages follow these two routes, the first being rather more private than the second. Each is presented only in outline to illustrate the approach; and other examples are, no doubt, possible.

Health maintenance organisations This is the case of private health care, private medical insurance and extensive regulation. The idea of a health maintenance organisation (HMO) is simple. Individuals pay a lump-sum annual contribution to a 'firm' of doctors (the HMO), which promises in return to provide the contributor and his/her family with a comprehensive range of medical services. The doctors provide primary care themselves, and buy in

---

[1] See, for instance, 'Private Health Treatment Not Necessarily Best, Survey Says', *The Times*, 7 June 1984, p. 4. The survey in question was by *Which?* magazine, a reputable consumer group.

(and monitor) hospital care as necessary. The HMO's income, which consists of the contributions of its members, is used to pay for health care, including the salaries of the doctors. Any surplus (like that of any firm) can be distributed to the doctors as additional income, or to members in the form of lower contributions, or ploughed back into the HMO to improve its service.[1]

An important theoretical advantage of HMOs is that the doctor provides both health care *and* medical insurance. The effect of an HMO is therefore analytically equivalent to merging the activities of doctor and insurance company; this internalises the externality caused by third-party payments (Chapter 12:4.1). As a result, doctors as managers of the 'firm' have an incentive to economise, e.g. providing preventive care or early treatment to nip any incipient problem in the bud. Empirical evidence supports this view. HMOs in the USA spend up to 40 per cent less per member than conventional insurance (Russell, 1983, p. 137) and use less hospital care without any reduction in the quality of treatment (McLachlan and Maynard, 1982a, p. 507). The only question mark in this context is that HMOs, in theory, do not *necessarily* prescribe the efficient quantity Q^* in Figure 12.3. We know that the quantity provided will be less than Q_1 but we do not know how much less; it might even be less than Q^*, i.e. inefficiently *low* (for further discussion see Luft, 1981; Brown, 1983b).

Any strategy based on HMOs would require non-trivial public involvement. *Production* of health care would be via HMOs. *Regulation* would be necessary in several forms: all HMOs would have to meet or exceed state-ordained minimum standards concerned with the range, duration and quality of service; HMOs would not be allowed to 'evict' high-risk members or individuals requiring expensive treatment; there would be a mandatory requirement on individuals to belong to an approved HMO (i.e. one which met minimum standards); and babies might have to be registered before birth. *Finance* by the state would have to include cash transfers to enable the poor to afford HMO membership. These could take the form of an untied income transfer; or the state could pay the subsidy directly to the HMO (cf. rent rebates for low income tenants in UK local authority accommodation). In addition, the state might subsidise everyone's health care in recognition of the external benefits created by certain kinds of treatment. The system which emerges has the general flavour of lines (1) or (2) in Table 4.2 for health care, and of lines (3)(a) or (4)(a) for health insurance.

A package of this sort has several advantages. Everyone would receive health care of an approved standard (because membership of an approved HMO supported by cash transfers would be compulsory). The fact of compulsory

---

[1] As McLachlan and Maynard (1982a, p. 507) point out, such organisations approximate labour-managed firms along the lines of the Yugoslav model.

membership starting before birth would alleviate problems of pre-existing or congenital ill health; it would also facilitate pooling the costs of GP visits and pregnancy, which raise potential problems of moral hazard. HMOs would have no incentive to oversupply. Finally, an element of consumer sovereignty is possible (subject to the regulations about minimum standards), in that each HMO can be thought of as a 'mini NHS'. Problems, however, remain. How is compulsory membership enforced? Might HMOs produce a sub-optimal output? There is also a problem with high-risk individuals who want to 'migrate' from one HMO to another because it offers a preferred package of health care; because they are moving to a different part of the country; or because their HMO goes out of business. Temporary or permanent immigrants raise similar problems.

Publicly financed medical care   This package of private production, public funding and extensive regulation embraces more public involvement than the previous one. *Production* of health care would be private, doctors being paid a fee for service. There would be *regulation* of the quality of treatment and, crucially, also of its quantity. This could be achieved by *thorough* inspection of doctors' bills (both quantity of treatment and prices charged), with the power to withhold payment for treatment or charges which were regarded as excessive. Alternatively, a broadly similar effect could be achieved through the imposition of a binding budget constraint. *Finance* would be through publicly provided health insurance, which would be organised as follows. *Production* of insurance would be public, i.e. the state would pay all medical bills (private, non-profit institutions, acting in effect as agents of the state, could achieve the same result). There would be *regulation*, in that membership would be compulsory. *Finance* could be arranged in one of two ways. With compulsory insurance, premiums could be income-related with little efficiency loss (Chapter 5:4.2), though they would, in effect, be no more than a specific health care tax. This may or may not be an advantage (see the discussion of the insurance principle in Chapter 11:5). Alternatively, the state could drop the idea of actuarial insurance because it does not fit health care very well, and finance the scheme from general taxation. The general thrust of these arrangements follows line (3)(b) of Table 4.2 for health care, and line (6) for health insurance. This is broadly the Canadian system, or medicare/medicaid with a binding output constraint.

The advantages of this approach are twofold. The problems of private insurance are largely avoided; and the incentive to oversupply, resulting from fee for service and third-party payments, is dealt with by policing doctors' decisions, either explicitly or by controlling total expenditure. The strategy rests crucially on the effective imposition of an output constraint. Such arrangements can undoubtedly be successful. A scheme of this sort has operated in Canada for many years; it works well and is widely popular (McLachlan and Maynard, 1982a, pp. 369–424; Brown, 1983c).

Possible improvements to the NHS   We have seen that the NHS strategy (approximately line (8) in Table 4.2) has powerful advantages. But it also has problems, so that some reforms are desirable. The first concerns macro efficiency. There is some evidence (though the issue is hard to quantify) that many problems (e.g. queues and old hospitals) are the result of under-funding. The solution is not to abandon the idea of the NHS, but to devote more resources to it. There are also problems of micro efficiency. We saw that priorities within the NHS, based largely on doctors' *implicit* criteria, are not always rational. This is inevitable, given the lack of technical information on the costs and benefits of treatment, and of clearly stated social priorities about different types of treatment and different classes of recipient. The solution is to gather more information of the type discussed in point (11). It is in this context that micro budgeting proposals (Enthoven, 1985) offer important prospects of improvement.

The NHS raises equity problems in two ways. Attempts have been made to equalise the geographical spread of resources by budgetary allocation and by financial incentives to doctors. These efforts should be continued and possibly intensified. The distribution of health care by social class could be made more equal by reducing the cost of treatment to the lower socio-economic groups, e.g. by compensating out-patients for transport costs and forgone earnings (as is done already with jurors). This process would be assisted by more general equalising measures, e.g. further income redistribution, and better education, including information about the benefits of health care.

The distribution of medical care by social class is probably the most intractable of the problems discussed, and the measures suggested may appear to some readers to be rather pale. It may be that we simply have to accept that inequality in health care, like inequality generally, cannot easily be reduced beyond a certain point. This does not mean that we should not try – merely that we should not expect easy answers. At a minimum we should not forget that the distribution of health care under the NHS, unequal though it might be, is more equal than that in many (if not most) other countries. The balance between realism and complacency is never easy.

2 The Educational System

2.1 INSTITUTIONS

This section discusses in turn the operation of school education (public and private) and the university system under the four heads of Table 4.2, i.e. production, the individual consumption decision, finance, and the aggregate production decision. The system is assessed in section 2.2, and various reforms considered in section 2.3.

Public expenditure on education approximately doubled in real terms between 1960 and 1976, when it reached a peak of nearly 7 per cent of gross national product. The increase was partly the result of increased birth rates in the late 1940s and mid-1960s, partly because expectations about educational standards rose, and partly because of the relative price effect.[1] Thereafter, expenditure fell slightly, partly because of economic conditions and partly because of a decline in the school-age population.

The Operation of School Education

The ultimate responsibility for education in England and Wales[2] rests with the Secretary of State for Education, who is responsible for the Department of Education and Science, and is accountable to Parliament. Under the Department there are 104 Local Education Authorities (LEAs) which build the schools, employ the teachers, and are the actual providers of educational services. In addition, a few schools are run by voluntary bodies, mostly religious, which provide the premises, but where most of the running costs are paid by the LEA. There is also a small private sector. Universities are not part of the legal framework established by the 1944 Education Act, nor are they the responsibility of LEAs. They are therefore discussed separately.

Schools are inspected by a central body, Her Majesty's Inspectorate of Schools, which is entirely independent of the Secretary of State and the Department of Education and Science so as to ensure that standards are policed without political influence. The inspectorate, which visits schools and publishes reports, is an important source of quality control by a central body of a locally provided service, a feature almost entirely lacking in the NHS.

The production of primary, secondary and further education   All children receive a compulsory primary education from age five to 11, usually at schools provided by LEAs. Teachers are employed and paid on an agreed national scale (the Burnham Scale) by the LEA. The total current cost of primary education in England in 1986/7 (Table 13.2) was £2748 million. Though at its best of high quality, primary education has been criticised. The Plowden Report (UK Central Advisory Council for Education, 1967) showed that some

---

[1] See p. 318, footnote 1.
[2] The Secretaries of State for Scotland and Northern Ireland are responsible *inter alia* for education in those countries. The Scottish educational system differs in some important respects from the system described here.

Table 13.2: Education and Science, UK, 1986/7 (est.) (£million)

	Current spending	Capital spending	Total
EDUCATION			
Schools			
Under fives	350	8	
Primary	2,748		
Secondary	4,088		
Special schools	421	209	
Other	310		
Transport	214		
Meals and milk	280		
			8,628
Higher and further education			
Universities	1,413	152	
Student awards	885		
Voluntary and direct grant	90	5	
Maintained sector	1,658	78	
			4,281
Miscellaneous	201	15	
Administration	578	1	
			795
Total education, of which			13,704
Central government	1,696	159	
Local authorities	11,541	308	
RESEARCH COUNCILS	540	74	
			615
TOTAL PROGRAMME			14,319
EXPENDITURE IN			
Scotland			1,792
Wales			730
Northern Ireland			666
TOTAL EDUCATION AND SCIENCE			17,508

Source: *The Government's Expenditure Plans, 1986–87 to 1988–89*, Cmnd. 9702-II, Tables 2.12 and 3.12.

primary schools fell well below acceptable standards, and recommended 'positive discrimination' by geographical area. Educational Priority Areas were established, with (limited) extra resources, and extra payments for teachers in the area. The Report also sparked off further research (Halsey, 1972).

Secondary education is provided by LEAs for children aged 11–19 years; it is free, and compulsory up to age 16. As with primary education, teachers are employed by the LEA and paid on an agreed national scale. Total current public expenditure on secondary education in England in 1986/7 (Table 13.2) was £4088 million.

The three major controversies over secondary education concerned the introduction of comprehensive schools; the raising of the school-leaving age; and the issue of private education. The 1944 Education Act (Chapter 2:5.1) established three types of secondary school for children of different ability – grammer schools (for the academically able), technical schools, and secondary modern schools (whose aim was to give a general education only until the minimum leaving age). The choice of school for any particular child was based on an examination at age 11 (the so-called 'eleven plus'). This structure was severely criticised. It was said to favour middle-class children, to be unequal by geographical area, and to waste the talent of many children from lower socio-economic groups (on the last point, see the Newsom Report (UK Central Advisory Council for Education, 1963)).

The debate over comprehensive schools was a political football for nearly 20 years. In 1965 LEAs were asked to submit plans for the reorganisation of secondary education on comprehensive lines. By 1980 all had done so, though in some cases only after considerable pressure. Many commentators argued that the fierce controversy over the best way of organising schools, despite its importance, obscured even more important educational objectives like the content and quality of teaching, especially in rapidly changing and increasingly technological times.

The minimum leaving age was raised from 15 to 16 in 1972, following the recommendation *inter alia* of the Crowther Report (UK Central Advisory Council for Education, 1959). The move was not a total success, partly because many LEAs had been too much taken up with the issue of comprehensive schools to devote sufficient thought to the development of curricula suitable for an extra year of schooling for non-academic adolescents. A second problem was the size of many of the new schools, and the fact that the new system had not had time to resolve its teething troubles. As a result, secondary education went through a difficult time in the 1970s. Matters improved somewhat thereafter as experience with the new system grew, and the number of children of school age started to decline. Remaining difficulties are argued to be attributable mainly to budget cuts.

Almost as heated as the debate over comprehensive schools was that over the place, if any, of private education. We return to this issue below.[1]

The third arm of the statutory system is further education, which covers the vocational, cultural, social and recreational needs of everyone over school-leaving age who is not in full-time secondary or higher (i.e. university) education. The system provides education relevant to people's working lives, and is often dovetailed with the practical training provided by industry (see Glennerster, 1985, Ch. 10). A second function is to provide for people's leisure. This involves a huge variety of courses, for many of which charges are levied.

This is not the place to discuss further education in detail (see Brown, 1985, Ch. 4) but one development in particular should be noted. A policy of rationalisation in the late 1950s culminated in a report (UK, 1966) which provided for the possibility of polytechnics (which are part of the LEA further education sector) offering degree courses. This introduction of higher education into the further education system was regarded as disturbing by some educationalists, by others as bringing welcome diversity. The result was a rapid concentration of resources at polytechnics. Degree courses by poly-technics increased, with standards supervised by a national body, the Council for National Academic Awards.

Finally, LEAs have several additional functions. They are permitted (but not compelled) to provide nursery education for pre-school children (despite ambitious policies (UK, 1972d) the service was available in 1985 only to 40 per cent of the age-group); they are obliged to provide special education for physically and mentally handicapped children; and they have a number of ancillary responsibilities involving school health activities, youth employment services, guidance for emotionally disturbed children and their parents, and some general welfare activities like free school milk and school meals.

The individual consumption decision We have seen that primary and secondary education is provided free, with compulsory attendance to age 16. A child normally attends a local primary school, and then proceeds to a local comprehensive school. Exceptionally, if a child is particularly gifted and/or with adequate financial resources he/she will go to a private school. Children who are less able or less ambitious usually leave school at 16 with no, or few, qualifications. A bright child will take the General Certificate of Secondary Education in six to eight subjects, both arts and sciences, at about the age of 16. The next step on the educational ladder is so-called Advanced Level ('A' level),

---

[1] For further discussion of the controversies over secondary education see Bosanquet and Townsend (1980, Ch. 13).

taken at about the age of 18, often in a narrow range of two or three related subjects, e.g. mathematics, physics, chemistry or French, German, English. Universities do not normally admit students unless they have two or three 'A' levels.

Individual choice arises in at least three ways. First, there is the decision to continue education beyond the minimum leaving age. This is the individual investment decision discussed in Chapter 12:2.2, to which we return later. Second, is the extent to which parents can choose which school their child attends. The 1944 Education Act allowed parents considerable discretion, but often the exercise of this choice conflicted with attempts by the LEA to balance numbers and quality of intake across schools within their jurisdiction. Parental dissatisfaction led to the introduction in 1980 of an appeals procedure, but where choice exists it is still the prerogative, more often than not, of middle-class families. Lastly, to what extent do (or should) parents and their children have any influence over the LEA and the teaching profession over the running of schools? After many years of debate (see UK, 1977b), legislation in 1986 extended parental representation on schools' governing bodies.

Finance The total cost of primary and secondary education in England in 1986/7 was £8628 million (Table 13.2). Since virtually no charges are levied, basic education is financed almost entirely by the state out of tax revenues. In contrast with the NHS, most expenditure takes place at a local level (Table 7.1), though it should be remembered that a large proportion of local revenues, particularly for education, derive from central government. Limited additional finance comes from other sources: to a small extent schools are able to raise funds through their own efforts to pay for 'extras' not financed by the LEA; and the voluntary sector contributes to the cost of some schools (see Glennerster, 1985, Ch. 10).

The aggregate production decision (i.e. setting budget limits). In principle, most decisions about educational expenditure are taken at a local level. But central government has come to exercise increasing influence over local spending totals, partly through central government grants to local authorities, and partly because of direct controls over local revenue raising (Prest and Barr, 1985, Chs 11 and 20; Glennerster, 1985, Chs 2–4). Nevertheless, local authorities retain some discretion over the composition of expenditure. The aggregate production decision in the case of education is therefore a complex mix of decisions at central and local levels.

Private Schools

Alongside the state sector a small number of private schools (often confusingly called 'public' schools) provide day and residential education. Some 6 per cent of children are involved, and about 10 per cent of expenditure on school education. The existence of a private sector causes considerable controversy. Private schools generally, and in particular the most prestigious, have come under heavy attack. It is argued that they cream off scarce resources of academically gifted children and teachers, and of finance, thus making it difficult for comprehensive schools to maintain high academic standards; and, through their hold on recruitment to key positions, that they perpetuate and accentuate economic and social divisions. The counter-arguments centre round their high quality, the beneficial effects of competition, and the freedom of parents to choose their favoured education. The debate has continued for many years, with no end in sight.

The finance of private education is more complex than might be apparent. The bulk of private schools' income comes from fees, though many have income from private endowments and from appeals to former pupils. They also benefit from public expenditure in a number of ways. Their charitable status gives them tax advantages; and they have received direct assistance. Under the 1902 Education Act so-called Direct Grant Schools received financial assistance from central government if they took a specified number of children from the state sector. This scheme was abolished in 1976. Since 1980 there has been a limited scheme under which central government pays for gifted children from the state sector to be educated at private schools.

Universities

Universities in Britain are independent, self-governing bodies. But they have close links with central and local government, in that a large proportion of their income derives directly or indirectly from public funds.

The individual consumption decision for British students is relatively straightforward. Universities offer places on the basis of academic quali-fications, usually 'A' levels. Students do not have a right to a place at university; they are carefully selected, and the drop-out rate is low by international standards. The tuition fees of any UK undergraduate at a UK university, polytechnic or other approved institution are paid out of public funds; in addition, most students receive a maintenance grant, inversely related to parental income, to cover living expenses.[1] University education is thus free for British students from poor families, and heavily subsidised for all. Overseas students are not generally eligible for public funding. They have to pay tuition fees (which rose very sharply in the early 1980s), and must finance their own living expenses.

---

[1] Students who have received a grant and completed an undergraduate degree will not normally be given a grant to do a second undergraduate degree, although they may for a postgraduate degree.

Finance for universities is complex. Total (current and capital) public expenditure on universities in England in 1986/7 was £1565 million, plus an additional £885 million on student maintenance grants (Table 13.2), making a total of £2450 million. Public funds flow to universities in two major ways. The average British university receives about 75 per cent of its income in the form of a recurrent grant from a central fund. These revenues are channelled through the University Grants Committee, which has three functions: it divides the total central government grant between the universities; it acts as a general link and a buffer between the Department of Education and Science and the universities; and it formulates a national policy for higher education. The Committee is an attempt to reconcile public funding with the independence of universities. The second source of public funds is through LEAs, which pay students' tuition fees and also their maintenance grants. Universities derive income also from the fees of privately funded UK students and of overseas students, from research grants, from a variety of commercial activities, and (in some cases) from their own endowments.

The aggregate production decision has grown considerably more complicated. In the past, somewhat to over-simplify, universities decided how many students they wished to admit, and the state made available sufficient funds to make this possible. A major event in the postwar history of British universities was the publication of the Robbins Report (UK, 1963), whose importance to higher education has been compared with that of the 1944 Education Act to general education. The Report advocated a dramatic expansion in the number of students in higher education, from 8 per cent of the relevant age-group in the early 1960s to 17 per cent in 1980/1, through the expansion of existing universities and the opening of new ones. Most of the Robbins recommendations were put into effect in the years until 1975. At the same time, as mentioned earlier, there was an increase in degree opportunities at polytechnics.

After 1975 these policies were to some extent reversed, or at any rate halted. By the late 1970s only about 12½ per cent of the relevant age-group started full-time degree courses at universities or polytechnics. The contraction had two separate aspects. Central government funding for universities through the University Grants Committee was reduced in real terms, with further cuts foreshadowed. Of equal importance, the University Grants Committee started to exercise a greater degree of influence on universities than hitherto. In particular, it told universities how many students it was prepared to finance, and indicated which types of course were favoured. What used to be virtually untied transfers to universities have become much more like tied grants. Universities are subject not only to the ordinary government budgetary process on aggregate expenditure, but also to an element of control over the disposition of public funds (for recent government policy see UK, 1985c).

In short, the production and finance of school education in the state sector are both public (approximating line (8) of Table 4.2). Private schools approximate to line (1), with elements of line (2). In the university sector production is private and finance for British students largely public (line (2)), but with increasing elements of line (4)(b).

2.2 ASSESSMENT

Efficiency in the UK educational system is even harder to assess than in the NHS, mainly because of the measurement problems outlined in Chapter 12:2.2. These apply equally to macro and to micro efficiency (see the Glossary). Much of the argument is therefore of necessity a priori.[1] Efficiency advantages and disadvantages are much more finely balanced than those of the NHS – one person's 'sign of a civilised society' is another's 'violation of individual freedom'. Discussion therefore concentrates on five areas, with no attempt at division into advantages and disadvantages.

(1) *The individual consumption decision* is substantially influenced by the state and the teaching profession both centrally and locally. Children must attend school until they are 16; and the LEA (see the Glossary) can influence (or in some cases control) the choice of school. This mitigates to some extent the problem of imperfect information, but only at the expense of consumer sovereignty. As discussed earlier (Chapter 12:4.2), there is heated debate about whether the LEA or the parent is better able to make decisions in the child's interests.

(2) *Primary and secondary education is free*, or nearly so; and university education is free for students from poor families, and subsidised for all UK students. Such subsidies avoid the externality problem and have equity advantages; but according to the screening hypothesis (Chapter 12:2.2) they are inefficient, at least for university education.[2]

(3) *Macro efficiency* There is little hard evidence about whether or not too few resources are devoted to education, save that it absorbs about the same proportion of national income as in most other industrial countries. A study of British secondary education by Blaug and Woodhall (1968) was severely qualified, as the authors make clear, by three measurement problems. First, there is no single definition of the purpose of education, and so it is not possible to measure output unambiguously. Second, though the quantity of inputs (teachers' and pupils' time, buildings, equipment) can be measured, their

---

[1] Other countries face similar problems in assessing their educational systems. See Peterson (1983) for description of a spate of reports on the American educational system in the early 1980s.

[2] And maybe also inequitable, see points (9) and (10) below.

quality is largely unmeasurable. Finally, it is not possible to relate the output to inputs. This is, first, because neither can be measured properly. Thus there is a tendency to measure output by the quantity of input, i.e. to assume that education is better simply because it costs more. It is thought, for example, that pupils do better if they are taught in smaller groups, although empirical evidence lends little support to this proposition. But even if output and inputs could be measured, there remains a second problem – that of establishing a *causal* relationship between the two. This brings us back to the screening hypothesis (Chapter 12:2.2). Is an individual productive because he/she is naturally able, or because he/she has been well educated – and if both, what are the proportional contributions?

An early study of high-school students in large American cities (Burkhead, Fox and Holland, 1967) found that variations in test scores depended almost entirely on factors unrelated to the school system, e.g. family income and the character of the neighbourhood. A study of fundamental importance by Jencks (1972) reached two even stronger conclusions: that differences in educational inputs offered no explanation of differences in educational attainment; and that differences in educational attainment made no independent contribution to explaining disparities in income. These results, taken together, suggest that attempts to equalise the distribution of educational inputs may do little to reduce inequality. Not surprisingly, these conclusions were controversial, and led to further research (for a British study see Rutter *et al.*, 1979), but the issue remains unsettled. Are Jencks's conclusions a statistical artefact arising out of measurement errors, or are factors other than education the dominant determinants of pupil achievement? The issue is crucial to reasoned decisions about the volume of resources to be devoted to school education.

The last point applies also to universities. Farmer and Barrell (1982) argue that the British university sector is too small, pointing out that Britain has a lower proportion of the relevant age at university than any other advanced country. In 1960/1 about 7½ per cent of the relevant age-group embarked on degree courses; 20 years later the figure was 12½ per cent, well below the 17 per cent target in the Robbins Report (UK, 1963), and far short of the comparable figure in most other industrial countries (see also UK Department of Education and Science, 1984). Farmer and Barrell argue that this is inefficient (and also inequitable – see point (9)), citing as evidence the fact that the earnings differential between graduates and non-graduates, though reduced by the post-Robbins expansion, is large by international standards. Such differentials, they argue, are the result of entry restrictions to university education, with effects on graduate earnings comparable to the result of efforts over the years in the USA to restrict entry to the medical profession. This evidence, though no more than indicative, lends at least qualified support to the view that the British university sector is too small.

(4) *Micro efficiency* Because of the measurement problems just discussed, little can be said about the efficiency with which resources are divided between different areas of education. A variety of government reports on different parts of the system were mentioned in section 2.1. They ranged over primary, secondary, further and higher education; without exception all gave plausible and laudable reasons why more resources should be devoted to 'their bit' of the system. Measurement problems make it impossible on a quantitative basis to choose between them; and resource constraints and current political realities make it impossible to implement all their recommendations. Criticism by the schools' inspectorate, however, carries weight because of its source. It was reported (UK Department of Education and Science, 1986) that many schools suffered shortages of equipment and neglected buildings, and that in some instances management was ineffective. This might be attributed in part to expenditure cuts (an issue of macro efficiency) – but micro inefficiency was also involved even if it could not fully be measured.

(5) *Administrative efficiency* There is some evidence (Lord, 1983) that the organisation and administration of the educational system could be improved. The switch to comprehensive schools is argued to have been less co-ordinated than it might have been. It is also argued that there was too little advance planning before the school-leaving age was raised. At a more technical level, Knight (1983) argues that localities gather too little detailed cost data, and do not make the best use of the data they have.

Equity, as we have seen (Chapter 4:2.2 and 4.3), is hard to define, and depends in part on one's political perspective. Following Chapter 12:2.1, horizontal equity is taken to imply that children A and B should have an equal *opportunity* (as defined in Chapter 6:3.1) to acquire an education of equal quality and duration, irrespective of whether A comes from a middle-class family and B from a low socio-economic group. Equality of opportunity does not necessarily imply equality of outcome, for at least three reasons: A may be luckier than B; A and B may have different tastes where (and the proviso is crucial) they are equally informed; and A may be more 'able' than B, where such differences are not related to educational and other circumstances earlier in their lives.

(6) *The role of income* The intention of the 1944 Education Act and subsequent policies, including the implementation of the Robbins Report, was that access to education at all levels should not be constrained by family income. This aim has not been fully achieved either for schools or universities. Though no fees are charged, school attendance still involves parental expenditure, e.g. on uniforms or sports gear (Bull, 1980); and many children leave school at 16 not because they want to or because they do not have the ability to proceed further, but because their family needs their earnings. It has been estimated (Piachaud, 1975) that the *absolute* costs of education for a child

between 15 and 17 are higher for low-income parents. School education after age 16 (for which maintenance grants are very limited), like health care under the NHS, is not 'free', but imposes a cost in forgone earnings which bears disproportionately on the lower socio-economic groups. This disproportion has major implications (discussed below) for university attendance.

(7) *The distribution of school education by quality is unequal by social class* Middle-class parents are better able to exercise choice within the state sector, and may further increase their choice by sending their children to private schools. At this point the conflict between equity and individual freedom is at its sharpest.

Some improvement has been sought. The idea of Educational Priority Areas (section 2.1) was to direct additional resources towards primary schools in areas with a disproportionate number of disadvantaged children; and the mechanism by which funds are channelled from central government via LEAs to individual schools can operate similarly (Glennerster, 1985, Ch. 10). The move to comprehensive secondary schools was motivated mainly by a desire to increase horizontal equity. Whether these policies are desirable, and whether they go far enough, depends on the importance attached to the aim of equality and on how one weights the relative claims on scarce resources of children from more and less fortunate backgrounds.

(8) *The distribution of school education by quantity is unequal by social class* There are persistent inequalities both in educational expenditures (i.e. inputs) and in outcomes. As measured by public expenditure, a child from socio-economic group 1 consumes on average about 1¾ times as much post-compulsory secondary education as a child from the lowest socio-economic group (Le Grand, 1982, Table 4.1). This figure, as Le Grand points out, understates the true difference in consumption of educational inputs because children (mainly from socio-economic group 1) attending private schools are not included. On the output side, the picture is similar. The children of better-off families disproportionately stay longer at school and obtain more and better qualifications than their less fortunate confreres.[1]

(9) *The distribution of university education is unequal by social class* This is not the place to discuss in detail why working-class attendance at UK universities is low. Reasons cited include poorer information about the value of education, lower quality schools, and the cost in terms of forgone earnings of post-compulsory education, all of which help to explain why children in lower socio-economic groups leave school earlier. In addition, it is argued that the nature of the 'A'-level system and the workings of the grant system itself (particularly the vexed issue of parental contributions) act further to reduce

---

[1] This *could* be entirely the result of differences in tastes – a point to which we return shortly.

working-class attendance. Whatever their cause, the results are clear enough. Farmer and Barrell (1982, p. 20) report that of the 12½ per cent of the relevant age-group attending university in 1979, only 22 per cent came from a working-class background (see also Universities Central Council on Admissions, 1985); in the USA in 1972, 36 per cent of the age-group attended college, of whom 42 per cent came from less-advantaged backgrounds.[1]

Le Grand (1982, Table 4.1) finds that public expenditure on university education for the average child from socio-economic group 1 is 5½ times that for a child from the lowest socio-economic group. As with school education this figure understates the true difference. His data relate to public expenditure, which is *lower* for the child of a wealthy family because he/she receives a lower maintenance grant. It follows that on average a child from a wealthy family is *more* than 5½ times as likely to go to university. Because of differential class take-up, free university education contributes less to occupational mobility than its proponents had hoped.

Despite data problems the evidence is thus overwhelming that education (measured simply in terms of quantity) beyond minimum school-leaving age is distributed highly unequally by social class. How should this finding be interpreted? Several issues arise. First, the difference *could* in principle be caused entirely by exogenous differences in tastes and abilities, in which case no issue of inequality arises.[2] A person would be brave (or foolish) to argue that this is the whole explanation. But to the extent that it is part of the story, a simple observation of outcomes tends to overstate inequality. Second, if this inequality is genuine, should we be concerned about it? Is education the engine of economic prosperity or the plaything of the rich? If the former, it is appropriate to be concerned about its distribution on efficiency as well as equity grounds. If the latter (i.e. if the screening hypothesis holds), post-compulsory education may have no *social* benefits, thereby diminishing the importance of the efficiency question. But since education confers *private* benefits, its distribution, if inequitable, remains a proper concern. Third, it is necessary to remind ourselves that a different system of education would not *necessarily* be

---

[1] It has been argued that the fact that the UK figure of 22 per cent remained largely unchanged by the Robbins expansion represents a considerable *success* in equity terms, in that one would expect a large and rapid expansion of the university system, ceteris paribus, to *reduce* working-class attendance as a proportion of the total.

[2] See Murphy (1981) for discussion from a sociological perspective. He sums up the issue neatly: 'though no necessary relationship exists between class *disparity* in education and class *inequality* in education, educational commentators have conventionally taken the existence of one to indicate the existence of the other' (p. 182, my emphasis).

more egalitarian. As with the NHS, it is not enough to argue that the present system is imperfect; it is also necessary to suggest an alternative which will do better. If none can be found, egalitarian goals must be pursued by other means.

These caveats notwithstanding, it is hard to resist the conclusion that the distribution of education is influenced by inequalities in society. Individuals from less fortunate backgrounds have less information about the value of education, and less of the *savoir faire* necessary to make the best use of 'the system'. They have lower incomes, and are therefore less able to afford the earnings forgone by continuing education. Nor should it be forgotten that education is an investment which, like all investments, takes time to pay off; but the pursuit of long-run goals requires *hope*; and hope, too, is distributed unequally by social class. The expectations of children are formed largely on the experience of their parents, whose lives may give little encouragement to long-run optimism. For all these reasons, children from low-income families tend to receive education of a lower quality, and to avail themselves of a smaller quantity. There is inequality in education, and the inequality is much greater than in health care.

(10) *Redistributive effects of the educational system* We have seen (Chapter 7:4.2 as qualified by Chapter 7:4.1) that education is financed progressively even if (rich) individual A consumes (say) twice as much education as (poor) individual B, so long as A (or his/her parents) pays more than twice as much as B in the taxes which pay for education. For the system as a whole, educational expenditure on a child of a family in socio-economic group 1 (henceforth for short a 'rich' child) is about 50 per cent higher than for a 'poor' child, i.e. one in the lowest socio-economic group (Le Grand, 1982, Table 4.1). Thus the system is financed progressively if on average the tax contribution towards education of an individual in the highest socio-economic group exceeds that of someone in the lowest by more than 50 per cent. As with the NHS (see the discussion in section 1.2) this is likely if we are prepared to assume that education is financed out of taxation generally, i.e. that if all public expenditure on education were withdrawn there would be, for example, a reduction in income tax, or an equi-proportionate reduction in all taxes, rather than a reduction of a regressive tax.

In contrast with the NHS, however, matters cannot be left there. The picture for different parts of the educational system must be discussed; and so must its inter-generational impact. The ratio of public expenditure on 'rich' children to 'poor' for education as a whole is about 1.5. For secondary education after age 16, for further education, and for university education the ratios are approximately 1¾, 3½ and 5½, respectively (Le Grand, 1982, Table 4.1). It is possible, subject to the caveats in the previous paragraph, to argue that post-compulsory secondary education might still be progressive; but the finance of further education is at best proportional, and that of universities almost certainly regressive. A similar conclusion was reached, for similar

351

reasons, by Hansen and Weisbrod (1969 and 1978) (see also Pechman, 1970) for the heavily subsidised system of public higher education in California.

The regressivity of university finance is compounded by noting that education, more than health care, has inter-generational aspects. One of the main conclusions of Atkinson, Maynard and Trinder (1983) is that nearly half of their sample of poor people came from poor parents. In part, this is because children of poor parents tend to have lower-quality education, and less of it. Thus the taxes of poor families contribute to consumption by the rich of a university education which helps to keep them rich.

2.3 REFORM

Four sets of reform are considered: radical privatisation; voucher schemes for school education; loans for university education; and possible improvements within the existing system.

Radical privatisation   Chapter 12:3.2 discussed the failure of many of the standard assumptions.[1] A priori we would therefore expect an unrestricted private market for school education (i.e. line (1) or (2) in Table 4.2) to be inefficient for technical reasons (Chapter 12:4.2), and also inconsistent with widely held views of social justice (Chapter 12:3.3). Complete privatisation offers no solution, and so it is not surprising that no advanced country has a system of school education which remotely approximates a pure private market. It is more useful to ask whether any mixed public/private package offers hope of improvement, considering separately the school and university systems.

Voucher schemes for school education   The idea is that parents receive an education voucher for each child, i.e. a form of tied grant which can be 'spent' by parents at a school of their choice. There are many variants (see the Further Reading), but Bosanquet (1983, Ch. 12) distinguishes two archetypal schemes.[2] Under the Friedman (1962) proposal (see also Maynard, 1975), the value of the voucher would be the average cost of a place in a state school, or a proportion of that cost. Parents would be free to spend the voucher at any school, public or private and, where it failed fully to cover fees, could 'top up' the voucher out of their own pockets; and schools would have complete freedom in their choice of pupils and organisation of waiting-lists. Jencks's (1970) scheme differs in several important ways. The basic voucher covers the

---

[1] I.e. the assumptions necessary for the market to allocate efficiently, see Chapter 4:3.2, or the Appendix to Chapter 4, paras 6–17.

[2] See Blaug (1984, pp. 161–5) for a more detailed breakdown of different voucher options.

full average cost of state education; topping up is not allowed, but low-income parents receive a compensatory increment to the basic voucher, thereby diverting resources to schools with a disproportionate number of children from poor backgrounds. The Jencks scheme, consequently, has more of an equalising effect on expenditure. In addition, schools for which demand exceeds supply must allocate at least half of the available places at random. Both Friedman and Jencks are concerned with consumer sovereignty and efficiency, but Jencks's scheme places more emphasis on distributional goals.

The essence of the voucher idea is that education is produced in the private sector, with intervention to increase efficiency and equity by subsidy (i.e. the voucher) and regulation (e.g. compulsory school attendance, minimum standards and, arguably, restrictions on topping-up and the allocation of places). The Friedman scheme is therefore a mixture of lines (1) and (2) of Table 4.2 (because parents can choose their child's school, and are free to top up the voucher) and line (4)(a) (since education up to a certain age is compulsory). The Jencks scheme is a combination of line (2) and line (4)(b), the latter because the 'no topping-up' rule imposes a constraint on total output.

Voucher schemes, it is argued, have the twin advantages of increasing efficiency and enhancing consumer sovereignty. Parents choose their child's school; education is privately produced and competitive, so that schools respond to parental demand more than state schools do at present; and voucher schemes avoid the present (arguable) inequity whereby parents who send their children to private schools receive no tax relief in respect of costs from which they thereby relieve the state system. To opponents of voucher schemes, their efficiency advantages are debatable and their equity effects almost certainly deleterious. The efficiency issue, as we saw in Chapter 12:4.2, hinges on whether parents are sufficiently well informed to police the standards of their child's school and, if not, whether a publicly organised inspectorate will be more effective with public or private production. In equity terms, it is argued that voucher schemes will increase inequalities in the distribution of education (both quantity and quality) by social class (though less so in the case of a Jencks type of scheme than under the Friedman proposals). Vouchers might well have advantages for middle-class families, but only at the expense of less well-informed choices by lower socio-economic groups. The equity issue therefore turns on the relative weight given to the claims of the two groups. Finally, voucher schemes are criticised because privately produced education is likely to reduce social cohesion.

Empirical evidence is scant. There has been one small, short-lived and inconclusive experiment with vouchers in the USA (see Bosanquet, 1983, pp. 167–70, and Blaug, 1984), and one feasibility study in Britain (Kent County Council, 1978). According to Bosanquet 'voucher schemes have not shown a robust Hayekian will to evolve. They have not been a socially selected institution which has grown' (1983, p. 170).[1]

Loans versus grants for university education It has been suggested that the British system of paying grants (i.e. gifts) out of tax revenues to students to finance their university education should be abolished and replaced by loans. One reason (see Farmer and Barrell, 1982) is the failure of the grants system to remove all financial barriers to university attendance, partly because inequalities in school education cause a disproportionately high attrition rate among children from disadvantaged backgrounds, and partly because of the grants system itself. The latter reason sounds paradoxical. The argument is that the reduction in the real value of the student maintenance grant by nearly 20 per cent between 1963 and 1982 eroded the differential between the grant and juvenile earnings (which rose substantially); and that the means-tested parental contribution caused disproportionate problems for working-class students, and probably also for women. Both factors tended to reduce working-class applications (i.e. demand) to universities. Additionally, on the supply side, grants are costly, and university places therefore rationed by controls on public spending. These problems, it is argued, would be ameliorated by a system of loans.

The following discussion does not look at any specific proposals (for which see the Further Reading), but sets out in turn the general way in which loans operate; some examples from other countries; and the issues which divide their supporters and opponents. Under most loan schemes, actual or proposed, university education remains partially subsidised, either through low (or zero) fees and/or by a residual grant to all students or, in some schemes, only to students from disadvantaged backgrounds. The loan can come from the state (as in Sweden), or predominantly from private lenders such as banks or universities themselves (as in the USA), either with or without a state loan guarantee. Repayment can follow two generic models: the 'mortgage repayment' model (i.e. the individual repays what he/she has borrowed, plus interest); or the 'graduate tax' model (Glennerster, Merrett and Wilson, 1968), in which the individual pays a surcharge on income tax (i.e. repayments are related not to the size of the loan but to eventual income).

Thus the price of the loan can be commercial (rarely), or at a subsidised interest rate (usually), or income-related (often). The essence of the loans strategy is that individuals pay for the private benefits of their university education, but are subsidised to the extent of the external benefit conferred on others. This is a valid approach to efficient resource allocation only where *inter*

---

[1] Discussion, nevertheless, continues – see 'Tories Give School Vouchers Priority', *The Times*, 24 February 1986, p. 1.

alia consumers have perfect information about the long-run value of education, and where capital markets are perfect. Loans bring about the latter condition; whether the first holds sufficiently is one of the central issues (to be discussed later) in the loans versus grants debate.

Loans systems of different types work well in a number of countries. Farmer and Barrell (1982) cite two schemes of particular interest: the Swedish system, which is a large state scheme in a country with a socialist tradition (see OECD, 1980 and 1981), and a much smaller private scheme run by Yale University (see Nerlove, 1972 and 1975). The original Swedish system consisted of a grant topped up by a loan. In 1964 it was decided to switch the emphasis towards loans by the simple expedient of freezing the nominal value of the grant and allowing its real value to be eroded gradually by inflation. By 1978 the grant covered just over 10 per cent of the total cost of a university education. It was topped up with a loan from the state, available to all qualified high-school students; an element of positive discrimination was later built in; repayments are income-related. Under the Yale scheme students were grouped into cohorts; each cohort was *jointly* responsible for repaying its loan, and repayments were income-related so that those with below-average earnings after they left university repaid less than they borrowed, and vice versa. The resulting system was self-financing and generally experienced low default rates. One of its most interesting features is that it provides a form of group insurance, so that individuals who are poor or unemployed after leaving university are not burdened by large debts.

The issues which divide supporters and opponents of loan schemes are varied, complex and sometimes contradictory. A number of efficiency issues arise. First, what is the effect of loans on the quantity of university education consumed? It is argued that grants distort the individual decision to acquire a university education by making it too cheap, thereby (in the absence of a budget constraint limiting the number of university places) causing over-consumption. A subsidy may well be justified if university education creates external benefits but, so long as private benefits are positive, this is no argument for a 100 per cent subsidy; and if the screening hypothesis is true there might be no efficiency justification for any subsidy at all. Loan schemes, it is argued, avoid the tendency to overconsumption associated with grants. A logically incompatible view is that loans avoid *underconsumption*. Farmer and Barrell (1982) argue that the expense of the grants system has kept the university sector below its optimal size. Loans, they argue, relax the budget constraint, and so enable an expansion of university education at no additional public cost. Other writers argue that loans, by reducing public expenditure, enable taxes to be reduced with beneficial incentive effects. It should be noted, however, that a *public* loan scheme, even if self-financing in the long run, is likely to *increase*

355

public spending in the short term, when the state will be issuing many loans and receiving few repayments.

A second set of issues concerns consumer sovereignty. Some writers argue that the need to repay loans would give students undue encouragement to take 'vocational' subjects. The US and Swedish experience lends little support to this view. It is also argued that students who finance their own education through loans are likely to be more assertive in demanding the kinds of courses they want, including more flexible opportunities for part-time study than currently exist at British universities.

A third efficiency (and equity) issue concerns the possibility that loans create a disincentive to women to acquire a university education, i.e. that women graduates burdened by repayments bring a 'negative dowry' upon marriage. Since women on average spend fewer years in the labour force than men they might be more reluctant to take out loans. This problem would be solved if repayments were income-related,[1] so long as the income in question was that of the woman herself rather than the joint income of husband and wife.

Loan schemes have two undoubted equity advantages: they solve the inequities arising from capital market imperfections; and they avoid the regressivity of the grants system resulting from differential consumption of university education by social class (point (10) on page 351). A third, and controversial, equity issue is whether loans contribute more than grants to equality of opportunity. Farmer and Barrell argue from a socialist perspective that loans, by making it possible for the university system to expand, open up opportunities for students from disadvantaged backgrounds, partly because more places in total would be available, and also because students no longer depend on parental contributions if they are not eligible for a full grant. But it does not follow that working-class take-up of university education would necessarily increase. The need to repay loans, even if repayments are income-related, and even if the loans are available on generous terms to students from poor families, might well increase inequality of university attendance by social class. It requires considerable optimism about one's future to take out a loan which, even if no tuition fees are charged, would amount at least to £7500 for a first degree. It might be advisable to introduce any UK scheme gradually, along Swedish lines, by freezing the nominal value of the current grant and allowing students to top it up with a loan as inflation eroded its real value (for a recent UK proposal see Glennerster and Le Grand, 1984).

Possible improvements within the existing system The strategy of public production, regulation and finance (line (8) in Table 4.2), at least for school education, is common to all industrialised countries. The evidence on the

---

[1] Though this might have efficiency implications.

efficiency of the British system is scant (section 2.2), so discussion of reform is concerned mainly with equity. The first issue is that imperfect information arises differentially by social class; partly as a result, the *quality* of school education varies with socio-economic status. Attempts to increase the information available to working-class parents are unlikely to have much impact. A more plausible approach, where disadvantage is concentrated by area, is to strengthen efforts to increase the resources available to primary and secondary schools, i.e. the Educational Priority Area strategy writ large.

The information problem is also one of the causes of the unequal distribution of the *quantity* of education. Again, efforts to improve information are unlikely to have much effect. Probably the most important inducement to children from poor families to stay at school until the age of 18 would be a grant, probably income-related, for those who remain at school after the minimum leaving age.

The regressivity of university finance has two roots: a system of grants financed out of tax revenues; and the fact that few children from a working-class background go to university. Loan schemes tackle the problem by altering the system of finance, which deals with the first root but not necessarily the second. Since low university attendance by working-class children is both inefficient (because it wastes talent) and inequitable, attempts to deal with the second root of the problem are desirable on their own account. This would involve improvements in the equity of the school system, both by equalising the quality of education and by income-related grants for 16- to 18-year-olds. Additionally, universities could make more strenuous efforts to recruit students from disadvantaged backgrounds.[1]

3 Conclusion: Health Care and Education

No system of health care or education can be perfect – the real issue is to choose the least inefficient and inequitable form of organisation. Radical privatisation (as defined in Chapter 4:5) is no way of doing so. This conclusion rests not on personal values but on the *technical* nature of health care and education as commodities, and particularly, though not exclusively, on information problems which are ignored in much of the pro-market literature.[2]

---

[1] The London School of Economics has an experimental scheme whereby, in liaison with the Inner London Education Authority, it attempts to identify gifted children from disadvantaged backgrounds. These children are encouraged to apply to the School, and may be offered a place conditional on lower 'A'-level marks than is the School's general custom. Once at the School they receive extra tuition. Several other universities have similar schemes.

[2] E.g. in the case of education see the classic piece by Friedman (1962, Ch. 6), and also Hayek (1960, Ch. 24).

Health care conforms only minimally with the assumptions necessary for market efficiency. The imperfect information and unequal power of consumers, externalities, and technical difficulties with private medical insurance cause serious problems on the demand side of a hypothetical private market; non-competitive behaviour by doctors can cause problems with supply, and third-party payments cause inefficiency via both demand and supply (Chapter 12:3.1). A priori there is an overwhelming presumption that an unrestricted private market will be highly inefficient, and also inconsistent with widely held notions of social justice. This view is confirmed by empirical observation (Chapter 13:1.1). Countries which have little public involvement in health care, or which have adopted ad hoc modifications to private systems, have typically experienced sharp, unplanned increases in expenditure. Efficiency requires, at a minimum, considerable regulation and state financial involvement (Chapter 12:4.1).

Because of information problems the NHS strategy has major advantages – an institution motivated largely by equity can be successful because it goes with the grain of efficiency arguments. On the demand side, decisions about treatment are made by doctors, thus alleviating the effects of consumer ignorance; the problems of private insurance are resolved by abandoning the insurance principle even as a fiction; and treatment is largely free at the point of use, which reduces the externality problem and goes a long way towards eliminating the influence of the income distribution on consumption. On the supply side, doctors are not as a rule paid a fee for service, thus removing the financial incentive to oversupply. Health care is rationed partly by administrative means and partly by the NHS budget. Furthermore, if public production and allocation can be defended on efficiency grounds, it is legitimate to finance health care redistributively for reasons of social justice (Chapter 4:6.1). In theory, therefore, the strategy is feasible in both efficiency and equity terms.

The practice (Chapter 13:1.2) is far from perfect. The NHS faces a shortage of resources; many hospital buildings are old; and there are waiting-lists for non-urgent (and even some urgent) conditions. The distribution of health care by social class and by region is less equal than many people would wish; and there is room for improvement in the administration of the system. However, a good deal can be said on the plus side:

The average quality of health care in Britain is good, in that health standards are not out of line with those in other countries.
The NHS is cheaper than the health care system of any comparable country, and considerably cheaper than most.
Doctors have no financial incentive to over-prescribe and (partly because of this) patients generally trust their doctor.

The variation in the quality and quantity of treatment by income level is smaller than in most other countries.

Treatment is free whatever the extent and duration of illness; no one is denied access because of low income; no one goes in fear of financial ruin.

The NHS thus has much to commend it, both *per se* and especially in comparison with the systems in many other countries; and most of its remaining problems could largely be resolved by giving it more resources and by gathering and using more and better information.

Its advantages notwithstanding, the NHS is not the only system of health care which makes sense, just as the governance of a country need not involve powers vested in a hereditary monarchy. But like the Crown the NHS is an institution which has served Britain well, is widely popular, and which can be drastically changed only at considerable risk of throwing out the baby with the bath water. The study of health care in other countries shows that the adoption of a different system is likely to raise problems very similar to those of the NHS, and additional and more intense problems as well. 'Privatisation' (whatever its proponents mean by the term) will not solve old problems, and is likely to create new (and probably larger) ones. To imagine otherwise (to put it no more strongly) is naïve dogmatism of the highest order. My preferred reform for Britain, therefore, is to keep the NHS; the principle should be retained, and the system improved within the existing strategy along the lines suggested in Chapter 13:1.3.

However, the political economy and the structure of the medical profession in many other countries make it unlikely that they would readily adopt a system of public production. This is especially true of the USA with its tradition of private markets. For them the mixed public/private arrangements described in Chapter 13:1.3 might be a more satisfactory solution. The Canadian model of privately produced health care has much to offer; and a system based on regulated health maintenance organisations buttressed by income transfers may prove an effective alternative. The crucial point is that any system of health care must constitute a genuine *strategy* – ad hoc tinkering is a guaranteed road to disaster.

Education raises very similar theoretical arguments (Chapter 12:3.2 and 3.3). Again, many of the assumptions necessary for market efficiency fail, the main problems being imperfect information, imperfect capital markets and external effects. From an equity viewpoint, the most important problem is that knowledge about the operation and value of education is likely to be correlated with socio-economic status. Substantial public involvement is therefore essential (Chapter 12:4.2) though, because the information problem is less acute than with health care, the theoretical arguments about public production (as opposed to regulation and finance) are rather more finely balanced. It is therefore not surprising that no advanced country has a system of school education which even remotely approximates a pure private market. State school systems universally are publicly regulated and financed; they are also all publicly produced. To the extent that this strategy is valid on efficiency grounds, it is legitimate for education to be financed in accordance with distributional goals (Chapter 4:6.1).

The practice of education in Britain is far from unblemished. The conclusion on the efficiency of the system is that we simply do not know (Chapter 13:2.2); and because measurement problems are so intractable (Chapter 12:2.2) it is unlikely that it will ever be possible to collect the information necessary to produce definitive answers. From an equity viewpoint, the educational system is less egalitarian than the NHS. There is strong (many would say irrefutable) evidence that the rich receive higher-quality school education and make considerably more intensive use of the system, particularly at the university level. The latter difference cannot be explained entirely by differences in tastes and ability. Additionally, though it can be argued that about four-fifths of educational expenditure is financed progressively or proportionately, the university sector is almost certainly regressive. For this sector at least, the hopes of the founders of the welfare state have not been met.

The performance of the educational system is thus more mixed than that of the NHS. But its critics have to show not that it is less than wholly efficient or equitable (which is not in dispute) but that a more market-oriented solution would do better. Opponents of the broad thrust of existing arrangements have (to put it no more strongly) yet to prove their case. The advocates of a mixed public/private system of school education offer only limited evidence in support of their views. The efficiency effects of vouchers are unclear a priori and not proven empirically. In equity terms they are likely to increase inequalities in the distribution of education, and in particular to benefit the middle class at the expense of lower socio-economic groups (Chapter 13:2.3).

Loan schemes might in the long run enable the university sector to expand, bringing it more into line with the size of university systems abroad. This might have efficiency advantages, though measurement difficulties, including the screening problem, make a definitive answer unlikely. The equity effects of loan systems would also be beneficial if they solved the problem of regressive university finance. But it is unclear whether they would encourage working-class attendance at university, even if repayments were biased in favour of children from disadvantaged families and/or those with low earnings after they left university. Loan systems on their own are unlikely to increase equality in university attendance by social class; but they might be useful in conjunction with other measures, particularly grants for 16- to 18-year-olds.

The essential first step towards equality of opportunity is to reduce inequalities in the quantity and quality of school education by social class in the ways described in Chapter 13:2.3. But there might be limits to which this can be achieved solely within the confines of the educational system. To the extent that inequalities in education are the result of broader inequalities, progress in the former will depend in part on improvements in the latter. International comparison suggests that the British record in education, in contrast with health care, leaves considerable room for improvement.

The issues raised by health care and education are genuinely complex, and raise much trickier problems of mixed public/private involvement than is the case with most cash benefits. Even in principle there are many threads to the argument; and matters are complicated by intractable measurement difficulties. In the face of these problems it is unfortunate that health care and education, more than most parts of the welfare state, are bedevilled by emotional polemics, most of which confuse aims and methods. The main purpose of these chapters has not been to give the 'right' answer, but firmly to establish the right battleground.

Further Reading

On the institutions of the NHS see Glennerster (1985, Ch. 8), Brown (1985, Ch. 3) and Aaron and Schwarz (1984) (an excellent comparison of health care in Britain and the USA, including a brief institutional summary). For an authoritative international survey see McLachlan and Maynard (1982a), for more specific discussion of cost containment Abel-Smith (1984), and for evaluations of the NHS Abel-Smith (1976), Culyer (1978), the Report of the Royal Commission on the National Health Service (UK, 1979b) and Black (1980). For arguments against the NHS (and state provision of education) see Friedman (1962, Ch. 6), Friedman and Friedman (1980, Chs 4 and 6) and Seldon (1981), and for a critique of their views Bosanquet (1983, Chs 11 and 12). A thoughtful (and sympathetic) discussion of reform within the NHS is by Enthoven (1985).

Institutional and other aspects of the educational system are discussed by Glennerster (1985, Ch. 10) and Brown (1985, Ch. 4). For the relationship (or lack of it) between educational inputs, educational attainment and the distribution of income see Jencks (1972) and Averch *et al.* (1972) in a US context, and Rutter *et al.* (1979) for a British study. Contrasting views of the British educational system and various voucher schemes are contained in Friedman (1962, Ch. 6), Jencks (1970), Maynard (1975), Friedman and Friedman (1980, Ch. 6) and Bosanquet (1983, Ch. 12); for a summary of the voucher issue and an assessment of practical experience see Blaug (1984). International comparisons of loan schemes are given in UK (1980) and Woodhall (1982); for a cogently argued UK proposal see Farmer and Barrell (1982). All these issues are discussed by Blaug (1970) and, more briefly, by Culyer (1980, Ch. 9). The arguments underlying the Robbins expansion of the university system are set out in UK (1963); for the demise of the policy see UK (1985c).

The detailed financial institutions of health care and education are analysed by Glennerster (1985). Le Grand (1982) discusses distributional aspects of both systems, and Le Grand and Robinson (1984b) look at the possibility of privatising different parts of the welfare state.

Housing

An Englishman's home is his tax haven. [*The Economist*, 1979.]

1 Introduction

This chapter argues that housing is the least successful part of the welfare state, largely because (with the wisdom of hindsight) it is apparent that policy-makers blurred the vital distinction between aims and methods. In part by historical accident the postwar Labour government chose a method of achieving its health care objectives which broadly accords with the predictions of economic theory; it is therefore not surprising that health care in Britain, by and large, has worked well. Housing policy, in contrast, has gone wrong not because its aims have been inappropriate, but because historically methods were chosen which have been unable to achieve them. The resulting problems are entirely predictable. The present system misallocates housing. Poor people can be homeless or overcrowded. At the same time, owner-occupiers and people living in local authority housing face incentives to consume inefficiently large quantities, so that the system simultaneously creates overoccupation and underoccupation, and at the same time subsidises the rich. To a Marxist this might be entirely predictable; from a liberal viewpoint, starting *tabula rasa*, no-one would knowingly devise such a system.

The main questions are concerned with the efficiency and equity of different ways of organising the housing market. A number of important matters are not discussed, particularly inner city problems, the planning of land use (other than consideration in a general way of the importance of regulation), and private rental outside the scope of the 1977 Rent Act (on all of which see the Further Reading). The aims of housing policy are discussed in section 2. Section 3 discusses in principle whether housing as a commodity accords with the standard assumptions[1] and, where it does not, what type of intervention might be appropriate; the conclusion is that economic theory offers no strong arguments for public production of housing, and powerful arguments against general subsidies of *housing* as opposed to subsidies of *income*. Section 4 assesses the practice, looking in particular at the inequities and inefficiencies resulting from past and present policies. This sets the scene for discussion in section 5 of possibilities for reform.

2 Aims

A Conservative White Paper (UK Department of the Environment, 1971) listed three objectives of housing policy.

(1) A decent home for every family at a price within their means.
(2) A fairer choice between owning a home and renting one.
(3) Fairness between one citizen and another in giving and receiving help towards housing costs.

A subsequent Green Paper under a Labour government (UK Department of the Environment, 1977a, para. 2.16) added six further aims.

(4) A better balance between investment in new houses and the improvement and repair of older houses.
(5) Housing costs should be a reasonably stable element in family finances.
(6) [Increased] scope for mobility in housing.
(7) A reasonable degree of priority in access . . . for people in housing need who in the past have found themselves at the end of the queue.
(8) [The necessity to] safeguard the independence of tenants.
(9) [The necessity to] ensure that the housing needs of groups such as frail elderly people, the disabled and the handicapped are met.[2]

It is helpful for subsequent discussion if some order is imposed on these objectives. Efficiency in the context of housing arises in three ways: the size and quality of the housing stock, tenure neutrality and mobility.

---

[1] I.e. the assumptions necessary for the market to allocate efficiently – see Chapter 4:3.2, and/or the Appendix to Chapter 4, paras 6–17.
[2] On the goals of US housing policy see Aaron (1981b, pp. 70–6) and Levine (1978).

The size and quality of the housing stock must be efficient. Housing faces the same trade-off as, for example, health care: clearly it is inefficient to spend nothing on housing; equally, if the whole of national income were devoted to accommodation there would be no resources for the production of food and health care. The optimal quantity lies somewhere in between – in principle where the value placed on the marginal unit of housing equals the marginal social cost of the resources used. This is the quantity $Q^\star$ in Figure 14.1 (see Chapter 4:2.1, and the Appendix to Chapter 4, paras 2–4). Part of this aim is captured by objective (4), above.

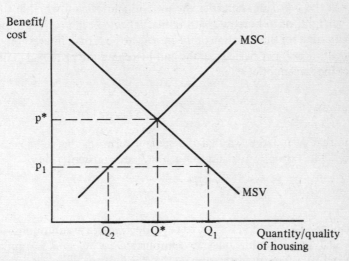

Figure 14.1   *Efficiency in the housing market*

Tenure neutrality (captured by objective (2)) exists when competitive markets leave individuals (on average and in the long run) financially indifferent between buying accommodation and renting it, with no artificial distortions (e.g. via the tax system) of their relative costs. An approximate example of tenure neutrality is the case of television purchase and rental in the UK. The concept, which has both efficiency and equity implications, is important and requires careful explanation (non-technical readers can skip the equations).

Formal analysis: consider the flow of housing services[1] (net of maintenance costs) $R_1, R_2, \ldots, R_N$ for a rational individual with a constant rate of time

---

[1] I.e. the value placed by occupants on housing of a given quality/type, as measured by the annual rent they would be willing to pay. The concept of the flow of services from physical wealth is discussed in Chapter 6:1.1.

preference, r. The present value of the benefit stream is

$$PVB = \sum_{t=1}^{N} \frac{R_t}{(1+r)^t} \qquad (14.1)$$

To simplify, let $R_t = R$ for all t. Then in perpetuity[1]

$$PVB = \frac{R}{r} \qquad (14.2)$$

and the individual will buy the house only if $R/r \geq P$ where P is the purchase price. On the cost side, consider the individual decision whether to buy the house outright, or to borrow P at the market rate of interest, i. Suppose, for simplicity, that for the duration of the mortgage he repays interest only (i.e. his repayments are iP per period); at the end he repays the principal. The present value of the stream of costs is

$$PVC = \sum_{t=1}^{N} \frac{iP}{(1+r)^t} + \frac{P}{(1+r)^{N+1}} \qquad (14.3)$$

Assume that N is large (so that the second term on the right-hand side of equation (14.3) drops out); and that i and P are constant. Then

$$PVC = \frac{iP}{r} \qquad (14.4)$$

Equations (14.2) and (14.4) have been derived via assumptions which are purely analytical. At this stage two important *behavioural* assumptions are introduced. Assume, first, that the market for housing is competitive for both purchase (so that $PVB = P$ in equation (14.2)) and rental, so that R (the flow of housing services per period) equals the competitive market rent R_c at the margin. Hence equation (14.2) becomes

$$PVB = \frac{R_c}{r} = P \qquad (14.5)$$

---

[1] The easiest way to prove equation (14.2) is to express the flow of benefits in continuous terms. Then (see also the discussion on page 249)

$$PVB = \int_0^\infty Re^{-rt}dt = -\frac{R}{r}\left[e^{-rt}\right]_0^\infty = \frac{R}{r}$$

For a simple exposition of the present value formula see Lipsey (1983, Ch. 28). For fuller discussion of cost-benefit analysis see Brown and Jackson (1982, Ch. 8), Musgrave and Musgrave (1984, Ch. 8) and Mishan (1982).

The second assumption is that capital markets are perfect; thus $i = r$. Two important results follow. First, from equation (14.5)

$$\frac{R_c}{i} = P \Rightarrow R_c = iP \tag{14.6}$$

i.e. *there is an economic relationship between the market rent, R_c and the purchase price, P,* i.e. between the flow and the stock prices. Thus there is no artificial incentive to rent or buy. Second, from equation (14.4)

$$\text{PVC} = P \tag{14.7}$$

Equation (14.7) shows that the cost of borrowing and the purchase price are equal; *a rational individual is indifferent between taking out a mortgage or making an outright purchase* – there is no artificial incentive to borrow.

Implications: equations (14.6) and (14.7) show that tenure neutrality requires two conditions: a competitive market for purchase and rental; *and* a perfect capital market, in the sense that mortgage finance should be available competitively and on a non-discriminatory basis. In practice, matters are complicated, *inter alia* by uncertainties about future rates of inflation, which may cause unforeseen variations in real interest rates and house prices. These factors make the relationship between purchase price, rent and borrowing costs more complex than equations (14.6) and (14.7) suggest. But the meaning of the condition remains unchanged – even in a world of uncertainty, tenure neutrality implies an undistorted economic relationship between purchase price and annual rent, and requires perfect capital markets.

Mobility (objective (6)) arises out of the fixed location of housing. The issue does not occur with (say) food. If an individual moves to another part of the country he simply buys his food in a different shop. But he cannot take housing with him, nor buy it off a supermarket shelf. If is therefore important that the housing market is sufficiently flexible to prevent persistent excess demand – a desirable aim for many reasons, and in the context of mobility because excess demand could hinder or prevent an individual who lives in area A from taking a job in area B.

Turning to distributional issues, the definition of horizontal equity, as we have seen (Chapters 4:4.3 and 6:3.1), is elusive. For housing it can refer to a minimum standard, or to equality of cost, equality of subsidy or equality of final outcome. All are different, and all lead to different results. For present purposes, as with health care and education, horizontal equity is defined in terms of equality of opportunity and minimum standards.

Equality of opportunity, as defined in Chapter 6:3.1, refers to access to housing of at least some minimum standard, analogous to the implicit but widely accepted aim for food, that everyone should have a healthy diet such that no one starves. Equality of opportunity applies in two ways: access to adequate housing generally (this is the 'decent home for every family' in objective (1), and also includes objectives (7) and (9)); and access to different tenures, i.e. tenure neutrality expressed in objective (2). If the price of different tenures or access to capital markets favour the better-off, then issues of equity as well as efficiency arise.

Minimum standards (objectives (1) and to some extent (8)) can be justified on efficiency grounds by imperfect information and by certain types of externality, and on equity grounds if information and power are systematically correlated with income (Chapter 4:3.2 and 4.3). They might also be necessary to protect children. There is considerable disagreement as to where the minimum standard should be set (see section 5.2).

Vertical equity   Once the efficient quantity/quality of housing and its equitable distribution have been decided, the remaining question is how housing should be financed. This concerns vertical equity (see the Glossary), expressed in objectives (3) and (5), and also in the second part of objective (1) ('at a price within their means'). The quotation is important. Vertical equity can be pursued *either* by reducing 'price' (cf. health care) *or* by increasing 'means' (cf. food). It was argued in Chapter 4:6.1 that in general the former is appropriate to achieve vertical equity only where there exist *efficiency* grounds for subsidy or for public production and allocation; in their absence, the latter policy (i.e. cash transfers) will generally contribute more to efficiency and social justice.[1] The extent of vertical redistribution will depend largely on one's political perspective (Chapter 4:2.2).

3 Methods

3.1 THE SIMPLE THEORY OF THE HOUSING MARKET

One of the key characteristics of housing is its durability. A family of four may

---

[1] Note the theoretical caveat in Chapter 4:6.1 that the optimal taxation approach can give a different result. The taxation necessary to finance income transfers may cause a substantial labour supply disincentive. If so, it may be possible to improve both efficiency and equity by subsidising the *prices* of goods consumed by the poor if (a) such goods are consumed only (or mainly) by the poor, and (b) the consumption of such goods is not strongly complementary to leisure. Since neither condition applies to housing the argument, even as a theoretical proposition, is not of immediate relevance.

over its lifetime spend £100,000 on (say) food. But consumption, expenditure and (crucially) production take place on a day-by-day basis, so supply can respond fairly rapidly to changes in demand. It is possible to make a loaf which lasts for two days; but it is not possible to build a two-day house, e.g. out of cardboard.[1] Though the consumption of housing *services* occurs on a daily basis, the *stock* (i.e. the building itself) can last a lifetime. New building is therefore only a small proportion of the existing housing stock, and so total supply can increase only slowly (in Britain at an annual average of less than 2 per cent). Thus short-run supply is highly inelastic, even though it may be elastic in the long run. The best representation of the housing market is therefore by a disequilibrium stock-adjustment model.

The left-hand diagram in Figure 14.2 shows the market for the *stock* of housing, the right-hand diagram, the *flow* of new housing (i.e. net additions to the housing stock). No distinction is made between accommodation for rent and for owner occupation. The curve D_1 shows the demand for housing at different prices, given the prices of other goods, the level of income and its dispersion, and the size and demographic structure of the population. The curve SRS_1 is the highly inelastic *short-run* stock supply of housing. The curve S in the right-hand diagram shows the supply schedule for new housing as a function of its price, based on two simplifications. First, building activity empirically depends less on current prices than on expectations about future prices (Robinson, 1979, Ch. 5); second, current completions depend on past decisions. The model at its simplest assumes that completions this period are a function of the stock price last period (Robinson, 1979; Muth, 1960; Whitehead, 1974). The net addition to the stock of housing in any period is total completions minus losses through depreciation and demolition.

Consider a point of initial equilibrium in Figure 14.2. With demand shown by D_1 and stock supply by SRS_1 the total housing stock is $Q^\star$. The price $p^\star$ serves two functions: it clears the market for the stock of housing; and it induces new building ($q^\star$ in the right-hand diagram) just sufficient to offset losses through depreciation. Thus the net stock of housing is exactly maintained, and the market remains in equilibrium. Now suppose that there is an increase in demand, shown by an outward shift in the demand curve to D_2. The stock price rises to p_1, so additions to the stock one period later rise to q_1 in the right-hand diagram; since this exceeds the rate of depreciation $q^\star$, the net stock of housing increases, as shown by the new short-run stock supply curve SRS_2. The new stock price is p_2, lower than p_1 but still higher than the equilibrium price $p^\star$. Net additions to stock therefore continue until the price

---

[1] Such dwellings do exist in less developed economies. But they are ruled out in industrial economies by prevailing attitudes, by legally binding minimum standards, and often also by the climate.

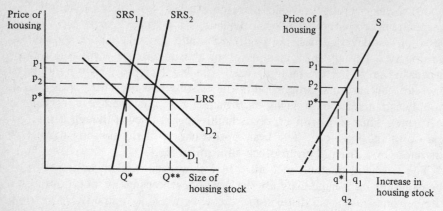

Figure 14.2 *A simple stock-adjustment model of the housing market*

returns to $p^\star$. With demand shown by D_2 this occurs with a housing stock of $Q^{\star\star}$. *Long-run* supply can therefore be represented by the curve LRS.

In practice, the market for a number of reasons is unlikely to converge smoothly to a new equilibrium. It is more realistic to think of the housing market as in continual disequilibrium as the result of random shocks, but generally tending towards equilibrium. Nevertheless, the stock-adjustment model, even in its simplest form, is useful because it illustrates the behaviour of a market where supply is inelastic in the short run but elastic over a longer period (for theoretical and empirical discussion of the UK and USA, see Robinson (1979, Chs 3–5)).

3.2 THEORETICAL ARGUMENTS FOR INTERVENTION 1: EFFICIENCY

The rest of section 3 discusses the theoretical arguments for public involvement in housing. We know (Chapter 4:3.2) that the market allocates resources efficiently only if the standard assumptions hold, i.e. perfect information, perfect competition and no market failures such as external effects, public goods or increasing returns to scale. The argument in this section considers the nature of housing as a commodity, and in particular the extent to which these assumptions hold; section 3.3 looks at equity arguments. The two sections taken together consider *why* the state intervenes. Section 3.4 discusses in principle *how* best it might do so (i.e. the question of method).

Perfect information   Are individuals well informed about the nature of the product, i.e. are their indifference maps well defined? If an individual inspects a house does he or she thereby acquire full information about its qualities? For many characteristics, e.g. size and location, the answer is yes; but most house buyers have highly imperfect information on technical matters like rising damp. This does not necessarily imply state intervention, because market institutions have developed (e.g. surveyors) to supply information. Furthermore, housing, from the viewpoint of the consumer, is not as highly complex a commodity as health care,[1] so that consumers generally understand the information they acquire. To that extent, market institutions deal more effectively with information problems with housing than with health care.

A second question is whether consumers are adequately informed about prices (formally, whether their budget constraint is well defined). This, typically, is the case for homogeneous commodities which are bought repeatedly (e.g. food), so that information is regularly updated. Where a good is bought infrequently but is homogeneous (e.g. train fares) out-of-date information can speedily be rectified. Housing, in contrast, is both an irregular purchase (taken to include renting) and highly heterogeneous, so that buyers will not have perfect knowledge. Again, however, the market has developed institutions such as estate agents to improve consumer information; or the buyer can commission a professional valuation from an independent expert.

The third information assumption concerns knowledge about the future. One problem is uncertainty about whether one's house will be destroyed, e.g. by fire. The market solution is to supply house structure insurance, which is efficient because it conforms with the technical conditions necessary for private insurance (Chapter 5:3). Other forms of uncertainty, e.g. a decline in property values, either generally or in one's locality, are not directly insurable, but by renting rather than buying, the worst of such risks can often be transferred to the landlord.

Though none of the information assumptions hold fully, the problems which arise are those which the market itself is often able to solve. The role of the state in this context is to regulate minimum standards for the surveying and valuation professions, and for house insurance policies.

Perfect competition Because housing is durable its short-run supply elasticity is low. As a result, an increase in demand (e.g. from D_1 to D_2 in Figure 14.2) can cause a short-run, sharp increase in price from $p^\star$ to p_1, though in the long-run, as new houses are built, the price will tend to return to $p^\star$. The fact that house prices and rents can change substantially in the short-run may cause equity problems (discussed below), but is neither uncompetitive nor inefficient (cf. the sharp rise in coffee prices after a bad harvest). Inelastic supply is not *per se* a violation of perfect competition. It is sometimes argued that supply is less than fully competitive in other respects,

---

[1] See Chapter 12:3.1 for the compexities of health care as a commodity.

because housing is heterogeneous, and because the construction industry is not fully competitive (Bowley, 1966). Nevertheless, the supply of housing displays no *major* violations of the competitive assumption.

Competition can, however, fail in two ways: the assumption of equal power; and the issue of perfect capital markets. The equal power assumption can be violated with rented accommodation because, in brief, a 'house' over time becomes a 'home', thus giving the landlord an element of monopoly power. Consider an individual who moves to a new area. At least in principle, he faces a competitive market, so that he pays a rent (say £50 per week) equal to his marginal valuation of the property. But once he has moved in, the house, for at least three reasons, becomes over time that mythical thing, a home. This is first because of the pictures and other personal effects he puts up (which features could all be transferred if he moved). Second he (or his landlord) might redecorate or improve the house; this is investment in physical capital, which raises the value of the property. Third (and crucially), he learns about the area (the best school, the best bakery), and makes friends. These last are investment in human capital; they do not raise the value of the property; nor are they transferrable if he moves elsewhere.

These factors, and especially the third, raise the marginal value (MV) of the house to the individual, i.e. MV (home) > MV (house). Ignoring inflation, the individual would be prepared to pay a higher rent (say £75) to stay there, both to protect his investment in human capital, and to avoid the substantial transactions costs (search time, removal expenses, etc.) of moving elsewhere.[1] At a rent of £50 he is intra-marginal, and this gives the landlord monopoly power,[2] though its strength is an empirical question.[3] If the problem is thought to be serious the simplest solution is regulation, not via rent control but

[1] On the general topic of mobility in the context of housing transactions costs see Venti and Wise (1984).

[2] A similar phenomenon can occur with owner-occupiers. An individual buys a house as a marginal decision. Over time it becomes a home, and its marginal value to the individual rises, and can often exceed the market price of the house (proof: try knocking on people's doors and asking if they would agree to sell their house at its market price plus moving costs, etc.). It is therefore iniquitous that governments can compulsorily purchase houses at their market price. Such an action steals from the individual the difference between MV (home) and MV (house) – it is a theft of the value of comfort, habit and of the human capital the individual has built up in the locality. Setting measurement problems to one side, the equitable compensation for compulsory purchase should in principle be that sum for which the individual would agree to move voluntarily. This would include not only the value of the garage which he has added (i.e. physical capital) but also his accumulation of human capital.

[3] There may be an element of monopoly power in the opposite direction, since landlords also face costs if a tenancy changes hands.

through a tribunal with the power to reduce rents if a landlord exploits his monopoly by raising the rent to £75, when *new* tenancies for similar property are fetching only £60.

In the case of owner-occupiers the assumption of perfect competition applies not only to the housing market *per se* but also to capital markets. As we have seen (equations (14.6) and (14.7)), both conditions are essential for tenure neutrality. But capital markets in practice may be (and often are) far from perfect, e.g. if lending institutions refuse loans to all but the safest cases. Intervention could take the form of public provision of loan finance, or of loan guarantees, i.e. the state would indemnify lending institutions against losses incurred if an individual defaulted on repayments. Such intervention could have equity as well as efficiency advantages.

The remaining assumptions Externalities[1] arise in several ways. Houses which are structurally unsafe or fire hazards threaten their occupants and neighbours, the fire hazard point being recognised in local by-laws as long ago as the Middle Ages. Similarly, a house with improper sanitation creates public health hazards (UK, 1842, discussed in Chapter 2:1.2). One solution is to subsidise the maintenance of building standards. But the aim in this case is not so much to encourage building quality as to ensure that it does not fall below a minimum standard. This might be achieved more directly through regulation of minimum standards of individual dwellings.

A related but different phenomenon is that housing can create a spatial externality. This arises in one form if I build a factory in my back garden, which imposes costs on my neighbours as an eyesore and a general reduction in the amenities they enjoy. There is a conflict between my freedom to do what I like on my land, and the freedom of others to be unaffected by my activities. This problem can sometimes be resolved by the market, if property rights are unambiguously assigned and enforceable (Coase, 1960). Another solution is a Pigovian 'eyesore tax' (see the Glossary), though this faces serious measurement problems. The most direct intervention is regulation of land use in the form of zoning and planning controls, though with room for disagreement as to their extent, e.g. should I be allowed to paint my house psychedelic orange?

A different type of spatial externality arises out of slums. A slum landlord (particularly if subject to rent control) faces incentives to reduce expenditure on his property (see section 4.2), which then deteriorates thereby reducing the value of surrounding property. Slum neighbourhood characteristics generally dominate attempts at improvement by any *individual* landlord because he cannot find tenants prepared to pay a rent high enough to cover the costs of improvement. Once the slum process has started, it tends to continue, creating

---

[1] See Chapter 4:3.2 and in the Appendix to Chapter 4, para. 15.

inter alia a public health problem. Two solutions are possible. If the houses are worth saving, subsidies (e.g. improvement grants) can lead to 'gentrification', and are therefore justifiable in efficiency terms. If the houses are not worth saving, because they are old or their density exceeds minimum standards, regulation in the form of planning controls may be appropriate (see Gauldie's (1974, pp. 279–80) description of how Birmingham in the nineteenth century purchased both houses and factories in areas it wished to improve).

A further problem, with the same analytical characteristics as externalities, arises if the private discount rate exceeds the social discount rate. In such cases, private markets tend to underinvest in terms of both quantity and quality. This gives rise to one of the few efficiency arguments for financial assistance with housing costs in the form of a general *price* subsidy.

The issue of public goods[1] arises over the provision of parks and open space. Though it is possible in principle to practise exclusion (i.e. to charge for admission to parks), the marginal cost of an extra user is zero if the park is not full. Thus the efficient price is zero, in which case private developers have no incentive to provide the efficient quantity of public open space, and may have no incentive to provide any at all. The most direct solution, again, is regulation in the form of planning controls, e.g. that at least x per cent of any development should be public open space.

Amenities such as sewers, drains, water and the distribution (though not the production) of domestic gas and electricity, face increasing returns to scale. If, for example, gas is supplied to a particular area, it is obviously cheaper to run a gas main down a whole street with a branch to each house than to supply each house separately. The solution is regulation – in this case that all property developments should include provision of these services.

Before proceding, it is worth spelling out a number of complexities which were implicit in earlier discussion. First, housing is a heterogeneous commodity so that there is not a single market, but a series of interrelated ones. Second, the longevity of housing, and its consequent nature as a capital asset, mean that the operation of the housing market is related to the availability of finance, and hence to financial markets. Third is the problem of indivisibilities, both in terms of the 'lumpiness' of much housing expenditure and in changing the quality of a given dwelling. Fourth, changing one's house can involve substantial transactions costs in both financial and utility terms. None of these features necessarily prevents housing markets from operating efficiently, but may well prevent them from operating quickly (as shown in the stock-adjustment model in section 3.1) and/or may necessitate regulation – policy design needs to take account of both possibilities.

---

[1] See Chapter 4:3.2 and in the Appendix to Chapter 4, paras 13 and 14.

The conclusion is that efficiency is likely to be enhanced by regulation in a variety of forms; by limited subsidies for specific reasons; and by public provision of loan finance or loan guarantees. It should be noted that none of the efficiency arguments points towards either public production of housing or state allocation to the individual.

3.3 THEORETICAL ARGUMENTS FOR INTERVENTION 2: EQUITY

Horizontal equity raises two issues: access to housing; and access to capital markets. The latter can be dealt with briefly. Capital market imperfections may bear disproportionately on the lower socio-economic groups. The problem is less that the poor are charged a higher interest rate (which would be justifiable on efficiency grounds to the extent that they were worse risks), than that those with lower and/or fluctuating incomes may not be able to borrow at *any* interest rate. Public intervention in the form of loans or loan guarantees may therefore be desirable to enhance tenure neutrality for equity as well as efficiency reasons.

Turning to access to housing *per se*, the crucial assumptions for horizontal equity (Chapter 4:4.3) are perfect information (to enable consumers to make rational decisions) and equal power (to enable them to enforce those decisions). If these assumptions hold there is little reason for the state to intervene. The question we need to ask, therefore, is why the state might wish to encourage or force people to consume more or better housing than they would voluntarily choose. Several reasons have been suggested. Individuals, it is argued, may not accurately perceive the benefits of housing (i.e. an aspect of imperfect information), and may therefore consume less than is efficient. If this problem disproportionately afflicts the lower socio-economic groups we have equity as well as efficiency grounds for intervention. Whether this is in fact the case is, in the final analysis, an empirical question and a crucial one. But it can be argued that imperfect information is not a *major* problem with housing – poor people live in sub-standard accommodation less because they misperceive the benefits of housing than because they cannot afford anything better. A second argument is that individuals may accurately perceive the value of housing to themselves, but fail to take account of the effects of their decisions on others, e.g. the public health argument. This problem is real and, where it affects the poor disproportionately, again gives equity as well as efficiency ground for intervention.

In either case, what intervention is appropriate? One form involves regulation of building standards and of land use generally. Alternatively, the state could seek to encourage consumption through subsidies applied either to prices or to incomes. The problems of price subsidies for housing (discussed in section 4) suggest that regulation will usually be more satisfactory.

Vertical equity involves intervention either via income redistribution, allowing individuals to make their own consumption decisions, or through direct transfers of housing. Consumption externalities (Chapter 4:4.2) offer one explanation of in-kind transfers: the utility of a representative rich individual, R, rises with his own consumption, rises with the 'good' consumption (e.g. housing) of a representative poor man, P, but falls with P's 'bad' consumption. In this situation, R might agree to an in-kind transfer to P of housing worth (say) £1000, but offer a cash transfer (which might be spent on 'bad' consumption) of only £200, in which case both rich and poor might prefer the in-kind transfer (see Figure 4.5).

The rich might also favour this approach for other reasons, including their own self-interest. They might believe that good housing improves the health and productivity of the workforce or that good housing prevents social unrest (Chapter 3:5.3). Another argument (discussed in Culyer, 1971b) is that housing is such an important part of community welfare that individuals should be compelled to consume at least some minimum quantity. This is the 'merit good' argument (Chapter 4:4.2) in its pure form. The poor may prefer direct transfers of housing either because of the generosity of the in-kind transfer in comparison with the cash offer they would otherwise receive, or because they feel less stigmatised by receiving benefits in kind than in the form of means-tested cash transfers. For all these reasons it may be politically easier to transfer housing in kind.

3.4 TYPES OF INTERVENTION

Pure market provision, according to the theoretical analysis, is likely to be inefficient and inequitable. Many of the assumptions necessary for efficiency can fail: landlords have potential monopoly power; capital markets may be imperfect; and housing creates a wide range of external effects. If these problems disproportionately afflict the lower socio-economic groups there is also a problem of horizontal equity; and in the absence of redistributive policies, inequalities in the distribution of income would lead to wider inequalities in the distribution of housing than most people would like. Proponents of a free market for housing (Friedman and Stigler, 1972; Friedman, 1962, pp. 178–80; Hayek, 1960, Ch. 22) point to the undoubted problems with housing in Britain. They are correct in attributing some of them to inappropriate intervention. But advocacy of unrestricted markets is implausible; a better solution is not to adopt a 'hands-off' policy, but to choose more effective policy instruments.

Mixed public/private provision involves the design of a theoretical package of regulation and subsidy such that private production and allocation is efficient and equitable. Such a scheme (whose policy aspects are discussed in section 5) would involve the following ingredients.

Regulation on the supply side would take various forms. There would be minimum standards, *inter alia* because of the public health externality; planning of land use (because of spatial and other externalities); regulation of professional standards for surveyors and valuers (thus improving information about the quality of housing); and regulation of landlords, as a counterweight to any monopoly power they acquired in the long run.

Finance: there is a strong case for public provision of loan finance or loan guarantees if capital markets are imperfect, not least to encourage tenure neutrality. In addition, price subsidies may be appropriate in strictly limited cases: in the presence of slum-type externalities; where there is a divergence between private and social discount rates; and possibly on equity grounds if short-run supply inelasticity causes financial hardship (though the latter subsidy would generally be of limited duration).

The arguments of principle suggest that state intervention along these lines could achieve efficiency and horizontal equity. Three major theoretical conclusions emerge. First, information problems are not overriding. Individuals (with professional assistance if necessary) generally have sufficient information about the quality and price of housing to make rational decisions. In the case of housing, much more than with health care (Chapter 12:3.1), one can argue that consumer sovereignty is useful (not morally better or worse, *useful*). Second, there is an efficiency justification for *general* price subsidies only if the private discount rate is thought to be inefficiently high. Together with the first point, this suggests powerful advantages if prices are kept at their efficient level, p^* in Figure 14.1, and vertical equity aims pursued through cash transfers (Chapter 4:6.1).[1] Third, the theory offers no efficiency justification for public production of housing (as opposed to regulation of private supply). This is *not* an argument against public production. But, taken together with the previous two points, it suggests that the aims set out in section 2 are more likely to be achieved if housing is allocated via efficient prices, supported by income transfers. If untied cash transfers are politically unacceptable, or if the untied transfer necessary to raise the consumption of housing to the desired level is too expensive, cash transfers could be tied to expenditure on housing. The kernel of the argument is its suggestion that *Britain's housing difficulties are not a market allocation problem but an income distribution problem*. In other words, as argued

---

[1] Though see p. 368, footnote 1.

in sections 4 and 5, the technical nature of housing makes it more like food than like health care.[1]

Public production and allocation to the individual at a zero or subsidised price (i.e. less than $p^\star$ in Figure 14.1) are theoretically defensible for health care (Chapter 12:4.1). Precisely the same theoretical considerations suggest that this approach is unlikely to work well with housing. First, there are problems with allocating accommodation to individuals by administrative decision. When faced with efficient prices, consumers are likely to make better decisions than housing administrators for two sets of reasons: because they have better information about their own tastes and requirements, and because tastes about housing vary widely across individuals. Both aspects contrast sharply with health care (Chapter 12:3.1).

A second problem arises if prices are inefficiently low. Unless the demand for housing is completely price inelastic, any subsidy of rents/prices greater than justified for efficiency reasons (e.g. p_1 instead of $p^\star$ in Figure 14.1) will raise demand to Q_1. One or both of two consequences follow: if supply increases to Q_1 the result is a housing stock larger than the efficient quantity/quality $Q^\star$; and if it remains at $Q^\star$ the result is excess demand, e.g. waiting-lists, immobility and/or homelessness as discussed in section 4.

The theoretical arguments therefore suggest that a strategy of public allocation of housing by administrative decision at a subsidised price will be inefficient and inequitable. There is a fundamental conflict between this approach and the mixed public/private strategy discussed previously, in which housing is allocated by individual consumption decisions constrained by efficient prices, and supported by income transfers. This conflict emerges repeatedly, both in assessing the British system in practice, and in considering options for reform.

4 An Assessment of British Housing Institutions

4.1 INSTITUTIONS

Public intervention in housing is far-reaching and diverse. It involves regulation, subsidy, and public production and allocation, though with

---

[1] The debate is an old one, going back at least as far as the Land Enquiry Committee (UK, 1914), whose long-term solution, according to Swenarton (1981, p. 41), 'was to ensure that everyone could afford an economic rent through minimum wage legislation; in the short-term, the housing shortage could be alleviated by state provision of houses, so long as they were built and let at a strictly economic rent'.

considerable variation between the three main types of tenure – owner-occupation, the local authority rental sector and private rented accommodation. Because of the complexity of these institutions it is impossible to give a comprehensive picture (see the Further Reading). This section seeks to sketch out the main institutional features. Section 4.2 assesses the extent to which different parts of the housing market meet the aims discussed in section 2, and the housing market as a whole is discussed in section 4.3. Throughout, the term 'house' is used to include flats, apartments, etc.

Housing as a Whole

The historical background is probably more relevant to the current situation in housing than in any other part of the welfare state. Government involvement at a national level began in the second half of the nineteenth century (Chapter 2:1.2) mainly out of concern with public health. Legislation established two powers: to set minimum standards for new houses; and to demolish unsafe or unhealthy dwellings. These simultaneously increased the cost of housing and reduced its supply. As a result, many families could not pay the market rent of minimum standard accommodation.[1] The main response in the nineteenth century was private philanthropy.

By the early twentieth century this approach was increasingly regarded as unsatisfactory. Two solutions were discussed: provision by local authorities of housing for the poor at subsidised rents; and income subsidies for the poor. The latter policy commanded little support at the time, partly for ideological reasons, and partly for lack of a suitable administrative structure to distribute income transfers. The Housing and Town Planning Act 1919 (the Addison Act) imposed on local authorities the duty of remedying housing deficiencies in their area (Chapter 2:3.1). Wartime exigencies had already led to the imposition of rent controls in 1915. The rejection of income subsidies at a time of acute housing shortage thus led over a four-year period to the adoption of two sets of policies: rent (i.e. price) subsidies in the form of rent control, and public provision of housing. These policies continued in various forms during the inter and post-war periods, and remain in force today.

Central and local government responsibilities Central government policy is formulated by the Department of Environment. Housing itself is provided by local authorities, housing associations and private landlords (for rent) and by private builders (for purchase). Local authorities have a general responsi-

---

[1] See the evidence presented to the Royal Commission on the Housing of the Working Classes (UK, 1885). This was, and still is, the last Royal Commission on housing in Britain, though see National Federation of Housing Associations (1985) for a non-governmental attempt, chaired by HRH The Duke of Edinburgh, to fill the gap.

bility for meeting housing need in their area, including the clearance of individual unfit dwellings, the exercise of planning controls to enforce minimum standards, and the building, managing and letting of housing.

Planning of the quantity, quality and location of housing is conducted by local authorities in consultation with central government. Under the Town and Country Planning Act 1968 each local authority submits to central government a general plan for land use, after public inquiry. Once the overall plan has been approved, its detailed implementation is the responsibility of the local authority. Any proposal to construct a new development or modify an existing one must be approved by the local authority. Unsuccessful applicants can appeal to the Minister, who has the power to reverse local decisions.

Public expenditure on housing is shown in Table 14.1. Current expenditure in 1986/7 was £1100 million, mostly in the form of subsidies to local authority housing; capital spending (net of sales and repayment of loans) was £1652 million. The total of £3904 million is a very narrow definition of public expenditure on housing. It omits income transfers such as housing benefit (Table 7.5), and also implicit spending in the form of various tax concessions to owner-occupiers (i.e. tax expenditures, discussed in Chapter 7:1.1).[1] Table 14.2 gives a more complete picture. Total spending on local authority and related housing, including price and income subsidies was £4937 million. The main tax expenditures on owner-occupation are mortgage interest relief[2] and relief from capital gains tax, amounting together to some £7250 million. Subsidies to the private rented sector consisted of £780 million for income subsidies, plus an unknown revenue loss due to rent control. Table 14.2 shows public expenditure on housing in 1986/7 of around £13 billion, mostly in the form of subsidies, and much of it subsidising prices rather than incomes. Given this vast expenditure what has been achieved?

The quantity and quality of housing There is a consensus that during the 1970s there was no *general* housing shortage (UK Department of the Environment, 1977a, para. 3.05). By the mid-1980s, however, pressure on accommodation was growing especially (though not only) in the London area (UK Department of the Environment, 1985a, Table 3). The average quality of housing in the mid-1970s was high by international standards (UK Department of the Environment, 1977a, para. 3.01; Lansley, 1979, p. 133), though with wide variation. Over one-quarter of the housing stock was old (i.e.

---

[1] It also omits the transfer to tenants resulting from rent control, which exemplifies a more general phenomenon – regulation as a form of implicit taxation/expenditure; for an analysis see Prest (1985).

[2] We discuss later whether the true tax expenditure is the revenue forgone because the imputed income of owner-occupiers is not taxed.

Table 14.1: Public Expenditure on Housing, UK, 1986/7 (est.) (£million)

CURRENT EXPENDITURE

Central government subsidies to local authority housing, new town and housing association housing	911	
Other current expenditure (including administration)	189	
Total current expenditure		1,100

CAPITAL EXPENDITURE

Local authorities			
Gross expenditure	2,532		
Total receipts	−1,435		
		1,097	
Housing corporation			
Gross loans and grants to housing associations	685		
Repayments of loans and grants to housing associations	−100		
		585	
New Towns			
Gross expenditure	31		
Total receipts	−65		
		−34	
Other		4	
Total net capital expenditure			1,652
of which			
Gross capital expenditure		3,253	
Total receipts		−1,601	
TOTAL PROGRAMME			2,752

EXPENDITURE IN

Scotland	657
Wales	140
Northern Ireland	355
TOTAL NET DIRECT EXPENDITURE ON HOUSING	3,904

Source: *The Government's Expenditure Plans, 1986–87 to 1988–89*, Cmnd. 9702-II, Tables 2.12, 3.9 and 3.9.2.

Table 14.2: Public Expenditure (More Broadly Defined) on Housing, UK, 1986/7 (est.) (£million)

PUBLIC HOUSING		
General current subsidies[a,d]	911	
Rent rebates[b,e]	2,374	
Capital expenditure (net)[a,d]	1,652	
Total public housing		4,937
OWNER-OCCUPATION		
Tax expenditures[c]		
Mortgage interest relief for owner-occupiers	4,750[f]	
Capital gains tax relief on principal private residence	2,500[f,g]	
Tax relief on life assurance premiums connected with mortgages	unknown	
Tax relief on gains disposal of life assurance policies connected with mortgages	unknown	
Total owner-occupation		7,250[h]
PRIVATE RENTED HOUSING		
Rent allowances[b,e]	780	
Rent control	unknown	
Total private rented housing		780[h]
TOTAL PUBLIC EXPENDITURE ON HOUSING		12,967[h]

Source:

[a]*The Government's Expenditure Plans, 1986–87 to 1988–89*, Cmnd. 9702-II, Table 3.9.

[b]*Ibid.*, Table 3.15.

[c]*Ibid.*, Table 2.24.

Notes:

[d]Excludes expenditure in Scotland, Wales and Northern Ireland.

[e]Excludes expenditure in Northern Ireland.

[f]Figure relates to 1985–86.

[g]This figure is very approximate.

[h]Figure only a lower bound.

pre-1914). There was rapid improvement over the 1960s and early 1970s; but from the late 1970s the condition of the housing stock declined sharply. The number of properties in serious disrepair increased, and slum clearance fell substantially despite persisting problems of unfitness (National Federation of Housing Associations, 1985, Ch. 2). As a partial response, consideration was given to improving the system of grants for home improvement (UK Department of the Environment, 1985b).

Tenure patterns have shifted dramatically over the postwar period from private rented accommodation to owner occupation and the local authority sector. In 1982, 59 per cent of houses were owner-occupied (30 per cent in 1950), 29 per cent rented from local authorities or new towns (18 per cent), and 12 per cent from private landlords (52 per cent).

Because the tenures are organised so differently they are discussed separately, using the same four heads as health care and education (see also Table 4.2), i.e. production, the aggregate production decision, the individual consumption decision, and finance.

The Owner-occupied Sector

Production of owner-occupied housing is by private individuals or property developers, subject to planning controls, and to considerable regulation of minimum standards of design and materials. The aggregate production decision is private, though again tempered by the need to obtain planning permission and by more general land policies.

The individual consumption decision is private in the sense that individuals can choose which house they want to buy. But decisions are generally constrained by the availability of mortgage finance which, as we shall see, is a greater problem for some people than others.

Finance for house purchase is generally private, though with heavy subsidies, mainly in the form of tax relief. The most common source of loan finance for owner-occupiers in Britain are the Building Societies (see Cullingworth, 1979, Ch. 1). They are non-profit institutions enjoying limited tax advantages, which make long-term (20–25 year) loans to individuals for house purchase or home improvement. In recent years banks have entered the mortgage market.

Owner-occupiers receive substantial tax relief. Mortgage interest repayments are deductible at the individual's marginal tax rate, which for most mortgage holders is the basic rate of income tax (30 per cent between 1979 and 1986); and relief at the basic rate is given also to individuals below the tax threshold.[1] Such tax relief applies to an individual's 'principal private

---

[1] This is administratively simple, since an individual whose tax rate is 30 per cent and who pays £100 gross mortgage interest sends £70 to the building society, which receives the remaining £30 from the tax authorities. For details of the UK system of income tax see Prest and Barr (1985, Ch. 9, section 2.1.1), and Kay and King (1983, Ch. 2).

residence' (i.e. not to second homes), and is restricted to the first £30,000 of any mortgage. A second major tax advantage is that no capital gains tax is charged on the increase in the real value of an individual's principal private residence.

These reliefs require explanation. Businesses pay tax on their net profits. Analogously, a landlord pays tax on his *net* rent receipts, i.e. the excess of his gross rent receipts over total costs, including maintenance and repair costs *and* any interest costs on borrowed money. Historically, if the landlord let the house to himself (i.e. was an owner-occupier) he would pay tax on a similar sum. He would have imputed to him the gross rent he would receive if he let the house to a third party; from this he could deduct maintenance costs and mortgage interest payments. So long as an owner-occupier paid tax on this imputed income (so-called 'Schedule A' receipts), it was entirely proper for mortgage interest to be deductible. But over time the income imputed to individuals was eroded, partly by inflation, partly because rent control made it difficult to estimate market rents, and partly because the tax was politically unpopular. It was abolished in 1962. It is thus open to debate whether the transfer to owner-occupiers is the deductibility of mortgage interest or the non-taxation of imputed housing income. However the tax advantages are measured, owner-occupied housing is favourably treated relative to most other investments and to other consumption goods, with important implications for tenure neutrality (see point (23) on p. 397).

These tax advantages all have the effect of offering owner-occupiers a price subsidy. In addition, poor homeowners are eligible for a limited range of income subsidies under housing benefit (Chapter 10:1).

Local Authority Housing

Production Local authority housing is publicly designed and planned, though its construction may be contracted to private builders. Maintenance is usually carried out by local authority employees. The aggregate production decision rests in principle with local authorities, but has latterly been severely constrained by past production decisions, and by current central government policy, notably that controlling local spending.

The individual consumption decision Local authorities have a statutory duty to meet housing need; but each has wide discretion in the way it allocates its housing stock in the face of excess demand, which persists despite the expansion of the local authority sector. Families signal their demand by asking to be put on an authority's waiting-list. There are two rationing devices. First, prospective tenants may not be eligible even to go on the waiting-list unless they have lived or worked in the area for a specified period; though no longer officially permitted, such residency requirements still occur in practice. Second, once a family is on the waiting-list, its housing need may be assessed by a 'points' system, which is used by about 50 per cent of authorities. Each local authority has considerable discretion both in constructing its weighting system and in interpreting it. In large measure, therefore, the local authority makes the individual consumption decision, though constrained to some extent by legal obligations.

The finance of local authority housing is a morass which will be touched on only briefly (see Glennerster, 1985, Ch. 11). Each local authority has a *Housing Revenue Account*, which shows all expenditure and revenue on a cash flow basis, including interest payments on past loans, and subsidies from central and local government (see UK, 1986a, Table 3.9.14). Historically, the account was required to break even, but latterly has been permitted to make a surplus. The former requirement that the account should balance on a current basis has had important implications: by 'pooling' its rent income a local authority can spread the high costs of new building across the whole of its housing stock; similarly, the interest charges to the Housing Revenue Account are the average 'pooled' interest rates paid by the local authority on its historical borrowing.[1] Rents in a given local authority therefore depend on two factors: the average age of the housing stock (which determines the historic cost of building, and hence interest charges); and the extent of subsidy from central and local government. The former implicit subsidy remains; the latter declined considerably in the years after 1980. The subsidy can be measured in different ways (see point (23)), and varies widely across individuals;[2] on average, however, local authority tenants receive a substantial, albeit latterly declining, *price* subsidy.

Local authority (and private) tenants are eligible also for *income* subsidies. Under the Social Security and Housing Benefit Act 1982, an earlier system of income-related benefits was replaced from April 1983 by housing benefit, as described in Chapter 10:1. The basic idea, in the words of an earlier debate, is 'to subsidise people rather than houses'; poor tenants in local authority and private rented accommodation receive assistance in paying their rent and rates. Such assistance is higher the lower the family's income, the higher its housing costs, and the larger the family size. Though sound enough in principle, the scheme experienced severe teething troubles, and was the subject of considerable criticism (see the Further Reading at the end of Chapter 10). Further reform is foreshadowed (UK, 1985k, Ch. 3).

---

[1] For details see UK Department of the Environment, 1977a, para. 4.07. Matters have latterly been further complicated in that central government grants to local authority Housing Revenue Accounts are based on deemed rather than actual rents and costs – see Glennerster, 1985, Ch. 11.

[2] Some tenants receive virtually no subsidy (whilst no owner-occupiers with a mortgage fail to benefit from their tax advantages).

The Private Rented Sector

Production of new housing for private rental is in principle decided by property developers, subject to planning controls and regulation of minimum standards, though in practice there has been little new building for private rental in the UK in recent years.[1] Total supply is determined privately, including decisions about building new rental property, and also whether new or existing stock is used for private rental or sold for owner occupation (though the latter decision is constrained by legislation giving certain tenants security of tenure).

The individual consumption decision is private in the sense that individuals can choose whether to seek a private tenancy. But choices are severely constrained by the availability of such accommodation for which, as we shall see, there is considerable excess demand in some areas.

The finance of private rented accommodation is private, subject to two major qualifications: poor tenants are eligible for housing benefit as described above; and some private tenancies are subject to considerable regulation concerned mainly with rent control and security of tenure. Rent control was first introduced in 1915.[2] Its history and institutions are complex (see Chapter 2:3.1, and the Further Reading). Two points are crucial for our purposes and have major implications: rent control is a form of implicit price subsidy; and it is financed not by government (i.e. the taxpayer) but is a transfer from landlord to tenant.

Conclusion

A key conclusion is the pervasiveness of subsidies to housing. The first point is their *scale*. From Table 14.2, public expenditure (including tax expenditures) on housing in 1986/7 was about £13 billion (expenditure on the national health service in England was £15 billion (Table 13.1)). Second, much of this expenditure was on *price* subsidies. Owner-occupiers receive substantial tax reliefs which serve, ceteris paribus, to reduce the cost of buying a house.[3] Though the relative importance of income subsidies in the local authority sector has increased, local authority rents are still generally reduced by

---

[1] The little that takes place is usually a spin-off from other developments, e.g. a new hospital must include accommodation for a caretaker.

[2] For a one-page summary of the history of rent control since 1915 see Robinson, 1979, Table 6.1.

[3] These tax advantages are likely at least partially to be capitalised in house prices, thereby reducing the subsidy element – see point (5) on p. 389.

subsidies from central and local taxation; and local authority tenants also benefit because rents are based on historic cost. Rents in parts of the private sector are reduced by rent control. The analysis of section 3.2 suggests that there is efficiency justification neither for such heavy price subsidies, nor for their application to such a large proportion of the housing stock.

Until recently there was no general housing shortage, and Britain had a higher average standard of housing than many richer countries. Yet many families live in poor housing, and homelessness is a growing problem. This suggests that the housing stock is misallocated, causing both inefficiency and inequity. The next two sections seek to explain how this has come about.

4.2 PROBLEMS IN INDIVIDUAL PARTS OF THE HOUSING MARKET

The owner-occupied sector   This section is concerned not with the detailed workings of different parts of the UK housing market, but with the overall pattern. The conclusion is that the substantial problems of the system conform strikingly with the predictions of economic theory. The major efficiency criticisms of the owner-occupied sector are:

(1) *Underoccupation*   Price subsidies to owner-occupiers, mainly in the form of tax reliefs, lead to overconsumption and underoccupation. The theory is simple. If house prices are p_1 rather than $p^\star$ in Figure 14.1, demand will be Q_1, greater than the efficient quantity/quality, $Q^\star$, unless price elasticity is zero. As an empirical matter, though not without their econometric difficulties, estimates agree that the elasticity of housing demand is greater than zero with respect to both prices and incomes, with a rough consensus round a price elasticity of 0.5 (Byatt *et al.*, 1973; MacLennan, 1982, Ch. 2; King, 1980); if the price of housing halves, demand will increase on average by 50 per cent. Furthermore, since the subsidy is paid out of tax revenues (rather than by private builders), supply will increase to Q_1. In practical terms the main effect is overconsumption. People tend to live in larger/higher-quality housing than they would if prices were set at $p^\star$. This is partly because at a subsidised price they choose to consume more housing services (a consumption motive). There is also an asset motive, to the extent that housing is treated more favourably than other forms of private asset accumulation. The result is underoccupation (UK Department of the Environment, 1977b, Ch. 2, especially paras 32–3).

(2) *Tax reliefs artificially raise the return to housing* above that on most other forms of saving available to private individuals. As a result, a disproportionate share of limited savings is attracted to housing finance, though this effect was

Table 14.3: Mortgage Interest Tax Relief and Subsidies for Local Authority Housing by Level of Pre-tax Income, 1974/5

Income of head of household and wife £s per year (1)	Average mortgage interest tax relief per owner-occupier £s per year (2)	Average subsidy per local authority tenant £s per year (3)
Under £1,000	59	168
£1,000–1,499	73	168
£1,500–1,999	91	159
£2,000–2,499	104	160
£2,500–2,999	101	137
£3,000–3,499	129	147
£3,500–3,999	129	154
£4,000–4,999	148	164
£5,000–5,999	179 ⎫	154
£6,000 and over	369 ⎭	

Source: *Housing Policy, Technical Volume 1*, Table IV. 34 and IV. 36 (HMSO, London, 1977).

probably reduced by tax concessions for other forms of private saving in the years after 1982.

There are also serious equity criticisms.

(3) *Access to mortgage finance is unequal* Lending policies of building societies and banks generally exclude individuals with low or irregular earnings and those without sufficient savings to pay the initial deposit on a house. This disproportionately affects the lower socio-economic groups, thereby causing inefficiency, and also inequity which is only partially mitigated because many local authority tenants, since the passage of the 1980 Housing Act, are able to buy the property they formerly rented. The result is a housing market which is largely segmented, with poorer families restricted for the most part to rented accommodation.

(4) *The tax reliefs to owner occupation are largely regressive* for two reasons: individuals with higher incomes generally have larger mortgages; and they often receive tax relief at a higher rate. The result is shown in column (2) of

Table 14.3. Families with high incomes in 1974/5 received on average 6¼ times as much mortgage interest relief as poor families. Le Grand (1982, Table 5.1), using the non-taxation of imputed income as a measure of the tax concession, reached a similar conclusion.[1] Official figures (*Hansard*, 3 February 1984) confirm the pattern: mortgage interest relief in 1983/4 was nearly 12 times as high, on average, for mortgage holders with incomes over £20,000 per year as for those with income under £5000. Capital gains tax relief is also regressive, since individuals with higher incomes tend to own larger houses and so make larger capital gains. Prima facie both forms of tax relief go mainly to the better-off.

A partial counter-argument is that subsidies lead to a 'filtering' process, whereby families who (partly because of tax reliefs) move into more expensive housing release cheaper accommodation to households with lower incomes. Empirical evidence, though limited, lends little support to the hypothesis (Robinson, 1979, pp. 30–1).

(5) *Tax capitalisation* A second counter-argument to the regressivity of tax reliefs is that they are capitalised; as a result, house prices are higher than they would otherwise be, thereby depriving owner-occupiers of the benefit of the tax concessions. The argument is best illustrated by example. Suppose that mortgage repayments consist only of interest, and that an individual wants to buy the largest house he can afford with mortgage repayments of £200 per month. In a world with no tax reliefs, suppose he can buy a house costing £25,000. If tax relief at 50 per cent is introduced, he can now afford monthly repayments of £400 (because the government pays half), and so can buy a house costing £50,000. But if the supply of housing is totally inelastic, his extra purchasing power (together with that of other similarly placed individuals) will double house prices, leaving him in exactly the same position as before. In this case, the introduction of tax relief does not benefit *new* house-buyers, but only *existing* home owners, who make large capital gains.

In practice, however the long-run supply of housing is not completely inelastic, so house prices in the previous example would not rise by 100 per cent. Thus tax reliefs do benefit owner-occupiers, though probably by less than the tax expenditure figures suggest.[2] The regressivity argument therefore stands. A different argument follows from the observation that the real burden

---

[1] The distribution of the tax concession differs substantially, depending on whether it is measured as mortgage interest relief, or as the non-taxation of imputed income – see point (23).

[2] If supply is not totally elastic, landowners and property developers will also benefit from the tax concessions.

of income tax has risen fairly steadily since 1948. This suggests that an *increasing* amount of tax relief has been capitalised, an argument strengthened by the gradual erosion and eventual abolition of the taxation of imputed income. As a result, the tax system can be argued to have exerted not a once-and-for-all effect on house prices, but a more or less steady upward pressure. The effect has been to confer capital gains on earlier house-buyers at the expense of more recent purchasers.

The conclusion on vertical equity is that various tax reliefs worth some £7250 million in 1986/7 have benefited mainly the better-off, though probably by less than the figures in Table 14.2 suggest; and to the extent that capital gains have accrued disproportionately to earlier buyers redistribution has also been arbitrary (see Whitehead, 1980, pp. 95–8, and Le Grand, 1982, pp. 90–5).

Local authority housing In efficiency terms there is little theoretical justification for price subsidies (section 3.2). Yet local authority rents in the early 1970s covered on average only 40 per cent of the historic cost of housing. Though the explicit subsidy declined after 1980, historic cost pricing remains. In most areas, therefore, local authority rents are almost certainly below their efficient level, though it is hard to say by how much. At least four consequential efficiency problems arise.

(6) *Subsidised rents lead to overconsumption/underoccupation* If rents are shown by $p_1 < p^*$ in Figure 14.1, people will wish to consume quantity/ quality $Q_1 > Q^*$. Local authority tenants will demand a larger/higher quality house than they would if they had to pay an efficient rent, p^*, which reflects the marginal social cost of housing. The crucial point for efficiency (given that demand, empirically, is price elastic) is that the *marginal* cost of rented accommodation should be p^*. Since administrative allocation is not, in practice, fully efficient (see point (10) below), subsidised rents create an incentive to overconsumption/underoccupation.

(7) *Excess demand* As another aspect of the same problem, subsidised rents lead to excess demand for local authority housing, thereby contributing to overcrowding (usually in the other sectors) and to homelessness.[1] If rents in Figure 14.1 are shown by p_1 people will demand Q_1. If local authorities increased the supply of housing to Q_1 demand would be satisfied, but only at the expense of overinvestment in housing (since $Q_1 > Q^*$). In practice this has not happened. As a result, there is excess demand for local authority housing,

---

[1] A rough association has been remarked between administrative allocation schemes and homelessness (UK, Holland, Germany), and between market allocation and overcrowding (USA, France).

as manifested by waiting-lists in most areas; many people want local authority housing (or want larger or higher quality housing) but are unable to obtain it. Frequently they are unable to move into the owner-occupied sector, because they cannot afford to do so, and/or because of inequalities in access to mortgage finance (point (3) above); nor can they find suitable private rented accommodation, because rent control leads to excess demand in that sector (point (15) below). Two results follow. Families who already have local authority housing but want more spacious accommodation (e.g. because their family has grown) suffer overcrowding; and families still on the waiting-list suffer from low quality (often private rented) accommodation and/or from overcrowding (e.g. if they are living with family or friends), or from homelessness, which is a growing problem (Donnison and Ungerson, 1982, Ch. 16; UK Department of the Environment, 1985a, Table 3).

Points (6) and (7) taken together show that unless there is *overinvestment* in housing, i.e. Q_1 in Figure 14.1, inefficiently low rents can *simultaneously* cause underoccupation, overcrowding and homelessness. The proponents of price subsidies had unimpeachable aims; but the method they chose is questionable, to say the very least.

(8) *Labour immobility* is a further consequence of excess demand. The argument is simple. The existence of excess demand leads to waiting lists; existing tenants, in consequence, may be unable to take up work in a different locality because they would have to go on the waiting-list in the new area. Immobility is reinforced, for the reasons given in point (7), by the inability of many local authority tenants to find accommodation in other sectors of the housing market. As cases in point, Lomas (1974) and Shankland, Willmott and Jordan (1977) describe how unemployed people in local authority housing in inner London are unable for this reason to move to areas with better job prospects. A more general study by Hughes and McCormick (1981) concludes that, ceteris paribus, local authority tenants have lower migration rates (except for moves within a locality) than owner-occupiers.

(9) *Hard-to-let* property (a related but different problem) results largely from charging rents on the basis of 'pooled' historic costs (section 4.1). The existence of hard-to-let property is telling evidence that not only absolute rents, but also rent *differentials* for different properties, are inefficiently small. Efficiency requires that if house P ('penthouse') is four times as attractive as house T ('terrace') in terms of quantity and quality, then its rent should be about four times as high. Because of rent pooling this is not the case in many localities. Furthermore, a family on the waiting-list knows that if it accepts house T, it is unlikely subsequently to be able to transfer to P. For this reason, and because the rent of T is not sufficiently lower than the rent of P (which is itself inefficiently low), the family is likely to refuse T in the hope of later being

offered P. Consequently, T is hard to let. This occurs only because both rents on average, and in particular rent relativities are inefficiently low. The problem is much smaller in the owner-occupied sector, because *relative* prices are determined by the market, even if absolute house prices are subsidised – long run problems of hard-to-sell are therefore minimal. Property which has remained on the market for several months is usually sold when the vendor adjusts the price downwards.

Local authority housing can also cause inequity.

(10) *Access to local authority housing in a given area can be arbitrary* The first source of the problem is the imperfect knowledge of housing administrators, who cannot have complete information about the circumstances of individuals on the waiting-list. Because they are unable to measure 'need' objectively they use proxies. The 'points' system (section 4.1) is unlikely, with the best will in the world, to produce optimal results (on the inefficiencies and inequities of administrative allocation, see Power (1984) and UK Audit Commission (1986)). Inequity arises, second, if housing allocation is influenced by extraneous considerations like racial prejudice (see Commission for Racial Equality, 1983); and some survey evidence suggests that the least desirable local authority housing tends to be occupied by the most disadvantaged people (Harrison, 1985). A third source of mismatch between 'need' and housing allocation arises over time. A needy family may quite properly be given local authority housing; but if the family's income rises substantially over the years it is possible neither to evict it nor to raise its rent to an efficient level.[1] This point is strengthened by the fact that in certain circumstances local authority tenancies can be transferred within a family from one generation to the next (i.e. tenancies can be inherited).

Local authority housing can fail to be allocated to those in greatest need for at least these three reasons. The result is arbitrariness, and hence horizontal inequity. Because of excess demand, the system benefits those who obtain local authority housing at the expense of those on the waiting-list, with no guarantee that the former group is necessarily the more needy.

(11) *Regional inequality in access to local authority housing* arises because waiting-lists vary by region. Some authorities, for historical reasons, have a large housing stock, but demand may be relatively low, e.g. because of out-migration. Elsewhere the situation is reversed. Thus it is easier to obtain local authority housing in some parts of the country than in others.[2]

---

[1] For a particularly lurid example see 'Council House Tenant's Rolls-Royce', *The Times*, 10 February 1983.

[2] It should be noted that waiting-lists, to the extent that they are longest in areas with the highest economic activity, are not arbitrary, but systematic. If so, waiting-lists are inefficient, but not as inequitable as point (11) suggests.

(12) *Redistribution via price subsidy* is arbitrary in at least three ways. Consider two areas A and B. A's housing stock for historical reasons is older than B's but of equal quality. The determination of rents on the basis of historic cost implies that rent in A will be lower than in B, even if tenants in the two areas have the same average income. Redistribution is thus arbitrary by region. Second, within a given area, the fact that housing costs are pooled can imply, depending on the precise method of rent setting, that tenants in newer (and hence higher-cost) housing are subsidised by those in older accommodation. The result of these two effects is that redistribution by income level can easily be arbitrary. Column (3) of Table 14.3 shows that average subsidies are virtually invariant to the income of tenants, though the greater emphasis on income subsidies in the 1980s is likely to have reduced this form of arbitrariness. Finally, because there is excess demand, families with local authority tenancies benefit at the expense of those on the waiting-list. The overall result has been described as redistribution by luck.

(13) *Redistribution via income subsidies* is progressive. Housing benefit is paid to low-income families, and is withdrawn as family income rises. The scheme, however, is not without its problems; in particular, both take-up and administration are patchy.

The conclusion on vertical equity is that the redistributive effects of rent rebates under housing benefit (£2374 million in 1986/7 – see Table 14.2) together with rate rebates were progressive, but that the distribution of other expenditure on local authority housing was largely arbitrary.

The private rented sector Many problems in this sector can be attributed to rent control (a form of implicit price subsidy), and to the fact that many individuals in regulated tenancies enjoy almost indefinite security of tenure.

(14) *Rent controls lead to overconsumption/underoccupation* The argument is similar to that in point (6). Rent control reduces rents to $p_1 < p^\star$ in Figure 14.1. Since demand is price elastic, people wish to consume more and/or higher quality accommodation, Q_1, than they would at the efficient rent, $p^\star$. The result, for tenants who are able to find regulated private rented accommodation, is overconsumption/underoccupation. At a minimum it is likely to reduce the downward adjustment which would normally be expected in the later stages of a family's life cycle.

(15) *Excess demand* is a related consequence, which aggravates overcrowding and homelessness. The argument is similar to that in point (7). Assume for the moment (the assumption is relaxed in point (16)) that the supply of rented accommodation is $Q^\star$. If rents in Figure 14.1 are shown by p_1, people will demand $Q_1 > Q^\star$. The result is excess demand. Many families want private

rented accommodation (or want larger/higher quality accommodation) but are not able to find any. Frequently they are not able to move into the owner-occupied sector because of unequal access to mortgage finance etc. (point (3)), nor into local authority housing because of the existence of waiting-lists (point (7)). Thus individuals who already have private rented accommodation, but want more space as their family grows, experience overcrowding; and families without accommodation may suffer homelessness.

The previous two points are accentuated by the fact that the price subsidy implicit in rent control is not paid from public funds, but by the landlord. This can have two effects.

(16) *Reduction in quantity supplied* The standard argument is that if controls reduce rents from $p^\star$ to p_1 in Figure 14.1, landlords will respond by reducing the supply of private rented accommodation from its optimum level, $Q^\star$ to Q_2, thereby accentuating excess demand. This argument is naïve even in theory. A more realistic picture is given by the stock-adjustment model in section 3.1 (see Figure 14.2). Suppose that the market rent in *long-run* equilibrium is $p^\star$. If demand increases from D_1 to D_2, the short-term equilibrium rent rises to p_1. In the absence of rent control, new houses are built at a more rapid rate, q_1 in the right-hand part of the diagram, a process which continues until the total stock has increased to $Q^{\star\star}$ restoring equilibrium rents to $p^\star$. If rents, instead, are held at p_2, new construction will be slower (q_2 in the right-hand diagram), but in the long run the housing market still returns to equilibrium, restoring rents to $p^\star$. The theoretical conclusion, therefore, is that rent controls do not reduce long-run supply so long as controlled rents exceed the *long-run* (though not necessarily the short-run) equilibrium. Only if rents are held below their long-run equilibrium, $p^\star$, does the conclusion of the naïve model hold.

Empirical investigation is complex and hampered by data problems. But there is consensus that for most (though not all) of the period since 1915 rents have been held below their long-run equilibrium; and that this has acted to reduce the supply of private rented accommodation, but is not the sole explanation of the dramatic decline in the private rented sector (Robinson, 1979, pp. 76–9 and 84–9).

(17) *Reduction in quality supplied* The fact that rent control is a subsidy from landlord to tenant is argued also to have reduced the *quality* of private rented accommodation below its optimum. The theoretical argument is shown in Figure 14.3.[1] A given house yields a flow of services, of which some are fixed (e.g. its size) and some variable (its state of decoration and repair); taken

---

[1] This approach is taken from Culyer (1980, Ch. 10).

together these services determine quality. The price of each unit of service, v, is measured on the vertical axis, and their quantity, R, on the horizontal axis. When the rental market is in long-run equilibrium the market rent $p^\star$ is shown in Figure 14.3 by the rectangle $0v^\star aR^\star$, i.e. $p^\star = v^\star R^\star$ shown at point a. If rents are restricted to $p_1 < p^\star$, the landlord's receipts are reduced to the rectangle $0v_1 bR^\star$, and the implied price per unit of service to v_1 as shown at point b.

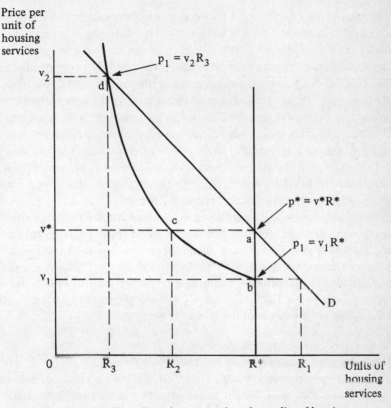

Figure 14.3 *The effect of rent control on the quality of housing*

A possible response by landlords, whilst observing the restriction of their receipts to p_1, is to reduce costs and hence to increase their profits by reducing the quality of the house by cutting expenditure on repairs and maintenance. The line bcd is a rectangular hyperbola; it therefore shows all combinations of v and R which yield the same revenue (i.e. rent) as the rectangle $0v_1 bR^\star$.

Suppose the landlord reduces quality to R_2. His receipts are shown by the rectangle $0v^\star cR_2 = 0v_1 bR^\star$. However, at this implied price per unit of service, $v^\star$, there will be excess demand (at price $v^\star$, demand will be $R^\star$, supply R_2). The market-clearing quantity is R_3, with an implied price per unit of service v_2. The landlord can obtain his required return at any price at or above $v^\star$, hence at any quality at or below R_2. If legislation on minimum standards prevents him from lowering quality to R_3 (but allows him to lower it below R_2), he will still obtain his required return, but there will be excess demand for rented accommodation.

The theoretical conclusion is that rent control creates incentives to reduce the quality of housing, but the reduction in quality may not prevent excess demand. Empirically, the average quality of housing in the private rented sector is dramatically lower than in the other tenures. It has been estimated that 40 per cent of occupied unfit dwellings are in the private rented sector (though it contains only 12 per cent of households), to which figure must be added dwellings in serious disrepair. This suggests that over half of all privately rented accommodation requires substantial expenditure to restore reasonable structural standards (Bovaird, Harloe and Whitehead, 1985, using data from UK Department of the Environment, 1982a, Tables 13, 21 and 28). Though causality is hard to establish, there is a strong implication that rent control has been a contributory, though not necessarily the only, factor.

(18) *Labour immobility* is a consequence of rent control to the extent that it creates excess demand. A tenant who leaves a controlled property may find no accommodation at a similar rent, and is therefore less likely to move. This reinforces the immobility caused by local authority waiting-lists (point (8) above), though its quantitative magnitude is smaller, partly because the sector is smaller, and partly because relatively few people in the controlled private rented sector are members of the labour force.

Equity effects can be listed more briefly.

(19) *Access to regulated tenancies is arbitrary*, with some tendency in addition to exclude those in greatest need. Rent control and security of tenure, by creating excess demand, benefit those tenants who already have controlled accommodation, at the expense of those who are not able to obtain a regulated tenancy. To some extent it is the most needy who find it hardest to obtain such accommodation. Because of security of tenure landlords choose tenants so as to minimise risk, which tends to exclude those who impose the greatest costs. These, disproportionately, are people in greatest housing need, for example people with low incomes, families with large numbers of children and individuals with personal handicaps.

(20) *Minimum standards are enforced least* in private rented accommodation, whose average standard (point (17)), is lower than in the other sectors. This quality differential disproportionately affects the lower socio-economic groups (point (25)).

(21) *The redistributive effects of rent control may be arbitrary* Not all landlords are rich and not all tenants poor. The transfer from landlord to tenant can therefore can be distributionally arbitrary in individual cases, even though on average it is probably progressive because most tenants in the regulated rental sector are poor.

(22) *Redistribution via income subsidies*, as with local authority housing, is progressive, though housing benefit is not without its problems.

4.3 HOUSING AS A WHOLE: TENURE NEUTRALITY AND THE DISTRIBUTION OF HOUSING

This section discusses three aspects of the housing market as a whole: the relative subsidy to the different tenures, and equality of access to different tenures (which are two aspects of tenure neutrality), and the distribution of housing.

(23) *The relative subsidy to different tenures is unequal* The subsidy to owner occupation is discussed by Robinson (1979, pp. 129–30) drawing on Rosenthal (1975). A renter and a home owner have pre-tax money incomes, Y_R and Y_O, respectively, and live in identical houses with the same market value, P. The owner-occupier receives an imputed income from his house of iE, where i is the (uniform) rate of return on capital and E his equity holding in his house. The two are assumed to have equal total (money plus imputed) incomes. Thus:

$$Y_R = Y_O + iE \tag{14.8}$$

The renter (ignoring maintenance costs, etc.) is assumed to pay a competitive market rent, iP. If we now introduce tax at a constant rate t on money income, but not on imputed income or mortgage interest payments, the disposable income (i.e. net of tax and housing costs) of the renter is

$$YD_R = (1-t)Y_R - iP \tag{14.9}$$

For the owner-occupier, income after tax and housing costs is

$$YD_O = (1-t)Y_O - i(P-E) + ti(P-E) \tag{14.10}$$

where $(P-E)$ is the size of the mortgage, $i(P-E)$ the mortgage interest payment and $ti(P-E)$ the mortgage tax relief. Comparing the disposable incomes of the two individuals by subtracting equation (14.9) from (14.10) gives

$$YD_O - YD_R = (1-t)(Y_O - Y_R) + (1-t)iE + tiP \qquad (14.11)$$

We know from equation (14.8) that $Y_O - Y_R = -iE$; hence substituting into equation (14.11) the first two right-hand terms cancel and

$$YD_O - YD_R = tiP \qquad (14.12)$$

The advantage to the owner-occupier, ceteris paribus, is tiP, the tax relief on the imputed income from his house.

The difference between the tax relief on imputed income and that on mortgage interest payments is much more than a technicality in two important respects. First, the relief on imputed income, iP, is related to the *current* market value of the house and will therefore rise as P appreciates, whereas mortgage interest payments, $i(P_0 - E)$, and hence the associated tax relief, are related to the *initial* purchase price, P_0, and so remain constant or decline over time. Thus, for any particular house, the tax base would be increased more by restoring the taxation of imputed housing income than by abolishing mortgage interest relief since $iP > i(P_0 - E)$, and the difference increases over time.[1] A second major difference is that taxation of imputed income applies not just to individuals with a mortgage (who could offset their interest payments against their imputed income), but to *all* owner occupiers, including the 50 per cent (largely the elderly) without a mortgage.

It is open to debate whether the tax relief on imputed income, tiP, or on mortgage interest, $ti(P_0 - E)$, is the better measure of the transfer to home owners. As so often, the answer depends on what is being compared with what. The tax relief on imputed income shows the advantage of owner occupation relative to renting; and the tax relief on mortgage interest is a measure of the advantage relative to investment in other consumer durables like cars, interest payments for which receive no tax concessions.

To these reliefs, however measured, is added the transfer to owner-occupiers due to the exemption from capital gains tax. The value of this relief has declined since 1984, when extensions to the indexation of capital gains reduced the impact of the tax on non-housing assets. It is possible at least approximately to measure the *actual* value of this relief; but it is much harder to measure the concession relative to 'true' capital gains, given the well-known difficulties of choosing an appropriate base for the tax (Prest and Barr, 1985, Ch. 13; Musgrave and Musgrave, 1984, Ch. 16). A complete measure of the tax benefit to owner-occupiers would have to resolve the ambiguities of all the various tax

---

[1] The widening difference is offset only in part by the tendency for P_0 to increase as individuals move to a larger house.

reliefs, as well as considering the extent to which they are capitalised in house prices (point (5)).

Transfers to local authority tenants can be discussed more briefly. The subsidy can be measured by comparing the actual rent (net of housing benefit) with *either* the historic cost of housing *or* the notional competitive market rent. The latter is the more appropriate in economic terms (Rosenthal, 1977; Robinson, 1979, pp. 132–3; Piggott, 1984) though much harder to measure. The former is more relevant to public expenditure, and is therefore the figure used in official publications.

The transfer due to rent control is the difference between the controlled rent (again net of housing benefit) and the market rent, though with ambiguity as to whether the comparison should be with the short-run equilibrium rent (p_1 in Figure 14.2) or the theoretical long-run equilibrium, p^*.

Though conceptually it is all but impossible to disentangle an unambiguous definition of equality of subsidy, empirical evidence suggests that owner occupation is favoured more than the other tenures (Whitehead, 1983, para. 5), and that the differential has widened in recent years (Glennerster, 1985, Ch. 11). Owner-occupiers have built up substantial wealth over the postwar period, in part through their own contributions. But they have also received two forms of transfer: from taxpayers generally (because of the non-taxation of mortgage interest and capital gains), and from savers. The latter transfer results from the redistributive effects of unanticipated inflation, which led to periods of negative real interest rates; and mortgage repayments for many individuals fell as a proportion of their income. Over the same period, tenants had to pay rising rents and built up no housing wealth.

(24) *Access to different tenures is unequal* This is a second aspect of tenure neutrality. Access to owner occupation is restricted by capital market imperfections, to the detriment of the worst-off (point (3)). The allocation of local authority housing is marred by the way tenants are selected from the waiting-list, and also because needy tenants may over time become less needy (point (10)); and regional inequalities cause further problems (point (11)). Excess demand for private rented accommodation and risk-averting behaviour by landlords together create arbitrariness in access to regulated tenancies, with particular difficulties for those in greatest housing need (point (19)).

Tenure neutrality is thus achieved neither in terms of equality of subsidy nor equality of opportunity. In both respects, the system tends to work to the advantage of the better-off, with an added element of arbitrariness. This conclusion is borne out by empirical evidence (UK Department of the Environment, 1977c, Ch. 5). We have already seen that the crude distribution of subsidies is unequal. Table 14.3 shows (column (2)) that mortgage tax relief disproportionately benefits the better-off, though these data are qualified in that tax advantages may partly be capitalised in house prices (point (5)). At the same time (column (3)), the distribution of subsidies to local authority tenants, at least until the early 1980s, was largely invariant to income. Le Grand (1982, Table 5.1) reaches similar conclusions.

The evidence on the relation between tenure and socio-economic status is also persuasive (though not conclusive). Table 14.4 shows that 82 per cent of households in the highest socio-economic group are owner-occupiers, whilst only 8 per cent are local authority tenants and 6 per cent private tenants. Column (1) shows that the higher socio-economic groups are disproportionately owner-occupiers whilst local authority tenants (column (2)) are concentrated among the less well-off. As a descriptive matter the housing market is not completely segmented (29 per cent of semi-skilled and unskilled manual workers are owner-occupiers), but differences in household tenure by socio-economic group are systematic and strong. In behavioural terms, these disparities can be explained by differences in tastes (in which case no issue of inequality arises), or by differences in constraints, or by a combination of the two. The difficulty of separating these effects qualifies the stark appearance of the data. The conclusion (Whitehead, 1980, p. 112) is that

> fiscal neutrality and 'appropriate' incentives are not obtained: between consumers, between different types of investment, within housing, between housing and other assets, or between consumption, saving and investment.

Table 14.4: Household Tenure by Socio-economic Group, Great Britain, 1978

Socio-economic group	TYPE OF TENURE (%)			
	Owner-occupied	Rented from local authority	Private rented	Other
	(1)	(2)	(3)	(4)
Professionals, employers and managers	82	8	6	5
Intermediate and junior non-manual	59	25	12	5
Skilled manual	49	40	9	3
Semi-skilled and skilled manual	29	56	11	3

Source: Le Grand (1982, Table 5.2).
Note: Percentages may not add up because of rounding.

Horizontal inequalities between tenures are particularly common and, especially for people living in the private rental sector, assistance helps to exacerbate the strong vertical inequities of the system.

(25) *The distribution of housing*   The lower socio-economic groups are twice as likely as better-off households to live at a density of more than one person per room (Le Grand, 1982, Table 5.4). Four per cent of households in 1977 had less than the 'standard' number of rooms given their size; the incidence of this type of overcrowding was six times as high for the lowest socio-economic groups as for households in the top socio-economic group (Reid, 1981, Table 5.30). Overcrowding also varies substantially by tenure. Only 0.5 per cent of owner-occupiers in 1971 lived at a density of more than 1½ people per room; for local authority tenants the proportion was 1.8 per cent, and for private tenants in furnished accommodation over 8 per cent (UK Department of the Environment, 1977b, Table II.14). The extreme case of shortage of space is homelessness. To an even greater extent than overcrowding this dispro-portionately afflicts the lowest socio-economic groups.

Similar variations occur in the quality of housing. In 1977, families in the top socio-economic group were more than twice as likely as the bottom group to have central heating, and nearly twice as likely to live in a detached or semi-detached house (Le Grand, 1982, Table 5.4). The distribution of housing by annual income shows even more marked inequalities (Townsend, 1979, Ch. 13; Le Grand, 1982, Ch. 5); and inequalities in tenure, density and amenities tend to persist across generations (Jenkins and Maynard, 1983).

The overwhelming conclusion is that though subsidies may have led to some equalisation, sizeable inequalities remain. Whether they are *too* large depends partly on whether the housing standards of the lower socio-economic groups are *inefficiently* low, and partly on the weight attached to equality.

5 Reform

5.1 THE DEBATE OVER REFORM

In view of the arguments in section 4 it is not surprising that proponents of the *status quo* are few, and their economic case weak. The argument that mortgage interest tax relief is not a subsidy does not bear close examination. As we have seen (Chapter 7:1.1), tax expenditures should properly be included in public spending.[1] Other arguments rest on very partial analysis. It is suggested that the abolition of higher rate tax relief for mortgage interest would distort the savings decisions of individuals with high incomes. This may be true of the policy considered in isolation but, precisely for that reason, is unconvincing. It is necessary to consider housing finance not piecemeal but as a whole, in which case such arguments become largely irrelevant. Possibly the only plausible argument for the *status quo* is that radical change may be impossible for political reasons because the interests of so many individuals would be affected. A fundamental reform of housing finance has been on the political agenda for a long time (UK Department of the Environment, 1971 and 1977a), but change has been very limited.

One of rather few coherent proposals for reform (Nevitt, 1966, subsequently echoed in part by the Housing Finance Act 1972, and more recently by the National Federation of Housing Associations, 1985) advocates tenure-neutral taxation together with a unified system of subsidies for all tenures, under which poor families receive subsidies scaled to their housing need, and better-off families receive no subsidy at all. The scheme suggested in section 5.2 is in many ways similar.

Donnison and Ungerson (1982) suggest a scheme which pays the full cost of housing for low-income families, the benefit to be withdrawn as family income rises. The problem with this proposal is its expense. If it were financed through the abolition of mortgage interest relief, the package would resemble the scheme in the previous paragraph. Lansley (1982) advocates a universal, flat-rate (i.e. non-means-tested) housing allowance based on family size and an index of regional housing costs, where the allowance covers the full cost of minimum standard accommodation. Conceptually, this scheme is a form of negative income tax, and so raises the problems discussed in Chapter 11. Its universal nature makes it immensely costly, and therefore requires a sharp increase in tax rates (on these and other proposals see Glennerster, 1985, Ch. 11).

The USA has also seen its fair share of reform proposals, concerned particularly with improving the housing conditions of the poor. Most schemes focus on income subsidies rather than public production of housing at subsidised rents. In 1973 the US Department of Housing and Urban Development funded a series of experiments in 12 cities to test the feasibility of housing allowances. For a variety of reasons the experiment met with mixed success (see Bradbury and Downs, 1981, especially the chapter by Aaron).

---

[1] Since 1983 mortgage interest in the UK has been paid net of tax (see p. 383 footnote 1). Thus tax relief for owner-occupiers is paid by the Inland Revenue to the building societies, etc. For local authority tenants, housing benefit is paid by the Department of Health and Social Security to local authorities. The latter payments appear in the public expenditure figures (UK, 1986a, Table 3.15), the former do not. See Barr (1986) for criticism.

5.2 DESIGNING A SYSTEM FOR A BRAND NEW COUNTRY

This section discusses how housing finance in Britain might be reformed, assuming that we start *ab initio* to design a system for a hypothetical brand new country. Section 5.3 considers how such a system might be introduced in practice.

Regulation is inevitable, and would be widespread. First, there would be minimum standards for individual dwellings, partly because of the public health externality and also (though more arguably) on the grounds of horizontal equity. Minimum standards to protect the poor 'for their own good' (i.e. the merit good argument discussed in Chapter 4:4.2) should not be accepted uncritically. If they are set at a level higher than is justified on *efficiency* grounds, the cost of minimum standard housing will (a) be inefficiently high for those who would rationally choose housing of lesser (but still efficient) quality, and (b) be beyond the reach of those with lower incomes. Given its longevity, there are enough unavoidable problems over the affordability of housing without aggravating them unnecessarily (though with the best of motives) by setting standards which can worsen the housing problem to the detriment particularly of the poor. It can be argued that the only *equity* justification for minimum standards is the protection of children and possibly also the elderly.

Zoning and planning controls over land use would be concerned with housing density (because of the public health externality); the separation of residential housing from factories (because of the spatial externality); and the provision of amenities such as public open space (which has public good attributes) and water, gas, electricity and sewerage (for reasons of public health, and because their distribution displays increasing returns to scale). Third, there would be some regulation of private landlords to prevent exploitation of monopoly power over tenants (see section 3.2), and to protect tenants against arbitrary eviction. This type of regulation is necessary for the fulfilment of the 'equal power' assumption (Chapter 4:3.2), thereby increasing both efficiency and horizontal equity. Finally, it may be necessary to regulate the professional standards of surveyors and valuers to ensure adequate consumer information about the quality and price of housing (cf. hygiene laws for food).

Production of housing would be subject to the relevant regulations; it could take place in either or both public and private sectors. In terms of economic efficiency the issues of public/private production of the housing stock and its ownership are much less important than its *price*.

Finance Three issues are important: the supply of mortgage finance; the price of housing; and vertical equity. *The supply of loan finance* could remain in the private sector, but with the addition of publicly provided loans or loan guarantees for individuals who have difficulty in obtaining an adequate mortgage in the private sector; and all mortgages would be fully indexed to the *real* value of the initial loan. These interventions would make access to capital markets more equitable, and would aid tenure neutrality; the supply of mortgages would not be artificially restricted; and there would be no arbitrary transfer from savers to mortgage holders.

House prices (both purchase price and rent) would be market prices with only three possible exceptions. There would be price subsidies in respect of a limited number of externalities, e.g. to prevent the spread of slums and/or to encourage 'gentrification' (see UK Department of the Environment, 1985b). Subsidies of this type are likely to be small in amount, and would apply only to a limited proportion of the total housing stock. The only argument for a *general* price subsidy is if it is believed that the private discount rate systematically exceeds the social discount rate. These two forms of subsidy perform an efficiency function.

The third exception is that it may be necessary for equity reasons to subsidise rents to prevent hardship if housing demand in an area rises, thereby (because short-run supply is inelastic) causing rents to rise sharply. These subsidies could be implemented in various ways: as additional income transfers to poor tenants in high-rent areas; or as a price subsidy paid by the *state* to prevent the contraction of private supply (measured in quantity and quality) resulting from rent control. Rent control is probably the least attractive method, and should be adopted, if at all, only as a temporary expedient;[1] and it is essential that controlled rents equal or exceed the long-run equilibrium, $p^\star$ in Figure 14.2, though they should obviously be below the (temporarily high) short-run market-clearing rent. This last solution has the disadvantages that it is likely to slow adjustment to the higher level of demand (point (16)), and also has arbitrary distributional effects (point (21)).

The adoption of market prices implies the removal of all price subsidies except in the cases just discussed. For owner occupation this should ideally take the form of taxing imputed housing income. If this is not possible for administrative or political reasons there should be no mortgage interest tax relief. In either case it would be necessary to apply capital gains tax, indexed in some sensible way, to owner-occupied houses. There would be no subsidies from central and local revenues to local authority housing, and local authorities would pay market interest rates on borrowed funds. In the private sector there would be no rent control except, possibly, in the circumstances just discussed,

---

[1] Though this was the intention in 1915. Income tax was also originally intended to be temporary.

in which case it should be strictly limited as to time and place. House prices and rents, in short, would be *market* prices, subject to long-run modification only for very specific reasons.

Income transfers would be the main vehicle for pursuing vertical equity. There would be one system applying to all tenures. Consider first the transfer to a householder with no income. He/she would receive £X per week, related to family size. In strict efficiency terms the subsidy would not vary regionally, so as to leave migration decisions undistorted. But housing costs vary so substantially in different areas that this policy conflicts with equity considerations. It can therefore be argued that the income subsidy should be higher in areas with higher *average* housing costs (ideally the transfer should not be directly related to a family's *actual* housing costs because this would interfere with marginal decisions). The transfer could be untied (i.e. paid in cash), or tied to expenditure on housing if this were necessary for political or other reasons (e.g. to protect children). The transfer would be reduced as family income increased, and above a certain income would cease entirely.

A veil is deliberately being drawn over the size of the basic transfer and its relation to family income, both of which require a great deal of detailed study. But the scheme is undoubtedly feasible in purely *financial* terms. Public expenditure (broadly defined) on housing in 1986/7 was around £13 billion (Table 14.2), much of it benefiting the better-off (Table 14.3). The scheme just described would use this sum to pay an income-related (i.e. unambiguously progressive) transfer. It follows as a proposition in pure logic that on a revenue-neutral basis the poor on average must benefit at the expense of the non-poor.[1] Herein lies the problem of the scheme, which is not its financial but its political feasibility.

The individual consumption decision Individuals would make a utility-maximising decision constrained by their income (including the housing transfer) and subject in all tenures to the (generally) market price/rent of housing.

These proposals are likely to sound abhorrent to those who regard the market as inherently inequitable. Such readers are asked to bear with the argument, and invited to remember the aims of housing policy outlined in section 2; to acknowledge (at least in part) the magnitude of the failure of the existing system to achieve them (section 4); and to consider the advantages of the scheme outlined above, advantages in terms of efficiency and, possibly even more, in terms of horizontal and vertical equity.

---

[1] The point in the income distribution at which people would receive less assistance than currently would depend on the precise details of the transfer.

In efficiency terms, market prices, modified if at all only for the three reasons discussed, avert incentives to underoccupy, thereby avoiding many of the forces contributing to overcrowding and homelessness. Owner-occupiers have no incentive to buy a large house as an artificially inflated asset; and the existence of market (or modified market) rents prevents systematic excess demand in both rental sectors, thus avoiding the worst of the problems discussed in section 4.2. Waiting-lists would no longer be a permanent part of the landscape, though it would be desirable for local authorities to have some housing under their control for emergency cases, and also because housing markets take time to adjust. Additionally, market pricing together with indexed mortgages result, at least approximately, in tenure neutrality.

The system also contributes substantially to horizontal equity. Access to mortgage finance would be more equal; arbitrariness in the allocation of rented accommodation in both public and private sectors would be reduced; and regional inequalities in access to local authority housing would be less important because there would be approximate neutrality between local authority housing and the other tenures. Access to housing would be determined not by administrative decision but by individual choice (see English, 1982); and the distribution of housing by income level could be adjusted via the size of the housing transfer and its relation to family income.[1]

In terms of vertical equity the housing transfer is unambiguously progressive. In comparison with the present system, transfers would go to those in greatest need, with no subsidy at all for the well-off. As a result, access to housing for the poor would be increased; for the rich it would be reduced. Additionally, the indexation of loans for house purchase eliminates the arbitrary transfer from savers to mortgage holders.

In terms of cost, the system would either be cheaper because individuals who were not poor would no longer receive subsidies; or if it were not cheaper, but revenue-neutral, would be more cost-effective because benefits would be focussed more systematically.

5.3 HOW TO GET FROM HERE TO THERE

The final part of the argument is to consider the major difficulties involved in changing the present UK system to a very different set of arrangements. Any such change would be a huge task, necessitating an immense amount of

---

[1] Another result is that council house sales would be less of a political hot potato. On the supply side, state intervention in mortgage markets would make owner occupation more generally available; on the demand side, tenure neutrality would remove the financial advantages of owner occupation relative to renting.

detailed work, and what follows is the barest of outlines (for a more detailed set of rather similar proposals see National Federation of Housing Associations, 1985). The sorts of changes envisaged would obviously set in train a series of long-run adjustments in all sectors of the housing market, implying that any new system should be phased in gradually.

Adjustment problems are likely to be particularly acute in the owner-occupied sector. The instant removal of all tax reliefs for owner-occupiers would at least partly be capitalised (Whitehead, 1983, paras 16–18). House prices would fall sharply, imposing heavy capital losses, with the result in some cases that house values would be lower than existing mortgages (i.e. an individual could find himself with a £30,000 mortgage on a house now worth only £25,000). It would therefore probably be necessary to phase out mortgage interest relief gradually, by reducing the amount of mortgage qualifying for tax relief (currently £30,000) by, say, £1500 per year, thereby removing the tax concession over a 20-year period;[1] or the rate at which tax relief is granted could gradually be reduced. Alternatively, mortgage interest relief could be retained, and the taxation of imputed housing income gradually reintroduced. The main difficulties with this approach are its administrative complexity, and the likelihood, for political reasons, that the assessment of imputed income would never reach the full market value of the flow of housing services, not least because such taxation would bear more heavily on the elderly than present arrangements. It might therefore be more realistic to abolish mortgage interest relief. The removal of capital gains tax relief could be phased in more easily, by bringing into tax only the real gains arising after some date subsequent to legislation (i.e. only gains arising *after* the market had at least partly adjusted to the new system).

The withdrawal of price subsidies for local authority housing would present no insuperable problems if accompanied by a suitable phasing in of the income-related housing transfer. For reasons of horizontal equity the time-scale might be the same as for the tax changes for owner-occupiers. Similarly, the gradual removal of rent control over the same period would be accompanied by the phased introduction of the housing transfer. In both cases, the only losers would be non-poor tenants with incomes too high to qualify for the income subsidy.

Several problems are harder to solve. First, an income-related housing transfer could aggravate the poverty trap, inasmuch as the transfer would be reduced as family income rose. To the extent that a solution exists it would depend on more general reform of income support along the lines discussed in Chapter 11. Second, the precise details of the transfer would need to take

---

[1] The proposals of the National Federation of Housing Associations (1985, p. 19) suggest that tax relief should be phased out over 10–12 years.

account of difficulties with take-up, links with other forms of income support, and similar such problems as arose with housing benefit (Chapter 10:1).

6 Conclusion: Housing

Housing fails in various ways to conform with the conditions necessary for an unrestricted private market to be efficient. The specific failures justify substantial regulation, price subsidies for strictly limited reasons, and public provision of loan finance or loan guarantees. The theoretical discussion in sections 3.2 and 3.3 suggests that state intervention along these lines would improve efficiency and horizontal equity.

Three conclusions follow (section 3.4). First, in sharp contrast with health care, the information problems which arise are of a type which the market itself is able to solve; individuals (with professional advice if necessary) are generally able to make rational choices. Second, the efficiency justification for *general* price subsidies is highly qualified. This point, together with the first, implies that there are powerful advantages to keeping prices at the level dictated by efficiency, and seeking to achieve distributional objectives through cash transfers. Third, no efficiency justification emerges for public production of housing (as opposed to regulation of private supply). This is not an argument *against* public production. But the three points taken together suggest that the aims of housing policy (section 2) are more likely to be achieved if housing is allocated via individual consumption decisions, subject to regulation on minimum standards and efficient prices, and supported by income transfers.

British housing institutions (section 4.1), characterised by substantial and pervasive subsidies, are strongly at variance with this model. Public expenditure, as set out in Table 14.2, is large (almost 70 per cent of spending on the national health service), and involves substantial *price* subsidies. Owner-occupiers receive considerable tax relief; local authority rents are subsidised in a number of ways including a pooled historic cost pricing principle; and private sector rents are generally reduced by rent control.

Many of these institutions date from decisions made during and just after the First World War (Chapter 2:3.1). For the reasons discussed in section 3 there is no efficiency justification for such large subsidies, nor for their application to such a large proportion of the housing stock. The result (section 4.2) is that price subsidies in each sector of the housing market create excess demand, which reinforces excess demand in the other sectors. In consequence, there is evidence simultaneously of underoccupation, overcrowding and homelessness; the quantity and quality of the regulated private rental stock has deteriorated; labour mobility is hindered; and the system is decidedly not tenure-neutral. The system also performs badly in terms of horizontal equity. Access to mortgage finance favours the higher socio-economic groups; and access to rental accommodation in both public and private sectors has a strong arbitrary element. The redistributive effects of housing finance can also be perverse. The tax advantages to owner-occupiers are regressive. The distributional impact of price subsidies to local authority tenants and (in a very different way) to households living in regulated private rented accommodation are largely arbitrary. Income subsidies to households in rented accommodation are progressive, but take-up and administration are still patchy.

These problems are an entirely predictable consequence of price subsidies introduced mainly to increase equity.[1] The conclusion is clear. The use of price subsidies *only* for equity reasons is a confusion of aims and methods which is almost bound to cause inefficiency and inequity (Chapter 4:6.1). In the absence of an efficiency justification, price subsidies are likely to cause excess demand and/or overconsumption unless demand can be rationed efficiently by administrative means. This is possible with health care but works less well with housing. In the latter case, equity (as well as efficiency) aims are more likely to be achieved by income subsidies. No policy-maker starting from scratch with the vast sum currently spent on housing would choose to spend it in the manner described in section 4.1.

The strategy for reform in section 5.2 draws on the theoretical discussion of section 3, supported by the analysis of section 4, which shows how the shortcomings just described are readily explicable in terms of the theory. The state would retain wide regulatory powers over individual dwellings and over land use generally; and there would be regulation to prevent private landlords from abusing their power. The production of housing, subject to regulation, could be private, public or both. Housing finance would be reformed in three ways. First, the state would take action to improve access to capital markets. Second, with only limited exceptions, house prices and rents would over time be brought into line with market-clearing prices by the phased withdrawal of tax reliefs for owner-occupiers, price subsidies to local authority tenants and the implied price subsidy of rent control. The revenue thereby released would be used to pay income-related transfers.

The result would come much closer than existing arrangements to tenure neutrality, and would greatly reduce underoccupation, overcrowding, immobility and homelessness. Vertical equity would be improved because

---

[1] Many other countries avoid at least some of these problems. It is noteworthy that a major American study of priorities for the 1980s in both foreign and domestic policy (Pechman, 1980) had a chapter on health care, another on education, another on the environment (pollution, safety, etc.). But in a volume of 500 pages there was scarcely a mention of housing (or of food).

subsidies would be systematically related to income, rather than arbitrary; and those with above-average incomes would no longer be subsidised at all.

These arrangements approximate more closely to the case of food than to the national health service model. The implied suggestion is that difficulties with housing are more an income distribution problem than a market allocation problem. The strategy is chosen *not* for ideological reasons, but because it is more likely to achieve the aims set out in section 2. The national health service strategy of free provision via administrative decision works well for health care, for the reasons given in Chapters 12 and 13; it does not work well in this case. Individuals have diverse tastes about housing, and can generally make better decisions than housing administrators because they have better information than officials (contrast the case of health care). The nature of housing as a commodity thus approximates more closely to food than to health care. This *technical* observation is the basis of the reforms proposed in sections 5.2 and 5.3. Their major difficulty is less an economic one than their requirement of a long-run policy based on widespread support. In political terms this may not be forthcoming, partly for ideological reasons and partly because the reforms produce losers as well as gainers. Despite the political problem, however, it is clear that Britain needs a *strategy* for the reform of housing finance, not just a series of ad hoc tinkering.

It is important, in conclusion, to be clear what I am *not* saying. I am not arguing for the abolition of subsidies to local authority housing, nor simply for the abolition of rent control, nor even for the abolition of all housing subsidies. What is being suggested, quite simply, is that over time *price* subsidies should be replaced by *income* subsidies in all sectors of the housing market.

Further Reading

For compendious discussion of British housing institutions see UK Department of the Environment (1977b, Ch. 2) for an overview, (1977b, Chs 6 and 7) for discussion of owner occupation, and (1977d, Chs 8 and 9) for local authority housing and the private rented sector, respectively. On the historical background see UK Department of the Environment (1977b, Ch. 1), Robinson (1979, Ch. 6), Gauldie (1974) and Swenarton (1981). On the quantity and quality of the housing stock see National Federation of Housing Associations (1985, Ch. 2). Details of housing benefit and its reform are contained in UK (1985g and 1985k, Ch. 3) (see also the Further Reading to Chapter 10). International comparisons of housing institutions are given in UK Department of the Environment (1977d, Ch. 11) and, for eastern Europe by Donnison and Ungerson (1982, Ch. 6). Cullingworth (1979) gives a good (though now partly out of date) general analysis of housing.

For more analytical discussion of financial aspects see Glennerster (1985, Ch. 11), Robinson (1979, Ch. 8) and Ermisch (1984). The planning process and its effects are discussed by Hall (1982), and inner city problems by Hall (1981), Donnison and Soto (1980) and Bassett and Short (1980).

The best discussions of housing economics, both theoretical and with a review of empirical evidence, are by Robinson (1979) and MacLennan (1982). Whitehead (1980) gives a brief and incisive assessment of the performance of the housing sector. For an up-to-date analysis of difficulties in the local authority sector see UK Audit Commission (1986); the private rental sector is discussed by Bovaird, Harloe and Whitehead (1985). On the distribution of housing see Le Grand (1982, Ch. 5).

The most complete early proposal for reform is by Nevitt (1966); a recent Inquiry chaired by HRH The Duke of Edinburgh (National Federation of Housing Associations, 1985) reached similar conclusions.

PART 4

EPILOGUE

15

Conclusion

A democratic capitalist society will keep searching for better ways of drawing the boundary lines between the domain of rights and the domain of dollars. And it can make progress. To be sure, it will never solve the problem, for the conflict between equality and economic efficiency is inescapable. In that sense, capitalism and democracy are really a most improbable mixture. Maybe that is why they need each other – to put some rationality into equality and some humanity into efficiency. [Arthur M. Okun, 1975.]

1 Arguments for a Welfare State

1.1 THEORY

The British welfare state is the outcome of diverse forces over nearly four centuries of developing social policy. Two aspects, in particular, stand out from the historical discussion in Chapter 2: debates about ideology (which are taken up in Chapter 3), and the welfare state's functional purposes, notably economic efficiency (Chapters 4 and 5). Ideological aims vary widely. To libertarians (Chapter 3:2) the primary goal is individual freedom, which is best achieved by unrestricted private markets. Empirical libertarians like Hayek and Friedman therefore espouse minimal intervention and oppose all but the most austere welfare systems, whose purpose is limited to the relief of destitution. Marxists (Chapter 3:4.2) regard the market system by its very nature as incompatible with their primary aim of meeting need. They therefore reject it, and give the state a primary role in production and allocation. Marxists have mixed feelings about the welfare state (Chapter 3:5.3). In part it accords with their aim of meeting need and is therefore to be applauded; yet it serves also to support a capitalist system which they regard as inherently unjust.

Liberals take a more eclectic view. The utilitarian aim (Chapter 3:3.1) is the maximisation of total welfare, leaving open the question of whether it is to be achieved by private markets, by public production and allocation, or by a mix of the two. Rawls (Chapter 3:3.2) argues that goods, liberty and opportunity should be distributed equally unless any other arrangement is to the advantage of the least well-off. Again, the issue of how this is best achieved is left open. For the purposes of this book the single feature which above all distinguishes liberal theories is the treatment of private property as an issue which is contingent, not dogmatic, i.e. the treatment of private property is not an end in itself but a means towards the achievement of stated aims (see Okun, 1975).

Society has functional as well as ideological goals, notably the achievement of economic efficiency, as defined in Chapter 4:2.1. Where there is a trade-off between efficiency and social justice their relative weights will vary between libertarians, liberals and Marxists. But an increase in efficiency which does not impair social justice is an unambiguous gain under *any* of these theories of society (Chapter 4:2.2).

Efficiency can be achieved as the outcome of a market-clearing process, notably in the presence of perfect information and perfect competition, and where there are no market failures such as external effects (Chapter 4:3.2). Similar conditions are necessary if insurance is to be efficient: at least some individuals must be risk-averse (Chapter 5:2.1), and there must be no technical problems with privately supplied insurance (Chapter 5:3). These conditions, referred to collectively as the *standard assumptions*, must all hold if the market is to be relied on to allocate efficiently.

The distinction between *aims* and *methods* is crucial. The ideological and functional aims of policy can be encapsulated in large measure in the twin goals of economic efficiency and social justice. Once the aims have been chosen, the next step is to select methods to achieve them, including (Chapter 4:3.1) no state intervention at all; intervention in the form of cash transfers; or interference with the market mechanism through regulation, through financial involvement and/or through public production. The approach can be summarised in two statements: (a) the proper place of ideology is in the choice of aims, particularly the definition of social justice and its trade-off with economic efficiency; (b) once these aims have been agreed, the choice of method should be treated as a *technical* issue.

Whether a good is better produced publicly or privately should be decided on the basis of which method more closely achieves specified aims; and a major purpose has been to give a rationale in any situation for choosing the method(s) most likely to do so. This was given, subject to a number of caveats, in the form of two propositions (Chapter 4:6.1).

(1) If the standard assumptions hold, market allocation will be efficient; in this case social justice is generally best pursued via income transfers (e.g. so that poor people can buy food at market prices).
(2) Suppose that public production and allocation can be justified on *efficiency* grounds; social justice may then appropriately be pursued through direct transfers in kind (e.g. free medical care under the national health service).

Whether a particular commodity should be publicly or privately produced is thus contingent on its technical characteristics, i.e. a liberal approach in the sense described above (for libertarian and Marxist counter-arguments see Chapter 4:6.2). The welfare state should be judged not in dogmatic terms, but supported only if it contributes more than alternative arrangements to the achievement of agreed policy objectives.

1.2 POLICY

Chapter 1 started with two questions: what theoretical arguments justify the existence of the various parts of the welfare state; and given these arguments of principle how well do the British and other systems perform? The answers are summarised in Chapter 4:6.1 for the underlying theory, Chapter 11:5 for cash benefits, Chapter 13:3 for health care and education and Chapter 14:6 for housing, so only the most important conclusions are set out here.

The aims of cash benefits include the relief of destitution (about which there is general agreement) and, more controversially, the protection of accustomed living standards and the reduction of inequality. Their achievement requires mechanisms to foster self-help and vertical redistribution.

Self-help is necessary for an individual/family who is self-supporting over his/her lifetime, but needs a system of redistribution from himself at one time (e.g. when working) to himself at another (e.g. when unemployed or retired). The answer in principle is voluntary private insurance. This, however, is not a tenable strategy (Chapters 8 and 9). On the demand side, non-insurance imposes external costs on various groups including taxpayers, giving an efficiency reason for making insurance compulsory (Chapter 8:2.1). On the supply side, the private market is unable for technical reasons to provide the efficient quantity and type of insurance against all causes of income loss; in particular, unemployment and inflation are not insurable risks.

Several important results follow. There are strong efficiency grounds for public provision of unemployment compensation (Chapter 8:2.2) and at least the indexation component of retirement pensions (Chapter 9:3.1). For these benefits at least, public involvement, whatever the form it takes, will not (because it cannot) be true insurance; and the same can be said of any private institutions in these areas. For the major risks covered by the state scheme the insurance principle is neither possible (except as a mimic of private institutions), nor necessary, and only arguably desirable. Various reforms of the insurance system are possible, but a substantial return to voluntary private insurance and pure, private, funded pensions is not one of them (Chapters 8:3.1 and 9:5.1). Social policy requires that individuals are protected against income loss; but strict adherence to market supply enables them to acquire protection only where risks are insurable. This puts the cart before the horse by making *social* policy subservient to *technical* considerations.

Vertical redistribution is relevant to those who cannot support themselves over their lifetime. In principle it can be organised through private charity or by the state. Partly because of the free-rider problem, redistribution through private charity is likely to be sub-optimal even by libertarian standards, and even further below the Rawlsian or socialist optimum (Chapter 4:4.1). Redistribution through the tax system may therefore be justified in both efficiency and equity terms (Chapter 10:2) under any theory of society, though with considerable disagreement as to how much redistribution is desirable (Chapter 4:4.4) or feasible (Chapter 11). The overall success of cash benefits in practice is also controversial (Chapters 8:3, 9:5 and 10:3). The UK has a wide-ranging system of insurance benefits whose effect, albeit imperfectly, is redistributive from rich to poor; these are buttressed by assistance benefits organised on a national basis, for which *everyone* is potentially eligible. Many other countries have much less comprehensive systems (Chapter 2:6). Nevertheless, poverty remains (Chapter 10:3.3). Nor is this simply because the poverty line has been moved up over the years; for many there is not just *relative* poverty, but a life of harsh discomfort which persists to the present.

Reform can follow one of two strategies. Benefits can be conditioned on income by an explicit means test or via a negative income tax (Chapter 11:2), though this approach can easily aggravate the poverty trap (see the Glossary), with important efficiency and equity costs. Alternatively, it may be possible to side-step the worst of the poverty trap by adopting the 'Back to Beveridge' approach (Chapter 11:3), under which benefits are conditioned on carefully chosen characteristics of recipients, such as being unemployed or retired, or having children. A judicious combination of the two approaches (Chapter 11:4) might be to raise the main national insurance benefits to the supplementary benefit level, to increase child benefit, and to make all these benefits taxable.

Benefits in kind   The theoretical discussion of public involvement in health care and education is set out in Chapter 12. The issues are complex, not least because of intractable measurement problems (Chapter 12:2.2). There are strong a priori arguments suggesting that unrestricted private markets for health care and education (Chapter 12:3) will be inefficient, and also inequitable to the extent that information, power and access to capital markets are correlated with socio-economic status. The precise form of public involvement has two aspects. The *allocation* issue rests crucially on whether individuals or 'experts' (doctors, teachers, etc.) are better informed and/or better able to act in the interests of consumers. The question of *production* depends largely on whether quality/quantity can be monitored more effectively with production in the public or private sector. The theoretical arguments for public production and allocation of health care and education (Chapter 12:4.1 and 4.2), though not irrefutable, are strong, largely because of information problems, particularly in the case of health care.

The national health service is not above criticism, but it has powerful advantages (Chapter 13:1.2). By international standards the system is cheap, provides high-quality care and, despite some inequalities, is remarkably egalitarian. Theoretical argument and international comparison both suggest that radical 'privatisation' (whatever its advocates mean by the term) will not solve old problems, and is likely to create new and larger ones. The evidence for Britain, overwhelmingly, is that the national health service should be retained, and improvement sought within the existing strategy by increasing its resources, and gathering and using more and better information. This is not to say that public production is the only possible model. Countries with different political traditions and different medical structures might adopt a sensible *strategy* of mixed public/private provision, e.g. private production and public funding subject to a budget constraint, as in Canada, or a system based on suitably regulated health maintenance organisations (Chapter 13:1.3).

The educational system fares less well (Chapter 13:2.2). The evidence suggests that middle-class children on average receive a disproportionate share of educational resources in terms of both quantity and quality; and that these differentials cannot be attributed solely to differences in tastes. In addition, the finance of university education is almost certainly regressive. It is open to question to what extent these features are *necessarily* an indictment of the present system. Opponents have to show not that the state sector is imperfect (which is not in dispute), but that a more market-oriented system would do better. Vouchers for school education (Chapter 13:2.3) offer no such prospect. Their efficiency effects are unclear a priori and unproven empirically; in equity terms they are likely to benefit middle-class children more than other groups. Loans for university education have also been suggested. It is argued that a well-constructed system would be an equalising measure, both because rich

419

students would no longer be financed by lower income taxpayers, and because a loan system might enable universities to expand to the advantage, *inter alia*, of students from poor backgrounds. Evidence from the Swedish system lends qualified support to this view.

Housing is the one major area where the welfare state has performed badly, not through choosing controversial aims (Chapter 14:2), but by adopting methods which are unlikely to achieve them. The theoretical arguments (Chapter 14:3.2) support a substantial efficiency role for the state through widespread regulation, via limited price subsidies for very specific reasons, and by intervention in the market for loans. There is little necessity for public production of housing, and no justification for state allocation to the individual. Equity objectives are thus likely to be met most effectively by market or near-market prices and regulation, supported by income transfers.

The historical strategy, however, has been based on price subsidies (Chapter 14:4.1), with substantial public production allocated by administrative means. The system has not worked well. It is explained (Chapter 14:4.2) how price subsidies in each sector of the housing market have led to excess demand and misallocation, with problems simultaneously of underoccupation, over-crowding, immobility and homelessness; the quantity and quality of the private rental housing stock has declined; and the system is nowhere near tenure-neutral (see the Glossary). The distributional effects of the subsidies are also largely perverse (Chapter 14:4.3): owner-occupiers (mainly in the higher socio-economic groups) benefit disproportionately; and the redistributive impact of rent control and subsidies to local authority housing, despite some shift towards income subsidies in the 1980s, retains an arbitrary element. The reforms set out in Chapter 14:5 therefore adopt a strategy in which *price* subsidies (i.e. mortgage interest relief, subsidised local authority rents and rent control) are gradually replaced by *income* subsidies. Housing would be allocated by individual choice in the face of efficient (i.e. for the most part market) prices, supported by income transfers.

One of the most important points I have tried to convey in this book is that the approach to housing (and to the other areas) is advocated *not* for ideological reasons but because it would have substantial advantages in terms of efficiency and, possibly even more, of social justice. Housing and health care are equally important from the viewpoint of *social* policy; but there are substantial differences in their *technical* natures. As a result, they require different solutions.

1.3 WHY HAVE A WELFARE STATE?

The welfare state has two purposes: one is redistributive, or compensatory, to enhance social justice, the other functional, e.g. to deal with market failures, thereby increasing economic efficiency. Virtually all parts of the welfare state display both aspects. Education from a functional perspective is a form of investment in the next generation of workers and citizens, but provided 'free' acts also to help the poor; and analogous arguments apply to health care. Publicly provided income transfers, similarly, have an efficiency role where the private market is unable to supply insurance (e.g. against unemployment) even to individuals who are able to support themselves on a lifetime basis.

Several important conclusions emerge. First, to the extent that the welfare state has a substantial functional aspect, opposition by writers like Hayek and Friedman is misplaced. The single theoretical issue which, more than any other, divides their arguments from those in this book is their failure to acknowledge the major implications of information problems, which affect consumers of increasingly complex products, and also arise in important ways in insurance markets. Information problems of this sort greatly strengthen the efficiency case for the welfare state. The debate with libertarians (Chapter 4:6.2), surprisingly, turns out to be at least as much technical as ideological. As a result, it is less public involvement *per se* which should be a matter for controversy, than its precise form and the choice of its distributional objectives.

Finally, and central to the argument of the book, the major efficiency role of social institutions makes them relevant to the population at large, not just to the poor. The welfare state is much more than a safety net; it is justified not simply by any redistributive aims one may (or may not) have, but because it does things which private markets for technical reasons either would not do at all, or would do inefficiently. We need a welfare state of some sort for efficiency reasons, and would continue to do so even if all distributional problems had been solved.

2 Broader Perspectives

2.1 OTHER REFORMS

This last section sets the subject-matter of the book into its broader perspective. Imagine a situation in which all the reforms discussed earlier had been implemented; that the public/private mix was optimal in all parts of the welfare state; the resources absorbed optimal for the welfare state as a whole and for its constituent parts; and market allocation and actuarially fair insurance applied where they contributed to efficiency and social justice, and rejected where they did not. Would the agenda for reform then be complete?

The answer, obviously, is no. The welfare state may make unemployment more bearable but it does little to reduce the number of people out of work; nor does it improve working conditions for those in employment; and many people, e.g. the disabled, ethnic minorities and women, are underprivileged for reasons not directly connected with poverty. There is room for debate about the nature of these problems and about appropriate ameliorative action, but little disagreement that each is a legitimate concern of public policy (for detailed discussion see Glennerster, 1983).

I shall not dwell on these problems, not because they are unimportant but because (with the exception of unemployment) economics has little to say about them. I want instead to turn to an issue which runs implicitly through the whole book. The welfare state, despite its faults, is an equalising force; but various writers argue that it is not sufficiently equalising and/or that on its own it cannot be. This raises the question of how to increase equality without creating incentive problems – the issue, in short, of the extent to which greater equality is compatible with a capitalist system. I make no attempt at any strategic answer to such a vast question. But I should like to suggest that, by exercising some imagination, the mixed economy can be made more flexible than many people (both libertarian and Marxist) believe.

It is conventionally argued that the advantage of capitalism is its dynamism, i.e. its tendency to encourage innovation and economic growth; its disadvantage is the inequality it creates. To Marxists the price of inequality is too high, so they reject capitalism; to libertarians the price of reducing inequality is too high, so they reject the aim of equality. Both solutions can be regarded as extreme. To avoid the disadvantages of capitalism by abandoning the market system entirely is to risk throwing out the baby with the bath water. A better solution might be to accept *some* price in inequality for the benefits of innovation and output growth, but to seek to minimise it.

To illustrate the argument I want to suggest that inequality could be reduced by two measures: the imposition of much heavier (but carefully designed) taxation of the transmission of wealth; and profit sharing. The standard argument against death duties and inheritance taxes is that they create disincentives, i.e. the price of greater equality in terms of lost output is high. This need not be inevitable. Consider two individuals: C (Chip) inherits nothing, but over his/her lifetime builds a computer business worth £100 million; D (Duke) inherits £100 million and earns nothing. C's enterprise has made him rich and has also benefited others. One way of retaining these benefits, whilst simultaneously reducing both the disincentive problem and the tendency of inherited wealth to perpetuate inequality, is to tax C's bequest less heavily than D's. Specifically, suppose that an individual is allowed to bequeath £X to his heirs, where X is a measure of his lifetime production as represented, for instance, by his lifetime earnings.[1] C could leave his fortune to his son or daughter on generous terms, whilst the greater proportion of D's wealth would be taxed away. C's son could leave a large fortune to *his* children only if he himself were productive. The resulting system would not tax the *creation* of wealth; and the taxation of its transmission, far from creating disincentives, would actively encourage economic growth by giving legatees a tax incentive to maximise their lifetime output.

A possible objection is that C's fortune is built on the backs of his workers who do not die rich. This might well be true – but again the solution may not be to throw out the benefits of capitalism to avoid its costs, but to share the benefits more equally. One way of doing so is to pay workers in part with shares in the firm where they work. They could, if they wished, sell these shares for cash; or they could build up an asset-holding, and share in C's fortune. In the latter case, workers would increasingly have the same incentives as owner-managers; in addition, as shareholders they would have some power in running the firm. The resulting system avoids conflict between labour and capital by creating worker-capitalists and manager-capitalists with shared interests;[2] and other ways of reducing the tension between distributional goals and dynamic efficiency are, doubtless, possible.

2.2 THE POLITICAL ECONOMY OF THE FUTURE

This book has concentrated on problems with the welfare state *qua* welfare state. But difficulties can arise also from much broader causes. These include a changed ideological climate, which has threatened the 'welfare consensus' on both sides of the Atlantic, and changes in external economic conditions, particularly the decline in growth rates, and sharp increases in unemployment in many countries since 1970. These problems give rise to two central controversies which transcend the boundaries of the book.

Is a welfare state compatible with high unemployment? We have seen (Chapters 5:3.2 and 8:2.2) that unemployment, for technical reasons, is an uninsurable risk. For this reason the Beveridge strategy had *two legs* – social insurance and high employment (which Beveridge rightly regarded as a precondition for the success of the insurance arrangements). There is general agreement that high levels of employment and rising living standards have been at least as much an equalising force as redistribution over the past 40

---

[1] Note that this would give a wealthy individual a powerful countervailing incentive not to cheat on his income tax (at least as regards earned income).

[2] See, for instance, 'John Lewis to Pay Worker-Partners Record £25 million Bonus', *The Times*, 9 March 1984; on analytical aspects see Meade (1984) and Weitzman (1984).

years. The postwar consensus was that welfare spending made a twofold contribution, through its redistributive impact, and through its multiplier effect on employment. Adherents of this view (broadly the Labour, Liberal and Social Democratic Parties in Britain, and Liberal Democrats in the USA) argue that current difficulties represent a failure not of the welfare state but of macroeconomic policy. The counter-view, espoused by so-called 'supply-siders', including the Conservative and Republican administrations of the 1980s, is that the causal chain goes the other way – that it is high public (and particularly social) spending which is a *cause* of high unemployment, rather than its cure (for an exposition and critique see Bosanquet, 1983). The debate is a continuing one.

The relation between the welfare state and economic growth is also complex. Spending on the welfare state in Britain rose fivefold in real terms between 1948 and the mid-1980s, from 10 per cent of gross domestic product to about 22.5 per cent (Table 7.2), and the experience of other countries, including the USA, Canada and Japan, has been similar. That social spending and consequently also taxation have increased is fact. What is controversial are the twin effects of (a) higher benefits on work effort and (b) higher taxation on economic growth. The answer to these questions, as we saw in Chapters 8:3.1 and 9:5.1, rests ultimately on empirical magnitudes which we do not, and may never fully know. The effect of the welfare state on capital accumulation and output growth, despite much research and strident polemics, remains largely *terra incognita*.

The opposite question – the effect of economic growth on welfare spending – is at least as much political as economic. There is a flourishing debate about whether Britain or other countries can afford a welfare state. The easy complacency of earlier years about the continued growth of social spending has been replaced by a growing literature on the 'crisis in welfare', from such diverse quarters as libertarians and Marxists (see the Further Reading). For the reasons discussed in Chapter 3:5 both groups question the compatibility of capitalism with a mixed economy comprising a substantial element of tax-financed public production, libertarians on the grounds of the disincentive effects of high taxation, Marxists because growing social spending has exposed what they regard as the inherent instability of capitalism (see Judge, 1982, and Heald, 1983). In direct contradiction, writers like Blake and Ormerod (1980) argue that, far from aggravating the problem of low growth rates, higher social spending exerts an ameliorative influence for traditional Keynesian reasons, especially during times of recession.

Glennerster presents a more agnostic analysis. Two crucial facts stand out. First, the level of taxation and social spending varies widely in otherwise similar Western economies (for comparative tax rates see Newman, 1985), and is not correlated in any obvious way with economic performance. These facts contradict the simple view that the present scale of the welfare state or something rather larger or smaller is incompatible with a substantial capitalist sector. Second, 'forty years ago in a ravaged economy when real incomes were far less than half of ours today, people voted for what came to be called a welfare state, and paid the price, and voted to continue affording it' (Glennerster, 1985, p. 235).

This brings out a final point – that the future of the welfare state depends not only on economic feasibility, but also very much on what people, through the political process, decide that they want.

None of the ideas in this book has been intended as a detailed blueprint, but more as an illustration of an approach which has been, throughout, to entertain moderately egalitarian aims but to avoid dogmatism about methods. The result shows how, with care, it is possible to create institutions both within the welfare state and more broadly which contribute to a society characterised simultaneously by economic efficiency and social justice.

Further Reading

For a classic defence of the mixed economy see Okun (1975). The 'crisis in welfare' is discussed by libertarians (Harris and Seldon, 1979; Seldon, 1981) and Marxists (Gough, 1979; Ginsburg, 1979). For more general discussion see Mishra (1984), Glennerster (1983 and 1985, Ch. 13), Heald (1983) and Klein and O'Higgins (1985).

Glossary

ABSOLUTE POVERTY: poverty line defined in terms of a subsistence standard of living; as opposed to **RELATIVE POVERTY**.

ACTUARIAL: an actuarial contribution is based on two factors: (a) the size of the benefit to be paid if the insured event (e.g. becoming ill) occurs; and (b) the probability of the event occurring. The probability needs to take into account mortality, morbidity, inflation and all other relevant factors. This is the way in which private insurance works.

ADVERSE SELECTION: situation in which an individual who is a poor risk can conceal the fact from the insurance company.

AFDC: AID TO FAMILIES WITH DEPENDENT CHILDREN.

AID TO FAMILIES WITH DEPENDENT CHILDREN: the main US **INCOME-TESTED BENEFIT** for families with no (or virtually no) other income.

ALLOCATIVE EFFICIENCY: see **ECONOMIC EFFICIENCY**.

ANNUITY: the payment of an income of £x per year for life; often given to an individual in exchange for a single, lump-sum payment at the time he/she retires. See Chapter 5:2.3.

BUILDING SOCIETY: UK financial institution which lends money to individuals for the purpose of buying a house. The US equivalent, broadly, is a savings and loan association.

CARDINAL UTILITY: if utility is *cardinally* measurable we can make statements like 'A gets twice as much utility from his first ice cream as from his second' or 'B gets the same utility as A from an ice cream'. When utility is measurable only *ordinally* we can say only that A gets *more* utility from his first ice cream than from his second, but not how much more; and it is not possible to make interpersonal comparisons between A's and B's utility. See also **UTILITY**.

CHILD BENEFIT: UK system of weekly, tax-free cash payment of £x for each child in the family, generally payable to the mother.

CHILD BENEFIT INCREASE: UK system of paying an addition to **CHILD BENEFIT** to a parent with single-handed responsibility for one or more children.

COLLECTIVIST: view which gives priority to the achievement of equality or meeting need. Can take various forms including **FABIAN SOCIALIST** or **MARXIST**.

COMPREHENSIVE SCHOOL: UK secondary school for pupils of all abilities, generally covering the age range 11–18.

426

CONTRIBUTORY BENEFIT: benefit payable only to individuals who (a) have a **NATIONAL INSURANCE** contribution record, and (b) are unemployed, retired, or suffering from ill-health, etc. See also **SOCIAL INSURANCE** and **NON-CONTRIBUTORY BENEFIT**.

CROSS-SECTION: series of observations on different entities during a single period of time, e.g. the Family Expenditure Survey gathers data on the expenditure patterns of a large number of families in a given week; as opposed to **TIME-SERIES**.

DHSS: UK Department of Health and Social Security.

DISREGARD: amount of earnings or other income which is disregarded (i.e. ignored) in calculating the benefit to which an individual or family is entitled.

DOE: UK Department of the Environment.

ECONOMIC EFFICIENCY: the allocation of scarce resources in such a way that no reallocation can make any individual better-off without making at least one other individual worse-off. Also referred to as efficiency, allocative efficiency, Pareto efficiency or Pareto optimality.

EFFICIENCY: see **ECONOMIC EFFICIENCY**.

EQUITY: a goal relating to the way in which resources should be distributed or shared between individuals, hence synonymous with **SOCIAL JUSTICE**; see also **HORIZONTAL EQUITY** and **VERTICAL EQUITY**. Equity *may* imply equality, but does not have to – see also **LIBERTARIAN, LIBERAL, COLLECTIVIST**.

ESTATE AGENT: institution to assist with the purchase and sale of property; in the US a realtor.

FABIAN SOCIALIST: view that **COLLECTIVIST** goals can be achieved within a mixed economy. See also **LIBERTARIAN, LIBERAL, MARXIST**.

FAMILY INCOME SUPPLEMENT: UK system of supplementing the incomes of low-income working families.

FIS: **FAMILY INCOME SUPPLEMENT**.

FUNDED: pensions paid from a fund built up over a period of years out of contributions of its members. Contrasts with **PAY-AS-YOU-GO** schemes.

GENERAL PRACTITIONER: family doctor.

GINI COEFFICIENT: a measure of the overall inequality in society; it takes on values between zero (when income is distributed equally) and one (when one individual has all the income).

GP: **GENERAL PRACTITIONER**.

GREEN PAPER: consultative document issued by UK central government, inviting discussion and comment; as distinct from a **WHITE PAPER**.

HEALTH MAINTENANCE ORGANISATION: a 'firm' of doctors, which charges individuals/families an annual premium, in return for which it provides the individual/family with a comprehensive range of medical services. See Chapter 13:1.3.

HMO: **HEALTH MAINTENANCE ORGANISATION**.

HMSO: Her Majesty's Stationery Office.

HORIZONTAL EQUITY: distribution in accordance with equal treatment of equals, e.g. the relative tax treatment of families of different sizes at a given level of income. See also **EQUITY** and **VERTICAL EQUITY**.

HOUSING BENEFIT: UK system of assistance with rent and **LOCAL RATES** for low-income householders.

HOUSING REVENUE ACCOUNT: shows housing revenue and expenditure in each local authority on a cash flow basis, including interest payments on past loans, rental income, and central and local subsidies.

HRA: HOUSING REVENUE ACCOUNT.

IMPLICIT TAX RATE: a tax which arises when a family in receipt of an **INCOME-TESTED BENEFIT** earns extra income, and as a consequence loses benefit. If benefit is lost pound for pound with earnings, the implicit tax rate is 100 per cent. See Chapter 10:3.

INCOME-RELATED BENEFIT: see INCOME-TESTED BENEFIT.

INCOME-TESTED BENEFIT: benefit awarded to individuals/families with low incomes, and withdrawn as income rises; as distinct from benefits awarded on the basis of other criteria, e.g. having a contributions record. Also referred to as income-related benefit or means-tested benefit. See also **CONTRIBUTORY BENEFIT**.

LAISSEZ-FAIRE: the term is used in this book in its most frequent sense as 'a belief in the efficiency of a free market economy' (Taylor, 1972, p. 11). See also **LIBERTARIAN**.

LEA: LOCAL EDUCATION AUTHORITY.

LESS ELIGIBILITY: condition that the standard of living of those in receipt of **POOR LAW** benefits should be lower than that of the poorest worker.

LIBERAL: view of property rights and income distribution as contingent matters rather than as items of dogma. Note the confusing ambiguity in the use of the word. In the nineteenth century it was used as a label for Classical Liberal thinkers like Bentham and Nassau Senior; and today a writer like Friedman, in calling himself a liberal, is using the term in the same way. Throughout the book such writers are referred to as **LIBERTARIANS**.

LIBERTARIAN: view which gives priority to individual liberty, usually associated with a belief in the free market and **LAISSEZ-FAIRE**. See also **LIBERAL** and **COLLECTIVIST**.

LOCAL EDUCATION AUTHORITY: the body which organises most forms of education at a local level, including building schools and employing teachers.

LOCAL RATES: UK system of local taxation, based on the annual rental value of property.

MACRO EFFICIENCY: concerns the proportion of national resources devoted to a particular activity such as health care or education; as opposed to **MICRO EFFICIENCY**.

MARKET FAILURE: impediment to the efficient working of the market, in particular externalities, public goods or increasing returns to scale (see Appendix to Chapter 4, paras 12–16).

MARXIST: view that **COLLECTIVIST** goals are incompatible with capitalism, and can be achieved only under state ownership of major productive resources. See also **LIBERTARIAN, LIBERAL** and **FABIAN SOCIALIST**.

MEANS TEST: income test on the basis of which **SOCIAL ASSISTANCE** benefits are awarded.

MEANS-TESTED BENEFIT: see INCOME-TESTED BENEFIT.

MICRO EFFICIENCY: concerns the division of total medical resources between the different parts of the health-care system, or that of educational resources between different areas of education, etc.; as opposed to MACRO EFFICIENCY.

MORAL HAZARD: situation in which an insured person can affect the insurance company's liability without its knowledge.

NATIONAL HEALTH SERVICE: UK system under which medical care is (a) provided by the state, (b) financed mainly out of general tax revenues and (c) supplied to patients without charge, apart from a contribution towards the cost of drugs (from which the young, the old and the poor are exempt).

NATIONAL INSURANCE: UK system of SOCIAL INSURANCE in respect, for example, of unemployment, ill health and retirement. See also CONTRIBUTORY BENEFIT.

NEGATIVE INCOME TAX: a system in which income support and income taxation are integrated by using the tax system, both to pay benefits to those with low incomes and to levy taxes on those with higher incomes.

NHS: NATIONAL HEALTH SERVICE.

NIT: NEGATIVE INCOME TAX.

NON-CONTRIBUTORY BENEFIT: benefit awarded without the need for a contributions record, and financed out of general tax revenues (in contrast with a CONTRIBUTORY BENEFIT). May be INCOME-TESTED, or awarded on the basis of non-income criteria, e.g. CHILD BENEFIT.

ORDINAL UTILITY: see CARDINAL UTILITY.

ORIGINAL POSITION: hypothetical situation (used by the philosopher John Rawls) in which rational negotiators behind the VEIL OF IGNORANCE negotiate a just constitution for a country in which they will all have to live.

OUTDOOR RELIEF: benefits paid under the POOR LAW to individuals, principally the elderly, who were not required to live in the WORKHOUSE.

PARETO EFFICIENCY: see ECONOMIC EFFICIENCY.

PARETO OPTIMALITY: see ECONOMIC EFFICIENCY.

PAY-AS-YOU-GO: pensions paid (usually by the state) out of current tax revenues, rather than out of an accumulated fund; contrasts with FUNDED schemes.

PAYG: PAY-AS-YOU-GO.

PIGOVIAN SUBSIDY/TAX: where an activity creates an external benefit, an unrestricted private market will supply an inefficiently small quantity. One way of restoring supply to its efficient level is to pay a so called Pigovian subsidy. Analogously, a Pigovian tax discourages excessive supply in the presence of an external cost. See Chapter 4:3.2 and/or the Appendix to Chapter 4, para. 15.

POOR LAW: UK system for the relief of destitution, from late sixteenth century; it was phased out over the first half of the twentieth century.

POVERTY TRAP: situation in which individuals/families earning an extra £1 lose £1 or more in income-tested benefits, and hence make themselves absolutely worse-off. See also IMPLICIT TAX RATE.

PROGRESSIVE TAXATION: tax system in which tax paid as a proportion of income is higher for individuals with higher incomes. See also PROPORTIONAL TAXATION and REGRESSIVE TAXATION.

PROPORTIONAL TAXATION: tax system in which tax paid is the same proportion of income at all income levels. See also **PROGRESSIVE TAXATION** and **REGRESSIVE TAXATION**.

RATES: see **LOCAL RATES**.

REGRESSIVE TAXATION: tax system in which tax paid as a proportion of income is lower for individuals with higher incomes. See also **PROGRESSIVE TAXATION** and **PROPORTIONAL TAXATION**.

RELATIVE POVERTY: poverty line defined relative to the average standard of living, e.g. as a proportion of average income. As opposed to **ABSOLUTE POVERTY**.

REPLACEMENT RATIO: ratio of income when unemployed, to income (post-tax and transfers) when in work.

REVENUE-NEUTRAL: a policy change is revenue-neutral if any resulting increase in expenditure is accompanied by a matching increase in taxation.

SB: **SUPPLEMENTARY BENEFIT**.

SERPS: state earnings-related pension scheme in the UK.

SOCIAL ASSISTANCE: state benefits paid out of general tax revenues without contribution condition, but usually subject to a **MEANS TEST**. See also **INCOME-TESTED BENEFIT**.

SOCIAL DIVIDEND SCHEME: form of **NEGATIVE INCOME TAX**.

SOCIAL INSURANCE: form of organisation, originally modelled on private insurance, under which individuals receive state benefits in respect of, for example, unemployment or retirement, often without any test of means or need, on the basis of previous (usually compulsory) contributions. See also **CONTRIBUTORY BENEFIT** and **NATIONAL INSURANCE**.

SOCIAL JUSTICE: a goal relating to the way in which resources should be distributed or shared between individuals. See also **EQUITY, HORIZONTAL EQUITY** and **VERTICAL EQUITY**. For different definitions of social justice, see **LIBERT-ARIAN, LIBERAL, COLLECTIVIST**.

SOCIAL SECURITY: all publicly provided cash benefits. Note that this standard British usage differs from the narrower American definition of social security as retirement benefits, and the broader EEC definition which includes health services. Throughout the book the term is used with its British meaning.

STANDARD ASSUMPTIONS: the assumptions under which the market will, in theory, allocate resources efficiently, viz. perfect information, perfect competition and no **MARKET FAILURES** (see Chapter 4:3.2 or the Appendix to Chapter 4, paras 5–17).

STIGMA: loss of **UTILITY** because income is received in the form of (usually) **INCOME-TESTED** benefits, rather than from some more congenial source (e.g. earnings or insurance benefits).

SUPPLEMENTARY BENEFIT: UK system of **MEANS-TESTED, NON-CONTRIBUTORY** benefits, for which individuals/families are eligible if their income from all other sources is less than the poverty standard.

TAKE-UP: the number of people receiving a particular benefit as a proportion of those potentially eligible.

TAX EXPENDITURES: public expenditure implicit in the granting of tax relief to certain activities, e.g. approved private pension contributions or mortgage interest payments, as opposed to explicit expenditure. See Chapter 7:1.1.

TENURE NEUTRALITY: an aim of housing policy, whereby individuals (on average and in the long run) are financially indifferent between buying accommodation and renting it. See Chapter 14:2.

THIRD-PARTY PAYMENT PROBLEM: situation in which the insurance company pays the whole of an individual's (e.g.) medical bill; as a result neither patient nor doctor have an incentive to economise. Technically, a form of **MORAL HAZARD**.

TIME-SERIES: series of observations on a single entity (or aggregate) over several periods, e.g. data on the level of unemployment benefits, the number of people out of work, etc. in a country each year from 1960 to 1980. As opposed to **CROSS-SECTION**.

UNEMPLOYMENT TRAP: situation in which an individual/family is better-off (or little worse-off) when unemployed than when in work. This situation arises particularly for those with low earnings and/or with large families.

UNFUNDED: see **PAY-AS-YOU-GO**.

UPRATING: increase in the value of almost all cash benefits, usually at annual intervals, and usually in line with changes in the price level.

UTILITY: individual well-being or satisfaction. See also **CARDINAL UTILITY**.

VEIL OF IGNORANCE: hypothetical situation in which rational individuals in the **ORIGINAL POSITION** have to negotiate a just constitution for a country in which they will all have to live, but *without knowing who they will be* (i.e. whether they will be born as one of the most or one of the least fortunate).

VERTICAL EQUITY: the extent of redistribution of income, consumption or wealth from rich to poor. See also **EQUITY** and **HORIZONTAL EQUITY**.

WELFARE: US usage for **INCOME-TESTED BENEFITS**.

WHITE PAPER: firm statement of government intent; as distinct from a **GREEN PAPER**.

WORKHOUSE: institution giving work and rudimentary accommodation to the destitute, under the **POOR LAW**.

WORKHOUSE TEST: condition that recipients of benefits under the **POOR LAW** must live in the **WORKHOUSE**.

References

AARON H J (1973), *Why is Welfare so Hard to Reform?* (The Brookings Institution, Washington DC).

AARON H J (1981a), 'Economic Aspects of the Role of Government in Health Care', in van der Gaag J and Perlman M (eds), *Health, Economics, and Health Economics* (North Holland Publishing Company, Amsterdam).

AARON H J (1981b), 'Policy Implications: A Progress Report' in Bradbury K L and Downs A (eds) (1981).

AARON H J (1982), *Economic Effects of Social Security* (The Brookings Institution, Washington DC).

AARON H J (1984), 'Social Welfare in Australia', in Caves R E and Krause L B (eds), *The Australian Economy: A View from the North* (The Brookings Institution, Washington DC).

AARON H J and BURTLESS G (eds) (1984), *Retirement and Economic Behavior* (The Brookings Institution, Washington DC).

AARON H J and PECHMAN J A (1981), *How Taxes Affect Economic Behavior* (The Brookings Institution, Washington DC).

AARON H J and SCHWARTZ W B (1984), *The Painful Prescription: Rationing Hospital Care* (The Brookings Institution, Washington DC).

ABEL-SMITH B (1964), *The Hospitals, 1800–1948* (Heinemann, London).

ABEL-SMITH B (1976), *Value for Money in Health Services* (Heinemann, London).

ABEL-SMITH B (1983), 'Economic Efficiency in Health Care Delivery', *International Social Security Review*, Vol. 36, No. 2, pp. 165–79.

ABEL-SMITH B (1984), *Cost Containment in Health Care*, Occasional Papers in Social Administration No. 73 (Bedford Square Press, London).

ABEL-SMITH B (1985), 'Who is the Odd Man Out?: The Experience of Western Europe in Containing the Costs of Health Care', *Health and Society*, Vol. 63, No. 1, pp. 1–17.

ABEL-SMITH B and TOWNSEND P (1965), *The Poor and the Poorest* (Bell & Sons, London).

ACTON J P (1973), *Evaluating Public Programmes to Save Lives: The Case of Heart Attacks* (Rand Corporation, Santa Monica, California).

AKERLOF G A (1970), 'The Market for "Lemons": Qualitative Uncertainty and the Market Mechanism', *Quarterly Journal of Economics*, Vol. 84, pp. 488–500, August.

ALTMEYER A J (1966), *The Formative Years of Social Security* (University of Wisconsin Press, Madison).

ANDERSON O W (1968), *The Uneasy Equilibrium: Private and Public Financing of Health Services in the United States 1875–1965* (College and University Press, New Haven, Connecticut).

APPS P F (1981), *A Theory of Inequality and Taxation* (Cambridge University Press).

ARROW K J (1963), 'Uncertainty and the Welfare Economics of Medical Care', *American Economic Review*, Vol. 53, pp. 941–73, reprinted in Cooper and Culyer (1973) and Diamond and Rothschild (1978).

ARROW K J (1965), 'Uncertainty and the Welfare Economics of Medical Care: Reply (the Implications of Transactions Costs and Adjustment Lags)', *American Economic Review*, Vol. 55, pp. 154–8.

ARROW K J (1968), 'The Economics of Moral Hazard: Further Comment', *American Economic Review*, Vol. 58, pp. 537–9.

ARROW K J (1970), 'Political and Economic Evaluation of Social Effects and Externalities', in Margolis J (ed.), *The Analysis of Public Output* (Columbia University Press, New York).

ARROW K J (1971), 'Models of Job Discrimination', in Pascal A H (ed), *Racial Discrimination in Economic Life* (Lexington), reprinted in Atkinson (ed.) (1980).

ARROW K J (1973), 'Some Ordinalist-Utilitarian Notes on Rawls's *Theory of Justice*', *Journal of Philosophy*, Vol. 70, May, pp. 245–63.

ARROW K J (1974), 'Limited Knowledge and Economic Analysis', *American Economic Review*, Vol. LXIV, No. 1, March, pp. 1–10.

ATKINSON A B (1970), 'On the Measurement of Inequality', *Journal of Economic Theory*, Vol. 2, pp. 244–63, reprinted in Atkinson (ed.) (1980, pp. 23–43) (including a non-mathematical summary).

ATKINSON A B (1973), *The Tax Credit Scheme and the Redistribution of Income* (Institute for Fiscal Studies, London).

ATKINSON A B (1974), *Unequal Shares* (Penguin, London).

ATKINSON A B (1981), 'Unemployment Benefits and Incentives', in Creedy J (ed.), *The Economics of Unemployment in Britain* (Butterworth, London).

ATKINSON A B (1982), *Social Justice and Public Policy* (Harvester Press, Brighton, Sussex).

ATKINSON A B (1983), *The Economics of Inequality*, 2nd edn (Oxford University Press).

ATKINSON A B (1984a), 'Take-up of Social Security Benefits', ESRC Programme on Taxation, Incentives and the Distribution of Income, Discussion Paper 65, London School of Economics.

ATKINSON A B (1984b), *The Costs of Social Dividend and Tax Credit Schemes*, ESRC Programme on Taxation, Incentives and the Distribution of Income, Discussion Paper 63, London School of Economics, reprinted in Atkinson (1987, Ch. 16).

ATKINSON A B (1984c), 'A Guide to the Reform of Social Security', *New Society*, 13 December, pp. 426–8.

ATKINSON A B (1986), 'Income Maintenance and Social Insurance', Welfare State Programme, discussion paper no. 5, (London School of Economics), forthcoming in Auerbach A J and Feldstein M S (eds), *Handbook of Public Economics*, Vol. 2 (North-Holland, Amsterdam).

433

ATKINSON A B (1987), *Poverty and Social Security* (Harvester Press, Brighton, Sussex).

ATKINSON A B (ed) (1980), *Wealth, Income and Inequality*, 2nd edn (Oxford University Press).

ATKINSON A B and FLEMMING J S (1978), 'Unemployment, Social Security and Incentives', *Midland Bank Review*, pp. 6–16.

ATKINSON A B and HARRISON A J (1978), *The Distribution of Personal Wealth in Britain* (Cambridge University Press).

ATKINSON A B and STIGLITZ J E (1980), *Lectures on Public Economics* (McGraw-Hill, London).

ATKINSON A B, GOMULKA J, MICKLEWRIGHT J and RAU N (1984), 'Unemployment Benefit, Duration and Incentives in Britain: How Robust is the Evidence?', *Journal of Public Economics*, Vol. 23, pp. 3–26.

ATKINSON A B, MAYNARD A K and TRINDER C G (1983), *Parents and Children* (Heinemann, London).

AUERBACH A J and KOTLIKOFF L J (1981), 'An Examination of Empirical Tests of Social Security and Savings', National Bureau of Economic Research, Working Paper 730 (National Bureau of Economic Research, New York).

AVERCH H A *et al.* (1972), *How Effective is Schooling? A Critical Review and Synthesis of Research Findings* (The Rand Corporation, Santa Monica, California).

BARR N A (1971), 'Public Assistance and Family Behaviour in the Urban United States' (PhD thesis, University of California, Berkeley).

BARR N A (1973), 'The Costs of Negative Income Tax', *Select Committee on Tax-Credit*, Session 1972–3, Vol. III, Appendices to Minutes of Evidence, HC 341-III (HMSO, London).

BARR N A (1975a), 'Labour's Pension Plan – A Lost Opportunity?', *British Tax Review*, Nos 2 and 3.

BARR N A (1975b), 'Negative Income Taxation and the Redistribution of Income', *Oxford Bulletin of Economics and Statistics*, Vol. 37, No. 1, February, as amended in Vol. 38, No. 2, May 1976.

BARR N A (1975c), 'Real Rates of Return to Financial Assets Since the War', *Three Banks Review*, No. 107, September.

BARR N A (1979), 'Myths My Grandpa Taught Me', *Three Banks Review*, No. 124, December.

BARR N A (1980), 'The Taxation of Married Women's Incomes', *British Tax Review*, Nos 5 and 6.

BARR N A (1981), 'Empirical Definitions of the Poverty Line', *Policy and Politics*, Vol. 9, No. 1.

BARR N A (1985), 'Economic Welfare and Social Justice', *Journal of Social Policy*, Vol. 14, No. 2, April, pp. 175–87.

BARR N A (1986), 'Revenue, Expenditure and the Government Accounts', *British Tax Review*, No. 6, pp. 340–46.

BARR N A and CARRIER J W (1978), 'Women's Aid Groups: The Economic Case for State Assistance to Battered Wives', *Policy and Politics*, Vol. 6, pp. 333–50.

BARR N A and HALL R E (1975), 'The Taxation of Earnings Under Public Assistance', *Economica*, Vol. 42, No. 168, pp. 373–84, November.

BARR N A and **HALL R E** (1981), 'The Probability of Dependence on Public Assistance', *Economica*, Vol. 48, No. 190, pp. 109–23, May.

BARR N A and **ROPER J F H** (1974), 'Tax-Credits: An Optimistic Appraisal', *Three Banks Review*, No. 101, March.

BARR N A, JAMES S R and **PREST A R** (1977), *Self-Assessment for Income Tax* (Heinemann, London).

BARRO R J (1974), 'Are Government Bonds Net Wealth?', *Journal of Political Economy*, Vol. 84, pp. 1095–1117.

BARRO R J (1978), *The Impact of Social Security on Private Saving: Evidence from the US Time Series* (The American Enterprise Institute for Public Policy Research, Washington DC).

BARRY B (1973), *The Liberal Theory of Social Justice* (Clarendon Press, Oxford).

BASSETT K and **SHORT J** (1980), *Housing and Residential Structure: Alternative Approaches* (Routledge & Kegan Paul, London).

BAUMOL W J and **OATES W E** (1979), *The Theory of Environmental Policy* (Prentice Hall, Englewood Cliffs, New Jersey).

BECKER G (1975), *Human Capital*, 2nd edn (National Bureau of Economic Research, Cambridge, Mass.).

BECKERMAN W (1979), 'The Impact of Income Maintenance Payments on Poverty: 1975', *Economic Journal*, Vol. 89, pp. 261–79.

BECKERMAN W and **CLARK S** (1982), *Poverty and Social Security in Britain Since 1961* (Oxford University Press).

BEESLEY M and **LITTLECHILD S** (1983), 'Privatisation: Principles, Problems and Priorities', *Lloyds Bank Review*, July.

BENTHAM J (1789), *An Introduction to the Principles of Morals and Legislation* (Payne, London).

BERTHOUD R (1984), *The Reform of Supplementary Benefit – Summary of Findings* (Policy Studies Institute, London).

BERTHOUD R (1986), *Selective Social Security* (Policy Studies Institute, London).

BERTHOUD R, BROWN J C and **COOPER S** (1981), *Poverty and the Development of Anti-Poverty Policy in the UK* (Heinemann, London).

BEVAN R G (1984), 'Organising the Finance of Hospitals by Simulated Markets', *Fiscal Studies*, Vol. 5, No. 4, November, pp. 44–63.

BEVERIDGE W H (1944), *Full Employment in a Free Society* (Allen & Unwin, London).

BLACK D (1980), *Inequalities in Health* (the Black Report), Report of a Research Working Group chaired by Sir Douglas Black (Department of Health and Social Security, London), published as Townsend P and Davidson N (eds) (1982) (Penguin, London).

BLAKE D and **ORMEROD P** (1980), *The Economics of Prosperity* (Grant McIntyre, London).

BLAUG N (1970), *An Introduction to the Economics of Education* (Penguin, London).

BLAUG M (1984), 'Education Vouchers – It All Depends on What You Mean', in Le Grand J and Robinson R (eds) (1984b).

BLAUG M and **WOODHALL M** (1968), 'Productivity Trends in British Secondary Education, 1950–63', *Sociology of Education*, Winter.

BOOTH C (1902), *Life and Labour of the People of London*, 17 vols (London).

BOS D (1984), 'Income Taxation, Public Sector Pricing and Redistribution', *Scandinavian Journal of Economics*, Vol. 84, pp. 166–83.

BOSANQUET N (1982), 'Living with Cash Limits: the Case of the National Health Service', *Public Money*, Vol. 2, No. 2, pp. 15–18, September.

BOSANQUET N (1983), *After the New Right* (Heinemann, London).

BOSANQUET N and TOWNSEND P (1980), *Labour and Equality: a Fabian Study of Labour in Power, 1974–79* (Heinemann, London).

BOSKIN M J (1977), 'Social Security and Retirement Decisions', *Economic Inquiry*, Vol. 15, pp. 1–25.

BOSKIN M J and HURD M D (1978), 'The Effect of Social Security on Early Retirement', *Journal of Public Economics*, Vol 10, pp. 361–77.

BOVAIRD A, HARLOE M and WHITEHEAD C M E (1985), 'Private Rented Housing: Its Current Role', *Journal of Social Policy*, Vol. 14, No. 1, January, pp. 1–23.

BOWLES S (1973), 'Understanding Unequal Economic Opportunity', *American Economic Review*, Vol. 63, pp. 346–56, reprinted in Atkinson (ed.) (1980).

BOWLEY M (1937), *Nassau Senior and Classical Economics* (Allen & Unwin, London).

BOWLEY M (1966), *The British Building Industry* (Cambridge University Press).

BRADBURY K L and DOWNS A (eds) (1981), *Do Housing Allowances Work?* (The Brookings Institution, Washington DC).

BRADSHAW J and PIACHAUD D (1980), *Child Support in the European Community* (Bedford Square Press, London).

BREAK G F (1957a), 'Effects of Taxation on Incentives', *British Tax Review*, June.

BREAK G F (1957b, 'Income Taxes and Incentives to Work', *American Economic Review*, September.

BRIGGS A (1961), *Social Thought and Social Action: A Study of the Work of Seebohm Rowntree, 1917–1954* (Longman, London).

BRITTAIN J A (1977), *The Inheritance of Economic Status* (The Brookings Institution, Washington DC).

BRITTAIN J A (1978), *Inheritance and the Inequality of Material Wealth* (The Brookings Institution, Washington DC).

BRITTAN S (1986), 'Privatisation: A Comment on Kay and Thompson', *Economic Journal*, Vol. 96, No. 381, pp. 33–8.

BROOME J (1978), 'Trying to Value a Human Life', *Journal of Public Economics*, Vol. 9, No. 1, and discussion in the same journal, Vol. 12, No. 2, 1979.

BROWN C V (1983a), *Taxation and the Incentive to Work*, 2nd edn (Oxford University Press).

BROWN C V and JACKSON P M (1982), *Public Sector Economics*, 2nd edn (Martin Robertson, Oxford).

BROWN C V and LEVIN E (1974), 'The Effects of Income Taxation on Overtime: The Results of a National Survey', *Economic Journal*, Vol. 84, No. 336, pp. 833–48, December.

BROWN L D (1983b), *Politics and Health Care Organization: HMOs as Federal Policy* (The Brookings Institution, Washington DC).

BROWN M (1985), *Introduction to Social Administration in Britain*, 6th edn (Hutchinson, London).

BROWN M C (1983c), *National Health Insurance in Canada and Australia: A Comparative Political Economy Analysis* (Health Economics Research Unit, Australian National University, Canberra).

BROWN R G S (1975), *The Management of Welfare* (Fontana, London).

BRUCE M (1972), *The Coming of the Welfare State*, 4th edn (Batsford, London).

BUCHANAN J M and TULLOCK G (1962), *The Calculus of Consent* (University of Michigan Press, Ann Arbor, Michigan).

BULL D (1980), *What Price Education?*, Poverty Pamphlet 48 (Child Poverty Action Group, London).

BURKHEAD J, FOX T G and HOLLAND J W (1967), *Input and Output in Large City High Schools* (Syracuse University Press, New York).

BURTLESS G and MOFFITT R A (1984), 'The Effect of Social Security Benefits on the Labor Supply of the Aged', in Aaron and Burtless (eds) (1984).

BYATT I C R, HOLMANS A E, LAIDLER D E W and NICHOLSON R J (1973), 'Income and the Demand for Housing', in Parkin M (ed.), *Essays in Modern Economics* (Longman, London).

CAVES D W and CHRISTENSEN L R (1980), 'The Relative Efficiency of Public and Private Firms in a Competitive Environment: The Case of Canadian Railroads', *Journal of Political Economy*, Vol. 88, No. 5, October, pp. 958–76.

CHESTER T E and ICHIEN M (1983), 'Health Care in Japan – Its Development, Structure and Problems', *Three Banks Review*, No. 137, pp. 17–26, March.

CHRISTOPHER A *et al.* (1970), *Policy for Poverty*, Research Monograph 20 (Institute of Economic Affairs, London).

COASE R H (1960), 'The Problem of Social Cost', *Journal of Law and Economics*, Vol. 3, pp. 1–44, October.

COLLARD D (1983), 'Economics of Philanthropy: A Comment', *Economic Journal*, Vol. 93, No. 371, pp. 637–8, September.

COMMISSION FOR RACIAL EQUALITY (1983), *Housing in the London Borough of Hackney: Report of a Formal Investigation* (Commission for Racial Equality, London).

COMMUNITY INCOME TAX SERVICE (1976), *Annual Report* (Winnipeg, Manitoba).

COOKE K and BALDWIN S (1984), 'How Much is Enough?', *New Society*, Vol. 70, No. 1138, 11 October, pp. 67–8.

COONS J and SUGARMAN S (1978), *Education by Choice: the Case for Family Control* (University of California Press, Berkeley).

COOPER M H and CULYER A J (eds) (1973), *Health Economics* (Penguin, London).

COOPER S (1985), *Family Income Support Part 5: The Health Benefits*, Studies of the Social Security System No. 7 (Policy Studies Institute, London).

COWELL F A (1977), *Measuring Inequality* (Philip Allan, Oxford).

CPAG (1984), *Double Discrimination: Racism in Social Security* (Child Poverty Action Group, London).

CPAG (1985a), *Rights Guide for Home Owners*, 5th edn (The London Housing Aid Centre and Child Poverty Action Group, London).

CPAG (1985b), *Burying Beveridge, A Detailed Response to the Green Paper: Reform of Social Security* (Child Poverty Action Group, London).

CPAG (1986a), *National Welfare Benefits Handbook*, Cohen R and Lakhani B (eds) (Child Poverty Action Group, London).

CPAG (1986b), *Rights Guide to Non-Means-Tested Social Security Benefits*, Smith R and Rowland M (eds) (Child Poverty Action Group, London).

CREEDY J (1982), *State Pensions in Britain* (Cambridge University Press).

CREEDY J and **DISNEY R** (1985), *Social Insurance in Transition* (Oxford University Press).

CREW M (1969), 'Coinsurance and the Welfare Economics of Medical Care', *American Economic Review*, Vol. 59, pp. 906–8.

CROSLAND C A R (1956), *The Future of Socialism* (Cape, London).

CULLINGWORTH J B (1979), *Essays on Housing Policy: the British Scene* (George Allen & Unwin, London).

CULLIS J G and **WEST P A** (1979), *The Economics of Health* (Martin Robertson, Oxford).

CULYER A J, (1971a), 'The Nature of the Commodity "Health Care" and Its Efficient Allocation', *Oxford Economic Papers*, Vol, 23, pp. 189–211, reprinted in Cooper and Culyer (1973).

CULYER A J (1971b), 'Merit Goods and the Welfare Economics of Coercion', *Public Finance*, No. 4.

CULYER A J (1976), *Need and the National Health Service* (Martin Robertson, Oxford).

CULYER A J (1978), *The British Health Service: An Economic Perspective* (University of York).

CULYER A J (1980), *The Political Economy of Social Policy* (Martin Robertson, Oxford).

CULYER A J (ed.) (1983), *Health Indicators* (Martin Robertson, Oxford).

DALTON H (1920), 'The Measurement of the Inequality of Incomes', *Economic Journal*, Vol. 30, pp. 348–61.

DANIELS N (ed.) (1975), *Reading Rawls* (Basil Blackwell, Oxford).

DANZIGER S and **PLOTNICK R** (1977), 'Demographic Change, Government Transfers and Income Distribution', *Monthly Labor Review*, Vol. 100, pp. 7–11.

DANZIGER S, HAVEMAN R and **PLOTNICK R** (1981), 'How Income Transfer Programs Affect Work, Savings and the Income Distribution: A Critical Review', *Journal of Economic Literature*, Vol. 19.

DANZIGER S, HAVEMAN R and **PLOTNICK R** (1984), *Antipoverty Policy: Effects on the Poor and Nonpoor*, discussion paper (University of Wisconsin).

DANZIGER S, VAN DER GAAG J, SMOLENSKY E and **TAUSSIG M** (1984), 'Implications of the Relative Economic Status of the Elderly for Transfer Policy', in Aaron and Burtless (eds.) (1984).

DAVIES B *et al.* (1983), *Kent Community Care Project: Final Report*, Personal Social Services Research Unit (University of Kent, Canterbury).

DAVIS E *et al.* (1985a), *1985 Benefit Reviews: The Effect of the Proposals*, Report Series No. 17 (Institute for Fiscal Studies, London).

DAVIS E *et al.* (1985b), 'The Social Security Green Paper', *Fiscal Studies*, Vol. 6, No. 3, August, pp. 1–8.

DAVIS O E and WHINSTON A (1965), 'Welfare Economics and the Theory of Second Best', *Review of Economic Studies*, Vol. XXXII, No. 89, January, pp. 1–14.

DAWSON R F F (1967), *Cost of Road Accidents in Great Britain* (Road Research Laboratory, Ministry of Transport, London), reprinted in Cooper and Culyer (1973).

DE MEZA D (1983), 'Health Insurance and the Demand for Medical Care', *Journal of Health Economics*, Vol. 2, pp. 47–54.

DEACON A and BRADSHAW J (1983), *Reserved for the Poor* (Martin Robertson, Oxford).

DEATON A S and MUELLBAUER J (1980), *Economics and Consumer Behavior* (Cambridge University Press).

DENISON E F (1962), *The Sources of Economic Growth in the United States and the Alternatives Before Us* (Committee for Economic Development, New York).

DENISON E F (1967), *Why Growth Rates Differ. Postwar Experience in Nine Western Countries* (The Brookings Institution, Washington DC).

DENISON E F (1969), 'The Contribution of Education to the Quality of Labor: Comment', *American Economic Review*, December.

DERTHICK M (1979), *Policymaking for Social Security* (The Brookings Institution, Washington DC).

DESAI M (1979), *Marxian Economics* (Basil Blackwell, Oxford).

DIAMOND P A and HAUSMAN J A (1984), 'The Retirement and Unemployment Behavior of Older Men', in Aaron and Burtless (eds) (1984).

DIAMOND P A and ROTHSCHILD M (eds) (1978), *Uncertainty in Economics: Readings and Exercises* (Academic Press, New York).

DILNOT A W and STARK G K (1986), 'The Poverty Trap, Tax Cuts, and the Reform of Social Security', *Fiscal Studies*, Vol. 7, No. 1, February, pp. 1–10.

DILNOT A W, KAY J A and MORRIS C N (1984), *The Reform of Social Security* (Clarendon Press, Oxford, for the Institute for Fiscal Studies, London).

DISABILITY ALLIANCE (1975), *Poverty and Disability: the Case for a Comprehensive Scheme for Disabled People* (Disability Alliance, London).

DISABLEMENT INCOME GROUP (1979), *Disablement Income Group's National Disability Income* (Disablement Income Group, London).

DONNISON D (1972), 'Ideologies and Policies', *Journal of Social Policy*, Vol. 1, Pt. 2, April, pp. 97–117.

DONNISON D and UNGERSON C (1982), *Housing Policy* (Penguin, London).

DONNISON D with SOTO P (1980), *The Good City: a Study of Urban Development and Policy in Britain* (Heinemann, London).

DOUGLAS P H (1925), *Wages and the Family* (University of Chicago Press).

DOUGLAS P H (1939), *Social Security in the United States: An Analysis of the Federal Social Security Act* (McGraw-Hill, New York).

DOWIE J (1975), 'The Portfolio Approach to Health Behaviour', *Social Science and Medicine*, Vol. 9, No. 11/12, November/December, pp. 619–31.

DOWNS A (1957), *An Economic Theory of Democracy* (Harper and Row, New York).

DUNCAN G J (ed.) (1984), *Years of Poverty, Years of Plenty* (Institute for Social Research, Michigan).

ENGLISH J (1982), 'Must Council Housing Become Welfare Housing?', *Housing Review*, pp. 212–13, November–December.

ENTHOVEN A C (1985), *Reflections on the Management of the National Health Service: An American Looks at Incentives to Efficiency in Health Services Management in the UK* (Nuffield Provincial Hospitals Trust, London) (a brief precis is contained in *The Economist*, 22 June 1985, pp. 19–20).

ERMISCH J F (1980), *Paying the Piper: Demographic Changes and Pension Contributions* (Policy Studies Institute, London).

ERMISCH J F (1981), 'Implications of Demographic Developments for the State Pension System', *Pensions World*, March, pp. 157–61.

ERMISCH J F (1983), *The Political Economy of Demographic Change* (Policy Studies Institute and Gower, London).

ERMISCH J F (1984), *Housing Finance: Who Gains?* (Policy Studies Institute, London).

FARMER M and **BARRELL R** (1982), 'Why Student Loans Are Fairer Than Grants', *Public Money*, Vol. 2, No. 1, pp. 19–24, June.

FEINSTEIN C H (1972), *Statistical Tables of National Income, Expenditure and Output of the UK, 1855–1965* (Cambridge University Press).

FELDSTEIN M S (1974), 'Social Security, Induced Retirement and Aggregate Capital Accumulation', *Journal of Political Economy*, Vol. 82, pp. 905–26.

FELDSTEIN M S (1979), 'Social Security Hobbles Our Capital Formation', *Harvard Business Review*, July–August.

FELDSTEIN M S and **POTERBA J** (1984), 'Unemployment Insurance and Reservation Wages', *Journal of Public Economics*, Vol. 23, pp. 141–67.

FIEGEHEN G C and **LANSLEY P S** (1976), 'The Measurement of Poverty', *Journal of the Royal Statistical Society*, Vol. 139, pp. 508–18.

FIEGEHEN G C, LANSLEY P S and **SMITH A D** (1977), *Poverty and Progress in Britain, 1953–73* (Cambridge University Press).

FINE B (1975), *Marx's Capital* (Macmillan, London).

FINER S E (1952), *The Life and Times of Sir Edwin Chadwick* (Methuen, London).

FISHER I (1930), *The Theory of Interest* (Macmillan, New York).

FLOREY C du V (1982), 'Diabetes Mellitus', in Miller D L and Farmer R D T (eds), *Epidemiology of Diseases* (Blackwell Scientific Publications, Oxford).

FOSTER C D, JACKMAN R, and **PERLMAN M** (1980), *Local Government Finance in a Unitary State* (George Allen & Unwin, London).

FOSTER J E (1984), 'On Economic Poverty: a Survey of Aggregate Measures', *Advances in Econometrics*, Vol. 3, pp. 215–51.

FRASER D (1984), *The Evolution of the British Welfare State*, 2nd edn (Macmillan, London).

FREEDEN M (1978), *The New Liberalism: An Ideology of Social Reform* (Oxford University Press).

FRIEDMAN M (1962), *Capitalism and Freedom* (University of Chicago Press).

FRIEDMAN M and FRIEDMAN R (1980), *Free to Choose* (Penguin, London).

FRIEDMAN M and KUZNETS S (1945), *Income from Independent Professional Practice* (National Bureau of Economic Research, New York).

FRIEDMAN M and STIGLER J (1972), 'Roofs or Ceilings? The Current Housing Problem', in Hayek F A *et al.*, *Verdict on Rent Control* (Institute of Economic Affairs, London).

GAULDIE E (1974), *Cruel Habitations: A History of Working-Class Housing, 1780–1918* (George Allen & Unwin, London).

GEORGE V and WILDING P (1976), *Ideology and Social Welfare* (Routledge & Kegan Paul, London).

GILBERT B B (1973), *The Evolution of National Insurance in Great Britain* (Michael Joseph, London).

GILBERT N (1983), *Capitalism and the Welfare State* (Yale University Press, New Haven).

GINSBURG N (1979), *Class, Capital and Social Policy* (Macmillan, London).

GINTIS H and BOWLES S (1982), 'The Welfare State and Long-Term Economic Growth: Marxian, Neoclassical and Keynesian Approaches', *American Economic Review*, Papers and Proceedings, Vol. 72, No. 1, pp. 341–5.

GLENNERSTER H (1985), *Paying for Welfare* (Martin Robertson, Oxford).

GLENNERSTER H (ed.) (1983), *The Future of the Welfare State: Remaking Social Policy* (Heinemann, London).

GLENNERSTER H and LE GRAND J (1984), 'Financing Students', *New Society*, 13 December, pp. 421–2.

GLENNERSTER H, MERRETT S and WILSON G (1968), 'A Graduate Tax', *Higher Education Review*, Vol. 1, No. 1.

GOLDFARB R S (1970), 'Pareto Optimal Distribution: A Comment', *American Economic Review*, Vol. LX, No. 5, pp. 994–6, December.

GORDON D M (1969), 'Income and Welfare in New York City', *Public Interest*, Winter.

GORDON R J and BLINDER A S (1980), 'Market Wages, Reservation Wages and Retirement Decisions', *Journal of Public Economics*, Vol. 14, pp. 277–308.

GOROVITZ S (1975), 'John Rawls: A Theory of Justice', in Crespigny A de and Minogue K R (eds), *Contemporary Political Philosophers*, pp. 272–89 (Methuen, London.

GOUGH I (1979), *The Political Economy of the Welfare State* (Macmillan, London)

GREEN C (1967), *Negative Taxes and the Poverty Problem* (The Brookings Institution, Washington DC).

GREENHALGH C (1977), 'A Labour Supply Function for Married Women in Great Britain', *Economica*, Vol. 44, No. 175, August.

GRONBJERG K, STREET D and SUTTLES G D (1978), *Poverty and Social Change* (University of Chicago Press).

GROSSMAN M (1972), *The Demand for Health: A Theoretical and Empirical Investigation*, Occasional Paper 119 (National Bureau of Economic Research, Cambridge, Mass.).

GRUBEL H G and MAKI D R (1976), 'The Effects of Unemployment Benefits on US Unemployment Rates', *Weltwirtschaftliches Archiv*, Vol. 112, pp. 274–97.

HALL P (1981), *The Inner City in Context*, Final Report to the Social Science Research Council Inner Cities Working Party (Heinemann, London).

HALL P (1982), *Urban and Regional Planning* (Penguin, London).

HALL R E (1973), 'Wages, Income and Hours of Work in the US Labor Force', in Cain G and Watts H (eds), *Income Maintenance and Labor Supply: Econometric Studies* (Markham, New York).

HALPERN J and HAUSMAN J A (1985), *Choice Under Uncertainty: A Model of Applications for the Social Security Disability Insurance Program*, Working Paper No. 1690 (National Bureau of Economic Research, Cambridge, Mass.).

HALPERN S (1985), 'What the Public Thinks of the NHS', *Health and Social Service Journal*, 6 June, pp. 702–4.

HALSEY A H (ed.) (1972), *Educational Priority, Vol 1: EPA Problems and Policies* (HMSO, London).

HAMERMESH D S (1977), *Jobless Pay and the Economy* (Johns Hopkins University Press, Baltimore).

HAMERMESH D S (1979), 'Entitlement Effects, Unemployment Insurance and Employment Decisions', *Economic Inquiry*, Vol. 17, pp. 317–32.

HAMERMESH D S (1980), 'Unemployment Insurance and Labor Supply', *International Economic Review*, Vol. 21, pp. 517–27.

HAMERMESH D S (1984), 'Life-Cycle Effects on Consumption and Retirement', *Journal of Labor Economics*, Vol. 2, pp. 353–70.

HANSEN W L and WEISBROD B A (1969), 'The Distribution of Costs and Direct Benefits of Public Higher Education: the Case of California', *Journal of Human Resources*, Vol. IV, No. 2, Spring, pp. 176–91.

HANSEN W L and WEISBROD B A (1978), 'The Distribution of Subsidies to Students in California Public Higher Education: Reply', *Journal of Human Resources*, Vol. XIII, No. 1, Winter, pp. 137–9.

HARBERGER A C (1962), 'The Incidence of the Corporation Income Tax', *Journal of Political Economy*, June.

HARRIS J F (1972), *Unemployment and Politics, 1886–1914* (Oxford University Press).

HARRIS J F (1977), *William Beveridge: A Biography* (Oxford University Press).

HARRIS R and SELDON A (1979), *Over-Ruled on Welfare*, Hobart Paperback No. 13 (Institute of Economic Affairs, London).

HARRISON A J (1979), *The Distribution of Wealth in Ten Countries*, Background Paper No, 7 Royal Commission on the Distribution of Income and Wealth (HMSO, London).

HARRISON J (1978), *Marxist Economics for Socialists* (Pluto, London).

HARRISON P (1985), *Inside the Inner City*, revised edition (Penguin, London).

HART J T (1970), 'Semicontinuous Screening of a Whole Community for Hypertension', *Lancet*, 1 August.

HAVEMAN R H and WATTS H W (1977), 'Social Experimentation as Policy Research; A Review of Negative Income Tax Experiments', in Halberstadt V and Culyer A J (eds), *Public Economics and Human Resources* (Cujas, Paris).

HAVEMAN R H and WOLFE B L (1984), 'Disability Transfers and Early Retirement: a Causal Relationship?', *Journal of Public Economics*, Vol. 24, pp. 47–66.

HAVEMAN R H, WOLFE B L and WARLICK J L (1984), 'Disability Transfers, Early Retirement and Retrenchment', in Aaron and Burtless (eds) (1984).

HAY J R (1975), *The Origins of the Liberal Welfare Reforms 1906–1914* (Macmillan, London).

HAYEK F A (1944), *The Road to Serfdom* (Routledge, London and Chicago University Press).

HAYEK F A (1960), *The Constitution of Liberty* (Routledge & Kegan Paul, London, and Chicago University Press).

HAYEK F A (1976), *Law, Legislation and Liberty*, Vol. 2, 'The Mirage of Social Justice' (Routledge & Kegan Paul, London).

HEALD D (1983), *Public Expenditure: Its Defence and Reform* (Martin Robertson, Oxford).

HEMMING R (1984), *Poverty and Incentives* (Oxford University Press).

HEMMING R and HILLS J (1983), 'The Reform of Housing Benefits', *Fiscal Studies*, Vol. 4, No. 1, pp. 48–65, March.

HEMMING R and KAY J A (1982a), 'Great Britain' in Rosa J-J (ed.) (1982).

HEMMING R and KAY J A (1982b), 'The Costs of the State Earnings-Related Pension Scheme', *Economic Journal*, Vol. 92, No. 366, June, pp. 300–19.

HICKS J R (1946), *Value and Capital*, 2nd edn (Clarendon Press, Oxford).

HIGGINS J (1981), *States of Welfare: Comparative Analysis in Social Policy* (Basil Blackwell and Martin Robertson, Oxford).

HIMMELFARB G (1984), *The Idea of Poverty: England in the Early Industrial Age* (Faber, London).

HIRSCH F (1977), *Social Limits to Growth* (Routledge & Kegan Paul, London).

HIRSHLEIFER J (1980), *Price Theory and Applications*, 2nd edn (Prentice-Hall International Inc., London).

HOBHOUSE L T (1909), *Democracy and Reaction*, 2nd edn (London).

HOBSBAWM E J (1964), *Labouring Men* (Weidenfeld & Nicolson, London).

HOBSON J A (1908), *The Problem of the Unemployed*, 4th edn (London).

HOBSON J A (1909), *The Crisis of Liberalism: New Issues of Democracy* (King & Son, London).

HOCHMAN H and RODGERS J (1969), 'Pareto Optimal Distribution', *American Economic Review*, Vol. LIX, No. 4, pp. 542–57.

HOCHMAN H and RODGERS J (1970), 'Reply', *American Economic Review*, Vol. LX, No. 5, pp. 997–1022, December.

HOLAHAN J (1984), 'The Effects of the 1981 Omnibus Budget Reconciliation Act on Medicaid Expenditures', Research Paper No. 3339-03 (The Urban Institute, Washington DC).

HONIG M (1974), 'AFDC Income, Recipient Rates, and Family Dissolution', *Journal of Human Resources*, Vol. 9, pp. 303–22.

HONIG M (1976), 'AFDC Income, Recipient Rates, and Family Dissolution: A Reply', *Journal of Human Resources*, Vol. 11, pp. 250–9.

HUGHES G and McCORMICK B (1981), 'Do Council Housing Policies Reduce Migration Between Regions?', *Economic Journal*, Vol. 91, No. 364, December, pp. 919–37.

HUME D (1770), 'Enquiry Concerning the Principles of Morals', in *Essays and*

Treatises on Several Subjects (Cadell, London).

HUNT E H (1981), *British Labour History, 1815–1914* (Weidenfeld & Nicolson, London).

HUNT S M *et al.* (1980), 'A Quantitative Approach to Perceived Health Status: A Validation Study', *Journal of Epidemiology and Community Health*, Vol. 34.

HURLEY S I (1985), 'The Unit of Taxation Under an Ideal Progressive Income Tax', *Oxford Journal of Legal Studies*, Vol. 4, No. 2, pp. 157–97.

ILLSLEY R (1980), *Professional or Public Health* (Nuffield Provincial Hospitals Trust, London).

INTERNATIONAL LABOUR OFFICE (1984a), *Introduction to Social Security* (International Labour Office, Geneva).

INTERNATIONAL LABOUR OFFICE (1984b), *Into the Twenty-first Century: The Development of Social Security* (International Labour Office, Geneva).

ISRAEL S and TEELING-SMITH G (1967), 'The Submerged Iceberg of Sickness in Society', *Social and Economic Adminstration*, Vol. 1, pp. 43–56.

JENCKS C (1970), *Education Vouchers: A Report on the Financing of Elementary Education by Grants to Parents* (Cambridge Center for the Study of Public Policy, Cambridge, Mass.).

JENCKS C (1972), *Inequality: A Reassessment of the Effect of Family and Schooling in America* (Basic Books, New York, and Allen Lane, London).

JENKINS S P and MAYNARD A K (1983), 'Intergenerational Continuities in Housing', *Urban Studies*, Vol. 20, No. 374, pp. 431–8.

JONES-LEE M (1969), 'Valuation of Production in Probability of Death by Road Accident', *Journal of Transport Economics and Policy*, Vol. 3, pp. 37–47, reprinted in Cooper and Culyer (1973).

JONES-LEE M (1976), *The Value of Life: An Economic Assessment* (Martin Robertson, Oxford).

JUDGE K (1982), 'The Growth and Decline of Social Expenditure' in Walker R (ed.), *Public Expenditure and Social Policy* (Heinemann, London).

KAHN A J and KAMERMAN S B (1983), *Income Transfers for Families with Children* (Temple University Press, Philadelphia).

KAIM-CAUDLE P (1973), *Comparative Social Policy and Social Security: A Ten-Country Study* (Martin Robertson, Oxford).

KALDOR N (1955), *An Expenditure Tax* (Allen & Unwin, London).

KATZNELSON I (1978), 'Considerations on Social Democracy in the United States', *Comparative Politics*, October.

KAY J A (1984), 'The Effects of Increasing Tax Thresholds on the Poverty and Unemployment Traps', *Fiscal Studies*, Vol. 5, No. 1, pp. 32–4, February.

KAY J A and KING M A (1983), *The British Tax System*, 3rd edn (Oxford University Press).

KAY J A and THOMPSON D J (1986), 'Privatisation: A Policy in Search of a Rationale', *Economic Journal*, Vol. 96, No. 381, March, pp. 18–32.

KEMP P (1984), *The Cost of Chaos: A Survey of the Housing Benefit Scheme* (The London Housing Aid Centre (SHAC)).

KENT COUNTY COUNCIL (1978), *Education Vouchers in Kent* (Kent County Council, Maidstone).

KINCAID J C (1975), *Poverty and Equality in Britain* (Penguin, London).

KING M A (1980), 'An Econometric Model of Tenure Choice and Demand for Housing as a Joint Decision', *Journal of Public Economics*, Vol. 14, No. 2, October, pp. 137–59.

KING M A (1983), 'An Index of Inequality: with Applications to Horizontal Equity and Social Mobility', *Econometrica*, Vol. 51, pp. 99–115.

KLAPPHOLZ K (1972), 'Equality of Opportunity, Fairness and Efficiency', in Peston M and Corry B (eds), *Essays in Honour of Lord Robbins* (Weidenfeld & Nicolson, London).

KLEIN R (1984), 'Privatisation and the Welfare State', *Lloyds Bank Review*, No. 151, pp. 12–29, January.

KLEIN R and O'HIGGINS M (eds) (1985), *The Future of the Welfare State* (Basil Blackwell, Oxford).

KNIGHT B (1983), 'Accounting for Educational Priorities', *Public Money*, Vol. 3, No. 3, pp. 37–40, December.

LAIDLER D (1981), *Introduction to Microeconomics*, 2nd edn (Philip Allan, Oxford).

LANCASTER T (1979), 'Econometric Model for the Duration of Unemployment', *Econometrica*, Vol. 47.

LANCASTER T and NICKELL S J (1980), 'The Analysis of Re-employment Probabilities', *Journal of the Royal Statistical Society*, Series A, Vol. 143, pp. 141–65.

LANSLEY S (1979), *Housing and Public Policy* (Croom Helm, London).

LANSLEY S (1982), *Housing Policy: New Policies for Labour* (Labour Housing Group, London).

LASKI H (1967), *A Grammar of Politics*, 5th edn (Allen & Unwin, London).

LAYARD P R G and PSACHAROPOULOS G (1974), 'The Screening Hypothesis and the Social Returns to Education', *Journal of Political Economy*, Vol. 82, pp. 985–98, October.

LAYARD P R G and WALTERS A A (1978), *Microeconomic Theory* (McGraw-Hill, London).

LAYARD P R G et al. (1978), *The Causes of Poverty*, Background Paper No. 5, Royal Commission on the Distribution of Income and Wealth (HMSO, London).

LAZEAR E P and MICHAEL R T (1980), 'Family Size and the Distribution of Real Per Capita Income', *American Economic Review*, Vol. 70, pp. 91–107.

LE GRAND J (1982), *The Strategy of Equality* (George Allen & Unwin, London).

LE GRAND J (1984), 'Equity as an Economic Objective', *Journal of Applied Philosophy*, Vol. 1, No. 1, pp. 39–51.

LE GRAND J (1985), 'On Measuring the Distributional Impact of Public Expenditure', in Terny G and Culyer A J (eds), *Public Finance and Social Policy* (Wayne State University Press, Detroit).

LE GRAND J and ROBINSON R (1984a), *The Economics of Social Problems*, 2nd edn (Macmillan, London).

LE GRAND J and ROBINSON R (1984b), *Privatisation and the Welfare State* (George Allen & Unwin, London).

LEES D S (1961), *Health Through Choice* (Institute of Economic Affairs, London).

LEIMER D R and LESNOY S D (1982), 'Social Security and Private Saving: New

Time-Series Evidence', *Journal of Political Economy*, Vol. 90, pp. 606–42.

LETWIN W (ed.) (1983), *Against Equality* (Macmillan, London).

LEVINE M D (1978), *Federal Housing Policy: Current Programs and Recurring Issues*, Congressional Budget Office, Background Paper (Government Printing Office, Washington DC).

LEVY F (1979), 'The Labor Supply of Female Household Heads, or AFDC Work Incentives Don't Work Too Well', *Journal of Human Resources*, Vol. XIV, No. 1, Winter, pp. 76–97.

LINDERT P H and WILLIAMSON J G (1982), 'Revising England's Social Tables 1688–1812', *Explorations in Economic History*, Vol. 19, pp. 385–408.

LINDERT P H and WILLIAMSON J G (1983), 'Reinterpreting Britain's Social Tables, 1688–1913', *Explorations in Economic History*, Vol. 20, pp. 94–109.

LINDSAY C M (1969), 'Medical Care and the Economics of Sharing', *Economica*, Vol. XXXVI, pp. 351–62, reprinted in Cooper and Culyer (1973).

LIPSEY R G (1983), *An Introduction to Positive Economics*, 6th edn (Weidenfeld & Nicolson, London).

LIPSEY R G and LANCASTER K (1956), 'The General Theory of Second-Best', *Review of Economic Studies*, Vol. XXIV, No. 63, January, pp. 11–32.

LISTER R (1983), *Poverty*, No. 54, April (Child Poverty Action Group, London).

LOMAS G (1974), *The Inner City* (London Voluntary Service Council).

LORD R (1983), 'Value for Money in the Education Service', *Public Money*, Vol. 3, No. 2, pp. 15–22, September.

LORENZ M C (1905), 'Methods of Measuring the Concentration of Wealth', *Publications of the American Statistical Association*, Vol. 9, pp. 209–16.

LUFT H S (1981), *Health Maintenance Organizations: Dimensions of Performance* (Wiley, New York).

LUKES S (1972), 'An Archimedean Point', *Observer Review*, 4 June.

LYDALL H F (1979), 'Some Problems in Making International Comparisons of Inequality', in Moroney J R (ed.), *Income Inequality: Trends and International Comparisons* (Lexington Books, Lexington, Mass.).

LYNES A (1981), *The Penguin Guide to Supplementary Benefit* (Penguin, London).

LYNES A (1984), 'Family Roulette', *New Society*, Vol. 70, No. 1138, 11 October, p. 74.

LYNES A (1986), *Paying for Pensions: the French Experience* (London School of Economics).

MACK J and LANSLEY P S (1985), *Poor Britain* (Allen & Unwin, London).

MacLENNAN D (1982), *Housing Economics: An Applied Approach* (Longman, London).

MAKI D R and SPINDLER Z A (1975), 'The Effect of Unemployment Compensation on the Rate of Unemployment in Great Britain', *Oxford Economic Papers*, Vol. 27, pp. 440–54.

MANDEL E (1976), 'Introduction' to Karl Marx, *Capital*, Vol. 1 (Penguin, London).

MARIN A (1983), 'Your Money or Your Life?', *Three Banks Review*, No. 38, pp. 20–37, June.

MARIN A and PSACHAROPOULOS G (1982), 'The Reward for Risk in the Labour Market', *Journal of Political Economy*, Vol. 90, No. 4, July/August.

446

MARSH D (1980), *The Welfare State*, 2nd edn (Longman, London).

MARSHALL T H (1975), *Social Policy in the Twentieth Century*, 4th edn (Hutchinson, London).

MARX K (1976), *Capital*, Vol. 1 (Penguin, London).

MARX K (1978), *Capital*, Vol. 2 (Penguin, London).

MARX K (1981), *Capital*, Vol. 3 (Penguin, London).

MAYER J E and TIMMS N (1970), *The Client Speaks* (Routledge & Kegan Paul, London).

MAYNARD A K (1975), *Experiment with Choice in Education* (Institute of Economic Affairs, London).

MAYNARD A K (1982), 'The Private Health Care Sector in Great Britain', in McLachlan G and Maynard A K (eds) (1982a).

McCLEMENTS L D (1977), 'Equivalence Scales for Children', *Journal of Public Economics*, Vol. 8.

McCLEMENTS L D (1978), *The Economics of Social Security* (Heinemann, London).

McCREADIE C (1976), 'Rawlsian Justice and the Financing of the National Health Service', *Journal of Social Policy*, Vol. 5, Part 2, April.

McDANIEL P R and SURREY S S (1984), *International Aspects of Tax Expenditures: a Comparative Study* (Kluwer, Deventer, The Netherlands).

McDONAGH O (1960), 'The Nineteenth Century Revolution in Government: A Reappraisal Reappraised', *Historical Journal*, II.

McKENNA C J (1986), *The Economics of Uncertainty* (Wheatsheaf Books, Brighton, Sussex).

McLACHLAN G and MAYNARD A K (eds) (1982a), *The Public/Private Mix for Health* (The Nuffield Provincial Hospitals Trust, London).

McLACHLAN G and MAYNARD A K (1982b), 'Public/Private Health Care: the British Scenario', *Public Money*, Vol. 2, No. 3, pp. 37–9, December.

MEADE J E (1972), 'Poverty in the Welfare State', *Oxford Economic Papers*, Vol. 24.

MEADE J E (1974), *The Inheritance of Inequalities* (Bristol Academy/Oxford University Press), reprinted in Atkinson (1980).

MEADE J E (1978), *The Structure and Reform of Direct Taxation* (Institute for Fiscal Studies and George Allen & Unwin, London).

MEADE J E (1984), 'Full Employment, New Technologies and the Distribution of Income', *Journal of Social Policy*, Vol. 13, No. 2, April, pp. 129–46.

MENSCHER S (1967), *Poor Law to Poverty Program* (University of Pittsburgh Press).

MERRETT S (1979), *State Housing in Britain* (Routledge & Kegan Paul, London).

MEYER P A and SHIPLEY J J (1970), 'Pareto Optimal Distribution: A Comment', *American Economic Review*, Vol. LX, No. 5, pp. 988–90, December.

MILIBAND R (1969), *The State in a Capitalist Society* (Weidenfeld & Nicolson, London).

MILL J S (1863), *Utilitarianism* (Parker, Son & Bourn, London).

MILLER D (1976), *Social Justice* (Clarendon Press, Oxford).

MILLER R (1975), 'Rawls and Marxism', in Daniels N (ed.) (1975).

MINARIK J J and GOLDFARB R S (1976), 'AFDC Income, Recipient Rates, and Family Dissolution: A Comment', *Journal of Human Resources*, Vol. 11, pp. 243–50.

MINFORD P (1984a), 'Response to Nickell', *Economic Journal*, Vol. 94, No. 376, December.

MINFORD P (1984b), 'State Expenditure: A Study in Waste', supplement to *Economic Affairs* (Institute of Economic Affairs, London).

MINFORD P, with ASHTON P, PEEL M, DAVIES D and SPRAGUE A (1985), *Unemployment: Cause and Cure*, 2nd edn (Basil Blackwell, Oxford).

MISHAN E J (1971), 'Evaluation of Life and Limb, A Theoretical Approach', *Journal of Political Economy*, Vol. 79, No. 4, pp. 687–705, July/August.

MISHAN E J (1982), *Cost-Benefit Analysis: An Informal Introduction*, 3rd edn (George Allen & Unwin, London).

MISHRA R (1981), *Society and Social Policy* (Macmillan, London).

MISHRA R (1984), *The Welfare State in Crisis* (Harvester Press, Brighton, Sussex).

MITCHELL O S and FIELDS G S (1981), 'The Effects of Pensions and Earnings on Retirement: A Review Essay', Working Paper 772 (National Bureau of Economic Research, Cambridge, Mass.).

MOFFITT R A (1983), 'An Economic Model of Welfare Stigma', *American Economic Review*, Vol. 73, pp. 1023–35.

MORGAN E V (1984), *Choice in Pensions: The Political Economy of Saving for Retirement* (Institute of Economic Affairs, London).

MOWAT C L (1969), 'Social Legislation in Britain and the United States in the Early Twentieth Century: a Problem in the History of Ideas', *Historical Studies*, Vol. VII.

MUELLBAUER J (1977), 'Testing the Barten Model of Household Composition Effects and the Cost of Children', *Economic Journal*, Vol. 87.

MUELLBAUER J (1979), 'McClements on Equivalence Scales for Children', *Journal of Public Economics*, Vol. 12.

MUELLBAUER J (1980), 'The Estimation of the Prais-Houthakker Model of Equivalence Scales', *Econometrica*, Vol. 48.

MUNNELL A H (1977), *The Future of Social Security* (The Brookings Institution, Washington DC).

MUNNELL A H (1982), *The Economics of Private Pensions* (The Brookings Institution, Washington DC).

MURPHY J (1981), 'Class Inequality in Education: Two Justifications, One Evaluation but No Hard Evidence', *British Journal of Sociology*, Vol. 32, No. 2, June, pp. 182–201.

MUSGRAVE R A (1970), 'Pareto Optimal Distribution: A Comment', *American Economic Review*, Vol. LX, No. 5, pp. 991–3, December.

MUSGRAVE R A and MUSGRAVE P B (1984), *Public Finance in Theory and Practice*, 4th edn (McGraw-Hill, London).

MUTH R F (1960), 'The Demand for Non-Farm Housing' in Harberger A C (ed.), *The Demand for Durable Goods* (University of Chicago Press).

MYERS R J (1965), *Social Insurance and Allied Government Programs* (R D Irwin, New York).

NARENDRANATHAN W, NICKELL S and STERN J (1985), 'Unemployment Benefits Revisited', *Economic Journal*, Vol. 95, No. 378, June, pp. 307–29.

NATIONAL CONSUMER COUNCIL (1984), *Of Benefit to All* (National Consumer Council, London).

NATIONAL FEDERATION OF HOUSING ASSOCIATIONS (1985), *Inquiry into British Housing: Report* (National Federation of Housing Associations, London).

NATIONAL SUPERANNUATION COMMITTEE OF INQUIRY (1976), *A National Superannuation Scheme for Australia* (Australian Government Publishing Service, Canberra).

NATIONAL SUPERANNUATION COMMITTEE OF INQUIRY (1977), *Occupational Superannuation in Australia* (Australian Government Publishing Service, Canberra).

NERLOVE M (1972), 'On Tuition and the Costs of Higher Education: Prolegomena to a Conceptual Framework', *Journal of Political Economy*, Vol. 80, No. 3, Part 2, pp. 1178–1218, May/June.

NERLOVE M (1975), 'Some Problems in the Use of Income-Contingent Loans for the Finance of Higher Education', *Journal of Political Economy*, Vol. 83, No. 1, pp. 157–83, February.

NEVITT A A (1966), *Housing, Taxation and Subsidies* (Nelson, London).

NEWFIELD J (1978), *Robert F Kennedy: A Memoir* (Berkley Publishing Corporation, New York).

NEWMAN K J (1985), 'International Comparisons of Taxes and Social Security Contributions in 20 OECD Countries 1972–1982', *Economic Trends* No. 376, February, pp. 82–93.

NICHOLSON J L (1974), 'The Distribution and Redistribution of Income in the United Kingdom', in Wedderburn D (ed.), *Poverty, Inequality and Class Structure* (Cambridge University Press).

NICHOLSON J L (1976), 'Appraisal of Different Methods of Estimating Equivalence Scales and Their Results', *Review of Income and Wealth*, Series 22, No. 1, March.

NICKELL S J (1979a), 'The Effect of Unemployment and Related Benefits on the Duration of Unemployment', *Economic Journal*, Vol. 89, No. 353, pp. 34–49, March.

NICKELL S J (1979b), 'Estimating the Probability of Leaving Unemployment', *Econometrica*, Vol. 47, pp. 1249–66.

NICKELL S J (1980), 'A Picture of Male Unemployment in Britain', *Economic Journal*, Vol. 90, pp. 776–94.

NICKELL S J (1984), 'A Review of *Unemployment: Cause and Cure*, by Patrick Minford with David Davies, Michael Peel and Alison Sprague', *Economic Journal*, Vol. 94, No. 376, December.

NISBET R (1974), 'The Pursuit of Equality', *The Public Interest*, Vol. 35, Spring, pp. 103–20, reprinted in Letwin (1983).

NOUMI K (1983), 'Financing of Social Security Medical Care Schemes and the Containment of Costs: The Japanese Experience', *International Social Security Review*, Vol. 36, No. 2, pp. 180–90.

NOZICK R (1974), *Anarchy, State and Utopia* (Basil Blackwell, Oxford).

O'CONNOR J (1973), *The Fiscal Crisis of the State* (St Martin's Press, New York).

O'HIGGINS M (1980), 'The Redistributive Effect of Public Expenditure and Taxation', in Sandford C, Pond C and Walker R (eds) (1980).

O'KELLY R (1985), *The Institute for Fiscal Studies and the Reform of Social Security* (The Fabian Society, London).

OECD (1977), *Public Expenditure on Health* (OECD, Paris).

OECD (1980), *Goals for Educational Policy in Sweden* (OECD, Paris).

OECD (1981), *Educational Reforms in Sweden* (OECD, Paris).

OFFICE OF HEALTH ECONOMICS (1985), *Measurement of Health* (Office of Health Economics, London).

OKUN A M (1975), *Equality and Efficiency: the Big Tradeoff* (The Brookings Institution, Washington DC).

ORSHANSKY M (1965), 'Counting the Poor: Another Look at the Poverty Problem', *Social Security Bulletin*, Vol. 28, pp. 3–29.

PALMER J L and PECHMAN J A (eds) (1978), *Welfare in Rural Areas: The North Carolina–Iowa Income Maintenance Experiment* (The Brookings Institution, Washington DC).

PARKER H (1982), *The Moral Hazard of Social Benefits* (Institute of Economic Affairs, London).

PARSONS D O (1980), 'The Decline in Male Labor Force Participation', *Journal of Political Economy*, Vol. 88, pp. 117–24.

PAULY M V (1968), 'The Economics of Moral Hazard: Comment', *American Economic Review*, Vol. 57, pp. 531–7.

PAULY M V (1974), 'Overinsurance and Public Provision of Insurance: The Roles of Moral Hazard and Adverse Selection', *Quarterly Journal of Economics*, Vol. 88, pp. 44–62.

PEACOCK A T (1952), *The Economics of National Insurance* (William Hodge, London).

PEACOCK A T (1984), 'Privatisation in Perspective', *Three Banks Review*, No. 144, December, pp. 3–25.

PEACOCK A T and SHANNON R (1968), 'The Welfare State and the Redistribution of Income', *Westminster Bank Review*, August, pp. 30–46.

PEACOCK A T and WISEMAN J (1967), *The Growth of Public Expenditure in the United Kingdom*, revised edition (George Allen & Unwin, London).

PECHMAN J A (1970), 'The Distributional Effects of Public Higher Education in California', *Journal of Human Resources*, Vol. 5, pp. 310–70.

PECHMAN J A (1985), *Who Paid the Taxes, 1966–85* (The Brookings Institution, Washington DC).

PECHMAN J A (ed.) (1980), *Setting National Priorities: Agenda for the 1980s* (The Brookings Institution, Washington DC).

PECHMAN J A (ed.) (1983), *Setting National Priorities: The 1984 Budget* (The Brookings Institution, Washington DC).

PECHMAN J A and TIMPANE P M (eds) (1975), *Work Incentives and Income Guarantees: The New Jersey Negative Income Tax Experiment* (The Brookings Institution, Washington DC).

PECHMAN J A, AARON H J and TAUSSIG M K (1968), *Social Security: Perspectives for Reform* (The Brookings Institution, Washington DC).

PELLING H (1979), *Popular Politics and Society in Late Victorian Britain*, 2nd edn (Macmillan, London).

PEN J (1971), 'A Parade of Dwarfs (and a Few Giants)', extract from *Income Distribution* (Penguin, London), reprinted in Atkinson (ed.) (1980).

PENCAVEL J (1984), 'Labor Supply of Men: A Survey', in Ashenfelter O and Layard P R G (eds), *Handbook of Labor Economics* (North-Holland, Amsterdam).

PETERSON P E (1983), 'Did the Education Commissions Say Anything?', *The Brookings Review*, pp. 3–11, Winter.

PIACHAUD D F J (1971), 'Poverty and Taxation', *Political Quarterly*, Vol. 41, January.

PIACHAUD D F J (1972), 'The Economics of Treating Varicose Veins', *International Journal of Epidemiology*, Vol. 1, Autumn.

PIACHAUD D F J (1975), 'The Economics of Educational Opportunity', *Higher Education*, Vol. 4, No. 2.

PIACHAUD D F J (1981), 'Peter Townsend and the Holy Grail', *New Society*, 10 September, pp. 419–21.

PIACHAUD D F J (1984), 'The Means Test State', *New Socialist*, October, pp. 53–4.

PIGGOTT J (1984), 'The Value of Tenant Benefits from UK Council House Subsidies', *Economic Journal*, Vol. 94, No. 374, June, pp. 384–9.

PIGGOTT J and WHALLEY J (1985), *UK Tax Policy and Applied General Equilibrium Analysis* (Cambridge University Press).

PIGGOTT J and WHALLEY J (eds) (1986), *New Developments in Applied General Equilibrium Analysis* (Cambridge University Press).

PINKER R (1979), *The Idea of Welfare* (Heinemann, London).

PIZZEY E (1974), *Scream Quietly or the Neighbours Will Hear* (Penguin, London).

POWER A (1984), *Local Housing Management, A Priority Estates Project Survey* (Department of the Environment, London).

PRAIS S J and HOUTHAKKER H S (1955), *The Analysis of Family Budgets* (Cambridge University Press).

PREST A R (1968), 'The Budget and Interpersonal Redistribution', *Public Finance*, Vol. 23, pp. 80–98.

PREST A R (1970), *Social Benefits and Tax Rates* (Institute of Economic Affairs, London).

PREST A R (1973), 'Proposals for a Tax-Credit System', *British Tax Review*, No. 1.

PREST A R (1979), 'The Structure and Reform of Direct Taxation', *Economic Journal*, Vol. 89, No. 354, pp. 243–60, June.

PREST A R (1983), 'The Social Security Reform Minefield', *British Tax Review*, No. 1, pp. 44–53.

PREST A R (1985), 'Implicit Taxes: Are We Taxed More than We Think?', *Royal Bank of Scotland Review*, No. 147, September, pp. 10–26.

PREST A R and BARR N A (1985), *Public Finance in Theory and Practice*, 7th edn (Weidenfeld & Nicolson, London).

PROJECTOR D S and MURRAY E G (1978), *Eligibility for Welfare and Participation Rates, 1970*, Studies in Income Distribution No. 7 (US Department of Health, Education and Welfare, Washington DC).

PRYKE R (1982), 'The Comparative Performance of Public and Private Enterprise', *Fiscal Studies*, Vol. 3, No. 2, July.

PSACHAROPOULOS G (1973), *Returns to Education: An International Comparison* (Elsevier, Amsterdam).

PSACHAROPOULOS G (1975), *Earnings and Education in OECD Countries* (OECD, Paris).

PSACHAROPOULOS G (1980), *Education and Income*, World Bank Staff Working

Paper No. 402 (World Bank, Washington DC).

RADFORD R A (1945), 'The Economic Organisation of a POW Camp', *Economica*, NS Vol. XII, No. 48, pp. 189–201, November.

RAWLS J (1972), *A Theory of Justice* (Oxford University Press).

REES P M and THOMPSON F P (1972), 'The Relative Price Effect in Public Expenditure: Its Nature and Method of Calculation', *Statistical News*, No. 18, August (HMSO, London).

REID I (1981), *Social Class Differences in Britain* (Grant McIntyre, London).

RICARDO D (1817), *On the Principles of Political Economy and Taxation* (Murray, London).

RIMLINGER G (1971), *Welfare Policy and Industrialisation in Europe, America and Russia* (Wiley, New York).

ROBBINS L C (1977), *Political Economy Past and Present: A Review of Leading Theories of Economic Policy* (Macmillan, London).

ROBBINS L C (1978), *The Theory of Economic Policy in English Classical Political Economy*, 2nd edn (Macmillan, London).

ROBERTI P (1978), 'Counting the Poor: a Review of the Situation Existing in Six Industrialised Nations', extract from *The Definition and Measurement of Poverty* (Department of Health and Social Security, London), reprinted in Atkinson (1980).

ROBINSON J and EATWELL J (1973), *An Introduction to Modern Economics* (McGraw-Hill, London).

ROBINSON R (1979), *Housing Economics and Public Policy* (Macmillan, London).

ROBSON W A (1976), *Welfare State and Welfare Society* (George Allen & Unwin, London).

ROSA J-J (ed.) (1982), *The World Crisis in Social Security* (Fondation Nationale d'Economie Politique, Paris, and Institute for Contemporary Studies, San Francisco).

ROSE M E (1972), *The Relief of Poverty 1834–1914* (Macmillan, London).

ROSEN S (1982), 'United States', in Rosa J-J (ed.) (1982).

ROSENTHAL L (1975), 'The Nature of Council House Subsidies' (PhD thesis, University of Essex).

ROSENTHAL L (1977), 'The Regional and Income Distribution of Council House Subsidy in the United Kingdom', *The Manchester School*, Vol. 45, pp. 127–40.

ROTHSCHILD M and STIGLITZ J E (1976), 'Equilibrium in Competitive Insurance Markets: An Essay on the Economics of Imperfect Information', *Quarterly Journal of Economics*, Vol. 90, pp. 629–49.

ROWLEY C K and PEACOCK A T (1975), *Welfare Economics: A Liberal Restatement* (Martin Robertson, Oxford).

ROWNTREE B S (1901), *Poverty: A Study of Town Life* (Longman, London).

ROWNTREE B S (1941), *Poverty and Progress: A Second Social Survey of York* (Longman, London).

ROWNTREE B S and LAVERS G R (1951), *Poverty and the Welfare State* (Longman, London).

RUNCIMAN W G (1972), *Relative Deprivation and Social Justice* (Penguin, London).

RUSSELL L B (1980), 'Medical Care', in Pechman J A (ed.) (1980).

RUSSELL L B (1983), 'Medical Care', in Pechman J A (ed.) (1983).

RUTTER M, MAUGHAN B, MORTIMORE P and OUSTON J (1979), *Fifteen Thousand Hours: Secondary Schools and Their Effects on Children* (Open Books, London).

SAMUELSON P A (1954), 'The Pure Theory of Public Expenditures', *Review of Economics and Statistics*, Vol. XXXVI, November.

SAMUELSON P A (1958), 'An Exact Consumption-Loan Model of Interest with or without the Social Contrivance of Money', *Journal of Political Economy*, Vol. LXVI, No. 6, December, pp. 467–82.

SAMUELSON P A (1980), *Economics*, 11th edn (McGraw-Hill, London).

SANDFORD C, POND C and WALKER R (eds) (1980), *Taxation and Social Policy* (Heinemann, London).

SCHELLING T C (1968), 'The Life You Save May Be Your Own' in Chase S B (ed.), *Problems in Public Expenditure Analysis* (The Brookings Institution, Washington DC), reprinted in Cooper and Culyer (1973).

SCHOTTLAND C I (1963), *The Social Security Program in the United States*, (Appleton-Century-Crofts, New York).

SELDON A (1981), *Wither the Welfare State* (Institute of Economic Affairs, London).

SEN A K (1970), 'The Impossibility of a Paretian Liberal', *Journal of Political Economy*, Vol. 78, No. 1, pp. 152–7, January/February.

SEN A K (1973), *On Economic Inequality* (Oxford University Press).

SEN A K (1976), 'Poverty: an Ordinal Approach to Measurement', *Econometrica*, Vol. 44, pp. 219–31.

SEN A K (1979), 'Personal Utilities and Public Judgements: Or What's Wrong with Welfare Economics?', *Economic Journal*, Vol. 89, No. 355, September, pp. 537–58.

SEN A K (1983), 'Poor, Relatively Speaking', *Oxford Economic Papers*, Vol. 35, pp. 153–69.

SHANKLAND G, WILLMOTT P and JORDAN D (1977), *Inner London: Policies for Dispersal and Balance*, Department of the Environment (HMSO, London).

SHAVELL S (1979), 'On Moral Hazard and Insurance', *Quarterly Journal of Economics*, Vol. 93, pp. 541–62.

SHORROCKS A F (1983), 'Ranking Income Distributions', *Economica*, Vol. 50, No. 197, February, pp. 3–17.

SIMONS H (1938), *Personal Income Taxation* (University of Chicago Press).

SINGH B and NAGAR A L (1973), 'Determinants of Consumer Unit Scales', *Economica*, Vol. 41, March.

SMITH A (1776), *An Inquiry into the Nature and Causes of the Wealth of Nations* (Clarendon Press, Oxford), reprinted 1976.

SMOLENSKY E, STIEFEL L, SCHMUNDT M and PLOTNICK R (1977), 'Adding In-kind Transfers to the Personal Income and Outlay Account: Implications for the Size Distribution of Income', in Juster F T (ed.), *The Distribution of Economic Well-Being*, Studies in Income and Wealth, Vol. 41 (Ballinger, Cambridge, Mass.).

SOLTOW L (1968), 'Long-Run Changes in British Income Inequality', *Economic History Review*, second series, Vol. 21, No. 1, pp. 17–29, reprinted in Atkinson (ed.) (1980).

SPENCE M (1973), 'Job Market Signalling', *Quarterly Journal of Economics*, Vol. 87, August, pp. 355–74, reprinted in Diamond and Rothschild (1978).

SPENCER H (1884), *The Man versus the State* (Appleton, New York).

STARK T (1977), *The Distribution of Income in Eight Countries*, Background Paper No. 4, Royal Commission on the Distribution of Income and Wealth (HMSO, London).

STEEL D and HEALD R (eds) (1984), *Privatizing Public Enterprises* (Royal Institute of Public Administration, London).

STEINER G V (1966), *Social Insecurity: The Politics of Welfare* (Chicago).

STEPHENSON G (1980), 'Taxes, Benefits and the Redistribution of Incomes', in Sandford C, Pond C and Walker R (eds) (1980).

STEVENS R B (ed.) (1970), *Statutory History of the United States: Income Security* (McGraw-Hill, New York).

STIGLITZ J E (1975), 'The Theory of "Screening" Education and the Distribution of Income', *American Economic Review*, Vol. 65, pp. 283–300, June.

STRACHEY J (1936), *The Theory and Practice of Socialism* (Gollancz, London).

SUGDEN R (1982), 'On the Economics of Philanthropy', *Economic Journal*, Vol. 92, No. 366, pp. 341–50, June.

SUGDEN R (1983a), 'On the Economics of Philanthropy: Reply', *Economic Journal*, Vol. 93, No. 371, p. 639, September.

SUGDEN R (1983b), *Who Cares? An Economic and Ethical Analysis of Private Charity and the Welfare State*, Occasional Paper 67 (Institute of Economic Affairs, London).

SUGDEN R (1984), 'Reciprocity: the Supply of Public Goods Through Voluntary Contributions', *Economic Journal*, Vol. 94, No. 376, December, pp. 772–87.

SURREY S S (1948), 'Federal Taxation of the Family—The Revenue Act of 1948', *Harvard Law Review*, Vol. 61, July, pp. 1097–1164.

SURREY S S (1958), 'The Federal Income Tax Base for Individuals', *Columbia Law Review*, Vol. 58, June, pp. 815–30.

SURREY S S and McDANIEL P R (1985), *Tax Expenditures* (Harvard University Press, Cambridge, Mass.).

SWEEZY P (1942), *The Theory of Capitalist Development* (Dennis Dobson, London).

SWENARTON M (1981), *Homes Fit for Heroes: the Politics and Architecture of Early State Housing in Britain* (Heinemann, London).

TAWNEY R H (1921), *The Acquisitive Society* (Fontana, London), reprinted 1961.

TAWNEY R H (1953), *The Attack and Other Papers* (Allen & Unwin, London).

TAWNEY R H (1964), *Equality*, 4th edn (George Allen & Unwin, London).

TAYLOR A J (1972), *Laissez-faire and State Intervention in Nineteenth-century Britain* (Macmillan, London).

THANE P (1982), *The Foundations of the Welfare State* (Longman, London).

THEIL H (1967), *Economics and Information Theory* (North-Holland, Amsterdam).

THUROW L C (1971), 'The Income Distribution as a Pure Public Good', *Quarterly Journal of Economics*, pp. 327–36, May.

TITMUSS R M (1956), *The Social Division of Welfare* (Liverpool University Press), reprinted in Titmuss (1976).

TITMUSS R M (1970), *The Gift Relationship* (Penguin, London).

TITMUSS R M (1976), *Essays on 'The Welfare State'*, 3rd edn (George Allen & Unwin, London).

TOBIN J (1968), 'Raising the Incomes of the Poor', in Gordon K (ed.), *Agenda for the Nation* (The Brookings Institution, Washington DC).

TOBIN J, PECHMAN J and MIESZKOWSKI P (1967), 'Is a Negative Income Tax Practical?', *Yale Law Journal*, Vol. 77.

TOLLEY (1986), *Social Security and State Benefits 1986*, Matthewman J (ed.) (Tolley Publishing Company, Croydon, Surrey).

TOWNSEND P (1979), *Poverty in the United Kingdom* (Penguin, London).

TOWNSEND P and DAVIDSON N (1982), see Black (1980).

TULLOCK G (1970), *Private Wants, Public Means* (Basic Books, New York).

TULLOCK G (1976), *The Vote Motive*, Hobart Paperback No. 9 (Institute of Economic Affairs, London).

UK(1842), *Inquiry into the Sanitary Condition of the Labouring Population of Great Britain* (HMSO, London).

UK (1885), *Report of the Royal Commission on the Housing of the Working Classes* (HMSO, London).

UK(1914), *The Land, Vol II:Urban*, Report of the Land Enquiry Committee (HMSO, London).

UK (1942), *Social Insurance and Allied Services* (The Beveridge Report), Cmd. 6404 (HMSO, London).

UK(1943), *Educational Reconstruction*, Cmd. 6458 (HMSO, London).

UK(1944a), *A National Health Service*, Cmd. 6502 (HMSO, London).

UK(1944b), *Employment Policy*, Cmd. 6527 (HMSO, London).

UK(1944c), *Social Insurance*, Pt. I, Cmd. 6550, and Pt. II (Workmen's Compensation), Cmd. 6551 (HMSO, London).

UK (1962), *A Review of the Medical Services in Great Britain* (HMSO, London).

UK (1963), *Higher Education* (the Robbins Report), Cmnd. 2154 (HMSO, London).

UK (1966), *A Plan for Polytechnics and Other Colleges* (HMSO, London).

UK (1968a), *Report of the Committee on Local Authority and Allied Personal Social Services* (the Seebohm Report), Cmnd. 3703 (HMSO, London).

UK (1968b), *The Administrative Structure of the Medical and Related Services in England and Wales* (HMSO, London).

UK (1970), *The Future Structure of the National Health Service* (HMSO, London).

UK (1972a), *Proposals for a Tax-Credit System*, Cmnd. 5116 (HMSO, London).

UK (1972b), *National Health Reorganisation: England* (HMSO, London).

UK (1972c), *Public Expenditure White Papers: Handbook on Methodology* (HMSO, London).

UK (1972d), *Education: A Framework for Expansion* (HMSO, London).

UK (1973), *Report and Proceedings*, Select Committee on Tax-Credit, Session 1972–3, HC 341-I, 341-II, 341-III (HMSO, London).

UK (1974), *Better Pensions Fully Protected Against Inflation*, Cmnd. 5713 (HMSO, London).

UK (1975), *Minutes of Evidence*, Select Committee on a Wealth Tax, Volume II, Session 1974–5, HC 696-II (HMSO, London).

UK (1976), *Local Government Finance, Report of the Committee of Enquiry* (The Layfield Committee), Cmnd. 6453 (HMSO, London).

UK (1977a), Royal Commission on the Distribution of Income and Wealth, *Report Number 5: Third Report on the Standing Reference*, Cmnd. 6999 (HMSO, London).

UK (1977b), *A New Partnership for Our Schools* (HMSO, London).

UK (1978a), *Report of the Committee of Inquiry into Normansfield Hospital*, Cmnd. 7357 (HMSO, London).

UK (1978b), *The Financing of Occupational Pension Schemes*, Evidence of the Government Actuary's Department to the Committee to Review the Functioning of Financial Institutions (HMSO, London).

UK (1978c), *Royal Commission on Civil Liability and Compensation for Personal Injury*, Cmnd. 7054 (HMSO, London).

UK (1979a), Royal Commission on the Distribution of Income and Wealth, *Report No. 7: Fourth Report on the Standing Reference*, Cmnd. 7595 (HMSO, London).

UK (1979b), *Report of the Royal Commission on the National Health Service* (HMSO, London).

UK (1980), *Fifth Report, Minutes of Evidence*, House of Commons Select Committee on Education, Science and the Arts, Session 1979–80, HC 787 (HMSO, London).

UK (1981), *Occupational Pension Schemes 1979. Sixth Survey by the Government Actuary* (HMSO, London).

UK (1983a), *The Structure of Personal Income Taxation and Income Support*, Third Special Report from the Treasury and Civil Service Committee, Session 1982–3, HC 386 (HMSO, London).

UK (1983b), *The Structure of Personal Income Taxation and Income Support, Minutes of Evidence*, Treasury and Civil Service Committee Sub-Committee, Session 1982–3, HC 20-I (HMSO, London).

UK (1983c), *The Structure of Personal Income Taxation and Income Support, Appendices*, Treasury and Civil Service Committee Sub-Committee, Session 1982–3, HC 20-II (HMSO, London).

UK (1985a), *The Government's Expenditure Plans 1985–86 to 1987–88*, Cmnd. 9428 (HMSO, London).

UK (1985b), *Employment: The Challenge for the Nation*, Cmnd. 9474 (HMSO, London).

UK (1985c), *The Development of Higher Education into the 1990s*, Cmnd. 9524 (HMSO, London).

UK (1985d), *Reform of Social Security*, Cmnd. 9517 (HMSO, London).

UK (1985e), *Reform of Social Security: Programme for Change*, Cmnd. 9518 (HMSO, London).

UK (1985f), *Reform of Social Security: Background Papers*, Cmnd. 9519 (HMSO, London).

UK (1985g), *Housing Benefit Review*, Cmnd. 9520 (HMSO, London).

UK (1985h), *The Government's Green Paper 'Reform of Social Security'*, Seventh Report from the Social Services Committee, Session 1984–5, HC 451 (HMSO, London).

UK (1985j), 'The Effects of Taxes and Benefits on Household Income 1984', *Economic Trends*, No. 386, December, pp. 99–115.

UK (1985k), *Reform of Social Security: Programme for Action*, Cmnd. 9691 (HMSO, London).

UK (1986a), *The Government's Expenditure Plans 1986–87 to 1988–89*, Cmnd. 9702 (HMSO, London).

UK (1986b), *The Reform of Personal Taxation*, Cmnd. 9756 (HMSO, London).

UK (1986c), *Primary Health Care: An Agenda for Discussion*, Cmnd. 9771 (HMSO, London).

UK (1986d), *Report of the Committee of Inquiry into Unnecessary Dental Treatment* (HMSO, London).

UK AUDIT COMMISSION (1986), *Managing the Crisis in Council Housing* (HMSO, London).

UK BOARD OF INLAND REVENUE (1983), *Cost of Tax Reliefs for Pension Schemes: Appropriate Statistical Approach* (HMSO, London).

UK CENTRAL ADVISORY COUNCIL FOR EDUCATION (ENGLAND) (1959), *Fifteen to Eighteen* (the Crowther Report) (HMSO, London).

UK CENTRAL ADVISORY COUNCIL FOR EDUCATION (ENGLAND) (1963), *Half our Future* (the Newsom Report) (HMSO, London).

UK CENTRAL ADVISORY COUNCIL FOR EDUCATION (ENGLAND) (1967), *Children and Their Primary Schools* (The Plowden Report) (HMSO, London).

UK DEPARTMENT OF EDUCATION AND SCIENCE (1984), 'International Statistical Comparisons in Higher Education', *Statistical Bulletin*, No. 9/84, July (HMSO, London).

UK DEPARTMENT OF EDUCATION AND SCIENCE (1986), *Report by Her Majesty's Inspectors on the Effects of Local Authority Expenditure Policies on Education Provision in England, 1985* (HMSO, London).

UK DEPARTMENT OF HEALTH AND SOCIAL SECURITY (1976a), *Sharing Resources for Health in England: Report of the Joint Resource Allocation Working Party* (HMSO, London).

UK DEPARTMENT OF HEALTH AND SOCIAL SECURITY (1976b), *Priorities for Health and Personal Social Services in Britain* (HMSO, London).

UK DEPARTMENT OF HEALTH AND SOCIAL SECURITY (1978a), *Social Assistance: A Review of the Supplementary Benefit Scheme in Great Britain* (HMSO, London).

UK DEPARTMENT OF HEALTH AND SOCIAL SECURITY (1978b), *Social Service Teams: the Practitioner's View* (HMSO, London).

UK DEPARTMENT OF HEALTH AND SOCIAL SECURITY (1979), *Patients First* (HMSO, London).

UK DEPARTMENT OF HEALTH AND SOCIAL SECURITY (1982), *Social Security Operational Strategy* (HMSO, London).

UK DEPARTMENT OF HEALTH AND SOCIAL SECURITY (1983), *Report of the NHS Management Enquiry* (HMSO, London).

UK DEPARTMENT OF THE ENVIRONMENT (1971), *Fair Deal for Housing*, Cmnd. 4728 (HMSO, London).

UK DEPARTMENT OF THE ENVIRONMENT (1974), *Land*, Cmnd. 5730 (HMSO, London).

UK DEPARTMENT OF THE ENVIRONMENT (1977a), *Housing Policy: A Consultative Document*, Cmnd. 6851 (HMSO, London).

UK DEPARTMENT OF THE ENVIRONMENT (1977b), *Housing Policy: Technical Volume, Part I* (HMSO, London).

UK DEPARTMENT OF THE ENVIRONMENT (1977c), *Housing Policy: Technical Volume, Part II* (HMSO, London).

UK DEPARTMENT OF THE ENVIRONMENT (1977d), *Housing Policy: Technical Volume, Part III* (HMSO, London).

UK DEPARTMENT OF THE ENVIRONMENT (1982a), *English House Condition Survey: Part 1, Report of the Physical Condition Survey* (HMSO, London).

UK DEPARTMENT OF THE ENVIRONMENT (1982b), *Housing Subsidies and Accounting Manual 1981* (HMSO, London).

UK DEPARTMENT OF THE ENVIRONMENT (1985a), *Homeless Households Reported by Local Authorities in England*, May (HMSO, London).

UK DEPARTMENT OF THE ENVIRONMENT (1985b), *Home Improvement – A New Approach*, Cmnd. 9513 (HMSO, London).

UK NATIONAL AUDIT OFFICE (1985), *National Health Service: Control of Nursing Manpower*, Report by the Comptroller and Auditor General (HMSO, London).

UNITED NATIONS (1982), *Economic Survey of Europe in 1981* (United Nations, New York).

UNIVERSITIES CENTRAL COUNCIL ON ADMISSIONS (1985), *Statistical Supplement to the Twenty-Second Report, 1983–84* (Universities Central Council on Admissions, London).

US (1969), *Poverty Amid Plenty: The American Paradox*, Report of the President's Commission on Income Maintenance Programs (Washington DC).

US ADVISORY COUNCIL ON SOCIAL SECURITY (1938), *Final Report*, (S. Doc. 4, 76 Cong. 1 sess. (1939)).

US DEPARTMENT OF HEALTH AND HUMAN SERVICES (1984), *Social Security Programs Throughout the World – 1983*, Research Report No. 59 (Washington DC).

US FEDERAL EMERGENCY RELIEF ADMINISTRATION (1942), *Final Statistical Report of the Federal Emergency Relief Administration* (Washington DC).

US NATIONAL RESOURCES AND PLANNING BOARD (1942), *Long Range Work and Relief Policies: Report of the Committee on Long Range Work and Relief to the National Resources Planning Board* (Washington DC).

US SUPREME COURT (1978), City of Los Angeles, Department of Water and Power *et al.* v. Manhart *et al.*, Case No. 76-1810.

VARIAN H R (1984), *Microeconomic Analysis*, 2nd edn (Norton, New York).

VENTI S F and WISE D A (1984), 'Moving and Housing Expenditure: Transactions Costs and Disequilibrium', *Journal of Public Economics*, Vol. 23, No. 1/2, February/March, pp. 207–43.

WALKER A and TOWNSEND P (eds) (1981), *Disability in Britain* (Martin Robertson, Oxford).

WARLICK J L (1981), 'Participation of the Aged in SSI', *Journal of Human Resources*, Vol. 17, pp. 236–60.

WEALE A (1978), *Equality and Social Policy* (Routledge & Kegan Paul, London).

WEAVER C L (1982), *The Crisis in Social Security: Economics and Political Origins* (Duke University Press, Durham, North Carolina).

WEBB M (1984), 'Privatization of the Electricity and Gas Industries', in Steel D and Heald D (eds), *Privatizing Public Enterprises* (Royal Institute of Public Administration, London).

WEBB S and WEBB B (1909), *The Break Up of the Poor Law*, Minority Report of the Poor Law Commission, Part I (Longman, London).

WEITZMAN M L (1984), *The Share Economy* (Harvard University Press, Cambridge, Mass.).

WEST E G (1970), *Education and the State*, 2nd edn (Institute of Economic Affairs, London).

WHITEHEAD C M E (1974), *The UK Housing Market: An Econometric Model* (Saxon House, Farnborough, Hants).

WHITEHEAD C M E (1980), 'Fiscal Aspects of Housing', in Sandford C, Pond C and Walker R (eds) (1980).

WHITEHEAD C M E (1983), 'Possible Effects of the Removal of Mortgage Interest Tax Relief', in UK (1983c).

WILENSKY H L (1975), *The Welfare State and Equality* (University of California Press, Berkeley).

WILENSKY H L and LEBEAUX C N (1965), *Industrial Society and Social Welfare* (The Free Press, New York, and Collier-Macmillan, London).

WILES P J D (1974), *Distribution of Income: East and West* (North-Holland, Amsterdam).

WILLIAMS A (1985), 'Economics of Coronary Artery Bypass Grafting', *British Medical Journal*, 3 August, pp. 326–9.

WILLIAMSON J et al. (1964), 'Old People at Home: Their Unreported Needs', *Lancet*, 23 May, pp. 1117–20.

WILLIAMSON J G (1980), 'Earnings Inequality in Nineteenth-Century Britain', *Journal of Economic History*, Vol. XL, No. 3, pp. 457–76.

WILLIS J R M and HARDWICK P J W (1978), *Tax Expenditures in the United Kingdom* (Heinemann, for the Institute for Fiscal Studies, London).

WINCH D M (1971), *Analytical Welfare Economics* (Penguin, London).

WISTOW G (1983), 'Joint Finance and Community Care: Have the Incentives Worked?', *Public Money*, pp. 33–7, September.

WITTE E E (1962), *The Development of the Social Security Act* (University of Wisconsin Press, Madison).

WOLFE B L, DE JONG P R, HAVEMAN R H, HALBERSTADT V and GOUDSWAARD K P (1984), 'Income Transfers and Work Effort: The Netherlands and the United States in the 1970s', *Kyklos*, Vol. 37, Fasc. 4, pp. 609–37.

WOODHALL M (1982), *Student Loans: Lessons from Recent International Experience* (Policy Studies Institute, London).

YOUNGHUSBAND E (1978), *Social Work in Britain 1950–1975* (George Allen & Unwin, London).

ZABALZA A and PIACHAUD D (1981), 'Social Security and the Elderly: A Simulation of Policy Changes', *Journal of Public Economics*, Vol. 16, pp. 145–69.

Author index

Subject index

466